MICROSOFT® ACCESS® 2010 24-HOUR TRAINER

INTRODUCTION xxxiii

LESSON 1	Installing Access 2010	1
LESSON 2	Getting Started in Access 2010	5
LESSON 3	Creating a New Database Application	9
LESSON 4	Access Database Objects	15
LESSON 5	The Access 2010 Ribbon	23
LESSON 6	The Access 2010 Backstage	31
LESSON 7	The Access 2010 Navigation Pane	37
LESSON 8	Creating a Table in Datasheet View	45
LESSON 9	Creating a Table in Design View	55
LESSON 10	Access 2010 Data Types	65
LESSON 11	Table and Field Properties	71
LESSON 12	Data Validation and Limiting User Input	79
LESSON 13	Creating Value List Fields	89
LESSON 14	Creating Lookup Tables	95
LESSON 15	Table Modifications	101
LESSON 16	Creating Table Relationships	107
LESSON 17	Creating Table Field Indexes	117
LESSON 18	Creating Tables from External Data	121
LESSON 19	Creating Linked Tables	129
LESSON 20	Collecting Data via E-mail	135
LESSON 21	Creating Queries with the Wizard	141
LESSON 22	Creating Queries in Design View	147
LESSON 23	Creating Select Queries	155
LESSON 24	Data Aggregation and Grouping	161
LESSON 25	Creating Parameter Queries	167
LESSON 26	Creating Append Queries	173
LESSON 27	Creating Update Queries	179
LESSON 28	Creating Delete Queries	185
LESSON 29	Creating Make Table Queries	191
LESSON 30	Creating Crosstab Queries	197

Continues

LESSON 31 Creating Forms in Layout View 205

LESSON 32 Creating Forms in Design View 215

LESSON 33 Access Form Properties 227

LESSON 34 Access 2010 Form Controls 233

LESSON 35 Working with Subforms and Subreports 243

LESSON 36 Embedded Macros in Forms 251

LESSON 37 Adding Code to Forms 259

LESSON 38 Access 2010 Form Types 269

LESSON 39 Creating PivotCharts 279

LESSON 40 Access Application Navigation 287

LESSON 41 Creating Reports in Layout View 293

LESSON 42 Creating Reports in Design View 301

LESSON 43 Access Report Properties 309

LESSON 44 Report Sorting, Grouping, and Totals 319

LESSON 45 Using Macros in Reports 327

LESSON 46 Creating Macros in Access 2010 335

LESSON 47 Macro Types and Security 341

LESSON 48 Macro Parts 347

LESSON 49 Building Macros 355

LESSON 50 Data Macros in Access 2010 363

LESSON 51 The Visual Basic Editor 367

LESSON 52 Introduction to VBA 379

LESSON 53 Using Operators in VBA 397

LESSON 54 Using Variables in VBA 409

LESSON 55 Creating Class Modules 421

LESSON 56 The Access Object Model 433

LESSON 57 Working with DAO 439

LESSON 58 Access Application Settings 457

LESSON 59 Customizing the Navigation Pane 463

LESSON 60 Customizing the Ribbon 469

LESSON 61 Customizing the Backstage 481

LESSON 62 The Access Runtime 489

APPENDIX What's on the DVD? 499

INDEX 503

Microsoft® Access® 2010
24-Hour Trainer

Geoffrey L. Griffith
Truitt L. Bradly

WILEY

Wiley Publishing, Inc.

Microsoft® Access® 2010 24-Hour Trainer

Published by
Wiley Publishing, Inc.
10475 Crosspoint Boulevard
Indianapolis, IN 46256
www.wiley.com

Copyright © 2011 by Wiley Publishing, Inc., Indianapolis, Indiana

Published by Wiley Publishing, Inc., Indianapolis, Indiana

Published simultaneously in Canada

ISBN: 978-0-470-59167-3

Manufactured in the United States of America

10 9 8 7 6 5 4 3 2 1

For general information on our other products and services please contact our Customer Care Department within the United States at (877) 762-2974, outside the United States at (317) 572-3993 or fax (317) 572-4002.

Wiley also publishes its books in a variety of electronic formats. Some content that appears in print may not be available in electronic books.

Library of Congress Control Number: 2010933471

*I dedicate this book to all the people who are just
learning to use Access for the very first time. I tried
my best to write this book so you would understand
it! And trust me, Access gets easier! And of course,
I wouldn't miss the opportunity to thank my wife
Jamie and my son Ryan. Without all of your
love and support, I would be nothing!*

— GEOFF GRIFFITH

*To my mother and father, my daughter Amy, my two
grandchildren Morgan and Logan, and my son Sean
for inspiring me; to my colleagues at FirstCare Health
Plans who allowed me to learn more about Access
by finding solutions to their database problems; to
the members, VIPs, Moderators, and Administrators
of UtterAccess.com for allowing me the opportunity
to help other Microsoft Office users; and to Teresa
Hennig for her friendship and encouragement.*

— TRUITT BRADLY

CREDITS

EXECUTIVE EDITOR
Robert Elliott

PROJECT EDITORS
Ed Connor
Tonya Maddox Cupp

TECHNICAL EDITOR
Kevin Marshall

PRODUCTION EDITOR
Kathleen Wisor

COPY EDITOR
Kimberly A. Cofer

EDITORIAL DIRECTOR
Robyn B. Siesky

EDITORIAL MANAGER
Mary Beth Wakefield

FREELANCER EDITORIAL MANAGER
Rosemarie Graham

ASSOCIATE DIRECTOR OF MARKETING
Ashley Zurcher

PRODUCTION MANAGER
Tim Tate

**VICE PRESIDENT AND
EXECUTIVE GROUP PUBLISHER**
Richard Swadley

VICE PRESIDENT AND EXECUTIVE PUBLISHER
Barry Pruett

ASSOCIATE PUBLISHER
Jim Minatel

PROJECT COORDINATOR, COVER
Katie Crocker

COMPOSITOR
Craig Woods,
Happenstance Type-O-Rama

PROOFREADER
Louise Watson, Word One

INDEXER
Robert Swanson

COVER DESIGNER
Michael E. Trent

COVER IMAGE
© naphtalina/istockphoto.com

ABOUT THE AUTHORS

 GEOFFREY L. GRIFFITH is a professional software developer from Boulder, Colorado, where he owns Imagine Thought Software (www.imaginethought.com), a small software consulting firm. He holds a Bachelor of Science in computer science from the University of Colorado, where he studied software engineering. He began his Access life working on several commercial database systems, starting in Access 2.0, and eventually worked on the Microsoft Access Team for the Access 2007 release. He was co-author on both the *Access 2010 Programmer's Reference* and *Access 2007 VBA Programmer's Reference*. Today, he continues his work with Access 2010 by consulting for companies that use Access, building applications that use Access, attending Access user groups, and providing Access help to all those who would seek it. He is also the founder of and a contributor to the Microsoft Office User blog (www.msOfficeUser.com), where he provides helpful information about building Microsoft Office solutions.

 TRUITT L. BRADLY is a sixth generation Texan, raised in West Texas, and graduated from Hereford High School and West Texas A&M University with a BBA degree in accounting. His first exposure to electronic databases was when he created a membership database for a Masonic lodge where he was lodge secretary in 1987. From that initial experience using PCFile II, a flat file database, he was hooked. He transitioned to Lotus Approach in the early '90s and reluctantly was forced to use Access 2 in 1996. Truitt quickly realized that Access had extremely robust capabilities, especially when used with other Microsoft Office products, and was soon creating databases that automated existing manual procedures. He added VBA to his skill set beginning with Access 97. Truitt works as an accountant for FirstCare Health Plans in Austin, Texas. He has created numerous applications, including a program used to calculate premium rates for group health insurance. He continues to use Access and develops solutions for the Accounting and Finance departments of FirstCare using Access, Visual Basic, and SQL Server. Truitt has been awarded the Microsoft Most Valuable Professional Award beginning in January 2007.

ABOUT THE CONTRIBUTING AUTHORS

 CRYSTAL LONG lives with her two boys, dog, and cat. She does remote training and programming for people all over the world. Crystal is a Microsoft MVP (Most Valuable Professional) and has been using Access on a near-daily basis since 1994. She builds applications, teaches, produces video tutorials (www.YouTube.com/ LearnAccessByCrystal), shares tips and tools on her website (www.AccessMVP .com/strive4peace), and posts on several forums, including MS_Access_Professionals (http:// groups.yahoo.com/group/MS_Access_Professionals), MrExcel (www.MrExcel.com/forum), and UtterAccess (www.UtterAccess.com).

 CHARLIE RANLETT is a technical writer by education, automotive handyman by hobby, and automotive support specialist at Cobalt by trade. Prior to contributing to *Microsoft Access 2010 24-Hour Trainer*, he helped create full support documentation for Microsoft's Live.edu implementation at Ohio State University and created development content for Microsoft's Pivot project. In his spare time he enjoys Android development, his Miata, and his family. He is lauded as an intuitive mechanic and an expert reader of Dr. Seuss.

ABOUT THE TECHNICAL EDITOR

 KEVIN MARSHALL is an accomplished software engineer with a Bachelor of Science in computer science from Western Washington University. His keen interest in computers and computer programming dates back to his childhood Commodore 64. Highlights of Kevin's career include time spent working at Microsoft, where he worked on Microsoft Access 2007, among other products. Kevin currently resides in beautiful Kirkland, Washington, along with his partner Cedric and their nearsighted Chinese water dragon. When not in front of a computer you'll find them sailing, scuba diving, bicycling, hiking, or enjoying good food and science fiction, but not all at the same time.

ACKNOWLEDGMENTS

WE'D LIKE TO TAKE THE TIME TO THANK all of the people who helped make this book possible. We'd like to thank our contributing authors, Crystal Long and Charlie Ranlett, for all of their contributions and work toward this book; your spirits are now part of this work. We'd like to thank Kevin Marshall for all of his technical editing, comments, and suggestions on this book; your efforts and attention to quality have greatly improved our content. We'd like to thank Rosemarie Graham, Tonya Cupp, and Ed Connor, our project editors; your editing and contributions to this book have been tremendous and it would not have been possible to complete this book without you. We'd like to thank Bob Elliott, our executive editor, and all of the other people from Wiley for working so hard and long on this book to ensure that it is of the highest quality possible. We'd like to thank the people on the Access Team at Microsoft for their continuing efforts on building such a great product and always trying to answer the tough questions. And last, but most importantly, we'd like to thank all of our friends and family members for all of their love and support over the years. You all mean a great deal to us. We appreciate your love and have not forgotten your generosity!

— GEOFFREY L. GRIFFITH and TRUITT L. BRADLY

CONTENTS

INTRODUCTION   *xxxiii*

LESSON 1: INSTALLING ACCESS 2010   1

  Lesson Setup   1
  How to Get Access 2010   1
    Purchasing Directly from Microsoft   1
    System Requirements   2
    Side-By-Side Installations   2
    Default Versus Complete Installations   2
  Installing Access 2010   3
  Try It   4
    Lesson Requirements   4
    Hints   4
    Step-by-Step   4
  Summary   4

LESSON 2: GETTING STARTED IN ACCESS 2010   5

  Lesson Setup   5
  Starting Access 2010   5
    Opening a Database from within Access   6
    Opening a Database File from Windows   6
    Microsoft Access File Types   6
  Try It   7
    Lesson Requirements   7
    Step-by-Step   7
  Summary   8

LESSON 3: CREATING A NEW DATABASE APPLICATION   9

  Lesson Setup   9
  Options for Creating Databases in Access 2010   10
    Creating a Blank Database   10
    Creating a Database from Template   11
  Try It   13
    Lesson Requirements   13
    Hints   13
    Step-by-Step   13
  Summary   14

LESSON 4: ACCESS DATABASE OBJECTS   15

Lesson Setup   15
Access Database Objects   15
    Access Tables   16
    Access Queries   16
    Access Forms   18
    Access Reports   18
    Access Macros   19
    VBA Code in Access   19
Try It   20
    Lesson Requirements   20
    Step-by-Step   20
Summary   21

LESSON 5: THE ACCESS 2010 RIBBON   23

Lesson Setup   23
Ribbon Overview   24
    Ribbon Tabs   24
    Contextual Ribbon Tabs   24
    Ribbon Sections   25
    Section Expanders   25
    The Quick Access Toolbar (QAT)   25
    Custom Ribbons   25
    Keyboard Shortcuts   27
Try It   27
    Lesson Requirements   27
    Step-by-Step   27
Summary   30

LESSON 6: THE ACCESS 2010 BACKSTAGE   31

Lesson Setup   31
The Backstage View   31
Touring the Backstage Features   32
    The Basic Backstage Controls   32
    Customizing the Backstage   34
Try It   34
    Lesson Requirements   35
    Step-by-Step   35
Summary   35

LESSON 7: THE ACCESS 2010 NAVIGATION PANE   **37**

Lesson Setup   37
The Navigation Pane Overview   37
    Navigation Pane Grouping Types   38
    Expanding and Collapsing the Pane   39
    Opening Database Objects   39
    The Navigation Pane's Context Menu   40
    Database Object Properties   40
    The Navigation Options Dialog   40
Try It   42
    Lesson Requirements   42
    Step-by-Step   42
Summary   44

LESSON 8: CREATING A TABLE IN DATASHEET VIEW   **45**

Lesson Setup   45
Creating Tables in Access 2010   45
    Terms   46
    Naming Schemes   46
Creating a Table in Datasheet View   47
    The Table Tools Ribbon   47
    Adding New Fields to a Table   48
    Setting Data Types   48
Application Parts in Access 2010   49
SharePoint Linked Tables in Access 2010   50
Try It   50
    Lesson Requirements   51
    Step-by-Step   51
Summary   53

LESSON 9: CREATING A TABLE IN DESIGN VIEW   **55**

Lesson Setup   55
Creating a Table in Design View   56
    The Table Tools Design Ribbon   57
    Adding New Fields   58
Try It   60
    Lesson Requirements   61
    Step-by-Step   61
Summary   63

LESSON 10: ACCESS 2010 DATA TYPES 65

Lesson Setup 65
Access 2010 Field Data Types 65
Text Fields 66
Memo Fields 66
Number Fields 66
Date/Time Fields 67
Currency Fields 67
AutoNumber Fields 68
OLE Object Fields 68
Hyperlink Fields 68
Attachment Fields 68
Calculated Fields 68
Multivalued Fields 69
Lookup Fields 69
Try It 69
Lesson Requirements 69
Step-by-Step 69
Summary 70

LESSON 11: TABLE AND FIELD PROPERTIES 71

Lesson Setup 71
The Table Property Sheet 71
Setting Table Properties 73
Field Properties 73
Setting Field Properties 75
Try It 76
Lesson Requirements 76
Step-by-Step 76
Summary 78

LESSON 12: DATA VALIDATION AND LIMITING USER INPUT 79

Lesson Setup 79
Data Validation Field Properties 80
The Default Value Property 80
The Allow Zero Length Property 82
The Required Property 82
The Validation Rule Property 82
The Input Mask Property 83
Try It 84
Lesson Requirements 85
Step-by-Step 85
Summary 87

LESSON 13: CREATING VALUE LIST FIELDS   **89**

Lesson Setup   **89**
List Fields in Access   **89**
    Creating Value Lists   90
    Allowing List Edits   90
    Creating Lookup Fields   91
    Creating Lists from Tables or Queries   91
Try It   **92**
    Lesson Requirements   92
    Step-by-Step   92
Summary   **93**

LESSON 14: CREATING LOOKUP TABLES   **95**

Lesson Setup   **95**
Lookup Table Theory   **95**
    Creating Lookup Tables   96
    Creating Lookup Controls via the Wizard   97
    Manually Setting Lookup Options   97
Try It   **98**
    Lesson Requirements   98
    Step-by-Step   98
Summary   **99**

LESSON 15: TABLE MODIFICATIONS   **101**

Lesson Setup   **101**
Renaming a Table   **101**
Table Locking Considerations   **102**
Modifying Fields   **103**
Data Integrity Considerations   **103**
Try It   **104**
    Lesson Requirements   104
    Step-by-Step   104
Summary   **105**

LESSON 16: CREATING TABLE RELATIONSHIPS   **107**

Lesson Setup   **107**
Relational Database Theory Primer   **107**
The Access Relationship Tools   **109**
    The Edit Relationships Dialog   109
    Creating Table Relationships   110
    Setting Referential Integrity   110
    Types of Relationships   111

Setting Join Types   112
Modifying Relationships   113
The Impact of System Relationships   113
Try It   **114**
Lesson Requirements   114
Step-by-Step   114
Summary   **116**

LESSON 17: CREATING TABLE FIELD INDEXES   **117**

Lesson Setup   **117**
The Role of Field Indexes   **117**
When to Use Indexes   **118**
Creating an Index Using Access 2010   **118**
Try It   **119**
Lesson Requirements   119
Step-by-Step   119
Summary   **120**

LESSON 18: CREATING TABLES FROM EXTERNAL DATA   **121**

External Data Sources   **122**
Importing from Excel   122
Importing from XML   123
Saving Imports   124
Modifying Saved Imports   125
Reusing Imports   125
Try It   **125**
Lesson Requirements   125
Step-by-Step   125
Summary   **127**

LESSON 19: CREATING LINKED TABLES   **129**

Lesson Setup   **129**
Linked Tables in Access   **130**
Creating Linked Tables to Other Access Databases   130
Creating Linked Tables to Excel   131
Creating Linked Tables to SharePoint   131
Try It   **132**
Lesson Requirements   132
Step-by-Step   132
Summary   **133**

LESSON 20: COLLECTING DATA VIA E-MAIL — 135

Lesson Setup	**135**
Prerequisites for E-mail Data Collection	**136**
Using the Data Collection Wizard	**136**
Working with Outlook	137
Requesting Data Updates	137
InfoPath Form E-mails	137
HTML Form E-mails	137
Try It	**138**
Lesson Requirements	138
Step-by-Step	138
Summary	**140**

LESSON 21: CREATING QUERIES WITH THE WIZARD — 141

Lesson Setup	**141**
Database Query Theory	**142**
Creating a Query with the Wizard	**142**
Query Types	143
Try It	**143**
Lesson Requirements	144
Hints	144
Step-by-Step	144
Summary	**145**

LESSON 22: CREATING QUERIES IN DESIGN VIEW — 147

Creating a New Query in Design View	**147**
The Show Table Dialog	148
The Query Design Ribbon	148
Adding Fields to the Query	150
Adding Criteria to Restrict Records	151
Sorting Results to Order Records	151
Adding Totals	151
Using the SQL View	152
Try It	**152**
Lesson Requirements	152
Hints	152
Step-by-Step	152
Summary	**153**

LESSON 23: CREATING SELECT QUERIES 155

Lesson Setup 155
Creating a Select Query 156
    Creating a Query from Multiple Tables 156
    Choosing Criteria for the Query 156
    Using Functions 157
    Creating a Select Query in SQL View 158
Try It 159
    Step-by-Step 159
Summary 160

LESSON 24: DATA AGGREGATION AND GROUPING 161

Lesson Setup 161
Grouping Data in Queries 161
Aggregate Data Queries 162
Sorting Multiple Columns 163
Uses for Crosstab Queries 163
Try It 164
    Step-by-Step 164
Summary 165

LESSON 25: CREATING PARAMETER QUERIES 167

Lesson Setup 167
Parameter Queries in Access 167
Creating Parameter Queries in Design View 168
Defining Parameter Data Types 169
Creating a Parameter Query in SQL View 169
Try It 170
    Step-by-Step 170
Summary 170

LESSON 26: CREATING APPEND QUERIES 173

Lesson Setup 173
Append Queries in Access 173
    Creating an Append Query in Design Mode 174
    Append Query Settings 175
    Creating an Append Query in SQL View 175
    Ramifications of Append Queries 175
Try It 176
    Step-by-Step 176
Summary 177

LESSON 27: CREATING UPDATE QUERIES   179

Lesson Setup	179
Update Queries in Access	179
Creating an Update Query in Design View	180
Update Query Settings	180
Creating an Update Query in SQL View	181
Ramifications of Update Queries	181
Try It	182
Step-by-Step	182
Summary	183

LESSON 28: CREATING DELETE QUERIES   185

Lesson Setup	185
Delete Queries in Access	185
Considerations for Delete Queries	186
Creating a Delete Query in Design Mode	187
Creating a Delete Query in SQL View	187
Ramifications of Delete Queries	188
Try It	188
Lesson Requirements	188
Step-by-Step	188
Summary	190

LESSON 29: CREATING MAKE TABLE QUERIES   191

Lesson Setup	191
Make Table Queries in Access	191
Creating a Make Table Query in Design Mode	192
Make Table Query Settings	192
Creating a Make Table Query in SQL View	192
Ramifications of Make Table Queries	193
Try It	193
Step-by-Step	193
Summary	195

LESSON 30: CREATING CROSSTAB QUERIES   197

Lesson Setup	197
Crosstab Queries in Access	197
The Crosstab Query Wizard	198
Creating a Crosstab Query in Design Mode	198
Crosstab Query Settings	199
Creating a Crosstab Query in SQL View	199

Try It	**200**
Step-by-Step	200
Summary	**203**

LESSON 31: CREATING FORMS IN LAYOUT VIEW — 205

Lesson Setup	**205**
Quick Forms in Access 2010	**206**
Switching to Layout View	**206**
The Form Layout Tools RibbonS	**207**
The Field List Pane	**208**
The Property Sheet Pane	**208**
The Record Source Property	**209**
Access Form Types	**209**
Try It	**210**
Lesson Requirements	210
Step-by-Step	210
Summary	**213**

LESSON 32: CREATING FORMS IN DESIGN VIEW — 215

Lesson Setup	**215**
Bound versus Unbound	**215**
Creating a Form in Design View	**216**
Design View Mode	**217**
The Form Design Ribbon	**217**
The Field List Pane	**218**
The Property Sheet Pane	**219**
The Navigation Pane	**219**
Try It	**219**
Lesson Requirements	220
Step-by-Step	220
Summary	**225**

LESSON 33: ACCESS FORM PROPERTIES — 227

Lesson Setup	**227**
The Property Sheet	**227**
The Property Sheet Tabs	**228**
Access Form Properties	**228**
Setting Form Properties	**229**
Try It	**229**
Lesson Requirements	229
Hints	229
Step-by-Step	230
Summary	**232**

LESSON 34: ACCESS 2010 FORM CONTROLS 233

Lesson Setup 233
The Built-in Access Controls 233
The Design Ribbon for Forms 235
Adding Controls to Forms 235
  Adding Controls from the Ribbon 235
  Adding Controls from the Navigation Pane 236
  Adding Controls from the Field List Pane 236
Setting Control Properties 236
  Using the Property Sheet 236
  Using the Access Designers 236
  Using VBA Code 237
  Default Properties for Controls 237
  Values for Control Properties 237
  Help with Controls and Control Properties 237
Try It 238
  Lesson Requirements 238
  Hints 238
  Step-by-Step 239
Summary 241

LESSON 35: WORKING WITH SUBFORMS AND SUBREPORTS 243

Lesson Setup 243
Subforms/Subreports in Access 243
  The Source Object Property 244
  Adding Bound Subforms 244
  Adding Unbound Subforms 244
Designing Subforms and Subreports 245
  Creating the Underlying Object 245
  Sizing the Subform/Subreport Control 245
  The Anchor Properties 245
  Modifying Properties of the Control 246
Try It 246
  Lesson Requirements 246
  Hints 246
  Step-by-Step 247
Summary 249

LESSON 36: EMBEDDED MACROS IN FORMS 251

Lesson Setup 251
Macros in Access 251
  Named Macros 251
  Embedded Macros 252

The Access 2010 Macro Designer 252
New Macro Features in Access 2010 253
Adding Macros to Forms and Controls 253
The Macro-to-VBA Code Converter 253
Enabling Macros in Access **254**
Safe Macros 254
Unsafe Macros 254
Try It **255**
Lesson Requirements 255
Hints 255
Step-by-Step 255
Summary **258**

LESSON 37: ADDING CODE TO FORMS **259**

Lesson Setup **259**
VBA Code in Access 2010 **260**
Code Modules 260
Embedded Code in Forms 260
The HasModule Property 260
Embedding Code in a Form **261**
Adding Code from the Property Sheet 261
The Visual Basic Editor 261
Writing VBA Code **262**
Referencing Objects Using VBA 263
Enabling Code in Access **264**
Try It **264**
Lesson Requirements 264
Hints 264
Step-by-Step 264
Summary **267**

LESSON 38: ACCESS 2010 FORM TYPES **269**

Lesson Setup **269**
Single Item Forms **269**
Single Item Form Property Settings 269
Creating a Single Item Form 270
Multiple Item Forms **270**
Multiple Item Form Property Settings 270
Creating a Multiple Item Form 270
Datasheet Forms **270**
Datasheet Form Property Settings 271
Creating a Datasheet Form 271
Split Forms **271**
Split Form Property Settings 271
Creating a Split Form 272

Pop-up Forms 272
Pop-up Form Property Settings 272
Creating a Pop-up Form 272
Modal Forms 272
Modal Form Property Settings 272
Creating a Modal Form 273
PivotChart and PivotTable Forms 273
PivotChart Form Property Settings 273
Creating a PivotChart Form 273
Try It 273
Lesson Requirements 274
Hints 274
Step-by-Step 274
Summary 277

LESSON 39: CREATING PIVOTCHARTS 279

Lesson Setup 279
Creating PivotCharts 279
Designing PivotCharts 280
The PivotChart Tools Ribbon 280
Adding Fields to a PivotChart 280
Setting PivotChart Properties 281
Displaying PivotCharts 281
PivotChart Form Properties 281
General Chart Settings 282
Try It 282
Lesson Requirements 282
Hints 282
Step-by-Step 283
Summary 285

LESSON 40: ACCESS APPLICATION NAVIGATION 287

Lesson Setup 287
Application Navigation Considerations 287
Navigation Pane Considerations 287
Ribbon Considerations 288
Access Runtime Applications 288
Creating Forms to Navigate 288
Using Buttons to Navigate 289
Using ComboBox Controls to Navigate 289
Using the Navigation Buttons 289
Setting a Startup Form 289
Try It 289
Lesson Requirements 290
Step-by-Step 290
Summary 292

LESSON 41: CREATING REPORTS IN LAYOUT VIEW 293

Lesson Setup 293
Quick Reports in Access 2010 293
Switching to Layout View 294
The Report Layout Ribbon 294
The Field List Pane 296
The Property Sheet Pane 296
Setting Report Design Properties 297
Try It 297
Lesson Requirements 297
Step-by-Step 297
Summary 299

LESSON 42: CREATING REPORTS IN DESIGN VIEW 301

Lesson Setup 301
Creating a New Report in Design 301
Bound versus Unbound Reports 302
The Report Design Ribbon 303
The Field List 304
The Property Sheet 305
The Group, Sort, and Total Pane 305
The Navigation Pane 305
Try It 306
Lesson Requirements 306
Step-by-Step 306
Summary 308

LESSON 43: ACCESS REPORT PROPERTIES 309

Lesson Setup 309
The Property Sheet Pane 309
Opening the Property Sheet 310
Docking/Undocking the Property Sheet 310
Resizing the Property Sheet 311
Using the Zoom Dialog 312
The Property Sheet Tabs 312
Access Report Properties 313
Setting Report Properties 313
Getting Information about Properties 314
Try It 314
Lesson Requirements 314
Hints 314
Step-by-Step 315
Summary 316

LESSON 44: REPORT SORTING, GROUPING, AND TOTALS   319

Lesson Setup   319
Showing Data in Access Reports   319
The Group, Sort and Total Pane   320
     Opening the Group, Sort and Total Pane   321
     Sorting Data in Reports   321
     Grouping Data in Reports   321
     Adding Totals to Reports   322
     Other Options on the Pane   323
Try It   323
     Lesson Requirements   323
     Step-by-Step   323
Summary   326

LESSON 45: USING MACROS IN REPORTS   327

Lesson Setup   327
Macros in Access   327
     Named Macros   328
     Embedded Macros   328
     The Access 2010 Macro Designer   328
     New Macro Features in Access 2010   329
     Adding Macros to Reports and Controls   329
Enabling Macros in Access   330
     Safe Macros   330
     Unsafe Macros   330
Try It   331
     Lesson Requirements   331
     Step-by-Step   331
Summary   333

LESSON 46: CREATING MACROS IN ACCESS 2010   335

Lesson Setup   335
The Theory of Macros   335
     Enabling Macros   336
     Creating a New Macro   336
The Access 2010 Macro Designer   336
     The Macro Tools Ribbon   336
     The Actions Catalog Pane   336
Executing Macros   336
Try It   337
     Lesson Requirements   337
     Step-by-Step   337
Summary   338

LESSON 47: MACRO TYPES AND SECURITY — 341

Lesson Setup	341
Macro Types	341
Macro Database Objects	341
Embedded Macros	342
Data Macros	342
Macro Security	342
Safe Macros	342
Unsafe Macros	343
Enabling Macros	343
Trusted Locations	344
Access Runtime Security	344
Try It	344
Lesson Requirements	344
Hints	344
Step-by-Step	345
Summary	346

LESSON 48: MACRO PARTS — 347

Lesson Setup	347
Macro Changes in Access 2010	347
Macro Names	348
Macro Actions	348
Macro Parameters	348
Macro Conditions	350
Macro Groups	350
Macro XML	350
Macro Comments	351
Macro Tempvars	351
Try It	352
Lesson Requirements	352
Hints	352
Step-by-Step	352
Summary	354

LESSON 49: BUILDING MACROS — 355

Lesson Setup	355
Creating Multi-Step Macros	355
Handling Errors in Macros	356
The MacroError Object	356
The OnError Action	357
The SingleStep Action	357
The ClearMacroError Action	357

Logic Branching in Macros   357
Looping in Macros   358
Debugging Macros   358
Try It   359
    Lesson Requirements   359
    Hints   359
    Step-by-Step   359
Summary   362

LESSON 50: DATA MACROS IN ACCESS 2010   363

Lesson Setup   363
The Theory of Data Macros   363
Events for Data Macros   364
Creating Data Macros   364
Running Data Macros   364
Try It   365
    Lesson Requirements   365
    Step-by-Step   365
Summary   366

LESSON 51: THE VISUAL BASIC EDITOR   367

Lesson Setup   368
Starting VBE   368
    The Code Window   368
    The Immediate Window   368
    The Object Browser   370
    The Project Explorer   371
    The References Dialog   371
Debugging Code   372
    Setting Breakpoints   372
    Debugging Step by Step   372
Try It   374
    Lesson Requirements   374
    Hints   375
    Step-by-Step   375
Summary   377

LESSON 52: INTRODUCTION TO VBA   379

Lesson Setup   379
Writing VBA Code   379
    Creating Modules   380
    Creating Subroutines   380
    Creating Functions   381

CONTENTS

VBA Keywords and Reserved Words 381
Adding Comments to Code 381
VBA Data Types 382
Variables in VBA 383
VBA Operators 384
Branching in VBA 385
Loops in VBA 388
Option Statements 390
Calling Subroutines 391
Calling Functions 392
Help with VBA Code 393
Try It **394**
Lesson Requirements 394
Step-by-Step 394
Summary **396**

LESSON 53: USING OPERATORS IN VBA **397**

Lesson Setup **397**
VBA Operators **397**
Assignment Operators 397
Comparison Operators 399
Arithmetic Operators 400
Bitwise Operators 401
Logical Operators 402
String Operators 403
Other Operators 405
Try It **405**
Lesson Requirements 405
Step-by-Step 406
Summary **407**

LESSON 54: USING VARIABLES IN VBA **409**

Lesson Setup **409**
Variables in VBA **409**
Global Variables 410
Local Variables 410
Accessing Variables 411
Creating New Instances for Complex Types 411
Literal Values 412
Constants 412
Enumerations 413

VBA Arrays   414
    Try It   417
  Lesson Requirements   417
  Step-by-Step   417
Summary   **420**

LESSON 55: CREATING CLASS MODULES   421

Lesson Setup   **421**
Creating a New Class Module   **421**
  Creating Properties   422
  Creating Methods   423
  Creating Events   423
Using a Class Module   **425**
  Creating a New Instance   425
  Accessing Properties   426
  Calling Methods   426
  Implementing Event Methods   427
Try It   **427**
  Lesson Requirements   428
  Step-by-Step   428
Summary   **431**

LESSON 56: THE ACCESS OBJECT MODEL   433

Lesson Setup   **433**
The Access Application Object   **433**
  The CurrentDb Function   434
  The CurrentProject Object   435
  The DoCmd Object   435
  The RunCommand Method   436
Try It   **436**
  Lesson Requirements   436
  Step-by-Step   436
Summary   **438**

LESSON 57: WORKING WITH DAO   439

Lesson Setup   **439**
The DAO Object Model   **439**
  Referencing DAO   440
  The DAO Database Object   441
  Using DAO to Work with Data   441
  More Information about DAO   450

Try It	**450**
Lesson Requirements	450
Step-by-Step	450
Summary	**456**

LESSON 58: ACCESS APPLICATION SETTINGS — **457**

Lesson Setup	**457**
The Access Options Dialog	**457**
Access Program Settings	458
Access Database Settings	459
Try It	**461**
Lesson Requirements	461
Step-by-Step	461
Summary	**462**

LESSON 59: CUSTOMIZING THE NAVIGATION PANE — **463**

Lesson Setup	**463**
The Navigation Options Dialog	**463**
The Navigation Pane Settings	464
Creating a Custom Category	464
Creating Custom Groups	465
Adding Objects to Custom Groups	465
Creating Custom Object Names	466
Try It	**466**
Lesson Requirements	466
Step-by-Step	466
Summary	**468**

LESSON 60: CUSTOMIZING THE RIBBON — **469**

Lesson Setup	**469**
The Customize Ribbon Options	**469**
Opening the Customize Ribbon Dialog	470
The Customize Ribbon Settings	471
Exporting the Current Ribbon Settings	471
Resetting the Ribbon	472
Importing Ribbon XML for a Database	473
Custom Ribbon Commands	**473**
Adding Controls to the Ribbon XML	473
Setting a Custom Ribbon for a Database	475
Try It	**476**
Lesson Requirements	476
Step-by-Step	476
Summary	**480**

LESSON 61: CUSTOMIZING THE BACKSTAGE   **481**

Lesson Setup   **481**
The Access 2010 Backstage   **481**
     The USysRibbons Table   482
     The <backstage> Tag   482
     Applying the Custom Backstage   484
     More Resources   485
Try It   **485**
     Lesson Requirements   485
     Step-by-Step   485
Summary   **487**

LESSON 62: THE ACCESS RUNTIME   **489**

Lesson Setup   **489**
The Access Runtime Overview   **489**
     Access 2010 versus the Access Runtime   490
     Considerations when Using the Runtime   490
     Benefits to Using the Access Runtime   491
Building Runtime Applications   **491**
     Getting the Access Runtime   491
     Enabling the Access Runtime   492
     Testing with the Access Runtime   494
Deploying Runtime Applications   **494**
Try It   **495**
     Lesson Requirements   495
     Step-by-Step   495
Summary   **497**

APPENDIX: WHAT'S ON THE DVD?   **499**

System Requirements   **499**
Using the DVD   **500**
What's on the DVD?   **500**
Troubleshooting   **501**
Customer Care   **501**

INDEX   *503*

INTRODUCTION

WELCOME TO THE *Microsoft Access 2010 24-Hour Trainer* book, and thank you for taking the time to read this material. Microsoft Access 2010 is a very exciting release with a ton of new features that both complement the existing features and provide completely new functionality. And, although Access 2010 has many new features, most of the preexisting features are still there. If you've used Access before, you should be right at home in this latest version. Truly, Microsoft Access 2010 is the most impressive and feature-rich release in Access history.

As such, we have worked tirelessly to try to cover all of the major features to help you dig deeper into the various components in which you are interested. We have tried our best to describe what they do within Access and explain how you can use them. It is our sincerest hope that after reading this book you will have a general understanding of what each part of the Access 2010 product does, how to use each within an Access database application, and how to create a fully functioning Access database application from scratch.

WHO THIS BOOK IS FOR

This book is designed to be a step-by-step guide to learning how to use each of the major Microsoft Access 2010 components. The content in this book is geared toward beginner- to intermediate-level users who want to learn how to develop database applications using Microsoft Access 2010, but do not know (or know very little) about Access 2010. Whether you have no experience whatsoever with Access 2010, or if you have general Access understanding and want to learn some of the basic features, this book provides step-by-step lessons.

HOW TO USE THIS BOOK

It is important to realize, before reading this book, that it has a very specific design and layout. The text appears with different types of formatting. Each lesson ends with a short video on the DVD so you can review the topics and step-by-step example. And each lesson in the book is designed to be a self-contained, standalone unit and can be completed separately, and in any order (for the most part), from other lessons. The following sections discuss the design of each of these parts of the *Microsoft Access 24-Hour Trainer* book in better detail.

The Design of the Chapters

Each of the lessons within this book are designed to teach you about Access 2010 in a very specific manner. Each chapter consists of three parts: The feature description, the step-by-step example, and the example video file. The feature description attempts to provide an overview of how the feature works, as well as how and why it can be used. The step-by-step example provides a detailed walkthrough of a specific example — how to implement and use the feature within a real database application. The video file for the lesson is included on the DVD. The video shows and narrates the step-by-step example onscreen. Sample files appear on the book's DVD and website.

The Conventions within the Book

Microsoft Access 24-Hour Trainer uses some conventions. Specifically, each of the lessons breaks down into a series of sections, many of which are common to all chapters, such as "Step-by-Step." Several text formatting techniques help you compartmentalize each of the concepts discussed. The following is a list of text formatting conventions used within the book:

➤ We italicize some key terms within the text like this: *key term*.

➤ We use a special font for code and file names that are embedded within a paragraph as `Code Term`.

➤ We use a special font for URLs that are embedded within a paragraph as `www.wrox.com`.

➤ We bold user input text (anything you'll type) within the example steps as **User Input**.

➤ We show keystroke combinations like this: Ctrl+C.

All side notes that are included with a topic are broken out into a special box that looks like this.

All warnings that are included with a topic are broken out into a special box that looks like this.

All direct reference to the DVD materials that are included with a topic are broken out into a special box that looks like this.

➤ All code samples that are not embedded within a paragraph are broken out into a separate section that looks like this:

```
' This is an example of the code snippet formatting
' It usually consists of multiple lines of code
```

➤ All tables within this book have the following formatting:

TABLE 1: Example Table

COLUMN 1	COLUMN 2
Record 1 column 1	Record 1 column 2
Record 2 column 1	Record 2 column 2

It is our sincerest hope that these bits of text formatting really help accentuate the key points of the lesson, as well as help break up each of the concepts into their separate components. We believe that by using these formatting techniques, the book is much easier to read overall.

The Video DVD

One of the most powerful *Microsoft Access 24-Hour Trainer* resources is the DVD included with the book. This DVD is physically placed between the back cover and the last page of the book in the plastic sleeve. This DVD provides video examples and sample files for each lesson in the book; the DVD is really one third of the book itself. As mentioned earlier, each lesson's video is a screen capture of the step-by-step example included in the second part of each lesson, along with narration explaining what is happening onscreen. We highly recommend reviewing the lesson's video after you read each lesson. The video may provide examples and comments that are not included in the written materials.

THE BOOK'S WEBSITE

Wrox provides additional support for *Microsoft Access 24-Hour Trainer* from their website. The Wrox website provides

➤ A detailed overview of the book

➤ The ability to purchase the book online

➤ All downloads and code associated with the book

➤ The Wrox P2P forums for getting help from the authors and other peers

➤ All error and errata information about the book

➤ Links to other Wrox books and resources

All of these resources contain valuable information about the *Microsoft Access 24-Hour Trainer* book or related information. We highly recommend exploring each of these resources.

Example Files and Sample Code

All of the examples files and sample code throughout this book are available for download from the book's DVD and the Wrox website, at www.wrox.com. Once you visit the Wrox website, you can search for this book by title and click the Download Code link.

 Because several books available on the Wrox website have titles similar to this book, you may find it easiest to search by ISBN: 978-0-470-59167-3.

When you find the download page for the example files and sample code, download the complete code package as a single ZIP file. Once you have downloaded the ZIP file, you need to unzip it to use the files.

 Although Access database files can be executed from within a ZIP archive, this application will be in read-only mode and may not have all functionality available. We always recommend unzipping any Access database applications before executing them to ensure they run correctly.

In addition to finding the download link for the example files and sample code on this book's home page, you can go to the main Wrox code download page at www.wrox.com/dynamic/books/download.aspx, where you can obtain files not only for this book, but all other code samples for all other Wrox books.

P2P.WROX.COM

We urge you to participate in the author and peer discussions in the P2P forums provided by Wrox at http://p2p.wrox.com. The Wrox P2P forums are a Web-based system that provides you, the reader, with the ability to communicate with the authors and other readers about related topics. Although the P2P forum allows anyone to read posts, you must register to be able to post messages. The forums also offer e-mail messages to be automatically sent when new posts have been added to the designated topics. These forums are extremely useful for interacting with authors, editors, industry experts, and, most importantly, other readers of the book. Best of all, the Wrox P2P forums are completely free and provide you with additional services and support when using this book.

To review and sign up for the Wrox P2P forums, go to http://p2p.wrox.com. Simply search for the *Microsoft Access 24-Hour Trainer* forum. Then, to join the Wrox P2P forums, complete the following steps:

1. Open your favorite browser and go to **http://p2p.wrox.com**.

2. At the Wrox P2P home page, click the Register Now link on the top right of the page.

3. Read the terms of use agreement and check the box to signify that you agree; then click the Register button.

4. Create a user name and provide your e-mail address and password. Optionally, set the referrer, time zone, and e-mail options.

5. Click the Complete Registration button. If everything is correct, you will be registered for the site.

6. Once you have completed initial registration, click the link in your confirmation e-mail.

After clicking the link, you will be taken to the Wrox P2P site and registration is confirmed. You can begin responding to posts and creating new ones as desired. If you would like to receive an e-mail each time a post is created for a particular discussion, complete the following steps:

1. From the Wrox P2P home page, find the discussion you wish to subscribe to. Click its link.

2. From the topics home page, click the Forum Tools menu at the top of the form. Choose the Subscribe to This Forum option.

3. You are taken to another page. Select the type of notification that you would like to receive.

4. Click the Add Subscription button.

You are returned to the topic's home page and are now subscribed. And if you need to unsubscribe from the topic at any time, simply repeat this process, but instead choose the Unsubscribe from This Forum option on the Forum Tools menu.

For more information about the Wrox P2P forum, as well as answers too many common questions about the P2P service and Wrox books, be sure to read the P2P FAQs page.

Errata and Errors within the Book

We make every effort to ensure that there are no errors in the text or code within this book. However, no one is perfect, and mistakes do occur. If you find an error in one of our books, such as a spelling mistake or faulty piece of code, we would be very grateful if you'd tell us about it. By sending in errata, you may spare another reader hours of frustration; at the same time, you are helping us provide even higher-quality information.

To find the errata page for this book, go to **www.wrox.com** and type the title into the Search box (or use one of the title lists). On the book details page, click the Book Errata link. On this page, you can view all errata that have been submitted for this book and posted by Wrox editors. A complete book list, including links to each book's errata, is available at `www.wrox.com/misc-pages/booklist.shtml`.

If you don't spot "your" error on the Book Errata page, go to `www.wrox.com/contact/techsupport.shtml` and complete the form to send us the error you have found. We'll check the information and, if appropriate, post a message to the Book Errata page and fix the problem in subsequent editions.

1

Installing Access 2010

Before you can begin using Access 2010, you must acquire a copy of the program and then install it on a machine. If you already have a copy of Access installed on your machine, you can easily skip this lesson and move on to the next. However, if you have never purchased or installed Access 2010 (or earlier versions), continue on with this lesson to find out more about getting and installing the most widely used database program in the world — Microsoft Access!

LESSON SETUP

This lesson explains some of the options available for purchasing a copy of Access 2010 and provides a step-by-step guide to installing Access 2010 as a part of Microsoft Office 2010. There is no previous experience or knowledge of Access required to complete this lesson.

HOW TO GET ACCESS 2010

You can purchase Microsoft Access 2010 as a standalone product or as part of Microsoft Office 2010 Professional (or higher versions of Office). Office 2010 Professional edition includes Access, Excel, PowerPoint, Publisher, Outlook, and Word. Office 2010 Professional Plus also includes Communicator and InfoPath. Office 2010 Enterprise adds Grove and OneNote. The Office 2010 Ultimate edition adds Outlook Business Contact Manager.

Purchasing Directly from Microsoft

Microsoft sells Access 2010 along with all of the Office editions at the Microsoft website (http://office.microsoft.com), go there to compare the features of each edition. Microsoft offers three basic plans to purchase retail software online:

➤ Purchase the product online, have the DVD shipped to your location, and use the product key included in the materials shipped to you.

➤ Purchase the product online, download the installation files to your computer, and use the product key that is provided at purchase to activate the software.

➤ Download and install a trial version that you can use for 60 days before purchasing.

Microsoft Office is also available in DVD versions at retail stores that sell computer software and at online software retailers. Check multiple outlets for the best price, but make sure you use a legitimate dealer. If a deal sounds too good to be true, it probably is; you don't want to get stuck with an illegal copy of Office 2010 for which you paid a substantial amount of money.

System Requirements

Before buying a copy of Access or Office, check the minimum system requirements for the version you are purchasing; that way you can ensure the software is compatible with your computer. The Office products are available in 32-bit and 64-bit versions. Your computer's CPU architecture *and* Windows operating system version will determine if you can use the 64-bit version of Access (or Office). The 64-bit version of Access requires that the system have a 64-bit processor and be running a 64-bit version of Windows.

Side-by-Side Installations

Note that Access 2010 can be installed side-by-side with older versions of Access. When installing Access with older versions, it is always recommended that you install older versions first and newer versions last. However, if you use an older version of Access and then go back to Access 2010 while both versions are installed side-by-side, it will retrigger a (somewhat) short installation process every time. This is because the last installed version of Access is the system default version, and that setting is updated if a different version of Access is run! Though this fact is important to consider because installation can be painfully time-consuming, it probably won't make much of a difference for most Access users.

Default versus Custom Installations

The Access (or Office) installation program provides a choice of installation options:

➤ Default installation installs features used by the majority of users and is sufficient for most installations. For both Office 2010 and Access 2010 installation programs, the default options install everything you need to start using Access.

➤ Custom installation allows you to select and install specific features (and programs, if installing Office). It also allows you to specify a location other than the default. Custom user information can also be entered.

Usually the default installation is all you need, and novice computer users may not want to attempt a custom installation. The default installation for both Office and Access is sufficient to complete the lessons in this book.

INSTALLING ACCESS 2010

Once you have acquired the Access 2010 software, installing it is easy. To start the installation process for Access (or Office), depending on the version that you are using, you need to execute the `setup.exe` file for Access or Office, respectively. If you have the DVD, simply inserting the disk into your computer should automatically start the installation process. If it does not, follow these steps:

1. Go to My Computer.

2. Right-click the DVD drive with the disk.

3. Choose the Explore option.

From the Explorer window, you can also navigate and manually run the `setup.exe` program provided on the root of the installation disk. Another option is right-clicking the DVD and selecting AutoPlay from the context menu.

If you downloaded the software, you may need to create an install DVD from the downloaded `.iso` file. Most CD/DVD writer software will create a disk to install the software from the `.iso` file. Also, several free programs are available for simply extracting `.iso` files to disk. Whichever method you choose, simply run the `setup.exe` file to begin the installation of Access (or Office):

1. After you begin, the installation program will extract the needed files from the installation disk.

2. You are prompted to enter the product key.

3. Enter the key. The installation program will verify the key before you can proceed. The key is a 25-digit key that consists of both numbers and letters.

4. There is a check box at the bottom of the dialog that allows Office 2010 to attempt to automatically activate the product online. Uncheck the box if you do *not* want to activate the product at this time.

5. Read the license agreement. If you accept the terms, check the box at the bottom of the pop-up signifying that you agree to the Microsoft software license terms. Acceptance of the terms is required before the installation can be completed.

6. Click Install Now (or click Customize to create a custom installation). Choosing the custom installation allows you to select products and file locations and to specify the user information.

7. After clicking Install Now, a progress bar appears on the Installation Progress dialog. Assuming no errors occur, installation will complete and Access will be ready to use.

Four types of component installation options exist: Run from My Computer, Run All from My Computer, Install on First Use, and Not Available. When either the Run or Run All option is selected for a feature, the installation program installs that feature completely to the machine. The Install on First Use option installs the feature the first time it is actually used within the program. The Not Available option specifies not installing the feature at all.

TRY IT

In this lesson you install the Office 2010 Professional Plus edition. Other editions of Office 2010 have similar installation processes.

Lesson Requirements

Verify that the computer on which you are attempting to install the Office 2010 products meets or exceeds the minimum technical requirements; otherwise the installation will fail. You also need the DVD included in the software package, a downloaded installation file that can be executed from a drive, or a DVD created after downloading the product files from Microsoft or a retailer.

Hints

Make sure you have the product key available to enter when prompted. Failure to provide the key results in failed installation.

Step-by-Step

1. Insert the program DVD and run the setup program.

2. Enter the 25-digit product key. The installation program will verify it is a valid key. If the verification fails, check the key and make corrections as necessary.

3. Read the software license terms. If you accept the terms, check the box at the bottom of the dialog.

4. Choose the desired installation options by accepting the defaults or selecting only the applications you want installed, accept the default or set a custom file location, and accept the defaults or enter user information.

5. Click the Install Now button to start the installation.

6. Wait for the installation to complete. Then remove the DVD and store it in the original packing with the product key in case you ever need to reinstall or repair corrupt program files.

SUMMARY

Installing Access 2010 or Office 2010 Professional on a computer that meets or exceeds the minimum technical requirements is usually very straightforward and easy. The simple installation discussed in this lesson is normally sufficient for most users. Custom installations provide more flexibility and allow you to select the options you wish to install. No matter which option you choose, Access 2010 is easy to set up and get going on your Windows machine!

 Please select Lesson 1 on the DVD to view the video that accompanies this lesson.

2

Getting Started in Access 2010

In this lesson, you learn how to start Access 2010 and open an existing Access database. In Access, as in other Windows programs, a user can open a program or a file in multiple ways: the Start menu, a desktop shortcut, and an icon on the Quick Launch Toolbar are all common methods. Another method of opening the Access program is double-clicking an Access database file. Windows also allows you to create a shortcut for a specific database and place it on the desktop or on the Quick Launch Toolbar. And finally, using Windows Explorer to browse to a database file and open it is yet another way to open a database. All of these options for creating and opening a database are easy to accomplish and are discussed in this lesson.

LESSON SETUP

In this lesson, you learn how to open an Access database using the different options available with Windows. No pre-existing knowledge of Access is required to complete this lesson.

STARTING ACCESS 2010

The Access 2010 program can be opened from the Windows Start menu. The Start menu is usually located in the bottom-left corner of the computer screen. In Windows 7 and Windows Vista the Windows Start button is the round button with the Windows logo. In earlier versions of Windows, it is a rectangular button labeled Start.

During installation, an Access 2010 shortcut was installed under Microsoft Office folder on the Start menu. Start Access by clicking the Start button on the Windows task bar or pressing the Windows key to open the Start menu. Click All Programs, ignoring the Microsoft Access 2010 entry at the top of the Start menu for now. Clicking Microsoft Office will drill down to show all of the installed Office products, including Access 2010. Clicking the Access 2010 shortcut starts the program without any database open and the Access 2010 Backstage is shown.

Opening a Database from within Access

Figure 2-1 shows the Access 2010 Backstage, which is found under the File tab on the Ribbon. Unless you have already opened a database using Access 2010, the Recent option will be empty. Normally it lists recently opened database files.

To open the database file, click the Open button in the Access 2010 Backstage. This invokes the Open dialog to allow you to browse to a database file. Once a database file has been selected, click the Open button.

Opening a Database File from Windows

To open an Access database from Windows, use Windows Explorer and browse to the file you want to open. You can double-click the file, or right-click the file and select Open from the context menu. The selected file will open in Access.

If you plan on using the file on a regular basis, you can create a shortcut and place it on your desktop or other easily accessible location. To create a shortcut on the Windows Desktop, follow these steps:

1. Browse to the database file using Windows Explorer.

2. Right-click the file and choose Send To Desktop (Create Shortcut).

FIGURE 2-1

To place the shortcut icon on the Quick Launch Toolbar or the taskbar (beginning with Windows 7), drag the icon onto the toolbar.

Microsoft Access File Types

By default, Microsoft Access 2010 uses the new file formats that were introduced in Access 2007. For backward compatibility, Access 2010 can open database files that were created in all previous versions of Access. However, if the database version is the 97 file format or older, then Access will prompt you to convert the file to a newer format; otherwise, the database file opens in read-only mode. Access 2010 does support creating and manipulating the older 2000, 2002, and 2003 MDB file formats, as well as the current ACCDB file format. The following is a list and short description of each of the file types that Access 2010 supports:

➤ **ACCDB** — This default database file format was introduced in Access 2007 and uses the ACE database engine instead of the JET engine.

➤ **ACCDE** — The Access Compiled Database file format is the new version of the old MDE file type. In an ACCDE file, the ability to create or modify forms or reports is removed, the VBA code is compiled, the original source code is removed from the file, thus creating and editing VBA code are disabled.

➤ **ACCDT** — This is the Access Database Template file type.

➤ **ACCDR** — This file type forces the database to open in runtime mode.

➤ **MDB** — This is the original Access database file extension and was used for databases created with versions prior to Access 2007.

➤ **MDE** — This extension was used by versions of Access prior to Access 2007 for an Access Compiled Database. Just as with the ACCDE file type, it provides full database application functionality, but with limited design capabilities.

➤ **ADP** — The Access Data Project file type was introduced in Access 2000 and utilizes SQL Server tables and other objects. ADP projects have no provision for local tables. Access 2010 continues to provide full support for the ADP file type.

➤ **ACCDA** and **MDA** — These file extensions are used in an Access database as an add-in component. ACCDA is used with the ACCDB (Access 2007 Database) file format only. MDA was the extension (and file format) used by versions of Access prior to Access 2007 originally for MDB files, but still works with the ACCDB file format as well.

TRY IT

In this lesson you create a new database from a template, open an existing database from within Access 2010, and open an Access 2010 database by using Windows Explorer. You also create a shortcut from Windows Explorer.

Lesson Requirements

You should have Access 2010 installed on your machine to complete this lesson. Otherwise, there are no other requirements for completing this lesson.

Step-by-Step

1. Click the Windows Start Button on the Windows Start menu. Click the All Programs option to show a list of the programs installed on the computer.

2. Click the Microsoft Office 2010 folder to expand and show the options it contains.

3. Click the Microsoft Access 2010 icon. The Access 2010 program will open.

4. When Access opens without a database file, you will automatically see the Backstage View. Click the New option on the left side of the Access Window. The options for creating a new database will be shown.

5. Click the Blank database option in the middle pane.

6. On the right pane of the Backstage, press the folder button found to the right of the File Name text box. The File New Database dialog will open.

7. In the File New Database dialog, click the Desktop option on the right side to select your desktop folder.

8. In the File Name text box of the File New Database dialog, type **Lesson02.accdb**. Then click the OK button to close the dialog and go back to the Access window.

9. Click the Create Button on the right pane of the Backstage to create the new database file.

Congratulations. You have created a brand new Access database file on your desktop. Close Access by clicking the X button in the top-right corner and you will be taken back to your Windows desktop. You should see the new database file that you've just created. Next, try a few different methods for opening this file by completing the following steps:

10. Start Access from the Windows start menu. The Access 2010 Backstage View will open.

11. On the left side of the Backstage, click the Open button. The Open dialog appears.

12. Browse to the desktop, which is where Lesson02.accdb was saved, by clicking the Desktop option on the left side of the dialog. The right side of the dialog will list files stored on the Windows Desktop that Access can open.

13. Click the Lesson02.accd database file shown in the list on the right side of the dialog. Then click the Open button.

Congratulations. You have opened a database using Access 2010 to browse to the file. Close the Access 2010 program window by clicking the X button in the top-right corner; you are taken back to the Windows Desktop. Next, try opening an existing database from Windows Explorer.

14. On the Windows Desktop, double-click the Lesson02.accdb file (or right-click it and select Open). Access 2010 will start and the database will be open in it.

15. Click the File button and then click Exit. This closes the Access program window.

16. You will be returned to the Windows desktop. Find the Lesson02.accdb file and right-click it to open the Windows context menu.

17. Select Send To and click Desktop (Create Shortcut). This will create a new icon, which is a shortcut for opening the database file, on the Windows desktop.

18. Find the shortcut on the Windows desktop and double-click it. Access should open the file.

Congratulations. You have successfully opened a database by double-clicking a file that is registered as an Access database file in Windows Explorer.

SUMMARY

Within the Windows environment, opening and closing programs works much the same way regardless of which program is being used. Navigation in Access is not much different than it is in any other Windows program you have used. As you've seen in this lesson, opening and closing the Access 2010 program, and the database files it supports, is extremely easy.

 Please select Lesson 2 on the DVD to view the video that accompanies this lesson.

3

Creating a New Database Application

This lesson discusses the options available for creating a new database using Access 2010. It discusses the different database file types available, and when you should use each. Also, you learn how to create a blank database and how to create a working application from a database template.

Microsoft Access has included database templates since Access 2.0, and in Access 2007, the template features were greatly improved. Access 2010 templates include multiple applications, such as the new and improved sample Northwind database application.

The official Microsoft Office website has many Access database applications and templates available for download. Some templates have been created by the Microsoft Access development team, and with the release of Access 2010, users and developers can submit templates to Microsoft to be shared with the community directly through the new Access 2010 Backstage. Creating new database applications from scratch or from a template is easier than ever using Access 2010.

LESSON SETUP

In this lesson you learn about the different options available in Access 2010 for creating database files. This lesson then provides examples for creating a blank database and creating a database from a template. To complete this lesson, you should have Access 2010 installed on your machine and be familiar with starting the program. Otherwise, no prior knowledge of Access is required for this lesson.

OPTIONS FOR CREATING DATABASES IN ACCESS 2010

Access 2010 can create new, blank databases in the Access 2000, Access 2002–2003, and Access 2007 database formats. If only you will be using the database application, we typically recommend using the latest database file format: ACCDB (Access 2007). This allows you to use all of the latest and greatest database features included in Access 2010.

However, if a database application needs to be used by versions of Access prior to 2010, you may need to create it using one of the earlier file formats; it depends on the minimum version of Access that will run the database application. Also, when building the application, ensure that any built-in features, macros, and VBA code that were not supported under the minimum required version of Access were not used in the database application. Otherwise, users running under older versions of Access get some unexpected results when running the database applications!

Creating a Blank Database

It is very easy to create a blank database using Access 2010. When Access opens, the Access Backstage is displayed. You have the option of opening an existing database file using the Open button or creating a new database. Figure 3-1 is an image of the Access 2010 Backstage when opened without using a specific database file.

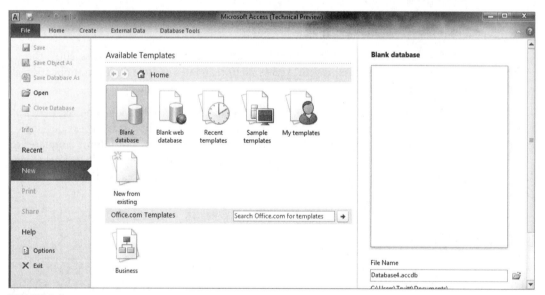

FIGURE 3-1

The New tab in the Access Backstage is selected and the button to create a blank database is highlighted in the middle section of the Access window by default. The other options available on the New tab are:

➤ Blank Web Database

➤ Recent Templates

➤ Sample Templates

➤ My Templates (empty if you have not created a template)

➤ New from Existing

➤ A section for online templates at Office.com

To create a new blank database, follow these steps:

1. Enter a file path and name for the new database on the right side of the Access window. Or, optionally, click the folder button to open the File New Database dialog box, browse to the desired location, and enter the new database name in the File Name field.

2. Click the Create button.

Access will create a database with a single table with a single ID field, which is automatically opened in Datasheet View mode when the database is created. Figure 3-2 shows an image of the Access 2010 window once a new blank database has been created. You have a blank database and you can begin creating a working database application. Although the physical database file has been created, the table that was created has not been saved.

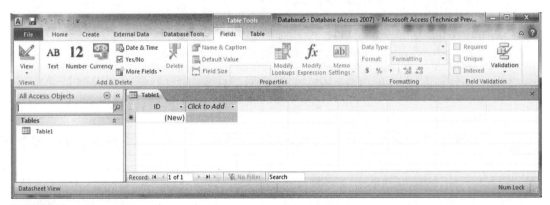

FIGURE 3-2

3. Save the table.

4. Close the database. The new blank database file has been created and saved on the local machine (or whichever location you designated) and is ready for use.

Creating a Database from Template

As mentioned, Access 2010 can use templates to create database applications. These applications can be extremely simple or very complex and depend on the specific template that is chosen. The Microsoft Office website has many Access templates that can be downloaded (for free) and created on your computer. The sample templates offer multiple database applications for both business and personal use. Other templates are created by individual developers and have additional features (such as technical support) available directly from the template's developer. These kinds of templates often have fees associated with the additional features and services.

Access 2010 includes the Northwind database as one of the templates available with the default installation. You use that template to create an application in this lesson. To create the Northwind database from a template, follow along:

1. Open Access.

2. Click the Sample templates button. The Available Templates section appears and displays available templates as buttons.

3. Click the Northwind button, enter the desired file name, and optionally browse to the desired folder.

4. Click the Create button.

Access will run the processes needed to build the database objects used to create the Northwind database. Figure 3-3 is an image of the Northwind startup screen after the database has been created from the template.

The Northwind database template contains code and macros which are disabled by default. To enable the functionality (which is perfectly safe in the case of the Northwind database application) and allow the database to run properly, the user must click Enable Content in the Security Warning bar (if the database was not created in an already trusted location).

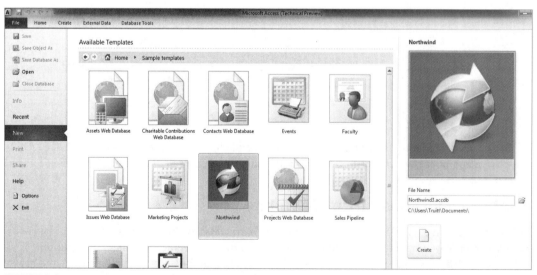

FIGURE 3-3

TRY IT

In this lesson you create a new blank database and then create the Northwind template from the new Access 2010 Backstage using the information discussed earlier in this chapter.

Lesson Requirements

This lesson requires that Access 2010 be installed and that you be familiar with starting the program. Otherwise, no previous knowledge of Access is required to complete this lesson.

Hints

➤ When naming your database (or objects in the database) do not use spaces or special characters — except the underscore — in the name.

➤ Manually browsing to a desired location for the database is not required and if none is selected, the database will be created in your default database folder. You can set that option in the Access options.

➤ Creating the database in a trusted location automatically enables the database application. The instructions for creating a trusted location and the explanation of the need for and uses of them are discussed in Lesson 46. We recommend creating templates in a trusted location only when you are *100 percent* sure of the source and contents of the template, due to possible security issues.

Step-by-Step

1. To create a blank database, open Access from the Windows Start menu. The Access 2010 Backstage will be opened.

2. From the Access Backstage, click the Blank database button. The blank database option will be selected for creation.

3. Optionally, enter a file name in the File Name field.

4. Optionally, click the folder button to browse to the desired output location for the new database file.

5. Click the Create button.

Congratulations. You have created a blank database and it is ready for you to start building a new application. Although somewhat different than creating a database in older versions of Access, it is just as easy, if not easier! Now close Access to close the new database you just created. Next, try creating a new database from an existing application template.

1. To create a database from a template, open Access from the Windows Start menu. The Access 2010 Backstage will be opened.

2. Click the Sample template button to show the sample template options.

3. Find the Northwind template button and click to select it.

4. Optionally, enter a file name in the File Name field.

5. Optionally, click the folder button to browse to the desired output location for the new database file.

6. Click the Create button. Access will create the Northwind application.

 If the template is from Office online, the Create button will actually be named Download and actually download the template to the local user folder before Access creates a new database application from it.

Congratulations. You have successfully created a database application from a template. The new application will open automatically in the Access window once it has been created and will then be ready for use.

SUMMARY

Creating blank databases and applications from templates is a simple process using Access 2010. Whether you are designing a database from scratch by creating a blank database file, or you are using a template to create the application, the process only takes a few mouse clicks and keystrokes using the Access Backstage features.

Using an existing template allows you to shorten the overall time needed to create a database. After Access has created the database from a template, you can extend the database by adding your own required features and functionality. No matter which kind of database you decide to create, using Access 2010 to create it will help you accomplish your tasks very quickly and efficiently.

 Please select Lesson 3 on the DVD to view the video that accompanies this lesson.

Access Database Objects

Database objects for Access 2010 can be generally defined as tables, queries, forms, reports, macros, and modules. The Access 2002–03 MDB database file format also supports Data Access Page (DAP) objects, which are no longer supported in the ACCDB database file format. These objects may use other objects as subcomponents of the parent objects. For example, forms use other forms as subforms and reports as subreports. Also, each of these database objects contains a collection of one or more subobjects. For example, tables have fields, indexes, and data; forms and reports contain controls, sections, and properties; modules store functions and subroutines. By using all of these database objects, you can build highly complex and robust database applications, but to do so, you must first understand how each of these object types works in the database.

LESSON SETUP

This lesson introduces the six major database object types allowed in the ACCDB (Access 2007) database file format and explains the basics of how each is used. You should have an existing knowledge of how to start Access and create new database files to successfully complete this lesson.

ACCESS DATABASE OBJECTS

The Access database file is the file that is physically stored on a drive and is visible from Windows Explorer. These files usually have (though they are not required) the .accdb or .mdb file extension. The database file is the container that stores all of the database objects. Each table, query, form, report, macro, and module created within the database application is defined in the main database file. You can create these objects using the Access user interface (UI) or by executing the proper VBA code. The Access UI includes designers for tables, queries, forms, reports, and macros. Access 2010, along with most of the other Office 2010 applications, also provides the Visual Basic Editor (VBE), which is used to create and edit

Visual Basic for Applications (VBA) code in module database objects. This section discusses each of these object types.

Access Tables

Access Table objects are one of the most common object types, as they are used to store data in the database application. An Access database has two main kinds of tables:

➤ *System tables* store information required by Access to manage the database file, but these tables are really just protected local tables in the database file. System tables are hidden by default, and although they are accessible, they are read-only and cannot be updated from within the Access database application explicitly. Access uses the prefix MSys in the names of these tables. We generally recommend not messing with or relying on the database's system tables too much, although they can be extremely useful for gathering information about each of the objects contained in the database application when necessary.

➤ *User (application) tables* can be local tables or linked tables. Linked tables are Access tables that are physically located outside of the database file, and can be other Access tables, SQL Server tables, SharePoint lists, Excel sheets, text files, and many other file types. The user tables are created to store information needed for the application.

Web tables are another type allowed in Access 2010. They are part of the new Access Web applications and specifically designed for use in conjunction with SharePoint. However, most Access tables are simply local tables that are physically stored directly in the database file, along with any data they contain, and are the type of table we examine in this lesson.

Access tables include fields and indexes, and each field has a specific data type, defined when the table is designed. (Lesson 10 discusses this further.) Indexes speed up and optimize the returning of data from the tables. Every table should have at least one index created for it, and some tables may have single field, multiple field, or compound field indexes.

Each table should have a primary key defined to uniquely identify each record in the table. Primary keys establish relationships with other tables. The Access Autonumber data type is commonly used to create a primary key. Foreign keys are fields in related tables used to identify a record as a related record by the value stored in the field.

Access also provides several different types of view modes for its tables. Design View mode allows you to build the structure of the table and interact with the design of the table's fields and their properties. Datasheet View mode allows the user to see the fields and the data stored in those fields in a standard tabular format. Datasheet View mode also allows limited interaction with the design of the table, through the use of the commands on the Ribbon. PivotTable and PivotChart View modes allow you to build charts and stylized pivot tables for providing graphical representation of the data stored in the table. With all of these features, Access tables are extremely powerful and flexible when compared to most other database products available.

Access Queries

Access has three types of queries: Select, Action, and Data Definition. Select and Action queries can be created using Access's Query Design View mode, from the SQL View mode, or from VBA code.

Data Definition queries, Union queries, and Pass-through queries must be created using SQL View mode or from VBA code.

Select queries are used to retrieve specific data from tables. The Record Source property for forms and reports can be a Select query, but Action queries and Data Definition queries are not allowed. The data that a Select query returns can be restricted by applying one or more criteria to the query. The criteria uses arguments, or values, to restrict what records are returned by the query. The criteria may require a value in a record to be equal to, not equal to, greater than, or less than the value supplied as the argument. The arguments for the query can be written into the query at design time by using functions to calculate the value of an argument, or by passing values to the query at run time.

Calculated fields create new fields in a query that is not included in the original tables and is typically a combination, or calculation, of other fields in the database. Math operations can be performed on one or more of the table's fields, strings can be combined using concatenation, and the results from functions called from a calculated field can be returned using calculated fields in a query.

Several kinds of Action queries are generally used to modify the data in a table in one way or another. Action queries append records to a table, update the field values in existing records, delete records, and create a new table from the records returned by a query. Calculated fields and criteria can also be used in Action queries to specify which records are to be modified as a result of the query.

Since Action queries can modify the database, and potentially harm the application or other files on the machine, the database must be trusted before Action queries can be executed. You must click the Enable button in the Access Security Warning bar, or the database must be saved in a Trusted location, before Access allows Action queries to be executed.

Data Definition queries can create, modify, or delete database objects, including tables, fields, and indexes in a database. Data Definition queries utilize (and require) a type of SQL called Data Definition SQL, which is specifically designed for database schema modification. However, it is important to note that one of the primary Access limitations when using a data definition query is that you can only create one table per query execution. Using data definition queries can be a powerful method for building database schema in your Access applications.

Much like tables, Access also provides a number of view modes for Access query database objects, although not all types of queries support all view modes. Datasheet View mode displays the results (if any) once a query has been executed. It is also important to note that anytime a query is opened in Datasheet mode, it is executed. Just as with tables, Datasheet View mode displays the output data and fields in tabular format. Query Design View mode displays the Access Query designer, which can build queries using a graphical user interface (GUI). SQL View mode allows the user to view and edit the exact SQL statement that the query uses in a text-based format. And finally, Access also provides PivotTable and PivotChart View modes for building pivot tables and charts from select queries, just as you can with Access tables.

Access Forms

One of the most important features that sets Access database applications apart from other database products is the built-in Forms package. Forms allow database application users to interact with the data and are much like other standard Windows application forms. Forms can be bound to a specific table or query, or they can be unbound and get the values from code behind the form or from the user. Access provides a number of built-in form types that are common to Access applications, but they all derive from the base Access form object.

Forms have properties, methods, and events that determine their overall characteristics such as how the form behaves, what it looks like, and any other physical trait of the form. A property stores a piece of data that determines a characteristic of the form. For example, the Record Source property determines if the form is bound or unbound. Form events are used with specific code or macro actions when some predefined action type occurs. For example, the On Load event might specify a macro or some code that should execute when the form is loaded. And form methods execute some built-in or user-defined functionality when explicitly called in a macro or code. Form properties, methods, and events are extremely useful and you will undoubtedly become familiar with them as you build Access database applications.

Access provides several different view modes for forms and even has two different form designers available. The most important view is Form View, which is the form's standard view and is designed to be where the user interacts with the form. Design View mode is the traditional view Access designer uses to build the form and allows the lowest level of design capabilities for forms that Access provides. Layout View mode is a second form designer, originally introduced in Access 2007, to allow the developer to see the data while building the form. Although it does not provide all of the design capabilities that the Design View mode designer does, being able to see the data the form will display (as you're building it) can be extremely useful. And finally, Access provides the PivotChart View mode for forms to present data in graphical format, just as with tables and queries. Access forms are extremely flexible and easy to work with, provide a lot of useful features for representing data, and are probably one of the most important parts of a good Access database application.

Access Reports

Another feature that sets Access database applications apart from other database products is the built-in reporting package. Reports display data for users to see onscreen and print on paper. Although reports are a lot like forms in many ways, reports provide a number of features for rendering data that are not supported by forms. For example, reports provide grouping and sorting features to order data to show the desired layout in the report. Also, after a report has opened, the user typically cannot change the report format or data. To alter the structure or data shown in the report, it must be reopened after the desired changes have been made to the data. As you may have realized already, reports are a method for creating visualizations of the data stored in the database application.

As with forms, Access 2010 provides a number of view modes for working with reports and also provides two different designers. The most important view for reports is Report View, which is the standard view and designed to be used to show the data in the report, directly from within the application. Print Preview View mode lets you see the report as it would be printed, and it provides the command to actually print the report. Reports also provide Design View mode, which is the traditional Access report designer and allows the lowest level of design capabilities for reports available in Access 2010. Layout View mode is the second report designer, originally introduced in Access 2007, and it allows the developer to see the data while they are building reports.

Access Macros

Macros in Access are common actions that are used in a database application, designed to be very easy for users to use. For example, you can use a macro behind the Click event of a Button control to open a form in the database. In addition to all of the existing macro features, Access 2010 now provides a completely redesigned Macro Designer, the only designer for macros in Access, and Microsoft has even added some new macro features, including data macros. Access 2010 now includes three types of macros:

➤ Embedded macros — Macros that are embedded, or stored, in the code modules of a form or report and are called from an event method of that object.

➤ Macro database objects — These types of macros, commonly known as named macros, are not necessarily associated with any other specific object and are considered separate standalone database objects. However, they are designed to be called from other objects in the database and can be used by multiple database objects simultaneously.

➤ Data macros — Macros that have been added to the ACCDB file format for Access 2010, these macros can be created for data level events and can modify data in the database. The functionality is very similar to table triggers used in database systems like Microsoft SQL Server. Data macros can execute in Disabled Mode where the same procedure using VBA will not run unless the database has been enabled.

Using the redesigned Macro Tools Design Ribbon, you can open the Action Catalog and see all of the program flow and action objects already available for use in a database.

Macros are placed behind an event and are executed when an event is fired. These can be events such as clicking a button, typing in a control on a form, and changing values in a control. The new data macros are used to interact with the data at the table level. They can function like triggers seen in a standard SQL database server, such as SQL Server or Oracle. For example, if a user inserts a new record, a data macro could be triggered to add data to the record, it could be set to validate the data, or the macro could create an audit trail. Macros in Access are extremely handy for accomplishing simple tasks programmatically, without having to know how to write code.

VBA Code in Access

Visual Basic for Applications (VBA) code is available for most of the Office 2010 applications, including Excel, Word, Outlook, PowerPoint, and most importantly for this book, Access. VBA is a powerful programming language that can enhance a database application and provide functionality not otherwise available. You can assign VBA code to the object events and the code will execute when the event fires. However, Access does not allow the execution of VBA code, unless the database is trusted. The Visual Basic Editor (VBE) is used to write the VBA procedures and can be opened directly from inside Access.

Standard modules are containers that hold functions, subroutines, type definitions, properties, and other objects. The modules themselves are not executed; the functions and subs contained *in* the standard modules are called and executed instead. Class modules are specialized and defined by using the module name specifically. And forms and reports can have code modules, if they use macros or VBA code, which is where the embedded macros and code are stored. Using VBA code is the most powerful method for providing custom functionality for a database application that is available in Access.

 VBA is an advanced feature of Access and it comes with a few security issues and considerations. Lessons 51 through 57 of this book are dedicated to discussing the intricacies of VBA.

TRY IT

In this lesson, you learn how to find and open some of the objects included in the Northwind database. You open objects and view them in their open state, as well as in Design View. To become more familiar with each object in Access, as you are exploring the objects in the Northwind database, look at the Property Sheet pane when forms and reports are selected and compare the property values with other forms and reports.

Lesson Requirements

For this lesson, you need the Northwind database created from the Northwind template in Lesson 3 (or simply create a new Northwind database from a template). You should be familiar with starting Access and creating databases. Otherwise, no previous knowledge of using Access is required for this lesson.

Step-by-Step

1. Open the Northwind database.

2. Find the Navigation Pane on the left side of the Access window. Click the chevron (>>) on the Shutter Bar (at the top of the Navigation Pane bar) to expand the pane.

3. Click the title bar at the top of the Navigation Pane and choose the All Access Objects option to organize the objects in groups based on their object type.

4. Click the Tables group header in the Navigation Pane to expand and show the tables in the database.

5. Right-click the Order Details table and open it in Design View. Look at the options available in the Data Type column and in the Field Property section.

6. To view the table data, click the View button on the Ribbon. This opens the table in Datasheet View mode.

7. To close the table without saving, click the X button on the top left of the table.

8. Continue exploring the objects shown in all of the object groups in Design View, and opening the object when possible. In Design View, pay close attention to the Property Sheet on the right side of the screen to see how the objects are designed and what property settings are available for each object. When you are finished viewing the objects you choose, close them without saving.

Congratulations, you have successfully opened a few database objects and seen their different view modes. Each of these objects will be very useful in your database applications and you are very likely to use each of them quite often. Continue with the rest of the lesson to learn more about each of the Access 2010 database objects.

SUMMARY

The Access 2010 ACCDB database file format supports six database object types: tables, queries, forms, reports, macros, and modules. Database objects are the tools from which you can create your database applications. Each of these objects (such as a table) can function alone or in conjunction with each other (such as a query using a particular table as its data source). In turn, that query can then be used as the record source for a form or a report. Regardless of the specific task, each of these database objects is a key component of an Access database application. As you continue through this book, each of the lessons is devoted to working with the database objects available in Access 2010 and you will become very familiar with tables, queries, forms, reports, macros, and modules, and the features and objects that each supports.

 Please select Lesson 4 on the DVD to view the video that accompanies this lesson.

5

The Access 2010 Ribbon

The Ribbon was introduced originally in Access 2007 at the same time it was released in the other core Office products, such as Word and Excel. The Ribbon is a replacement for the Windows-style toolbar menu system and custom command bars that are standard in most Windows programs. More importantly for Access users, the Ribbon is a menu system that is proprietary to the Microsoft Office applications and supplies much of the functionality for building database applications in Access 2010.

Ribbons are context driven and change depending on the state of the program or what action has been taken. In theory, this design puts the commands needed to perform common tasks just a mouse click away. The Ribbon can also be customized by the developer of a database application and, using VBA code or macros, can provide custom functionality right in place with the standard Access menu commands, or even all alone on separate Ribbons.

If you are not familiar with the Ribbon, finding items on it may seem awkward. As you continue using it, navigating Access using the Ribbon becomes second nature. In this lesson, you learn about the basic parts of the Access 2010 Ribbon and use some of the commands it provides in the examples.

LESSON SETUP

In this lesson you become familiar with the Ribbon's basic features. This lesson describes how the Ribbon is organized, its functions and features, and how to use the keyboard short-cuts. You should be familiar with Access database files and the major database objects that Access 2010 supports for this lesson. Otherwise, no prior knowledge of Access is required to complete this lesson.

RIBBON OVERVIEW

The *Ribbon* is the menu bar across the top of the Access 2010 program window that is shown when a database is open. The Ribbon is divided into tabs, and each tab contains a separate and distinct Ribbon object. Each Ribbon is broken into sections, and in each section are several types of controls; button commands are the most prevalent. The tabs organize tasks into functional areas, and the groups further organize the areas by locating them in logical groups.

The Ribbons in Access 2007 and Access 2010 differ in a couple of ways. Access 2010 no longer has an Office button. Instead, the Office button has been replaced with the File tab, which opens the Access Backstage. Second, many of the tools from the Database Tools tab have been relocated to the Office Backstage. Although these differences are important, they are minor, and these Ribbon improvements should increase your productivity in Access over the long run.

Ribbon Tabs

The default Ribbon for Access 2010 has five standard tabs. These five are shown all the time (except in a few select cases) and are the standard Ribbons used for working with Access 2010 features. The default Ribbon includes the following tabs:

> **File** — Opens the Access Backstage. The File button replaces the Office button used in Access 2007, and opens the Backstage View. It includes an array of functionality and information about the current database, and includes commands formerly found on the File menu, such as Save and Print. The Access Options dialog is opened from the Access Backstage. See Lesson 6 to learn more about the Backstage View.

> **Home** — Includes commands for switching view modes, Clipboard, Sort & Filter, Records, Find, and Text Formatting sections. The Home tab includes general commands used to copy, paste, sort, and for record manipulation, navigation, and text formatting.

> **Create** — Includes templates, tables, queries, forms, reports, and macros & code. The Create Ribbon contains commands to create Access database objects.

> **External Data** — This Ribbon has the Import & Link, Export, and Collect Data sections. The External Data tab has commands used to allow Access to use external data, either by importation or linking, and to export Access data to external locations.

> **Database Tools** — Includes the Tool, Macro, Relationships, Analyze, Move Data, and Add-ins sections. The Database Tools tab includes commands to open the Visual Basic Editor (VBE), run macros, create relationships, document and analyze a database, move data, and work with add-ins.

Contextual Ribbon Tabs

In addition to the five basic Ribbons, many additional Ribbons only appear when Access is in a certain state. For example, when a user opens a form in Design View, the Form Design Tools Design Ribbon will open and show some of the commands available for designing a form. If the user then opens a report, the Report Design Tools Design Ribbon is automatically opened. As you work with Access, you discover a lot of contextual Ribbons for all sorts of features in Access. Contextual Ribbons help reduce the clutter.

Ribbon Sections

Each Ribbon is divided into sections and each section contains controls that perform similar or related actions in that section group. For example, all of the commands for formatting text are located in the Text Formatting section on the Home Ribbon. The sections are specific for each Ribbon and some Ribbons may even reuse sections from other Ribbons. Some of these sections have section expanders to expose additional features, such as the legacy dialogs or other panes that are associated with the particular features for that section. The Ribbon sections are pretty self-explanatory, and exploring the Access Ribbon is the best method of getting to know each section.

Section Expanders

Some sections in Access have section expanders, which are small diagonal arrow controls that are found just to the right of the name of some sections. Clicking these section expanders often opens a feature-specific dialog or pane that is not available otherwise from the Ribbon. For example, clicking the Text Formatting section expander on the Home Ribbon will open the Access Font dialog. Section expanders can be added to Ribbon sections manually or programmatically when building custom Ribbons. Figure 5-1 is an image of the Clipboard expander on the Home Ribbon. Clicking the expander arrow opens the Office Clipboard pane.

FIGURE 5-1

The Quick Access Toolbar (QAT)

The *Quick Access Toolbar* (QAT) is a customizable toolbar that allows the user to put frequently used commands in one place. The benefit of using the QAT is that all commands on it are shown all the time. And, the really nice part is that you can customize QAT as an Access 2010 program setting (so Access will show those commands all the time) or as a database setting (so Access only shows those customizations when the specific database file is open).

The default placement of the QAT is just above the Ribbon's File button in the top left of the Access 2010 window, and the default commands are Save, Undo, and Redo. The QAT can also be moved below the Ribbon by clicking the QAT and selecting Show Quick Access Toolbar Below the Ribbon.

There are actually a couple of methods of adding commands to the QAT. The first, and probably easiest, is to simply right-click the exact command on any Ribbon you wish to add, and then choose the Add to Quick Access Toolbar option that is shown on the context menu. A second method is using the Quick Access Toolbar dialog found in the Access Options. The More Commands option on the QAT's drop-down menu takes the user to the Quick Access Toolbar dialog, which provides an editor for working with the QAT.

Custom Ribbons

Starting in Access 2007, the ACCDB file format provides users the ability to add custom Ribbons in an Access database application as a replacement to the Custom Command Bars feature in previous versions. The Access Options dialog, which is found in the Backstage, provides the Customize Ribbon tab as a launching point for creating user-defined custom Ribbons. You can also get to this dialog by clicking the Ribbon and selecting the Customize the Ribbon option. The Customize Ribbon tab on the

Access Options dialog allows you to add or remove commands, add new tabs, and add new groups as desired, import and export Ribbon settings, and even reset the Ribbon back to its initial state. As with the QAT settings, custom Ribbon settings can be on the Access program level or database application level. Figure 5-2 shows the Customize Ribbon dialog in the Access Options.

FIGURE 5-2

Access allows the developer to create custom Ribbons using existing commands and allows the user to build custom commands and functionality using macros, VBA code, and/or XML code. To find out more about creating custom Ribbons, see Lesson 60 of this book, which discusses the basics of customizing the Access 2010 Ribbon and using the Customize Ribbon dialog.

There are a number of additional references that discuss working with the Ribbon, both in Access and Office. The following books are additional references for designing custom Ribbons in Access.

➤ *Access 2010 Programmer's Reference (Programmer to Programmer).* Hennig, Cooper, Griffith, Dennison. Published by Wrox.

➤ *Access 2007 VBA Programmer's Reference (Programmer to Programmer).* Hennig, Cooper, Griffith, Stein. Published by Wrox.

➤ *RibbonX: Customizing the Office 2007 Ribbon.* Martin, Puls, Hennig. Published by Wiley.

Keyboard Shortcuts

Almost all Windows-based programs support *hotkeys*, which are keyboard shortcuts for common commands. Hotkeys perform specific actions through a series of keystroke combinations. For example, the key combination Ctrl-C will copy the selected text and Ctrl-V will paste the contents of the clipboard.

To see the available keyboard shortcuts in Access 2010, press the Alt key; Access will display characters over each Ribbon tab. Press the key with the letter for the Ribbon you wish to activate (it is not necessary to continue holding the Alt key when pressing the letter) and the Ribbon will open. All of the commands on that Ribbon will display their specific hotkey codes. Pressing the next key (or set of keys) to complete the key combination code will execute the desired command. Figure 5-3 provides an example of the letters that appear on the Ribbon after pressing the Alt key in the Access program window.

FIGURE 5-3

The familiar Ctrl-C for copy, Ctrl-V for paste, and other Windows standard shortcuts are still available. For additional shortcuts, search Access Help using the keywords **Keyboard Shortcuts** or hover the mouse over a button. If there is a shortcut associated with the button, the drop-down menu will include the combination.

TRY IT

In this lesson you examine some of Access 2010's standard built-in Ribbons, their tabs, groups, and sections. The example walks you through the steps for customizing the QAT and creating a custom Ribbon using the Access Options dialog. With each new Ribbon shown in this lesson, please take some time to explore its functionality.

Lesson Requirements

For this lesson you should be familiar with starting Access and creating a new database. Otherwise, no other knowledge of Access is required. This lesson uses the Northwind database (created from a template) to complete the steps for this lesson.

Step-by-Step

1. Start Access 2010 from the Windows Start menu.

2. In the Access Backstage, select the Northwind template and create a new database from it, as explained in Lesson 3.

3. Create and open the database in the Access window. Close any forms that may have opened when the database was started.

4. Expand the Navigation Pane by clicking the pane on the Shutter Bar. The Home Ribbon is displayed by default, but many commands are disabled because no objects are open in the Access window.

5. In the Navigation Pane, right-click the Customers table and select the Design View option from the context menu. This will open the table in Design View. Notice that the Table Tools Design Ribbon has been opened, so that you can quickly access the table tools used to modify tables.

6. On the Table Tools Design Ribbon, click the View button to switch the table to Datasheet View. Observe the Ribbon switching back to the Home tab. Most of the commands are enabled now that an object is open.

7. Close the table without saving.

Congratulations; you've just observed how the Ribbon is context sensitive and how it behaves when certain database objects are opened in the Access window. Next, you examine the Query Tools Design Ribbon.

8. In the Navigation Pane, right-click the Customers Extended query and choose the Design View option from the context menu. The query will be opened in Design View mode.

> *Notice that the Query Tools Design Ribbon opens automatically, which presents commands specific to designing and running queries.*

9. On the Query Tools Design Ribbon, click the Run button to execute the query and see the results that it produces. Close the query without saving.

Congratulations, you've observed the Query Design Tools contextual Ribbon in action. Next, try adding some commands to the Quick Access Toolbar.

10. Open the Access Backstage by clicking the File button on the Ribbon.

11. Click the Options button on the bottom left of the Backstage window to open the Access Options dialog.

12. Click the Quick Access Toolbar option (on the left side of the Access Options dialog) to show the options for customizing the QAT.

13. Click the Copy command in the list on the left; then click the Add button located center screen between the lists. The Copy command button will move to the list on the right and be added to the QAT.

14. Close the Access Options dialog by pressing the OK button. You will be able to see the changes to the QAT and the Copy command should be available.

To see additional commands, use the options from the drop-down list labeled Choose Commands From on the Quick Access Toolbar dialog. The default view for the commands shown in the left list is Popular Commands, but choosing the All Commands option shows all built-in commands available for the QAT.

Congratulations; you have customized the QAT. Since you made the changes for all documents (the default, as specified in the drop-down menu above the right list in the Quick Access Toolbar options dialog), these commands will be shown in Access every time it is opened. Of course, you could have easily applied the changes to only this database using the settings in the Quick Access Toolbar options dialog. Next, try removing a command from the QAT.

15. In the Access window, click the down arrow button on the QAT to show the context menu for the QAT. Click the More Commands option to open the Quick Access Toolbar Options dialog.

16. To remove a command from the QAT, click the Copy command from the list (on the right side of the screen) to select it and then click the Remove button.

17. When finished, click OK to close the Quick Access Toolbar options dialog and save the changes. Verify that the QAT no longer contains the Copy commands.

Congratulations; you have removed the Copy command button from the QAT that you added in the previous steps. Adding and removing items on the QAT is extremely easy and only takes a few mouse clicks. Next, try an example that uses a section expander in the Ribbon.

18. In the Navigation Pane, double-click the Customers table to open the table in Datasheet View mode.

19. On the Home Ribbon, the Clipboard section and the Text Formatting section should have the small diagonal arrow (just to the right of the name of the section) that indicates additional features available for that Ribbon section.

20. On the Home Ribbon, click the section expander for the Text Formatting section. The Datasheet Formatting dialog presents additional formatting options. Click the OK or Cancel button to close the dialog.

21. Click the section expander on the Clipboard section. The Office Clipboard pane is shown, and any items currently stored on the Clipboard can be viewed.

Congratulations; you successfully opened a dialog using the Ribbon section expanders. The section expanders provide a quick method for accessing common functionality and dialogs related to that particular Ribbon section. Finally, try customizing the Home Ribbon by adding a built-in command to it:

22. Click the File button on the Ribbon to open the Access Backstage.

23. Click the Options button on the bottom left of the Access Backstage window. The Access Options dialog will open.

24. On the left side of the Access Options dialog, click the Customize Ribbon tab. This will open the Customize Ribbon options dialog.

25. To add a command to a built-in Ribbon, it must be added to a custom section group. Click the Home tab option (on the right side of the Customize Ribbon dialog) and click the New Group button (at the bottom of the list). A new section group will be added under the Home Ribbon tree list.

26. Click the Rename button to open the Rename dialog for the new group. Type in the value **Export** and press the OK button. The new group is renamed and the changes are added to the Customize Ribbon options dialog.

27. Click the Saved Exports command option from the list on the left to select it and click the Add button to add it to the new Export section group.

28. Click the OK button on the Access Option dialog to save the changes and close it. The Home Ribbon will now have the Saved Exports command button shown under the Export section.

Congratulations; you have customized the Home Ribbon by adding an Export group and placing the Saved Exports command button in it. These changes are shown when databases are opened in Access on your current computer. Customizing Ribbons for Access is sure to be quick and easy when using the Access Options dialog.

SUMMARY

The elegance of the Ribbon in Access 2010 is that it is complex in its functionality, provides superior customization flexibility, and yet is simple in appearance and usage. New options can be added quickly and easily to an existing Ribbon, to new custom Ribbons, or even to the QAT. The Ribbon is context sensitive and only shows the tools that are required for a specific task appear when needed. Custom Ribbons are easily added using the Access Options dialog and can add functionality specific to the application. These custom Ribbons can also be context sensitive and extend the elegance to custom database applications. Keyboard shortcuts provide users fast access to menu items, without taking their hands away from the keyboard. Truly, the Access 2010 Ribbon is a vast improvement over the previous menu system and command bar features.

One final note about the Ribbon: The Ribbon in Access is used in the same fashion as in any Office product that supports it. So, as you become familiar with the Ribbons in one product, you are also learning concepts that apply equally to the other Office products. The more comfortable you become with the layout and design of the basic Ribbons, the easier it will be to work with the built-in functionality Access 2010 provides.

 Please select Lesson 5 on the DVD to view the video that accompanies this lesson.

The Access 2010 Backstage

The Backstage View is a new feature of Access 2010. It replaces the File menu as a one-stop source for important information about the program and access to commands in the current database, as well as working with many of the features of the Access program itself. The Office button in Access 2007 introduced some of the same features as the Backstage, but 2010 moves even more Access program functionality to a central location.

LESSON SETUP

In this lesson you explore the features available in the Access 2010 Backstage. Many of the commands from the Database Tools Ribbon in Access 2007, or the Tools menus prior to Access 2007, have been moved to Access Backstage. This lesson provides an overview of the Backstage, its features, and some examples of how it can be used in Access 2010.

THE BACKSTAGE VIEW

The Backstage View in Access 2010 is a single-stop site for many commands that were previously scattered throughout the Ribbon, or other menus, in the previous versions of Access. Everything needed to open an existing database, create a blank database, create a database from a template, set options for the current database, or set options for the Access program itself are presented in the Backstage. The Backstage provides a number of tools for working directly with database files, such as converting the file format, working with relationships, compacting and repairing the database, publishing the database to SharePoint, packaging and signing the database file for transfer, or creating a setup package for the database. The Backstage can even be programmed to provide custom options and functionality, which we discuss in Lesson 61. The Access 2010 Backstage View is an extremely powerful and flexible feature, and becoming familiar with it will help you greatly increase your productivity.

TOURING THE BACKSTAGE FEATURES

The Backstage is comprised of a number of tabs, buttons, and screens to provide all of its features. Much like the Ribbon controls, only enabled commands are available and any control whose functionality is not currently available will be disabled. The main window is broken into several different sections, and always shows a left-hand panel. The left panel contains a set of tabs and buttons that are the launching point for all of the Backstage functionality, and will display different Backstage views depending on what functionality has been selected and if there is currently a database open. Just as with the Access Ribbon, the Backstage is also designed to be context sensitive.

The Basic Backstage Controls

The left panel of the Access 2010 Backstage provides seven buttons and five tabs in the default configuration, which hosts the basic functionality that the Backstage provides. Some of these buttons or tabs are disabled at certain times during program execution, depending on whether a database is currently open in Access. The Backstage also displays recently opened files, which are denoted by the Access database icon and their respective file names and found just below the Close Database button (assuming files have been opened previously). Each of the Backstage tab and button controls provide some very useful functionality.

The Basic Backstage Buttons

As noted, the left panel of the Backstage contains seven button controls in the default configuration. However, these buttons are broken into two sections: five on the top and two on the bottom. The buttons host most of the basic functionality that the Backstage provides and are context sensitive, so they are enabled only when their commands are available. The following is a list of the top five buttons and a description of their functionality:

➤ **Save** executes the Save command for any unsaved objects that are currently open in the Access program.

➤ **Save Object As** executes the Save Object As command for the database object that is currently in focus in the Access program. This allows the database object to be saved as one of the supported formats.

➤ **Save Database As** creates a new copy of the database that is currently open in the Access program to the specified location and file format. This command is most commonly used to convert file formats in Access.

➤ **Open** invokes the Open dialog to allow the user to open a database file, or any other Access-supported file formats, in the Access program.

➤ **Close Database** closes any files that are currently open in the Access program.

In addition to the previous buttons, two other button controls are found at the bottom of the left panel:

➤ **Options** opens the Access Options dialog for setting the database and program options.

➤ **Exit** closes the Access program itself, along with any files that are currently open.

The Basic Backstage Tabs

The Backstage provides six basic tab controls in the default configuration: Info, Recent, New, Print, Save & Publish, and Help. When you click any of these tabs, the tab's options are shown on the right panel of the Backstage. The following sections review each of the Backstage's tab controls and the functionality each provides.

The Info Tab

The Info tab is enabled when a database file is open in the Access program. The Info tab contains a number of options, which are also context sensitive, and options are shown based upon the database file that is currently open. The following is a list of the most common options that are shown on the right panel of the Info tab in the Access 2010 Backstage:

➤ **Enable Content** — Just as with the Access Security bar, the Enable Content button on the Info tab will enable unsafe code and macros in the current database.

➤ **Publish to Access Services** — This option appears if the current database is a Web database. It opens the Publish dialog to allow the user to publish the current database to Access services on SharePoint 2010.

➤ **Compact & Repair Database** — Compacts the current database file by deleting temporary objects and removing deleted records, then repairs the indexes in the file.

➤ **Encrypt with Password** — Encrypts the current database file with a specified password, requiring all users to provide the password before they can open the database file. This function requires that the database be open in Exclusive mode.

The Recent Tab

The Recent tab provides links to recently opened database files. When the Recent tab is clicked, the right panel of the Backstage displays a longer list of recently opened files. A single click opens the selected database. The number of recently opened database files to be displayed can be set in the Access Options, under the Show This Number of Recent Documents setting. Of course, the links shown on the Recent tab are in addition to the four most recently opened files that are shown in the left panel of the Backstage.

The New Tab

When no files are open in the Access program, the New tab is enabled and available for the user. The New tab presents the user with options for creating new databases files in the right panel of the Backstage. The New tab provides options for creating a database from scratch or from a template, and even allows the user to select and download templates from Office.com. The New tab in the Backstage is opened by default whenever the Access 2010 program is opened *without* a database file.

The Print Tab

The Print tab provides three options for quickly printing a database object that is open in the Access window and consists of the following buttons: Preview, Quick Print, and Print. The Preview button allows the user to view the object in the Print Preview dialog before sending it to the printer. Quick Print automatically sends the print job to the default printer without asking for options. And finally, the

Print button opens the Print dialog and allows the user to select the printer and set the printing options. The Print tab is only enabled when there is a printable database object open in the Access window.

The Save & Publish Tab

The Save & Publish tab provides a number of options for saving and publishing the database file that is currently open in Access. When clicked, the Save & Publish tab shows three panels in the backstage: the left (which is always shown), and new middle and right panels. The middle panel provides three tabs: Save Database As, Save Object As, and Publish to Access Services. The Save Database As tab provides options for saving the current database file to a specified location and file format, which are shown on the right panel when the tab is clicked. The Save Object As tab provides options on the right panel for saving database objects to supported formats, just as with the button on the left panel of the Backstage. Finally, the Publish to Access Services tab provides options on the right panel for publishing the database to SharePoint.

The Help Tab

The last tab on the left panel of the Backstage is Help. The Help tab also consists of two panels: a middle and a right panel. The middle panel presents two groups of tabs: Support tab group and the Tools for Working with Office tab group. By default, the right panel shows the version number, type, and product ID, and links to Microsoft customer service and support. Both the Support tab group and Tools tab group provide very useful features for Access 2010 users.

➤ **Support** is under the Help tab in the Backstage. It provides three options for getting support in Access 2010. The Microsoft Office Help tab opens the online Help dialog or opens the local help files (when no internet connection is present). The Getting Started tab opens a browser window online so the user can see what is new and see links to resources for Access 2010. The Contact Us tab opens a browser window to the Microsoft Support website to assist the user in resolving issues regarding the purchase, installation, or implementation of Access 2010.

➤ **Tools for Working with Office** provides two very common options for Access 2010: Options and Check for Updates. The Options tab simply opens the Access Options dialog when clicked. The Check for Updates tab opens a browser window to the Windows Update site, allowing the user to check for available updates for Access 2010 and other Office products.

Customizing the Backstage

One last item to mention is that the Access 2010 Backstage is fully customizable. You can add, disable, or even provide a completely customized Backstage by building the proper XML and placing it in the USysRibbons table in the database. Lesson 61 of this book discusses the basics of building a customized Backstage. Building a custom Backstage for any database application is fairly simple and can provide a really nice touch to any Access database application.

TRY IT

In this lesson, you explore the Access 2010 Backstage View features. The best way to learn what is offered in a product is to test the different options and see the features. The following steps walk you through some of the basic functionality of the Access 2010 Backstage.

Lesson Requirements

For this lesson you should have Access 2010 installed and you should have a database file. You can use the Northwind database from Lesson 5, found on the book's DVD and website, or simply create a new database from a template.

Step-by-Step

1. Start Access 2010 and open a database file.

2. Click the File button on the Ribbon to open the Backstage View.

3. Click the different tabs and experiment with the available options; observe the changes.

4. Use the information provided in this lesson to remind yourself where various features are located. Continue exploring and experimenting with the Backstage options. The tabs and features become easier to find the more you use Access.

5. Customize the features to suit your needs.

SUMMARY

The Access 2010 Backstage View provides the tools to create, manage, and customize a database application, all from a single location. Although many of the tools found in the Backstage are also located on various Ribbons for easy access, the Backstage provides a single known location that can be opened from anywhere within Access. The Access 2010 Backstage View is a huge improvement over previous versions of Access in terms of providing a single location for program features, customizing the start-up screen for database applications, and providing information about the Access product.

 Please select Lesson 6 on the DVD to view the video that accompanies this lesson.

7

The Access 2010 Navigation Pane

The Navigation Pane was originally introduced in the Access 2007 release as a replacement to the database window in prior versions. The Navigation Pane is the feature that allows database users to view and open the objects of a database, such as tables, queries, forms, reports, macros, and VBA code modules. The Navigation Pane is the panel on the left side of the Access program window. The Access 2010 Navigation Pane has features that help organize these objects into generic groups, as well as provide the ability to customize and build different views for the database application user. The Navigation Pane can also be hidden from the users. In custom applications, preventing users from seeing or using the Navigation Pane is considered standard practice, and this is discussed more in Lesson 59. This lesson is dedicated to discussing the basic features that the Access 2010 Navigation Pane provides as well as providing a step-by-step example of how to work with the Navigation Pane and the objects it contains. Learning how to effectively use the Navigation Pane's features can greatly increase the robustness of any Access database application.

LESSON SETUP

In this lesson, you learn about the basic features of the Access 2010 Navigation Pane and how to use them. The Navigation Pane is a very important, albeit simple, part of building Access database applications and becoming familiar with its functions is important to efficient use of Access. You should be familiar with starting the Access 2010 program and creating database files to complete this lesson.

THE NAVIGATION PANE OVERVIEW

The Navigation Pane is an extremely important part of the Access user interface, especially from the database developer's standpoint. Since the Navigation Pane provides access to the various database objects, you will use it all the time, primarily for developing the database application.

However, it is worth noting that it is possible to enable and disable the pane from the normal view in the database application, and in some cases (such as when running an Access application under the Access Runtime), the Navigation Pane will not be shown at all. The Navigation Pane also allows the developer to customize the views of the pane and how the database objects are grouped and displayed. By using the Navigation Options dialog, you can further customize the Navigation Pane views, including creating and modifying groups, showing Hidden and System Objects, and selecting either Single-click or Double-click actions to open Objects in the pane. Figure 7-1 provides an illustration of the Navigation Pane after opening the sample Northwind database application.

Navigation Pane Grouping Types

The default grouping shown in the Navigation Pane for new databases is the All Access Objects view option, which is denoted by the text in the pane's title bar. Figure 7-2 shows an image of the Navigation Pane in the default grouping type for a new database.

However, one of the more powerful features is that the Navigation Pane provides multiple grouping options, which means that it will display database objects based on the desired settings. The Navigation Pane's grouping menu can be shown by clicking the arrow button found to the right of the pane's title text. The Navigation Pane's grouping menu shows the current grouping options available for the pane in the current database. Since all Navigation Pane settings and options are stored in System Tables for the current database, each database application can have its own settings that do not affect other database applications. Figure 7-3 shows an image of the Navigation Pane's grouping menu.

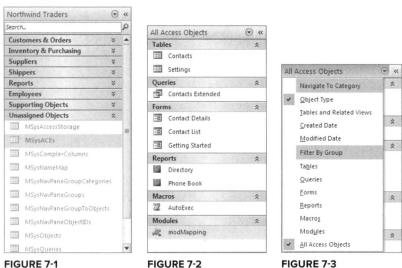

FIGURE 7-1   **FIGURE 7-2**   **FIGURE 7-3**

The Navigation Pane comes with a number of predefined group settings, which have names that are more or less self-explanatory. When one of the grouping options is selected, the Navigation Pane switches to the selected view. These predefined options are as follows:

➤ Object Type

➤ Tables and Related Views

  Created Date

- ➤ Modified Date

- ➤ Tables

- ➤ Queries

- ➤ Forms

- ➤ Reports

- ➤ Macros

- ➤ Modules

- ➤ All Access Objects (Default)

For example, selecting the Object Type grouping option on the grouping menu will group the database objects shown in the Navigation Pane by the type of object, under headers that are categorized by the specific object names, such as Tables or Macros. If a particular group does not contain any objects, the Navigation Pane will hide the empty group header. However, as soon as there is at least one object for a group, the group header for that object type will appear in the pane. Selecting the Tables and Related Views grouping option will group the database objects by the tables and queries that make up their specific record sources and all remaining objects are dumped into the Unrelated Objects group. All of the built-in grouping types can be extremely useful, depending on how you want the database's users to interact with the database objects.

Expanding and Collapsing the Pane

The Navigation Pane can be expanded and collapsed. Instead of completely hiding it from the user, you can leave only the Shutter Bar for the user to see. The Shutter Bar is the vertical bar along the left side of the Access program window, providing an open button of sorts for the pane. Collapsing the pane frees up screen space in the main Access program window, allowing more of the database objects to be shown when opened. If needed, clicking the Shutter Bar, or pressing the F11 key, expands the Navigation Pane to full view again. Although a minor feature, it can be useful when a user needs to free up space in the Access window, but still needs to be able to use the Navigation Pane to interact with the database application.

Opening Database Objects

As mentioned, the Navigation Pane's primary purpose is to let the user see and open the various objects contained in the database. The pane provides a few different methods of opening database objects, which are as follows:

- ➤ **Double-clicking an object** – Double-clicking any object in the Navigation Pane will open the object in its normal view mode.

- ➤ **The Navigation Pane context menu** – Right-clicking any object will reveal a menu with one or more options for opening the database object.

- ➤ **Pressing the Enter key** – Pressing the Enter key when a database object in the Navigation Pane is selected and the pane has focus will open the object in its normal view mode.

The Navigation Pane's Context Menu

The Navigation Pane's context menu can be shown by right-clicking any database object. The Navigation Pane's context menu provides options to Open, Export, Rename, Hide, Delete, Cut, Copy, Paste, View Properties, and Check Web Compatibility when opened for any object. Selecting any of these options for a database object will cause Access to execute that functionality on the given database object. In addition to the context menu for database objects, right-clicking the Navigation Pane's title bar reveals the context menu with slightly different options: Category, Sort By, View By, Show All Groups, Paste, Navigation Options, and Search Bar. The first four options pertain to the grouping and view options for the Navigation Pane, and the final three options are the same as before. In either case, both context menus for the Navigation Pane will be extremely useful when working with the Navigation Pane or the database objects.

Database Object Properties

If you choose the View Properties option from the context menu for any database object in the Navigation Pane, the Properties dialog for that object will be opened. While the Properties dialog for any object only shows a fraction of the object's actual properties, it does provide the ability to set that database object as Hidden, hiding the database object in the Navigation Pane in the default view. The Properties dialog for the database object also provides information about the created and modified dates, as well as the type, description (if any), and owner of the database object. Figure 7-4 shows the Properties dialog for the Contact Details form in the sample Contacts database application (created from a template).

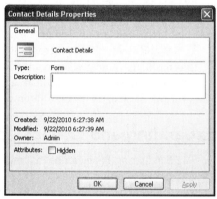

FIGURE 7-4

The Navigation Options Dialog

Selecting the Navigation Options choice from the Navigation Pane's context menu opens the Navigation Options dialog. The Navigation Options dialog is where you can modify the Navigation Pane's settings and create custom groups. The Navigation Options dialog provides options for managing existing grouping options, creating new groups, showing and hiding the system and hidden tables, showing and hiding the Search Bar, and toggling between Single-click and Double-click settings. Figure 7-5 shows the Navigation Options dialog.

The Search Bar

The Navigation Pane includes a Search Bar, which can be used quickly to filter the items displayed in the Navigation Pane. Hidden by default, the revealed Search Bar is near the top of the pane just above the first object group. If the Search Bar is not visible, selecting the Show Search Bar option on the Navigation Options dialog will reveal the Search Bar.

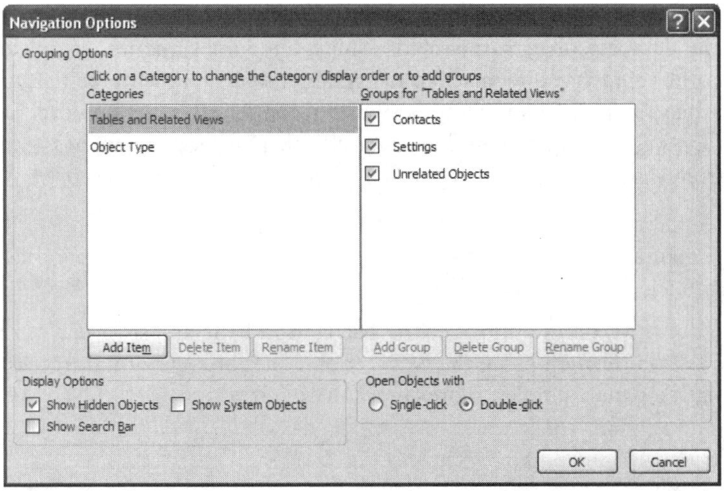

FIGURE 7-5

To search for an object using the Search Bar, type the name of the object in the search box. As you type the name, Access narrows the search by removing items from the Navigation Pane that are not matches to the text being typed. Access will not return the object being searched if the object is hidden (in the current view of the Navigation Pane) or if the object group is not currently visible.

Custom Groups

Probably the most important feature that the Navigation Options dialog provides is the ability to add, modify, delete, and rename categories and groups in the Navigation Pane. Custom groups can be used to group related database objects together, hide objects from the user, or organize objects in the desired manner. When database objects are assigned to a custom group, you will see shortcuts that refer to the actual objects in custom groups, instead of to the actual database objects. Deleting the shortcut to a database object will not delete the object itself. Instead, the shortcut will be removed from the group and the actual object will be shown in the Unrelated Objects group. Using shortcuts also allows Access to show a single object in multiple categories and even have different display names for a single base object. See Lesson 59 for more about building custom Navigation Pane settings.

Hidden and System Objects

Hidden objects have been hidden by specifying the Hidden option on the object's Properties dialog. It is considered good practice to only expose what is needed through forms and reports. Hiding the objects in the Navigation Pane prevents the average user from breaking something inadvertently. If objects are hidden, users don't tend to notice or tinker with them.

> *However, hiding database objects does not secure them in any way and should not be used as a method of application security. Access provides other true security features to make your databases more secure.*

System tables are used by Access to manage almost everything about the database file itself. System tables store information about the database objects, the relationships, temporary queries, complex data, the Navigation Pane, and other database information. All system tables start with the text MSys to denote that they are system tables. System tables can be very useful for determining low-level information about the database, but it is recommended you *do not* modify them directly in any way; and, they should not be modifiable from the Access UI.

TRY IT

In this lesson, you learn how to use the general options of the Navigation Pane and set a few of the options. The following steps walk you through using the Navigation Pane for any normal Access database application, illustrating the pane's simpler, more common operations.

Lesson Requirements

For this lesson, Access 2010 must be installed. This lesson uses the sample Northwind database application, which you can create from a template if you do not already have it available.

Step-by-Step

1. Start Access 2010 and open the Northwind database.

2. If the Navigation Pane is collapsed, open it by clicking the Shutter Bar.

3. Double-click the Customer Details form (or any item) option in the Navigation Pane to open the form in its normal view mode. The form will be opened for the user to see. Click the X button in the top-right corner of the form to close it.

4. Right-click the Customer Details form (or any item) option to show the context menu for the database object.

5. Select the Design View option from the context menu. The form will open in Design View mode for editing and design. Close the form by clicking the X button in the top-right corner of the form.

Congratulations; you have opened a form in two different view modes by using the Navigation Pane. Next, try adjusting the views of the Navigation Pane by completing the following steps.

6. Click the down arrow button on the title bar of the Navigation Pane to show the grouping menu for the pane.

7. On the Navigation Pane's grouping menu, click the Tables option to select it. This hides all objects except the table objects, and the Shutter Bar will now have the label Tables, indicating which objects are available in the current grouping mode.

8. To change the grouping mode to see the reports, select the Reports option from the grouping menu. Repeat this process to see the other object groups.

9. Right-click the Navigation Pane's title bar to show the context menu. Select the View By option to show its submenu and click the Details option. Each object in the Navigation Pane now shows the created and modified date information, along with an icon and the object name.

10.   To switch back, click the Icon option from the View By submenu on the grouping menu. The created and modified date information is removed from the objects in the Navigation Pane, leaving only the icon and the object name again.

11.   To change the Navigation Pane grouping to see all objects related to a particular table under each header, by table name (including Queries, Forms, and Reports), click the down arrow button on the Navigation Pane title bar. The grouping menu is shown, so select the Tables and Related Views option. Now the Navigation Pane shows database objects related to a particular table or query in a group based on that object, and all other, non-related objects are grouped together in the Unrelated Objects group.

Congratulations; you have selected several different grouping option modes in the Navigation Pane. Notice that each time you select a different option, the database objects shown in the Navigation Pane change in one way or another, based upon the grouping option that was selected. Next, complete the following steps to try a few other features that the Navigation Pane has to offer.

12.   Change the grouping mode back to All Access Objects by right-clicking the Navigation Pane's title bar and selecting the All Access Objects option. All of the database objects will be shown under groups by database object type.

13.   Right-click the title bar and click Navigation Options in the menu. The Navigation Options dialog will be opened.

14.   In the Categories column, click the Object Type option to select it. All of the object types (which are the grouping options) will be shown in the Groups column. Uncheck the Tables option and click the OK button to close the Navigation Options dialog. Notice that the Table group is now hidden in the Navigation Pane.

15.   To unhide the Table group, right-click the Navigation Pane's title bar and click the Navigation Options item on the context menu. Again, the Navigation Options dialog will be opened.

16.   In the Categories column, click the Object Type option to select it. All of the object types will be shown in the Groups column again. Check the Tables option and click OK to close the Navigation Options dialog. Notice that the Tables group is visible in the Navigation Pane once again.

17.   You can hide individual objects instead of entire groups by setting the Hidden property for the database object. Right-click any object in the Navigation Pane and choose the View Properties option to open the Properties dialog for the object.

18.   On the Properties dialog, check the Hidden attribute and then click the OK button to save the changes and close the dialog. The object will now be hidden in the Navigation Pane's default view mode and should not be visible (assuming hidden objects are not shown in the Navigation Pane).

19.   To show hidden objects in the Navigation Pane, right-click the title bar and click the Navigation Options item from the menu. The Navigation Options dialog will open.

20.   In the Navigation Options dialog, click the Show Hidden Objects option so that it is checked and then click the OK button to close the dialog. All hidden database objects should be visible in the Navigation Pane, although they will be grayed out to denote that they are marked as hidden.

21. Right-click the object that you marked as hidden in the previous steps to show the context menu for the object. Select the View Properties option to show the Properties dialog for the object again.

22. Click the Hidden attribute to deselect it. Then click the OK button to save the changes and close the Properties dialog. The object will now be unhidden, as any normal database object is by default.

23. Try the search tool to look for a database object. If the Search Bar is not enabled, open the Navigation Options dialog and check the Show Search Bar option.

24. In the Search Bar, type **cu** in the text box. Access filters all objects in the Navigation Pane and removes any object that does not begin with the letters *cu*.

Congratulations; you have opened the Navigation Pane using the Shutter Bar, opened database objects from the pane, switched to different view modes, used the search tool, and changed a database object's attributes to hide or unhide it. Working with objects in the Navigation Pane is really just that simple. Although you haven't exhausted all of the options, you should now have a good understanding of the basic functionality for the Navigation Pane and how it can be used to work with an Access database application.

SUMMARY

It is important that you become familiar with the Navigation Pane because it is how you, as the application developer, organize every object in the database. It is the central repository of database objects and you can choose to organize the objects with the custom tools provided in Access 2010. Often, simple database applications do not have a user interface with custom application navigation other than the Navigation Pane, and in that event, the user accesses all of the database objects through the Navigation Pane. Therefore, customizing the Navigation Pane can provide a useful interface for both the developer and user of an Access database application.

Aside from just working with database objects, the Navigation Pane also provides a number of other features. It enables the ability to organize database objects into predefined or custom, user-created categories. The major benefit is that the developer can create multiple views for the database user to work with. Second, the Search Bar is used to look for individual database objects, which expedites a search — especially when the database has a large number of objects. Instead of having to sort the objects by name or date and then scrolling through them individually, the search tool quickly narrows the search by showing only the objects that have the selected text. Finally, the ability to hide both selected database objects and system objects reduces the amount of clutter in the Navigation Pane and is a great way to obscure from the user's view database objects that are normally not used directly from the Navigation Pane. Access 2010 makes it easier than ever to use and work with the Navigation Pane features and the database objects in any Access application.

 Please select Lesson 7 on the DVD to view the video that accompanies this lesson.

8

Creating a Table in Datasheet View

Tables are probably the most important part of a database. Tables are made up of sets of fields (columns) that are defined as specific data types. Tables store data in these fields in the form of individual records (rows) in the table. Access makes it very easy to create new tables and edit existing ones, and a number of methods exist for doing so in Access 2010, such as Datasheet or Design View modes. This lesson discusses the basics of building tables for a database application using Datasheet View mode in Access 2010.

LESSON SETUP

In this lesson, you learn how to create a table using the Datasheet View designer in Access 2010. Datasheet View allows you to quickly add fields, set the data type of the field, and enter data into the table, all in a tabular layout that is similar to an Excel worksheet.

CREATING TABLES IN ACCESS 2010

The Create Ribbon offers three basic methods for creating tables. The Table button creates and opens a new table in Datasheet View mode. The Table Design button opens the table in Design View mode and is the traditional method of creating tables. Design View also provides easy access to all the properties of the fields in the table. This allows you greater control when designing the table. The SharePoint Lists button allows the user to create linked tables to a new SharePoint list. This lesson discusses creating Access table objects in an ACCDB database file using the Table Design button to create the table in Datasheet View mode.

Terms

The following is a list of terms that you should be familiar with to complete this lesson. The terms will help you understand the basics of working with database tables:

➤ Access is a *relational database* system and it creates databases with a collection of tables that often link dimensions of data in one table to others. For example, you have a database that houses all of your customer information for your business, and you need to create a newsletter mailing list. At a minimum, the database applications should contain a `Customer` table, which contains data about your customers, and a `Mailing List` table, which contains at least one field that stores the ID values of records in the customer table that are to be sent the mailing list.

➤ *Primary keys* and *foreign keys* are table fields used in a relational database system to relate data from one table to another. A primary key is a table field that contains unique values that Access uses to identify the record. A foreign key is a field in a table that contains values from a primary key field in a related table. Primary keys come in two types: natural and surrogate.

   ➤ *Natural keys* are values that are derived from the data being compiled and stored. Social Security numbers (SSNs) are examples of natural keys. SSNs are usually unique to a single employee and unlikely to be issued to more than one employee. Notwithstanding the security issues of storing an employee's SSN, it is a candidate for use as a primary key. The values from multiple fields can be combined to form a natural *compound key*. The number of the department that hired the employee, the hire date, and the last four digits of the SSN could be used to uniquely identify the employee. Though SSNs are usually unique to a single person, uniqueness cannot be guaranteed. Avoiding the possibility of encountering duplicate key values is very important. Surrogate keys are an alternative method used to enforce unique values.

   ➤ *Surrogate keys* are values created by the database that have no meaning outside the database. In Access, the `AutoNumber` data type is used to create a unique value to use as a primary key. The `AutoNumber` data type should not be used as a number that a user will see or to which someone will apply meaning. The Access `AutoNumber` data type can be used with a natural key to form a compound key to ensure a unique value.

Naming Schemes

Numerous naming schemes are used with Access databases. There is not a single correct scheme, but you should be consistent in how objects are named throughout your database. There are some things you should not use when naming Access objects. Although Access will allow their use, *do not use* special characters, with the exception of the underscore, to name any object. *Do not use* reserved words as the name of an object. Reserved words are loosely defined as any word used by Access as a function or built-in object name.

A couple pseudo-standardized naming schemes are available. The *camel case* is a method used to distinguish words in a phrase without using spaces; instead of a space, capitalize the first letter of each word in a phrase. `NameFirst`, `NameLast`, and `PostalCode` are examples. This allows the use of more descriptive names without using special characters. Prefixes to object names also serve to identify the type of objects: `tbl` for tables, `frm` for forms, and `qry` for queries. These practices are for the database developer's benefit and Access does not require using naming schemes or prefixes. No matter which naming convention scheme you choose will be sure to make it easier when creating and maintaining the database application over the long term.

CREATING A TABLE IN DATASHEET VIEW

Creating a table in Datasheet View mode is the quickest, simplest method to create a table and add fields. This is accomplished by using the Table button on the Create Ribbon. The options on the Table Tools Ribbon allow most common table properties and features to be set without a need to access the table's properties in the table designer. Figure 8-1 shows a new table created in Datasheet View mode in the Access 2010 program window.

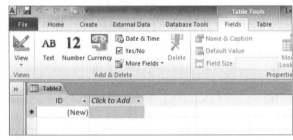

FIGURE 8-1

Complete the following steps to create a new table in Datasheet View mode:

1. Click the Table button on the Create Ribbon. In Datasheet View mode, Access opens a table with a single field named `ID`. The field is an `AutoNumber` data type and has been defined as the primary key for the table.

2. In the cell under the Click to Add Field Header, type the name for the new field.

3. Click the Click to Add Field Header drop-down menu to select the data type. A new column appears to the right of the field just created.

4. Add other fields as needed and save the table.

The Table Tools Ribbon

By default, the Table Tools Ribbon appears when a table is opened in Datasheet View mode. The Table Tools Ribbon provides a number of options for working with the fields and settings for the table. The Table Tools Fields Ribbon is shown in Figure 8-2.

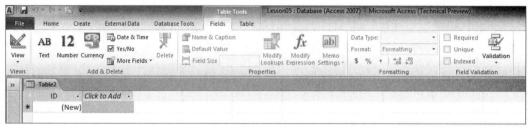

FIGURE 8-2

Adding New Fields to a Table

Once a table has been created, you need to create fields in the table to store the parts of the data in each record. The Table Tools Ribbon provides a number of tools for working with the fields and settings. The following is on the Table Tools Fields Ribbon for working with field settings:

➤ The Add & Delete section of the Table Tools Fields Ribbon adds a new field. Each new field is named by using its corresponding data type. Refer again to Figure 8-2.

➤ The More Fields button opens a drop-down list of options available for creating fields of different data types.

➤ The Delete button completely removes the field that is currently selected in the datasheet.

You can add fields by using the buttons on the Ribbon, or by clicking the Click to Add drop-down in the table itself, which presents a list of the Access data types. You must choose a data type to create a new field, and in most instances the data type can be changed later if an incorrect type was chosen. Access tries to determine the data type by the data that is added, but can be wrong. For example, if you enter a value of 5, Access will make this a `Number` data type, but you may have wanted a `String` data type.

Setting Data Types

Access 2010 provides these defined data types for table fields:

➤ Text

➤ Number

➤ Currency

➤ Date/Time

➤ Yes/No

➤ Memo

➤ Attachment

➤ Hyperlink

➤ Calculated

Also, the Number data type provides a further subtype that is defined by using the Field Properties settings of the table when it is opened in Design View mode. The Number field subtypes, which are set by using the Field Size property, follow:

➤ Byte

➤ Integer

➤ Long Integer

➤ Single

➤ Double

➤ Replication ID

➤ Decimal

The first three subtypes are integers: Byte, Integer, and Long Integer. Integers are whole numbers and cannot store any values to the right of the decimal. The Byte type is limited to unsigned integers from 0 to 255 (8-bit). The Integer type can be signed integers with a range of –32,678 to 32,767 (16-bit). The Long Integer type has a range of –2,147,483,648 to 2,147,483,647 (32-bit).

Single and Double are floating-point decimals. Single, a 32-bit number, can hold values from -3.402823^{38} to 3.402823^{38}. Double, a 64-bit number, can store large values between -1.79769313486231^{308} and -4.94065645841247^{-324} for negative values and 1.79769313486231^{308} and 4.94065645841247^{-324} for positive values. Floating-point types are approximations of the actual number. The approximation of numbers is necessary due to the way the computer's microprocessor handles numbers.

The Decimal data type is a fixed-point number and can hold numbers from $-10^{28}-1$ through $10^{28}-1$. *Precision* is the total number of digits that the type can hold, and *scale* is the number of digits to the right of the decimal point. A Decimal number with a precision of 28 and a scale of 10 could have a maximum of 18 numbers to the left of the decimal and 10 to the right. Table Datasheet View mode does not allow the user to set the subtype of a Number field data type; these settings must be set in Table Design View.

APPLICATION PARTS IN ACCESS 2010

New to Access 2010, the Templates section of the Create Ribbon provides a single button called Application Parts. When the Application Parts button is clicked, a drop-down menu lists available Template objects and is divided into two sections: Blank Forms and Quick Start. The Quick Start section provides a list of table template options which, when selected, create a set of new tables and related forms for that Template object set. The Create Relationship Wizard is launched when one of the Quick Start options is selected, allowing the user to select a relationship to be created between the new table and any existing table in the database. You can create your own Application Part templates by saving a copy of the Template objects in the Quick Start section.

SHAREPOINT LINKED TABLES IN ACCESS 2010

To create a SharePoint List from an Access database (which requires access to an existing SharePoint server), Access 2010 provides the Create New List Wizard. You can invoke the wizard by choosing one of the options from the SharePoint Lists button in the Tables section of the Create Ribbon. Clicking the SharePoint Lists button presents the user with six choices:

➤ **Contacts** creates a SharePoint contacts list.

➤ **Tasks** creates a SharePoint tasks list.

➤ **Issues** creates an SharePoint issues list.

➤ **Events** creates a SharePoint events list.

➤ **Custom** allows you to create a customized SharePoint list.

➤ **Existing SharePoint List** creates a linked table to an existing SharePoint list.

The first four choices are Microsoft-designed lists that correspond to list templates on SharePoint 2010. The Custom option allows you to use an existing SharePoint list. Figure 8-3 shows the options available when creating a SharePoint list from an Access database.

Selecting the Issues list opens the Create New List Wizard and requests information for the SharePoint site, the name for the new list, and a description for the list, all of which are stored in the list settings on the SharePoint server. Once the name and SharePoint site have been specified, and the OK button is clicked on the wizard, Access takes the following actions:

➤ Creates the new list on the SharePoint server.

➤ Creates a linked table in the database to that new list on the SharePoint server.

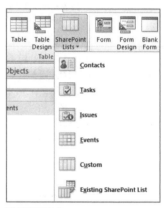

FIGURE 8-3

 When the name of the list specified in the Wizard is already used for a list name on the SharePoint site, SharePoint will create the new list with an ordinal number on the end, so that the original list is not overwritten or used incorrectly.

Figure 8-4 shows the Create New List Wizard dialog used to create a SharePoint linked table using Access 2010.

TRY IT

In this lesson, you create a table, add fields, set the data types of those fields, and require that a field have data in it before saving the record. Now that you are familiar with Table objects in an Access database and know about the different supported field data types, the following steps walk through creating a new table in Access 2010. All of these steps are completed using the Datasheet View mode designer for tables in Access 2010.

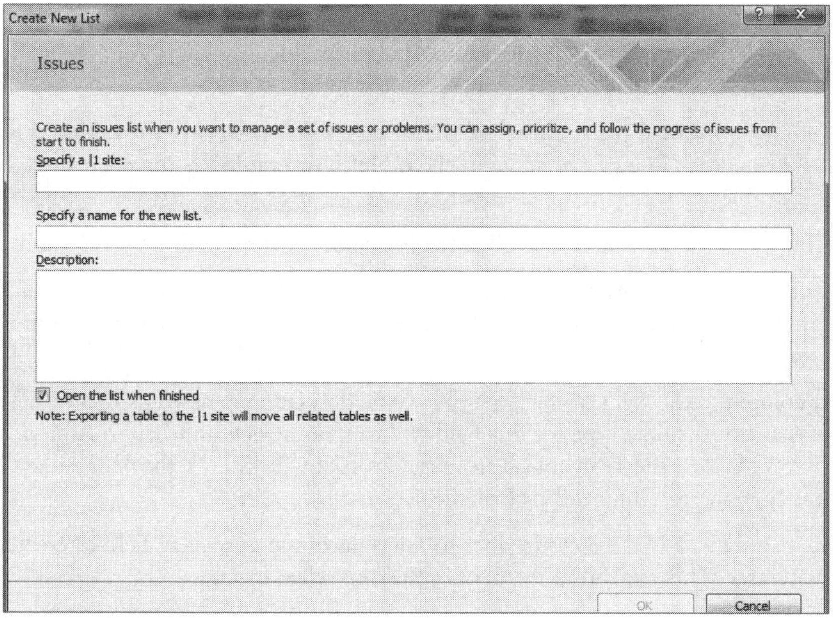

FIGURE 8-4

Lesson Requirements

For this lesson, Access 2010 must be installed and you need to either create a new, blank database or use one of the existing databases from the previous lessons. You should be familiar with creating new databases and new database objects (described in the previous lessons). This lesson uses a blank database, so there are no special prerequisite database objects or data necessary for completing this lesson. This example focuses on building a new table, completely from scratch, in a new Access database.

Step-by-Step

1. Start Access 2010 from the Windows Start menu. The Access 2010 Backstage will be opened.

2. On the Backstage, click the Blank Database option under the Available Templates section in the middle of the screen to select it.

3. Optionally, choose a name and folder location for the new database.

4. Click the Create button on the right side of the Backstage screen to create the new, blank database file. The new database will be created and opened in Access.

5. By default, when a new database is created, a new table is created and opened in Datasheet View mode (which is the mode you want to use here). For the purpose of this lesson, close the default table by clicking the X button on the top right of the table. This will remove the

table, but you will create a new one (in a few steps) in the manner consistent with this lesson's earlier discussion.

6. Click the Create tab to open the Create Ribbon.

7. Click the Table button on the Create Ribbon to create a new, blank table in Datasheet View. The new table will be created and opened in the Access window.

8. Click the Save button in the top-left corner of the Access window to save the table. This opens the Save As dialog. Change the name of the table to **tblEmployee** and click the OK button. The new table is saved.

9. Click the ID column in the table and then click the Name & Caption button on the Ribbon.

10. Change the text in the header of the field from ID to **EmployeeID**, and add a description for the field. Right-click the Field Header, select Rename from the menu, and change the name of the field.

11. Click the next column to the right of the EmployeeID field to create a new Last Name field. Because a name is text, the data type for this field will be Text. Click on Click to Add in the Field Header and select the Text option from the drop-down. Change the field name to **LastName** directly in the column header of the field.

12. Click the Click to Add text in the Field Header to the right of the LastName field to create a field for the first name. This expands a menu of options to select from.

13. Select the Text option. A new Text type field will be added to the table and the field name text will be selected.

14. While the field name is selected, type in **FirstName**. The name of the field will be updated to be FirstName and shown in the Field Header.

15. Create a field to store the employee's birth date. Click the Field Header of the next column and this time select Date & Time to make the field a DateTime data type. Change the name of the field to **DateOfBirth**.

16. Save and close the table.

17. Create a second table by repeating Step 7 and name the table **tblAddress**.

18. Change the ID field name to **AddressID**.

19. Add a field that will be a foreign key to the Employee table, select Number as the data type, and name it **EmployeeID**. Remember, the AutoJoin feature in Access automatically creates a join between two tables when the tables share a field with the same data type and the same field name. One of the fields must be a primary key for AutoJoin to work.

20. Add six fields: **Address1, Address2, City, State, PostalCode,** and **Country**. For this example, all of these fields should be the Text data type. The last four fields could also be foreign keys to lookup tables; this would be a more normalized table design.

21. Close the table and choose Yes when prompted to save the table.

Congratulations; you have created a table in Datasheet View mode. To verify that the table is working, double-click either of the tables you created in the Navigation Pane to open it back up in Datasheet View mode. The table is now ready to begin having data added to it.

SUMMARY

Creating a table and adding fields using the Access 2010 Table Datasheet View mode is a simple and easy process for new users of Access. The Datasheet View mode allows the user to create the fields of a table in a tabular layout, much like an Excel spreadsheet. However, although you can build the fields for the table, the Datasheet View designer does not expose a way to define many of the field properties, including a field's specific number subtype, so it is not the perfect solution to building tables in Access 2010. Still, building tables in Datasheet View mode using Access 2010 is extremely easy and can be much faster for building tables in some cases.

 Please select Lesson 8 on the DVD to view the video that accompanies this lesson.

Creating a Table in Design View

In Lesson 8, the previous lesson, you learned how to create tables using Datasheet View mode and the built-in table wizards in Access 2010. However, Access 2010 offers another, more important table designer, which is the Table Design View designer. As the original method for creating tables in an Access database, most developers still use the Table Design View designer to create and modify tables. The Table Design View designer provides Access's richest design experience for tables. The tools to add or delete fields and to set the many field properties are all exposed to the developer in Table Design View. This lesson focuses on creating tables using the Table Design View designer.

Becoming familiar with the Table Design View designer and its tools is very important for an Access developer. Learning how to use the Table Design View will make creating custom tables much easier for you in the long run. Before creating your tables, it is highly recommended to first design your database tables and relationships to show how each table relates to the other tables. This is the core design for the database application, because the database will store all of the data. Database design can be done using a pencil and paper or with software tools like Microsoft Visio. By first visualizing how the data will be stored, and how each table and each field in the tables will relate to the other tables, you get a better understanding of how the data should be stored and accessed. This is typically done long before you ever open Access. Proper planning leads to fewer design changes during the development stage. This lesson is devoted to discussing the Access 2010 Table Design View designer and how it can be used to build tables in an Access database application.

LESSON SETUP

In this lesson you learn how to create a table using the Access 2010 Table Design View designer. You then use the designer to modify the table to meet your design specifications. You should be familiar with starting Access 2010, creating databases, and what tables in a database do to complete this lesson successfully.

CREATING A TABLE IN DESIGN VIEW

Once a database file has been created, you can begin creating the tables for the application. The Table Design button is located in the Tables section of the Create Ribbon. Clicking the Table Design button creates a new table and opens it in Design View, showing a form with the field designer as a grid at the top that contains three columns:

➤ Field Name — Where the field name is defined.

➤ Data Type — The data type for the field is set here.

➤ Description — This describes how the field is used, what kind of information is stored, or other information to document the field's purpose.

On the bottom of the table designer form, beneath the grid, is a section named Field Properties. This section has two tabs for setting the various field properties:

➤ General — Context-sensitive and displays the properties based on the data type of the field that is selected.

➤ Lookup — Context-sensitive and contains the properties needed to create lookup fields.

The Field Properties section provides access to most of the properties for any table field and can be used to manipulate their settings. Figure 9-1 shows a new table opened in Table Design View.

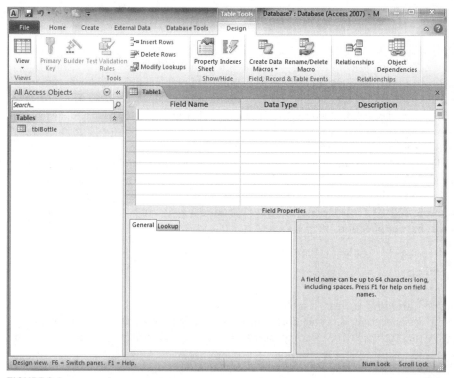

FIGURE 9-1

Becoming familiar with these sections of the Table Design View designer is **vital to the efficient cre**ation and maintenance of the tables in an Access database application.

The Table Tools Design Ribbon

The Design Ribbon holds the tools used to set and modify the table properties. **It is divided into** five sections:

➤ Views

   ➤ Datasheet View — Opens a table in Datasheet View.

   ➤ PivotTable View — Opens a table in PivotTable View.

   ➤ PivotChart View — Opens a table in PivotChart View.

   ➤ Design View — The Design View is used to create or modify **a table.**

➤ Tools

   ➤ Primary Key — Sets the selected field as the primary key.

   ➤ Builder — Starts the Builder for the selected field.

   ➤ Test Validation Rules — Checks the validation rules of the table **for all data in the table.**

   ➤ Insert Rows — Inserts a row(s) above the field(s) selected.

   ➤ Delete Rows — Deletes one or more of the currently selected **fields.**

   ➤ Modify Lookups — Starts the Lookup Wizard for the **currently selected field and** converts that field to a lookup field if it is not already.

➤ Show/Hide

   ➤ Property Sheet — Shows or hides the Property Sheet for the **table's properties.**

   ➤ Indexes — Shows or hides the table's Index dialog box.

➤ Field, Record & Table Events

   ➤ Create Data Macros — Data macros are a new feature introduced **in Access 2010.** They are similar to Triggers in Microsoft SQL Server and allow **limited table event** procedures to execute when certain table-level events take place.

   ➤ Rename/Delete Macro — Does just what its name implies.

➤ Relationships

   ➤ Relationships — Opens the Relationship Tools Design View **dialog. The Relationship** Tools Design View dialog is used to create relationships between **tables and to edit** the settings of the relationships in the database.

   ➤ Object Dependencies — Opens the Object Dependencies pane. **The Object Dependencies** pane shows which database objects depend on, or are dependent **on, the current table** opened in Design View.

Adding New Fields

Unlike Table Datasheet View mode, when a table is created in Design View, Access does not automatically add an `AutoNumber` field (named `ID`) that it designates as the primary key. Instead, the developer must manually add all fields and set all properties without the assistance of a wizard. Each row in the design grid represents a field in the table, and to add a field to the table you simply type a name for the field.

Choosing a Field Name

Access imposes a couple of small requirements when creating a name for a field in a table. The following is a list of requirements for the field name:

➤ The name must contain between 1 and 64 characters.

➤ The name must *not* contain:

   ➤ A period (.) character.

   ➤ An exclamation point (!) character.

   ➤ A square bracket ([or]) character.

   ➤ A tab, carriage return, or other non-printable character.

   ➤ A space as the starting character of the name.

Other than those few basic requirements, you can choose just about any set of characters as a field name that you wish. However, we highly recommend considering a few other things when choosing a field name: The field names should be as descriptive and self-documenting as possible. Using cryptic field names will probably cause confusion over the life of the database. A good tip is to avoid the use of spaces and other special characters when names are applied to fields and tables. For example, when creating a field name, instead of using a value of `Last Name`, use `LastName`. The camel case convention value excludes the space and uses capital letters for the first letters of the two words. All a user needs to do is look at the field name to determine what should be stored there. Moreover, you can always set the Caption property for the field to the value of `Last Name`, so that the field name header in Datasheet View will show a value of `Last Name` (with a space between the words), instead of `LastName`. And no matter which naming convention you decide to use (if any), be as consistent as possible.

Setting Data Types

After naming the field and entering the description, the developer must either accept the default data type or select a desired data type. The default data type is Text with a default field size value of `255`. You can change the default data type for new fields from the Backstage by using the Access Options dialog. Lesson 10 discusses each of the following data types in detail, but in general the data types available in an Access 2010 ACCDB file are:

➤ Text

➤ Memo

➤ Number

➤ Date/Time

➤ Currency

➤ AutoNumber

➤ Yes/No

➤ OLE Object

➤ Hyperlink

➤ Attachment

➤ Calculated

With the exception of the Text and Number data types, once the type is selected from the drop-down list in the Data Type column, there are no additional type attributes to set. With the Text data type the field size value may be set and it can be any length between 1 and 255. The Number data type has seven sub-data types that range from Byte to Decimal. You set these properties, and all additional field properties, in the table designer's Field Properties section. The Number field subtypes available in Access 2010 are:

➤ Byte

➤ Integer

➤ Long Integer

➤ Single

➤ Double

➤ Replication ID

➤ Decimal

All of these Number subtypes and their specific supported values are discussed in Lesson 10 in detail. Be sure to review that lesson for more information about the Number subtypes.

New in Access 2010 is the Calculated data type for tables. If a calculated total needed to be displayed in a record in previous Access versions, the total was calculated in a query, a form, or a report. In Access 2010, the new Calculated data type allows table-level calculations and are activated when the record is opened. Because the calculation occurs at the table level, the results are not stored directly in the table. This makes calculated fields extremely useful, simply because they do not consume the amount of space that their calculated values normally would. Lesson 10 discusses Calculated data type in detail.

Setting Field Properties

Once the data type has been selected, the Field Properties section of the Design View dialog is activated with the properties that are related to the specific data type of the field. Figure 9-2 shows a portion of the Field Properties General tab. When a particular field type has a lot of properties, a scroll bar is provided to view all of the properties.

Format styles, input masks, default values, validation rules, whether an entry is required, or if the field has an index are all set on the General tab. Lesson 11 discusses in detail the properties available for each data type.

The Lookup tab is used to create a field-level lookup. The process of creating lookup fields is simple. You have the option of creating a value list for the field or to look up the values in another table. And with slightly more effort, you can establish a lookup table, which utilizes a relationship between a lookup table and the current table. A lookup table is generally recommended over using just a value list for the field.

General	Lookup	
Field Size	255
Format	
Input Mask	
Caption	
Default Value	
Validation Rule	
Validation Text	
Required	No
Allow Zero Length	Yes
Indexed	No
Unicode Compression	Yes
IME Mode	No Control
IME Sentence Mode	None
Smart Tags	

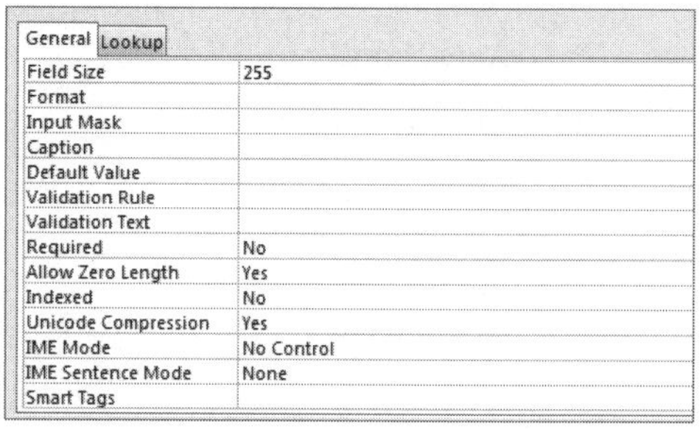

FIGURE 9-2

Adding a Primary Key

It is recommended — required if you intend to have system relationships between this table and others — that each table have a primary key field. A *primary key* is a field, or combination of fields, whose values are guaranteed to be unique within the table fields. The most common primary key field type in Access databases is a single field with an AutoNumber data type. Other examples of primary keys could be a customer account number; an employee number; or a compound key using last name, first name, middle initial, and date of birth. The principal requirement for a primary key is that the value be unique within the scope of the table.

To add a primary key to a table using Access 2010, select the field (or set of fields) and then click the Primary Key button on the Table Tools Design Ribbon. However, you should know that a few data types cannot be used for a primary key: Memo, OLE Object, Attachment, and Calculated data types. Behind the scenes, Access will create a unique index for the fields that comprise the key. Figure 9-3 shows the primary key indicator, which Access adds next to the field name in the table. Access will prompt you to add a primary key if one has not been created the first time the table is saved.

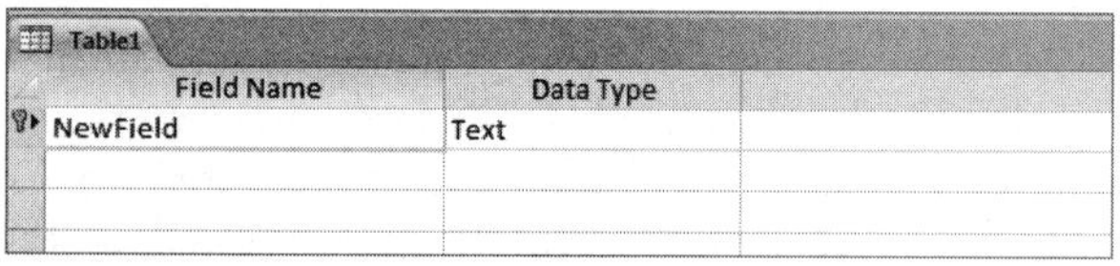

	Field Name	Data Type	
▶	NewField	Text	

FIGURE 9-3

TRY IT

In this lesson, you create a table using the Table Design View designer to track bottles of wine in a personal wine cellar. You add multiple fields, create a single field primary key, create an index, change the type of primary key to a compound primary key, and set field properties. Complete the following step-by-step example to accomplish this task.

Lesson Requirements

For this lesson, Access 2010 must be installed. You should be familiar with opening a database in Access 2010 and the basics of working with Access tables and fields, as discussed earlier, to complete this lesson successfully. This lesson uses a new, blank database to complete the following steps.

Step-by-Step

1. Open Access 2010 and create a new, blank database.

2. If Access opens with a blank table in Datasheet View, click the X button on the top right of the table to close it without saving.

3. Click the Create tab of the Ribbon.

4. Click the Table Design button in the Tables section of the Create Ribbon to open a new table in Design View. Notice that the Ribbon switches to the Table Tools Design Ribbon.

5. Add a field to the table by typing the desired field name into the first row of the Field Name column in the design grid for the table. Type in a field name of **BottleID**.

6. On the Table Tools Design Ribbon, change the data type by selecting the AutoNumber option from the Data Type drop-down list.

7. Type the value **Primary Key** in the Description field to identify it as the primary key.

8. Add a field named **Winery** and select Text from the Data Type drop-down list.

9. Click the Primary Key button on the Ribbon to make the field the primary key for the table.

In a working application, this field would probably be a foreign key to a winery table. In that case the data type would need to match the data type of the winery table's primary key. There will be additional fields in this table that are candidates for their own table, but for this "Try It" you will not use lookup tables.

10. Add a field named **WineColor** and choose Text data type.

11. Add a field named **LabelName** and choose Text data type.

12. Add a field named **Appellation** and choose Text data type.

13. Add a field named **Varietal** and choose Text data type.

14. Add a field named **Vintage** and choose Number data type.

15. Set the Field Size to the Long option in the Field Properties section of the table designer.

16. Add a field named **Date Acquired** and choose Date/Time data type.

17. Add a field named **DateRemoved** and choose Date/Time data type.

18. Save the table as **tblBottle**.

19. Open the table in Datasheet View by clicking the View button. Notice the option to add a new field, since the table is in Datasheet View.

> *To remove the Click to Add option for a table in Datasheet View, uncheck the Enable Design Changes for Tables in Datasheet View option in the Access Options dialog (under the Current Database tab).*

20. Click the File tab on the Ribbon to open the Backstage. In the Backstage, click the Options button (on the bottom left of the screen).

21. Select Current Database and uncheck Enable Design Changes for Tables in Datasheet View. Click OK to close the dialog and return to the table.

> *The database must be closed and reopened for this change to be activated for the database session. After closing and reopening the database, you can open the table to see that the Click to Add field option has been removed.*

22. From the Navigation Pane, open the table tblBottle in Design View to modify some field properties. Place the cursor in the WineColor field; in the Field Properties section, change the Field Size property value to **15**.

23. Place the cursor in the Validation Rule row of the Field Properties. Invoke a builder by clicking the Builder button on the Ribbon.

24. For the Validation Rule property value, type **Red or White or Rose**.

25. In the Validation Text row type **Valid entries are Red, White, or Rose**. Then click the Save button on the top left of the Access window to save the table.

26. Add an index to the Vintage field by placing the cursor in the Vintage row and change Indexed property value to **Yes (Duplicates OK)**. Then click the Save button on the top left of the Access window to save the table.

27. Move the DateAcquired field by selecting the DateAcquired field and dragging it to just under the BottleID row.

28. Select both the BottleID row and the DateAcquired row and click the Primary Key button on the Design Ribbon to create a compound primary key. Then click the Save button on the top left of the Access window to save the table.

29. Add a field named **Cost**, and choose the Currency data type.

30. Open the table by clicking the View button. To test the Validation rule, type a value other than Red, White, or Rose directly in the WineColor field. You should receive an error message.

31. Complete a record by entering values into a record in the tblBottle table, but do not enter a date in the DateAcquired field and take note of the error raised.

Congratulations; you have created a table in the Access 2010 Design View mode. Lesson 10 discusses the data types used in Access. Figure 9-4 is a view of the completed tblBottle table.

tblBottle		
Field Name	**Data Type**	**Description**
BottleID	AutoNumber	Primary Key
DateAquired	Date/Time	Date that wine was aquired
Winery	Text	Name of Winery
WineColor	Text	Color of the wine
LabelName	Text	The name of the wine as printed on the label
Appelation	Text	Region where the wine is grown
Varietal	Text	Type of grape or blend
Vintage	Number	Year harvested
DateRemoved	Date/Time	Date bottle was removed from the cellar.
Cost	Currency	Cost of the bottle of wine.

Field Properties

General | Lookup

Field Size	Long Integer
New Values	Increment
Format	
Caption	
Indexed	Yes (Duplicates OK)
Smart Tags	
Text Align	General

FIGURE 9-4

SUMMARY

Access 2010, like previous versions of Access, includes the Access Design View mode designer, which is a powerful, easy-to-use tool that builds and modifies database tables. The data types include the new Calculated type, which adds the functionality of runtime calculations each time a table is opened or accessed programmatically (instead of requiring the calculation to be in a query, form, or report). The Field Properties section of Table Design View allows a developer to add table-level data validation, set the field size, and add indexes, formats, and other field properties.

This brief lesson has shown several important steps to building the tables for a working database. It, and the lessons to follow, lay the foundation for your database. An excellent way to enhance your learning experience is to explore the property settings and other tools available on the Ribbon. Change settings, add features, and generally play with all of the table objects to learn what happens when you do. You will not break Access while you are experimenting with the tables in a sample database, so enjoy!

 Please select Lesson 9 on the DVD to view the video that accompanies this lesson.

10

Access 2010 Data Types

Access 2010 (and other databases systems for that matter) define different representations of data, such as numbers, text, and other common items stored in a database table field, as specific *data types* to be stored within the field. Common data types are numbers, strings of characters, and date and time values. Access has special data types, such as OLE Object, Calculated, and Attachment fields, which hold specific types of objects or perform table-level calculations. As you have seen in the previous two lessons, each field in an Access database must have a data type defined for that field. Selecting the correct data type to match the characteristics and use of the data being stored is an important part of the design process. This lesson is dedicated to discussing the different data types supported for Access table fields and is designed to help define which values each of those data types can represent.

LESSON SETUP

In this lesson you learn about the different data types available for table fields in Access 2010. You should be familiar with creating tables and understand the basics of how they work. Each of the supported Access 2010 table field data types is discussed in detail.

ACCESS 2010 FIELD DATA TYPES

As noted earlier in this lesson, Access table fields are defined as specific data types and the data type selected for the field will determine the data values that can be stored in that field. The following list shows each of the Access 2010 data types, as well as a couple of other specific field settings that determine the type of data stored in the field:

- ➤ Text
- ➤ Memo
- ➤ Number

➤   Date/Time

➤   Currency

➤   AutoNumber

➤   Yes/No

➤   OLE Object

➤   Hyperlink

➤   Attachment

➤   Calculated

➤   Multivalued

➤   Lookup

Although Multivalued and Lookup are not specific field data types themselves, it is worth discussing them in more detail. Each of the types in the preceding list is discussed in depth in the following sections.

Text Fields

Text fields are used to store alphanumeric characters. Any character in the Access adopted ASCII character set can be stored using the Text data type. The length of the field can be any length between 0 and 255 characters. For example, a name or an address can be stored in this field type. Numbers that are stored in this data type cannot have mathematical operations performed on them. A good example of numerical data that should be stored in a Text field type are Social Security or phone numbers. Text fields are the perfect data type for storing text data values that are up to 255 characters in length.

Memo Fields

Memo field types also store text data values, but can store much longer amounts of text. Memo fields hold up to a maximum of 63,999 characters (as opposed to the 255-character limit of the Text data type). The uses for the Memo data type include detailed freeform comments that exceed the 255-character limit of the text type and combinations of text and numbers. However, the major limitation of the Memo data type is that only the first 255 characters of this field are searchable by queries.

Number Fields

The Number type includes seven subtypes, which are set by using the Field Size property. The first three subtypes: Byte, Integer, and Long, store integer value types. Integers are whole numbers and cannot store any values to the right of the decimal.

➤   Byte supports unsigned integer values from 0 to 255 (8 bit).

➤   Integer supports signed integers with a range of values of –32,678 to 32,767 (16 bit).

➤   Long supports values from –2,147,483,648 to 2,147,483,647 (32 bit).

The next two `Number` subtypes, `Single` and `Double`, store floating-point decimal value types.

➤ `Single` supports 32-bit floating-point numbers and can hold values from -3.4×10^{38} to 3.4×10^{38} and up to 7 significant digits of precision.

➤ `Double` supports 64-bit floating-point numbers and can store values between -1.797×10^{308} and 1.797×10^{308} for large numbers and values between $-4.94065645841247 \times 10^{-324}$ and $4.94065645841247 \times 10^{-324}$ for small numbers, with up to 15 significant digits of precision.

Floating-point types are approximations of the actual number, because the precision of the number is limited.

 For a detailed white paper about floating-point issues, see Intel and Floating Point at `www.intel.com/standards/floatingpoint.pdf`*.*

➤ `Replication ID` supports data type values that represent a 128-bit globally unique identifier (GUID). It is used to identify replicas, replica sets, tables, and records when using Access replication. The `Replication ID` type is used to share information between replicated Access database applications. These types of applications are typically used where users do not have continuous access to a shared database; the database is replicated to allow multiple users to work in multiple, separate copies of the database simultaneously.

➤ `Decimal` supports data type values that are fixed-point numbers and can store values from -10^{28} through $10^{28} - 1$. In this case, the precision is the total number of digits that the type can hold, and *scale* is the number of digits to the right of the decimal point. A Decimal number with a precision of 28 and a scale of 10 could have a maximum of 18 numbers to the left of the decimal and 10 to the right.

Choosing the correct `Number` subtype when designing a table for the database application is extremely important and depends upon the types of values that need to be stored in the field.

Date/Time Fields

The `Date/Time` data type can store date values that range from Jan 1, 100 to Dec 31, 9999. Under the covers, the `Date/Time` data type is really a `Double` number that is used as an offset from the base date. The date part of the `Date/Time` type is stored as the number of days from Dec 30, 1899. For example, the value of 1 corresponds to Dec 31, 1899 and the value 40359 corresponds to June 30, 2010. The time part of the `Date/Time` data type is stored as the fractional decimal value of the number. This value corresponds as a fraction of the day, in microseconds. For example, 0.5 represents noon, 0.75 corresponds to 6:00 PM, and 0.3681712963 is 8:50:10 AM. The `Date/Time` data type is the perfect solution to storing dates after Jan 1, 100 in a database application.

Currency Fields

The `Currency` data type is a fixed-point number that has a precision of 19 digits and a scale of 4. In other words, it can hold a number with 15 digits to the left of the decimal point and 4 digits to the right. The `Currency` data type is used for financial and other numeric data that requires accurate and unchanging decimal values. Some consider the name `Currency` for this data type to be a little misleading, because it displays a default currency indicator; the indicator can be removed for non-financial numeric value storage.

AutoNumber Fields

The `AutoNumber` data type provides an integer number generated internally by Access in a consecutive ordering, starting from the value 1. For this reason, `AutoNumber` fields contain data values that are unique to other rows in that table, which is the reason they are typically used as primary key fields. Under the covers, these values are stored in a `Long` data type field. Their most common usage is a system-generated primary key, and they are extremely common in Access database applications.

OLE Object Fields

The `OLE Object` field data type stores either linked data or embedded objects from other applications, such as an Excel spreadsheet. There is a 1-megabyte limit per record. The `OLE Object` fields have a tendency to cause the database to grow in size very quickly as records are added to the table, so it is usually better to store the actual object in a local folder and use the `OLE Object` field's linking ability to store the object externally from the database. The newer `Attachment` field type is typically a better choice to store file objects internally in the database file.

Hyperlink Fields

The `Hyperlink` data type stores data values like a URL, a path to a file on disk, or to a UNC path on a network. A text string is stored in the field with information that specifies the text to display, address, path, sub-address, and the optional screen tip text. `Hyperlink` fields are extremely useful when you want to store clickable links to content.

Attachment Fields

Introduced originally in Access 2007, the `Attachment` data type can store many file types directly in the database file. The file can be viewed and manipulated in a manner similar to the way e-mail attachments are used (since the attachments are stored in their native formats). Image file attachments can show a preview of the image in the `Attachment` control. In addition, the `Attachment` control UI provides all the features necessary to allow the user to upload and download files from the application, which saves you, the developer, the time and expense of having to develop this UI for the application yourself. The `Attachment` data type is extremely useful for storing multiple files in a table field that are associated with a single record.

Calculated Fields

The `Calculated` field data type is a new ACCDB database file in Access 2010. `Calculated` fields display values that are calculated from an expression, which can be based on one or more fields in the record. This is done at the table level and the data value is recalculated whenever the underlying values in the expression are modified. The actual data type that a `Calculated` field returns is determined by the value result of the field's underlying expression.

Multivalued Fields

Added as part of the Access 2007 release, Multivalued fields are used to simplify the storing of multiple values of a value list or lookup field. Multivalued fields also integrate with SharePoint lists, which also allows multivalue lookups. Use the Lookup Wizard to create this data type or set the Allow Multiple Values property in the field properties. Multivalued fields are only supported in the ACCDB file format.

Lookup Fields

Lookup fields are used to allow values from one field to be related to records in another table. The Lookup Wizard will guide you through the Lookup creation process or you can manually create the settings in the field properties. A Lookup field's actual data type is determined by the primary key type of the records in the lookup.

TRY IT

In this lesson, you create a new table and create a new field for each of the Access 2010 field data types, and explore which values can and cannot be used for the specified type. Now that you are familiar with the different field data types in Access 2010 and know which data types represent which values, the following steps walk you through creating table fields in Access.

Lesson Requirements

For this lesson you need Access 2010 installed and a new blank database. To successfully complete this lesson you should be familiar with the basics of Access table objects and how they are created.

Step-by-Step

1. Start Access 2010 from the Windows Start menu and create a new, blank database from the Backstage with the name **Lesson10.accdb**. The new database will open in Access.

2. Click the Create tab on the Ribbon to open it. Then click the Table Design button on the Create Ribbon. A new table will be opened in Design View mode.

3. Create a new field and name it **FieldText**. Select the Text data type.

4. Continue adding fields in the order of the Data Type drop-down list, naming each **FieldMemo**, **FieldLongInteger**, **FieldByte**, and so on. Use the name of the data type or subtype for each of the supported data types. When a `Number` data type is selected, add a field for each subtype in the Field Size property drop-down list.

5. Click the Save button to save the table. For a name, use the value **tblFieldTypes**. The table is saved and shown in the Navigation Pane.

6. Close the table.

7. In the Navigation Pane, double-click the `tblFieldTypes` to open it in Datasheet View.

8. Enter some sample data values into each field for the first record. Use values that are suitable for the selected data type and use values that are unsuitable. Observe the behavior of Access when you attempt to use improper values.

Congratulations; you have successfully created a new table with all of the different types of Access field data types. Understanding the field data types in Access 2010 is vital to building robust database applications. And working with the various fields of a table and their data types is best accomplished in the Access Table Design View designer!

SUMMARY

Access 2010 supports more field data types for tables than ever before when using the ACCDB file format. Learning which data type is correct for your application is critical to efficient table and database application development. Selecting the correct type early in the design stage of development will help prevent last-minute design changes and type mismatch errors.

When designing a database, take a few minutes to look closely at the data values that you expect to store in each field and compare that with the field type specifications to ensure that you are using the correct type. Using the proper field data types in your applications will save a lot of time and effort.

 Please select Lesson 10 on the DVD to view the video that accompanies this lesson.

11

Table and Field Properties

Access table and field properties are used to control how objects appear and behave at run time. Every Access table has two types of properties: table properties and field properties. Table properties are set to make the table behave in the manner desired by the developer. All tables in Access 2010 have the same set of properties. Field properties are used to set how the fields in the table behave. In contrast to the properties of a table, each data type has a unique set of properties associated with it. This lesson discusses both table and field properties and provides some examples of how these can be applied to an Access database application.

LESSON SETUP

This lesson lists most of the Access table and field properties and provides an explanation of how they are used and set from the Table Design View mode designer. Note that table and field properties can be set using VBA code at run time, but that is beyond the scope of this lesson and is discussed later on in this book. You should be familiar with creating tables and fields in Access 2010 to complete this lesson successfully.

THE TABLE PROPERTY SHEET

When a table is open in Design View, the Table object's Property Sheet can be activated by clicking the Property Sheet button on the Table Tools Design Ribbon. When activated, the Property Sheet is located on the right side of the table design grid by default. This is the standard Property Sheet used to work with forms and reports and to control object properties in Access.

When a table is open in Design View mode and the Property Sheet is shown, there is only one tab available: the General tab. The General tab contains all of the table properties that can be set by the developer at design time. Table 11-1 lists all the table properties, their default settings, and their functions, that are provided on the General tab of the Property Sheet.

TABLE 11-1: Table Properties

PROPERTY	DEFAULT SETTINGS	DESCRIPTION
Read Only When Disconnected	No	Specifies making SharePoint linked tables read-only when no connection to the server is available.
Sub datasheet Expanded	No	Specifies if the records in a related table have an expander control, so they can be viewed from the current table.
Sub datasheet Height	"0"	Sets the viewing height of the sub datasheet when expanded.
Orientation	Left to right	Changes the orientation of how fields are displayed in Datasheet View and how the cursor moves from field to field.
Description		Provides a description of the table's purpose; does not affect the control's behavior.
Default View	Datasheet	Specifies in which view the table will be opened under the default open behavior. Can be Datasheet, Pivot Table, or Pivot Chart.
Validation Rule		An expression to evaluate the data in the table to only allow data in that field that passes the validation rule.
Validation Text		Text to display when the data does not pass the validation rule.
Filter		Filter to restrict records displayed when the table is opened. The filter works like a WHERE clause in a query.
Order By		Used to specify which fields are to be sorted either ascending or descending, if any. Multiple field names should be separated by commas. For example: LastName DESC, FirstName
Sub datasheet Name	[Auto]	Sets the name of the sub datasheet object, or disables sub datasheets for the table when cleared.
Link Child Field		Specifies how Access links fields in child tables. Link Child/Master fields are used to update related records in a related table.
Link Master Fields		Specifies how Access links fields in master tables.
Filter On Load	No	Specifies filtering the dataset when the table is opened, if a filter has previously been applied.
Order By On Load	Yes	Specifies if the table should be sorted by the Order By property when the table is opened.

SETTING TABLE PROPERTIES

The table properties are set in Table Design View from the Property Sheet. To open the Property Sheet, click the Property Sheet button on the Table Design Tools Ribbon. Each property allows free-form entries, both freeform and predefined values, or only predefined values. Some properties include a Builder to assist you with setting the property. To add a value to a property, choose from the list, start a builder (if available), or type in the value that you like. But be sure to save the object once you have updated its properties. Some properties may require that the object be closed and reopened to take effect. Otherwise, setting table properties using the Access Property Sheet is just that easy!

FIELD PROPERTIES

Each field has associated properties which can be set from the Field Properties section of the Table Design View designer. Several unique field properties are used for all of the Access 2010 data types. Only one field property, the Caption property, is common to all 11 data types. Table 11-2 lists most of the Access field properties available and each data type that uses those properties.

TABLE 11-2: Field Properties

FIELD PROPERTY	APPLIES TO DATA TYPE	DESCRIPTION
Allow Zero Length	Text, Memo, and Hyperlink	Specifies whether the field allows a zero-length (empty) string as input.
Append Only	Memo and Hyperlink	Specifies whether the field should append or overwrite data values that are stored in these fields.
Caption	All	Specifies the value that is displayed for the field header when the table is open in Datasheet View.
Decimal Places	Number and Currency	Specifies the number of decimal places for the field.
Default Value	Text, Memo, Number, Date/Time, Currency, Yes/No, and Hyperlink	Specifies the default value of the field for a new record in the table. Built-in functions can be used to create the value. The `Date()` function is an example of setting today's date as the entry in the field. The user can override the default value when entering the record.
Expression	Calculated	Specifies the formula used to calculate the value of the `Calculated` field.
Field Size	Text, Number, and AutoNumber	For the `Text` type, specifies the number of characters allowed in the field. For the `Number` and `AutoNumber` types, specifies the numeric subtype.

continues

TABLE 11-2 *(continued)*

FIELD PROPERTY	APPLIES TO DATA TYPE	DESCRIPTION
Format	Text, Memo, Number, Date/Time, Currency, AutoNumber, Yes/No, Hyperlink, and Calculated	Specifies how the data is to be formatted in the field. Access provides several built-in formats or the user can create custom formats.
IME Mode	Text, Memo, Date/Time, and Hyperlink	Specifies how the user can enter Japanese or Korean character text.
IME Sentence Mode	Text, Memo, Date/Time, and Hyperlink	Specifies the type of IME sentence mode to use.
Indexed	Text, Memo, Number, Date/Time, Currency, AutoNumber, Yes/No, Hyperlink	Specifies setting an index for the field. Single field indexes can be set using this property. Choices for allowing unique or duplicate values can be set.
Input Mask	Text, Number, Date/Time, and Currency	Specifies the input mask that is to be applied to the field. The input mask defines the format of the data value that is accepted by this field. You can invoke the Input Mask Wizard to use one of the built-in masks or a user-defined custom mask can be applied. The input mask forces the user to enter data in the specified format, while the Format property displays the data in the field in the specified format.
New Values	AutoNumber	Specifies how new values for the field are to be generated. Options include Increment or Random.
Required	Text, Memo, Number, Date/Time, Currency, OLE Object, Hyperlink, and Attachment	Specifies whether a value is required in the field when the record is saved. If set to Yes the field must contain an entry before the record can be saved. The default property value is No.

TABLE 11-2

FIELD PROPERTY	APPLIES TO DATA TYPE	DESCRIPTION
Result Type	Calculated	Specifies the data type returned by the calculation in a `Calculated` field type.
Show Date Picker	Date/Time	Enables or disables the date picker with the choices of For dates or Never. Never disables the date picker while For dates enables it with date values. The date picker is a calendar control that allows the user to select dates from a calendar.
Smart Tags	All except Yes/No, OLE Object, and Attachment	Specifies which type of Smart Tags are to be used for the field, if any. Smart Tags allow action tags to be created for the field. Smart Tags give Access the ability to link text in the table to other features of Office and its programs.
Text Align	All except Attachment	Specifies the alignment and how the values in the field are displayed in table Datasheet View.
Text Format	Memo	Specifies the type of data stored in the field and how it should be displayed, as one of two options: Plain Text or Rich Text. Plain Text is text without any ability to embed any formatting. Rich Text has the ability to add basic formatting within the text.
Unicode Compression	Text, Memo, and Hyperlink	Specifies whether Unicode compression should be used for the field. The default value is Yes.
Validation Rule	Text, Memo, Number, Date/Time, Currency, Yes/No, and Hyperlink	Specifies the expression used to restrict which values can be entered in the field. When this property is empty, any valid data for the field type can be entered into the field, which is the default.
Validation Text	Text, Memo, Number, Date/Time, Currency, Yes/No, and Hyperlink	Specifies the text for the error message returned when the entry does not pass the Validation Rule.

SETTING FIELD PROPERTIES

All of the Access built-in field properties are set from the Field Properties section of the Table Design View. The properties displayed depend on which data type is selected. Most of the field properties have drop-down lists or wizards associated with them and the values are limited to the choices presented.

When there is no predefined set of options (such as the Validation Rule or Default Value), the user must type in a value. Once the field property has been set in the Table Field Properties section of the table designer, save the entry to ensure it is persisted to the database file; but of course, you will be prompted to save the table upon closing it. Setting the field properties for a field is pretty much the same as working with other Property objects, even though the Field Property section of Table Design View is used to set these properties instead of the Property Sheet.

TRY IT

In this lesson, you create a table and set a series of table and field properties. The steps stress some of the important aspects of the Number data type settings. You also create a Calculated field type and set the Expression and Result Type properties for the field.

Lesson Requirements

For this lesson you need Access 2010 installed and a blank database. You should be familiar with starting Access and creating a new blank database, and have a basic understanding of tables and fields in Access 2010 to complete this lesson.

Step-by-Step

1. Start Access 2010 and create a new blank database in the Access 2010 Backstage.

2. Click the Create tab to show the Create Ribbon; click the Table Design button. A new table is created and opened in Design View.

3. Create some fields to experiment with the property settings. Add an AutoNumber field, two Text fields, a Number field, a Date/Time field, and a Yes/No field. Name the fields **ID**, **TextField, SSN, NumberField, DateField**, and **YesNo**, and save the table as **Table1**.

4. Click the Property Sheet button on the Table Tools Design Ribbon to open the Property Sheet for the table.

Congratulations; you have created some fields using the Access 2010 table designer. Next you set some properties for the fields to get the hang of working with the field properties in Access 2010.

5. In the Field Properties section of the table designer for the NumberField field that was just created, click the drop-down for the Indexed property. The menu reveals three choices: No, Yes (Duplicates OK), and Yes (No Duplicates).

If the NumberField field had been set as the primary key, an index would have been created and the value in the Indexed Property would have been Yes (No Duplicates).

6. Set the Indexed property to **Yes (No Duplicates)** for the NumberField field in the Field Properties.

Congratulations; you have created a Number field that is indexed and does not allow duplicate values to be placed in it. This means that each record in this table must have a different value in this field. Next, you create a Calculated field for your table in the following steps.

7. Add a new field and type in the name **CalcField.** For the fields data type, select the Calculated type.

8. Once the Calculated data type has been selected, the Expression Builder starts automatically. Set the Expression property to *concatenate* the values from two other fields in the table. Type the following into the Expression Builder: [**TextField**] & " " & [**DateField**].

9. Click OK.

10. In the Field Properties section of the table designer, set the Result Type property value to Text by selecting it from the drop-down menu for the property.

11. Save the table and open it in Datasheet View. Add some test data (such as names and dates of birth) to the fields of a few records and notice what appears in the Calculated field.

12. Change one of the values in the Text field or Date/Time field and see the updates of the Calculated field.

Congratulations; you have created a Calculated data type field, by setting its properties using the Field Properties section of the table designer. Finally, set the Input Mask property on the SSN field to display Social Security Numbers (SSNs) to require data be entered in the standard SSN format of xxx-xx-xxxx.

13. Open the table in Design View mode and click the SSN field to select it.

14. In the Input Mask property, invoke the Builder by clicking the ellipsis (…) button (on the right side of the property field). If the table has not been saved since it was last modified, you will be prompted to allow the table to be saved.

15. The Input Mask Wizard will be invoked. Select the Social Security Number option. To test it, enter **123456789** in the Try It text box. Then click the Next button.

16. Change the Placeholder character to an asterisk using the Placeholder character drop-down.

17. Click in the Try It text box to see that asterisks are now used as placeholders. Then click the Next button.

18. Choose to store the data without storing the symbols used in the mask by selecting that option. Click the Next button and then click the Finish button. The field's settings are added to the field and the wizard closes.

19. Save the table by clicking the Save button (on the top left corner of the Access 2010 window). Then open the table in Datasheet View.

20. Enter **123456789** and **abc123xyz** into the SSN field. The all-numeric string is accepted as valid input, but the string with alpha characters will not be accepted.

Congratulations; you have created a table and a Calculated field type and set multiple field properties. Creating table fields with any of the Access data types is extremely easy to do using Access 2010 and only takes a few minutes of your time.

SUMMARY

Working with table and field properties in Access 2010 is accomplished using the Access Table Design View mode. Using the Input Mask and Validation Rule properties (to ensure data entries into the field meet the predefined requirements for a field) helps reduce the risk of bad data and ensures that normalized data is being stored in the application. Using the Default Value property to automatically enter values allows actions such as adding a timestamp to a record without exposing that field directly to the user in a form. By carefully choosing the table and field properties settings in a database application, the developer can enhance and improve the database design at very little cost and effort.

 Please select Lesson 11 on the DVD to view the video that accompanies this lesson.

12

Data Validation and Limiting User Input

A very important part of Access table design is determining how data values can be entered into the database application. Providing methods that permit the user to enter only values that are appropriate for the records in the table is a fundamental problem of storing data in any type of database. Moreover, it is often desirable to have the data being entered formatted consistently throughout the records. For example, consider a phone number field. The format in which values are entered into this field could be very different, especially if multiple users are entering the data. One user might enter the value **3035551234**, while another user might enter the value **303-555-1234**, and even a third user might enter a value of **(303)555-1234**. And this doesn't even consider all of the other data entry mistakes that could occur, such as missing or invalid digits in the phone number. The sheer number of problems with data entry can be a bit overwhelming. If no constraints are enforced by the application, users can easily enter incorrect, improper, or non-uniform data values, which can result in inconsistent search results and other unexpected behavior in the application. This lesson is dedicated to discussing the field properties that can be used to validate, limit, and format data values for table records using Access 2010.

LESSON SETUP

In this lesson, you examine the field properties used to ensure the data values for records have been validated. You should have a basic knowledge of how to create tables and add fields to them using Access to complete this lesson. You should also be familiar with the Access 2010 field data types and know how to work with field properties in the table designer.

DATA VALIDATION FIELD PROPERTIES

Access tables have several field properties that are specifically designed to validate the data being entered by the user, to help the developer ensure the data is complete, correct, and uniform. The following is a list of the Access field properties that can be used to validate data:

➤ Default Value

➤ Allow Zero Length

➤ Required

➤ Validation Rule

➤ Validation Text

➤ Input Mask

Using some, or all, of these field properties allows the developer to fine tune which values can be entered into a record. Any restriction applied to a field requires that the data entered into the field from *any* source conform to the defined specifications. This includes data entered directly into the table's Datasheet View, through a form, using queries, and through macros or VBA code. The following sections discuss each of these properties in detail.

The Default Value Property

Setting default values at the field level is one way to help the user ensure that the correct values are being saved in the record. Using the Default Value property is a good way to provide a common value for the field for a new record, as well as provide the user a visual clue about what kind of data the field will accept. Another use for the Default Value property is to enter a value without having to show that particular field to the user on a form. Because the default value is entered into the field automatically when the record is created, regardless of user interaction, the record can be saved even when the field is required.

The Default Value property value for a field can be a hardcoded value or even a function or expression. Examples of a hardcoded default value could be the City or State name used primarily for a dataset that contains data values from a single city and state. But, even when a default value is used, the user can override this value if desired, assuming the field is visible and updated by the user. Essentially three types of values can be provided for the Default Value property setting. These options include entering the specific text or a number value to provide a literal value, using a single function to return a value, or building a complex expression to calculate a value at the time the record is created. Of course the value provided for the Default Value property setting must return the appropriate data type for the field, otherwise you will most likely run into problems.

Using Hardcoded Values for Default Values

Using a hardcoded value for the Default Value property is very common in Access database applications. To enter a text or numeric value as the value of the Default Value property setting, enter the desired value directly in the Default Value property value field in the Field Properties section of the table designer for the field. The following three entries are some examples of hardcoded values that could be used for a field:

```
=10
="The default string value"
=#03/10/2010#
```

The preceding example shows three hardcoded Default Value property settings. The first is the numeric value of 10, the second is a string of text, and the third is a date value. Remember, the Default Value property setting should be appropriate to the data type of the field, or you may encounter errors when saving the record and the default value has been unmodified.

Using Functions for Default Values

Using functions for the Default Value property setting, among other properties, allows the default value to be dynamically calculated at run time. For example, using one of the VBA date functions is a common method of supplying a Date/Time field type with the appropriate value. You can even write your own VBA function to return the desired default value, and then set it to the Default Value property for a field. When entering a function in the Default Value property, the syntax requires an equal sign before the function. The following code provides an example of setting the Date() function to the Default Value property:

```
=Date()
```

 To create a field that works as a timestamp for a record, create the Date/Time *field and use the* Now() *function for the Default Value property setting. The* Now() *function returns both the current date and time for a field.*

Using Expressions for Default Values

The final property setting type to discuss is using an expression. Expressions can consist of constants, operators, and functions to calculate a value for the property. Expressions can be entered by typing the expression string value or by using the Access Expression Builder. Expressions can produce complex results. Text, numeric, and date values can be combined to form a new value, which is evaluated at run time of the application, and without any user interaction required. The following is an example of using an expression to dynamically build a string to display date information for 10 days after the record is created:

```
="Ten days after this record is created is " & DateAdd("d", 10, Date()) & ".".
```

In the preceding code, the Date() function is used to get the current date by the DateAdd() function, which adds 10 days to it and returns the new date. Building an expression string by hand for a property is really just that simple.

To create an expression using the Expression Builder, click the Builder button on the Tools section of the Table Tools Design Ribbon, or click the ... (ellipsis) button, found on the right side of the property's text box in the Field Properties section of the table designer. This will open the Expression Builder in a separate dialog. Figure 12-1 shows the Expression Builder.

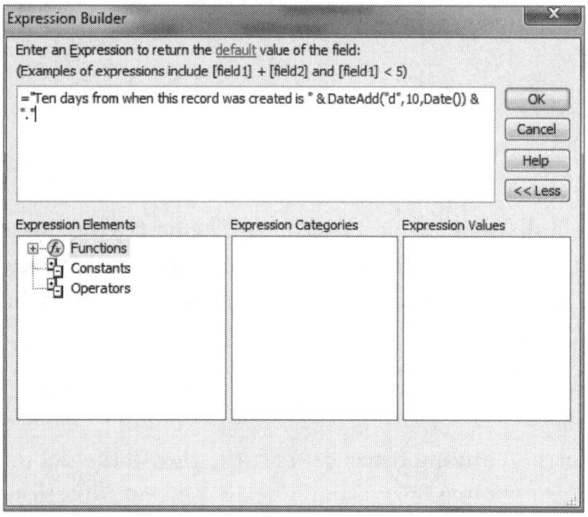

FIGURE 12-1

The Allow Zero Length Property

The Allow Zero Length Property applies to Text and Memo type fields and its name is pretty self-explanatory. When set to a value of Yes, the Allow Zero Length property ensures that an empty string or null value has not been placed in the field when it is saved. If an empty string or null value has been placed in the field, the record cannot be saved and an error will be displayed for the user. Using the Allow Zero Length property setting to disallow empty strings is a great method of ensuring that the user of the application has entered a value into the field for Text and Memo field types.

The Required Property

To ensure that data is entered into a field, you can set the Required property to Yes to require that an entry has been made into the field before the record can be saved. In this situation, it is also common to set the Allow Zero Length property value to No for Text data type fields, so that empty strings are not entered into required data fields. Requiring that a field be populated with data is a great way to ensure that a user has entered all of the necessary data before the record can be saved and the data is committed to the database.

The Validation Rule Property

The Validation Rule property is used to validate the user's input and is specified as an expression. This expression is executed when the user attempts to save data to the field and, if validation fails, the record is not saved and the user sees an error message containing the text stored in the Validation Text property value. The Validation Rule property allows the developer to use some logic to determine the validity of the data that has been entered and is the preferred method of ensuring valid data values in your records.

The Validation Rule property setting can be a number of different items. The expression can be a list of words that are valid entries for the field, a function that returns a value, and/or comparison operators to compare the entry with the value in the rule. An example of an expression for a validation rule might be a business rule that requires the record date to be less than, or before, today's date. The less than operator (<) is entered in the property, followed by the `Date()` function. For example, in this case, the Validation Rule property setting would be:

```
<Date()
```

Another example of a validation rule would be that the sales price of an item entered into a table might be required to be at least $10. In this case, the Validation Rule could be entered as the value:

```
>=10
```

Finally, to allow only characters to be entered into a `Text` or `Memo` field, you could use a Validation Rule property value of:

```
Like "*[a-z]*" Or Is Null
```

The companion property to the Validation Rule property is the Validation Text property. As noted earlier, the Validation Text property is used to supply the error message to the user when the entry does not pass the validation rule's requirements. For example, the property setting for the Validation Text property for the `<Date()` validation rule might be `="The date entered in this field must be a date before today's date.".`

Comparison operators, such as =, <, >, <=, >=, and <>, can be used to validate the entry. Lesson 53 discusses the comparison operators used in Access and VBA in more detail. And, just as with other property settings, Access's built-in functions can also be used as part of a validation rule. As you've seen in the previous example, using the less than operator with the `Date()` function is an example of how to require that the user enter date values that are before the current date. Regardless of exactly how you design the Validation Rule property settings, this property is the recommended method for limiting user input in a field.

The Input Mask Property

The Input Mask property is used to both show the user what type of entry is expected and control the format of the data that is entered into the field. Using the Input Mask property can be helpful to the user when entering data by requiring that the information be entered in a specific format. Phone numbers, Zip codes, and Social Security numbers are all examples of formatted text that should be entered into the table in a consistent format. This makes searching and querying much easier when the data is consistent between records.

 The Access 2010 Customize Input Mask Wizard helps the developer provide guidance to the user when entering the data. The Microsoft Office website has a detailed discussion about Input Masks in Access 2010 at `http://office .microsoft.com/en-us/access-help/control-data-entry-formats-with- input-masks-HA010096452.aspx.`

Access provides the Customize Input Mask Wizard, which includes a number of the predesigned input masks or allows creation of a new user-defined input mask. Otherwise, the user can just enter the desired input mask value directly into the Input Mask property. The Access 2010 Help shows the characters you can use to limit or require a specific type of input:

➤ **0** — User must enter a digit (0 to 9).

➤ **9** — User can enter a digit (0 to 9).

➤ **#** — User can enter a digit, space, plus or minus sign. If skipped, Access enters a blank space.

➤ **L** — User must enter a letter.

➤ **?** — User can enter a letter.

➤ **A** — User must enter a letter or a digit.

➤ **a** — User can enter a letter or a digit.

➤ **&** — User must enter either a character or a space.

➤ **C** — User can enter characters or spaces.

➤ **. , : ; - /** — Decimal and thousands placeholders, date and time separators. The character you select depends on your Microsoft Windows regional settings.

➤ **>** — Converts all characters that follow to uppercase.

➤ **<** — Converts all characters that follow to lowercase.

➤ **!** — Causes the input mask to fill from left to right instead of from right to left.

➤ **** — Characters immediately following will be displayed literally.

➤ **" "** — Characters enclosed in double quotation marks will be displayed literally.

Figure 12-2 shows the Customize Input Mask Wizard with the phone number input mask selected for editing.

A part number mask for a hypothetical part number composed of two alpha characters and six numeric characters might be made using this string: LL000000.

FIGURE 12-2

TRY IT

In this lesson, you create a table in an Access database and learn how to set the Default Value, Validation Rule, Required, and Input Mask properties. This lesson walks you through each step necessary to accomplish these tasks.

Lesson Requirements

For this lesson you will need Access 2010 installed and you can download the sample file for Lesson 12 from the book's DVD and website at www.wrox.com. This is also the database file that was created as part of the previous lesson, so you can use that database if you have already completed Lesson 11.

Step-by-Step

1. Start Access 2010 and open `Lesson12.accdb`.

2. From the Navigation Pane, Open `tblSample` in Design View.

3. Select the `YesField` field by clicking anywhere on the field's row.

4. On the General tab of the Field Properties section, change the Default Property from `0` to `-1`. Access stores the value `False` as `0` and `True` as `-1`, so the default value will be `Yes` and because the Format is set to `True/False`, a check box will have a check mark in it.

5. Press **Ctrl+S**, reopen the table in Datasheet View, and view the value of the `YesField` in the new record.

Next you use a function to set the Default Value property value for the `Date/Time` field named `DateField`.

6. In Table Design View, select the `DateField` field and enter **=Date**() in the value field for the Default Value property in the Field Properties section. This sets the default property of the field to the current date at the time the record is entered.

7. Open the table in Datasheet View mode, saving the table when prompted. Notice that the `DateField` value in the new record displays today's date.

In this case, assume that you want to set the Default Value property to use a default value for a date other than today. Do this via an expression for the Default Value property by using a combination of the `Date()` function and the `DateAdd()` function. The `DateAdd()` function's syntax is `DateAdd(interval, number, date)`. The business rule you will use for this field requires that the entry be a date that is 10 days before the date the record is entered.

8. In Table Design View, select `DateField` and in the Default Value property value field, type **=DateAdd("d",10, Date())** in the field as the function for the Default Value property.

9. Open the table in Datasheet View by clicking the View button on the Ribbon and save the table when prompted. Observe that a date shown in the new record for the `DateField` field is 10 days from the current date. Also note that you can change the date entry to show that it will allow changes to the default date.

Next you set the Default Value property to require that the user enter a value that is not a zero-length string for the `TextField` field.

10. In Table Design View mode, select `TextField` and set the Required property to the value **Yes** and the Allow Zero Length to **No**.

11. Open the table in Datasheet View mode by clicking the View button on the Ribbon and save the table when prompted. After the table is open in Datasheet View mode, attempt to add a record without an entry in the `TextField` field or with a zero-length string as the entry. Notice that you are prompted and the entry is not allowed.

Next you set field properties to validate user input for a numeric field type. The business rule for this example requires that the value be greater than 999, but less than or equal to 2,000,000.

12. In Table Design View mode, select the `NumberField` field and in the value field for the Validation Rule property, enter the expression **>999 And <= 2000000**. Values entered into this field now must be greater than 999 and less than or equal to 2,000,000.

13. Set the Validation Text property value to **The value must be greater than 999, but less than or equal to 2,000,000.** This will inform the user that they have entered a value that is not valid for this field.

14. Open the table in Datasheet View by clicking the View button on the Ribbon and save the table when prompted. Now try to enter a value of 10. Notice that you are prompted with the message that was created in the previous step.

Next you set the Input Mask property for the `TextField` field. For this example you use the Zip Code mask from the Input Mask Wizard.

15. Select the Input Mask property for the `TextField` field and invoke the Input Mask Wizard by clicking the Builder button on the Table Tools Design Ribbon. The Input Mask Wizard dialog opens.

16. Click the Zip Code option to select the predefined Zip code mask type. Type **078501147** in the Try It box in the wizard to see how the mask acts. You'll get an error, because it does not conform to the rules created by the wizard.

17. Click the Finish button to close the wizard. The field will now be ready for testing.

18. Open the table in Datasheet View mode by clicking the View button on the Ribbon and save the table when prompted. Try entering both numbers and letters into the `TextField` field to see the result. The field will now allow only ZIP code format input.

19. Switch back to Table Design View and edit the Input Mask property by removing everything but the zeros, by typing the value **00000**.

20. Open the table in Datasheet View by clicking the View button on the Ribbon and save the table when prompted. Now notice how the data is displayed and see how the mask's behavior is changed by entering some new values. The Input Mask should now allow only entry of a 5-digit Zip code, instead of the Zip+4 code as set by the wizard in the previous steps.

Congratulations; you have set the Default Value property for several different field types. In the preceding steps, you created default values by using a hardcoded value, by using the `Date()` function, and by using an expression. You changed the Allow Zero Length property, created a Validation Rule, and created an Input Mask. These are the standard properties used to validate and limit user input in an Access database table and you should now have a good understanding of what they do and how to use them.

SUMMARY

Gently requiring users to enter consistent and complete data is a desirable goal for all database developers. Access 2010 provides several options, in the form of built-in field properties, to attempt to help meet your needs. The ability to use rules, functions, and expressions to create default values at the table level is a powerful tool provided by the Access table designer. The Validation Rule property provides control over what values are allowed to be entered into a field. The Input Mask property forces the correct format of data entered into a field. Because these properties are applied at the field level, any fields changed, including those from Append or Update queries, or through VBA code, are subject to the rules in the properties. Building Access tables that limit user input right from the start is the best way to ensure data validation in your application so that your data is clean, consistent, and concise.

 Please select Lesson 12 on the DVD to view the video that accompanies this lesson.

13

Creating Value List Fields

Tables in Access often have fields that contain a value list of options for the user to choose from (instead of having users type the text). Access 2010 makes it very easy to create value list fields and even provides built-in dialogs to allow the user to update the values in the list. The values can be static and typed into the Row Source property of the lookup field, or from values that are either in a table or returned using a query as a data-driven list.

One of the main reasons for using a lookup field (data-driven list field) is to provide a method to increase the consistency of data being entered into a field. If the three choices allowed for a city name field for a retail outlet store are Tallahassee, Talladega, and Tuscaloosa, relying on the users' spelling skills will probably result in hundreds of spelling variations, making any searches for individual city names virtually impossible. Providing a drop-down list that includes only the correct options ensures that the correct spellings (and data formats) are used. This lesson discusses the various options for building list fields for tables using Access 2010.

LESSON SETUP

In this lesson, you learn how to create list fields using both value lists and values from tables or queries. The Lesson 13 files should be downloaded from the book's website to complete this lesson, and you should be familiar with creating database objects and working with tables.

LIST FIELDS IN ACCESS

Access has two list types available for fields: value list fields (which allow a static list of option values to be entered into the field) and lookup fields (which use a table or query as the source and only allow values that are included in the source object).

> ➤ **Value list field** items are manually entered in the Row Source property of the field by the developer during the design phase and are more or less static. (However, Access 2007 and higher provides a built-in dialog to allow the user to update the values at

run time, if desired.) Lookup fields are always computed at run time by using data from the source tables or queries to generate the list of values for the field. The listed items change when the records in the source tables change. The best candidates for a value list are values that are relatively few in number and are relatively stable. An example of a good hardcoded value list option is a person's sex. There are usually only two choices — Female and Male — but a third choice is possible if you want to allow an unknown sex. Because the options are limited and unchanging, marital status is another candidate for a value list field (for example: Single, Married, Divorced, It's Complicated, and Unknown). However, managing a list of employees in a value list would require changing the value list each time an employee is hired or terminated, so that kind of data is *not* a good candidate for a value list field.

➤ **Lookup fields** use tables or queries to populate the field, simplifying the regular maintenance of the list items. A list of employees from the `Employee` table can show every employee in a field list. If only active employees need to be displayed, a query that returns only active employees is a better choice as the source of a lookup field.

Creating Value Lists

To create a value list for a table field, enter the values into the Row Source property for the field. In Table Design View, create a new field, or select an existing field, and select the Lookup tab from the Field Properties section. Set the Display Control property to either the List Box or Combo Box option. Change Row Source Type to the Value List option. The values can now be entered using a builder or via the Row Source property. The builder can be started from the Tools section of the Ribbon or by clicking the ellipsis on the right edge of the Row Source property. When using the builder, as shown in Figure 13-1, you are prompted to enter each item on a separate line in the Edit List Items form. You are also given the option to set the default value by using the drop-down list below the main entry field.

FIGURE 13-1

To enter the items manually, enter each value in the Row Source field, separating each item with a semicolon. To set a default value, return to the Field Properties General tab and enter the desired value in the Default Value property.

Allowing List Edits

Situations exist in which the user may want to edit the value list for a field at run time. The decision to allow changes to these values at run time is based on the application's requirements and should be made on a case-by-case basis, depending on the needs of the particular application. Assume you are using a City field. If management decides that only three cities are listed in the value list, the user should be prevented from adding new cities and from editing the list. If the user may need to add the cities Tulsa or Tucumcari, and changes to the list are allowed by policy, the developer can set properties to allow edits or additions to the value list.

To allow a user to edit the items in a value list at run time, set the Allow Value List Edits property to Yes. After this property has been set, by default whenever a user sets focus to the list box or combo box, a floating Edit List Items button appears. This feature and field property are only allowed in ACCDB files and was introduced as part of the Access 2007 release. Figure 13-2 shows the button as it appears when editing is enabled.

Clicking this button opens the Edit List Items dialog. Or, if a custom list edit form name was specified in the List Items Edit Form property, your custom form opens instead.

FIGURE 13-2

Two types of display controls can be used for field list fields: list boxes and combo boxes. The list box display control allows a user to enter a value that is not on the list, whereas the combo box properties can be set to either limit the entry to the existing list or allow the user to enter a new value. The developer should select the correct control based on the application's requirements.

Creating Lookup Fields

Lookup fields use the information stored in a table to produce the values used in the list box or combo box for a field. Using tables to store the items makes maintaining the items a simple task, but requires more work on the part of the developer. Using queries to restrict data and using field expressions in queries to create calculated values at run time provide additional options to display items in a lookup field. A list that displays an employee's full name is an example of a calculated field in a query adding value to a list. The employee's name is stored in the table in three fields: FirstName, MI, and LastName. The application specifications for the list require the name to be displayed as last name, first name, and middle initial and the list needs to be sorted in alphabetical order. The list should also be restricted to active employees.

Prior to Access 2010, a query was the only way to concatenate one or more fields in a table. Access 2010 introduced calculated fields as another powerful option for manipulating data at run time.

Creating Lists from Tables or Queries

To create lists from a table or a query, you first need to create the field in a table and select either List Box or Combo Box from the Lookup tab in the Field Properties. The Row Source Type property must be set to Table/Query. The Row Source property is where the table or query is designated or a SQL statement is created to return the desired items.

The remaining properties on the Lookup tab define which data element will be stored, what information will be displayed, how it will be displayed, and whether or not edits are allowed. Unless the table or query being used has only one field, you need to carefully choose which field is *bound*, or stored, in the record. In most instances the bound column will be the primary key for the record.

Create a query field that uses an expression to concatenate the three name fields and then set the query to sort the results. The alias and the expression for the field (as well as the Order By clause of the query) would look like this:

```
EmpName:LastName & ", " & FirstName & " " & MI
ORDER BY LastName, FirstName, MI
```

The name of the saved query or the query's SQL statement is then set as the Row Source property for the lookup field.

TRY IT

In this lesson you create a list box that uses a value list as its record source and a combo box that uses a query as the record source using Access 2010.

Lesson Requirements

For this lesson you need Access 2010 installed and the Lesson13.accdb file from the book's DVD and website. You should be familiar with creating database objects and working with queries to complete this lesson successfully.

Step-by-Step

1. Open the Lesson13.accdb database file, and then open the tblEmployee table in Design View.

2. Add a field named **Gender**.

3. Click the Lookup tab in the Field Properties section for the table designer.

4. Change the Display Control property value to the List Box option.

5. Change the Row Source Type property to the Value List option.

6. Click the Builder button to start the List Builder.

7. Add entries for both **Female** and **Male** to the Edit List Items form, typing each one on a separate line.

8. If desired, set one of the values as the default. Click OK to close the Edit List Items dialog.

9. Save and open the table to verify the value list field works as expected.

Congratulations; you have successfully created a Value List field for a table using Table Design View. Now users can select from a list of values when entering data into the Gender field. Next, try creating a lookup field for a table.

1. Using the database Lesson13.accdb, open tblEmployee in Design View mode.

2. Add a field named **City**.

3. Click the Lookup tab in the Field Properties section.

4. Change the Display Control property value to the Combo Box option.

5. Change the Row Source Type property value to the Table/Query option.

6. Click the Builder button to start the List Builder.

7. Add tblLocations to the Query Builder.

8. Add the City field to the query.

9. In the Property Sheet of the query, change the Unique Values property to Yes.

10. Set the City field to Sort Ascending.

11. Run the query to see if it returns the records you expected.

12. Click Yes when prompted to save the changes made to the SQL statement and update the property. The SQL statement should be visible in the Row Source property for the field.

13. Save the changes and open the table to verify that the lookup field functions properly.

Congratulations; you have successfully created a lookup field for a table in Table Design View. Now when users enter values for records in the City field, all the values available in the tblLocations table will appear for the user to choose from.

SUMMARY

In this lesson, you learned about some of the different Access 2010 options for creating a value list and lookup fields. Value lists are hardcoded values that are stored in the field's Row Source property and should only be used when the list has a relatively low number of items and when the values in the list are not subject to routine changes. A lookup field, which uses tables or queries for its source data, should be used as the Row Source property when the items in the list frequently change, when the total items will be more than just a few, or when the values of the list need to be calculated at run time. Regardless of which type is chosen, using list fields for tables is the perfect way to provide the application user with a list of options, while simultaneously reducing the amount of possible data entry errors.

 Please select Lesson 13 on the DVD to view the video that accompanies this lesson.

14

Creating Lookup Tables

In Lesson 13 you learned how to create and use the value list and lookup fields in a table using Access 2010. In this lesson you learn how to create and use lookup tables, so that you can easily attach lookup fields to them. The uses of lookup tables are similar to the lookup fields Access makes available directly in a field of a table. However, the primary difference between the two is that lookup tables are used in most relational database systems, and as such make converting to other systems much easier, whereas the value list fields are a proprietary feature of Access and are not recognized by most other major database systems. Unlike the value list fields, all the data in a lookup field is contained in a separate table. This lesson discusses the basics of building lookup tables and attaching lookup fields to them.

LESSON SETUP

For this lesson you need Access 2010 installed and the Lesson 14 files from the book's website. You should be familiar with creating database objects and working with tables to complete this lesson successfully.

LOOKUP TABLE THEORY

Lookup tables are used to store data that is needed to support one or more fields in other tables. Examples of lookup tables include lists of cities, states, membership levels, ticker symbols, manufacturers, brand names, and many other types of data that might have other records related to them. Essentially, a lookup table is a list of unique values in one table that is used by fields in other tables to populate a *foreign key* field value in the primary table.

The structure of the lookup table can be as simple as a single field or it can be multiple fields. In Access databases, a lookup table is usually comprised of at least two fields: an `Autonumber` primary key field and at least one other field used to store the data values in the lookup table.

For example, in a manufacturer lookup table for a `Products` table, the fields are `ManufacturerID` and `ManufacturerName`. In the `Products` table, the field name is also `ManufacturerID`. In this example, when a record is created, instead of storing the actual name of the manufacturer, the `ManufacturerID` is saved as the foreign key value in the `Products` table.

In a relational database, a primary key uniquely identifies each record in a table. It can consist of a single field or multiple fields in combination. A foreign key is a field or a combination of fields that points to the related primary key in another table. It is a referential constraint between two tables.

Access automatically adds an index to any field that begins or ends with `ID`, `key`, `num`, *or* `code`. *The default prefixes and suffixes can be modified using the Object Designers section in the Access Options dialog. Access also automatically creates a join between two fields that share a common name when the two tables are added to the Query Designer. By naming primary keys in lookup tables, and foreign keys in the related tables, with identical names, Access automatically creates the joins for you when you add tables to a query in Design mode.*

A lookup table can also be used in Access as a means of restricting the input to a finite set of options. Access developers typically use an `Autonumber` primary key in addition to the lookup values. An example is a list of the states and territories of the United States. The primary use of the lookup table in this instance is to provide consistency of the abbreviation of the name. The state abbreviation field is also designated as the primary key and the actual abbreviation is stored in the related table. An example of this structure is a list of states used in an address table and a store location table. The lookup table is used to provide a list of the abbreviations of the allowable states stored in the address or store location tables.

Lookup tables can also have additional fields and provide multiple variations of the information returned. Using the previous example of a state table, additional fields may be added to include the `ID` as the primary key, state abbreviation, state name, and geographical region. By adding these additional fields, more options are available to control how much detail is available to forms and reports and add options for grouping and aggregating the data.

Creating Lookup Tables

Lookup tables are created like any other table in Access 2010. There is nothing special about a lookup table except in the manner they are used. Other than the fields included in the table, the most important design considerations for lookup tables are the index and primary keys. For example, a `States` table with two fields, the `StateName` field and the `ID` field (the primary key), is an `Autonumber` type field by default and automatically includes an index and enforces no duplicates. The `StateName` field might need to have an index added for the field to optimize searches and queries, depending on how long the list is or becomes over time. Although the primary key value for the lookup field record is stored in, for example, the Address table, the StateName field in the States table can still be used as the criterion in a query when the tables are shown and joined in the Query Designer.

To create a Lookup table for a State field in a hypothetical Address table, a new table should be created containing an Autonumber field named ID (and designated as the primary key) and a Text field named StateName. These are the two basic fields needed to create a States Lookup table. Add an index to the StateName field by changing the Indexed property value to Yes (No Duplicates) in the Field Properties section of the Table Design View. Once you have changed the settings for the table, be sure to save the changes to ensure that the updates have been persisted.

Creating Lookup Controls via the Wizard

Lesson 13 discussed using the wizard to create Lookup Fields using tables. In this lesson, you learn how to create a similar Lookup Field on a form that is not directly in the field of a table. The Combo Box or List Box control wizards are invoked when the control is drawn on a form in Design View. The wizard asks a few simple questions that are necessary to construct the lookup to do what you want it to do.

Using the frmLocations form, draw a Combo Box. As it is drawn, the Combo Box Wizard opens. The wizard asks you to have values from another table or query so the Combo Box will look up the state abbreviation from tblStates so that it can be stored as a foreign key in tblLocations. The wizard leads you through the process, which is very similar to the List Field Wizard for a field in a table. The wizard for creating a List Box works the same way.

After the data has been entered using the Combo Box or List Box controls, the information is available to use in queries. Typically, a query with the main table and the lookup table is created to view and manipulate the data. The two tables usually have an Inner join between the foreign key of the main table and the primary key of the Lookup table. In the database for Lesson 14 (Lesson14.accdb) on the DVD and website for this book, qryLocations is an example of a query using tblLocations and tblStates to return the City and Zip Code from tblLocations and the State abbreviation from tblStates. Figure 14-1 shows the Query Design View of qryLocations.

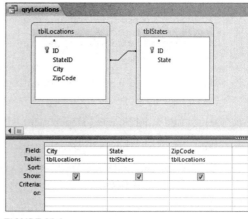

FIGURE 14-1

Manually Setting Lookup Options

To manually set the lookup options, open the form in Design View, select the Combo Box, and open the Property Sheet. The properties include all of the properties in the List Field properties of tables with some additional properties that are form-specific. To set the Combo Box in this example to look up and select specific states, follow these steps:

1. Set the Control Source to **StateID** to bind the selection to the StateID field in tblLocations.

2. Set the Row Source to **tblStates** or click the ellipsis to start the Query Builder and create a query to use as the Row Source.

3. The Bound Column property designates which column in the Row Source is stored in `tblLocations`. In this example the `ID` field is the primary key of `tblStates` and `StateID` is the related foreign key in `tblLocations`. Column 1 is the bound column.

Figure 14-2 shows the Property Sheet for a Combo Box control.

From the Property Sheet you can change how the control acts and what it displays.

TRY IT

In this lesson, you create two lookup tables, one with two fields and a second with four fields. You also create queries for both examples. The Try It illustrates how the lookup tables are structured and how they are used.

Lesson Requirements

You should be familiar with creating database objects and designing both tables and queries using Access 2010 to complete this lesson successfully.

FIGURE 14-2

Step-by-Step

1. Start Access 2010 and open the `Lesson14.accdb` sample database file.

2. On the Create Ribbon, click the Table Design button to create a new table in Design View mode.

3. Add a field named **DepartmentID** with a Data Type of `Autonumber` and set the field as the primary key.

4. Add a field named **Department** with a Data Type of `Text`.

5. Save the table as **tblDepartment**.

6. Open the table in Datasheet View and add five department records: **Grocery**, **Produce**, **Meat**, **Drug**, and **Beauty**.

7. Create a query using the existing `tblSales` table and the `tblDepartment` Lookup table. On the Create Ribbon, click the Query Design button to create a new query in Design View mode.

8. Add the `tblSales` and the `tblDepartment` tables to the query. You will notice that a join is automatically created between the `DepartmentID` fields in both tables. To see the sales information by department, add the `Department` field from the `tblDepartment` table and the `DateSales` and the `AmtSales` fields from the `tblSales` table.

9. Save the query as **qrySales** and run the query to show the results. Now that the query for the lookup field is ready, you can create a field in another table with the four lookup fields.

10. On the Create Ribbon, click the Table Design button to create a new table in Design View mode.

11. Add a field named **StateID** with a Data Type of `Autonumber` and set the field as the primary key.

12. Add a field named **StateAbbreviation** with a Data Type of `Text`.

13. Add a field named **StateName** with a Data Type of `Text`.

14. Add a field named **Region** with a Data Type of `Text`.

15. Save the table as **tblState4**.

16. Open the new `tblState4` in Datasheet View mode. Add four state records: **TX, NM, WA,** and **VA,** filling in the abbreviation, full name, and geographical region in the proper fields.

17. Create a query using `tblCity` and `tblState4`. First add the fields **City** and **StateName** and run the query.

18. Return to Query Design View, change `StateName` to **Region**, and run the query again, observing that the query now displays the region instead of a state.

Congratulations, you have now successfully created a lookup field to a table and a query. In both cases, the lookup fields function in the same manner. The difference is that with the query, you have the ability to filter the records as desired, whereas with the table, you will see all records that are stored in it. Both of these types of lookup fields are extremely common in Access and the method you decide to use will usually be dependent on your specific task at hand.

SUMMARY

Lookup tables are a vital part of building relational database applications and extremely common in Access databases. Using tables to store lists of frequently used information, which can easily be related to one or more tables, allows for more efficient data storage, and with less duplication of your data. Lookup tables also enforce data normalization and integrity by requiring the correct spelling of frequently used data, like cities, states, departments, and so on. Whether you are using them for table fields or list controls, lookup tables can be useful for any Access database application.

 Please select Lesson 14 on the DVD to view the video that accompanies this lesson.

15

Table Modifications

In a perfect world, designing the tables that make up your application would be completed before the Access 2010 table design tools are ever opened. Once a table is designed, created, and saved, the design should not need to be changed. However, in common practice, that is rarely the case and you may often need to make minor, and sometimes major, modifications. The modification can range from changing a field or property or even renaming the table altogether, and these changes can occur pretty much anytime after the original table has been built.

The first, and probably the most important, step is to always make a backup copy of the database file before making changes to the design of the application. You can make modifications manually using the table design tools in Access, programmatically using Visual Basic for Applications, or by executing SQL DDL (Data Definition Language) queries. This lesson discusses only the methods accessible using the Access 2010 built-in table design tools. Visual Basic for Applications and DDL queries are beyond the scope of this lesson.

LESSON SETUP

In this lesson, you learn how to rename a table, add and modify the locking schemes, modify existing fields, and add new fields. You should be familiar with working with tables using the Access 2010 table tools to successfully complete this lesson.

RENAMING A TABLE

Changing a table name seems like a simple process, but you should consider that the change may affect other database objects inadvertently. Tables are often used as the record sources for other objects, such as queries, forms, reports, macros, and VBA functions and subs. If you change the table name, how will you know what is going to break? Fortunately, Access 2010 includes a couple of features to help make this process easier for you. The Name AutoCorrect feature is automatically turned on in an ACCDB file database and attempts to make updates to related objects when possible. Secondly, Access 2010 provides a tool to check the dependencies of objects in the database. The Object Dependencies button on the Database Tools Ribbon opens the Object Dependencies pane and allows the user to check if any object uses or is being used by the current object that is open in the Access window.

To change the name of a table using Access 2010, complete the following steps:

1. Close the database and make a complete backup of the file.

2. Open the database in Access 2010.

3. In the Navigation Pane, right-click the table you want to rename. This will show the table's context menu.

4. Select the Rename option from the context menu. This opens a text box over the name of the table directly inside of the Navigation Pane.

5. Type in the new name for the table and press the Enter key to save the changes. The table's name will be updated.

6. Update the table name in any related objects, if you are not using the Name AutoCorrect feature.

7. Test the other database objects in the application to ensure that they are working correctly once the table's name has been updated.

When updating a table name, you must always close the table itself. It is always a good idea to close all other database objects to ensure the related objects are updated by the Name AutoCorrect feature (if you are using it).

 Some developers do not use the Name AutoCorrect feature for at least two reasons: first, when the feature is enabled, Access is prone to run slower; and second, it does not always change every instance related to each object. This is especially true as the application gets larger and more complex. You can enable or disable the Name AutoCorrect feature from the Backstage under the Current Database tab in the Name AutoCorrect Options section.

After the table name has been changed, you should always test all queries, forms, reports, macros, and VBA procedures that use the table to ensure that they are still working correctly. Once all of the name changes have been made, it is a good practice to thoroughly test every object in the application to be sure nothing was missed.

TABLE LOCKING CONSIDERATIONS

Tables in Access do not employ locking schemes by default. This is not a problem if the database is used by only a single user. There is a chance of conflicts arising when more than one user is attempting to simultaneously edit the same record. Using locking schemes can prevent or reduce the chances of multiple users editing the same record simultaneously. To change the locking method, go to the Advanced section of the Client Settings tab of the Backstage and choose one of the three locking options:

➤ No Locks — This option is also called Optimistic Locking. When two users are editing the same record and one user tries to save the changes, an Access message tells the user that the record cannot be saved. The user attempting to save the record has an opportunity to save the values to the clipboard and save it later, once the other user has left the record.

➤ All Records — This means that all records in the table or query are locked every time they are accessed and only the first user can make any edits; other users can still see records in read-only mode.

➤ Edited Records — This option is also more commonly known as Pessimistic Locking; a page of records is locked, but the remainder of the records are available for other users to edit. By default, Access 2010 creates an ACCDB file with the No Locks option enabled.

MODIFYING FIELDS

Modifying field names is just as dangerous as, and probably more common than, modifying a table name and will also affect dependent objects that use that field. Again, dependent objects can be existing forms, reports, queries, and VBA code that already uses the current field. Even changing a field property can cause failure in other parts of your application. The procedure to prepare for changing field names is exactly the same as when a table name is changed. First make a backup of the database, change the field name or properties in Table Design View mode, update the field's name in any related objects (if Name AutoCorrect is not used), and then thoroughly test the application to ensure it is still working correctly.

DATA INTEGRITY CONSIDERATIONS

Data integrity is probably the most important thing to consider when modifying the fields of a table. If the data type of a field is changed, extreme caution should be used to prevent the loss of data that may already exist in the table. In some cases, the change may not even be allowed until the data is modified or removed first. For example, changing a data type of Text to a Number data type may cause data loss in the table, if the Text type field already contains non-numeric character data. Changing the length of a Text data type can cause the data to be truncated, resulting in some lost data. When changing a data type, you should always back up the database before making a change. Instead of simply changing the data type, an alternative is to add a new field with the new data type and then use a query to update the new field with the existing data. When you are satisfied that the data is intact in the new field, delete the original field and rename the new field to the original field name. And always, make a complete backup of the database structure and data before making any modifications to a table or its fields!

TRY IT

In this lesson, you learn the steps necessary to change a table name, a field name, and a data type. You learn how each change affects other objects in the database and learn the proper procedures for making post-design changes to an existing database application using Access 2010.

Lesson Requirements

For this lesson you should have Access 2010 installed and the Lesson15.accdb file from the book's DVD and website. You should be familiar with creating database objects and working with tables to successfully complete this lesson.

Step-by-Step

1. Download and create a backup copy of the Lesson15.accdb file for later use.

2. Open Lesson15.accdb and open the tblLocations table in the Access window.

3. On the Database Tools Ribbon, click the Object Dependencies button to open and run the Object Dependencies tool. It should report that qryLocations and frmLocations are dependent on the table.

4. Change the name of tblLocations to **tblLocation** by right-clicking the table name in the Navigation Pane and choosing the Rename option from the context menu.

5. If Name AutoCorrect was enabled, both qryLocations and the Record Source of frmLocations should have automatically updated the table name. If it is not enabled, you will need to manually change the name of the table in both the query and the form.

Next, change the name of a field in the database application.

6. Open the tblLocation table in the Table Design View.

7. Change the field name ZipCode1 to **ZipCode**. Close and save the table.

8. Check qryLocations and frmLocations to ensure the changes in the field names have been made to reflect the change in the table.

Next, change a data type of a field in a table.

9. Open tblLocation in Table Design View again.

10. Change the data type of the ZipCode field from Text to Number data type.

11. Close and save the table. Choose Yes in the dialog, noting that some data may be lost. The updates will be completed.

12. Open the tblLocation table in Datasheet mode and inspect the data to ensure it was converted correctly.

Congratulations; you have successfully modified the data types of an existing field in a table. Although this example has been fairly simple, it has tried to stress the importance of checking related objects once a structural change has been made to a table.

SUMMARY

Making modifications to objects in your database can be a simple, but tricky, and possibly even dangerous, process. Whenever changes are made to the structure of a database, you should always plan for those changes ahead of time and ensure you understand the scope of the objects affected by the change. Your plan should also include testing all objects after the changes have been made to ensure all database objects are still working as expected. And remember, the more complex your database, the greater the chance that an object will be adversely affected by a change, which can possibly cause the database to fail unexpectedly. Remember to always plan before you make any changes and always back up your database before you begin making structural changes.

 Please select Lesson 15 on the DVD to view the video that accompanies this lesson.

16

Creating Table Relationships

Access 2010 is a *Relational Database Management System* (RDMS), as are all previous versions of Access. The heart of RDMS is the ability to eliminate or limit the need to store redundant data. The method used to eliminate duplicated data requires conforming to the rules of normalization, rules that were originally defined by Edgar F. Codd in 1971. Normalization works because data in one table is related to data in one or more other tables. The relationships can be implicitly created in a SQL statement, or explicitly created and enforced by the RDMS.

Relationships between tables in an Access database can be explicitly created in the Relationship Tools designer on the Database Tools Ribbon. Access relationships can be defined to require *referential integrity*. Referential integrity is the primary way to require that a parent record exists for each child record and to prevent the deletion of parent records when related child records exist. Deleting the parent record and leaving the related child records results in what are called *orphan records*, which cause reporting anomalies because the information is not intact. Referential integrity is used to help prevent orphan records within a database system.

LESSON SETUP

In this lesson you learn about the different types of relationships and how to create them in Access 2010. You learn how to use the Access 2010 Relationship Tool to create and modify relationships between tables in an Access database.

RELATIONAL DATABASE THEORY PRIMER

Normalization of the data is required for a relational database to work as it was intended. The purpose of the rules of normalization are to:

➤ Reduce data redundancy

➤ Store data as efficiently as possible

➤ Limit data inconsistencies and instability

➤ Limit the need to modify or delete existing records and to prevent anomalies that such modifications can cause

➤ Provide for a consistent method to update and maintain parts of the database system

Normalization also requires that each row have a unique value field to use as a primary key. As noted in previous lessons, primary keys are unique values and are used to link values in child tables through a foreign key. A foreign key stores the value of the parent's primary key to relate the two tables. Keys can be a single field or multiple fields in combination. The Access 2010 `Autonumber` data type is an ideal candidate to use as the primary key. It is guaranteed to be unique, it has no meaning outside of the database, and it is simple to implement and use. Compound keys require additional effort and skill to implement and may or may not produce unique values.

Keys, both primary keys and foreign keys, are essential for a relational database to function. *Keys* are the process by which records in one table are mapped, or related, to records in another table. In a flat data file, such as an Excel spreadsheet, all of the data for a single record is stored in that physical row in the file. If elements of data are missing from the record, the cells are blank, but the blank space is still stored in that row in the file itself. In a database system where there may be millions of records, it is inefficient to store blank, or null, records, simply because it is a waste of space that could otherwise be used to store real data.

However, in a relational database system, instead of one table storing all the data for the entire application, multiple tables are used to logically break up and composite the data more efficiently. Instead of storing lots of null values and empty strings in fields, a relational database attempts to structure the tables so that all fields in any given table are used (store data when a record is entered). Fields that are used to store a predefined set of values store those values in a separate, but related, table. An example of this might be a customer's phone numbers; you need to store a home phone number, a cell phone number, and a work phone number. A flat file would have three fields, one for each phone type. If the customer only has a home phone, the other two fields would be blank, thus storing data inefficiently in the file. However, in a relational database, the phone numbers could be stored in a separate `PhoneNumbers` table, with a field to indicate what type of phone the number is tied to and a `CustomerID` foreign key field to relate any particular phone number record back to a record in the `Customers` table. In this case, a record would be added to the `PhoneNumbers` table only if there was a specific type of phone number for that customer, such as a cell phone or work phone. The benefit is that the relational database does not store any values for phone numbers unless they actually exist.

Once the data structure is divided and broken into a logical grouping that will form the tables in the database, the developer still needs a method for getting the data back in the manner that is useful for the application. This is where system relationships and queries come into play, to allow the developer to join the database back together again. System defined relationships allow Access to automatically know the relationships between fields in tables and how to join fields automatically in the query designer. Defining and using keys to create an identifiable link between two tables creates a relationship.

THE ACCESS RELATIONSHIP TOOLS

Open the Access Relationships dialog by clicking the Relationships button on the Database Tools Ribbon. The Relationships dialog allows the developer to design the system relationships between tables in the current database and is yet another visual designer provided by Access. The developer can add tables to the Relationships window by dragging them from the Navigation Pane or selecting them from the Show Table dialog. Dragging from a primary key field in one table to the foreign key field in another creates a one-to-many system join between the fields. Dragging from a primary key to another primary key creates a one-to-one system join between the fields. Figure 16-1 shows the Relationships window with six tables and the three types of joins: one-to-many, many-to-many, and one-to-one.

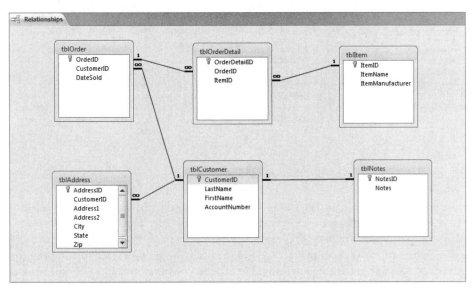

FIGURE 16-1

The symbols at each end of the join indicate the type of relationship, or join, that is in use. A join with a 1 on one end and a ∞ on the other end indicates a one-to-many join. Joins with 1 on both ends are one-to-one joins. There is no specific symbol for a many-to-many join, because many-to-many joins are actually two one-to-many joins, and use an intermediate table, or junction table, to create the relationship.

The Edit Relationships Dialog

The Edit Relationships dialog opens when a join is created or edited, and allows you to define the join type, enforce referential integrity, enable or disable cascade updates and deletes, and add relationships to multiple fields. You can open the Edit Relationships dialog for an existing relationship by double-clicking the line that shows the join between the two table fields. Figure 16-2 shows the Edit Relationships dialog open in the Relationships window.

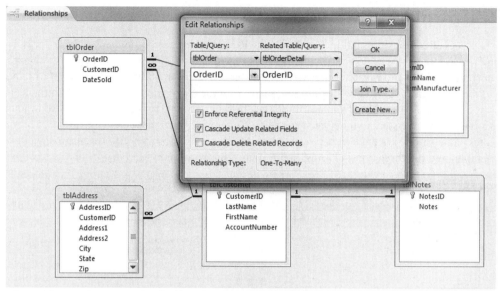

FIGURE 16-2

In Figure 16-2 notice that the relationship between the `tblCustomer` table and the `tblNotes` table is a one-to-one relationship. The `tblCustomer` table has three relationships defined, and two are one-to-many relationships: one to the `tblOrder` table and the other to the `tblAddress` table. The third relationship, to the `tblNotes` table, is a simple one-to-one relationship. The last relationship shown in Figure 16-2 is a many-to-many relationship and involves three tables: `tblOrder`, `tblItem`, and `tblOrderDetail`. Many-to-many relationships require the use of a junction table to complete the relationship and `tblOrderDetail` is the junction table. The Access Relationships window provides the location for viewing and modifying the system relationships for the current database.

Creating Table Relationships

The procedure for creating system relationships in an Access database is similar to creating joins in the Access query designer. Simply drag a field in the list from one table to the corresponding field in a second table field list with which you wish to create the system join. This will open the Edit Relationships dialog and allow you to create a new system relationship between the tables. The Edit Relationships dialog, as mentioned, is where you will set all the properties of the relationship. Once you have set all of the desired properties for the relationship, which we discuss shortly, simply click the Create button on the Edit Relationships dialog and the new relationship will be created. Access makes it extremely easy to create and modify system relationships using the visual designer.

Setting Referential Integrity

Three check boxes on the bottom of the Edit Relationships dialog allow the developer to specify the types of referential integrity the relationship should use. It is usually recommended to at least select

Enforce Referential Integrity. Referential integrity requires child records in related tables to have parent records in the primary table matching the child records. In this example, there needs to be a customer record in tblCustomer, the parent table, before an address can be entered for a customer into tblAddress, the child table. If referential integrity is not enforced, a child record can be entered and assigned to a non-existing customer. The resulting address record is called an orphan record because it has no parent record. Enforcing referential integrity prevents orphans.

Once the developer has chosen to enforce referential integrity, he will have the additional options to allow cascade updates and deletes for the relationship. Cascade updates allow the records in the child, or right, table to be updated along with changes to the parent, or left, table. The cascade updates option for a relationship is set by checking the Cascade Update Related Fields check box at the bottom of the Edit Relationships dialog, but requires that the Enforce Referential Integrity option is selected. The Cascade Deletes option removes child records when a parent record is deleted, so that orphan records are not left behind in the child, or right, table. Using these options in your database is usually recommended and will help ensure the data integrity within the database application.

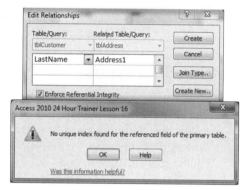

One last thing to mention about creating a system relationship in Access is that you may receive an error when trying to create a relationship that is invalid. Figure 16-3 shows the error you will receive if you attempt to create a relationship, and choose to enforce referential integrity on a primary (parent) table that does not have a unique index defined on the field you want to use in the relationship.

FIGURE 16-3

Types of Relationships

When the fields are chosen for the system relationship that is to be created, the Access Edit Relationships dialog determines the type of relationship that it is and displays that for you to see at the very bottom of the dialog. Access databases support three different types of relationships:

➤ One-to-one

➤ One-to-many

➤ Many-to many

A one-to-one relationship requires that each record in the parent table can have only one related record in the related child table. When the two tables are joined in a query, returning all fields, the resulting recordset appears to be a single table with all of the fields from both tables.

A one-to-many relationship allows each record from the parent table to have zero or more records in the child table, related by the primary key field from the parent table to the foreign key field in the child table. For example, an Orders table will have one record for each overall order, and an OrderItems table could contain many order item records for each single order record. Again, the relationship uses the primary key field from the parent table and a foreign key field in the child table to determine the relationship between the records.

A many-to-many relationship is not directly creatable as a specific relationship type in Access 2010 (or earlier versions), but is possible to simulate using a third table. The third table, which is sometimes called a *junction table*, is used as a link between the parent and child tables, containing two fields, one for each of the primary keys from each table. Records are then added to the junction table for each instance of a record in one table being related to a record in the other table. For example, you might have a Customers table and a CarModels table, for which you could use a junction (third) table to link each of the people records in the Customers table to each of the car models they own from the CarModels table. In this case, a record would be added to the junction table for each customer's car model record, effectively creating the many-to-many relationship between the Customers and CarModels tables. In addition to using a junction table to simulate a many-to-many relationship, Access also allows the multivalued field type, which can also simulate certain types of many-to-many relationships. Although both of these methods are available for simulating a many-to-many relationship in an Access database, neither option is really the same as a true many-to-many relationship, because you will still have to account for the junction table or multivalued field when building queries that join the parent and child tables.

Setting Join Types

The type of join determines how the records will be returned by queries that use that system relationship. You can edit the type of join in the Join Properties dialog, which you can open by clicking the Join Type button on the Edit Relationships dialog. Access 2010 (and earlier versions) support the following types of system joins: inner, left, and right. Table 16-1 provides a description of each of the join types available in Access.

TABLE 16-1: Access Join Types

JOIN TYPE	DESCRIPTION
Inner	Returns all records in the parent table that contain corresponding key values from the child table. All other records from both tables are excluded.
Left	Returns all records in the parent table that contain corresponding key values from the child table, plus all other parent table records. All other child table records that do not correspond to parent table records are excluded.
Right	Returns all records in the parent table that contain corresponding key values from the child table, plus all other child table records. All other parent table records that do not correspond to child table records are excluded.

There is also a fourth join type that is not supported by Access 2010 or earlier versions, which is the Outer join type. The Outer join type actually includes all records from both tables. This is basically a combination of Left and Right joins, where the corresponding records in the left and right tables are joined, and the non-corresponding records in the left and right tables are included as additional records in the resulting record set.

Modifying Relationships

The Access Relationships window allows you to modify existing relationships. As mentioned earlier, double-clicking an existing relationship opens the Edit Relationships dialog for that particular system relationship, where you can edit the properties of the relationship. However, the Access Relationships window also allows a number of other operations for working with the current system relationships. Clicking a join line to select it and then pressing the Delete key deletes an existing relationship, though it requires that the database be open in exclusive mode and that the related table objects are not currently open or in use. Right-clicking the join line opens a context-sensitive menu with choices to edit the relationship or delete the relationship. Clicking the Edit Relationship button on the Relationships Tool Design Ribbon opens the Edit Relationships dialog for the currently selected relationship in the Relationships window. The Access Relationships window, although simpler than many of the other Access designers, provides all of the necessary functionality for modifying existing system relationships.

However, it is important to consider the impact of modifying an existing relationship and, in some cases, that it may not be possible without other modifications to the database first. Although the Edit Relationships dialog allows the user to modify the options of the relationship without deterrence, upon saving the changes, the user may be warned, or the operation may not be able to complete due to the current state of the other objects in the database. For example, if there is data in the tables affected by the relationship change to the referential integrity settings, the data must be in compliance with the new referential integrity rules before Access will allow changes to be successfully completed. Some examples of the rules for referential integrity are:

➤ If there is no value in the primary key for the parent table, no record can be entered in the foreign key field of the related child table.

➤ A record from the parent table cannot be deleted if there are matching records in the related child table.

➤ Both tables are required to be located in the same database. Linked tables cannot have referential integrity enforced.

➤ The joined fields between the parent and child tables must be of the same data type.

The good news is that Access will tell you if there is an issue encountered when trying to create a new, or modify an existing, system relationship. That way you do not have to worry about remembering or trying to analyze all of the possible problems that could occur before you try to create or edit a relationship.

The Impact of System Relationships

Relationships allow the developer to better control the data integrity by enforcing relationship rules at the table, but they come at a cost, constraining how records can be added, modified, or removed from the database. The following are a few rules of thumb to consider when working with relationships between tables:

➤ For relationships to be most effective, the database structure should be properly normalized, to ensure the table design is sound and will work as expected for the application with the intended relationships.

➤ Enforcing referential integrity impacts the data integrity in the database by preventing orphan records, but will incur additional computational time when adding or removing records from the tables.

➤ Cascading updates and deletes ensure that all related child records from a parent record are updated or deleted when an action is taken on the parent record, but will also incur an even larger performance decrease when adding, modifying, or removing records from the related tables.

➤ In some cases when referential integrity is enforced, it will be impossible to add or remove records in one table, without first adding or removing other records from the related table.

Remember, a system relationship between two tables in an Access database defines how those two tables interact with each other. Although these relationships provide great power to other parts of the database, such as building queries, system relationships are designed to constrain how the data can be used and often block operations that would otherwise be possible, such as deleting a record from the parent table. We highly recommend designing the system relationships while developing the database application. Adding relationships to an existing database as an afterthought may prove to be extremely difficult and much more costly than had you properly planned during the design phase of the project!

TRY IT

In this lesson, you create two different types of relationships: a one-to-one and a one-to-many, both using the Access Relationships window. This example also explores options for enforcing referential integrity, and some of its repercussions are demonstrated by using the data provided in the sample database file.

Lesson Requirements

For this lesson, you need to download the Lesson16.accdb sample database file from the book's DVD and website and complete the following steps. You should be familiar with creating database objects and working with table and query objects using Access 2010 to successfully complete this lesson.

Step-by-Step

1. Start Access 2010 and open the Lesson16.accdb file.

2. On the Database Tools Ribbon, click the Relationships button to open the Relationships window for the database.

3. Drag the tblCustomers table and the tblNotes table from the Navigation Pane onto the Relationships window to show the tables to the designer.

4. Drag the CustomerID field from the tblCustomers table to the NotesID field in the tblNotes table. The Edit Relationships dialog will open to create the new relationship. Observe that the Relationship Type (shown at the bottom of the dialog) shows the relationship as a one-to-one type.

Once you have created the join, observe the table and field names listed in the grid on the Edit Relationships dialog. It can sometimes be difficult to drag and drop the fields from one table to the other through the visual designer and you should be aware that the fields in the dialog can be adjusted through the grid as needed.

5. Once the join has been created, click each of the check box controls at the bottom of the form to enable the Enforce Referential Integrity, the Cascade Updates, and the Cascade Deletes options. Then click the Create button to exit the dialog and create the new system relationship in the database.

6. Close the Relationships window and choose to save changes to the Relationships layout when prompted.

You have created a one-to-one system relationship between the tblCustomers and the tblNotes tables. Because referential integrity is enforced for this relationship, every record in the tblNotes table requires a related record in the tblCustomers table.

7. Open the tblCustomers table in Datasheet View and add a customer record to the table. Then close the table.

8. Open the tblNotes table in Datasheet View and add a note record for the customer record that was added in the previous step. Then close the table.

9. Open the tblCustomer table and delete the customer record that was added two steps ago. Then, reopen the tblNotes table in Datasheet View and observe that the note record was also deleted as a result of the Cascade Deletes option being enabled.

Congratulations, you have now observed the results of the cascade delete operation occurring as a result of the system relationship that you previously defined. It is important to realize the impact of this operation and how you can inadvertently delete the data from a related table, simply by deleting the data in the current table, when the Cascade Deletes option is enabled. Next, try creating a one-to-many system relationship for the database application.

10. From the Database Tools Ribbon, click the Relationships button to open the Relationships window.

11. Drag the tblAddress table from the Navigation Pane into the Relationships window to show the table in the Relationships window.

12. Drag the CustomerID field in from the tblCustomers table to the CustomerID field in the tblAddress table. The Edit Relationships dialog will open.

13. Once the Edit Relationships dialog has opened, verify that the Relationship Type shown at the bottom of the dialog is one-to-many.

14. Check the Enforce Referential Integrity option and both of the Cascade options to enable them all again.

15. Click the Create button to create the new system relationship and close the Edit Relationships dialog.

16. In the Relationships window, observe that the new join line between the `tblCustomers` and the `tblAddress` tables shows the 1 and ∞ symbols on each end of the join. These symbols indicate the relationship type is one-to-many.

17. Double-click the join line between the `tblCustomers` and `tblAddress` tables to open the Edit Relationships dialog for the join.

18. Uncheck the check box control for the Enforce Referential Integrity option to deselect it.

19. Click OK to close the Edit Relationships dialog and save the change. In the Relationships window, observe that the 1 and ∞ symbols are now missing from the join. This is the graphical method Access uses to indicate whether referential integrity is enforced in the relationship.

Congratulations; you have successfully modified an existing relationship and have seen how the Access Relationships designer displays the different types of joins. Using the Edit Relationships dialog, you can create new, and edit existing, relationships with minimal effort.

SUMMARY

Access 2010 makes it extremely easy to create and maintain system relationships, using the Relationships designer. The Relationships window can be opened from the Relationship Tools Ribbon and provides all of the tools necessary for working with the system relationships of an Access database. The Edit Relationships dialog allows the user to set the properties for the relationship and is the primary dialog used to create and modify system relationships. The layout in the Relationships window provides visual clues about the relationships that are displayed. Using system relationships and enforcing referential integrity can greatly improve the overall data integrity as well as provide robust functionality for almost any Access database application.

 Please select Lesson 16 on the DVD to view the video that accompanies this lesson.

17

Creating Table Field Indexes

Table field indexes can be a vital component to a high-performance database application. As the number of records in a table grows, the amount of time to search for a given piece of data in that haystack of records can start to become expensive. An index can be added to a field in a database to map the records in that field, so they can be accessed more quickly by the database engine during a search. Indexes in a database system help the database engine find records by creating and sorting key fields of the index. The index helps to speed up the search by using techniques to quickly isolate the specific piece of information's location in a table. This lesson discusses how to create table field indexes using Access 2010.

LESSON SETUP

This lesson introduces Access table field indexes and discusses why, when, and how they can be used in a database application. You learn how to create indexes for a field using Access 2010.

THE ROLE OF FIELD INDEXES

As noted, table field indexes can be used to help decrease the overall search time required by ACE (the Access database engine) to find records in large tables. Fields that are indexed can be unique or may include duplicates. When an index is defined as unique, it will not allow duplicate records in the field, or combination of fields, defined in the index. You may have also noticed already, in Access, that any field designated as the primary key is automatically set to allow unique values only. Access also allows the creation of multi-field indexes. If these indexes are set as unique, the combination of all of the included fields comprises the unique value.

However, although adding indexes to large tables may increase search performance, you have a few other things to consider. When records are added, modified, or deleted, the index must be recalculated, so that the records stored in the field are mapped correctly. This might cause a degradation in overall application performance and a noticeably slow response time during add, update, or delete operations on the table. So, even though field indexes may speed up searches, they may not always be worth the extra time needed to compute the data mappings if the records in the table are frequently changing. Therefore, when adding indexes to a table, it is important to be certain that an index is needed and that the extra overhead to compute the index when a record is added, modified, or deleted is necessary before adding it.

WHEN TO USE INDEXES

Generally, indexes should be used on any field used in a relationship or join, or on any field that will be used as criteria in a query. For fields that will only rarely be used in a join or as criteria in a query, adding an index will usually not benefit performance. Adding indexes to fields where there are not many distinct values, such as Access's Boolean, or Yes/No, fields, will not add any performance increase. In a Yes/No field only two possible values are allowed; in a table with millions of records an index would not improve the performance. On the other hand, a Text field for names, or a field for order numbers, will have many possible distinct values, is a great candidate for an index, and would likely improve the performance of a search.

A simple way to determine whether a field is a candidate for an index is to create an aggregate query that counts the distinct values in the field. Then calculate what percentage each value is of the whole. If the majority of the values have high percentages, more than 10 percent of the total, which would indicate few distinct values, the field may not be a good candidate for an index. However, if the percentages are low, less than 10 percent of the total, the field may be a good candidate.

CREATING AN INDEX USING ACCESS 2010

Access 2010 provides multiple methods to create a table field index. Single-field indexes can be added and removed using the Indexed property for a table open in Table Design View. The choices are Yes (No Duplicates), Yes (Duplicates OK), and No. Yes (No Duplicates) creates an index on a single field and will prevent duplicate values from being entered in that field. Yes (Duplicates OK) creates an index on the field that will allow duplicate values to be entered in multiple records. If the Indexed property is set to No, Access does not create any index for that field.

Another method available from Table Design View is the Indexes dialog. You can open it by clicking the Indexes button on the Table Tools Design Ribbon. The Indexes dialog is the interface used to create compound indexes that use multiple fields.

Compound indexes can be used as constraints on the table to prevent duplicate entries. An example of a constraint is a business rule that requires that all orders made on a single day for a single customer be combined into one order — multiple orders are not allowed. To create a unique compound index, open the Indexes dialog and enter a name for the index. Select a field name from the drop-down and select Ascending or Descending. On the next row leave the Index Name blank and select the next field and the sort option desired. Set the Unique property for the named row to Yes. Figure 17-1 shows the Indexes dialog for the tblOrder table after creating a compound index named OneOrderDaily.

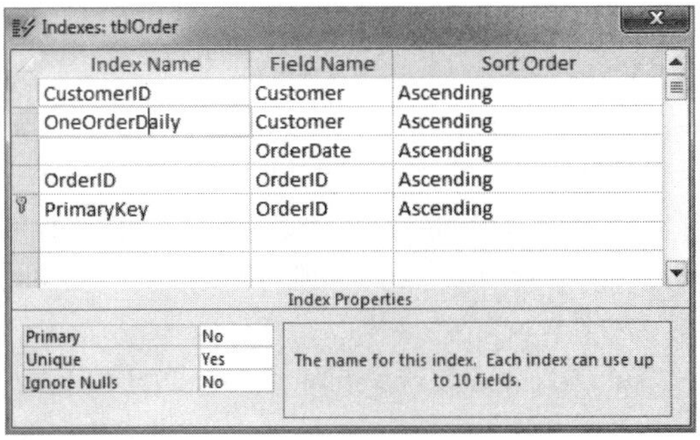

FIGURE 17-1

Additional methods exist for creating field indexes in Access, such as using SQL DDL (Data Definition Language) queries or VBA (Visual Basic for Applications) code, but these methods are beyond the scope of this lesson and more advanced concepts than this book teaches. The Access 2010 Programmer's Reference book, published by Wrox, provides much more information about these topics and is recommended reading if you want to learn more about adding indexes to tables programmatically.

TRY IT

In this lesson, you create a single-field index using the Field Properties in Table Design View, a single-field index using the Indexes dialog, and a compound index.

Lesson Requirements

For this lesson you will need the Lesson17.accdb file from the book's DVD and website. You should be familiar with creating database objects and working with tables in Design View mode using Access 2010 to complete this lesson successfully.

Step-by-Step

1. Start Access 2010 and open the Lesson17.accdb file.

2. Open the tblTestIndex table in Design View mode. The MemID field has a wide range of unique values and will be a good candidate for an index.

3. In the table designer, set the Indexed property of the MemID field to the Yes (Duplicates OK) option.

4. Save the table to ensure the changes are persisted to the database file.

You have created an index for a table field using Table Design View mode. Next, try creating a single-field index on the `Suffix` field in `tblTestIndex`.

1. Open `tblTestIndex` in Table Design View and then open the Indexes dialog by using the Indexes button on the Ribbon.

2. In the Indexes dialog, type in a name for the new index in the Index Name column. Select the `Suffix` field from the Field Name column. The Sort Order should default to Ascending. Close the Indexes dialog.

3. Save the table to ensure the changes are persisted to the database file.

You have created a field index using the Access Indexes dialog. Finally, create a compound unique index using the `Customer` and `OrderDate` fields in `tblOrder`.

1. Open `tblOrder` in Table Design View and open the Indexes dialog again.

2. Add `OneOrderDaily` as the name of the index in the Index Name column.

3. Select the field `Customer` from the Field Name column and accept the default sort order.

4. For the second field, do not enter a name in the Index Name column. In the Field Name column select `OrderDate`.

5. Set the unique property to the value `Yes`. Close the dialog, save the table, and close it.

6. Open the table and attempt to add two orders using the same customer and order date in both. If you get an error message you successfully created a unique compound index.

Congratulations, you have now successfully set three different types of field indexes using Access 2010. No matter which kinds of indexes you choose to use, Access 2010 makes it quick and easy using the tools provides by the UI.

SUMMARY

Indexes can play a critical role in Access databases. By properly designing indexes, you can greatly improve the search times in a database application. But be careful; a poorly designed index can degrade the overall performance of the database. Know your data and use the tools that Access 2010 provides to analyze whether an index might help the performance of the database. Fields with limited distinct values may not see an increase in performance, whereas fields with many distinct values will probably increase performance, if that field will be used in a relationship, join, or as criteria in a query. Indexes can be a powerful method for improving the search performance for large tables in almost any Access database application.

 Please select Lesson 17 on the DVD to view the video that accompanies this lesson.

18

Creating Tables from External Data

Another very powerful feature in Access is the ability to import data from a multitude of data sources. Access 2010 supports a variety of external data types. For example, a text file in excess of 100,000 records would require hours to enter by hand, one record at a time; fortunately, Access provides wizards to help you import many different types of data in just a few minutes. In Access, data imports into a table can be a simple one-time loading of a list of data into a blank database, or it can be as complex as millions of records from a flat file that need to have additional data cleaning or other manipulation, using temporary tables and multiple queries, before importing the data.

Some examples of external data types that are easily imported into, or exported from, Access follow:

- ➤ Access
- ➤ Excel
- ➤ SQL Server
- ➤ Text
- ➤ CSV
- ➤ XML
- ➤ SharePoint
- ➤ ODBC

The purpose of providing methods to import data from external sources is to allow data sharing between multiple users, application types, and data formats as quickly and easily as possible. In Access 2010, no programming experience is necessary to import most types of data. The Import

Wizard guides you through the import process, providing you with instructions. This lesson is dedicated to discussing how to do simple data imports into a database using Access 2010 for a variety of common data types.

EXTERNAL DATA SOURCES

Access 2010 has built-in tools that enable the import of data and database objects from other Access databases, Excel files, data from ODBC databases like SQL Server, text files, XML files, SharePoint Lists, HTML documents, Outlook folders, and dBase files. Additional ODBC third-party drivers can be installed for an unlimited number of file types. Figure 18-1 shows the Import & Link section of the External Data Ribbon. Pressing any one of the buttons will invoke an Import Wizard.

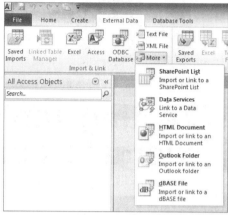

Importing from Excel

FIGURE 18-1

The need to import data from an Excel spreadsheet is very common for many users. If the data is not already formatted in defined columns and rows, some *data scrubbing* may be necessary to get it in the proper form for import. If you do not need to import the entire worksheet, you may be able to define a named range in Excel and only import that range.

Click the Import Excel button and browse to the Excel workbook you want to import. The Import Spreadsheet Wizard takes you through the steps needed to select a specific worksheet or a named range for import as illustrated in Figure 18-2. On the next screen you indicate whether the first row has column headings. In the screen that follows, you can change the field names or data types, specify an index, and exclude field(s) from the import.

 Allowing you to change an imported column's data type was introduced in Access 2007. In previous versions of Access, the Import Wizard would attempt to determine the data type based upon the data in the Excel spreadsheet, which could be quite frustrating at times.

The next screen is where a primary key is set for the table, followed by a screen that asks you to name the table or to accept the default table name, which is usually the name of the workbook, spreadsheet, or range being imported. The final screen lets you save the import for future reuse.

Always check the data after a first-time import to be sure the correct number of records and all of the data was imported properly. If possible, compare the original file with the new table created from the imported data.

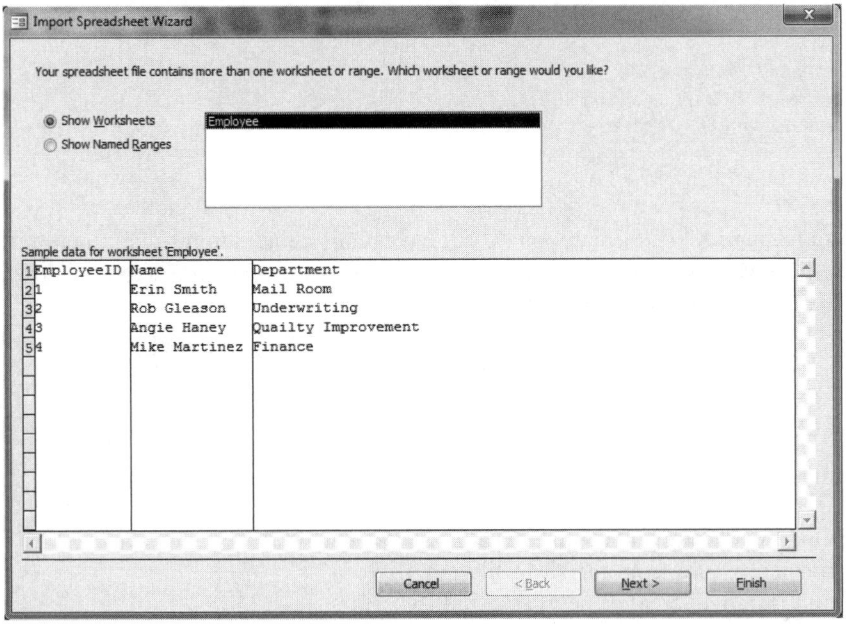

FIGURE 18-2

Importing from XML

XML (Extensible Markup Language) data is text data provided in a very specific format; it is quickly becoming the world standard for transferring data in standardized format.

The following text is an example of a simple XML file and is the file used in the "Try It" portion of this lesson.

```
<?xml version="1.0"?>
<wclass>
  <!-- Employees -->
  <Employee>
    <EmployeeID>1</EmployeeID>
    <Name>Erin Smith</Name>
    <Department>Mail Room</Department>
  </Employee>
  <Employee>
```

```
    <EmployeeID>2</EmployeeID>
    <Name>Rob Gleason</Name>
    <Department>Underwriting</Department>
  </Employee>
  <Employee>
    <EmployeeID>3</EmployeeID>
    <Name>Angie Haney</Name>
    <Department>Quality Improvement</Department>
  </Employee>
  <Employee>
    <EmployeeID>4</EmployeeID>
    <Name>Mike Martinez</Name>
    <Department>Finance</Department>
  </Employee>
</wclass>
```

When importing data from an XML format, you do not have many choices to make in the wizard. Once you browse to the XML file, the next screen is a Tree View, which allows you to drill down to see the fields to be imported, and to select the Import Options. The Import Options are:

➤ Structure Only

➤ Structure and Data (The default choice)

➤ Append Data to Existing Table(s)

Selecting Structure Only will create a new table in the database, but not append any data from the XML file. Selecting Structure and Data will create a new table and append the data from the XML file. If Append Data to Existing Table(s) is selected, Access will not create a new table and the data will be added to an existing table or tables. Figure 18-3 provides an image of the Import XML dialog showing what the previous XML code will look like in this window.

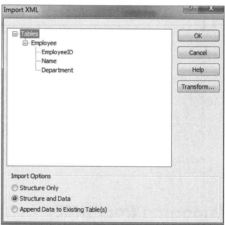

FIGURE 18-3

Saving Imports

Access allows you to save your import steps for future use. Once the import is saved, the next time the file is ready to be imported again, just a few simple clicks are required. The saved import definition stores the information about the file that is to be imported and other information that will be used for the same schema as the original file. However, if the schema for a saved import changes, the import will fail and you will have to re-run the wizard on the new data to set up the saved import again. Schemas don't change very often, though; for example, the weekly file you receive from the payroll system will usually be formatted the same as the last one. All you need to do is save the import and use it each time to import the file.

To save an import file, simply check the Save Import Steps check box when the final screen of the Import Wizard is displayed, add a meaningful name, and add a description. Save the import and it is ready to use.

Modifying Saved Imports

Access allows a user to edit the saved import name, the path of the import file, and the description, but the actual import steps cannot be edited; the saved import must be recreated if a change is made to the import steps in the wizard. To modify a saved import, click the Saved Imports button on the External Data Ribbon. On the Saved Imports tab of the Manage Data Tasks form, click the saved import you want to edit, then click in the name, file, or description section and make your edits.

Reusing Imports

After an import has been saved, it is available from the External Data Ribbon in the Import & Link section. Clicking the Saved Imports button opens a list of all the saved imports in the current database. If the file you are importing has the same file name and path as the last time it was used and the file is structured the same, you are ready to select the saved import and click Run. If the original saved import created a new table on import, it will (on subsequent use) create a new table. If the original table exists, the next time the saved import is used, the same name will be used, but a unique numeric suffix added to the table name. When creating the saved import, you have the option to append the records to an existing table instead of adding another table.

An import specification, which is created by using the dialog opened by clicking the Advanced button of the Text Import Wizard, can be selected each time the import is created. It can also be used when importing text data using VBA. You can schedule an import to run automatically, eliminating the need for a user to initiate the import.

TRY IT

In this lesson, you import a comma-delimited text file, an Excel spreadsheet, and an XML file. When importing the Excel spreadsheet, you will save the import and append the data to an existing table.

Lesson Requirements

For this lesson, you should have Access 2010 installed. You also need three files to import: `Employee.txt`, `Employee.xlsx`, and `XMLImport.xml`. The database and files can be downloaded from the book's DVD and website.

Step-by-Step

1. Open Access 2010 and the `Lesson18.accdb` database.

2. From the External Data Ribbon, click the Text File button to open the Import Wizard for text files.

3. Browse to the file `Employee.txt` and select it, and click Open.

4. Select the option to import the source data into a new table in the current database. Click OK.

5. Access should detect that the file is comma delimited. If it doesn't, select Delimited and click Next.

6. Check the First Row Contains Field Names box. The data should be neatly lined up in columns. If it is not, make sure Comma is selected as the delimiter. If the data appears to be correct, click Next.

7. Clicking the Advanced button allows you to select additional items, save an import specification that can be used in VBA code, or select an import specification to use or modify. In this example you skip the Advanced option and complete the import. Click Next.

8. Select Let Access Add a Primary Key and click Next.

9. The default table name is Employee. Accept the default name and click Finish. Click Close at the Save Import Steps screen.

10. Open the Employee table; it should have four records with four fields. Close the table.

Congratulations; you have successfully imported a text type file. Next you will import an Excel spreadsheet and append it to the Employee table you just created in the preceding steps.

11. Click the Excel button in the Import & Link section of the External Data Ribbon. Browse to the Employee.xlsx file and select it.

12. Choose Append a Copy of the Records to the Table and select the Employee table.

13. The Show Worksheets option should be selected and the Employee table highlighted. Click Next.

14. If the data looks correct, click Next.

15. Import to Table should be Employee. Click Finish.

16. Check the Save Import Steps box. Accept the name Import-Employee and click Save Import.

17. Open the Employee table and determine if the four records from the Excel file were appended to the table. There should be a total of eight records in the table. Close the table when done.

Congratulations; you have successfully appended an Excel spreadsheet file to your table. Next, you will import the Excel file a second time using the saved import you created.

18. Click the Saved Imports button on the External Data Ribbon.

19. Select Import-Employee and click Run.

20. Click OK in the Success dialog and click Close.

21. Open the Employee table. There should now be 12 records in the table. Close the table.

For the last exercise, you import an XML file into a new table.

22. Click the XML File button on the External Data Ribbon.

23. Browse to the file XMLImport.xml and select it. Click Open and then click OK.

23. Expand the Employee table in the Tree View and make sure three fields are in the file.

24. Check the Structure and Data option and click OK. Click Close.

25. Open the Employee table to ensure there are four records in the table. Close the table.

Congratulations. You have successfully imported a text file and an Excel spreadsheet file, created a saved import, used the saved import to import data from an Excel file again, and imported an XML file.

SUMMARY

Access 2010 has incorporated powerful tools to assist with importing a variety of external data types. One-time ad hoc imports are easily completed by novice users with the Import Wizard. Text files, spreadsheets, other Access databases, SQL Server databases, XML files, and other types of data can be imported with the click of a button. The Import Wizard guides you through the simple process of importing a data file, allowing you to save the steps if the process will be repeated. Because Access has made the import process so simple, anybody with rudimentary computer skills can import external data using Access 2010: it is that easy!

 Please select Lesson 18 on the DVD to view the video that accompanies this lesson.

19

Creating Linked Tables

Access 2010 lets you create and use linked tables to a wide variety of data sources. A *linked table* in an Access database is a table of data that can be used as though it is a local table in the database, even though the data actually resides in another location. In most cases a linked table is updatable through manipulation in the Access database, but a table must at least be readable to be usable as a linked table.

In some ways, linking is not much different than importing external data, except that the data remains in the external file and not in the Access database. It reduces the database size by not needing to physically store the data in the MDB/ACCDB file. Linking also helps eliminate duplicate data. If the linked tables are used by multi-user applications, the data is located in a single database file — not in each user's local database. Linking can be used when you want to import only records that meet certain criteria. Linking also allows Access applications to gather, use, and manipulate data in an external data source without actually storing that data within the Access database.

The primary use for linked tables in Access is to create multi-tiered database applications. A typical multi-user Access database application is a two-tiered application. The first tier is the user interface (front end), which is distributed to all the application's users. The front end typically contains the database objects that the user interacts with, such as the forms, reports, queries, some macros, and some modules. The back end typically contains the actual tables and data used by, and shared between, the users, along with the relationship definitions and common code and macros. Access can link to any number of external data sources simultaneously; it is not uncommon to link to other Access databases and/or SQL Server databases at the same time. This lesson discusses the benefits of using linked tables to create back-end database applications using Access 2010.

LESSON SETUP

In this lesson, we discuss creating linked tables to external data sources using Access 2010. Creating linked tables to Access databases, Excel spreadsheets, and SharePoint lists can be accomplished using the Get External Data Wizard.

LINKED TABLES IN ACCESS

A majority of the professionally designed Access applications are implemented as two-tier applications, front-end applications that use linked tables. Many reasons exist to use linked tables in an Access application:

➤ Using a back-end database allows for centralized data storage. While all the application users are using a separate, and in some cases different, front-end application, the data being stored in the back-end database will always remain in sync.

➤ Access 2010 has a 2 GB size limit on the MDB/ACCDB file. When using linked tables, this limitation can be mitigated by using more database files.

➤ If more than one user or more than one computer will be using the database, linked tables should be used, instead of users attempting to use the same MDB/ACCDB file. Record-locking issues and data corruption problems may occur otherwise.

➤ Fewer maintenance issues occur when the application is split. Modifying the forms or reports in the front end on a split database will not require methods to sync the data for all users, because the data is not contained in the local front-end database and the data is not affected.

➤ Security concerns can be addressed by using tables linked to a client/server database like SQL Server or SharePoint lists. Most client/server systems have robust user-level security and the permissions are enforced when a linked table is used. A user cannot view or modify data in a linked table without the proper permissions to the server.

The primary reason for separating the front end, back end, and (in some instances) other parts of the database is to reduce the chance of record-locking issues in multi-user database applications. It also makes it much simpler and safer to update the front-end application.

Creating Linked Tables to Other Access Databases

Access 2010 supports linking all versions of Access databases from Access 2.0 through Access 2010. The linking process is effectively the same as importing data from tables in an Access database. One difference between import and link is you are not able to link any objects except tables. You can only *import* forms, reports, and so on using the Import option. To create a linked table, complete the following steps:

1. Click the Access button on the External Data Ribbon.

2. At the first screen of the Get External Data Wizard, browse to the database you want to link.

3. Choose the option titled Link to the Data Source by Creating a Linked Table.

4. The next screen lists all the tables in the database that are available for linking. Select at least one table and click OK. The Navigation Pane should now list all the tables you selected as tables in your database.

If you no longer need a linked table, you can remove it by selecting the table and deleting it. The link is all that is deleted; the data in the original table remains intact and available for others to use.

Creating Linked Tables to Excel

Linking to an Excel spreadsheet can be a valuable tool. One drawback to using Excel as a linked table is that the Excel data is read-only. If you need to update the data in the spreadsheet, consider other options (including importing the data or using VBA automation). Using a linked Excel spreadsheet allows Access to use information that was calculated in Excel and see any changes made in Excel in real time from Access.

You can create a linked table to an Excel spreadsheet by clicking the Excel button in the Import group on the External Data Ribbon to open the Get External Data - Excel Spreadsheet Wizard. The first page of the wizard allows you to browse to the Excel file and presents three options:

➤ Import as a new table.

➤ Import and append to an existing table.

➤ Link to the data source by creating a linked table.

In this case, because you want to create a linked table, select the Link option, browse to a file, and then click the Next button to specify creating a linked table. The next page of the wizard allows you to select either Worksheets or Named Ranges to import as a linked table.

➤ The Worksheets option uses the entire worksheet as a linked table.

➤ The Named Ranges option only uses a predefined Excel range.

The wizard's third screen lets you specify that the first row contains the column headings. And finally, the last screen lets you create a name for the linked table. Using the External Data Wizard to create a linked table using Access 2010 only takes those steps!

Creating Linked Tables to SharePoint

It is also possible to create linked tables to SharePoint lists, or even move existing tables to a SharePoint site. This concept is functionally the same as linking to other Access databases or to SQL Server tables. Linking to Access databases on a WAN can introduce extremely poor performance results. However, a linked SharePoint list's performance will usually be equivalent to the performance of an Access web application.

Follow along to link to a SharePoint list:

1. Click the More button on the Import & Link section of the External Data Ribbon.

2. Choose SharePoint List from the drop-down. The Get External Data - SharePoint Site Wizard opens and allows the user to enter the site address of the SharePoint Site and select the Link to the Data Source by Creating a Linked Table option.

3. Enter your credentials for the SharePoint site. A screen opens with the lists available to link.

4. Select the list(s) you are linking to and click the Next button. A message box opens and reports that an attempt at linking to the lists is in progress.

5. When Access reports a successful link, test the link by opening the table from the Navigation Pane.

TRY IT

In this lesson, you learn how to link to external tables in other Access databases, link to Excel spreadsheets, and link to SharePoint lists. You need to create a blank database for this lesson. There will not be any local tables or objects besides the linked tables you will create. Use the database and Excel spreadsheet with this book's sample files as the source of the external data.

Lesson Requirements

For this lesson you should have Access 2010 installed, the database and spreadsheet sample files, and you also need the rights and credentials to connect to a SharePoint site to complete the portion of the "Try It" that demonstrates linking to a SharePoint list. You can download the sample files from the book's DVD and website.

Step-by-Step

1. Start Access and create a new blank database. Open the External Data Ribbon and click the Access button. Notice that the External Data Wizard opens.

2. On the first page of the wizard, browse to the sample database.

3. Select Link to the Data Source by Creating a Linked Table and click OK.

4. On the second page of the wizard, select the `SampleEmployee` table and click OK. Then click the Finish button. The new table will be created in the Access database, which is linked to the table in the file.

5. From the Navigation Pane, open the `SampleEmployee` table and verify that it has four records. Then close the table.

Congratulations; you have successfully created a linked table to another Access database. This table will now show up in the Navigation Pane for the current database, but will have a different icon than the standard local Access tables. Linking to an Excel spreadsheet is your next task. In this example, you will link to an Excel spreadsheet and to a named range within the Excel workbook.

 To create an Excel named range, highlight the Excel data in the Excel spreadsheet that you want to include. For this example, select the header row and two records, and click the Define Name button on the Formulas Ribbon and name the range **EmployeeRange**. *Save the workbook and close Excel.*

6. Open the database created at the beginning of this "Try It" and click the Excel button in the Import & Link section of the External Data Ribbon.

7. Browse to the `Employee.xlsx` spreadsheet. Select Link to the Data Source by Creating a Linked Table. Click the OK button.

8. The Get External Data - Excel Spreadsheet Wizard opens. Select the Show Worksheets option, select the Employee worksheet, and click the Next button.

9. Check First Row Contains Column Headings and then click the Next button. Then click the Finish button on the last page of the wizard without changing the table name.

10. If you haven't created a named range, do so as shown in the preceding note. Then repeat Steps 6 and 7 to start the Get External Data Wizard.

11. This time, select the Show Named Ranges option and select EmployeeRange. Click the Next button, check First Row Contains Column Headings, and click the Next button again. Then click the Finish button without changing the table name.

12. From the Navigation Pane, open the new `EmployeeRange` table and check to see that it only contains the two records.

Congratulations; you have created a linked table to a named range in an Excel spreadsheet. Finally, if you have access to lists on a SharePoint site, this last example will show you how to create a linked table to a SharePoint list.

13. Open the database created at the beginning of this "Try It" section. Click the External Data tab to show the External Data Ribbon. Click the More button in the Import section, then click the SharePoint List button. The Get External Data - SharePoint List Wizard is opened.

14. Enter the site address of the SharePoint site and select Link to the Data Source by Creating a Linked Table. Click the Next button.

15. A login dialog pops up and requests your credentials. After entering your username and password, click OK.

16. The second page of the wizard shows all the lists visible to the user for the SharePoint site. Select one or more lists to create linked tables for in your database. Click OK. The new linked tables will be created and shown in the Navigation Pane.

17. In the Navigation Pane, open the tables and see that they are actually linked to the SharePoint site. Close the table and exit Access.

Congratulations; you have successfully linked to an external Access database, an Excel spreadsheet, and a SharePoint list (if you had access to a SharePoint server). Creating linked tables to almost any type of external data source requires only a few minutes and clicks.

SUMMARY

As you see, linking to external data is a very simple and straightforward process and the Access wizards make it almost foolproof. The practice of creating multi-tier Access database applications is not only a means to get external data into the application, but also a tool to provide a more robust database application for your users. And in most cases, splitting a database into multiple tiers helps prevent the possibility of record-locking issues occurring when the application is being used by multiple users simultaneously. Using data sources other than Access is very popular and provides a lot of flexibility to end users who need to import data.

Microsoft is investing a large amount of resources to allow SharePoint 2010 and Access 2010 to work well together; SharePoint is becoming more common in the business world, and adding the ability to link to and use the data is a very powerful tool for Access users. Access 2010 makes it simple and supports a wide variety of data types to create linked tables in a database application.

 Please select Lesson 19 on the DVD to view the video that accompanies this lesson.

20

Collecting Data via E-mail

The Collect Data Through E-Mail Messages Wizard, often called the *Data Collection* feature, allows users to collect information from one or more recipients via e-mail messages that automatically populate the database records when returned to Outlook. Originally introduced in Access 2007, the Data Collection feature creates an e-mail containing a form that the recipients can return with the requested information. When the e-mail is received by Outlook, the data stored in the form is either appended to the table or the existing records are updated, depending on which option has been selected. To use this feature, the originator of the request must be using Outlook and the recipients will need to have e-mail applications that can receive HTML messages or, if the sender chooses to use Microsoft InfoPath forms, all the recipients will need to have both Microsoft Outlook and Microsoft InfoPath installed, both of which are included with Office 2010 Professional.

To provide an example of how the Data Collection feature can be used, consider a scenario for a small business user. A Human Resources manager needs to create a phone number list of each of the employees that currently work for the company. Instead of sending a standard e-mail requesting the data and manually transferring the records from the returned e-mails, the Access 2010 e-mail Data Collection feature could be used to create the e-mails and input the records automatically, effectively doing all of the work and reducing the chance of human errors. The Data Collection feature can save a lot of time and effort if used correctly.

LESSON SETUP

In this lesson, you use Outlook, InfoPath, and Access 2010 to create an e-mail that gathers data from recipients. Outlook 2010 should be installed and preconfigured before starting this lesson. You should be familiar with working with tables and queries, and be familiar with sending e-mail using Outlook 2010, to successfully complete this lesson.

PREREQUISITES FOR E-MAIL DATA COLLECTION

Before using the wizard to set up data collection, you need to set up the tables that will receive the data. The data source can be either a table or a query. If the data source is a query, it must be an updatable query, otherwise the wizard will fail.

Depending on the structure of the tables in your database, it may be necessary to create a temporary table to use to import the data. For example, if you are requesting the current mailing addresses and phone numbers of employees, and your database design stores addresses in one table and phone numbers in another table, a simple solution is to use a temporary table. After the data is received, a query, or series of queries, can be used to append the imported data from the temporary table to the normalized tables in your database.

One other item to be aware of when using data collection is that, although the data collection e-mail can accept all Access data types, if a person enters a data value that is not compatible with the table's data type, the data collection process for that user will fail when the e-mail is received by the original sender's Outlook. For this reason, it is important *not* to include AutoNumber fields in the data collection e-mail. Appending to an AutoNumber field will cause the append process to fail, because you can't append a value to an AutoNumber data type.

USING THE DATA COLLECTION WIZARD

The Collect Data Through E-Mail Messages Wizard is very complex for an Access wizard and consists of a number of different pages. The following are the minimum steps:

1. Click the table or query you want to use for the data collection e-mail in the Navigation Pane.

2. Click the Create E-mail button on the External Data Ribbon.

3. The page of the wizard displays a list of the steps needed to set up data collection by e-mail from Access. Click Next to continue.

4. The second page of the wizard offers two choices:

   ➤ **Use an HTML Form.** Most e-mail applications can support HTML, including most web-based e-mail clients.

   ➤ **Use an InfoPath Form.** Each recipient will need Microsoft Office InfoPath installed on his or her individual computer to use InfoPath forms. Use the InfoPath option only if you are certain that all recipients have InfoPath.

5. The third page asks you to choose between collecting new data and updating existing data:

   ➤ The New Data option is used to create new records.

   ➤ The Update option allows you to send recipients information to review and return the message to you, updating the information in the table.

6. The fourth page allows you to select, arrange, and rename the fields to include in the e-mail form.

7. The fifth page offers the option to automatically process replies and add the data to your table.

8. The sixth page offers the choice of typing or pasting the e-mail addresses in Outlook or using e-mail addresses stored in the database.

9. The seventh page allows you to modify the Subject and Body of the e-mail as needed.

10. The last page creates and sends the e-mails.

Although quite a few steps are involved in setting and configuring the data collection e-mail through the wizard, overall this process can save a lot of time when the e-mails are returned and the records are automatically entered into the tables by Outlook.

Working with Outlook

The first time you send a data collection e-mail from Access, Outlook creates a folder named Access Data Collection Replies and a search folder of the same name. As the replies are received, Outlook routes the e-mails to this folder. If you selected the option to apply the data to the database on receipt, Outlook sends the data to the database. If you did not select the option to apply the data to the database, the Data Collection Status of the e-mail should read Message Unprocessed. To manually send the data to the table, locate the Export to Access button on the message's Ribbon in Outlook, or right-click the message in the Access Data Collection Replies folder and select Export Data to Microsoft Office, Access and you are done.

Requesting Data Updates

Each time a request for data is created, Access saves it and allows you to edit, resend, or delete the data collection message. From the Manage Replies button on the External Data Ribbon you can select the message you want to reuse and then click the Resend This E-mail Message button. You can modify the import settings by clicking the message options. To delete the message, click the Delete This E-mail Message button.

Clicking the Resend button starts the wizard and guides you through the steps to re-create the message, including allowing you to change the recipients and the message's text. After adding the e-mail addresses, click Send and the request is sent.

InfoPath Form E-mails

Creating InfoPath forms for data collection is as simple as creating HTML forms; the only limiting factor is the necessity of having InfoPath installed on the computer creating the e-mail, as well as those of all of the recipients. One feature of InfoPath data collection forms that is not available with HTML forms is the ability of the recipient to add additional rows of data to the returned e-mail. This ability can also be disabled prior to sending the data request e-mail.

HTML Form E-mails

The HTML form option is probably the safer of the two choices, because it is hard to know if a recipient has InfoPath installed. The end user does not need any special software installed, other than an Internet browser, such as Internet Explorer, and the ability to receive and send e-mails with embedded HTML code. The recipient is limited to one record per e-mail, but that should not be too big of a problem.

TRY IT

In this lesson, you create two "collect data through e-mail messages" forms: an HTML form and an InfoPath form. You will see how Outlook sends and receives the information and how the data can be automatically applied to the database when the e-mail is received. You use a saved e-mail and then delete a saved e-mail using the Manage Replies button.

Lesson Requirements

For this lesson you should have Access 2010, Outlook, and optionally, InfoPath installed, and you should have an e-mail address available for you to both send and receive e-mails to see how the actual data is sent and received. You should also have the sample `Lesson20.accdb` file, which you can download from the book's DVD and website.

Step-by-Step

1. Open the `Lesson20.accdb` file in Access 2010.

2. Click the `tblContacts` table in the Navigation Pane to select it.

3. On the External Data Ribbon, click the Create E-mail button to start the wizard. The wizard will open.

4. On the first page of the wizard, read the steps listed on the screen and click Next to continue.

5. Select the HTML Form option and click Next to continue.

6. Select the Collect New Information Only option and click Next to continue.

7. Add all of the fields from the table to the e-mail message and click Next to continue.

8. Check Automatically Process Replies, add data to `tblContacts`, and click Next to continue.

9. Select the Enter the E-mail Addresses in Microsoft Office Outlook option and click Next to continue.

10. In this screen you have the choice of accepting the default text, or you can modify the text to meet your requirements. For example:

    Please provide your current mailing address, phone number, and Employee ID in the form below.

11. Click Next to continue.

12. On the last page of the wizard, click the Create button to create the e-mail. An Outlook e-mail with an HTML form in the body of it will open.

13. Add at least one valid e-mail address in the TO line of the e-mail, preferably one to yourself so you can respond with test data, and then click the Send button on the e-mail to send it.

14. Once you have received the e-mail (from yourself), reply to the e-mail to create an e-mail for the response (as you would if you were normally responding to an e-mail). The new e-mail will open.

15. In the response e-mail, complete the HTML form and submit the response by clicking the Send button on the e-mail. The response will be sent.

16. Once the response has been received by Outlook, it should appear in the Access Data Collection Replies folder and will be processed automatically.

Congratulations, you have now successfully created, completed, and returned a data collection e-mail using Access 2010. Open the tblContacts table to verify the new data was added. If it was not, add the data by opening the returned mail and clicking the Export to Access button on Outlook's Message Ribbon.

Next, if you have InfoPath installed, try creating an e-mail using an InfoPath form. Remember, InfoPath must be installed on both the originating and receiving computers for this scenario to work correctly. Otherwise, skip ahead to the next series of steps to finish this lesson.

17. Repeat Steps 2–4.

18. This time, on the second page of the wizard, select the InfoPath Form option and click Next to continue.

19. Repeat Steps 5–14 to complete the data collection e-mail, send it, and create the e-mail reply.

20. Enter the responses in the form and the click the Insert a Row button at the bottom of the e-mail. Add a second set of responses and click the Send button to send the e-mail.

21. Once the e-mail has been received, the response should appear in the Access Data Collection Replies folder in Outlook and the data will be processed automatically.

Congratulations, you have now created a data collection e-mail that uses an InfoPath form. Open the tblContacts table to verify the new data was added. If it was not, add it by clicking the Export to Access button on Outlook's Message Ribbon.

Finally, try deleting a saved e-mail message and resending another using the Manage Replies dialog that Access provides:

22. Click the Manage Replies button on the External Data Ribbon to open the Manage Replies dialog.

23. Select a saved e-mail and click the Delete This E-mail Message button. Choose Yes at the prompt.

24. Select another e-mail and click Resend This E-mail Message, following the steps in the wizard, and click the Create button when done to create the new e-mail message.

25. Add one or more e-mail addresses and click the Send button to send the new e-mail message.

26. Once the e-mail has been received, open the e-mail and use the Reply option to create a response e-mail. Complete the HTML form and submit the response by clicking the Send button.

27. The response should appear in the Access Data Collection Replies folder in Outlook and be processed automatically once received.

Congratulations, you have now successfully resent a data collection e-mail using the Manage Replies dialog. Regardless of whether you are updating existing data or need new data, using the Data Collection feature can save you a lot of time and effort.

SUMMARY

When there is a need to collect data from multiple users, such as requesting contact information from existing customers, creating an e-mail to automatically collect data can simplify the process. When set up correctly, the Data Collection feature can request the information from everyone on the mailing list, provide a form that allows the user to enter the requested information, and then add the data collected to a table in the database automatically on receipt of the e-mail.

The Data Collection Wizard guides you through the process to create and send the e-mail. To reuse a previously created and saved e-mail, all that is needed is a few clicks in the Manage Replies dialog and then supplying the recipients again. Data that needs processing prior to importing into a properly normalized database can be appended to a temporary table using the Collect Data Through E-mail Messages Wizard, and then processed with predefined queries or VBA code to add it to the working tables of the database.

When used properly, the Data Collection feature is a powerful data gathering tool. Data collection is easy to implement and can be used in both large and small applications, and in both large and small organizations, using Access, Outlook, and InfoPath 2010.

 Please select Lesson 20 on the DVD to view the video that accompanies this lesson.

21

Creating Queries with the Wizard

The query is the workhorse of a database, and without queries to retrieve the data from tables, every search for a specific record would be a manual walk through the records in a table. Queries are formed from SQL (Structured Query Language) statements, which are a kind of programming language for data manipulation in standardized database systems, which Access understands. Select queries can be used to gather data from multiple tables and join the related fields to form the data into a structure that is useful for the task at hand. Action queries, such as Add, Update, and Delete, can be used to modify the table data directly. Select queries are often used in Access to gather, structure, and sort data into certain formats for presentation, allowing the developer to use those queries for the Record Source properties of Form or Report objects. And learning how to create really good queries will make building Access database applications much easier and more efficient!

Becoming proficient in the creation of queries is essential to an Access database developer, but they can be extremely complex and often difficult, even for advanced Access developers. Because queries are such a complex feature of the product, Access provides several tools for building and working with Query database objects. The Access Query Wizard, Query Design View, and the SQL View are all designers that Access provides for building Query objects in Access 2010. Because this is the first lesson in this book to explorer Query objects directly, it examines creating an Access Query object using the Access Query Wizard.

LESSON SETUP

In this lesson you learn how to create an Access Query object using the Access Query Wizard in Access 2010. You should be familiar with creating database objects, working with tables, and have a basic understanding of table relationships (as described in previous lessons) to successfully complete this lesson.

DATABASE QUERY THEORY

Before we jump into building Access Query objects, it is important to have a good understanding of exactly what queries do and how they can benefit your application. As discussed in Lesson 16, relational databases use joins between key fields to identify records that are related to other records. The *primary key* of a table is a unique identifier for that one record in a table. A *foreign key* is used to relate single or multiple records to a primary key in another table. A *join* is the definition of how two related fields are connected. Access 2010 allows *inner joins*, *left joins*, *right joins*, and *Cartesian joins* to be created and used in Query objects. Except for Cartesian joins, all these join types are discussed in detail in Lesson 16.

A Cartesian join, sometimes called a *cross join*, is actually the absence of a defined system join, and produces the Cartesian product of the combination of records between the tables. In common terms, this means that each record in the primary table will join with each record in any secondary tables included in the query. For example, a primary table with 100 records and a secondary table with 75 records will return a whopping 7,500 records with a Cartesian join.

If a query containing a Cartesian join for tables containing large amounts of records is executed, the Access database engine may grind away for hours to build the resulting data set, while eating up all of the memory and resources on the machine. For this reason, it is a good idea to be careful before constructing and using Cartesian joins, and these can often be the result of a mistake that has been made when designing the query.

Because Select queries can be used to gather specific records, join the fields between tables into a single structure, and sort data in different formats, they are often used as the Record Source property for a form or report, instead of the table itself. The theory is that once you get the data in the desired format in the Query object, you can tie the form object to the query to allow a method for editing the data, or tie the query to a report object to show and print the data in the desired layout. So, the trick is to properly build the query to get the specific data from the collection of tables and order it in a manner that will be useful for your task. And this is where Access makes your life really easy, by providing the Query Wizard to help you build queries quickly and in the format you need.

CREATING A QUERY WITH THE WIZARD

Included as part of the query design tools is the Access Query Wizard, which can be used to create several different types of queries. The Query Wizard can create simple Select queries, Find Unmatched records, Find Duplicates records, and Crosstab queries. The benefit to using the wizard to create queries is that you do not need to know how to write SQL statements to create the query. Instead, the wizard's dialogs ask a series of questions onscreen to help you select the necessary parameters to build the query and then the wizard takes care of putting together the SQL statement and creating the actual query database object for you. To create a query using the Query Wizard, click the Query Wizard button on the Create Ribbon, and follow the steps on the wizard to create what you want to use.

Query Types

The Access Query Wizard enables you to create the following types of queries:

➤ Select queries

➤ Crosstab queries

➤ Find Duplicates queries

➤ Find Unmatched queries

Select queries return recordsets to display in forms or reports, or to use in VBA code. Although there are no options for creating Action queries by using a wizard, once a Select query is created and it is returning the results desired, in most cases, it is a simple matter to change it to an Append, Update, or Delete query. Crosstab queries aggregate data using the Sum, Min, Max, or other aggregate functions, then group those values by at least two sets of values. An example of a Crosstab query would be totaling sales by department and sales month. The department would be listed as records in the first column on the left and the sales month would be columns across the top of the query. The total of sales for each month and department is calculated at the intersection of the rows and columns. Figure 21-1 shows the results of a Crosstab query.

qrySales_Crosstab					
Department ▾	Total Of Amt ▾	Jan ▾	Feb ▾	Mar ▾	Apr ▾
Beauty	$3,038.00	$881.00	$657.00	$222.00	$451.00
Drug	$5,854.00	$776.00	$1,112.00	$1,010.00	$986.00
Grocery	$13,193.00	$1,245.00	$2,215.00	$1,446.00	$2,524.00
Meat	$9,102.00	$1,245.00	$1,789.00	$1,952.00	$1,540.00
Produce	$9,930.00	$1,812.00	$1,678.00	$1,996.00	$1,402.00

FIGURE 21-1

 The Crosstab Wizard allows you to add only three fields to use as Row Headings in a Crosstab query. Crosstab queries can have more than three Row Headings, but you must add the headings in Design View or in SQL View.

Find Duplicates queries are used to find values, in a single table or query, that are duplicated values. The wizard will create a query that returns the records suspected to be duplicates. It creates a subquery that groups and counts the number of duplicated records. Then the subquery is used as the criterion for the main query, returning only the records where the count from the subquery is greater than one.

The Find Unmatched query is used to find records that are in one table, but not in another. A Find Unmatched query is actually a query with a left join on the related fields and criteria to return null records on the right side of the join.

TRY IT

In this lesson, you use the Access Query Wizard to create several queries based on the Lesson21 .accdb file, which you can download from this book's DVD and website. You create both a simple

Select query and a more advanced Crosstab query to show how these types of queries can be created using the Query Wizard in Access 2010.

Lesson Requirements

For this lesson, you will need to download the `Lesson21.accdb` sample database file from the book's website to complete the following steps. You should be familiar with creating database objects and working with Table and Query objects; have Access 2010 installed and seek out Lesson 21 from the website at `www.wrox.com` to successfully complete this lesson.

Hints

The following is a short list of hints to help complete this lesson:

➤ You can launch the Query Wizard from the Create Ribbon in Access 2010.

➤ You will need at least one table, ideally with some sample data in it, to create a Select query.

Step-by-Step

1. Open the `Lesson21.accdb` file in Access 2010.

2. On the Create Ribbon, click the Query Wizard button to launch the New Query dialog.

3. On the New Query dialog, click the Simple Query Wizard option and click OK. This will close the New Query dialog and launch the Simple Query Wizard.

4. On the first page of the Simple Query Wizard, choose the `tblPatient` table from the Tables/Queries drop-down list. This will show the fields from the `tblPatient` table in the Available Fields list just below.

5. Click the `PatientNumber` field to select it and then click the > button to add the field to the Selected Fields list.

6. Repeat that process for the `PatientLastName`, `PatientFirstName`, and `PatientSex` fields to add them to the Selected Fields list and click the Next button to continue.

7. Change the title of the query to be **qryPatient**. Then ensure that the option to Open the query to view information is selected and click the Finish button.

You have created a Select query using the Access Simple Query Wizard. The new query will be opened automatically and will show you all of the records from the four fields you added to the query. Next, try creating a Crosstab query using the Query Wizard.

8. Close the `qryPatient` query that was created and opened by the Simple Query Wizard.

9. On the Create Ribbon, click the Query Wizard button to open the New Query dialog.

10. Click the Crosstab Query Wizard option in the list to select it and click the OK button to close the dialog and open the Crosstab Query Wizard.

11. On the first page of the Query Wizard, click the `tblPatientUtilization` table to select it in the list and click the Next button to continue.

12. On the second page of the Query Wizard, add the `PatientID` field to the Selected Fields list and click the Next button to continue.

Notice that when you select the `PatientID` field in the wizard, the sample grid at the bottom of the wizard shows how the results of the query will look in the datasheet.

13. On the third page of the wizard, select the `DateService` field as the Column Heading and click the Next button.

14. On the fourth page of the wizard, select the Date/Time option as the interval you want to group the `DateService` information on and click the Next button.

15. On the fifth page of the wizard, select the `TypeVisit` option from the Available Fields list and choose the `Count` option from the Functions list. Then click the Next button.

16. On the last page of the wizard, change the title of the query **qryCountPatientsServicedByDate** and click the Finish button to save and execute the query. The results of your new Crosstab query will be shown.

Congratulations; you have successfully created a Crosstab query using Access 2010. Creating queries using the wizard is extremely quick and easy, because Access does all the work for you to create the SQL statement for the query, using just the information that you provide the wizard.

SUMMARY

Creating queries in Access 2010, regardless of whether they are simple or complex, can be accomplished very easily by using the Query Wizard. The Access Query Wizard can be used to create four different types of queries with just a few mouse clicks. And because queries do the work to gather records in a database, you will likely create many queries in every database application you create. Using the Query Wizard to speed up the process of building queries can save you lots of time and the headache of getting the SQL statement for the query correct. However, many developers often find the Query Wizard somewhat limiting, because you cannot always build the exact query you desire using just the wizard. This is where the Query Design View mode comes into play — to allow the developer even further manipulation of the query using the Access query designer, which is the topic of our next lesson. And now that you know how to create queries using the Access Query Wizard, you are ready to delve deeper into the query features that Access 2010 provides.

Please select Lesson 21 on the DVD to view the video that accompanies this lesson.

22

Creating Queries in Design View

After becoming more familiar with creating queries using the Access 2010 Query Wizard (explained in Lesson 21), you might want to begin creating queries directly from Query Design View mode. The Access 2010 Query Design View allows more control over a query's final design than the wizard allows. A proficient user can easily open a new query in Design View and add single or multiple tables, create and define joins, drag and drop all fields (or only add specific fields), create field expressions, add sorting to single or multiple fields, and create aggregate or group by queries.

This lesson shows you how to use the Query Design View to create a query. The lesson familiarizes you with the Show Table dialog and the Query Design Ribbon. You learn how to add fields to the query, add criteria to restrict returned records, sort the results to order the records, and add totals to the query. You also get an introduction to the query's SQL view to show what the query designer is creating in the background.

One of the major strengths of Access 2010 is its ease of learning and use. With only a few clicks and limited typing, you can design a simple query to return records that meet specific criteria. In addition to queries that return records, Access allows the user to create Action queries that modify, or manipulate, data by using the Design View. Action queries include Append, Update, Delete, and Make Table queries. This lesson discusses the basics of creating an Access query database object using Query Design View mode.

CREATING A NEW QUERY IN DESIGN VIEW

The Create Ribbon includes the Macros & Code section, which contains the two buttons used to create queries in Access 2010. To create a query in Design View, open an existing database and click the Create tab on the Ribbon to show the Create Ribbon, as illustrated in Figure 22-1.

FIGURE 22-1

Click the Query Design button on the Create Ribbon. This opens a blank query and opens the Show Table dialog shown in Figure 22-2.

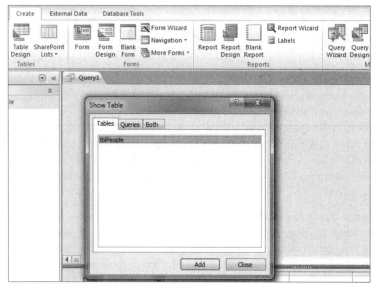

FIGURE 22-2

The Show Table Dialog

The Show Table dialog has three tabs: Tables, Queries, and Both. You can add tables or other queries to a query by selecting a single table or query and clicking the Add button. Alternatively, you can add single tables or queries by double-clicking them. The dialog also allows you to select multiple tables or queries. Click the Add button to add the selections to the query. After you've added the needed tables or queries to the query grid, close the Show Table dialog.

The Query Design Ribbon

When the Show Table dialog closes, the Query Design Ribbon is displayed, as shown in Figure 22-3. The Query Design Ribbon has four sections: Results, Query Type, Query Setup, and Show/Hide.

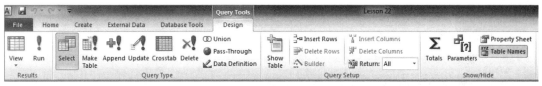

FIGURE 22-3

Results

The Results section has two buttons — View and Run:

➤ **View** allows the user to preview the results of select and action queries without appending records, making a table, updating fields, or deleting the results of an action query. View has five buttons:

    ➤ **Datasheet View** opens the query.

    ➤ **PivotTable View** opens a Query Design View for a pivot table.

    ➤ **PivotChart View** opens a pivot table in a Chart Query Design View.

    ➤ **SQL View** shows the queries' underlying SQL statements.

    ➤ **Design View** opens the Query Design View.

➤ **Run** executes action queries including appending, deleting, and so on.

Query Type

The Query Type section has buttons to create specific query types:

➤ **Select** sets the type of query to a Select query, used to return records only and not perform any actions.

➤ **Make Table** sets the type of query to a Make Table query, used to return records and insert the records into a new table.

➤ **Append** sets the type of query to an Append query, used to append records to an existing table.

➤ **Update** sets the type of query to an Update query. Update queries are used to change the value of specific fields in a record.

➤ **Crosstab** sets the type of query to a Crosstab query. Crosstab queries are special queries that transform rows of data into columns, aggregating the data if desired.

➤ **Delete** sets the type of query to Delete, which deletes all the records returned by the query.

➤ **Union** opens a blank query in SQL View mode. Union queries cannot be created in Query Design View.

➤ **Pass-Through** opens a blank query in SQL View mode with the property set to a pass-through query. Pass-through queries are used to query a client/server database, such as Microsoft SQL Server, directly at the server without using any client-side processing.

➤ **Data Definition** opens a blank SQL tab where you can write the SQL to create or drop tables, add or drop an index, add or drop fields, and so on.

Query Setup

The Query Setup section has seven buttons:

➤ **Show Table** opens the Show Table dialog.

➤ **Insert Rows** adds rows to the query grid.

➤ **Delete Rows** deletes rows from the query grid.

➤ **Builder** opens the Expression Builder dialog.

➤ **Insert Columns** adds columns to the query grid.

➤ **Delete Columns** removes columns from the query grid.

➤ **Return** activates the top predicate and allows the user to select how many records are returned by a query. A fixed number of records or a percentage of the records can be selected.

Show/Hide

The Show/Hide section has four buttons:

➤ **Totals** changes the query to a Group By or an Aggregate query.

➤ **Parameters** allows explicit declaration of parameters and the data types of parameters used in a query.

➤ **Property Sheet** shows or hides the Property Sheet associated with the query.

➤ **Table Names** shows or hides the Table row of the query grid.

Adding Fields to the Query

The tables or queries added using the Show Table dialog show all available fields that can be added to the query. Figure 22-4 shows all of the fields in a table named `tblPeople` in the Query Design View of a query named `qryPeople`.

FIGURE 22-4

Fields can be added to a query by dragging and dropping them individually to the grid, selecting multiple fields and dragging and dropping them into the query grid, double-clicking individual fields, or by using the drop-down in the Field row of the query. If multiple tables are used there is also a drop-down in the Table row. Selecting a table restricts the available fields in the Field drop-down to the fields in the selected table.

Selecting the asterisk and placing it in the query grid creates a query that returns all fields in the table. It is usually not good practice to use the asterisk because it is less efficient than returning only the minimum number of fields needed.

Calculated fields can be created and used in a query. A *Calculated field* is a column that a formula uses to create a value. Adding two fields, multiplying price by units sold to return total sales, performing concatenation operations, and parsing strings are examples of Calculated fields. The builder can be used to create an expression or they can be created manually.

Adding Criteria to Restrict Records

To add criteria to a query, enter the desired criteria in the Criteria row of the query grid. The criteria can be literal values such as names, dates, and ranges of values, or the criteria can be calculated from values in other fields or from functions like the Date() function. Access allows query criteria to be either hardcoded in the query or entered at run time by prompts or from values on forms passed to the query when it is opened.

➤ Typing the value to return in the Criteria row in the Query Design View of the query hardcodes the query to return that value.

➤ Using square brackets to surround text for a prompt for the user allows a user to enter the value in a prompt at run time. An example of using the prompt method is [Enter Last Name] entered in the Criteria row of the LastName field.

➤ Using form references that use values entered in controls on a form is another way to pass criteria values to a query at run time. The syntax for a form reference is Forms!FormName!ControlName and is entered in the Criteria row of the query.

Sorting Results to Order Records

The Sort row in the query grid is where a query's sort order is set. Three options are available in the Sort drop-down:

➤ Ascending

➤ Descending

➤ (not sorted)

Setting Ascending or Descending sorts the records in either ascending or descending order. If multiple columns are required for ordering, Access sorts the column on the left first and then sorts the column to the right next, until all sorting-enabled columns have been processed.

Adding Totals

Adding totals includes all of the aggregate functions, including Sum, Avg, Min, Max, and Count. Total queries are sometimes also called Group By queries. They are used to group or aggregate columns with like values and they use a function like Sum to total one or more columns.

To create a query that totals a column, select the Totals button in the Show/Hide section of the Query Design Ribbon. A Total row will be displayed on the query grid with a default value of Group By in each column. It is here that columns are selected to be used to group by and those used to sum or count and so on. Use the minimum number of fields necessary to produce the results; using more than necessary may not allow the correct aggregation of data. Figure 22-5 shows a totals query that counts the number of males and females in the recordset.

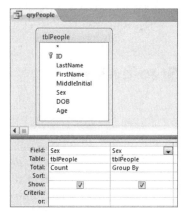

FIGURE 22-5

Using the SQL View

Every query created using the Query Wizard or Query Design View designer creates an underlying SQL statement for the query. SQL (Structured Query Language) is the native language that Access understands for executing queries and manipulating data. Access allows the SQL statement for a query to be viewed from SQL View mode.

To view or create a query in SQL View, use the SQL button located on the Results section of the Query Design Ribbon. The query shown in Figure 22-5 is written in SQL like this:

```
SELECT Count(tblPeople.Sex) as CountOfSex, tblPeople.Sex
FROM tblPeople
GROUP BY tblPeople.Sex
```

Some types of queries cannot be created in Query Design View and must be created in SQL View. Union queries, queries that use non-equi joins (<>, >=, <=, and so on), and queries that use functions on fields to create joins are examples of SQL-only queries. As long as any of these features are in the query, the user cannot go back to Query Design View to modify the query; changes must be made in SQL View.

TRY IT

In this lesson, you learn how to create a simple query using the Query Design View.

Lesson Requirements

A single table is all that is needed to create this query. The sample database, found on the book's DVD and website, has a table named tblPeople, which has seven fields: ID, LastName, FirstName, MiddleInitial, Sex, DOB, and Age. You use this table to create a query that returns all records in the table, and add criteria to restrict the results of the query.

Hints

After each query is completed, open the query in the SQL View to observe how the statement has been constructed. After modifying the query, look again and find the changes. Learning how the SQL statement produces the results in the query will put you well on your way to learning how to write SQL statements without using the Access designer or wizards.

Step-by-Step

1. Create a new database and add a table called **tblPeople**. In the table, create seven fields: **ID, LastName, FirstName, MiddleInitial, Sex, DOB,** and **Age.** Then save and close the table.

2. On the Create Ribbon, click the Query Design button to create a new query in Design View mode.

3. From the Show Table dialog that is opened automatically, add the tblPeople table to the query grid by double-clicking it. Then close the Show Table dialog.

4. Drag and drop each of the fields in the `tblPeople` table into a separate grid in the query designer.

5. Save the query as **qryPeople** and run the query. The query should return all the records in the table.

6. Try adding some criteria to the query to return only the records for people who are female. Type **Female** in the Criteria row in the `Sex` column and run the query. Check the results to see if all records are for females.

7. Add criteria to the query to prompt the user for females younger than **40. Type < [Enter Maximum Age]**.

8. Run the query, enter 40 when prompted, and ensure all records returned show an age under 40.

Congratulations; you have created an Access Query object using the Query Design View designer in Access 2010. The Design View mode designer is one of the most powerful designers that Access has to offer, and probably one of the most widely used. Building queries is likely to be a necessity for almost any Access database application.

SUMMARY

By using the Query Design View instead of only using query wizards, the developer can have greater control of how a query is constructed. Additional features can be added to the query that will make returning the required results easier. Control of how the query's results are sorted, how the data is aggregated, adding field expressions to create calculated values, and using prompts or form references to supply the values for criteria are all benefits of using the Query Design View to create and modify queries. Using the SQL View allows the developer to create more complex queries than are available from wizards or Query Design View. Queries are essential to all properly designed databases, and learning to use the tools available in Access helps the database designer create robust and efficient applications.

 Please select Lesson 22 on the DVD to view the video that accompanies this lesson.

23

Creating Select Queries

Select queries are the most common type of query used in an Access database. A Select query simply gathers a group of records but does not modify them in any way. Select queries are often used as the record source for forms, reports, and other queries, and in addition, many built-in VBA functions and macros can use Select queries as their record source. Select queries are an everyday part of life in an Access database application.

Single-table queries are the simplest of Select queries. Adding tables to the query, using joins to link one table to another, creates more complex queries by using the power of a relational database. Adding criteria, or parameters, to a query limits the records returned. Queries can also have parameters to serve several purposes: to return single records only, to return a range of records, and to exclude records that meet specific criteria. Access's built-in functions, as well as user-defined functions, can be added to queries by creating a Calculated field.

Writing SQL statements without the assistance of a wizard or the graphical user interface is also permitted in Access using SQL View mode. Writing SQL code directly allows for the greatest amount of control on how the query is formed. In fact, using the SQL View mode is the only way Union queries can be written. Regardless of the method you use to build your Select queries, Access 2010 makes it very simple.

LESSON SETUP

For this lesson you need Access 2010 and the Lesson 23 files from the book's website at www.wrox.com. You should be familiar with how to create database objects and work with queries to complete this lesson successfully.

CREATING A SELECT QUERY

A Select query in Access is one of the easiest types of queries to create and work with. Using a single table in a query is accomplished by adding the table to the query pane in Query Design View. Once the table, and the available fields, show up in the table Field List, select the desired fields and arrange them in the desired order in the query. You can select certain fields to be used to sort the data. Access always sorts the columns from left to right. A query with a sort of three columns — LastName, FirstName, and MiddleName — would sort LastName, then FirstName, and finally MiddleName. Moving any of the fields to the left or right changes the sort order of the fields. There is also a Show check box that allows you to toggle between hiding the field and displaying it in the recordset.

Additional options can be set using the query's Property Sheet. The Top Values property limits the results of the query to the top N values or percentage of the records in the recordset. The Unique Values property aggregates like records, very similarly to a Group By query. Whatever options or query design features you use, always test the data produced by the query, and check it often when changing the query's design. You will not regret performing the tests, but you will regret not doing them.

Creating a Query from Multiple Tables

Using multiple tables in a query introduces joins into the query design. Joins are similar to creating relationships between primary and foreign keys in the Relationships window, with the joins being created as needed for each query and not enforced at the table level. Joins can be created using non-key fields. If a non-key field is used, care must be taken to ensure that duplicate records are not created because of a Cartesian join.

In most instances, you will use key fields to create joins. To create a multiple-table query in Query Design View, add the tables that are required for the query to the Query Designer. Create a join, or joins, by dragging a field in the first table and dropping it on the corresponding field in the second table, and repeat if using multiple tables. Add any fields required to complete the query.

Access automatically creates a join between two tables when the tables share a field with the same data type and the same field name. One of the fields must be a primary key for AutoJoin to work.

Choosing Criteria for the Query

Criteria used in a query can be equal to a single value, or it can be greater than, less than, greater than or equal to, less than or equal to, or not equal to a value, or between two values. You can also use functions in the criteria. You have multiple ways to apply criteria to the query. The following two statements will evaluate the same:

```
(MyDate >= #6/4/1976# AND MyDate <= #11/22/1983#)
Between #6/4/1976# and #11/22/1983#
```

Both are seeking records that are equal to or between the two dates. The first uses the >= (greater than or equal to) and the <= (less than or equal to) operators with the AND operator. The AND operator indicates that the MyDate field can be any value within the range. Other examples include:

```
MyDate = #2/29/1952#
MyDate > #7/31/2010# and MyDate < #9/1/2010#
MyDate <> #12/25/2009#
MyDate IN (#12/25/2009#, #1/1/2010#, #5/31/2010#)
```

The first will return any record with a MyDate of Feb 29, 1952. The second will return any records where MyDate is in August 2010. The third uses the <> (not equal to) operator to return all dates that are not Christmas Day 2009. The last uses the IN operator to choose from a list of possible values that can be matched to the value in MyDate.

The criteria are specified in the Criteria row in the Query Designer. Additional OR lines can be used to add more conditions, or the additional conditions can be typed in a single Criteria row. Entering Criteria in multiple rows for two columns creates two distinct conditions. For example, entering = "M" in the Sex field and >= #2/1/1978# in the DOB field on one OR row, and = "F" in the Sex field and >= #2/1/1965# in the DOB field on another OR row, will create this criteria:

```
((Sex="M" AND DOB>=#2/1/1978#) OR (Sex="F" AND DOB>=#2/1/1965#))
```

Access creates two AND conditions and then ties them together with an OR operator, requiring both conditions using the AND operator to be True. If either of the AND conditions are True, the entire clause will evaluate to True.

Using Functions

Functions add powerful functionality to queries in Access 2010. Functions, either functions built into Access or user-defined custom VBA functions, can be used to create Calculated fields to perform complex calculations to help filter results when used in a criteria statement, and to create joins.

A common use of functions in Access queries is in Calculated fields. Date and time math functions simplify calculating intervals of time. An example of this might be a due date determined by a project assignment date. The project is due 10 days from the date it was assigned. A Calculated field to calculate the due date at run time might look like this:

```
DueDate:DateAdd("d", 10, [DateAssigned])
```

This expression is typed into a blank column in the query. The field DateAssigned must be a field that is included in one of the tables used in the query. You can now use the column to apply criteria to the results of the calculation. Another commonly used function is the Format() function. The Format() function, and the other related format functions (FormatCurrency(), FormatPercent(), and so on) are used to format numbers into specific number formats, format dates and times to the desired format, and to create left- or right-filled fixed-width numbers for export.

The Date() function is used in criteria to calculate date ranges frequently. A simple example is to subtract 10 days from today's date and return all dates between and including the two dates:

```
Between Date()-10 and Date()
```

The value returned by a function used as the criteria must be a compatible data type with the field to which the criteria are being compared; otherwise a type mismatch error will be raised. In the preceding example, the Date() function returns a DateTime data type, so the field type should also be that type.

Creating a Select Query in SQL View

Writing Select queries using SQL is actually easy to learn. A Select SQL statement is composed of seven major parts, or clauses:

➤ SELECT determines which fields are included in the output.

➤ FROM designates the table to use.

➤ JOIN or JOINS, which are optional, designate the additional tables to be used and defines which fields are to be joined.

➤ WHERE applies criteria to the query.

➤ GROUP BY is used in a query with aggregate functions to indicate how to aggregate the data.

➤ HAVING applies criteria to aggregate functions.

➤ ORDER BY defines how a query is sorted.

A simple Select query must have at least a SELECT and a FROM clause; anything else depends on what is expected as the result of the query.

```
SELECT Field1, Field2, Field3
FROM YourTable
```

This is a fully formed SQL statement. It will return every record in YourTable and display the contents of the three listed fields. If you need to sort the results by Field3, and then by Field2, you will need to add an ORDER BY clause to the query:

```
SELECT Field1, Field2, Field3
FROM YourTable
ORDER BY Field3, Field2
```

If you need to add a field from a lookup table, you must add a JOIN and specify the table and how to relate it:

```
SELECT Field1, Field2, Field25
FROM YourTable
INNER JOIN YourOtherTable
ON YourTable.Field3 = YourOtherTable.Field22
ORDER BY Field3, Field2
```

A great teaching tool provided in Access is being able to view the SQL created when a query is created in Design View or with a Query Wizard. Each time you create a query, take a few minutes to open the query in SQL View to see how it was constructed and attempt to make changes to the design directly to a copy of the SQL.

TRY IT

In this lesson, you create a query in Query Design View, modify the query in Design View, and then modify the query again in SQL View.

Step-by-Step

1. Open Access 2010 and then open the `Lesson23.accdb` file from the book's DVD and website.

2. Create a new query in Design View mode by clicking the Query Design button on the Create Ribbon. The Query will be opened.

3. Add the `tblReceivable` table to the query by selecting it in the Show Table dialog and clicking Add. Close the Show Table dialog.

4. Add the fields `CustomerID`, `DateBilled`, `AmtDr`, and `AmtCr` to the query grid by double-clicking the field or dragging and dropping the field to the desired column in the query grid.

5. Save the query as **qryReceivable** and run it. Check the results to see that the records you expected to be returned were actually returned.

 It is considered good practice to test the data on the initial design of the query, and then retest each time a change is made to the design. If a simple query returns 1,000 records and the sum of the records is 1,234,242, adding a lookup table to show more detail should not change the query to return more records and should still sum to 1,234,242.

6. Next, add a field expression and use the string `Balance` as an alias (field name) for the expression.

7. Return to Design View and in the column to the right of `AmtCr`, type **Balance:AmtDr+AmtCr.**

8. Save the query and run it.

9. Check the results for accuracy and completeness.

Add criteria to return only records that have a balance of other than 0.

10. Return to Design View and in the Criteria row of the `Balance` column, type **<> 0.**

11. Save the query and run it.

12. Check to see that records with a value of 0 are not included in the results.

Add an Aggregate function to the query.

13. Return to Design View. Remove the field `DateBilled` from the query. Click the Totals button on the Design Ribbon to create an aggregate query.

14. Change the Total row on the `AmtDr`, `AmtCr`, and `Balance` fields to Sum.

15. Save and run the query.

16. Check the results to see if the results are as expected.

Add a Sort using SQL View.

17. Switch to SQL View.

18. Delete the semicolon at the end of the SQL statement.

19. Add the ORDER BY clause after the HAVING clause: **ORDER BY Sum(AmtDr+AmtCr) Desc.**

You need to repeat the formula in the ORDER BY clause and not use the alias. The Desc keyword sorts the records in descending order. Save and run the query. Look at the results to see if the records are sorted in the order you specified. Next, add the tblCustomer table to the query.

20. Return to Design View. Using the Show Table button on the Design Ribbon, add tblCustomer to the query.

21. A join should automatically be created between the two CustomerID fields. Open the query in SQL View and notice how the join was created. Save the query and run it.

Congratulations; you have created a Select query and modified it several ways to get different results from your dataset. Building queries using both the Design View and SQL View designers is extremely easy to do and will get you the results you need from your data.

SUMMARY

Knowing how to create Select queries to present the data in the manner necessary for the task at hand is crucial to building a working database application. Adding a table to a query can cause unexpected results if the tables are not joined correctly. Improperly applied criteria can cause the query to fail, or return invalid results. The better acquainted a database developer is with Access's Query Design View designer, the better the resulting application will be.

Testing the accuracy of your queries as you create them is a vital part of building an application. Test your queries thoroughly before you deploy the database. And don't forget that there are many built-in Access functions that can enhance the output of the query, as well as provide a method to apply complex criteria.

Learning to write and modify queries in SQL View can give a developer more precise control on how a query is constructed and how it ultimately performs. Taking time to see how changes made in Query Design View affect the SQL statement in SQL View can be a great tool in learning to write SQL statements. Although it may look extremely complex, SQL is actually simple and elegant. Learning to create well-formed queries is one of the better ways to simplify database development using Access 2010.

 Please select Lesson 23 on the DVD to view the video that accompanies this lesson.

24

Data Aggregation and Grouping

When we refer to data being aggregated and grouped, we are describing a process of grouping like items, or fields, and summing, counting, averaging, or using any of the aggregate functions available in Access 2010 queries. A simple example of a query using aggregation and grouping is a query designed to count the number of widgets each department sold in the previous week. A more complex example is using a Crosstab query to track the sale of those same widgets by department, but also displaying the sales of the widgets made on each day of the previous week.

The ability to quickly summarize data into meaningful segments is available using the power of Access 2010 queries. In this lesson you are introduced to the concepts needed to design successful aggregation, or Totals, queries.

LESSON SETUP

For this lesson you need Access 2010 and Lesson 24 files from the book's website at www.wrox.com. You should be familiar with creating database objects and working with queries to complete this lesson successfully.

GROUPING DATA IN QUERIES

Two different methods are available to aggregate, or group, data in an Access query. If no aggregate functions are used in the query, and the goal is to return unique records from many possible duplicated values, the DISTINCT keyword will combine all duplicate records into single records. Each field included in the SELECT clause is evaluated and all fields in the records must exactly match the fields in the other records to be combined.

```
SELECT DISTINCT TypeVisit
FROM tblPatientUtilization;
```

If, in the preceding example, there were 10 records with Office and 12 records with Inpatient, the result would be two records returned by the query: Office and Inpatient.

The same results can be obtained by using the second option, which is a totals, or GROUP BY, query instead of using the DISTINCT keyword:

```
SELECT TypeVisit
FROM tblPatientUtilization
GROUP BY TypeVisit;
```

Usually a query using the DISTINCT keyword will run faster than using a GROUP BY clause in a query, but the difference in execution speed may not be noticeable in any but very large tables. Remember, when multiple fields are included in the SELECT clause, the combination of all the fields must be unique to be combined. Each field included in the SELECT clause that is not part of an aggregate function needs to be included in the GROUP BY clause; otherwise an error will be generated.

Queries provide two ways to limit the results of the query using criteria. You can use either a WHERE clause or a HAVING clause. A WHERE clause is used to limit data that is not going to be aggregated, whereas a HAVING clause is used to limit data using an aggregate function. Using WHERE clauses instead of HAVING when possible will yield better performance than attempting to only use the HAVING clause. The improved performance of using a WHERE clause when possible is because the WHERE excludes records before the data is aggregated, which reduces resources needed to process the aggregate functions.

AGGREGATE DATA QUERIES

Using aggregate functions on fields to count, sum, or average the data is another powerful function of queries. The need to calculate the sales figures for each product, each sales person, each department, and each store, or a thousand variations of this example, arises all the time in organizations. The Totals query (found in the sample database file) was created to easily summarize and group data for just this purpose.

The Lesson24.accdb database file on the website has a table named tblPressures. Among others, there is the Date/Time field called SampledAt and a numeric field called Systolic. Using the Totals query, you will learn how to get the average systolic pressure reading for each day that a pressure was recorded. Notice that there are 44 records in the table, and all records have a date and a time recorded.

Create a query using tblPressures and click the Totals button on the Query Tools Design Ribbon. In the first attempt at this query just use the SampledAt field without removing the time portion and use the Avg() function on the Systolic field.

```
SELECT SampledAt, Avg(Systolic) as AvgOfSystolic
FROM tblPressures
GROUP BY SampledAt;
```

When you run this query it should return all 44 records with the systolic reading the same as in the original record, that is, not averaged. If you try to group on a date with times entered, you will not get the expected results when you group the records. Each date will probably be a separate record because the entire field is not equal. Use one of Access's date functions or the Format() function to remove the time portion of the `Date/Time` field. Try it again, but this time use the `DateValue()` function to remove the time portion from the `SampledAt` field:

```
SELECT DateValue(SampledAt) as SampleDate,
       Avg(Systolic) as AvgOfSystolic
FROM tblPressures
GROUP BY DateValue(SampledAt);
```

This time when you run the query it should return 36 records, one for each unique date in the table. The `Avg()` function will now return an average reading for each date. Now change the `DateValue()` function to the `Month()` function to only return the integer value of the months. In this sample table, you should only return 2 records:

```
SELECT Month(SampledAt) as SampleDate,
       Avg(Systolic) as AvgOfSystolic
FROM tblPressures
GROUP BY Month(SampledAt);
```

It will sometimes be necessary to parse strings to "clean the data" before you can group it. Examples of this might be a part number that consists of a three-letter prefix code and a five-digit number. The prefix indicates a slight variation of the part, but you need all variations of a part to be grouped into a single number. `Mid(PartNumber,4,5)` will return only the five-digit number and all records can be grouped on that number.

SORTING MULTIPLE COLUMNS

Sorting in Totals queries is not much different than non-aggregating queries. From the Query Design View you set the sort options in the Sort row, and if you are sorting multiple columns, arrange the columns left to right in the order you want the columns to be sorted. One trap you need to watch for is when you are using Calculated fields, especially if you are writing the query in the SQL View, always make sure that the sort will work and not create an error. The best method is to repeat the complete expression in both the GROUP BY and ORDER BY clauses. It is important in a Totals query because each field used in the SELECT or ORDER BY clauses, except those fields where an aggregate function was used, must also be in the GROUP BY clause and it must use the same syntax.

USES FOR CROSSTAB QUERIES

Crosstab queries are specialized queries used to aggregate and group data. The results are presented with field values as Row Headings, Column Headings, and Values. Row headings are the values listed up and down the left side of the query, the column headings are presented across the top of the query, and the values are either grouped or are calculated using an aggregate function.

The uses for Crosstab queries are much the same as those for Excel's Pivot Tables. It is a way to present data to make it easier to visualize the data. In the health insurance industry, Crosstabs are used to create Lag Triangles. Lag Triangles use at least three fields: the date a patient was treated, the date the claim was paid, and the dollar amount of the claim. Optionally, a claim category, location code, or other value that further identifies where the claim originated can be used. Usually the date paid is the

Row Heading, the date incurred is the Column Heading, and the amount paid is the Value and uses the Sum() function. Actuaries use the resulting lag reports to visualize how quickly, or slowly, claims for a given month are being reported and paid.

Sales by department and days of a month can be presented using a Crosstab. Any time you need to group data by values, like a department or postal code, and with a date or by sales person and so on, using a Crosstab query might be an option for you.

TRY IT

In this lesson, you create a totals query, modify it, and create a Crosstab query using the Query Designer and without the help of a wizard.

Step-by-Step

1. Open Access 2010 and open the Lesson24.accdb from the book's DVD and website. Click the Query Design button on the Create Ribbon.

2. Add the table named tlbPressures to the Query Designer.

3. Add the SampledAt field and the Systolic field to the query grid. Click the Totals button on the Design Ribbon.

4. SampledAt should be set to Group By and you will need to change Systolic to Avg.

5. Save the query as **qryGroupBySampledAt** and run the query.

Modify the query to use distinct dates using the DateValue() function.

6. Open the query qryGroupBySampledAt in Design View and save it as **qryGroupBySampledAtDateValue**.

7. Add the DateValue() function to the SampledAt field by renaming the field, aliasing, and typing in the function. To give the field an alias, at the beginning of the field type the new name, followed by a colon. In the first field, replace SampledAt with **SampleDate:DateValue(SampledAt)**. Save the query and open it.

Modify the query to sort the SampleDate field descending.

8. Open the query qryGroupBySampledAtDateValue and save it as **qryGroupBySampledAtDateValueSorted**.

9. Change the Sort row in the SampleDate field to Descending.

10. Save and run the query to see that the sort is working. Open the query in SQL View and notice that the complete expression was used in the sort, and not the alias.

Create a Crosstab query in Query Design View. The query will show how many customers were billed each month and by year.

11. Click Query Design on the Create Ribbon. Add `tblReceivable` to the designer.

12. Add the `Trans`, `Recorded`, and `Amount` fields to the query grid.

13. Click the Crosstab option on the Ribbon.

14. In this example the `Trans` and `Recorded` fields are in year/month format and you want to use a Row Heading for the year and a Column Heading for the month. To do this you will need to parse the year and month values from the existing value.

15. For the year value use this expression as the Row Heading: **TransDate:Left(Trans,4)**.

16. For the month value use this expression as the Column Heading: **RecordMonth:Right(Recorded,2)**.

17. Add the `Amount` field, setting `Total` as Count and `Crosstab` as Value. Save the query as **qryCrosstab** and run the query.

SUMMARY

Using Aggregation and Grouping queries in Access is usually a design requirement for any application. The ability to present summarized information instead of the raw data greatly enhances the usefulness of Access. Without the Totals query, the only means to summarize data would be using VBA code, using the power of an Access report, or using Office automation and sending the data to Excel for processing in that application.

Whether you need to produce a list of unique values from a table, create a detailed list of departments and the sales figures related to each department, or if you need a complex Crosstab query, with Access you can easily create the summarized data you need. And the data can usually be produced, using real-time data, on demand and as it is needed, unlike most spreadsheet applications where it is necessary to refresh the data and then make sure the correct ranges are being used.

A totals query in Access 2010 can, and will, save time, reduce errors, and give novice users access to the data, if the queries are designed correctly and implemented using the powerful user interface Access allows you to create.

 Please select Lesson 24 on the DVD to view the video that accompanies this lesson.

25

Creating Parameter Queries

Parameter queries are used in Access when the values for criteria in the query are required to be passed to the query at run time instead of when the query was created. There are other ways to supply runtime arguments to queries, such as building the SQL string with the criteria or modifying the query's QueryDef, but these methods require the developer to know how to use VBA.

Access 2010 provides two simple ways for the developer to request that a user enter values, such as a date or an invoice number, before executing the query. In this lesson you learn how to use a simple popup *Parameter Request dialog* and use controls on a form with a command button to pass arguments to a query. You also learn how to explicitly define the data type of the parameter using the Query Parameters dialog.

LESSON SETUP

For this lesson you need Access 2010 and Lesson 25 files from the book's website at www.wrox.com. You should be familiar with creating database objects and working with queries to successfully complete this lesson.

PARAMETER QUERIES IN ACCESS

A Parameter query in Access is any query designed to accept user input to supply the values to be used as criteria in the query at run time. The easiest method to prompt a user to supply a value in a Parameter query is to use square brackets to surround a prompt for the user, such as [Enter the Customer Number] in the Criteria row of the CustomerNumber field. Each time the query is executed, a Parameter Request dialog is shown and prompts the user to input a value. In simple applications this method may suffice, but this method lacks the ability to validate the input data. In this example, it is possible for the user to press the Enter key, enter a date instead of a customer number, or place many other inappropriate values into the Parameter dialog. If the query does not then fail outright, the user may not realize that the results are probably incorrect.

Access uses the same popup dialog when a field is missing or the field name is misspelled. Reports can generate the same dialog when an orphan reference to a deleted field remains in the sorting and grouping tool. Anytime you receive an unexpected Parameter Request dialog, check your query and, if necessary, your report for orphan field references.

The preferred technique to ask a user to input a value, or values, is to create a form with various controls to collect all the information needed for a query and then use a command button to cause the query to run. By using a form to collect and pass the parameter values to the query, the code behind the form can be used to validate the parameter value when it is entered, instead of waiting until the query fails or returns invalid results. The form must be open as the query executes or the query will fail because the form is not available to pass the parameters to the query. An example of this is using a form to return the customer records of a single customer. For this example you have a form named `frmEmployeeRecordInput` with a `TextBox` control named `txtEmployeeNumber`. To pass the form value to the query, you would enter a form reference in the Criteria row of the `EmployeeNumber` field using the form name and control name like this:

```
Forms!frmEmployeeRecordInput!txtEmployeeNumber
```

The controls you have available to collect information can be text boxes, list boxes, combo boxes, and more. Having multiple values entered in a single location, instead of requiring multiple popups, presents a more professional interface to the user, and helps eliminate some of the user's confusion.

CREATING PARAMETER QUERIES IN DESIGN VIEW

Adding Parameter query prompts to a query using Design View is usually an easy task. The first step is to create the query: It can be a `SELECT` query, a Crosstab, or one of the Action Queries. For this example you use a `SELECT` query. In the `Lesson25.accdb` file (found on the book's website), open `qryParameter` in Design View. The `CustomerID` field is the primary key for the table and each record has a unique number to identify a specific customer. You will use that field to add a prompt for the user to enter a customer number when the query is executed. In the criteria row of `CustomerID`, type the following value:

```
[Enter the Customer Number]
```

Save and run the query and when prompted enter any number between 1 and 4,206. The query should return a single customer record with a customer number that matches what you entered. To add a parameter to return all records of a single name, first clear the Criteria value for `CustomerID` and type this in the `LastName` field:

```
[Enter the Last Name]
```

Save and run the query, entering **Smith** as the last name. The resulting recordset should include all customers with the last name Smith. You can also use a Parameter query to do a wildcard search. For example, you want to see all customers with a last name that begins with Bra. To do this you will need to combine the parameter prompt with the `Like` operator and the asterisk. Change the text entry in the previous parameter to [Enter a Partial Last Name], then add the `Like` operator and concatenate the * to the right end of the string:

```
Like [Enter a Partial Last Name] & *
```

Save and run the query and when prompted, enter **Bra**. All last names beginning with Bra should be returned.

The preferred method of passing the parameters to a query is to have the users enter the values in a form. The `Lesson25.accdb` file has a form for passing values to two queries and then running the queries using a command button. Change the Criteria Row text in `qryParameter` to use a form reference. Type this:

```
Forms!frmParameter!txtCustomerID
```

Save the query and open the form named `frmParameter`. Enter **123** in the `CustomerID` text box and click the Customer Number button. The query should open with a single record with the `CustomerID` of 123.

DEFINING PARAMETER DATA TYPES

If a query is used with VBA code, or as the source of a Crosstab query, it is usually necessary to explicitly define the parameter data type, otherwise the query will fail. To explicitly define the query's parameters, click the Parameters button on the Query Tools Design Ribbon. This opens the Query Parameters dialog. In the Parameter column, type or paste the parameter text exactly as it is in the query. Then select the correct data type from the drop-down list. In the case of the `CustomerID`, which is an `AutoNumber`, the correct data type would be a `Long Integer`.

CREATING A PARAMETER QUERY IN SQL VIEW

Creating a Parameter query in SQL View requires inserting a `PARAMETERS` clause and adding either the Parameter Request or form reference to the `WHERE` clause; otherwise, the rest of the SQL is the same. The `PARAMETERS` clause consists of the `PARAMETERS` keyword, the text of the parameter or form reference, the data type, and a semicolon. Although the semicolon is usually the terminator of the SQL statement, when using a `PARAMETERS` clause it is required after the last parameter. Each `PARAMETER` is separated by a comma.

The `WHERE` clause needs to refer to the same parameters or form references included in the `PARAMETERS` clause, otherwise the rest of the criteria are the same as for non-parameter queries. An example of the SQL for a Parameter query would look like this:

```
PARAMETERS Forms!frmParameter!txtCustomerID Long,
Forms!frmParameter!txtLastName Text (255);
SELECT CustomerID, LastName, FirstName
FROM tblCustomer
WHERE CustomerID = Forms!frmParameter!txtCustomerID
      And LastName = Forms!frmParameter!txtLastName;
```

TRY IT

In this lesson you add a Parameter Request dialog to a query and then explicitly define the parameter in the query using Query Design View, and then convert the Parameter Request and PARAMETERS clause to a forms reference using SQL View.

Step-by-Step

1. Open Access 2010 and open the `Lesson25.accdb` file from the book's DVD and website.

2. Open `qryParameterTryIt` in Query Design View.

3. In the `LastName` field add a Parameter Request to the Criteria Row: **[Enter the Last Name]**.

4. Copy the text **[Enter the Last Name]** and open the Query Parameters dialog by pressing the Parameters button on the Query Tools Design Ribbon.

5. Paste the text into the Parameter column of the Query Parameters dialog, and choose Text from the Data Type column. Click OK.

6. Save and run the query. Enter a name — Adams, Bell, or Chapman will work for this example — in the prompt when it is displayed.

Convert the parameter to a form reference using SQL View.

7. Open `qryParameterTryIt` in SQL View.

8. Change the PARAMETERS clause to `Forms!frmParameter!txtLastNameTryIt`.

9. Change the WHERE clause to also read `Forms!frmParameter!txtLastNameTryIt`.

10. Save the query.

11. Open the form named `frmParameter`.

12. Enter a name in the Last Name Try-It control and click the Last Name Try-It command button.

SUMMARY

Access 2010 gives the developer tools to simplify passing runtime arguments to queries. The Parameter Request dialog can be an easy method that lets the user enter a value as the query is running. However, this method may be confusing and cumbersome to users because the prompt is unforgiving; it does not allow for validation of the entry made by the user before being passed to the query. Improper values will cause the query to fail or to return incorrect results.

The preferred method to request values from the user at run time is to use a form to request the values before running the query. The code behind the form can then be used to validate the entries for correctness before the query is executed. If there are incorrect values, the code should ask the user for the correct information and allow the user to cancel the query request if the correct information is unavailable. The form reference has another benefit: When opening a report, the query the report is based on may run several times before the report is displayed or printed.

If the query is using a Parameter Request dialog, the value, or values, must be entered each time the query runs. Using the forms reference method, as long as the form used to enter the needed values remains open, the query will reuse the original values, eliminating the need to enter the same value multiple times.

 Please select Lesson 25 on the DVD to view the video that accompanies this lesson.

26

Creating Append Queries

Append queries are Action Queries used to add a row, or multiple rows, of data to a table as new records. The records can originate in a single table, multiple tables, from values pulled from a form, or from hardcoded values in the query. Append queries are one of many methods used to add records to a table:

➤ Add records to the table using form controls bound to the table.

➤ Add records from a table or tables using an Append query.

➤ Add single records using a single-record Append query.

➤ Add records using macros or VBA code.

Learning how to use Append queries should make your database perform better. In this lesson, you learn how to create and use both types of Append queries available in Access 2010, and use Query Design View and SQL View to design your query.

LESSON SETUP

For this lesson you need Access 2010 and the Lesson 26 files from the book's website at www.wrox.com. You should be familiar with creating database objects and working with queries to successfully complete this lesson.

APPEND QUERIES IN ACCESS

Access 2010 has two types of Append queries: the multi-record Append query and the single-record Append query. The multi-record Append query uses records that originated from pre-existing tables available to the database. A single-record Append query will get its values from fields that are either literal values or calculated values. Remember that when inserting values into a table that uses an `AutoNumber` primary key, you will need to be certain that the `INSERT INTO` clause, or the Append To row, does not include the `AutoNumber` field to prevent a possible runtime error.

Creating an Append Query in Design Mode

To create an Append query using the `SELECT … FROM` syntax, you first need a Select query. Create the Select query as you would any other query, either from a single table, or from multiple related tables. You can use Calculated values, criteria, sorts, Totals queries, or a simple Select statement to create an Append query, remembering the prohibition of appending to an `AutoNumber` field.

Although Access allows the use of calculated values in an Append query, best practices in a properly normalized database discourage storing almost any calculated values. The value should be calculated at run time to minimize data anomalies due to the stored calculated value not being updated when the underlying values are changed.

Once the query is returning the records that you expect to be returned, it is time to change the query to an Append query. From the Query Tools Design Ribbon, click the Append button in the Query Type section. Set the Append To Table Name option to the desired table name when the Append prompt appears; then click OK. A new row in the query grid will appear. The Append To row is used to designate to which field the column will be appended. If the field names in the `FROM` clause and the field names in the `INSERT INTO` clause are the same, Access will auto populate the field names in the Append To row; if they are not you will need to select the correct fields from the Append To row drop-down lists. Once the fields are mapped to the correct destination you can view the results by clicking the View button on the Design Ribbon. No records will be appended when you use the View button. To execute the Append query and append the data, you must click the Run button. Unless warnings have been turned off, Access will show a pop-up dialog that requires the user to confirm the append action. Also, Append queries require that the database be in trusted mode before they can be executed.

Although it is possible to programmatically turn off warnings before running an Action Query and then turn the warnings back on after the action is completed, it is not a best practice to do it. If an error occurs that causes the database to shut down, the warnings may not be turned back on. This can cause problems when users are expecting a warning before the Action Query executes and no notification when errors occur during the append operation. One method to run an Action Query without the conformation dialog and still receive error messages is the `CurrentDB Execute` *method:* `CurrentDB.Execute "YourQueryName", dbFailOnError`. *The* `Execute` *method is the preferred way to execute an Action Query, one that does not require turning off the warnings.*

To create a single-value Append query, open the Query Design View but do not add any tables to the query. Click Append on the Design Ribbon and specify the table to which you want the values to be appended. Enter the field expressions, which may include Forms References, or prompts using the Parameter Request syntax. The View and Run buttons will view or execute the Append query as shown previously.

Append Query Settings

An Append query allows most of the properties that are included in Select queries; you can use the TOP predicate to restrict the records being returned. The DISTINCT keyword is also available to return unique records. Access also provides a method to append the records to a table in another database by using the IN clause. You can also turn off warnings for Action queries, but it is not recommended.

Creating an Append Query in SQL View

To create an Append query using the SQL View, you need to use the INSERT INTO clause and the VALUES clause. For a multi-record Append query, first write the SQL for the SELECT query. When it is complete, add the INSERT INTO clause preceding the SELECT clause, as shown in the following SQL statement:

```
INSERT INTO tblPatientUtilizationNew ( PatientID, DateService, TypeVisit )
SELECT PatientID, DateService, TypeVisit
FROM tblPatientUtilizationOld;
```

To create a single-record Append query, you need to write both the INSERT INTO and the VALUES clauses:

```
INSERT INTO tblPatientUtilizationNew ( PatientID, DateService, TypeVisit )
VALUES 3 as PatientID, Date() as DateService,"Office" as TypeVisit
```

In the preceding SQL statement, the value of 3 is used for the PatientID field, the Date() function returns the current date for the DateService field, and the string value Office is used for the TypeVisit option for the appended record. Remember, the VALUES clause can include Form References to pull information from an open form.

Ramifications of Append Queries

The properties that have been set for the table will be enforced when an Append query is attempting to insert records into the table:

➤ **Validation Rules** — All defined rules will be enforced.

➤ **Required Property** — If the required property is set to Yes, a value must be provided in the Append query.

➤ **Allow Zero Length** — Zero-length strings cannot be appended if this property is set to No.

➤ **Indexed** — If no duplicates are selected, duplicate entries will be allowed.

➤ **Key Violations** — If the primary key is not an AutoNumber, a valid value will need to be provided. If the primary key is an AutoNumber, do not insert a value into that field and the AutoNumber field will create one.

TRY IT

In this lesson you learn how to create multiple-value and single-value Append queries in Query Design View. Use the `Lesson26.accdb` file (from the book's DVD and website) to complete these steps.

Step-by-Step

1. Open Access 2010 and open the `Lesson26.accdb` file.

2. Open Query Design View and add **tblCustomer** to the query.

3. Click the Append button on the Query Tools Design Ribbon, select `tblCustomerArchive`, and click OK.

4. Drop all three fields into the query grid. The Append To row should auto populate with the correct fields. In `tblCustomerArchive` the primary key field is `CustomerArchiveID` and not `CustomerID`, so the original ID field will append correctly.

5. Add criteria to limit the query to only the last names **Smith** and **Jones**.

6. View the query using the View button and determine that the correct records are being returned by the query. Run the query to append the records. Check `tblCustomerArchive` to see if the records were inserted. Save the query and close it. Next add a `DateArchived` field to the `tblCustomerArchive` table.

7. Open `tblCustomerArchive` and delete all the records, then open it in Design View and add a **DateArchived** field and set the data type as **Date/Time**. Save and close the table.

8. Open the previous query in Design View.

9. Create an expression in the first open column:

```
DateArchive:Date()
```

10. Set the Append To row for the new field to **DateArchived**.

11. Save and run the query. Check the destination table to see if the records were appended, including the value from the field expression. Close the query and table. Next create a single-value Append query in Design View.

12. Open the Query Design View. Close the Show Table dialog without adding any tables.

13. Click the Append button and set the Append To table to `tblCustomerArchive`.

14. Append the following values for the four fields:

➤ CustomerID: 101

➤ LastName: "Houston"

➤ FirstName: "Sam"

➤ DateArchived: #12/29/1845#

15. Set the Append To row to the appropriate fields in the table.

16. Run the query and check the results in `tblCustomerArchive`. Save the query.

Congratulations; you have successfully created an Append query and appended a record to the `tblCustomerArchive` table. If you open the table you will now see that the record has been placed in the table and will be stored as part of the data in the application.

SUMMARY

Append queries are used frequently in an Access 2010 database. They are easily created and executed using the tools Access offers. From appending single records pulled from unbound forms to appending large recordsets that were imported to a temporary table, scrubbed, normalized, and then appended to the working tables in your database, you have many opportunities to use Append queries. Access can append records taken directly from other tables, append both data from a table and data from a field expression in the Append query, append data from expressions, and append data pulled from a form or external source. As a database developer, the Append query is a very important tool and you should familiarize yourself with the many capabilities available to you. Creating Append queries in Access 2010 will make adding data to your tables very easy and is an important part of building your Access database applications.

 Please select Lesson 26 on the DVD to view the video that accompanies this lesson.

27

Creating Update Queries

Update queries are used to modify the values in a specific field in one or more existing records for a given table. An Update query can change the value in a single record or modify multiple records. In most normalized database systems, standard practice is to add new records to modify data, instead of modifying existing records.

However, at times updating information is necessary, and an Update query is the tool to use. A simple example is a part number that has been stored with a single-letter prefix. Management would like to remove the prefix and just store the basic part number. If you are using a normalized data structure, the part number should be stored in a part number table, with foreign keys for the part stored in a transaction table. In the case of a normalized database, you would develop an Update query to update the part number, probably using the Mid() function.

In this lesson, you learn how to create and use Update queries, how to set some of the settings, and the ramifications of using them.

LESSON SETUP

For this lesson you need Access 2010 and the Lesson 27 files from the book's website at www.wrox.com. You should be familiar with creating database objects and working with queries to complete this lesson successfully.

UPDATE QUERIES IN ACCESS

An Update query in Access is like a Find & Replace command on steroids. The query performs much the same function, but with many more capabilities. With capabilities like updating multiple fields with a different value in each field, updating every record in a table, or updating only records that meet your criteria, the field values can be updated using the power of functions. The power provided in an Update query should to be used wisely. If you routinely need to update data in a production application, you may need to change the table structure or provide data validation to prevent the need to update a field.

The following few are things an Update query *cannot* do:

➤ Perform updates on a Totals query or a query using the DISTINCT keyword.

➤ Perform updates on a Crosstab query.

➤ Update a query with a many-to-many Join using a junction table.

➤ Update a Union query.

➤ Update a query with a Cross Join.

➤ Update a Calculated field.

➤ Update a recordset that is not updateable.

It is also important to note that an Update query, just like other Action queries, requires that the database be trusted before it can be executed. Because the query can modify data in the database, it is considered an unsafe object and thus requires the database to be enabled before it can be used.

Creating an Update Query in Design View

To create an Update query in Design View, click the Query Design button on the Create Ribbon. Add the table that includes the field you need to update. Add any criteria needed to limit the updates to only records that you want to update. Run the query and check the results of the query while it is still a Select query to be certain the records it returns are the records to be updated.

 It is highly recommended to back up the database before running any Update queries. Once the Update query has been run, it cannot be undone and any old values for the records that were modified will not be recoverable. Therefore you should always make a complete backup of the database before modification from the Update query takes place.

Once you are satisfied with the records being returned, change the query to an Update query by clicking the Update button on the Query Tools Design Ribbon. Set the Update To row to the new value by entering a literal string as the value, or enter a function to calculate the new value. Click the Run button to execute the query. Once the Run button has been clicked, the specified records will be updated and the action will be complete. Remember that clicking the Run button for an Update query is the point of no return!

Update Query Settings

You can set several of the Update query's properties in Query Design View: Use Transactions and Record Locks are two examples. The Use Transactions property determines whether the Action query runs as a single transaction or in multiple transactions. The default is a single transaction and causes Access to cache the updated records, degrading the query's performance. The Record Locks property determines whether only the edited record is locked or whether all records are locked while the Update query is running.

Creating an Update Query in SQL View

The Update query consists of an UPDATE clause and at least one SET clause. It can optionally include a WHERE clause. To write a query to update the field MyDate to tomorrow's date in the Product table (found in the Lesson27.accdb file) you need to specify the table to update, the field to update, and the new value:

```
UPDATE Product SET MyDate = DateAdd("d", 1, Date());
```

If there are multiple fields to update repeat the field name = new value syntax for each field and separate each field with a comma:

```
UPDATE Product SET MyDate = DateAdd("d", 1, Date()), MyMonth = "May";
```

To add criteria, add a WHERE clause as you would with any other query:

```
UPDATE Product SET MyDate = DateAdd("d", 1, Date())
WHERE VendorID = 1234;
```

Ramifications of Update Queries

The primary ramification of running an Update query is the possibility of data loss. The first step before the use of any Update query is to back up the data; this is especially important with ad hoc updates and new Update queries. The unintentional loss of data by changing critical values with an Update query that had the wrong criteria or the incorrect value in the SET clause is actually a common occurrence with novice users. It is not as common with users who have had to reconstruct the data in an incorrectly updated table. To prevent having to learn about data reconstruction the hard way, back up your data before attempting to update it.

Always test your query before using it on live data — simple syntax errors can completely destroy anything in a field. The Access Query Design View has a small quirk where it adds double quotes around field names used in a function if the field name does not have square brackets surrounding it. An example is using the Mid() function to remove a single-letter prefix from a PatientNumber. If you type in the function correctly in the Update To row, Access will change it to this:

```
Mid("PatientNumber",2)
```

However, it should be this:

```
Mid([PatientNumber],2)
```

In an Update query the first function will update the affected record's PatientNumber field to this literal string:

```
PatientNumber
```

Not too much of a problem with one or two records, but if it is a global update, you are in trouble. This is an instance when the square brackets are required. Double-check this each time you use a function in an Update query, but more importantly, back up the database before attempting an update and inspect the result afterwards.

TRY IT

In this lesson you learn how to create an Update query using Query Design View. You then modify the completed query to update two fields. You need the `Lesson27.accdb` file found on the book's DVD and website to complete this lesson.

Step-by-Step

1. First, make a backup copy of the `Lesson27.accdb` file.

2. Open Access 2010 and open the `Lesson27.accdb` file.

3. Create a new query in Query Design View mode by clicking the Query Design button on the Create Ribbon.

4. Add the table named `tblCustomer` to the Query View.

5. Add the `LastName` and `FirstName` fields to the query.

6. In the `LastName` column add **Smith** to the Criteria row and test the query to see that only records with the last name of `Smith` are being returned.

7. Click the Update button on the Query Tools Design Ribbon to change the table to an Update query.

8. Add this function to the Update To row of the `FirstName` field, being sure to use the square brackets to surround the field name: `StrReverse([FirstName])`.

9. Save and run the query. Check to see if the first names were reversed. If they were successfully updated, rerun the query to return the first names to the correct spellings.

Next, modify the query to add Jr. to all last names in the table.

10. Open the query in Design View.

11. Remove the criteria from the LastName field.

12. Use concatenation to add Jr. to all last names by setting the Update To row to **[LastName] & " Jr."**.

13. Save and run the query. Check to see that Jr. was added to all records and the first name was reversed.

14. Switch back to Design View and change the Update To row to **Replace([LastName]," Jr.","")** to remove the Jr. from the name.

15. Save and run the query. The Jr. should be removed and the first name should be back in the correct order.

Congratulations; you have created an Update query and modified data in the `tblCustomer` table to change the value of the records. Again, we highly recommend always creating a complete backup of the database prior to executing Update queries in your Access database applications. Remember, once an Update query has been executed, it cannot be directly undone!

SUMMARY

As you have seen in the lesson, the Update query can be a powerful tool for the database developer and its users. However, with that power there may also be pitfalls. The prudent user will always back up the data before attempting to execute an Update query. As soon as you skip that step, you will be distracted just as you run the query and confirm that you want to update 9,235,986 records. You immediately realize that you only needed to update five records, but forgot to add any criteria to the query. Please remember to always back up your data before running an Update query. However, the recordset of the query must be updateable for an Update query to execute.

Creating Update queries in Design View is an easy task — if you can create a Select query, you can usually modify it to become an Update query. The UPDATE and SET syntax used in SQL View is very simple to learn to write. When used properly, Update queries can add functionality to your application, but if you are frequently updating production data, it may be an indication that you have design problems and are using Update queries to overcome those problems. Update queries will be an important part of building your database applications, and using Access 2010 to create Update queries is very easy to do using either Design View or SQL View mode.

 Please select Lesson 27 on the DVD to view the video that accompanies this lesson.

28

Creating Delete Queries

Delete queries are used to remove records from a table. You can use criteria in Delete queries to limit the records that are to be removed; otherwise each time a Delete query is executed all records in the table will be deleted. For example, assume you have a `Customers` table and you want to remove one of the customer records from it. You could use a Delete query to programmatically remove the record from the table. Delete queries can be an important piece of your database application, and at the same time, they can be one of the most destructive tools allowed in a database. With the exception of import and export operations, Delete queries should rarely be used in a properly normalized database application. We highly recommend always creating a complete backup of the database before ever running a Delete query, because once it has been executed, the records will be gone forever!

LESSON SETUP

This lesson discusses the basics of creating Delete queries. You should be familiar with creating database objects and working with tables and queries using Access 2010 to complete this lesson successfully.

DELETE QUERIES IN ACCESS

Access 2010 allows Delete query objects to be created and executed in a database application. Because Delete queries are considered Action queries and can modify the data stored in the tables, you must trust the database file, so that Access will run in Enabled mode before you can execute a Delete query properly. Creating Delete queries is much like creating other queries in Access 2010, but you should be aware of a number of considerations and limitations when using Delete queries in your Access database applications.

Delete queries, like Update queries, need to be used with caution and with thorough testing. When designing and testing a Delete query, always back up the data before the query is executed, or at the very least, always use a test database before applying the query to a production environment. Test the query as a Select query before converting it to a Delete query. An incorrect criteria value in a Delete query can cause the query to permanently delete all, or some, of the data you planned on retaining in your database.

Considerations for Delete Queries

The use of Delete queries in a database application is often quite controversial. Some database designers believe that a record should never be removed from a database, whereas others believe that if the data is worthless and no longer necessary, it should be removed. Regardless of your position on the subject, everyone can agree that Delete queries should be used with great caution, because of the power that they provide. And, in some cases, a Delete query may not execute properly under certain conditions.

The first condition to consider when building Delete queries is that the Select statement for the Delete query must be updatable. If the statement is not updatable, the Delete query will fail when executed. Be aware that this means that the Select statement should not be an aggregated data query or use the DISTINCT keyword. If formed correctly, queries using Joins can be the source of a Delete query, but again, the query must be updatable to work.

The second condition to consider when building a Delete query is any child records that may be related to the record, when Referential Integrity is enforced in the system relationships. If the Cascading Delete option is selected for the relationship between the tables, executing a Delete query on the one side of the relationship will delete the related records on the many side of the relationship. Be certain you really know and understand both the primary table and related tables, and their system relationships, before executing a Delete query. Otherwise, you may end up deleting child records or creating orphan records inadvertently.

Sometimes deleting records in Access will cause the database file to grow in size a little! This is because when Access deletes a record, it only marks the record for deletion and the record is fully deleted only when Access's Compact and Repair tool is executed. After running the Compact and Repair tool, the database will be reduced to its smallest possible file size, removing all deleted records and temporary tables and queries.

Creating a Delete Query in Design Mode

Creating a Delete query in Design View mode using Access 2010 is typically accomplished using the following steps:

1. The most important step is to first make a complete backup copy of the database file. This is one step that you do not want to learn the hard way and it always applies.

2. Open the database in Access 2010.

3. On the Create Ribbon, click the Query Design button to create a new query in Design mode.

4. Write a Select query to select the specific records you want to delete. Run the query to ensure that you have the correct records, and only the correct records, to be deleted.

5. Once you are certain that the Select query contains the correct records, convert it to a Delete query by clicking the Delete button on the Query Tools Design Ribbon.

6. Execute the query by clicking the Run button on the Query Tools Design Ribbon. You will be required to verify that you want to run the query from a dialog. This is the point of no return! Select the Yes button to execute the Delete query or No to not execute the query.

Once you have clicked the Yes button, the query will be executed and the records will be deleted. Once the query is executed, you will no longer be able to use those records.

Creating a Delete Query in SQL View

Usually Delete queries have three clauses: DELETE, FROM, and the optional WHERE. When creating a query in SQL View mode, it is not necessary to provide specific field names or the asterisk in the DELETE clause. The FROM clause tells the query in which table the records are located, and the WHERE clause is used to apply criteria to restrict the recordset to the specific records. Once you have the SQL statement to be used for the Delete query, it is a simple process to create the query itself:

1. The most important step is to first make a complete backup copy of the database file.

2. Open the database in Access 2010.

3. On the Create Ribbon, click the Query Design button to create a new query in Design mode.

4. On the Query Tools Design Ribbon, click the View button and choose the SQL View option to switch to SQL View mode.

5. Type the SQL statement into the SQL View window to create the query and click the Save button.

6. Execute the query by clicking the Run button on the Query Tools Design Ribbon. You will be required to verify that you want to run the query from a dialog. This is the point of no return! Select the Yes button to execute the Delete query or No to not execute the query.

And again, once you have clicked the Yes button, the query will be executed and the records will be deleted and no longer usable, so be sure you know which records you want to remove.

An example of the SQL statement for a query to delete all records from an `Employees` table would look like this:

```
DELETE
FROM Employees
```

To add criteria to the query to delete only records with a transaction date more recent than yesterday would look like this:

```
DELETE
FROM Employees
WHERE DateTransaction > DateAdd("d", -1, Date())
```

Ramifications of Delete Queries

The primary ramification of running a Delete query, like the Update query in Lesson 27, is the possibility of unintentional data loss. The first step before using any Delete query is to back up the data; this is especially important with ad hoc Delete queries and new Delete queries. Database bloat is another problem associated with deleting records — the records cannot be restored after deletion, but Access leaves them in the database file. To actually remove the records from the database file, a Compact and Repair must be run. We highly recommend being extremely careful when using Delete queries to remove data from a database application.

TRY IT

In this lesson, you learn how to create a Delete query using Query Design View. You then modify the completed query by adding criteria to restrict the records to be deleted, and then create and modify a simple Delete query using the SQL View.

Lesson Requirements

For this lesson, you should be familiar with creating queries using Access 2010. You should also have the sample `Lesson28.accdb` database file, which you can download from the book's DVD and website.

Step-by-Step

1. Create a (backup) copy of the `Lesson28.accdb` file.

2. Open Access 2010 and the `Lesson28.accdb` file.

3. On the Create Ribbon, click the Query Design button to create a new query in Design View mode. A new query will open in Design View mode and the Show Table dialog will open.

4. In the Show Table dialog, add the table named `tblCustomer` to the query and click the OK button to close the dialog.

5. From the `tblCustomer` field list, double-click each of the three fields to add them to the query grid.

6. Click the Delete button in the Query Type section of the Query Tools Design Ribbon to switch the Select query to be a Delete query.

7. Save the query as **qryDelete**.

8. Click the Run button to run the query and delete all records in the table.

Congratulations, you have now created a Delete query using Access 2010. Open the `tblCustomer` table and verify that all of the records have been removed. Now that you know how to create a Delete query, modify the query to restrict the deleted records to anyone with a last name of Adams:

9. Open `qryDelete` in Design View.

10. Add criteria to the `LastName` field to limit that field to Adams. Type **Adams** in the criteria row of the `LastName` field.

11. Save the query and close it.

12. In the Navigation Pane, right-click the `tblCustomer` table and choose the Delete option to delete the table from the database.

13. From the backup database you created in step 1, import the `tblCustomer` table and save it as **tblCustomer**.

14. Now, in the Navigation Pane, double-click `qryDelete` to execute the Delete query.

Congratulations, you have now created a Delete query to remove a specific set of records from a table. Open the `tblCustomer` table and verify that all of the records with the last name of Adams have been removed from the table. Finally, create a simple Delete query in SQL View mode:

15. On the Create Ribbon, click the Query Design button to create a new query in Design View mode.

16. On the Query Tools Design Ribbon, click the View button and Select the SQL View option from the dropdown to open the query in SQL View mode.

17. In the SQL View window, type the following SQL statement:

```
SELECT *
FROM tblCustomer
WHERE CustomerID Between 46 and 95;
```

18. Click the Run button to execute the Select query to verify it returns only records with a `CustomerID` between the values of `46` and `95`.

19. Assuming the correct records are returned, click the View button and choose the SQL View mode option to switch the query back to SQL View. Change the `SELECT *` to a `DELETE`, so that the query text appears as:

```
DELETE
FROM tblCustomer
WHERE CustomerID Between 46 and 95;
```

20. Click the Save button and close the query.

21. In the Navigation Pane, double-click the `qryDelete` query to run the query and delete the records.

Congratulations; you have created a Delete query using SQL View mode. If you open the `tblCustomer` table, you will see that the proper records have been deleted. Access 2010 makes it very easy to create and modify Delete queries, so always be careful which data you decide to delete!

SUMMARY

Delete queries are used to remove records from a table. The query can be limited to deleting a single record or it can delete all records. From its power to easily delete records comes major risks. One mistake in the design of the query can result in all records being deleted inadvertently. Again, we highly recommend backing up the database file any time you execute a Delete query. Also, always test new Delete queries before using them in a production environment, and always back up the production database data regularly. Regardless of whether you are creating the Delete query in Design View or SQL View mode, Access 2010 makes it very easy to accomplish!

Please select Lesson 28 on the DVD to view the video that accompanies this lesson.

29

Creating Make Table Queries

Make Table queries are used to create new tables from the recordset returned by a query. The source query can use expressions and perform calculations as well as return the values from the fields in one or more tables. In this lesson you learn that some of the uses of Make Table queries are to store the results of complex queries or summarized data in a temporary table for further use, to archive data from existing tables, and to create a temporary table with mail merge data to use with Microsoft Word.

LESSON SETUP

For this lesson you need Access 2010 and the Lesson 29 files from the book's website at www.wrox.com. You should be familiar with creating database objects and working with queries in Access 2010 to complete this lesson successfully.

MAKE TABLE QUERIES IN ACCESS

Make Table queries in Access 2010 are much like other Action queries in Access. A Make Table query has many uses:

- ➤ Storing the results of a complex query for more efficient or further processing of the data.

- ➤ Archiving all, or a subset, of the existing data in a table should be to a new table.

- ➤ Creating temporary staging tables to hold data that is to be exported.

- ➤ Creating temporary tables to use as a source for a mail merge to an external program, such as Microsoft Word.

- ➤ Exporting data to an external Access database.

- ➤ Creating a new table with the same design as an existing table, but without any data.

A Make Table query is an Action query and can cause a loss of data, thus it requires that the database be in a trusted state before it can be executed. If the table named in the Make Table query already exists when the query is run, confirmation is required to overwrite the existing table, except when the warnings have been disabled. It is still the best practice to back up your data before testing a Make Table query.

Creating a Make Table Query in Design Mode

Usually, the first step in creating a Make Table query is creating a Select query to use as the source. If an existing query returns the records needed in the new table, you can create a copy of that query to use; otherwise, you will need to create a new query. Once you have a query that returns the correct fields and records, you can convert it to a Make Table query.

Click the Make Table button in the Query Type section of the Query Tools Design Ribbon to change the query to a Make Table query using the Access 2010 designer. The Make Table dialog allows you to select a table name or type a new table name. You also have a choice of designating the destination database as the current database or using another database. If you choose the Another Database option, you can type in or browse to the database to which you want to send the results of the Make Table query. Test the query by clicking the View button and if it runs correctly, click the Run button to execute the query and create a new table. Access will present a confirmation dialog box asking if you want to paste rows into a new table and give you a chance to abort the operation.

Make Table Query Settings

Make Table queries can be based on single tables or multiple tables, Totals queries or queries using the DISTINCT keyword, Pass-Through queries, and Union queries. To use Pass-Through or Union queries as the source, you must create a query based on them instead of converting the Pass-Through or Union queries to a Make Table query. As with other Action queries, you can bypass the warning and confirmation dialogs, but it is not recommended.

Creating a Make Table Query in SQL View

A Make Table query has a SELECT clause, an INTO clause and the table name (or the IN operator), a database path and database name, a FROM clause, and optional JOIN WHERE, GROUP BY, HAVING, and ORDER BY clauses as required. A simple Make Table query might look like this:

```
SELECT *
INTO tblYourNewTable
FROM tblYourTable
```

This example returns all records and all fields from tblYourTable and uses them to populate the new table in the current database named tblYourNewTable. To create a query that summarizes data through the last day of the previous month and makes a table in another database, the SQL resembles this:

```
SELECT CustomerName,
       CustomerAccountNumber,
       Sum(Amount_Transaction) as
           AccountBalanceINTO tblBalances IN 'C:\Databases\Sample.accdb'
```

```
FROM tblTransactions
WHERE DateTransactions <= DateSerial(Year(Date()),Month(Date()),0)
GROUP BY CustomerName, CustomerAccountNumber
HAVING Sum(Amount_Transaction) <> 0
ORDER BY CustomerName
```

The syntax used to create the destination table in another database is IN 'database\pathname'. Note that the database path and name are enclosed in single quotes.

Ramifications of Make Table Queries

Unlike other Action queries, Make Table queries usually are not destructive to existing data, unless they overwrite an existing table. Compared to Delete queries, which can delete entire tables of records, and Update queries, which change the data of multiple specific records, Make Table queries are considered somewhat safer. A Make Table query can destroy an entire table and the data in it only when it creates a new table with the same name as an existing table, but not single or multiple records. If the warnings are enabled, two mouse clicks will replace an existing table with the new data; if the warnings are disabled, running the query will replace the table without any warning. Create safeguards in your application to prevent inadvertent loss of data.

Anytime data is being added and removed in an Access database, the size of the database will begin to increase, or bloat. Compact & Repair will complete the deletion process and reclaim the space, and reduce the size of your database.

TRY IT

In this lesson, you learn how to create a Make Table query using Query Design View. You then modify that query and create another Make Table query in SQL View. You need file Lesson29.accdb from the book's DVD and website to successfully complete this lesson.

Step-by-Step

1. Open Access 2010 and open the Lesson29.accdb database file.

2. Create a new query in Query Design View mode by clicking the Query Design button on the Create Ribbon.

3. Add the table named tblCustomer from the Show Table dialog.

4. Add all three of the fields in the table to the query.

5. Click the Make Table button on the Query Tools Design Ribbon to convert the query to a Make Table query.

6. Enter a name for the new table, such as **tblCustomerStepByStepA**.

7. Save the query as **qryMakeTable1**.

8. Test the query by clicking the View button to open the query and see if the records in the table have been returned properly.

9. Once you are sure the query is working properly, click the Run button to execute the query and create the new table. Click the Yes button when prompted to confirm pasting records into a new table.

10. Check the new table to see if all the records from the original table were added to the new table.

11. Verify the design of the new table by clicking the Design View button on the Ribbon. Notice that the `CustomerID` field was created as an `AutoNumber` data type, but the field was not made the primary key and it was not indexed. You must manually create the primary key and indexes, or use a Data Definition query to complete the new table each time the Make Table query is run. Close the table and the query.

Next, create an empty table by modifying `qryMakeTable1` to not return any records.

12. Open `qryMakeTable1` in Design View. Save it as **qryMakeTable2** by using the File tab and clicking Save Object As, entering the new query name, and selecting Query in the As box.

13. Change the name of the destination table to **tblCustomerStepByStepB**. You can click the Make Table button on the Query Tools Design Ribbon and change the name in the Make Table dialog, or open the Property Sheet of the query and change the value in the Destination Table property.

14. Add criteria to the Criteria row of the `CustomerID` field that will ensure no records will be returned. You can use a value that is not in the table or an expression that will not ever evaluate to `True`, such as `1=2`.

15. Click the View button to verify that the query does not return any records. If the query does not return any records, save the query and click Run to execute it. The new table will be created.

16. Open the new table to verify that it did not have any records created. When you are satisfied, close the query.

Next, create a Make Table query in SQL View mode that will make a table of unique last names that are currently in the table.

17. Click the Query Design button in the Create Ribbon and close the Show Table dialog without adding a table.

18. Click the SQL button and compose the SQL statement by adding a `SELECT` clause, an `INTO` clause, a `FROM` clause, a `GROUP BY` clause, and an `ORDER BY` clause.

19. The `SELECT` clause will include only the `LastName` field:

        SELECT LastName

20. The `INTO` clause will use the table named `tblUniqueNames`:

        INTO tblUniqueNames

21. The `FROM` clause designates `tblCustomer`:

        FROM tblCustomer

22. The GROUP BY clause and the ORDER BY clauses will both use only the LastName field:

```
GROUP BY LastName
ORDER BY LastName
```

23. The final SQL statement for the query should look like this:

```
SELECT LastName
INTO tblUniqueNames
FROM tblCustomer
GROUP BY LastName
ORDER BY LastName
```

24. Click the View button to test the results, and then click the Run button to execute the query. The new table will be created. Close and save the query as **qrySQLMakeTable**.

Congratulations, you have created several Make Table queries using both the Access 2010 Design View and SQL View mode designers. Make Table queries can be very useful when you need to build tables on-the-fly in your Access database applications.

SUMMARY

Make Table queries can be used to create tables that can be used for a variety of reasons, from simply creating a new blank table, to storing the results of a complex series of joins that build a brand new table, to creating a local table for the purpose of making the end users' queries run faster and more efficiently to improve performance on the database. Make Table queries can be used to move a table, and all of its data, to another database by adding an IN operator and the path and database name to the INTO clause. If the destination table named in the query is an existing table, Access will overwrite the original table and data with the new data. Use this feature with caution because it is possible to permanently remove your data when clicking Yes instead of No at the warning dialog. As with the other Action queries, regular backups of the database are a necessity to safeguard your data. Building Make Table queries using Access 2010 is extremely easy to do in both Design View and SQL View modes and can be an important part of almost any Access database application.

 Please select Lesson 29 on the DVD to view the video that accompanies this lesson.

30

Creating Crosstab Queries

A Crosstab query is a query that transforms rows of data into columns of data; most often it includes aggregation of some of the data elements. If you need to show the total sales by customer and by month in a matrix, a Crosstab query is a good choice. Crosstab queries transform normalized records into a matrix and display aggregated data at the intersections of the rows and columns. The Crosstab Wizard is a good place to start creating Crosstab queries, but the wizard has limitations and cannot create queries with more than three row headers. Query Design View and SQL View can both be used to make modifications that are not available from the wizard. This lesson discusses the basics of building Crosstab queries using Access 2010.

LESSON SETUP

For this lesson you need Access 2010 and Lesson 30 from the book's website at www.wrox.com. You should be familiar with creating database objects and working with queries using Access 2010 to complete this lesson successfully.

CROSSTAB QUERIES IN ACCESS

A Crosstab query will transform the records (rows) of data from a table into columns in a new table. The Crosstab query can generate a result set of aggregate data in a table typically in the form of True/False values, or the sums of values indicating the number of records that were contained in the previous table and are now a column in the new table. For example, if you have a Customers table that contains a State field, you could use a Crosstab query to generate a table consisting of State name fields that match the customer State name records, with a single record containing a number indicating the number of customers in each state.

In addition to converting the records from one table into the columns of a new table, the Crosstab query can be used to merge two different sets of records, containing a related field, into a new table containing some data aggregation of those records. For example, if you have a Customers table and an `Orders` table, you could use a Crosstab query to generate a new table of the number of orders per state, where each record in the table denotes a specific date for the orders. The possibilities for the uses of Crosstab queries are limitless, yet many developers tend to shy away from them because they are complex, often hard to build, and typically misunderstood. Fortunately, Access 2010 provides three different methods for creating Crosstab queries: the Crosstab Query Wizard, the Query Design View designer, and the Query SQL View designer.

The Crosstab Query Wizard

The Crosstab Query Wizard helps the user to create a Crosstab query with a few clicks of the mouse. To activate the Crosstab Query Wizard, click the Query Wizard button on the Create Ribbon. The New Query dialog presents the Crosstab Query Wizard as one of its options. Select it, click OK, and select the fields desired from the table or query you need. To select fields from multiple tables, you must first create a query that presents the records and fields that are needed and then use the query as the basis of the crosstab. Select the field, or fields — the wizard allows you to select up to three row headings. The next choice is the Column Heading; there can be only one column heading. If a date field is selected, the next screen gives you the option of selecting an interval to group the date values:

➤ Year

➤ Quarter

➤ Month

➤ Date

➤ Date/Time

The next screen is where you select the field to be aggregated and select which aggregate function to use. The wizard will save and open the query for you to examine.

Creating a Crosstab Query in Design Mode

Creating a Crosstab query using the Design View allows the user to have more control over the design of the query and eliminates the restriction of three row headings in a query. Multiple tables or queries can be added to the Crosstab query in Design View, eliminating the single table restriction when using the wizard. When activated, the query grid in Design View will have two additional rows: the Total row and the Crosstab row. The options for each row are listed here:

➤ Total

    ➤ Group By

    ➤ The Sum function and all of the aggregate functions associated with Totals queries

    ➤ Expression

    ➤ Where

➤　Crosstab

➤　Row Heading

➤　Column Heading

➤　Value

➤　(not shown)

Creating a Crosstab query is much like creating any other query: Create the new query in Query Design View mode, select the table or query you will be using in the query, and click the Crosstab button in the Query Type section of the Design Ribbon. Add the fields you are going to use as Row Headers to the query. Change the Crosstab row to Row Heading for each field added as a Row Heading. Add the field to be the Column Heading to the grid and change the Crosstab row to Row Heading. Add the field you want to use as the aggregated field and change the Crosstab row to Value and the Total row to the aggregate function you will be using; it cannot be left at the default setting of Group By. If you need a Totals column for each row, add a field expression with a unique name and set the Total row to Sum and the Crosstab row to Row Heading. This will add totals for each row.

Crosstab Query Settings

If you are used to using parameter queries that use the square bracket syntax or use form references, you will find that a Crosstab query will fail unless the parameters are explicitly declared using the PARAMETERS clause. You can do this using the Query Parameters dialog in Query Design View or by writing code in SQL View.

If it is necessary to display columns for data not in the database, such as a column for each month of the year, Access allows you to do this either by using the Column Headings property in the Property Sheet of the query, or by adding an IN clause to the SQL. A list of all possible values in the Column Heading field is added to the Column Headings property, text values are enclosed in quotes and comma delimited, dates are enclosed using the # sign, and numeric data is comma separated. Access will display the data in the order entered in the list, and will also omit any data not included in the list. In SQL View, the list is added using the IN operator following the PIVOT clause:

```
IN ("Jan","Feb","Mar","Apr","May","Jun",
    "Jul","Aug","Sep","Oct","Nov","Dec")
```

In addition to the online Access 2010 help, Access MVP Allen Browne at http://allenbrowne .com/ser-67.html and Access MVP Duane Hookom at http://www.access.hookom.net/ DynamicMthlyCrosstabRpt.htm have additional Crosstab query resources on their websites.

Creating a Crosstab Query in SQL View

Creating a Crosstab query in SQL View mode allows you to write the specific SQL statement you wish to use for the query, providing you with the greatest amount of flexibility. A Crosstab query is constructed from the following SQL statement clauses:

➤　PARAMETERS (Optional) — Explicitly defines the query parameters.

➤　TRANSFORM — Specifies the field used as the Value field and the aggregate function to be used.

➤ SELECT — Lists the fields used as Row Headings, including the field and aggregate function used as the Total row.

➤ FROM — Joins to multiple tables or queries are optional. Specifies the table or query to use.

➤ WHERE (Optional) — Any criteria are listed here.

➤ GROUP BY — The non-aggregated Row Header fields in the SELECT clause are listed here.

➤ PIVOT — Specifies the Column Header field. An optional predicate is the In predicate. The In predicate is used to list all possible values that may be returned by the Value field in a Crosstab query that may return Null values, and it also will order the values in the same order as the list.

The following example is a Crosstab query that you can write in the Access 2010 SQL View mode designer:

```
TRANSFORM Sum(Amt_Transaction) AS Total_Transaction
SELECT DepartmentID, Sum(Amt_Transaction) AS TotalTransaction
FROM tblTransaction
GROUP BY DepartmentID
PIVOT Format(Date_Transaction,"mmmm")
    IN("January","February","March","April",
        "May","June","July","August","September",
        "October","November","December")
```

An alternative to a Crosstab query is the Excel Pivot Table. The Pivot Table is more flexible to the user because the design can be changed at run time with a few mouse clicks. By using an Excel data connection to an external data source, a Pivot Table can retrieve current data at run time to populate tables. The data source can be an Access table or query, any ODBC-compliant database system, or any of the external data types included on the External Data Ribbon. Allowing the end user the ability to modify the output increases the productivity of the end user, and frees up the time the analyst or developer previously used to modify the output.

TRY IT

In this lesson, you learn how to use the Query Wizard to create a Crosstab query, create and modify a Crosstab query in Design View, and create a Crosstab query in SQL View. You need the Lesson30.accdb file from this book's DVD and website to complete this lesson successfully.

Step-by-Step

1. Open Access 2010 and open the Lesson30.accdb database file.

2. Click the Query Wizard button on the Create Ribbon.

3. Select Crosstab Query Wizard from the list of choices and click OK.

4. Select tblStudents to use as the table in the query and click the Next button.

5. Add the LastName field as a Row Heading and click the Next button.

6. Add Sex as the Column Heading and click the Next button.

7. Add Fees as the field to use as the Value and select Sum as the function. Click the Next button.

8. Change the name of the query to **tblStudents_Crosstab_Wizard**.

9. Click the Finish button to save and view the query.

Congratulations, you have now successfully created a Crosstab query using the Crosstab Query Wizard. Next, create a Crosstab query in Query Design View mode.

10. Click the Query Design button on the Create Ribbon to create a new query in Design View mode.

11. Add the table named tblStudents from the Show Table dialog to the query. Click the Close button on the Show Table dialog.

12. Click the Crosstab button in the Query Type section of the Query Tools Design Ribbon.

13. Add the LastName field to the first column. Set the Total row to Group By and the Crosstab row to Row Heading.

14. Add the Sex field to the next column. Set the Total row to Group By and the Crosstab row to Column Heading.

15. Add Fees to the third column. Set the Total row to Sum and the Crosstab row to Value.

16. Save the query as **tblStudents_Crosstab_DesignView** and open the query to view the results.

Congratulations, you have now created a Crosstab query using the Query Design View designer. The query created by using the wizard and the query using Design View should return the same results, with the exception of the Total row included in the one created using the wizard. Next, you add the Total row to the second query.

17. In the Navigation Pane, make a copy of the tblStudents_Crosstab_DesignView query and save it named as **tblStudents_Crosstab_DesignView_Modified**.

18. Add the Fees field and use the alias of **Total Of Fees**.

19. Set the Total row to Sum.

20. Set the Crosstab row to Row Heading.

21. Save the query and run it to see the result. Then switch back to Design View mode.

22. Add the FirstName field to the right of the LastName column, setting the Total row to Group By and the Crosstab row to Row Heading.

23. Save the query and open it to view the results.

Next you create a simple Crosstab query using SQL View that returns the fee collected by students, by the sex of the student. It includes the student's last name and a total student fee column.

24. Create a new query by clicking the Design View button and do not add any tables to the query, just close the Show Table dialog. Open the query in SQL View mode.

25. The first line of SQL in a Crosstab query is usually the TRANSFORM clause. Use the Fees field in the Sum() function for this clause:

```
TRANSFORM Sum(Fees) AS StudentFees
```

26. The next clause is the SELECT clause. Include the fields used as Row Headers in this line, which are the LastName field and the Fees field. Add the Sum() function to the Fees field. Use the alias TotalStudentFees for the Fees field expression:

```
SELECT LastName, Sum(Fees) AS TotalStudentFees
```

27. The FROM clause designates the table you are using:

```
FROM tblStudents
```

28. The next clause is the GROUP BY clause. Because there is only one non-aggregated field in the SELECT clause, only one field is in this clause, the LastName field:

```
GROUP BY LastName
```

29. The last line is the PIVOT clause. The goal is to list the fees of female students in one column and the fees of male students in another. To do that you need to use the Sex field as the PIVOT field:

```
PIVOT Sex
```

30. The completed query should look like this:

```
TRANSFORM Sum(Fees) AS StudentFees
SELECT LastName, Sum(Fees) AS TotalStudentFees
FROM tblStudents
GROUP BY LastName
PIVOT Sex
```

31. Save the query as tblStudents_Crosstab_SQL and run the query. The results should be the same as the queries completed using the wizard and Query Design View.

32. To require the Male column to be before the Female column in the query, add an In predicate to the PIVOT clause:

```
PIVOT Sex In ("M","F")
```

33. Run the query to see that the column order is now reversed. Save the query as **tblStudents_Crosstab_SQL_In.**

Congratulations, you have now created several Crosstab queries using the Access 2010 Crosstab Query Wizard, Design View, and SQL View mode designers. Use Crosstab queries to build tables of data on-the-fly and yield powerful results for any Access database application.

SUMMARY

A Crosstab query is probably the most misunderstood and underutilized query included in Access. With a little practice, the database developer can begin creating robust Crosstab queries. Crosstab queries can be valuable when the data needs to be presented by units displayed as rows or field values used to create columns, and when the intersection of the data is an aggregate function to sum or count the values.

The Crosstab Query Wizard is limited in what it can create, but it will get you started. Create a simple query using the wizard and then either use Query Design View or SQL View to make modifications to the query. Once you are familiar with each piece of the Crosstab query puzzle, it becomes much easier to design and create complex queries and use the results in Access reports. Access 2010 makes it very easy to quickly build Crosstab queries, no matter which method you choose to create them with!

 Please select Lesson 30 on the DVD to view the video that accompanies this lesson.

31

Creating Forms in Layout View

One of the most powerful features of Microsoft Access 2010 is the Access Forms package. Access Forms enable developers to create Windows-style forms directly within an Access database application. These forms are very versatile for working with data in Access and provide a number of modes, settings, and events with which developers can utilize. Creating and designing forms are important parts of building any Access database application because that is how you typically want users to interact with your application. The uses for forms are endless.

Several designers (and other methods) are available for creating and building forms in Access, one of which is the Form Layout View designer. Introduced originally in Access 2007, the Layout View designer enables the developer to create and manipulate the form and its objects while seeing actual data in the form. The benefit to using the Layout View designer is that it makes it very easy to perform simple adjustments to controls on the form. It is also nice to see actual data while the form is being designed, especially when sizing controls. The Layout View designer is very useful when creating custom Access forms, such as Split Forms. The only drawback to using the Form Layout View designer is that you cannot use every available option for forms in this mode, but it does allow manipulation of most objects and settings. This lesson discusses the basics of building Access forms using the Layout View designer in Access 2010.

LESSON SETUP

To begin using the Access Form Layout View designer, you really only need two things:

1. A table that contains some sample data.
2. A form that has a row source set to a table (or other data source, such as a query) containing data.

As long as you have the table with data, you can just create a new form in the database to begin using the Layout View designer.

QUICK FORMS IN ACCESS 2010

One very powerful and productive feature of Access is the ability to create quick forms. Quick forms in Access are a great way to create new, fully functioning forms from specific sets of data. These forms have all of the necessary settings and controls for working with the various fields of the data source and are ready to use with only a few clicks in Access. Imagine creating a complete form with controls to all the fields in a data source in just 5 seconds. This is not only possible, but a common operation in Access 2010!

To create a quick form in Access 2010, simply click any Table, Query, Form, or Report in the Navigation Pane to select it. Then click the Create tab on the Ribbon and click any of the Form buttons (except Form Design). A brand new form will be created, with its Data Source property based on the item selected in the Navigation Pane. Also, you could have chosen any of the options from the More Forms pull-down on the Create Ribbon to choose one of the custom form options. Creating quick forms in Access is fast and easy to do for any Access user.

SWITCHING TO LAYOUT VIEW

To start working in the Form Layout View designer, all you need to do is open the form in Layout View. Simply double-click any form in the Navigation Pane to open it. Once a form is open (and it is the current object selected), the View button on the Home Ribbon will be available for use. To switch to Layout View, click the View button's down arrow to see all of the choices and then click the Layout View option. Figure 31-1 shows an example of the View button options in Access 2010.

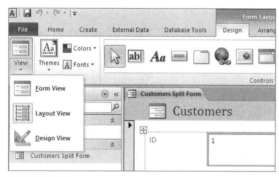

FIGURE 31-1

Once the form is in Layout View, you will see it in the main section of the Access window as normal, except that now all controls on the form will be selectable. You can begin editing the form's controls and properties in Layout View.

THE FORM LAYOUT TOOLS RIBBONS

Once a form has been opened in Layout View, Access provides three new Ribbons that were not previously visible. These are the Form Layout Tools Ribbons, which contain the Design, Arrange, and Format tabs. The Form Layout Tools Ribbons contain options for working with the form in Layout View.

The first tab of the Form Layout Tools Ribbon is the Design Ribbon. The Design Ribbon provides options for working with Controls, Themes, and Headers and Footers, and provides buttons for changing the Form View and for turning on and off the Property Sheet and Field List panes. Figure 31-2 is an example of this Ribbon.

FIGURE 31-2

The second tab of the Form Layout Tools Ribbon is the Arrange Ribbon. The Arrange Ribbon provides options for setting control layouts and adjusting rows, columns, and general positions of controls. Figure 31-3 is an example of this Ribbon.

FIGURE 31-3

The third tab of the Form Layout Tools Ribbon is the Format Ribbon. The Format Ribbon provides options for setting the formats of controls, such as quick style and objects. It also provides the ability to set font settings, data formatting, and background and alternating row colors. Figure 31-4 is an example of this Ribbon.

FIGURE 31-4

To use any of these Ribbon options, simply click the control you want to manipulate and choose the Ribbon option. To add controls, simply click the control type in the Ribbon to select it and click the desired location in the form, and the control will be added. Using the Form Layout Tools Ribbons is just that simple!

THE FIELD LIST PANE

The Access Field List pane is very useful for working with fields in the various tables contained in the database. Specifically, the Access Field List allows the user to drag and drop existing fields into a form (or report) that is in Layout View. To open the Field List pane, click the Add Existing Fields button of the Design tab of the Form Layout Tools Ribbon. The Field List can also be opened by using the Alt+F8 keystroke combination. Figure 31-5 is a screenshot of the Field List pane.

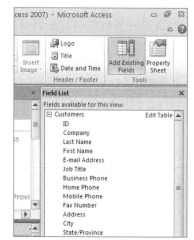

To add a field from the Field List, simply click the field you want to add and then drag it onto the form at the location you want to add it. You can double-click a field in the Field List to add it to the default location on the form, and you can right-click the various fields of the form to see the context menu options for the field.

The Field List shows not only the fields for the current record source of the form, but also Related tables and Other tables in the database. It is important to consider that if you add fields from Related or Other tables, the Field List will modify the Record Source property query to accommodate this change. Beware that this can inadvertently break other items on the form if they depend on the Record Source property.

FIGURE 31-5

THE PROPERTY SHEET PANE

The Access Property Sheet is very useful for working with the properties of the form and its controls. To open the Property Sheet pane, click the Properties button on the Form Layout Tools Design Ribbon. The Property Sheet can also be opened by using the F4 key. Figure 31-6 is a screenshot of the Property Sheet.

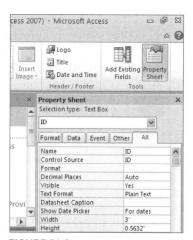

To modify the properties of a particular control, simply click the control to select it. Once a control has been selected, all of its properties are shown in the Property Sheet. To set the property value, click the property in the Property Sheet and either type or adjust the property from its drop-down menu (some properties have a drop-down menu to select a value from). To save the modification to the property, simply save the current form and the new values will be persisted to the database file.

FIGURE 31-6

THE RECORD SOURCE PROPERTY

The Record Source property is probably the single most used and important property of any form. The Record Source property is used to specify the object that the form is tied to and can be a number of different things, including:

1. A Table name
2. A Query name
3. A SQL statement that returns rows

To set the Record Source property for a form, select the entire form object. You can do this by selecting Form in the Property Sheet's selection type drop-down menu. Once the form has been selected, the Record Source property is listed as the first property on the All tab of the Property Sheet. If you click the value for this property, you will see a list item button and builder button appear in the value field. These allow you to select objects already in the database or to open the Query Builder. Or, you can also just type the specific text you want to use into this value field. Once the Record Source property has been set, all controls on the form can automatically reference fields contained within the record source. The Record Source property is the most commonly used way of binding a form to a particular dataset.

ACCESS FORM TYPES

Access 2010 provides a number of different built-in form types that can be created in any application. Each of these different form types provides a specific purpose, relative to some kind of functionality in Access. Although these different form types can be useful for working with various Access features, there isn't any real requirement to use one form type over another for a given situation. These types are just provided to make certain tasks easier to do in Access. The following table lists each kind of Access form and provides a description of that type.

FORM TYPE	DESCRIPTION
Single Form	Typically used for forms where the number of records on the form is fixed, usually to work with one individual record.
Continuous Form "Multiple Items"	Typically used to display a set of records. Provides a repeating section to display each record in the form's Record Source property.
Datasheet	Provides a standard Access datasheet to show all the records in from the Record Source. Useful for showing records in a tabular format.
PivotChart	A form for creating Charts in Access.
PivotTable	A form for creating Pivot Tables in Access.
Split Form	A form that is really two forms in one. One part of the form is a datasheet that displays all the records in the record source. The second part is a single form that provides the data from currently selected records from the Datasheet form.
Modal Dialog	A message box dialog form contained in its own window that is always on top of all other windows in the database.

You can implement any one of these forms by building the form manually from a new blank form, but this would require a great deal of work in most cases. Thus, choosing the right type of form can save a lot of time and effort when building an Access database application.

TRY IT

Now that you know how to open a form in Layout View mode and have learned about the Layout View tools that Access 2010 provides, this lesson walks you through a step-by-step example of how to create a form using the Form Layout View designer.

Lesson Requirements

The sample database file provided for this chapter on the book's DVD and website has the `Contacts` table and data provided by the Northwind sample database template from Access 2010, as well as a Split Form created from this table. For this lesson, the examples reference this sample database.

Step-by-Step

1. Open the `Ch31_Sample.accdb` database file included with the lesson by double-clicking the file. This starts Access and opens the database in the Access window.

2. Click the `Customers` table in the Navigation Pane to select it.

3. Click the Create tab on the Ribbon to see the create options. Click the More Forms pull-down menu in the Form group and choose the Multiple Items option. This creates a new multiple item form and opens it in Layout View, as shown in Figure 31-7.

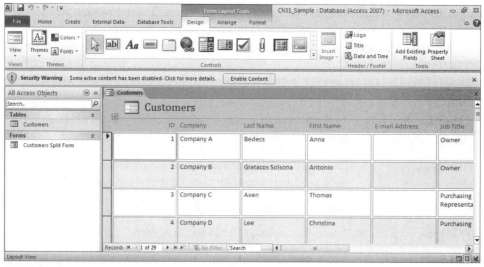

FIGURE 31-7

4. Press the F4 key to open the Property Sheet if it is not open already. Choose Form in the Selection Type pull-down menu on the Property Sheet and then click the All tab to see all of the properties for the form. Note that the `Record Source` property (the first property listed here) shows a value of `Customers`. This means that the form is tied to the `Customers` table, which is correct, so press F4 again to close the Property Sheet pane.

5. Click the line between the `TextBox` controls for the first and second records of the `ID` field. (The cursor changes when you hover over this area, but the cursor has to be in the exact position.) Drag the control to resize the entire row to make it only one line of text tall (so that more records can be shown in a smaller area).

6. Click the line between the `ID` and `Company TextBox` controls for the first record and drag it to the left to make the `ID` column smaller, thus removing unused space in the field. Notice that this automatically adjusts all of the `TextBox` controls in the column.

7. Right-click the text box for the first record of the `E-mail Address`. This opens the context menu for the Layout View designer, so choose Select Entire Column. Then press the Delete key. The entire column is deleted from the form and the others are shifted left.

8. Repeat the previous step for all columns except `ID`, `Company`, `Last Name`, `First Name`, `Job Title`, and `Business Phone` to delete all of the fields except those from the form. Figure 31-8 provides an example of what your form should look like now.

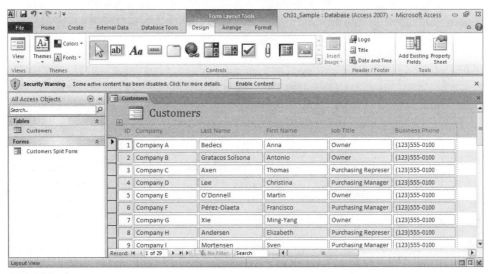

FIGURE 31-8

9. Right-click the `ID` label column header and choose the Select Entire Row option to select all of the column header labels for the form. Click in the Format tab of the Form Layout Tools and choose the Bold and Center options under the Font group. All of the labels should be bolded and centered appropriately.

10. Click the Design tab of the Layout Form Tools Ribbon and choose one of the themes from the Theme pull-down menu. All of the controls, fonts, and colors on the form should be adjusted to match the selected theme.

11. Right-click the `First Name` field and choose the Select Entire Column option. Drag the entire column left one column, so that it is now between the `ID` and `Last Name` columns.

12. Press the Alt+F8 key combination to open the Field List. Drag the `Fax Number` field back onto the form, between the `First Name` and `Job Title` fields. Press Alt+F8 again to close the Field List.

13. Resize the `Fax Number` column so that the data and label fit correctly, using the method described in Step 6.

14. Drag the `Fax Number` column all the way to the right on the form, using the method described in Step 11. The form should now look similar to Figure 31-9.

FIGURE 31-9

15. Click the Close button for the form.

16. Choose Yes when you are prompted to save the form. For the form name, type **Customers Form**. The new form is saved to the database file and ready to use! Just to confirm its existence, you should see the new form listed in the Navigation Pane.

Congratulations, you now have successfully created a brand new, fully functional, multiple item form in your Access database using the Form Layout View designer! To verify everything is working, you can simply double-click the form in the Navigation Pane to open it and see it in action. As you can see, the Access 2010 Form Layout View designer is quite efficient for building Access forms.

SUMMARY

The designer provides all of the tools necessary to modify, add, and delete controls on the form, as well as set the formats for those controls. The Property Sheet allows the user to manipulate the properties for the form and the controls on the form. The Field List pane allows the user to drop fields onto the form and place them visually without having to set any properties for the controls. The Access Form Layout View designer is a truly powerful way to create and modify forms in Access 2010.

 Please select Lesson 31 on the DVD to view the video that accompanies this lesson.

32

Creating Forms in Design View

As you saw in the preceding lesson, several designers (and other methods) are available for creating and building forms in Access, one of which is the Form Layout View designer. Now that you understand some of the basics of building forms, this lesson explores the traditional approach to designing forms in Access: using the Form Design View designer.

Form Design View goes all the way back to the beginning of Access; it was the original designer created for working with forms in Access. Design View enables the developer to create and manipulate the form and its objects in a grid-based format. Although you won't be able to see specific data from the Data Source in the form while designing it, the true power of this designer comes from the granularity you have when working with controls in this mode. This lesson discusses the basics of building Access forms using the Form Design View designer provided in Access 2010.

LESSON SETUP

To begin using the Access Form Design View, you really don't need anything at all; you can just create a blank form in a blank database and start building from there. However, it might be easier to get started if you have a table with a few fields in it. The discussion in this lesson assumes that the database file has a couple of tables in it.

BOUND VERSUS UNBOUND

In the previous lesson, you created a quick form from an existing table, which automatically set the Record Source property of the form to the specified table. When a form has its Record Source property set, it is regarded as a *Bound* form. Conversely, when the Record Source property of the form is blank, the form is called *Unbound*. Although the differences are minor, you should note some important distinctions.

Bound forms have a couple of benefits. First, controls on this form can reference fields in the data source strictly by field name, which means that you do not have to build code or a SQL statement to populate data in the control and that many Access features, for example, the Record Selectors at the bottom of an Access form, can be used without having to do anything else. Also, because so many Access features set the Record Source automatically, Bound forms are the de facto standard Access form.

However, Unbound forms have several benefits as well and are required for a couple of special situations. First, forms have many uses that do not require being tied directly to any specific object, and in some cases you may even want the Record Source for the form to be changing. Second, some types of controls, like ADO (ActiveX Data Objects) Recordsets, cannot be tied directly to the Record Source of a form. In this case, the user would be required to write some code to manually bind the data to the controls on the form.

Either way, it doesn't really matter whether or not the form is Bound. If you need to bind the form to data, simply set the Record Source property. If you need the form to be Unbound, simply clear the Record Source. It is just that easy to create Bound and Unbound forms in Access!

CREATING A FORM IN DESIGN VIEW

Creating a form in Design View is very simple and can be done with a single button click from the Ribbon. To create a new form in Design View, click the Create tab on the Ribbon, and under the Forms group, click the Form Design button. Once this button is clicked, a new, blank form is created and opened in Design View. The form is Unbound when created in this manner; that is, the form does not have any preset Record Source value, nor any existing controls on it. Once created, the Access window looks something like Figure 32-1.

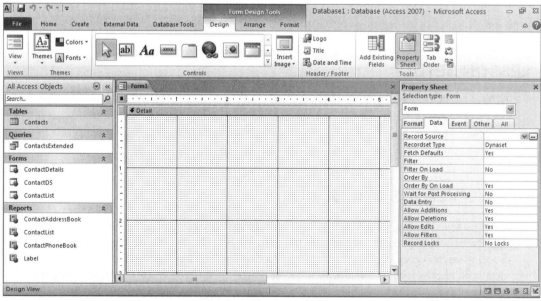

FIGURE 32-1

Although the form has been created and opened in the main window, you might have noticed that it has not appeared in the Navigation Pane. You are required to save the form to the database before it will show up here, and are prompted to do so when closing the form. If you do not save the form when closing it, all changes to the form are discarded, and in the case of a new form, the form itself is discarded.

DESIGN VIEW MODE

When you create a form in Design View, Access automatically opens it in Design View. But, of course, you can always open any form in Design View (except Web Forms, in which case it is not available). You have several ways to open a form in Design View:

➤ Right-click the form in the Navigation Pane and choose the Design View option.

➤ Open the form. Then choose the Design View option on the View menu of either the Home or the Form Tools tab of the Ribbon.

➤ Open the form, right-click the Document tab (or form title bar if it is a dialog), and choose Design View from the context menu.

Once the form is in Design View, you will see it in the main section of the Access window, except that it will have grid dots and you can see each of the sections of the form. All controls on the form will be selectable and you can begin editing the form without discretion. When the form is open in Design View, the status bar (on the bottom left of the Access 2010 window) will say Design View when the form is selected.

Working in Design View offers several benefits. First and foremost, anything that can be done with a form can be done from Design View. Design View provides gridlines and a ruler to help make the control positioning and sizing easy. Each of the sections of a form has tabs for quick selection, which are not available in Layout View. However, you will not see any data in this form when it is in Design View, which is different than Layout View. If you've used Access prior to the 2007 version, you are probably much more familiar with this design mode. Design View is the classic Access designer for forms and you should find it very easy to use.

THE FORM DESIGN RIBBON

Once a form has been opened in Design View, Access provides three new Ribbons that were not previously visible. These are the Form Design Tools Ribbons, which contain the Design, Arrange, and Format tabs. The Form Design Tools Ribbons contain options for working with the form in Design View. These Ribbons are very similar to the Layout Design Tools Ribbons discussed in the previous lesson, with a few minor differences.

The first tab of the Form Design Tools Ribbon is the Design tab. The Design Ribbon provides options for working with Controls, Themes, and Headers and Footers, and provides buttons for changing the Form View and for turning on and off the Property Sheet and Field List panes. For Design View, this tab also provides buttons for setting the tab order, opening the code for the form, and a button for converting macros to VBA code. Figure 32-2 is an illustration of this Ribbon.

FIGURE 32-2

The second tab of the Form Design Tools Ribbon is the Arrange tab. The Arrange Ribbon provides options for setting control layouts and adjusting rows, columns, and general positions of controls. In addition to the tools that are provided in Layout View, the Arrange Ribbon provides some additional sizing and ordering tools when in Design View. Figure 32-3 is an illustration of this Ribbon.

FIGURE 32-3

The third tab of the Form Layout Tools Ribbon is the Format tab. The Format Ribbon provides options for setting the formats of controls, such as quick style and objects. It also provides the ability to set font settings, data formatting, and background and alternating row colors. There is no difference between the Format tabs in Design or Layout View modes. Figure 32-4 is an illustration of this Ribbon.

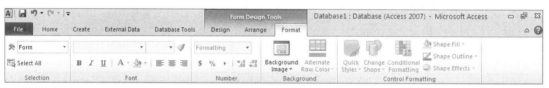

FIGURE 32-4

To use any of these Ribbon options, simply click the control on the form that you want to manipulate and click the Ribbon option you want to use. To add controls, simply click the control type in the Ribbon to select it, click the desired location in the form to place the control, and it will be added to the form. Using the Form Design Tools Ribbon is just that simple!

THE FIELD LIST PANE

As discussed in the previous lesson, the Access Field List pane is very useful for working with fields in the various tables contained in the database. However, the Field List is context sensitive to the Record Source property of the form, so when creating a form in Design View (and it has not already been bound to a data object), the Record Source will be blank and the Field List will not show any fields.

However, the Field List does provide the option to start adding fields to the form. If you click the Show All Tables link, the Field List shows a list of tables in the database. From there, you can expand any given table and drop fields onto the form, just as you could in Layout View. When you add fields in this manner, the Field List creates a query for the Record Source property of the Field List. Also, any time you use the Field List to add new fields, the Record Source property for the form may be modified. We discuss how the Field List creates and modifies a form's Record Source in a later lesson.

THE PROPERTY SHEET PANE

The Access Property Sheet is very useful for working with the properties of the form and its controls. To open the Property Sheet pane, click the Property Sheet button on the Form Design Tools Design Ribbon. The Property Sheet pane can also be opened by using the F4 key. Get used to using the Property Sheet if you will be designing a lot of forms and reports in Access; it is a guarantee that you will be using this pane a lot!

To modify the properties of a particular control, simply click the control to select it. Once a control has been selected, all of its properties are shown in the Property Sheet. To set the property value, click the property in the Property Sheet and either type or adjust the property from its options menu (some properties have an options menu to select a value from). Also, some properties have a builder button that will open one of the various Access designers to help set the property value. To save the modification to the property, simply save the current form and the new values will be persisted to the database file.

THE NAVIGATION PANE

The Navigation Pane replaced the Database window in Access 2007 and it provides some useful form-building functionality that was not possible with the old Database Window. Specifically, objects in the Navigation Pane can be dropped onto a form to add a subobject of that type. If the object being dropped from the Navigation Pane is a Form or Report, a subform or subreport for that object will be added to the form. If the object dropped from the Navigation Pane is a Table or Query, Access will launch the Subform Wizard to help build a subform for the given data object, and then place it on that form. The Navigation Pane can be extremely useful for quickly creating subform and subreport objects for forms in Design View.

To add a subform or subreport from the Navigation Pane, simply click a form or report in the Navigation Pane and drag it onto the form. Once the object has been dropped, you will have a control for that subobject. From there, the size and position of the control can be adjusted, but it does not require any further modification. The object will work without having to set any other properties or settings. Dropping controls from the Navigation Pane is just that easy!

TRY IT

In this lesson you create a form using the Access 2010 Design View designer. Now that you know how to open a form in Design View and have learned about the Design View tools that Access provides, you should understand the basics of using the Design View designer. You create a Customers form that shows the order details for a selected customer in a subform. This subform is made so that any order detail item that is clicked opens in a new `Order Details` form (which you also create here). This kind of functionality is very common in Access database applications and is typically called a drill-down form.

Lesson Requirements

For this lesson, the example steps use the Northwind database application created from the template. However, the Northwind database is not necessarily required for this lesson; you can use just about any database application. These steps are general enough that you could use just about any database that has some tables that contain data, but to see the exact functionality, including how the drill through to the `Order Details` form works, it is recommended you use the Northwind tables when completing these steps.

Step-by-Step

1. Open the `Ch32_Sample.accdb` database file, found on the book's DVD and website, by double-clicking it. This starts Access and opens the database in the Access window.

2. Click the Create tab on the Ribbon and click the Form Design button. A new form is created in Design View.

3. Press the F4 key to open the Property Sheet, if it is not already open.

4. From the All tab on the Property Sheet, set the following property values.

PROPERTY NAME	VALUE
Record Source	Order Details
Caption	Order Details
Pop Up	Yes
Default View	Datasheet
Allow Form View	No
Allow PivotChart View	No
Allow PivotTable View	No
Navigation Buttons	No

5. Once those properties have been set, press the Alt+F8 key combination to open the Field List.

6. From the `Order Details` table on the Field List, drag the `Order ID` field onto the form. A new `TextBox` and `Label` control for the `Order ID` is added to the form.

7. Click the Arrange tab on the Ribbon and click the Stacked button. This creates a Stacked Layout for the control, and any controls dropped on top of it will be added to the stack.

8. Drag the `Quantity`, `Unit Price`, and `Discount` fields from the `Order Details` table in the Field List onto the `Order ID` control stack. These three fields will be added to the control stack.

9. From the `Products` table in the Field List, drag the `Product Name` field onto the stack, between the `Order ID` and `Quantity` `TextBox` controls. The `Product Name` controls will be added to the stack (and the Record Source for the form will be updated to a new query, but you do not need to worry about that just yet).

10. Resize the form to make it a little smaller by adjusting the edges of the form. This form will only have records for one customer at a time when you are done.

11. Click the Save button on the top-left corner of the Access window. This invokes the Save As dialog. For the form name, type **Order Details** and click OK. The form will now be saved and show up in the Navigation Pane.

12. Close the form. Your `Order Details` form is now complete!

You can double-click it in the Navigation Pane to open it. The new `Order Details` form should look similar to Figure 32-5.

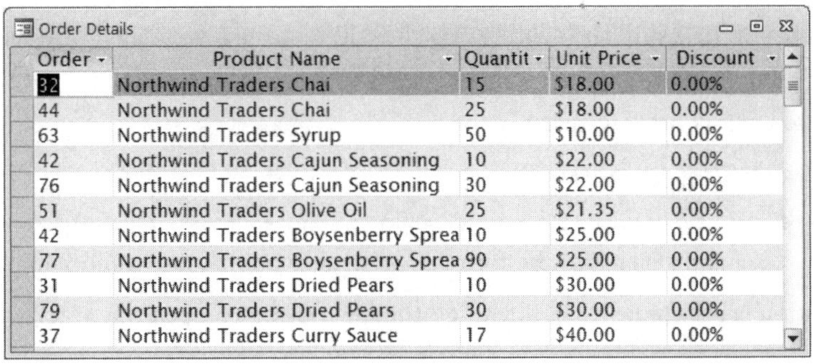

FIGURE 32-5

But, you are not done just yet. You are going to add two more forms to use with this form, so you can look at the specific order details for a particular order, based on the customer. Next you will build an orders subform.

13. Click the Create tab on the Ribbon and click the Form Design button. A new form is created in Design View.

14. Press the F4 button to open the Property Sheet, if it is not already open.

15. From the All tab on the Property Sheet, set the following property values.

PROPERTY NAME	VALUE
Record Source	Orders
Default View	Datasheet

continues

(continued)

PROPERTY NAME	VALUE
Allow Form View	No
Allow PivotChart View	No
Allow PivotTable View	No
Navigation Buttons	No

16. Once those properties have been set, press the Alt+F8 key combo to open the Field List.

17. From the `Orders` table on the Field List, drag the `Order ID` field onto the form.

18. Click the Arrange tab on the Ribbon and click the Stacked button. This creates a Stacked Layout for the new control.

19. Drag the `Order Date`, `Ship Date`, and `Paid Date` fields from the `Orders` table in the Field List onto the `Order ID` control stack.

20. Resize the form to make it a little smaller by adjusting the edges of the form. This form will only have records for one customer at a time when you are done.

21. Click the `Order ID` `TextBox` control to select it.

22. Press the F4 key to open the Property Sheet.

23. Click the Event tab of the Property Sheet to show the events for the `TextBox`. Click the "…" (Builder) button for the `On Click` event for the form. This invokes the Choose Builder dialog.

24. The Macro Builder option is selected by default. Click the OK button to open the Macro Builder.

25. In the Macro Builder action pull-down menu, choose the OpenForm option and apply the following settings:

SETTING NAME	VALUE
Form Name	Order Details
View	Datasheet
Where Condition	="[Order ID]=" & Nz([Order ID])
Data Mode	Read Only
Window Mode	Dialog

26. Once those settings have been completed, close the Macro Builder and choose Yes to save the new macro created for the `On Click` event for the `TextBox`.

27. Repeat Steps 21–26 for each `TextBox` on the form. That way, any time one of these `TextBoxes` is clicked from the subform, the `Order Details` form will be opened for that `Order ID`.

28. Click the Save button on the top-left corner of the Access window. This invokes the Save As dialog. For the form name, type **Orders Subform** and click OK. The form is saved and shows up in the Navigation Pane.

29. Close the form. Your `Orders Subform` is now complete!

You can double-click it in the Navigation Pane to open it. The new `Orders Subform` should look similar to Figure 32-6.

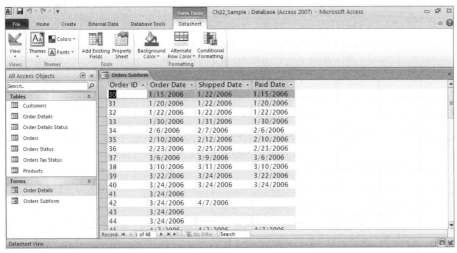

FIGURE 32-6

Finally, you will create one last form, your `Customers` form. From the `Customers` form, you will show your `Orders Subform` and be able to select the `Order Details` for any order selected for your customer.

30. Click the Create tab on the Ribbon and click the Form Design button. A new form is created in Design View.

31. Press the F4 key to open the Property Sheet, if it is not already open.

32. From the All tab on the Property Sheet, set the following property values.

PROPERTY NAME	VALUE
Record Source	Customers
Caption	Customer Details
Allow Datasheet View	No
Allow PivotChart View	No
Allow PivotTable View	No
Record Selectors	No

33. Once those properties have been set, press the Alt+F8 key combination to open the Field List.

34. From the Customers table on the Field List, drag the First Name field onto the form. A new TextBox and Label control for the First Name field will be added to the form.

35. Click the Arrange tab on the Ribbon and click the Stacked button. This creates a Stacked Layout for the control, and any controls dropped on top of it will be added to the stack.

36. Drag the Last Name, Company, and E-mail Address fields from the Customers table in the Field List onto the First Name TextBox control stack. These three fields will be added to the control stack.

37. From the Navigation Pane, drag the Orders Subform onto your new form, just below the TextBox control stack. This adds a subform control for your Orders Subform to your Customers form.

38. Adjust this subform so it fits nicely and resize the Customers form's edges so that everything fits well.

39. Click the Save button on the top-left corner of the Access window. This invokes the Save As dialog. For the form name, type **Customer Details** and click OK. The form will now be saved and show up in the Navigation Pane.

40. Close the form. Your Customer Details form is now complete!

You can double-click it in the Navigation Pane to open it. The new Customer Details form should look similar to Figure 32-7.

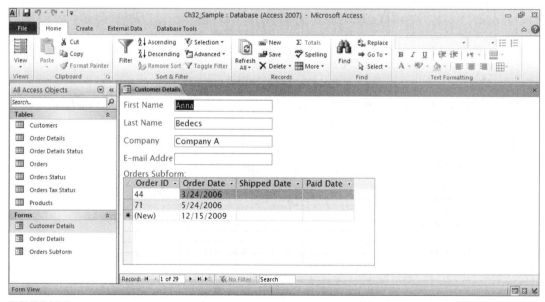

FIGURE 32-7

Congratulations, you have successfully created three brand new, fully functional forms in your Access database using the Design View designer. To verify that everything is working, you can simply double-click the `Customer Details` form in the Navigation Pane to open it and see it in action. Notice that if you move through records, the orders in the `Orders Subform` are updated based on the current customer selected. Also, if you click one of the orders for a customer, the `Order Details` form will be opened with the details for the order automatically selected. And all of this functionality was created with about 10 minutes of work!

SUMMARY

Using the Form Design View designer is a very simple and productive way to design forms in Access. The designer provides all of the tools necessary to modify, add, and delete controls on the form, as well as set the formats and layouts for those controls. The Property Sheet allows the user to manipulate the properties for the form and the controls on the form. The Field List pane allows the user to drop fields onto the form and place them visually without having to set any properties for the controls or manually build the Record Source for the form. The Navigation Pane allows the user to drop subform and subreport objects right onto the form. The Access Form Designer is a truly powerful way to create and modify forms in Access 2010.

 Please select Lesson 32 on the DVD to view the video that accompanies this lesson.

33

Access Form Properties

As you have already seen in the previous two lessons, working with Access form properties is an important part of building forms. The form's properties specify the individual settings for a form. For example, the Record Source property for a form determines which data is bound to a form. Although you have been setting these properties statically through the Property Sheet (for the most part) up until now, these properties can also be set through macros or code, as you will see in this lesson. Form properties play a vital role in every Access form, and this lesson will examine several more commonly used properties.

LESSON SETUP

To begin working with form properties, you must have a form to work with in the database. Every form has the same properties, so it doesn't really matter what kind of form you use (except for Web forms; they are completely different). You can easily create a new form or just use an existing one that is already in a database — it doesn't really matter for the purpose of viewing the form's properties.

THE PROPERTY SHEET

As you've seen in previous lessons, an easy method for working with a form's properties is through the Property Sheet pane. Part of Access since the very beginning, the Property Sheet lists each of the various properties that an object contains, providing a list of item names and values that can be modified by the user. The pane consists of five tabs to help categorize each of the types of properties.

The Property Sheet pane can be opened in one of three ways:

➤ Click the Property Sheet button on the Design tab of either the Form Layout Tools or Form Design Tools Ribbons.

➤ Use the F4 hotkey.

➤ Right-click a form, or a control on a form, and choose the Properties option.

Once the Property Sheet pane is opened, it remains open for any supported objects whenever they are selected, until the pane has been closed. For example, if the Property Sheet is opened while a form is in Design View and the form is closed, the Property Sheet is closed. But if you open another form in Design View, the Property Sheet will be opened again automatically, without pressing F4 or the button on the Ribbon.

THE PROPERTY SHEET TABS

The Property Sheet is broken up into five tabs to help categorize all of the properties of any given object. There are actually four categories: Format, Data, Event, and Other, plus an All tab that includes every property the object supports. Each of these tab names tries to be as descriptive as possible. The Format tab is for the format settings, such as the position, size, fonts, colors, and other such properties of a form (or any control). The Data tab contains the settings that are related to data in the form, such as the record source, filter, and other properties for the form. The Event tab lists all of the event methods available for the form. Finally, the Other tab provides a location for all of the other miscellaneous properties that don't fall in one of the first three categories. And, again, the All tab hosts every available property for the form or control. The Property Sheet tabs will become your best friends as you develop database applications in Access, and knowing which properties are on which tab can save a lot of time and effort.

ACCESS FORM PROPERTIES

Access forms provide a multitude of functionalities, most of which are exposed through the various properties that a form supports. A property is really nothing more than a setting for the form that serves some purpose related to the form. For example, in the previous lesson, you set the form's Type property to get the form to be the desired type. To do anything with forms, you pretty much have to utilize these properties to make it happen!

To know what any given form property does in Access, simply select the property you want to know more about, and a description of the property is displayed in the Access status bar, located on the bottom left of the Access window. In addition to the status bar, Access help provides a lot of information about common properties. Press the F1 key to open Access help at any time and simply search for the name of the property that is desired.

 If the status bar and Access help do not provide enough information, you can always find a complete list of the Access form properties in the MSDN library at `http://msdn.microsoft.com`*.*

Once you know what property you want to use, you only have to set the desired value — it is just that simple!

SETTING FORM PROPERTIES

If you've completed previous lessons throughout this book, you have already set lots of properties. A number of methods are available for setting properties, either through the Property Sheet, Macros, or VBA code. Depending on the property, the values that it can be set to will be dependent upon the specific property that is being employed.

To set a property on the Form level using the Property Sheet, you must first select the entire form. This can be accomplished by choosing the Form option in the Selection Type pull-down menu on the Property Sheet. Once the form is selected, all of its properties automatically appear in the Property Sheet. Simply click the value field (the field to the left of the property name) and one of several options will be available for setting the property:

> ➤ Type the value text. In some cases, you can type in the specific string or value you want the property to have. Sometimes this will be the only method available for setting the control.

> ➤ Choose from an option list. Some properties provide a list of options available for the property. If this is the case, the value field for the property will have a pull-down menu to select the option from.

> ➤ Use an Access Builder. Some properties provide a Builder button option, which is labeled by the ellipsis (...), to help set the value for the field. The three most common builders utilized from the Property Sheet are the Macro Builder, the Expression Builder, and the Code Builder (the Visual Basic Editor, or VBE).

No matter which method is used, Access is likely to make the job as easy as possible for you. Once the property value has been selected and placed in the value field for that property, the property will be set and you will be ready to use it!

TRY IT

Now that you have a basic understanding of what the Access form properties are and how to utilize them, this lesson provides a few examples for setting some form properties. These steps cover setting properties using each of the three methods discussed earlier.

Lesson Requirements

The sample database file provided for this chapter contains several forms, among other database objects. You can use either the database from the sample files provided on the book's DVD and website for this lesson, the Contacts template in Access 2010, or any database that contains a form.

Hints

Here are a few tips for working with properties:

> ➤ When an Access form is in Design View mode, you can quickly select the Form object by clicking the Form Selector. The Form Selector is the little square box on the top-left corner of a form where the rulers intersect when the form is opened in Design View.

➤ Use the F4 hotkey to open the Property Sheet at any time (but it must be supported in the current context).

➤ To see the properties for any object, simply click the object to select it and its properties will automatically be shown in the Property Sheet.

Step-by-Step

1. Open the `Ch33_Sample.accdb` database file by double-clicking it. This starts Access and opens the database in the Access window.

2. In the Navigation Pane, right-click the `Contact Details` form and choose the Design View option. This opens the form in Design View, as shown in the Figure 33-1.

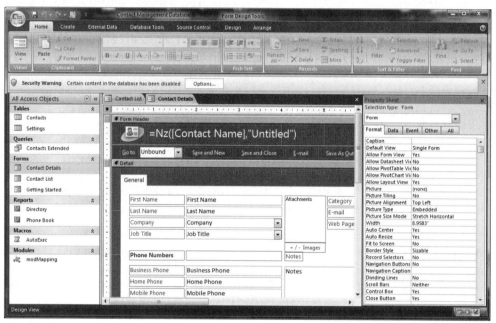

FIGURE 33-1

3. Press the F4 key to open the Property Sheet, if it did not open automatically when the form was opened in Design View.

4. Click the Data tab on the Property Sheet. Click the value field for the Record Source property to show the pull-down menu button.

5. Click the pull-down menu to see the options for the Record Source property. Select the Contacts option. The `Contacts` table will now be selected as the Record Source for the Details form.

Good work, you have set a property by selecting it from a list. Next, to set a property by typing in the value you want:

6. Click the Format tab of the Property Sheet to select it.

7. For the `Caption` property, type in **My Test Form**.

8. Right-click the Document tab for the `Contact Details` form and choose the Form View option. The form will now show My Test Form as the caption at the top of the form, as shown in Figure 33-2.

FIGURE 33-2

Finally, to set a property using an Access Builder, complete the following steps:

9. Right-click the `Contact Details` form in the Navigation Pane and choose the Design View option. This opens the form in Design View again.

10. Click the Event tab of the Property Sheet to select it.

11. For the `On Load` event, click the "…" (Builder) button. This invokes the Choose Builder dialog. Choose the Macro Builder option.

12. In the pull-down menu in the Macro Builder, choose the Close Window option. For the Object Type, choose Form. For the Object Name, choose Contact List.

13. Close the Macro Builder by clicking the X on the top right of the form. Choose Yes for the Save prompt.

The macro will now be applied to the On Load event for the form. The next time you open the Contact Details form from the Contact List form, the macro will run and the Contacts List form will be closed, which is a common form navigation technique used in Access. The Access Macro Builder, as well as the other built-in builders, makes building and setting form properties very simple!

14. For the On Dirty event, click the "..." (Builder) button in the Property Sheet. This invokes the Choose Builder dialog. Choose the Code Builder option.

15. VBE opens and an event method called Form Dirty is automatically created. Add the following code to this event:

```
If (MsgBox("Change this record?", vbYesNo, "Modify Record?") <> vbYes) Then
    Cancel = True
EndIf
```

16. Close the VBE by clicking the X on the top right of the window. The event method is automatically added, but it is a good idea to click the Save button to save all changes to the form.

The next time that the data on the Contact Details form is modified, the user is prompted with a message box asking "Change this record?" If they choose No, the change to the form is cancelled; if they choose Yes, the change is accepted. Of course this requires that the database be enabled. Adding code to a form using the Code Builder option in the Property Sheet is just that simple!

Congratulations, you now have successfully set some the form properties using the Property Sheet. As mentioned previously, you can also use code to set the values of properties, but we will save that for a later lesson. The important thing to take away from this lesson is getting used to working with the Access UI, the Property Sheet, to set and modify the various properties.

SUMMARY

Setting form properties, or any object properties in general, is a big part of building database applications in Access. Using the Property Sheet to set form properties is quick and easy to do. As you become more familiar with the Access form properties, you'll also become more accustomed to using the Property Sheet and may find that one day you cannot live without it! And don't forget, if you ever want to know what a specific property does, just click the property and read the message in the Access status bar. Working with form properties in Access couldn't be easier!

 Please select Lesson 33 on the DVD to view the video that accompanies this lesson.

34

Access 2010 Form Controls

One of the most powerful features of the Access Forms package is the built-in control set that Access 2010 provides. These controls supply the Access developer with some very common control types for building robust, professional-looking Windows Forms very quickly. As part of the new features of Access 2010, a couple of new controls have been added to improve upon this already solid set of controls. This lesson discusses the Access 2010 Form Controls and provides some examples about how these controls can be used in a database application.

LESSON SETUP

This lesson discusses controls in Access 2010 Form objects. You should be familiar with creating forms in databases and their basics as discussed in the previous lessons. Otherwise, no prior knowledge of Access Form controls is required for completing this lesson.

THE BUILT-IN ACCESS CONTROLS

Access 2010 has about 20 built-in controls, which can be placed on forms to provide some specific functionality to that form. For example, you could place a Button control on a form that a user could click to open another form or maybe even submit some data on that form. Regardless of the task that needs to be accomplished, Access 2010 provides a multitude of very common and flexible Windows-style controls. The following is a list of common controls that are included in Access 2010 (but this is by no means a complete list):

➤ **TextBox Control** — A standard Windows-style text box that a user can type text into.

➤ **Label Control** — A control that displays some text, but cannot be manipulated by the user. Labels are commonly paired with another control, such as a TextBox, and used to display the name of that control.

➤ **Button Control** — Also referred to as Command control in Access, this control provides a standard Windows-style Button control that a user can click.

➤ **Tab Control** — The `Tab` and `TabPage` controls provide tabular-style features that show different nested forms depending on which tab is selected.

➤ **Web Browser Control** — Updated in the Access 2010 release. This control provides a custom browser window that allows web pages to be loaded inside of it.

➤ **Navigation Control** — New to Access 2010. Provides a standard web-style navigation menu for web forms, which provides breadcrumbs to other web forms.

➤ **Option Group Control** — A Windows-style grouping area for a form, which will have some other controls, such as several `OptionButton`, placed within it.

➤ **Option Button Control** — A Windows-style radio button control that shows a dot in it when selected.

➤ **Combo Box Control** — A text box that can be typed in, but also has a pull-down menu that provides list items.

➤ **List Box Control** — A text box that contains a list of items from which the user can select.

➤ **Toggle Button Control** — A `Button` control that has an on/off-style interface. When the button is clicked, it shows as on until it is clicked again to turn it off.

➤ **Line Control** — A simple line that can be placed in a form. Often this control is used to visually separate the different sections of a form.

➤ **Rectangle Control** — A simple box of lines that can be placed on a form. This control is very similar to the `Line` control.

➤ **CheckBox Control** — A Windows-style check box control that shows a check mark when selected, otherwise it shows as empty.

➤ **Bound Object Frame Control** — The Bound Object Frame control is tied to a particular OLE object, such as an embedded Word Document, PDF, or image viewer.

➤ **Unbound Object Frame Control** — Similar to the Bound Object Frame, the Unbound Object Frame is a placeholder that can be dynamically tied to objects during the execution of the database application, and can have a changing data source.

➤ **Attachment Control** — Specifically for `Attachment` data types in Access, the `Attachment` control allows the user to work with Attachment record data stored in a table.

➤ **Subform/Subreport Control** — This control allows other database objects, including Forms, Reports, Queries, and Charts, to be shown in the current form.

➤ **Image Control** — A simple control for displaying images in the form.

➤ **Calendar Control** — Specifically for `Date/Time` data types, the `Calendar` control provides the user with the ability to select dates in a calendar-style format control.

In addition to these extremely useful controls, which are shown on the Ribbon, Access supports ActiveX and COM controls. This includes (if you have Office installed) any user controls that are built into Office, as well as pretty much any controls built in .NET or previous Windows-based platforms. This is truly an amazing feature of Access, because it provides the developer with the flexibility to add almost any control to a database application.

Knowing the Access control set well is very important for building solid database applications, but once the control has been placed, you may want to add some custom functionality behind it. One of the benefits to Access 2010 is that Access Macro features provide a lot of functionality that can be called from the events of a control. And in addition to macros, VBA (Visual Basic for Applications) code, the programming language that is included in Access and many other Office 2010 programs, allows the user to add a broad range of functionalities to the control. This lesson provides both macro and simple VBA code examples, but for more information about programming VBA code, please refer to the later lessons in this book, starting with Lesson 51.

THE DESIGN RIBBON FOR FORMS

The first tab of both the Form Design Tools and Form Layout Tools Ribbons is the Design tab. The Design tabs for both of these Ribbons provide options for working with the built-in controls used in Access forms. These controls are found under the Controls section of this Ribbon, as shown in Figure 34-1.

FIGURE 34-1

As you build more Access applications, you are likely to become very familiar with this Ribbon tab. From here, you can drop the different built-in controls right onto the form that you currently have opened in either Layout or Design mode. The Ribbon also provides the ability to quickly switch between the different Form View modes, as well as open the Property Sheet, Field List, and VBE (Visual Basic Editor), three very common actions taken by a developer when building Access Forms. Get to know the Design Ribbon well; it will definitely be your friend in Access 2010.

ADDING CONTROLS TO FORMS

Several methods exist for adding controls to a form using Access 2010, several of which are described in the following sections.

Adding Controls from the Ribbon

Adding any of the built-in controls to a form is quite simple to do through the Ribbon. In general, while the form is open in Design or Layout View, simply click the control option on the Ribbon and then click the location in the form where you wish to place the new control. However, some of the built-in control options, when accessed from the Ribbon, have a wizard or builders associated with them and when you choose that option, you will be prompted to supply more information when creating the control. Fortunately, these Access builders make it very easy and you can just follow the on-screen steps to complete the task.

Adding Controls from the Navigation Pane

Subform and Subreport controls can be added to a form in Access directly from the Navigation Pane, as you have seen in previous lessons. To add a Subform or Subreport on the Navigation Pane, simply click it and drag it onto a form that is open in either Layout or Design View mode. A Subform or Subreport object will be added to show the selected object directly within the parent form. This means that all of the properties for the Subform or Subreport control were set automatically by Access when it created the control on the form. This shows the true power of the Access 2010 designers, because Access makes it just so simple!

Adding Controls from the Field List Pane

The Field List pane is specifically designed to make it easy to add TextBox and Label controls for a specific data field for any given table or query in the database. To add a control from the Field List, click the desired field name and drag it into a form that is open in either Layout or Design View mode. A new TextBox and Label control will be added to the form, which are tied directly to the selected field in the Field List. This means that all of the properties needed to make this TextBox control work with that field in the database have already been set for you automatically and are ready to begin using.

SETTING CONTROL PROPERTIES

Once a control has been added to a form, you often will need to set some of its properties to get the desired behavior from the control. You have several methods for setting control properties and each of these methods is described here.

Using the Property Sheet

As you have already seen in previous lessons, using the Property Sheet is a very common method for setting the properties in forms. Because the Property Sheet provides a list of all of the properties that the control supports, it is very easy to find the desired property and set it. Although using the Property Sheet is the most common method for setting properties, it is not the only method.

Using the Access Designers

When you use the Access visual designers to create a form, either Layout or Design View mode, Access is really just setting the properties of the form "under the covers." For example, when you drop a Report object from the Navigation Pane onto a form opened in Layout or Design View mode, it creates a Subreport control and sets all of the properties to make that control work correctly for the specified form. Modifying controls with the visual designers is no different! When you move the control around the form or resize it, the Access Form Designer is simply setting the control's properties. Using the Access Form Designer to work with controls is probably the easiest method for setting control properties.

Using VBA Code

The most flexible, and also very common, method for setting properties for controls is by using VBA code. Though it may take some effort to write the code to set the control property, the benefit is that these properties can be set dynamically at run time and allow the developer to specify the conditions and values to which the control is set. This can be extremely handy when building the logic for an application and has an immeasurable number of uses. The only trick is that you have to know how to program VBA, which we talk much more about later in this book, starting with Lesson 51.

Default Properties for Controls

One other thing to know about the Access built-in control set is that most of the controls have what is called a default property. The default property of a control is the property that is implicitly referenced when setting or retrieving the value of a control. The default property for a control is special because it can be referenced without having to set focus to the control first. In addition, you don't even have to reference that property to get or set the value; you can just get or set it from the base control. The default property for any given control is usually the most commonly used property. For example, the default property for the TextBox control is the Text property. Although it probably doesn't make a lot of difference to you now, this is actually an important fact about controls that you will probably employ often as you learn to develop more with VBA.

Values for Control Properties

The actual values that can be set on a control are dependent upon the specific type of control. If you are setting these values through the Property Sheet, it is fairly intuitive to know what data type an object is and what values it can be set to, because often the control's description and purpose are descriptive enough to figure it out. As you've seen in previous lessons, the Property Sheet will often provide lists, builders, or wizards for setting various properties. But even then, the data type for the property may not always be clear, and it can be rather confusing at times to figure this out.

A quick way to know the exact data type of a property is to look up the object in the VBE (Visual Basic Editor) Object Browser. The VBE Object Browser allows the user to search and examine any VBA object's methods, properties, events, and collections. To open the Object Browser at any time, simply use the Alt+F11 keystroke combination to open VBE and then press the F2 hotkey to open the Object Browser. From there, you can search the name of the control; once you have found and selected it, the first line on the very bottom pane will tell you the data type for the control. For example, if you were to find and select the Text property for the TextBox control, this text would say "Property Text as String," with String being the data type for the property. Figure 34-2 provides an example of what this would look like.

Help with Controls and Control Properties

Sometimes even knowing the value type, the description, and what the control can do is still not enough information to know what value to set for a property. Fortunately, Access 2010 provides fairly comprehensive help and tutorial features that can be called on at any time. To find out more about what a specific control or property does, select that control and press the F1 hotkey. This will open the Help menu, and if available, in the specific context of the referenced control. The Access help provides tons of information about the built-in Access controls as well as some examples for setting these controls, including sample code. If all else fails, `http://office.microsoft.com`, the Office homepage, and `http://msdn.microsoft.com`, the MSDN homepage, both provide an enormous amount of information and resources for Access 2010. There is literally 15 years' worth of information and code samples available on the web.

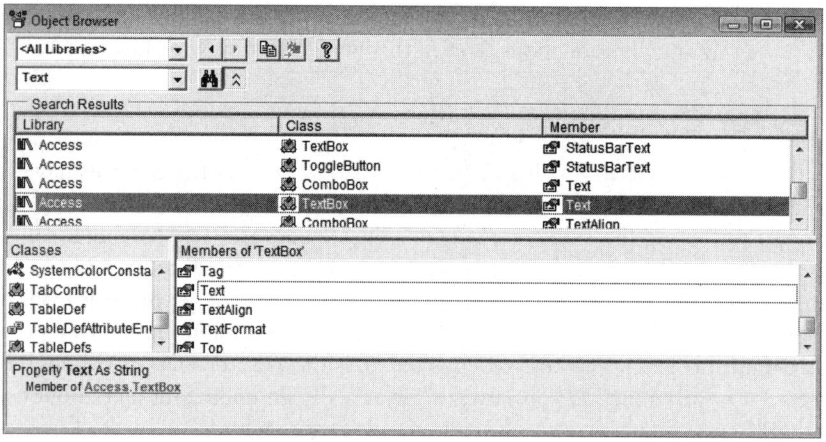

FIGURE 34-2

TRY IT

In this lesson you build a form by adding some controls to it to provide some custom functionality to the form. By now you should understand the basics of what a control is in Access, where they can be added from, and how to set their values. However, the best way to really get to know these controls is to practice with them. The following step-by-step example walks you through each of the steps necessary to accomplish this task. Sample files are available on the book's DVD and website.

Lesson Requirements

The example steps use the Northwind 2010 database application created from a template. However, Northwind 2010 is not required for this lesson; you can use just about any database application that has some tables in it. In either case, this example focuses on adding and setting some controls for a form, based on a normal Access table object.

Hints

The following is a list of some common hotkeys that can make it easier to navigate through the Access UI and find the information you need:

➤ The F4 hotkey opens the Property Sheet.

➤ The Alt+F8 keystroke combination opens the Field List.

➤ The Alt+F11 keystroke combination opens VBE.

➤ The F2 hotkey in VBE opens the Object Browser.

➤ Click a property in the Property Sheet to shows its description in the Access status bar.

Remember, controls can only be added and modified in a form when it is open in either Design or Layout View modes.

Step-by-Step

1. Open Access 2010 from the Windows Start menu. The Access Backstage will open in the Access window.

2. In the Backstage, click the New option on the left-hand menu and then click the Sample Templates option to show a list of the built-in templates.

3. Choose the Northwind option from the list of templates and click the Create button on the right side of the screen to create the sample database application. The new Northwind database will open in the Access window.

4. Click the Create tab on the Ribbon and choose the Form Design option. This opens a new form in Design View. Notice that the Ribbon automatically switches to the Design tab on the Form Design Tools Ribbon.

5. Click the `TextBox` control (the second control from the left in the Controls section) and then click in the top-left corner of the form to add the control to it. Notice that both `Label` and `TextBox` controls have been added to the form.

6. Click the `Label` twice to select it and begin editing its text, and type in **Name**. The Access designer automatically sets the `Caption` property for the `Label` to the value Name.

To verify the `Label Caption` property has indeed been modified by the Access Form Designer, press F4 to open the Property Sheet (if it is not already open). While the `Label` is selected, click the All tab of the Property Sheet and examine the `Caption` property; it is set to the value "Name."

7. Next, click the `TextBox` control to select it and change its `Name` property to **txtName** in the Property Sheet. The `Name` property for a control specifies by which name the control can be referenced.

8. In the Design Ribbon, click the `Button` control and then click to the right of the `TextBox` control on the form to place the `Button` control to the right of the `TextBox`. This invokes the Command Button Wizard, but just cancel this for now.

9. For the button you just dropped on the form, set the `Name` property to **btnFilter** and the `Caption` property to **Filter** via the Property Sheet.

10. From the Navigation Pane, switch the view mode to Object Type, and drag the `Customers` table onto the form. This creates a subform for the `Customers` table to be shown in Datasheet mode.

11. Set the `Name` property for this subform to **subCustomers** from the Property Sheet. Notice that the object `Source` property is set to `Table.Customers`, which is how the subform knows how to display the `Customers` table.

12. Click the `btnFilter` button to select it again.

13. In the Property Sheet, click the Events tab. Click the ... (Builder) button for the `On Click` event. This invokes the Choose Builder dialog, so choose the Macro Builder option.

14. Once the Macro Builder is open, choose the SetFilter option from the pull-down option list. This opens up three new options to set.

15. Set the `Where Condition` property to:

```
= "[First Name] LIKE '" & Nz([txtName], "*") & "'"
```

16. Although this statement may look pretty strange, you are simply building the Where condition for a SQL statement to filter on, using the value that the user has typed into the `txtName` `TextBox` control. The `Nz()` function is simply saying that is there is no data there, so use the `*` operator, which, combined with the `LIKE` keyword, will show all records in the table.

17. Set the `Control Name` property to **subCustomers** to tell the macro to filter this subform.

18. Close and save the new macro by clicking the X directly to the right of the Macro Builder tab. The macro will now be added to the `On Click` event for the `Button` control.

19. Now, adjust all of the controls on the form so that they fit nicely by using the designer and dragging and adjusting the controls with the mouse cursor.

20. Click the Save button on the top left of the Access window to save to the form. It is now complete and ready to use!

Your form should look similar to Figure 34-3.

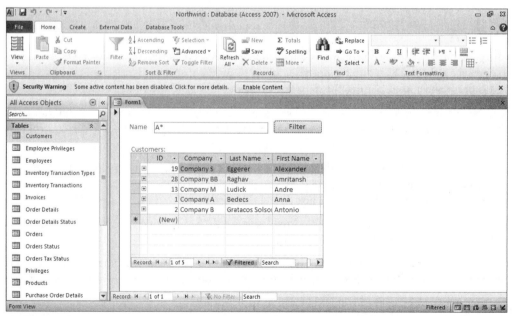

FIGURE 34-3

There should be a `TextBox`, a `Button`, and a `Subform` control on the form. Switch the form to Form View to try it out. Once in Form View, type **A*** into the `TextBox` control and then click the Filter button. Voilà, the `Customers` subform is filtered to people whose first names start with A. If you remove the text from the `TextBox` and then click the Filter button again, it shows all of the records in the `Customers` table once again. Congratulations, you now have successfully added controls to forms and set their properties, and you have created a form that can filter on a subform in fewer than 10 minutes!

SUMMARY

Using the various controls in Access is very easy to do and, in most cases, can be done with just a few mouse clicks. Using the Ribbon and the various Access panes, the developer can quickly add the desired controls to a form. Using the Property Sheet and VBA code, the properties for these controls can be set in a snap. If you do not know, or cannot figure out, what type of values a property can be set to, you know how to look in the VBE Object Browser to find out. Using controls on your forms will enhance your database application in untold capacities, just waiting to be discovered by you!

 Please select Lesson 34 on the DVD to view the video that accompanies this lesson.

35

Working with Subforms and Subreports

Subforms and Subreports are used every day in Access 2010. The `Subform/Subreport` control enables the developer to show other database objects directly from within the parent form. The `Subform/Subreport` control is extremely flexible and provides a lot of functionality for working with subobjects, as you will see in this lesson.

LESSON SETUP

This lesson is designed to provide an overview of working with Subforms and Subreports in Access Forms. Now that you have a basic understanding of working with Access Forms, you will explore the `Subform/Subreport` control to illustrate how easy it is to work with the visual controls of Access.

SUBFORMS/SUBREPORTS IN ACCESS

Access Subforms and Subreports are nothing more than object frames that can be used to display other database objects. Like forms, Subforms and Subreports can be *Bound* or *Unbound*, depending on what functionality is desired. Binding the control really only means that the `Object Source` property has been set to some valid database object. The `Subform/Subreport` control can be bound to tables, queries, forms, reports, PivotCharts, and PivotTables.

The type of database object that is bound to a `Subform/Subreport` determines the view for what is to be displayed in the `Subform/Subreport` control. In the case of a table or query, the default view is the Access Datasheet View, showing the data that would be shown in that object. For a report, PivotChart, or PivotTable, the default normal view for the object is shown. But as for a form, that is a little trickier, because the view shown is dependent upon the form's default view and type settings, but in general, it will be the default view for the form, which is Form View. A quick way to check the default view for any object is to double-click it in the Navigation Pane to open it in its normal view mode.

Finally, the most powerful feature of the Subform/Subreport control, as with all controls, is the various properties, methods, and events it provides the developer. Often, reading and manipulating these properties during the execution of the application will be useful to provide functionality for the application. For example, you might want to filter a Subform on values that have been typed into the parent form by the user. Whatever the case, using macros and VBA code make it possible to manipulate a Subform/Subreport, or any control's properties, at run time.

The Source Object Property

The most important property of the Subform/Subreport control is the Source Object property. The Source Object property is a text string that determines the object that will be displayed within the Subform/Subreport control. The Source Object property can be any table, query, form, report, PivotTable, or PivotChart that is a member of, or linked to, the current database. This property can be set at design time using the Property Sheet or set at run time using macros or VBA code.

Adding Bound Subforms

As discussed in the previous lesson, Subform/Subreport controls can be added directly from the Navigation Pane. When they are dropped on the parent form in this manner, all the properties needed to make the control work with the selected object are set automatically by the Access designer. Because a Subform has its Source Object property set when it is dropped on the form, it is considered a Bound object. The term *Bound* means that the control is now connected to the source object and it can now show its data. That is, the Subform/Subreport control will automatically show the object that its Source Object property is set to, when the parent form is open in its normal view mode. However, you can always change the value of the Source Object property to whatever value is desired, at run time or otherwise, thus binding the Subform to a different object.

Adding Unbound Subforms

Unbound Subform controls can also be created very easily. If you drop a Subform/Subreport control from the Control section in the Design Ribbon, the resulting control that is placed on the form will not have its Source Object property set, making it Unbound. There are many reasons why you might want to use an unbound Subform or Subreport to an application; for example, you might plan to set it at a later time when the form is created or you want to set it dynamically during application execution. Regardless of the reason, when the Subform is not bound to anything and the parent form is open in its normal view mode, the Subform/Subreport control will simply show a blank space in its place. Remember, you can always bind the control at any time by setting its Source Object property, or for that matter, unbind the control by clearing its Source Object property. Creating Unbound Subform and Subreport controls is easily accomplished when adding the control from the Ribbon.

DESIGNING SUBFORMS AND SUBREPORTS

There are really two pieces to working with a `Subform/Subreport` control: the control itself and the Subform(s) and/or Subreport(s) that will be displayed within the control. We have already talked about placing and working with the control itself, but what about the source object that it will display? Presumably, once a `Subform/Subreport` control has been placed on a form, it will be set to some database object to display its data, at design time or at runtime. There are several factors to take into consideration when working with the `Subform/Subreport` control, each of which is discussed in this section.

Creating the Underlying Object

Often it is easiest to create the underlying object that will be shown in the `Subform/Subreport` control first, before adding the control to a different, parent form. Creating the source object first allows you to get everything working correctly on the source object, before creating the parent object. However, it is often good to consider that the object will be used as a subobject on a different form when deciding on its design.

Also, if the object is another form or report, it can be designed directly within the parent form, when it is in Design or Layout View mode. The Access designer is smart enough to detect if the underlying subobject is the right type and thus open the underlying object in Design or Layout View mode when its parent is opened in that mode. This can be extremely handy for quickly modifying the underlying object. But remember, any changes that are made to this object and are saved, are saved to the underlying object, and will be reflected in instances of that object.

Sizing the Subform/Subreport Control

It is important to consider that that size of the `Subform/Subreport` control does not determine the size of the of the source object. If the source object is larger than the `Subform/Subreport` control, the control will have scroll bars for moving around the subobject. On a personal note, we find these very undesirable in most cases, so it can be useful to size the subobject to fit the space that the `Subform/Subreport` control will consume. Setting the size appropriately for both the `Subform/Subreport` control and the object it will display can reduce the confusion for the application user and can make it look a lot more professional.

The Anchor Properties

One exception to the sizing rule is the various Anchor properties of the `Subform/Subreport` control. You should be aware of two Anchor properties that were originally added in Access 2007: the `Horizontal Anchor` property and the `Vertical Anchor` property. These anchoring properties, which are properties of all of the Access Form controls that are visual, allow the developer to set a relative location for one or more of the borders for the control. That means that if the form size is changed, the control size will scale with it, depending on how the anchors are set. This is important in Access, especially in Tabular Document mode, because depending on the size of the screen of the user, the overall size a database object, such as a form, will be displayed will be different. Setting the `Vertical Anchors` will lock the top, bottom, or both borders of the controls to their relative positions on the forms, and the `Horizontal Anchors` will lock the left, right, or both borders to their relative positions on the form. But remember, if and when the subobject is larger than the area that the Subform/Subreport control takes up, you will have scrolling bars for viewing the full area of the subobject.

 Tabular Document mode is the Access window mode where each form has a tab at the top of the Access window instead of each object being in its own separate window.

Modifying Properties of the Control

It is also important to understand that modifying the properties of the Subform/Subreport control does not affect the underlying control itself. For example, if you set a filter on the Subform/Subreport control, this filter is not placed on the underlying object, and will only be reflected on the data that is displayed by the control. However, if you place a filter on the underlying object itself, that change will be reflected by any Subform/Subreport controls that display that underlying object. Remember, the Subform/Subreport control itself is a separate entity from the underlying object that it is displaying, and thus changes made to the control do not directly affect the underlying object.

TRY IT

In this lesson you create a form that contains a Subform control that displays a second form. By now you should have a pretty good understanding of what the Subform/Subreport control does in Access and how it can be used. The best way to really understand the Subform/Subreport control is to put the knowledge to use and try it yourself. The following steps walk you through an example of creating a form that uses a Subform/Subreport control. Sample files are available on the book's DVD and website.

Lesson Requirements

For this lesson, the example steps use the Northwind database application created from a template. However, the Northwind database is not necessarily required for this lesson; you can use just about any database application that has some tables in it. In either case, this example focuses on working with a Subform/Subreport control, and not necessarily the data displayed within the control.

Hints

The following is a list of some common hotkeys that can make it easier to navigate through the Access UI and find the information you need:

➤ The F4 hotkey opens the Properties Sheet.

➤ The Shift+F2 keystroke combination opens the Zoom dialog.

➤ Click a property in the Property Sheet to show its description in the Access status bar.

Remember that controls can only be added and modified in a form when it is open in either Design or Layout View mode.

Step-by-Step

1. Open Access 2010 from the Windows Start menu. The Access Backstage will open in the Access window.

2. In the Backstage, click the New option on the left-hand menu and then click the Sample Templates option to show a list of the built-in templates.

3. Choose the Northwind option from the list of templates and click the Create button on the right side of the screen to create the sample database application. The new Northwind database will open in the Access window.

4. Click the Create tab on the Ribbon and choose the Form Design option. This opens a new form in Design View. Notice that the Ribbon automatically switches to the Design tab on the Form Design Tools Ribbon.

5. In the Controls section of the Design Ribbon, click the pull-down menu for the controls and choose the Combo Box option. Then click in the top middle of the form's design surface. The ComboBox and a Label controls will be added to the form and the Combo Box Wizard will be invoked.

6. Click the Cancel button on the wizard; the properties for this control will be set manually.

7. Double-click the Label control to edit its text, and type in **Choose Report** as the new value.

8. Press the F4 button to open the Property Sheet and then click the ComboBox control so that it is selected and its properties are shown in the Property Sheet.

9. Click the All tab of the Property Sheet and change the Name property to **cboReports** to change the name of the control.

10. Click the Data tab of the Property Sheet, click in the value field for the Row Source property, and press the Shift+F2 keystroke combination. This invokes the Zoom builder for the Row Source property.

 The Zoom dialog is extremely helpful for working with properties that contain long string values. The Zoom dialog allows the developer to see much more text at one time than just the bit that is displayed in the Property Sheet.

11. Type the following SQL statement in the Zoom builder to set the Row Source property:

```
SELECT [MSysObjects].[Name]
FROM [MSysObjects]
WHERE ([MSysObjects].[Type]=-32764)
ORDER BY [MSysObjects].[Name];
```

This query will select all of the names of the report objects in the database, and binding the query to the Control Source property will display them in the ComboBox control.

12. Make sure that the Row Source Type property is set to Table/Query (which should be the default setting).

Congratulations, you now have a `ComboBox` that displays all of the reports in the database automatically, by querying the `MSysObjects` table, the Access system table that stores information about the object in the database. Next the `Subform/Subreport` needs to be added and the `ComboBox` needs to be hooked up to modify the Subreport when a different value is selected. To accomplish this task, complete the following steps:

13. In the Controls section of the Design Ribbon, click the pull-down menu for the controls and choose the Subform/Subreport option. Then click just below the `Label` for the `ComboBox` control to add the `Subform/Subreport` control to the form's design surface.

14. Double-click the new control's `Label` control to edit its text, and type in **Report** as the new value.

15. Click the `Subform/Subreport` control to select it, such that its properties are shown in the Property Sheet.

16. Click the All tab of the Property Sheet and change the `Name` property to **subReports** to rename the control.

17. Click the Format tab of the Property Sheet and change the `Horizontal Anchor` property to Both to set the left and right control border anchors on both sides of the form.

18. Click the `ComboBox` control to select it, such that its properties are shown in the Property Sheet.

19. Click the Event tab of the Property Sheet and click the "..." (Builder) button for the `On Change` event. This invokes the Choose Builder dialog; click the Code Builder option and click OK. This invokes VBE (the Visual Basic Editor) and creates a subroutine for the event automatically, called `cboReports_Change()`, which is the change event for the `ComboBox` control.

20. Inside this subroutine, add the following line of code:

```
Me!subReports.SourceObject = "Report." & Me!cboReports.Value
```

This code simply sets the `Source Object` property of the `Subform/Subreport` control to the text string "Report." plus the name of the selected report in the `ComboBox`. This event will be triggered any time a person selects a different report, and thus it will automatically be displayed for them in the parent form.

21. Close VBE once you have added this code. It will be automatically added to the form.

22. Now adjust all of the controls to fit the form nicely.

23. Click the Save button in the top-left corner of the Access window and click OK for the default name, which is `Form1` in this case.

24. Because this form now actually has code in it, you must enable code in the database by clicking the Enable Content button on the Security Warning bar across the top of the Access window. Once the code has been enabled in the database, you should be able to see your new form in action, and it should look something like Figure 35-1.

Congratulations, you now have successfully created a form that displays different reports in a `Subform/Subreport` control that can be updated on the fly. Along the way, you learned a little something about the `ComboBox` control and even wrote a little VBA code. Not as hard as one would expect! In fact, you created this brand new form in less than 10 minutes using Access 2010.

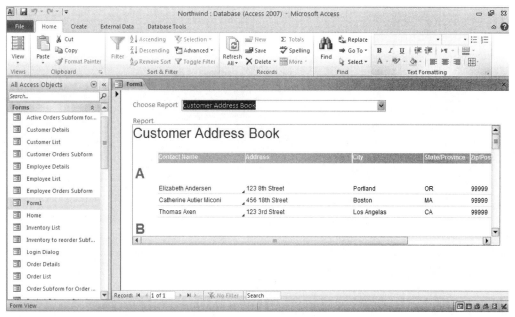

FIGURE 35-1

SUMMARY

The `Subform/Subreport` control is an extremely useful and widely used control in Access database solutions. In this lesson, you learned about what the `Subform/Subreport` control is and how it can be used within an Access application. The most important property of the control, the `Source Object` property, determines which database object is displayed in the control. And you learned that working with the properties of this control is extremely easy to do, both through the Property Sheet and through VBA code. The `Subform/Subreport` control is definitely a handy feature of forms that is found only in Access.

 Please select Lesson 35 on the DVD to view the video that accompanies this lesson.

36

Embedded Macros in Forms

Macros is one of the major Microsoft Access features that has been greatly improved upon in the last several releases of the product. Access 2010 has a completely revamped Macro Designer that makes it easier than ever to create macros in a database application. Using macros can be extremely easy, especially considering you do not need to know any special code to make them work. Using macros in forms can be a very simple, yet extremely effective method for enhancing the functionality of forms in an Access database.

LESSON SETUP

This lesson provides an overview of working with embedded macros in Access Forms. Now that you have a basic understanding of working with Access Forms and the controls that can be used on them, you explore the building of some embedded macros in a form to show how easy it is to build macros for forms using Access 2010.

MACROS IN ACCESS

The term *macro* in Access refers to a type of functionality that can be executed when the macro is called. A macro can have one or more actions that execute in sequence. The best part about them is that building macros is as easy as choosing items from a list, like in the Property Sheet. Basically two types of macros can be used in forms: Named Macros and Embedded Macros. These types of macros are basically the same, with a few distinct differences.

Named Macros

Named Macros, also known as *standalone macros,* are created as database objects. This is really the base type of macro object. A Named Macro object, as its moniker suggests, has a name attached to it, so that the macro is referred to by name. Named Macros can be called from any place in the database application where macros are allowed to be called. Named Macros are separate entities from other objects in the database and exist in their own context, without necessarily depending on other objects (though in most cases, they do).

Although Named Macros are a huge part of the Access product, this lesson focuses mainly on Embedded Macros in Forms. But do not worry: Lessons 46 through 50 of this book are devoted to discussing, in depth, building macros. This chapter is really about adding Embedded Macros using the Access Form designer.

Embedded Macros

Embedded Macros live directly within another database object, such as a form or report. These macros also consist of one or more actions, but these macros are part of the parent object and execute actions based upon the events occurring within the parent object. The nice part about using Embedded Macros is that the Access Form designer makes it very easy to embed macros in any object with just a few clicks, as you have seen in previous lessons. However, one drawback to Embedded Macros is that you may find yourself making the same macro over and over again, with just minor differences in the objects. In any event, the Access form designer makes it quick and easy to build Embedded Macros right into your forms, and the functionality is sure to be astounding!

The Access 2010 Macro Designer

Redesigned in Access 2010, the Macro designer is the place to build Macros. The Access Macro designer has been made to make it easy to create macros, either Named or Embedded, and works very well for building Macros on the fly in your forms and reports. The Access Macro designer provides a user interface where all of the possible macros can be selected from a list, and then, once selected, the designer provides a list of parameters, as well as the possible settings for many of these parameters. This designer is shown in Figure 36-1.

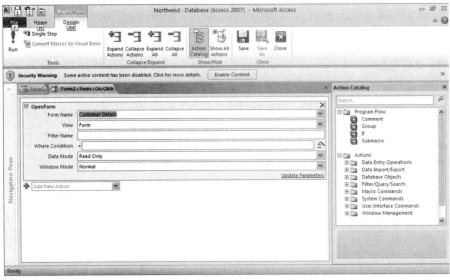

FIGURE 36-1

When an Embedded Macro is created, it is always immediately tied to the event of some database object or control on that database object. For example, you might create an Embedded Macro to open a form when the `On Click` event of a button is fired. Once the particular event is triggered, the macro's actions are executed in sequence from top to bottom, as they are shown in the Access Macro designer. Data can be passed between these macros using `TempVars`, temporary variables for use in macros. Of course, if the macro only consists of one action, this doesn't really matter, but if there are multiple actions, and there often are, you can specify the order of actions by ordering the macro procedures from top to bottom appropriately.

New Macro Features in Access 2010

In addition to these previously existing features of macros, Access 2010 provides a couple of brand new features to macros: Conditional branching, an updated designer UI (user interface), IntelliSense in the Access Macro designer, and an enhanced Action Catalog. The conditional branching features are provided in the forms of if/else if/else actions that can be built directly into the macro. The new layout and look of the Access Macro designer make it easier to read and build macros very quickly, as well as provide a host of new features, such as some new builders that are included with the designer. The IntelliSense feature both increases productivity and reduces the chances of error by providing a list of available options when typing text into the fields in the Access Macro designer. The Action Catalog is easier than ever to choose the macro actions from. Although it may not sound like all that much on paper, these new features in Access 2010 make a world of difference when building macros.

Adding Macros to Forms and Controls

Embedded Macros are always added to form and control events, which is easily done using the Property Sheet. In fact, you've already created a number of Embedded Macros if you followed all the steps in the previous lessons. To add an Embedded Macro to a form or control event, simply click the "…" (Builder) button in the Property Sheet for the desired event and choose the Macro Builder option. The Access Macro designer will be opened to create a new macro, if there is not one already existing for this event. If a macro already exists for the event, the Access Macro designer will open the existing macro in edit mode, so that it may be modified. When you are done adding the macro actions and setting the various properties, simply close the Access Macro designer and the macro will be added to the form. Once you save the modified form, all changes to the macro will be persisted to the form object.

The Macro-to-VBA Code Converter

Novice users of Access prefer to use the Access Macro designer over writing VBA code, because it offers a lot more simplicity for quickly building the desired functionality. But, it is important to know that anything that can be done in a macro can also be done in VBA code. For this reason, Access 2010 continues to provide the Macro-to-VBA converter, which will convert any macro directly to its VBA code. The Macro-to-VBA converter button is under the Tools group on the Form Design Tools Design Ribbon. This can be very helpful when first learning VBA, especially when you don't know how to write the code for a function that you know a macro can perform. You can simply convert the macro to code to see how to create a same functionality in VBA. Though macros are much easier to build through the Access UI than VBA code, VBA code provides a lot of flexibility overall.

ENABLING MACROS IN ACCESS

Actually running macros in Access 2010 may prove to be trickier than you might expect. As mentioned in previous chapters in the book, the security features of Access, by default, block VBA code and unsafe macros from executing until the database is in a Trusted state. However, this does not block all macros from running; only unsafe macros are blocked from executing when the database is in disabled mode. Once the database is placed in a Trusted state, typically by clicking the Enable button on the Access 2010 Security Bar, all code and macros can run freely, without deterrence from Access application security. The following sections describe some of the differences between safe and unsafe macros.

Safe Macros

Safe, or Trusted, macros do not actually change the objects or data in the database; neither can they modify or change settings on the machine that the application is running on. For example, opening an Access form, all else being equal, does not actually change any data in the database, nor by itself does it modify or change any settings on the machine. It simply displays the form for the user to see. Therefore, a macro such as this can be considered Trusted, because it cannot actually affect the database or machine in any way.

The major benefit to using Trusted macros is that the database is not required to be Trusted to actually execute these macro actions. Because they are deemed safe, Access will run them regardless of the Access application security state. If your database can function without VBA code or unsafe macros, this will potentially save the user of the application one extra step of having to enable the database every time the application is invoked. However, the scope and overall feature set of Trusted macros is fairly limited; you might need to use unsafe macros to get the most power out of your database application.

Unsafe Macros

Unsafe, or Untrusted, macros can perform actions that can potentially change the database objects, data in the database, or the settings on the machine that the database is running on. This is truly the essence of the power of unsafe macros, though — they can do so much, with so little effort. These macros can add/modify/delete data, run action queries, save changes to database objects, and so forth. Though unsafe macros are powerful, they come at the cost of requiring the database to be enabled before these actions can be executed. You can always spot an unsafe macro in the Access Macro designer by the warning icon to the left of the name of the macro action, as shown in Figure 36-2.

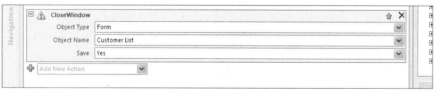

FIGURE 36-2

TRY IT

In this lesson you create a form and some Embedded Macros for it. By now you should have a pretty good understanding of what Embedded Macros are in Access and how they can be added to form and control events. But the best way to get to know Embedded Macros and the Access 2010 Macro designer is to try to build a few macros. The following steps walk you through how to build a form that uses Embedded Macros to perform its actions. Sample files are available on the book's DVD and website.

Lesson Requirements

For this lesson, the example steps use the Northwind database application created from a template. However, the Northwind database is not necessarily required for this lesson; you can use just about any database application that has some tables in it. This example focuses on building Embedded Macros in forms and controls, and does not necessarily require the data or database objects in the Northwind database.

Hints

The following is a list of some things you might find helpful when creating Embedded Macros:

➤ The F4 hotkey opens the Property Sheet.

➤ Closing the Macro designer automatically adds the Embedded Macro to the form.

➤ The Embedded Macro will be saved, once the parent form has been saved.

Remember, Embedded Macros can only be added and modified in a form when it is open in either Form Design View or Form Layout View mode.

Step-by-Step

1. Open Access 2010 from the Windows Start menu. The Access Backstage will open in the Access window.

2. In the Backstage, click the New option on the left-hand menu and then click the Sample Templates option to show a list of the built-in templates.

3. Choose the Northwind option from the list of templates and click the Create button on the right side of the screen to create the sample database application. The new Northwind database will open in the Access window.

4. Switch the Navigation Pane grouping setting to Object Type.

5. In the Navigation Pane, under the Tables group, click the Customers table to select it.

6. Click the Create tab on the Ribbon and choose the Split Form option from the More Forms pull-down menu on the Forms section of the Ribbon. This opens a new Split Form in Layout View, with the Customers table set to its Record Source property.

7. Click the View pull-down in the View section of the Design Ribbon and choose the Form Design option to switch the form to Design View mode.

8. Delete all of the `TextBox` and `Label` controls on the form, except the `ID`, `Company`, `First Name`, `Last Name`, and `Job Title` `TextBox` and `Label` controls. Adjust the form and the controls to fit nicely here.

9. Click the `TextBox` control for the `ID` field to select it.

10. Press the F4 key to open the Property Sheet, if it is not already open. The `ID` `TextBox` control properties should be selected in it.

11. Click the Event tab of the Property Sheet and click the "…" (Builder) button of the `OnClick` event to invoke the Choose Builder dialog. Choose the Macro Builder option and click the OK button. The macro builder will open for the `TextBox` control's `OnClick` event.

12. In the pull-down menu for the first macro action in the Access Macro designer, choose the `OpenForm` action. This opens up six new fields for the parameter settings of the `OpenForm` macro.

13. For the Form Name, choose `Customer Details`. For the Where Condition, type in the following text:

```
="ID=" & NZ([ID], -1)
```

For the Data Mode, choose the Edit option.

14. Close the Macro Builder and choose Yes when prompted to save changes to the macro. The macro will now be added to the `OnClick` event for the `TextBox` control.

15. Repeat Steps 11 through 14 for the `Company`, `First Name`, `Last Name`, and `Job Title` `TextBox` controls. The macro should now be applied to each of these controls.

16. Click the Save button in the top-left corner of the Access window to save the form. Choose a name, such as Form1, and click OK to save the form.

Congratulations, you have successfully created an embedded macro for the `OnClick` event for each of the `TextBox` controls on this new form. This form should look similar to Figure 36-3.

To see this Macro in action, simply open the form in Form View mode by double-clicking it in the Ribbon. Once the form is open, if you click any of the `TextBox` controls, the `Customer Details` form will open filtered to the selected record in the Split Form. This is done by the `Where Condition` property that was specified when the macro was created. Essentially, the `Where Condition` is telling the underlying query for the form to filter the record to the `ID` of the record that was selected in the Split Form. The beauty of this example is that no matter which record is selected in the Split Form, Access always opens the `Customer Details` form filtered to the correct customer.

While this is an excellent example of an embedded macro, this was a safe macro action, and thus did not require that the database be trusted to allow the macro to execute. Try creating an unsafe macro to see the differences between the two types of macros. Complete the following steps to build an unsafe macro:

17. Click the Home tab of the Ribbon and switch the Split Form back to Design View mode, using the View pull-down menu on the Home Ribbon.

18. In the Controls group of the Design Ribbon, click the Button control to select it.

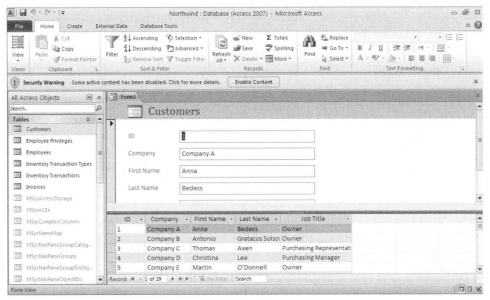

FIGURE 36-3

19. Click the area of the form to the right of the TextBox controls (or wherever there is room to add this new Button control, it doesn't really matter). This invokes the Command Button Wizard, so just hit the Cancel button to close it.

20. Press the F4 key to open the Property Sheet, if it is not already open. The new Button control properties should be selected in it.

21. In the Property Sheet, click the "…" (Builder) button for the OnClick event of the Button control.

22. This invokes the Choose Builder dialog, so select the Macro Builder option and click the OK button. The Macro designer will now be opened for the OnClick event.

23. In the pull-down menu for the first macro action in the Access Macro designer, choose the CloseWindow action. This opens up three new fields for the property settings of the CloseWindow macro.

24. For the Object Type, choose the Form option. For the Object Name, choose the name of the Split Form, in this case, Form1. For the Save option, choose Yes.

> *Notice that as soon as the Yes option is selected for the Save property, a warning icon is displayed just to the left of the macro action's name. This is to denote that the macro is an unsafe macro action and that the database will need to be enabled for the macro to execute.*

25. Close the Macro Builder and choose Yes when prompted to save changes to the macro. The macro will now be added to the `OnClick` event for the `TextBox` control.

26. Click the Save button in the top-left corner of the Access window to save all changes to the form.

Congratulations, you have now successfully created an unsafe embedded macro for the `OnClick` event of the `Button` control of your Split Form. To verify that this function only works when the database is Trusted, open `Form1` in the Form View mode and click the button, while the database is not enabled. Access will show an error message saying that the database needs to be enabled before the macro can run correctly. Just dismiss the message by clicking the OK button and close the Macro Single Step dialog.

Next, click the Enable button in the Access Security Bar. Close any Northwind forms that open and double-click `Form1` in the Navigation Pane to open it in Form View mode. Now try clicking the button again. This time the form will be promptly closed, and all changes along with it will be saved. Hopefully now you can see the differences between running safe and unsafe macros. Building Embedded Macros in Access 2010 Forms is quite a simple task, no matter which type of macros you use!

SUMMARY

Embedded Macros can be a great benefit to any Access user, from novice to advanced. Macros can be built very easily and quickly using the new Access 2010 Macro designer. The Access Macro designer provides a wide range of Macro actions, both safe and unsafe, that afford the developer a wide range of functionalities. Though a database must be enabled to run unsafe macros, these macros can provide an even greater scope of features for building robust database applications. Now that you have had the chance to learn about Embedded Macros, I encourage you to use them in your applications when possible. Embedded Macros can provide great functionality, at a very low cost, to any database application.

 Please select Lesson 36 on the DVD to view the video that accompanies this lesson.

37

Adding Code to Forms

Microsoft Access 2010 continues to provide support for VBA (Visual Basic for Applications) code, which is the programming language built into most of the Office 2010 programs, including Word, Excel, Outlook, and PowerPoint. Arguably, VBA code provides the Office application developer with the most flexible and extensible tools built into Office 2010. You can use VBA code to create almost any functionality imaginable, but it comes at a cost. The VBA language is fairly complex, and learning to write code and build high-quality programs often requires a tremendous amount of time and effort. Just learning the language and how to make it work in your application can be quite a daunting task for the novice Access user.

Although this lesson provides a brief overview of adding code to Access forms, Lessons 51 through 57 of this book are devoted to providing much more information about the VBA programming language. This lesson discusses building forms that utilize VBA code and provides some very basic examples of how to embed VBA code in forms using Access 2010.

LESSON SETUP

To begin this lesson, it is assumed that you have a basic knowledge of forms in Access 2010 and how to design and use them. Although understanding the VBA programming language is not required for this exercise, the more you know about VBA code and its functionality, the easier it will be to apply this lesson to your own database applications. However, for this lesson, it is assumed that you do not have any previous knowledge of VBA. Lessons 51 through 57 discuss working with VBA code in much more depth and we recommend reviewing those lessons for more information about VBA. This lesson provides a simple discussion of embedding VBA code in forms using Access 2010.

VBA CODE IN ACCESS 2010

Access 2010 provides the same code support for VBA as previous versions of Access, and VBE (Visual Basic Editor) remains relatively unchanged as well. So, writing code for forms is essentially the same as before, if you have written VBA code in previous versions of Access. Also, the code in any of your existing applications should work the same way as it did with Access 2007, the previous version of Access.

If you have never used VBA code before, the idea of creating it is fairly simple. *VBA code* is a series of commands that Access will execute to perform certain functionality when the database application is running (much like Access Macros objects do). Unlike macros, however, VBA code is much more flexible and provides the entire world of functionality that macros only begin to touch on. You can add and use custom code, written in other programs or even other programming languages, using VBA code. And the best part is that the VBA code and all of this functionality can be added directly to forms in your Access database applications!

Code Modules

All VBA code (and macros for that matter) written in Access are contained inside an Access Code Module, and there are several kinds of modules to be aware of. Access has basically three kinds of modules that are similar, but have minor differences: Modules, Class Modules, and Form/Report Modules. Access Modules and Class Modules are actually Access database objects that live directly in the database and do not necessarily depend or rely on any other database objects. These kinds of modules are discussed more in the VBA section of this book. Embedded code in Access Form objects uses the Form Module, which is discussed here.

Embedded Code in Forms

Form and Report Modules are different from other Access modules, because they are tied directly to the form or report and are contained directly within that object in the database. Form Modules are part of the Access Form object, and any form that contains VBA code must have a module to store that code in. Embedded code in forms is often, but not always, applied directly to events for the form, or the controls that are contained in that form. And, using VBA code, you can extend the functionality of that form to make your own custom functionality to fit your desired tasks. Embedded code in Access Forms is part of that form, can extend the form, and resides in the module tied to that form.

The HasModule Property

All forms in Access have the `HasModule` property. This property is both readable and writable, and can be used to determine if the form already has a module associated with it and can be used to specify turning on the module of a form. By default, forms do not have a module when created, until code or macros are applied to it, which helps improve the performance of the form. Forms that do not have a module associated with them are considered *Lightweight Form* objects. Otherwise, if they do have a class module, they are considered *Heavyweight Form* objects. Remember, only forms that have a module can have embedded VBA code in them.

If the form has a module, the `HasModule` property will return a value of `True`; otherwise `False`. If this property's value is set to `False`, and the form already has a module, the module will be removed and any code (and macros) in the form will be deleted. The `HasModule` property can be read in any form mode, but it can only be set when the form is in Design View mode.

 Be very careful when setting a form's `HasModule` property to `False`. If the form already has code in it, the code will be deleted and may be lost forever if that database has not been properly backed up.

EMBEDDING CODE IN A FORM

A couple of methods exist for actually adding code to a form, but they all involve using the VBE, which is the built-in code editor for VBA language. However, Access does include some tools for helping you design the VBA code for forms, reports, and controls, which will set up some of the code to get you started. Code can be added to the project by directly opening the desired module in VBE or by using the Property Sheet's builder button to build the event methods for the selected form or control event. Although these methods are slightly different, the result is the same, and code written in the Access Form Module will be embedded in the form.

Adding Code from the Property Sheet

The fastest method for adding code to an event of a form, or to the event of a control on that form, is to use the "..." (Builder) button on the Property Sheet value field for that event. As you've seen before, this invokes the Choose Builder dialog that Access 2010 provides. If you choose the Code Builder option in this dialog, you will be taken to VBE and the code needed to create the specific event method will be added to the module for the form. In fact, if the form does not already have a class module, Access will even add the Access Form Module to the form automatically when this option is used. Adding event methods from the Property Sheet is probably the quickest way to start adding code to a form.

Once the event method has been generated by Access, VBE will automatically be opened to that code and you will be ready to begin writing code for that event. Although you have been taken to that particular event method in VBE, you can write code anywhere you want to within that module. Each Access Form Module object is a single code file, so any code contained in that form (aside from the built-in methods of a form) will be in that one module. Simply typing the desired code in the module will add the code to that mode, and it can be run and modified at any time. However, the code will not actually be saved in that module until you hit the Save button in VBE or Access, or until you close VBE and are prompted to save the code changes.

The Visual Basic Editor

The Visual Basic Editor is really the only way to work with VBA code in Access or otherwise. VBE provides all of the tools necessary to develop VBA code and is a very powerful tool in

Access. VBE provides an integrated code debugger, so you can step through your code at run time to see that it is working or to help you debug problems in the code. VBE's Object Browser provides a tool for viewing all of the objects, methods, events, collections, and properties available in that Access Code Project. You will definitely become very familiar with VBE as you write more VBA code. Figure 37-1 provides an example of what VBE looks like in Access 2010.

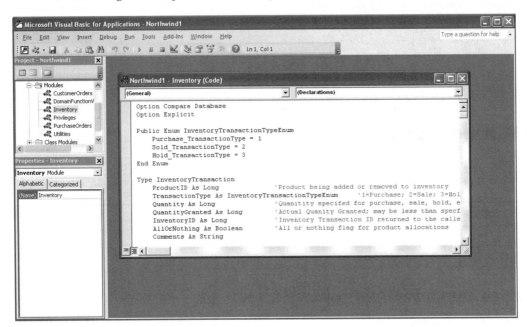

FIGURE 37-1

WRITING VBA CODE

Often, one of the most difficult things for beginners about writing code is getting the code syntax correct for the specific language. *Code syntax* is a set of rules detailing how to write a specific type of code, so it can be understood by a compiler (or in the case of Access, the VBA interpreter). This can be compared to the English language, which has rules about how sentences and paragraphs are formed. Although you must follow the syntax rules, the rules don't determine the meaning of the words. In this chapter we provide the basics of writing some very simple VBA code. We brush up on a few key concepts such as variables, operators, and events to illustrate this example.

As noted earlier, Access does all the work of creating the code to define event methods in the Form Module when you use the Property Sheet to create code for an event. Once you have created a function or subroutine for an event, you can begin writing code inside the function. The function can be called later or when the event is fired, and the code is executed. Additionally, inside the Access Form Module you can create other functions, subroutines, and variables that are outside of any specific event method, and that can be called by any other code within the module. This section discusses the basics of writing code behind an event method of a form

Referencing Objects Using VBA

All variable objects in VBA code have specific names that can be used in code to manipulate the specific object stored in that variable. Objects are referenced by variable name and the methods and properties of those objects can be called by using the . (dot) operator format. That is, if you want to call the Open() method for an Access Form object stored in a variable named frmCustomers, you would write the following VBA code:

```
frmCustomers.Open()
```

Object properties can be accessed in this same manner, but when you are accessing a property, you are either reading from it or setting its value. The following provides an example of both reading from and writing to the Text property of a TextBox control variable named txtName:

```
Dim sText as String
sText = Me!txtName.Text
Me!txtName.Text = "Geoffrey Griffith"
```

When you type the . (dot) after the object name (in this case txtName), you are presented with a list of methods, events, and properties for that object. This is the IntelliSense feature and it can save you the effort of looking up methods and properties for objects.

Notice that the second and third lines of the preceding code use an operator that we have not previously discussed: the ! (bang) operator. The ! operator specifies to Access that the property following it is part of, and belongs to, the object that precedes the operator. In this case, this means that to reference the txtName control variable within this Access Form, denoted by the keyword Me, we use the ! operator to specify that the control belongs to the current form. In this case, this is done so that we do not have to explicitly set focus to the control before accessing its value.

Lesson 53 discusses in more detail the ! (bang), . (dot), and other operators in VBA language.

Although the second and third lines in the preceding code are reading from and writing to the Text property, the first line of code is slightly different. The first line of code is declaring a new variable — a piece of memory that can temporarily store data during program execution. To define a new variable, use the keyword Dim, the name of the new variable, the keyword as, and then the name of the type. If you want to create an instance of a class or a type that is not one of the primitive types built into VBA, use the keyword new between the keyword as and the type. The following code shows a couple of examples of declaring variables in Access:

```
Dim iCount as Integer
Dim dPercent as Double
Dim oMyObject as New Object
Dim frmNewForm as New Form
```

ENABLING CODE IN ACCESS

After writing code, you will want to run it as a normal functionality of the database application. You should be aware of the Access 2010 application security features. By default, Access 2010 (as well as Access 2007) blocks any unsafe code or macros on application startup. Access won't execute this code until the user has either enabled code in the application or trusted the database solution. The easiest way to enable code is to enable the database by clicking the Enable button in the Access Security Bar at the top of the Access window, just below the Ribbon. Once the database has been enabled, all code (and macros) should run, assuming you've written the code correctly.

TRY IT

In this lesson, you create some embedded VBA code for an Access Form object. Now that you know the basics of VBA code and how it applies to forms, practice writing code yourself. The following step-by-step instructions walk you through creating a new form, adding some controls to it, and writing some embedded code to work with the Access Form controls. Sample files are available on the book's DVD and website.

Lesson Requirements

For this lesson, the example steps use the Northwind database application created from a template. However, the Northwind database is not necessarily required for this lesson; you can use just about any database application. This example focuses primarily upon writing some embedded code for forms and controls, and does not require the data or database objects in the Northwind database.

Hints

The following things might be helpful when creating embedded code for forms:

➤ The F4 hotkey opens the Property Sheet.

➤ The Alt+F11 keystroke combination opens VBE.

➤ The Ctrl+G keystroke combination opens the VBE Immediate window.

➤ The embedded code is saved once the parent form has been saved or once VBE is closed.

Remember, embedded code can only be added and modified in a form when the form is open in either Design or Layout View modes.

Step-by-Step

1. Open Access 2010 from the Windows Start menu. The Access Backstage will open in the Access window.

2. In the Backstage, click the New option on the left-hand menu and then click the Sample Templates option to show a list of the built-in templates.

3. Choose the Northwind option from the list of templates and click the Create button on the right side of the screen to create the sample database application. The new Northwind database will open in the Access window.

4. Click the Enable button in the Access Security Bar just below the Ribbon. This enables code and reopens the Northwind database application.

5. Close the `Login` form that is opened by default.

6. Click the Create Ribbon tab. Click the Form Design button in the Forms group to create a new form in Design View mode.

7. Once the new form has been opened in Design mode, click the Text Box button in the Controls group (in the Design Ribbon) and click the top left of the next form to drop a new `TextBox` control onto the form.

8. On the Design Ribbon, click the Button control to select it and then click the top right of the form to place the new control. This invokes the Command Button Wizard, so just click the Cancel button on the wizard.

9. On the Design Ribbon, click the Web Browser control to select it and then click just below the new Text Box to place a new Web Browser control on the form. This invokes the Insert Hyperlink dialog; just click the Cancel button to add the control to the form unbound.

10. Double-click the label for the form to edit the text and type in the word **Address**.

11. Make the `TextBox` control almost as wide as the form, leaving enough room to fit the button between it and the right edge of the form.

12. Press F4 to open the Property Sheet, if it is not already open.

13. Click the `TextBox` control and change the `Name` property to **txtAddress** in the Property Sheet. Set the `Horizontal Anchor` property to the Both option.

14. Click the Button control and change the `Name` property to **btnGo** in the Property Sheet. Then change the `Caption` property to **Go**. Set the `Horizontal Anchor` property to the Right option.

15. Click the Web Browser control to select it and change the `Name` property to **wbBrowser** in the Property Sheet. Set the `Horizontal Anchor` property to the Both option. Set the `Vertical Anchor` property to the Both option.

16. In the Property Sheet's Selection Type pull-down menu, choose the Form option to select the entire form. For the `Caption` property, type **Web Browser** as the value. For the `Record Selectors` property, choose the No option. For the `Navigation Buttons` property, choose the No option.

Figure 37-2 shows what your form should look like at this point. The form has almost been completely designed; there just needs to be some code added to hook up all the functionality for your `Web Browser` form.

17. Click the `Button` control to select it and show its properties in the Property Sheet. Click the Event tab and then click the "..." (Builder) button for the `On Click` event. This invokes the Choose Builder dialog, so choose the Code Builder option and click the OK button.

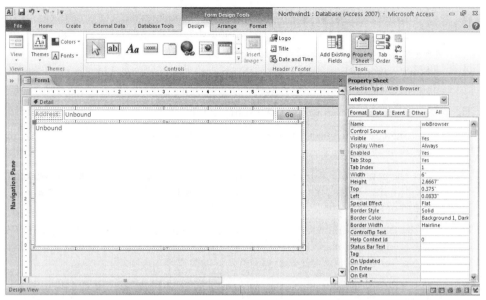

FIGURE 37-2

18. VBE will open with a new Event subroutine for the `Click` event of the `btnGo` control. This is where the code is added to set the destination address of your `Web Browser` control.

19. Add the following code inside the `btnGo_Click` subroutine:

```
Me.wbBrowser.ControlSource = "=""http://" & Me.txtAddress & """"
```

20. This code sets the `ControlSource` property value for the `wbBrowser` control to a Web address that is typed into the `txtAddress` `TextBox` control.

21. Click the Save button on the top-left corner of the Access window. This invokes the Save As dialog, so choose Browser as the name and click the OK button. The form is saved in the database.

22. Close VBE.

23. Now switch the form to Form View, type **www.microsoft.com** into the `TextBox`, and click the Go button. The Web browser opens the Microsoft.com page directly in your database application form.

Congratulations, you have now created embedded code in an Access form. Adding embedded code to forms in Access 2010 is a very simple task. In just 10 minutes and with only one line of code, you built a fully functioning Web browser form from scratch, using only the built-in tools in Access 2010.

SUMMARY

Embedded code can provide a world of functionality to any database application. You can embed code in the events of a form or its controls by using the Property Sheet's Builder button. The Visual Basic Editor program allows the user to write code and find out more about the code objects in the current Access database solution. Once the code has been written and embedded in a form and the database application's trusted mode has been enabled, code can be executed as desired through the normal execution of the database application. Embedding code in forms is a quick and easy way to get the form to provide the functionality that your application needs.

 Please select Lesson 37 on the DVD to view the video that accompanies this lesson.

38

Access 2010 Form Types

In Microsoft Access 2010 you have many types of forms to choose from, and the differences can be confusing. Any form in Access can be derived from any other by setting the correct properties for the form. This lesson is devoted to discussing the different types of forms available in Access 2010 and how they vary from one another.

LESSON SETUP

To begin this lesson, it is assumed that you have at least some knowledge of how to design and use forms in Access 2010, as discussed in the previous lessons. This lesson discusses the differences between the Access form types in terms of properties, so you should understand what form properties are and how they work.

SINGLE ITEM FORMS

The most basic form in Access is the standard Single Item form. Single Item forms are particularly useful for displaying a single record. Because Access forms are equipped with built-in record selectors and navigation buttons, creating a Single Item form to navigate through a set of records is very easy. Single Item forms are probably the most commonly used type of form in Access because they have such a wide variety of uses, and because they are really the base form type in Access.

Single Item Form Property Settings

For the most part, a Single Item form can have any property settings that you desire, but two settings are required for a Single Item. The first required setting, the `Default View` property, should be the value of `Single Form`, which automatically makes the form a Single Item form type. The second required setting, the `Allow Form View` property, should be a value of `Yes` to allow the form to be opened in Single Item form mode. Otherwise, the form can have any other settings that may be required to fulfill the form's task.

Creating a Single Item Form

Several methods exist for creating a Single Item form in Access 2010. From the Create Ribbon's Forms group, choosing any of the following options creates a (type of) Single Item form: Form, Blank Form, Form Design, or Modal Form. The Form Wizard can also be used to create a Single Item form, depending on the options selected. You could also create any other type of form and set the `Default View` and `Allow Form View` properties to convert the alternate form type to a Single Item form. And, you can write VBA code to create a new form and set the `DefaultView` property to the value of `0` (the predefined value for a Single Item form). No matter which method you choose, creating Single Item forms in Access 2010 is sure to be a snap!

MULTIPLE ITEM FORMS

Multiple Item forms are the first of the Access-specific form types. Multiple Item forms are designed to make it easy to display a set of records, by automatically repeating the Detail section of the form for each record in the set. Multiple Item forms in Access are also very common, because they have been part of the product since the beginning, even though their uses are somewhat more limited than the Single Item form's.

Multiple Item Form Property Settings

Just as with Single Item forms, Multiple Item forms can have pretty much any property settings that you desire, but two settings are required for a Multiple Item form. The first required setting, the `Default View` property, should be the value of `Continuous Form`, which automatically makes the form a Multiple Item form type. The second required setting, the `Allow Form View` property, should be a value of `Yes` to allow the form to be opened in Multiple Item form mode. Otherwise, Multiple Item forms can have any other settings that may be required for the form.

Creating a Multiple Item Form

Several methods exist for creating a Multiple Item form in Access 2010. Simply choosing the Multiple Item form from the Create Ribbon's Forms group will create a brand new Multiple Item form. The Form Wizard can also be used to create a Multiple Item form, depending on the options selected. A form of any other type could be created and then have the proper values set for the `Default View` and `Allow Form View` properties, to convert the form to a Multiple Item form. And, you can write VBA code to create a new form and set the `DefaultView` property to the value of `1` (the predefined value for a Continuous form). Any of these methods can be easily utilized to create a Multiple Item form using Access 2010.

DATASHEET FORMS

Datasheet forms are an Access staple; they harness the power of the Access datasheet (the form type that is displayed when you view a table or query open in Datasheet View mode). Datasheet forms are designed to provide the Access developer with the ability to utilize the Access datasheet to show multiple records in this format. Datasheet forms are very common in Access, because they have also been part of the product since the beginning.

Datasheet Form Property Settings

The property settings for a Datasheet form, and which form properties are available in Datasheet View mode, are slightly different from those for the Single Item and Multiple Item forms. The Datasheet View is its own separate view mode for a form, and so really, the only required property setting is to set the Allow Datasheet View property to the value of Yes. However, if you want to force that form to always open in this mode by default, the `Default View` property should also be set to the value of `Datasheet`. Otherwise, the user or developer will somehow have to manually, or through code, open the form in Datasheet View mode to make this view possible when the form is opened.

Creating a Datasheet Form

Several methods exist for creating a Datasheet form in Access 2010. Choosing the Datasheet option from the Create Ribbon's Forms group will create a brand new Datasheet form. The Form Wizard can also create a Datasheet form, depending on the options selected. A form of any other type could be created and the `AllowDatasheetView` property value could be set to `Yes` to allow the form to be shown in Datasheet View mode. And, as always, you could create some VBA code to create a new form and set the `AllowDatasheetView` property to a value of `True`. Any of these methods can create a Datasheet form; and remember, the key to Datasheet forms is opening the form in Datasheet View mode.

SPLIT FORMS

Originally part of the Access 2007 release, Split forms are quickly becoming a very popular form; they provide two forms in one and are an Access-specific form type. Split forms are a hybrid form that is one part Datasheet form and one part Single Item form. The idea is that the form's Datasheet portion shows all of the records in the set, and then whichever record is selected in the Datasheet is also shown in the Single Item form part of the Split form. Before this kind of form was created, Microsoft found that this kind of custom design for a form was very common in the industry, thus this form type was added as a result to make it easy to create these types of Split forms.

Split Form Property Settings

The required property settings for a Split form are very similar to the required settings for the Single Item and Multiple Item form properties. The first required setting, the `Default View` property, should be set to the value of `Split form`. The second required setting, the `Allow Form View` property, should be set to a value of `Yes` to allow the form to be opened in Split Form View. However, when a Split form is opened in Design View mode, only the Single Item part of the form is shown and can be designed in this mode. The Datasheet, or Splitter Bar, cannot be modified in this mode. To modify the Datasheet and Splitter Bar, use the Layout View mode designer to make adjustments to these controls with the Access visual designer tools.

Creating a Split Form

Several methods exist for creating a Split form in Access 2010. Choosing the Split Form option from the Create Ribbon's Forms group creates a brand new Split form. A form of any other type could be created and the `Default View` property could be set to `Split Form` to allow the form to be shown in Split Form mode. And, you can write VBA code to create a new form and set the `DefaultView` property to the value of 5 (the defined value for a Split form as noted in the Access Programmer's Reference). Any of these methods is sufficient to create an Access Split form.

POP-UP FORMS

Pop-up forms are very popular in Access. They are often used to provide Windows-style pop-up message dialogs. The Pop-up form is always contained within its own window, and not a tabbed document, even if tabbed document mode is being used (which is the default for ACCDB file format databases). Pop-up forms are a great way to implement a custom message dialog in Access.

Pop-up Form Property Settings

The required property settings for a Pop-up form are also slightly different than the required settings for the Single Item and Multiple Item form properties. The only required setting, the `Pop Up` property, should be set to the value of `Yes`, which automatically makes the form a Pop-up type. Because any form type can be a Pop-up form just by setting the `Pop Up` property value, any `Default View` property setting and all other form View settings are valid for Pop-up forms.

Creating a Pop-up Form

Several methods exist for creating a Pop-up form in Access. Creating any type of form and setting its `Pop Up` property to `Yes` will make it a Pop-up form. Also, choosing the Modal Form option from the Create Ribbon's Forms group will create a Modal form which, by default, is a Pop-up form. And, as always, you could create some VBA code to create a new form and set the `Pop Up` property to `True`. Any of these methods can quickly create a Pop-up form.

MODAL FORMS

Modal forms in Access are much like Pop-up forms, except that they are always on top and must be dismissed before the user can interact with any other objects. Modal forms are used to implement a form that requires input to continue execution of the program. Any type of form can be Modal, but often Pop-up forms are set to be Modal to implement a message box that requires some user input before you can proceed further in the program.

Modal Form Property Settings

The required property settings for a Modal form are much like those of a Pop-up form. The only required setting for Modal forms is the `Modal` property, which should be set to `Yes`. This automatically makes the form a Modal Form type. Because any type of form can be a Modal form just by setting this property, any setting for the `Default View` is valid for a Modal form.

Creating a Modal Form

Several methods exist for creating a Modal form in Access 2010. Choosing the Modal Form option from the Create Ribbon's Forms group will create a Modal form with some common settings. Also, creating any type of form and setting its `Modal` property to `Yes` will make it a Modal form. And, as always, VBA code can be created to create a new form and set the `Modal` property to the value of `True`. Any of these methods can be used to easily create a Modal form.

PIVOTCHART AND PIVOTTABLE FORMS

PivotChart and PivotTable forms are similar to each other. PivotChart and PivotTable forms, as their names suggest, are used to provide different methods of representing sets of data in a visual sense. In fact, PivotChart and PivotTable forms are great ways to enhance the visual appearance of any database application by providing attractive visualizations of charted data.

PivotChart Form Property Settings

The property settings for PivotChart and PivotTable forms are what make these form types similar to a Datasheet form type. PivotCharts and PivotTables have their own separate View mode for a form, and only require the `Allow PivotTable View` and `Allow PivotChart View` properties (respectively) to be set to the value of `Yes`. Additionally, tables and queries allow the PivotTable and PivotChart View modes. But, if you want to force an object to always open in this mode by default, the `Default View` property should also be set to the value of `PivotChart` or `PivotTable` (respectively).

Creating a PivotChart Form

Several methods exist for creating a PivotChart or PivotTable form type in Access 2010. Because PivotCharts and PivotTables are View states for a database object, you can use any form and create a PivotChart or PivotTable for it by switching the View settings appropriately. The Chart Wizard can also create a PivotChart and do much of the work to quickly get the chart up and running. And, you could create some VBA code to create a new form and set the `AllowPivotChartView` or `AllowPivotTableView` property to a value of `True`. Each of these methods will accomplish the task of creating either a new PivotChart or PivotTable object.

TRY IT

In this lesson, you use Access 2010 to create several different form types. You should have a fairly good understanding of the different types of forms in Access 2010 and what makes these forms different from each other. The following instructions walk you through the steps necessary to create several different Access 2010 form types. Sample files are available on the book's DVD and website.

Lesson Requirements

For this lesson, the example steps use the Northwind database application created from a template. However, the Northwind database is not necessarily required for this lesson; you can use just about any database application. This example focuses primarily upon the different types of Access forms, and does not require the data or database objects in the Northwind database.

Hints

The following things might be helpful when creating embedded code for forms:

➤ The Create tab on the Ribbon is the fastest way to create the different types of form objects.

➤ Selecting a database object in the Navigation Pane before clicking one of the form buttons in the Create Ribbon makes a form based upon the selected object.

➤ The F4 hotkey opens the Property Sheet.

➤ All of the form properties discussed in this lesson can be found near the top of the All tab of the Property Sheet.

Step-by-Step

1. Open Access 2010 from the Windows Start menu. The Access Backstage will open in the Access window.

2. In the Backstage, click the New option on the left-hand menu and then click the Sample Templates option.

3. Choose the Northwind option from the list of templates and click the Create button on the right side of the screen to create the sample database application. The new Northwind database will open in the Access window.

4. Click the Navigation Pane to expand it. Then switch the Navigation Pane view type to the All Access Objects option.

5. Under the Tables group, click the Customers table to select it. You will create a form based on this object.

6. On the Create tab of the Ribbon, click the Form option to create a new Single Item form based on the Customers table. Notice that all of the data from the first record is displayed and that you can use the record selectors at the bottom of the form to navigate through all the records in the Customers table. Figure 38-1 provides an example of what this form looks like.

7. On the Design Ribbon, choose the Design View option on the View menu to switch the form to Design View.

8. Press the F4 key to open the Property Sheet, if it is not already open. Set the Selection Type pull-down menu to Form to select the entire form in the Property Sheet.

9. Set the form's Pop Up property to Yes. The form is now a Pop-up form.

10. On the Design Ribbon, choose the Form View option on the View menu to switch the form to normal view. Notice that the form is now in Windowed mode. Figure 38-2 provides an example of what this form might look like.

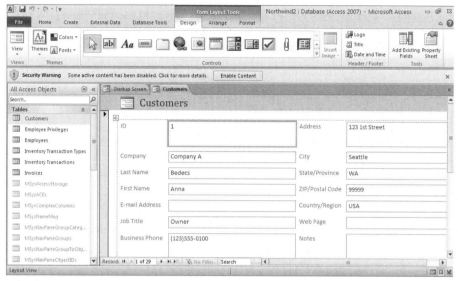

FIGURE 38-1

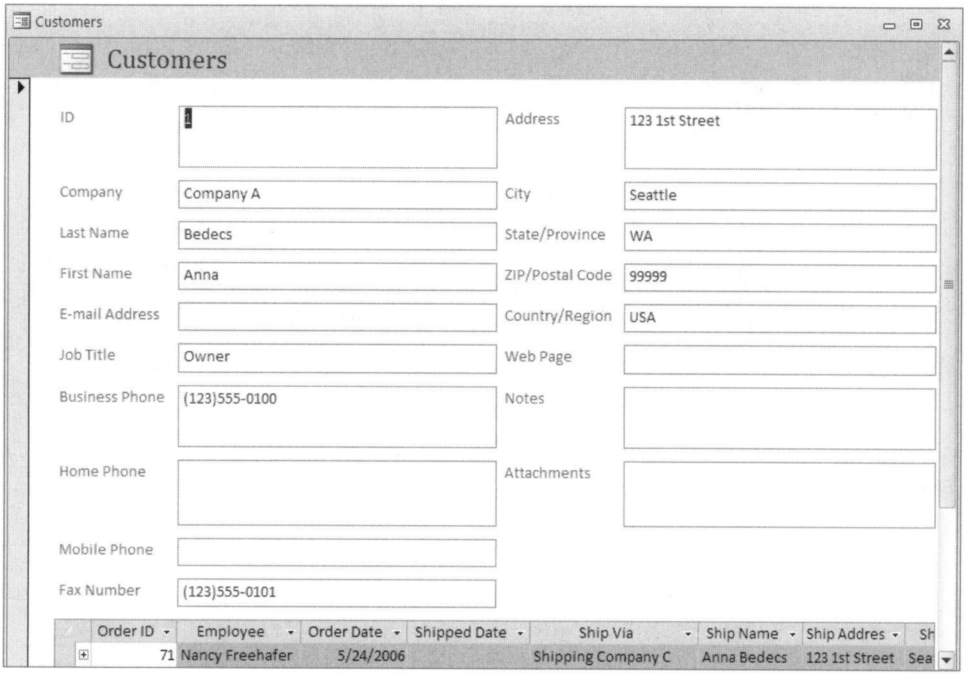

FIGURE 38-2

11. On the Design Ribbon, choose the Design View option on the View menu to switch the form to Design View.

12. Set the form's `Modal` property to `Yes`. The form is now a Modal form.

13. On the Design Ribbon, choose the Form View option on the View menu. Notice that nothing else in the Access window can be interacted with until the form is closed. Close the form. Discarding the changes is fine; this form is no longer needed.

14. Under the Tables group in the Navigation Pane, click the `Customers` table to select it.

15. On the Ribbon's Create tab, click the Split Form option under the More Forms pull-down menu to create a new Split Form based on the `Customers` table.

The new Split Form is created. Notice that half of the form is a Datasheet form, containing all the records from the `Customers` table. The other half of the form is a Single Item form that shows the data for the record that is selected in the datasheet portion of the form. Figure 38-3 provides an example of how this form might look.

Congratulations, you have now created several different types of Access forms. Creating any of the Access form types can be accomplished with just a few mouse clicks using Access 2010.

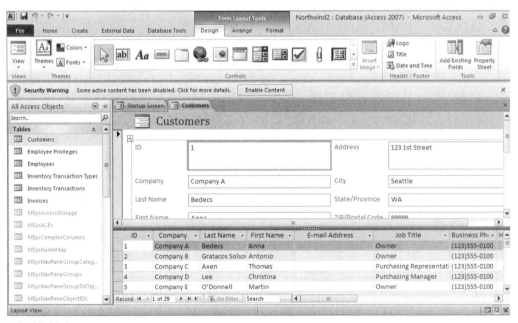

FIGURE 38-3

SUMMARY

Access 2010 provides a wide variety of different form types to make it easy for a developer to quickly create common types of forms. Single Item forms are used to show a single record. Multiple Item forms show a set of records. Datasheet forms provide the developer with the ability to utilize the Access datasheet. Split forms are a combination of a Single Item and Datasheet form. Pop-up forms are forms that are always in Windowed mode. Modal forms are forms that halt all other executions of an application, and must be dismissed before the application can continue. And finally, PivotCharts and PivotTables are used to provide additional visual representations of a dataset. Most of these form types are specific to Access and are what make Access such a powerful tool for application developers. The Access forms package is truly one of the best features of Access 2010.

 Please select Lesson 38 on the DVD to view the video that accompanies this lesson.

39

Creating PivotCharts

Microsoft Access 2010 continues to provide support for Access PivotCharts. PivotCharts can be a great way to provide users with a visual representation of data, and is often used to represent sets of data for easy visual comparison. PivotCharts are a great way to spruce up your forms and reports, because almost every database has some kind of data that can be charted. Best of all, PivotCharts in Access 2010 can be built with just a few clicks of the mouse!

LESSON SETUP

To begin this lesson, it is assumed that you have at least some limited knowledge of how to design forms in Access 2010. This lesson discusses how to build PivotCharts, which are essentially a certain type of form in Access. However, this lesson does assume that you have no prior knowledge of building Access PivotCharts.

CREATING PIVOTCHARTS

Several methods exist for creating PivotCharts in Access. The most common method is to simply choose the PivotChart button from the Create Ribbon under the Forms group. However, it is possible to use the Chart Wizard, which is launched automatically when you drop a Chart control from the Design Ribbon onto a form or report that is in Design or Layout View mode. Finally, both tables and queries contain storage space for PivotCharts directly within their definition, so you can build PivotCharts directly from these base objects. However, one possible method that might be expected for creating PivotCharts — using VBA code — does not exist.

DESIGNING PIVOTCHARTS

Creating PivotCharts using the Access 2010 Chart Designer is much the same as working with a form in Design View. However, unlike forms, PivotCharts only have one view mode for working with and viewing the chart: PivotChart View. Although Design View mode is available for a PivotChart that is a form, this is just to set the base form properties, like the `Record Source` for the data. All the design work for the PivotChart itself is done through the PivotChart View mode, which is the exact same view mode in which the chart is displayed.

The PivotChart Tools Ribbon

Once a PivotChart has been opened in PivotChart View mode, the PivotChart Tools Ribbon becomes available. The PivotChart Tools Ribbon is the primary set of options available for designing the chart, and all of the functionality for a chart can be accessed using this Ribbon or through one of the options that it provides. However, most of the actual options for PivotCharts are set by using the Chart Property Sheet, which is discussed shortly. Figure 39-1 shows the PivotChart Tools Ribbon menu.

FIGURE 39-1

Adding Fields to a PivotChart

Once you have selected a data source and created a new chart, you need to add the desired fields to the chart to start showing data from the data source. The purpose of a chart is to provide a visual representation of one or more sets of data in such a way that one group of values is displayed upon another group of related categories so that they can be compared. You will need to add the desired fields to the form, in the manner that you wish to display the data. This task is accomplished by using the Chart Field List.

The Chart Field List

Although different than the Form Designer Field List pane, the Chart Field List control behaves in much the same way. The Field List can be toggled on and off from the Field List button on the PivotChart Tools Ribbon. When the Field List is visible, fields can be dragged and dropped onto the chart's design surface to add their data to the chart. However, adding fields to a chart is slightly different than a form in terms of where the fields are dropped on the PivotChart. For PivotCharts, fields are placed on the *drop zones*, special locations on the PivotChart form. Figure 39-2 shows the Chart Field List.

FIGURE 39-2

Chart Drop Zones

You can add fields to a PivotChart in four drop zones: Category, Data, Filter, and Series. The Category drop zone is the x-axis of the chart. The Data drop zone is the y-axis of the chart, and it displays the values chosen for the Category drop zone. The Filter fields are data that the chart is to be filtered on. The Series is a list of different values in the record to group the items categorically. Additionally, PivotCharts support adding multiple items to the Data drop field, for showing multiple dimensions of that data, per Category filter. New users often find it difficult to build PivotCharts in Access because deciding which fields to drop on any of these four drop zones is confusing and may take a couple of tries to figure out the exact combination.

The best way to learn about any of the four drop zones in a PivotChart is to play around with them using some sample data that you know and understand well, and have ideas about how you would like to visualize that data. Also, the Chart Wizard can be a great resource for seeing how a chart is built. The wizard definitely makes it easy to quickly build a PivotChart by answering a few simple questions.

Setting PivotChart Properties

The PivotChart Property Sheet, which lives in its own modal window outside the main Access user interface, is also very different than the Access designer Property Sheet. The PivotChart Property Sheet is where most of the properties and settings for the chart can be adjusted. One key item to note about the PivotChart Property Sheet is the Select pull-down menu on the General tab. The Select options allow the developer to select any individual item, or collection of items, in the PivotChart to adjust their formatting properties (either individually or as a group). Whatever you choose in the Select drop-down menu is modified when adjusting the properties on the Property Sheet's other tabs. Figure 39-3 shows the Chart Properties Sheet.

FIGURE 39-3

DISPLAYING PIVOTCHARTS

Once you have created the PivotChart, you can display it for the user by simply opening it in PivotChart View mode. (Opening the PivotChart designer and opening it in a read-only view are the same.) But often PivotCharts in Access are displayed as subforms on other forms or reports. No matter which way you show charts, some key properties about and some general settings for the chart should be set before showing the PivotChart to the user.

PivotChart Form Properties

A couple of general form properties are set by Access when using Form Design View mode automatically for building a PivotChart. The first is the `Default View` property for the form, which is typically set to the `PivotChart` option, but is not necessarily required, depending on the specific form design. However, if `PivotChart` is not the `Default View`, you must open the form specifically in PivotChart mode to see the chart. Secondly, and more importantly, the `Allow PivotChart View` property must be set to `Yes` to open a form in PivotChart mode. These two properties are the most important for actually opening and viewing the PivotChart form.

General Chart Settings

Because the PivotChart designer and normal View mode are the same mode for PivotCharts, a couple of settings are useful when displaying the chart for viewing. First, it is always nice to turn off the drop zones by clicking the Drop Zones button in the Ribbon. This removes them from view and helps the chart formatting look better. Also, displaying the Legend, which can be turned on from the Ribbon as well can be a nice touch. The Legend provides a list of the corresponding Series field names for the chart. And finally, at a minimum, it is always nice to add names for the chart axes and maybe even add a title, which can be set under the Format tab in the Chart Property Sheet. Once these general settings for the chart have been selected, the chart should be ready for users!

TRY IT

In this lesson, you create a new PivotChart from existing data using Access 2010. Now that you have a good idea of what PivotCharts in Access are, how to design them, and how they can be displayed, you create a fictional calls table to build a PivotChart that provides a visual representation of the data in this table. The following example provides a step-by-step walk-through of building a PivotChart from scratch using Access 2010.

Lesson Requirements

For this lesson, the example steps create a blank database and a new table, with data for that table. However, this particular data and table are not required for this lesson; you can use just about any database application. This example focuses primarily on building the PivotChart itself, although not using the given data may make it difficult to see the chart visualization. Sample files are available on the book's DVD and website.

Hints

The following things might be helpful when creating PivotChart forms:

➤ The Create tab on the Ribbon is the fastest way to create a PivotChart object.

➤ Selecting an object in the Navigation Pane before clicking the PivotChart Form button creates a PivotChart Form based on the selected object.

➤ The F4 hotkey opens the PivotChart Property Sheet.

➤ The PivotChart will become broken and not show any data if the fields dropped on the PivotChart do not calculate to a value and the results of the PivotChart settings are invalid.

Step-by-Step

1. Open Access 2010 from the Windows Start menu. The Access Backstage will open in the Access window.

2. In the Backstage, click the New option on the left-hand menu and click the Blank Database option. Then click the Create button on the right side of the screen to create a new blank database. The new database will open in the Access window and a default table will be created.

3. Add the following fields to the table (in addition to the field that is already there):

FIELD NAME	FIELD TYPE
CallDate	Date/Time
Operator	Text
Status	Text

4. Once the fields have been added to the table, save the table and name it **Calls**.

5. Add the following data to the table:

ID	CALLDATE	OPERATOR	STATUS
1	1/26/2010	Geoff	Open
2	1/26/2010	Truitt	Closed
3	1/26/2010	Geoff	Open
4	1/27/2010	Truitt	Closed
5	1/27/2010	Truitt	Open
6	1/27/2010	Geoff	Closed
7	1/27/2010	Geoff	Open
8	1/28/2010	Truitt	Closed
9	1/28/2010	Truitt	Open
10	1/28/2010	Geoff	Closed
11	1/28/2010	Geoff	Open
12	1/28/2010	Geoff	Closed

6. Close the table. You are now ready to begin building the PivotChart.

7. Click the new Calls table in the Navigation Pane to select it.

8. On the Create tab of the Ribbon, choose the PivotChart option under the More Forms pull-down menu. A new PivotChart form will be created.

9. On the PivotChart Tools Ribbon, click the Field List button to open the Chart Field List if it is not already open.

10. From the Field List, drag the `CallDate` field down to the Category drop zone at the bottom of the chart. The field should be added to the chart.

11. From the Field List, drag the `CallDate` field up to the Data drop zone at the top of the chart (just below the Filter Fields drop zone). The `Count of CallDate` should be added to the chart. At this point, you should see some data on the chart.

12. From the Field List, drag the `Operator` field down to the Series drop zone on the right side of the chart. The field should be added to the chart.

13. Finally, from the Field List, drag the `Status` field down to the Category drop zone at the bottom of the chart, where the `CallDate` field already resides. This will break down each call date by the status of the call. The field should be added to the chart.

14. Close the Field List and press F4 to open the PivotChart Property Sheet.

15. On the General tab in the Select pull-down menu, choose the Chart Workspace option to select the entire chart.

16. On the General tab, under the Add section, click the Title button. This adds a title bar to the Chart called `Chart Workspace Title`.

17. Click the new title bar in the chart to select it in the Property Sheet. Then, under the Format tab of the Property Sheet, change the caption to **Employee Call Status by Date**.

18. Click the Axis Title at the bottom of the chart to select it in the Property Sheet. Then, under the Format tab of the Property Sheet, change the caption to **Call Status by Date**.

19. Click the other Axis Title on the left of the chart to select it in the Property Sheet. Then, under the Format tab of the Property Sheet, change the caption to **Number of Calls**.

20. Close the Property Sheet.

21. On the PivotChart Tools Ribbon, click the Legend button to show the Legend in the chart. Then click the Drop Zones button to hide the drop zones. Figure 39-4 provides an illustration of what this chart might look like.

Congratulations, you have now successfully created a PivotChart form using the Access 2010 PivotChart designer. In less than 10 minutes, you were able to create a brand new PivotChart table completely from scratch and make it look presentable for a database application. The PivotChart tools in Access provide an enormous benefit in time, effort, and development cost when charts need to be implemented in a database application.

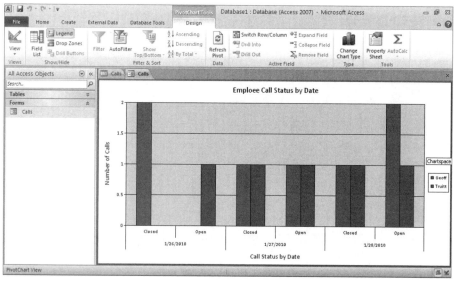

FIGURE 39-4

SUMMARY

Access 2010 provides the ability to quickly and easily build professional-looking charts through the use of the PivotChart feature. PivotCharts can be added to any table, query, or form by switching the object to PivotChart View mode. The Access 2010 PivotChart designer provides all of the necessary tools to build these charts, namely the PivotChart Tools Ribbon, the Chart Field List, and the PivotChart Property Sheet. Once the proper form properties have been set, opening and viewing charts is no problem. PivotCharts provide a great set of features for viewing graphical representations of data in Access 2010.

 Please select Lesson 39 on the DVD to view the video that accompanies this lesson.

40

Access Application Navigation

The Microsoft Access 2010 user interface provides a host of tools for working with any supported database object. But often it is desirable to build custom navigation into an Access database application for any number of reasons. Moreover, in some cases, custom navigation is required to operate the database application. This lesson provides an overview of building custom application navigation and some examples of how these methods can be applied.

LESSON SETUP

Before beginning this lesson, it is assumed that you have at least some knowledge of the different types of database objects available in a database, as well as the Access 2010 UI tools, such as the Navigation Pane and the Ribbon. This lesson discusses the considerations of building custom navigation into your database applications, but does not necessarily require an in-depth knowledge of any particular type of database object.

APPLICATION NAVIGATION CONSIDERATIONS

When any database file, say an ACCDB file, is opened, the Access program is already doing a lot of work for you and it is all too easy to take these tools for granted. For example, the Navigation Pane automatically displays all the objects in the database (or some other custom view that the Navigation Pane provides). You can open, close, create, save, and modify all of the database objects using the Ribbon and the various Access designers. You can even set properties on the database file by using the Access Options dialog. But, all of these tools aren't really part of the database application; they are actually part of the Access program. There are a number of things to understand and to consider about these Access tools when building a database application.

Navigation Pane Considerations

When a database application only has a few database objects, it is very easy to use the default settings in the Navigation Pane. However, once a database starts to grow larger, with say, 20 or more objects, it gets more and more difficult to rely strictly on the Navigation Pane, or the Database window in versions of Access prior to 2007, to get between forms and reports. Access 2010 offers several solutions to this problem. The foremost and safest method is to build custom navigation right into the application's forms, primarily through the use of buttons. This option is very common and is discussed shortly. However, a second option, available starting with the release of Access 2007, is providing custom Navigation Pane settings. Customizing the Navigation Pane is easy to do and can enhance the ease of navigation by hiding, grouping, and creating custom names for database objects. However, it is important to realize that the Navigation Pane is not available when an Access database application is executed using the Access Runtime. Additionally, it is possible to turn off the Navigation Pane in the database properties. So, when it is available, the Navigation Pane provides a nice set of tools for navigating an Access application. But, in the cases when it cannot be used, you will need to develop other methods of navigation to suit your application.

Ribbon Considerations

The Access 2010 Ribbon provides a host of options that are also easy to forget about until they are no longer present. The Access Backstage provides tons of tools for opening, closing, and saving database files, as well as tools for analyzing and compacting the database. The various Ribbons provide all of the tools for creating new database objects, switching View modes for those objects, and working with those objects. However, in some cases most of the Ribbon functionality is not available. When a database application is run using the Access Runtime, most of these options are not available. However, Custom Ribbons can be built and will be shown in Runtime mode, which is another method for providing your users with a means of application navigation. As with the Navigation Pane, the main Access Ribbons can also be turned off by setting the proper database property settings. The best way to rely on the Ribbon for application navigation in any environment is to create custom Ribbons to ensure they will always be present.

Access Runtime Applications

The Access Runtime is a royalty-free, redistributable package provided by Microsoft that allows Access application developers to distribute their applications to users who do not have Access installed on their machines. This means that the user can install the Access Runtime and run an Access application, without ever having to purchase Access or Office. However, when a database application is in Runtime mode (which is discussed more in Lesson 62), the Navigation Pane and standard Access Ribbons are unavailable to the user. In this case, the database application must have its own custom navigation built in; otherwise, the user will not be able to open objects in the database.

CREATING FORMS TO NAVIGATE

The most common method of providing custom navigation in an Access database application is by programming the functionality right into the forms in the database. It is common to have a start page that opens automatically when the database is opened, as a launching point for the user to begin working in the application. This start page usually provides buttons, or some other means for opening and viewing the objects of the application. This can also be useful for keeping users from seeing, or even accessing, objects in the database that they do not need to work with directly. Several common methods exist for providing custom navigation via the use of forms.

Using Buttons to Navigate

The easiest and most common method for providing navigation on a form is by adding a `Button` control. `Button` controls are very familiar to almost any level of computer user and they are easy to program — everybody loves buttons! Slap a `Button` down on a form, add some code or a macro to the `OnClick` event, and presto — you can open any object in the database with a simple mouse click.

Using ComboBox Controls to Navigate

Another very common, but a little more savvy, method for adding navigation to a form is by using a `ComboBox` (or a `TextBox` or `ListBox`) control. These controls can be bound to multiple items, so the user can choose from a list. These controls also expose a number of events to work with and can provide a more dynamic experience with less work than might be required with a `Button` control. The `ListBox` control is a good method for providing a lot of options in one small area that the user can choose from.

Using the Navigation Buttons

Specific to Access Forms, the Navigation Buttons (the buttons on the bottom of a form) do exactly as their name suggests; they allow the user to navigate across the sequence of records that are bound to the form. When the Navigation Buttons property for an Access Form is set to `Yes`, the bottom of the form will show a series of record navigation buttons. Those buttons automatically know how to work with the recordset that is bound to the form, without any additional programming required. You can toggle these buttons on and off just by setting the Navigation Buttons property. Writing the code to create buttons to do the same work yourself would be much more time-consuming. However, it is worth noting that all of the functionality found in the Navigation Buttons can be created using the Button Control Wizard. Navigation Buttons are a very easy method for building record navigation into a form.

Setting a Startup Form

How does the user open the first form in a database application if the Navigation Pane is not present? Access databases support the `StartUpForm` database property (called the Display Form in the Access Options dialog), which is simply the name of the form to be opened when the database is opened via Access or the Access Runtime. It is common to use this form as the starting point of a database application and is the preferred, but not only, method for launching a form on startup.

TRY IT

In this lesson you create some custom application navigation for a database application using Access 2010. Now that you have a basic understanding of most of the methods for creating custom navigation in a database application, you create a custom startup form for a database application that opens a second form, which is the hypothetical starting form for the application. The following step-by-step example guides you through every action necessary to accomplish this task. Sample files are available on the book's DVD and website.

Lesson Requirements

For this lesson, the example steps use the Northwind database application created from a template. However, the Northwind database is not required to complete this lesson; you can use just about any database application. This example focuses primarily on building custom navigation in a database, and does not necessarily require the data or database objects in the Northwind database.

Step-by-Step

1. Open Access 2010 from the Windows Start menu. The Access Backstage will open in the Access window.

2. In the Backstage, click the New option on the left-hand menu and then click the Sample Templates option to show a list of the built-in templates.

3. Choose the Northwind option from the list of templates and click the Create button on the right side of the screen to create the sample database application. The new Northwind database will open in the Access window.

4. On the Create tab on the Ribbon, click the Form Design option. This creates and opens a new form in Design View mode.

5. On the Design Ribbon tab, click the Combo Box control option to select it and then click the top left of the form to drop the new control onto the form. This invokes the Combo Box Wizard.

6. Choose the I Will Type in the Values That I Want (second) option on the wizard and click the Next button.

7. On the second page of the Combo Box Wizard, there will be a grid that you can just start typing values into. These values are what will be displayed in the ComboBox control's pull-down list. Type in the following list of values:

   ➤ **Login Dialog**

   ➤ **Inventory List**

   ➤ **Order List**

8. Click the Next button on the wizard.

 These values will be added to the RowSource *property of the* ComboBox *control and the* RowSourceType *property will be set to Value List. Also, the* ControlSource *property should be blank. You can verify this by viewing these properties in the Property Sheet with the* ComboBox *control selected.*

9. On the last page of the wizard, type in the value **Choose Form:** for the label option. Click the Finish button and the new ComboBox control will be added to the form.

10. Click the new ComboBox control, so that only it is selected, and press the F4 key to open the Property Sheet to view the properties for the new control.

11. On the Other tab of the Property Sheet, change the `Name` property to **cboForms**.

12. On the Event tab, click the "..." (Builder) button for the `On Click` event. This invokes the Choose Builder dialog. Click the Macro Builder option and click OK. The Macro Designer will be opened.

13. In the Macro Designer's action pull-down menu, choose the OpenForm option. This opens six new fields to set the properties for the OpenForm macro.

14. For the Form Name parameter, type in the value **=cboForms.SelText**. This automatically sets whichever form name is selected in the `cboForms` ComboBox as the form to open with the OpenForm macro.

15. Close the Macro Builder and choose Yes when prompted to save the new macro. You will be taken back to the new form.

16. On the Design Ribbon tab, click the Combo Box control option to select it and then click the top left of the form, just below the previous ComboBox control, to add another new ComboBox to the form. This invokes the Combo Box Wizard.

17. Click the Cancel button on the Combo Box Wizard to dismiss it; you'll set the properties manually this time.

18. Double-click the new `Label` control that came with the new ComboBox to select its text and type in **Choose Report:** as the new text.

19. Click the new ComboBox control to select it and press the F4 key to open the Property Sheet (if it is not already open).

20. On the All tab of the Property Sheet, change the `Name` property for the new ComboBox control to **cboReports**.

21. On the Data tab, click in the value field for the `Row Source` property, and press the Shift+F2 keystroke combination to open the Zoom Builder dialog.

22. Type the following SQL statement in the Zoom Builder dialog to set the `Row Source` property:

```
SELECT [MSysObjects].[Name]
FROM [MSysObjects]
WHERE ([MSysObjects].[Type]=-32764)
ORDER BY [MSysObjects].[Name];
```

23. Once this query text has been added to the Zoom builder control, click OK to add the data to the ComboBox. The ComboBox will show all of the reports in the database.

24. On the Event tab, click the "..." (Builder) button for the `On Click` event. This invokes the Choose Builder dialog. Click the Macro Builder option and click OK. The Macro Designer will be opened.

25. In the Macro Designer's s action pull-down menu, choose the OpenReport option. This opens six new fields to set the properties for the OpenReport macro.

26. For the Report Name parameter, type in the value **=cboReports.SelText**. This automatically sets whichever form name is selected in the `cboReports` ComboBox as the report to open with the OpenReports macro.

27. Close the Macro Designer and choose Yes when prompted to save the new macro. You will be taken back to the new form.

28. On the Design tab of the Ribbon, click the Button control, and then click to the right of the new ComboBox controls to place a new button there. This invokes the Command Button Wizard dialog.

29. On the first page of the Command Button Wizard, for the Categories section, choose the Application option. Notice that the only action for this Category is Quit Application, so click the Next button on the wizard.

30. The second page of the wizard lets the user choose between text and a picture for the button, so choose the default image and click Next.

31. On the last page of the wizard, for the button name, type **btnExit**, and then click the Finish button on the wizard. The new Button control will be added to the form and ready to use.

32. Click the Save button on the top left of the Access window to save the new form. For the name of the form, type in **Start** and click OK. The form will now be saved in the database.

33. Click the File Ribbon and, in the left-hand pane, choose the Options option. This invokes the Access Options dialog.

34. Click the Current Database option on the left-hand pane of the Access Options dialog. In the right-hand pane, choose the Start form as the Display Form option. Then click OK to apply the setting to the database.

35. A message box pops up saying that the changes won't take effect until the database has been reopened. Click OK to dismiss the message.

Congratulations, you have now successfully created a form that has several options for navigating the forms and reports of the Northwind database application. To verify that this functionality is working correctly, close and reopen the Northwind database — the new Start form should open automatically. Click the pull-down menu for the Forms and click any option. The form is promptly opened. The same will work for the reports ComboBox as well. If you click the Exit button, the application will be closed. You should now have a good understanding of how to build custom application navigation into an Access database.

SUMMARY

Building the proper navigation is one of the keys to a successful database application. As your application grows, the need for simplifying its navigation will become increasingly evident. It is important to consider that the Navigation Pane and Ribbon will not be available if the user plans to execute the database application in Access Runtime mode, or if the corresponding database settings are turned off. Building the proper custom navigation directly into your database design greatly adds to the robustness of any Access database application.

 Please select Lesson 40 on the DVD to view the video that accompanies this lesson.

41

Creating Reports in Layout View

Microsoft Access 2010's Reports package makes it easy to create reports for your databases. A report can be a simple one-click creation, or built from scratch with full control over Record Sources and report styling. You can approach building a report in several different ways, including the focus of this lesson, the Report Layout View designer. Originally introduced in Access 2007, the Layout View designer allows the user to manipulate objects and control formats while seeing the actual data in the report. This lesson discusses the basic features of the Layout View designer and how to create reports.

LESSON SETUP

Creating basic reports is very easy in Access 2010. You should be familiar with Access basics such as selecting tables, entering data, creating new database objects, and navigating the program, but you do not need to know much more for this lesson. To create a new report in Access, all you need is at least one table containing data.

QUICK REPORTS IN ACCESS 2010

One of Access's most productive and time-saving features is the ability to create Quick Reports. These reports are just like blank reports built from scratch, but with the table fields automatically added and formatted for you. With Access 2010, a complete, ready-to-present report is literally just a few clicks away. To create a Quick Report in Access 2010, click any table in the Navigation Pane to be used as the Record Source for the report and then, on the Create Ribbon, click the Report button. A new, fully functional report will be created, complete with fields based on the source selected in the Navigation Pane. This report will be opened in Layout View mode for further modification. Figure 41-1 provides an example of what a report open in Layout View looks like in Access 2010.

FIGURE 41-1

SWITCHING TO LAYOUT VIEW

To switch to the Report Layout View, double-click any report in the Navigation Pane to open it. Once a report is open, the View button on the Home Ribbon becomes active. To switch to Layout View, click the down arrow of the View button to bring up the drop-down menu, and then click the Layout View option. Once the report is in Layout View, it will appear in the main section of the Access window as before, only now all elements of the report are selectable. You can begin editing the report's content and visual properties in Layout View.

THE REPORT LAYOUT RIBBON

Once a report has been opened in Layout View, the Report Layout Tools Ribbons become available. These four Ribbons appear as the Design, Arrange, Format, and Page Setup tabs. Each of these Ribbons contains a different set of tools for working with different aspects of the report in Layout View.

The first tab of the Report Layout Tools Ribbon is the Design tab. The Design Ribbon provides options for working with themes, groupings & totals, controls, and headers and footers. It also provides buttons for changing the Report View, and for turning on and off the Property Sheet and Field List panes. Figure 41-2 shows the Report Layout Tools Design Ribbon.

FIGURE 41-2

The second tab of the Report Layout Tools Ribbon is the Arrange tab. The Arrange Ribbon provides options for setting control layouts and adjusting rows, columns, and general positions of controls. Figure 41-3 shows the Report Layout Tools Arrange Ribbon.

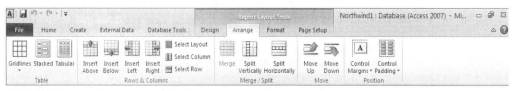

FIGURE 41-3

The third tab of the Report Layout Tools Ribbon is the Format tab. The Format Ribbon provides options for setting the formats of controls, such as font settings, conditional formatting, and background images. Figure 41-4 shows the Report Layout Tools Format Ribbon.

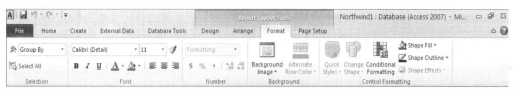

FIGURE 41-4

The fourth, and final, tab of the Report Layout Tools Ribbon is the Page Setup tab. The Page Setup Ribbon provides options for setting basic print options for a report, such as margin sizes and layout orientation. The Page Setup button on this Ribbon provides quick access to all of these options in the legacy Page Setup dialog provided in Access 2003 and earlier versions of Access. Figure 41-5 shows the Report Layout Tools Page Setup Ribbon.

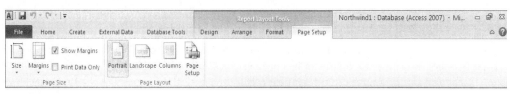

FIGURE 41-5

To use the commands from the first three of these Ribbon tabs, simply click the control you want to manipulate and choose the Ribbon option. To add controls, simply click the control type in the Ribbon to select it and click the desired location in the report, and the control will be added. The Page Setup Ribbon can be selected at any time while in Layout View.

THE FIELD LIST PANE

The Access Field List pane is an easy and simple way to work with the data fields in the various tables and queries within a database. The primary feature of the Access Field List is the ability to drag and drop controls onto forms and reports, with the resulting controls being bound directly to their fields within the data source. To open the Field List pane, click the Add Existing Fields button of the Design tab of the Report Layout Tools Ribbon. You can also open the Field List by using the Alt+F8 keystroke combination.

To add a field from the Field List, simply click the field you want to add and then drag it to the location on the report where you want to add it. You can double-click a field in the Field List to add it to the default location on the report (typically to the right of the currently selected control), or you can right-click the various rows, columns, and cells of the report to see the context menu options for the field for more specific placement options.

The Field List not only shows the fields for the current Record Source of the report, but also related tables and other tables in the database. It is important to consider that if you add fields from related or separate tables, the Field List will modify the Record Source property query to accommodate this change. But beware, the Field List does not discriminate as to which fields can be dropped into the report, and dropping the wrong combination of fields between unrelated tables can inadvertently break the report and cause it to display data incorrectly.

Because Access is creating a SQL statement in the Record Source property for a form, it is impossible to explain all the reasons that the SQL statement might cause the form not to show any data. Generally, however, this is caused by two or more tables in a record source with a combination of fields that do not return any resulting records. Be cautious when adding fields from multiple tables to the same form and be sure you understand the relationships between those fields and tables.

THE PROPERTY SHEET PANE

The Access Property Sheet pane provides access to the properties of a report and its controls, all in one place. To open the Property Sheet, click the Properties button on the Design tab of the Report Layout Tools Ribbon. You can also open the Property Sheet by using the F4 key.

To modify the properties of a particular control, simply click the control to select it in the report while the Property Sheet is open. Once a control has been selected, all of its properties are shown in the Property Sheet and can be adjusted. To set a property value, click the property in the Property Sheet pane and adjust the property from its drop-down menu (if applicable) or type in the desired value. To save modifications to the property, just change the focus away from the property's value field. But, always save the current form to ensure the new values will be persisted to the database file; without actually saving the report, the property will be reverted in some cases when the report is closed.

SETTING REPORT DESIGN PROPERTIES

The Layout Tools Design Ribbon makes it easy to quickly change the visual theme of a report or add new elements to the report layout, such as text boxes or images. To set the theme for a report, simply open it in Layout View and select the Design Ribbon. Click the Themes button to view the drop-down menu of available theme options, and then click the theme of your choice. The color and font properties for all of the controls in the report will be automatically changed. To choose the overall color scheme or font style of a report by hand, simply use the Colors or Fonts buttons to the right of the Themes button. The Design Ribbon also allows controls to be inserted outside of tabular data, such as text boxes, hyperlinks, logos, and images. These controls are generally confined to the gridline format of the report — free-floating text boxes and images are not possible.

TRY IT

In this lesson you create a report with the Access 2010 Report Layout View designer, using the Northwind database application included with Access 2010. The following example walks you through the steps necessary to accomplish this task. Sample files are available on the book's DVD and website.

Lesson Requirements

For this lesson, the example steps use the Northwind database application created from a template. However, the Northwind database is not necessarily required to complete this lesson; you can use just about any database application that contains a table with some fields and data. This example focuses primarily on building the report itself, and not necessarily the objects or data in the database being used.

Step-by-Step

1. Open Access 2010 from the Windows Start menu. The Access Backstage will open in the Access window.

2. In the Backstage, click the New option on the left-hand menu and then click the Sample Templates option to show a list of the built-in templates.

3. Click the Northwind template option in the middle of the list of templates to select it.

4. In the right panel of the Backstage, optionally select a name and location for the new database application.

5. Click the Create button to create the new database application from the template. The Northwind database application will open in the Access window.

6. Close any forms that are open, so that no database objects are open in the Access window.

7. Click the down arrow at the top of the Navigation Pane to show the grouping options available and select the Object Type option. The Navigation Pane will show the database objects grouped by type.

8. Click the Tables header in the Navigation Pane to expand it and show the tables in the database.

9. Click the Orders table in the Navigation Pane to select it.

10. Click the Create Ribbon to show the create options. Click the Report button. This creates a new report based on the Order List table's fields and opens it in Layout View.

11. Right-click any cell in the Taxes column to bring up the context menu. Choose Delete Column to remove the column and shift the remaining columns to the left.

12. Repeat the previous step for the Employee ID and Customer ID columns.

13. Right-click the Status column. Choose the Equals "Closed" option. This will filter all rows except for those whose status is Closed. This is much quicker than selecting and deleting individual rows.

14. Click the Design tab of the Report Layout Tools Ribbon, then click the Add Existing Fields button in the Tools group. The Field List will appear to the right of the report.

15. Click the Paid Date field in the Field List and drag it to the space in between the Shipped Date and Shipping Fee columns. The Paid Date column will be inserted into the report in this location.

16. Again on the Design Ribbon, click the Themes button and choose one of the themes from the menu that appears. All of the controls, colors, and font styles in the report will be changed to match the selected theme.

17. Change the color and font styles individually by using the two respective menus to the right of Themes. All related elements in the report will be changed to match the color or font style selected.

18. Right-click the Order Total column to bring up the context menu. Select the Total Order Total submenu and then select the Sum option. This inserts a cell at the bottom of the column showing the total value of the Order Total column.

19. Notice that the new sum cell is not showing its value in Currency format. Click the sum cell, and then click the Property Sheet button in the Design Ribbon to open the Property Sheet.

20. On the Property Sheet, click the Format tab to select it. Choose the value of Currency from the pull-down list in the value field of the Format property in the Property Sheet. The control will now display values in Currency format.

21. Move the mouse cursor to the right border of the cell until the cursor turns into a double-ended arrow. Click and drag to the right to widen the cell enough to show the full contents of the value in the Totals row. Note that the rest of the controls in the column are widened automatically.

22. Click the Save button on the top left of the Access window and type in a name when prompted. Click OK to save the report.

Congratulations, you have now successfully created a brand new report using the Access 2010 Report Layout View designer. To verify this report is working correctly, simply double-click the report in the Navigation Pane. The report will be opened in Report View mode and will show all of the data that was shown in Layout mode, but without the design grid lines or other designer features.

SUMMARY

Quick Reports are the easiest way to get started on a report in Access 2010, if detailed control over the `Record Source` property is not needed. The Report Layout Tools Ribbon provides all of the tools and options necessary to create, delete, edit, and modify controls in a report. The Field List pane allows easy additions of fields from tables and queries in the database to a report. The Property Sheet allows modification of control properties and the report itself. Visual properties of the report are easily modified with the tools in the Design and Format tabs of the Ribbon. The Access 2010 Report Layout designer makes it extremely easy to create robust, professional-looking reports in Access 2010.

 Please select Lesson 41 on the DVD to view the video that accompanies this lesson.

42

Creating Reports in Design View

The original report designer and traditional method for creating reports in Access is the Report Design View designer, and it has been around since the beginning of Access. The Report Design View designer allows the user to place controls of the report's design surface in a grid-based layout. Each report section provides a specific purpose in the report, such as a Header or Footer for the report. The Report Design View mode provides a number of tools and panes for working with reports, such as the Property Sheet, the Field List, the Group, Sort, and Totals Pane, the Navigation Pane, and all of the controls found on the Ribbon. The Report Design View designer is different than the Layout View designer in a number of ways, but most notably, the major difference is that the data from the data source is not shown at design time. This lesson discusses the basics of using the Report Design View designer to create reports for an Access database application.

LESSON SETUP

The lesson is designed to provide a basic overview of building Access reports as well as a step-by-step walk-through of how to create a report using the Design View designer. You should be familiar with opening and creating new objects in an Access database and be aware that reports are used to display the data contained in database tables.

CREATING A NEW REPORT IN DESIGN

Creating a new report in Design View mode is extremely easy to do in Access 2010. Complete the following steps to create a new report in Design View mode:

1. Open any database in Access 2010.

2. Click the Create Ribbon to select it.

3. Click the Report Design button under the Reports group. A new report is created and opens.

Once the new report has been created, you can begin building it by adding controls and manipulating their properties. Figure 42-1 is an example of a report that has been opened in Design View mode in Access 2010.

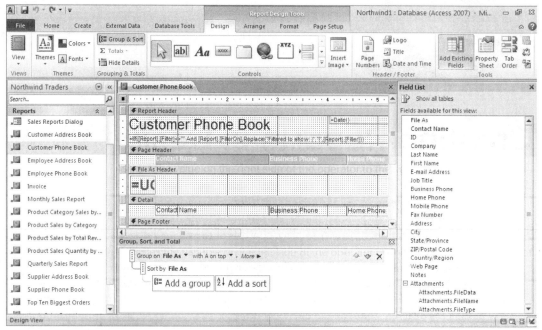

FIGURE 42-1

BOUND VERSUS UNBOUND REPORTS

Just as with forms, reports also have a `Record Source` property that determines whether a form is *Bound*. One of a report's most important properties is the `Record Source` property. Just as with forms, the `Record Source` property determines what source the report is getting data from by default. Controls on the report can refer to the fields in that dataset of the `Record Source` property by name. This allows the records in the dataset to automatically display in the report. Simply set the `Control Source` property of a control to the name of the desired table field, without adding any special code. When a report's `Record Source` property is set to a value that represents a dataset, the report is said to be bound to the data source. This value of the `Record Source` property can be the name of a table, query, expression, or even a SQL statement, and pretty much anything in Access that returns records. And, of course, the `Record Source` property can be set using VBA code or by using the Property Sheet to set the value.

When the `Record Source` property is empty, the report is said to be *Unbound*. When the report is unbound, it will still function as normal; the only difference is that the report does not have an underlying dataset attached to it. For example, you might want to have a report in your database that simply displays some static text. Rather than building a table to store this text and adding the fields to a report, it is often simpler and faster to type the static text into a control on the report. In addition to static reports, you might want to create a report that has changing data sources. In this case, you might bind and unbind the report to several data sources throughout the execution of your application. Setting and clearing the `Record Source` property is very easy to do, either using the Property Sheet through the Access UI or through VBA code.

THE REPORT DESIGN RIBBON

Once a report has been opened in Design View, Access 2010 provides four Ribbons that were not previously visible. These are the Report Design Tools Ribbons, which consists of the Design, Arrange, Format, and Page Setup Ribbons. The Report Design Tools Ribbons contain options for working with the report in Design View. These Ribbons are very similar to the Layout Design Tools Ribbons discussed in the previous lesson, with a few minor differences.

The first tab on the Report Design Tools Ribbon is the Design Ribbon. The Design Ribbon provides options for working with controls, themes, and headers and footers, a button for changing the report's View mode, and buttons for toggling on and off the Property Sheet and Field List panes. This Ribbon also has buttons for quickly creating page numbers, a title, adding a logo, adding totals, and opening VBE. Figure 42-2 shows the Report Design Tools Design Ribbon.

FIGURE 42-2

The second tab of the Report Design Tools Ribbon is the Arrange Ribbon. The Arrange Ribbon provides options for setting control layouts and adjusting rows, columns, and general positions of controls. In addition to the tools that are provided in Design View, the Arrange Ribbon provides some additional sizing and ordering tools when in Design View. Figure 42-3 is an example of this Ribbon.

FIGURE 42-3

The third tab of the Report Design Tools Ribbon is the Format Ribbon. The Format Ribbon provides options for setting the formats of controls and the report, such as quick styles, background images, font settings, data formatting, and background and alternating row colors. There is no difference between the Format Ribbons in Design and Layout View modes. Figure 42-4 shows the Report Design Tools Format Ribbon.

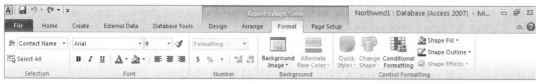

FIGURE 42-4

The fourth, and final, tab of the Report Design Tools Ribbon is the Page Setup Ribbon. The Page Setup Ribbon provides options for working with the report's page settings, such as the margins, page size, and page layout, and even provides a button for entering the legacy Page Setup dialog that was included with Access 2003 and earlier versions. There is no difference between the Page Setup Ribbons in Design and Layout View modes. Figure 42-5 shows the Report Design Tools Page Setup Ribbon.

FIGURE 42-5

To use any of these Ribbon options, simply click the control on the report that you want to manipulate and click the Ribbon option that is to be applied. In the case of adding controls to a report directly from the Ribbon, simply click the control type in the Ribbon to select it and then click the desired location in the report to place the control and it will be added to the report. Using the Report Design Tools Ribbon could not be any easier!

THE FIELD LIST

As discussed in previous lessons, the Access Field List pane is very useful for working with fields in the various tables contained in the database. However, the Field List is context-sensitive to the `Record Source` property of the report. The Field List does not show any tables for the data source for unbound reports, although the Field List does show data sources available in the database.

The Field List does provide the option to start adding fields to the report, even when they are unbound. If you click the Show All Tables link, the Field List will show a list of tables in the database. From there, you can expand any given table and drop fields onto the report, just as with forms. When fields are added in this manner, the Field List will create a SQL statement query for the `Record Source` property of the report automatically. But beware: Any time the Field List is used to add new fields to a report (or form), the `Record Source` of the report may be modified if the field being added does not already exist in the `Record Source` SQL statement. Also, because the Field List tries to create a SQL statement for any set of fields added to the report, modifying the report with fields from the Field List may cause the SQL statement to become an invalid query, causing the report to not show any data. In general, the Field List can be very handy for quickly dropping fields directly onto a report, adding the proper controls to make the report work in just a few clicks.

THE PROPERTY SHEET

The Access Property Sheet is very useful for working with the properties of the report and its controls. To open the Property Sheet, click the Property Sheet button on the Design tab of the Report Design Tools Ribbon. You can also open the Property Sheet by pressing the F4 key whenever the report is open in Design View (or Layout View) mode.

To modify the properties of a particular control, simply click the control to select it. Once a control has been selected, all of its properties will be shown in the Property Sheet. To set the property value, click the property value field to the left of the property's name in the Property Sheet and either type or adjust the property, depending on the options allowed for that particular property. Some properties have a "…" (Builder) button, which will open one of the various Access designers to help create and set the property's value. Once the cursor has been moved away from the value field, the new property value will be applied, but always be sure to save the report to ensure that all property changes are persisted.

THE GROUP, SORT, AND TOTAL PANE

Unique to reports, the Group, Sort, and Total Pane allows the user to visually manipulate the groups, sorting, and totals for the various controls on the report. Originally introduced with Access 2007, the Group pane allows group levels added to a report, which adds a new `Detail` section directly to the report, containing the control for the field that was selected for grouping. Sorting can be applied to any of the fields within the `Record Source` property and, of course, each sort can specify a number of different types of sorting and filtering for the records in the report. Totals can be added to each group level and even the entire report, so that the set of values shown can provide a total for the values, such as the count of the items or the sum of the values. Figure 42-6 shows the Group, Sort, and Total Pane in Access 2010.

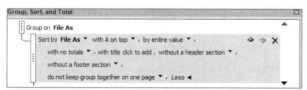

FIGURE 42-6

THE NAVIGATION PANE

By this point in the book you should be very familiar with the Access 2010 Navigation Pane. The Navigation Pane provides the user with the ability to drag and drop database objects directly onto the report, to add them as Subreport objects. This was not possible in Access 2003 and earlier versions, because the Navigation Pane did not exist. When creating a Subreport in this manner, the Access Design View designer does all the work to set the Subreport's properties to make it integrate with the current report. The Navigation Pane is a quick and easy method for adding Subreports or other supported database objects to a report open in Design View mode.

TRY IT

In this lesson you create a report using the Access 2010 Report Design View designer. The following example walks you through the steps necessary to build a simple report in Design View mode using the Northwind database application created from a template. Sample files are available on the book's DVD and website.

Lesson Requirements

For this lesson, the example steps use the Northwind database application created from a template. However, the Northwind database is not necessarily required to complete this lesson; you can use just about any database application that contains a table with some fields and data. To complete this lesson you should be familiar with creating a database from a template, creating database objects, and working with the Ribbon. This example focuses primarily on building the report itself, and not necessarily the objects or data in the database being used.

Step-by-Step

1. Open Access 2010 from the Windows Start menu. The Access Backstage will open in the Access window.

2. In the Backstage, click the New option on the left-hand menu and then click the Sample Templates option to show a list of the built-in templates.

3. Click the Northwind template option in the middle of the list of templates to select it.

4. In the right panel of the Backstage, optionally select a name and location for the new database application.

5. Click the Create button to create the new database application from the template. The Northwind database application will open in the Access window.

6. Close any forms that are open, so that no database objects are open in the Access window.

7. Click the Create tab of the Ribbon to select it. The Create Ribbon will be shown.

8. Click the Report Design button to create a new report. A new report will be opened in Design View mode.

9. On the Report Design Tools Design Ribbon, click the Add Existing Fields button to open the Field List.

10. Because the Record Source property for the report is currently empty, the Field List does not show any fields. Click the Show All Tables link in the Field List to show the tables and fields in the database.

11. Click the expander to the left of the Orders table to show the fields in the list.

12. Click and drag the Order ID field from the Orders table in the Field List onto the Page Header section of the report. New TextBox and Label controls will be created for the field, and the report's Record Source property will be updated with a new SQL statement.

13. Right-click the new `TextBox` control and select the Layout option from the context menu, and then choose the Tabular option. This will change the `TextBox` and `Label` to a Tabular Layout, so that the `Label` control is in the `Page Header` section and the `TextBox` control is in the `Detail` section of the report.

14. On the Field List, click and drag the `Order Date` field on top of the existing `Order ID` Label control on the report and drop it. Because the existing `Label` control is already in a Tabular Layout mode, the new `Order Date TextBox` and `Label` controls will be added to the layout, just to the right of the `Order ID` controls.

15. In the Field List, click the expander to the left of the `Customers` table to expand and show the fields available in the table.

16. Click the `First Name` field and drag it onto the existing Tabular layout, so that it will be added. The new controls will be created, the `Record Source` for the report will be modified again to include the new table, and the `Customers` table will be moved to the top section of the Field List.

17. Click the `Last Name` field and drag it to the position beneath `First Name`, so that the field will be added to the report. The new controls will be created and the `Record Source` for the report will be modified again to include the new field.

18. Click the expander to the left of the Invoices table in the Field List to expand and show its fields.

19. Click the `Amount Due` field and drag it into the Tabular layout on the form. The new controls will be added to the report.

20. If the Group, Sort, and Total Pane is not turned on already, click the Group & Sort button on the Report Design Tools Design Ribbon. The pane will open at the bottom of the Access window.

21. In the Group, Sort, and Total Pane, click the Add a Group button in the middle of the pane. A Field List will appear, so click the `First Name` field. This creates a group level and shows a `First Name` header section in the report.

22. Click the `First Name` Label control and press the Delete key to remove the `Label` and `TextBox` controls from the report.

23. In the Field List, click the `First Name` field again and drag it into the report, but this time, drop the field into the `First Name Header` section of the report.

24. Click the `First Name` Label control that was created to select only it, then press the Delete key to remove the `First Name` Label control from the report, leaving only the `First Name` `TextBox`.

25. Drag the `First Name` TextBox all the way to the left edge of the `First Name Header` section.

26. Repeat steps 22 through 25 for the `Last Name` Label and `TextBox` controls. The report will now group and sort by the first name of the customer.

27. Press F4 to open the Property Sheet.

28. Click the `First Name Header` to select it. From the Format tab of the Property Sheet, choose the Black option to make the background color for this section black.

29. For the First Name and Last Name TextBox controls, make the background color **Black**, the font color **White**, and the font weight **Heavy**. The names will now show in white for this section of the report.

30. Pull the report's Footer section all the way up to the bottom of the TextBox controls in the section to collapse it. This way, that record will not show so much space between them.

31. Click the Design tab of the Report Design Tools Ribbon to open the Design Ribbon.

32. Click the Amount Due TextBox controls and click the Totals button on the Design Ribbon to show the different total options for the field.

33. Choose the Sum option from the list and a couple of new Totals controls will be added at the bottom of the report. These controls now provide a sum of all the Amount Due fields shown in the report.

34. Click the Title button on the Design Ribbon. A new Title control will be added to the report.

35. For the report title, type in the value **Orders by Customers**. Then press the Enter key to commit the changes.

36. Click the Save button to save the changes and the report. For the Report Name, choose Orders by Customers and then click OK. The new report will be saved to the database.

Congratulations, you have now successfully created a brand new report using the Access 2010 Design View mode designer. You created this form completely from scratch, building each of the pieces using the various tools in the designer. To verify the report is working correctly, click the View button on the Design Ribbon to switch to Report View mode. The report will be shown, broken down by each customer, showing each of the orders for that customer.

SUMMARY

Creating a report using the Access 2010 Design View designer is a very simple and productive way to design reports in Access. The designer provides all of the tools necessary to modify, add, and delete controls on the report, as well as setting the formats and layouts for those controls. The Property Sheet pane allows the user to manipulate the properties for the report and its controls. The Field List pane allows the user to drop fields onto the report and place them visually without having to set any properties for the controls or manually build the Record Source for the report. The Navigation Pane allows the user to drop Subreports and other database objects directly onto the report. The Report Design View designer is the most powerful and traditional method of building reports in Access 2010.

 Please select Lesson 42 on the DVD to view the video that accompanies this lesson.

43

Access Report Properties

A strong knowledge of report properties is very important to building robust reports in Access. As you probably know already, all the settings on a report and its controls are called *properties*. When building reports, you set many properties using the Access Property Sheet, which is the Access UI (user interface) tool that exposes most of the properties for many different objects in an Access database. This lesson discusses the basics of Access's report properties and how you can apply them in Access 2010.

LESSON SETUP

To begin working with report properties, you must have a report to work with in a database. Every report has the same properties, so it doesn't really matter what kind of report you use — except for Web Report objects, which are different and are for use with SharePoint Web Applications specifically. You can easily create a new report or just use an existing one that is already in a database — it doesn't really matter for the purpose of viewing the report's properties for this lesson.

THE PROPERTY SHEET PANE

As you've seen in previous lessons, the only method for working with report properties is the Property Sheet. Part of Access since the very beginning, the Property Sheet lists each of the properties that an object contains, providing a list of property names and their values. The pane consists of five tabs to help categorize each of the property types.

Opening the Property Sheet

You can open the Property Sheet pane in one of two ways:

➤ Click the Property Sheet button on the Design tab of either the Report Layout Tools or Report Design Tools Ribbon.

➤ Press the F4 hotkey.

By default, the Property Sheet is located on the right side of the Access client window when opened, as shown in Figure 43-1. Once the Property Sheet pane is opened, it will remain open for any supported object whenever it is selected, until the pane has been closed. If a report is closed with the Property Sheet open, then the Property Sheet automatically reopens when the report is opened again in Design or Layout View mode. For example, if the Property Sheet is opened while a report is in Design View and the report is closed, the Property Sheet is closed as well. But if you open another report in Design View, the Property Sheet will open again automatically, without hitting F4 or the button on the Ribbon again.

It is important to note that the Property Sheet can only be opened in certain cases, and not for every object or just at any time when using Access. In general, the Property Sheet is available for forms and reports when they are in either Design or Layout View modes and that object is selected in the main Access window. Otherwise, the Property Sheet cannot be opened in many cases, such as when a report is open in Report View mode.

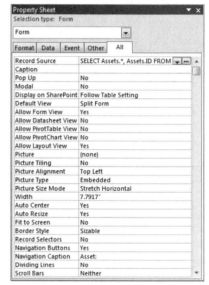

FIGURE 43-1

Docking/Undocking the Property Sheet

By default the Property Sheet is docked on the left side of the Access window, but it is possible to undock and move it to any desired location in the window. To undock the Property Sheet, complete the following steps:

1. Click and hold the title bar of the Property Sheet.

2. Drag the title bar away from the side of the Access window to which the Property Sheet is docked.

The Property Sheet will be undocked and have its own window. To once again dock the Property Sheet back to the Access window, complete the following steps:

1. Click and hold the title bar of the Property Sheet.

2. Drag the title bar back to the left or right side of the Access window, depending on where you want the Property Sheet redocked.

Once completed, the Property Sheet pane will be redocked to the Access window. Note that it is possible to dock this pane to either the left side or the right side of the Access window.

Resizing the Property Sheet

The Property Sheet can be resized by the user at any time during its use, when it is open. You have two methods for resizing the Property Sheet, depending on whether it is docked or undocked. This section examines both methods.

Resizing the Property Sheet when Docked

When the Property Sheet is docked with the Access window, it can be resized horizontally. To do so, complete the following steps:

1. Click and hold the edge of the Property Sheet that is farthest from the side of the Access window. By default, this will be the left edge of the Property Sheet.

2. Drag the edge of the Property Sheet left or right to make it larger or smaller.

Note that when you move the mouse cursor over the edge of the Property Sheet, the cursor bar switches to a splitter bar to denote that you can resize the pane. Resizing the Property Sheet when docked is just like resizing any other docked form in any other Windows application.

Resizing the Property Sheet when Undocked

The process for resizing the Property Sheet pane when it is undocked is slightly different, but also very intuitive. To resize the Property Sheet when undocked, complete the following steps:

1. Click and hold the bottom-right corner of the undocked Property Sheet pane. Note the grip marks on the edge of the window to denote where to click and hold.

2. Drag the corner of the Property Sheet pane in any direction to change its size.

That is all you need to do to resize the undocked Property Sheet pane. In this case, instead of using the edge of the pane, you use the handle of the undocked window to modify its size, just like other standalone Windows forms.

Resizing the Name and Value Fields

In addition to changing the size of the Property Sheet itself, it is also possible to change the size of the Name and Value fields inside of the Property Sheet. To do so, complete the following steps:

1. Click and hold the bar between any property name and value in the Property Sheet.

2. Drag the bar left or right to resize either the Name or the Value field.

Again, note that when you hover the mouse cursor over this bar, the cursor changes to a Splitter Bar, denoting that the element can be resized.

Using the Zoom Dialog

Often it is the case in Access that some property values are very long strings and difficult to see in their entirety in the Property Sheet. For this situation, Access provides the Zoom Builder tool, which is really nothing more than a dialog with a box that allows multiple lines of text to be displayed for a property value, as shown in Figure 43-2.

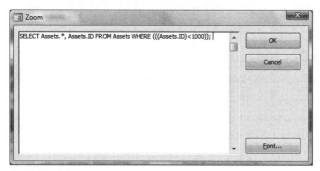

FIGURE 43-2

The easiest method for opening the Zoom dialog is by using the Shift+F2 key combination when you have the desired property selected in the Property Sheet. Complete the following steps to open the Zoom dialog:

1. Open the Property Sheet so a report is selected and the report's properties are shown.

2. Click the value field of any property that takes a string value. For this example, I used the `Record Source` property.

3. Press the Shift+F2 key combination while the property value field is selected, and the Zoom dialog will open.

Once the Zoom dialog is opened, it will show the property value currently stored in the field, if any. From there you can modify the value in any way you like and then click OK to save the changes. Working with the Zoom dialog is just that easy!

The Property Sheet Tabs

The Property Sheet is broken into five tabs to help categorize all the properties any given object provides. These tabs consist of Format, Data, Event, and Other, as well as an All tab that provides all available properties.

➤ Format is for the design formatting properties of a Report (or any object).

➤ Data contains the properties related to the data that is bound to an object.

➤ Event lists all the event methods available for the object.

➤ Other provides a location for all the miscellaneous properties that don't fall in one of the first three categories.

➤ All provides a list of every available property for the object, which is a culmination of all the properties listed on the other tabs. Using the Property Sheet to set property values, and knowing which properties are on which tabs, can save a lot of time and effort when building reports in Access.

ACCESS REPORT PROPERTIES

Access Report objects provide a multitude of functionality, much of which is exposed through the various properties that the report supports. A property is nothing more than a setting for the report that serves some purpose related to the report. For example, in the previous lesson, you set the report's Record Source property to determine which data source is tied to the report — this is a good example of how a property works. You supply the property with the desired data setting and, based on what is selected, the report behaves in a specific way. Doing anything with reports pretty much requires you to utilize these properties to make it happen!

Setting Report Properties

If you've completed the previous lessons in this book, you have already set lots of properties. A number of methods exist for setting properties, either through the Property Sheet or VBA code. Depending on the property, the values that can be set depend on the specific property that is being employed.

Using the Property Sheet

When using the Property Sheet to set a property on the Report object, you must first select the entire report. You can do this by selecting the Report option value in the Selection Type drop-down menu on the Property Sheet. Once the Report is selected, all of its properties automatically appear in the Property Sheet. Simply click the value field in the Property Sheet and then you will be able to complete one or more of the following actions:

➤ **Type the Value Text** — In some cases, you can type in the specific string or value you want the property to have. In many cases, this will be the only method available for setting the value.

➤ **Choose from an Option List** — Some properties provide a list of options available for the property. If this is the case, the value field for the property will have a pull-down menu from which to select the option. IntelliSense is also provided to show object names when typing in a specific value.

➤ **Use a Builder** — Some properties provide a builder option to help set the value for the field. The three most common builders utilized from the Property Sheet are the Macro Builder, the Expression Builder, and the Code Builder (the Visual Basic Editor, or VBE).

No matter which method is used, Access attempts to make the job as easy as possible for you. Once the property value has been chosen and placed in the value field for that property, the property will be set and ready for use.

Getting Information about Properties

Access Reports and their controls have tons of different properties to choose from, far too many to go into each of them in this lesson. However, lots of documentation is available on each of these properties and Access provides a couple of methods for finding out what any particular property does. The following is a list of several options for finding more information about each property:

➤ **The Access Status Bar** — A quick method for getting a short description for any property is to view the Access Status Bar, in the bottom left of the Access window, when a property is selected in the Property Sheet. The Status Bar displays a short description of the property.

➤ **The Access Help** — For a more in-depth description of a given property, the Access help often provides information and even some examples of using the property in many cases. Although these are often code examples, they can provide a more detailed description about properties than the Access Status Bar does.

➤ **The MSDN Library** — If the previous two methods don't produce enough information, the MSDN library is Microsoft's definitive online resource to find out more information about Microsoft products. See more at `http://msdn.microsoft.com`.

Once you know what property you want to use, you only have to set the desired value. Working with Report and other object properties in Access could not be any easier!

TRY IT

In this lesson, you set the values of several report properties using the methods described earlier. Although these aren't the only methods for setting property values, they are the most common, and getting familiar with using the Property Sheet and the other Access UI property tools will greatly improve your efficiency in building Access database applications. Sample files are available on the book's DVD and website.

Lesson Requirements

For this lesson, the example steps use the Northwind database application created from a template. This example focuses primarily on setting properties in a new report that is derived from the tables and data found in the Northwind database.

Hints

The following is a list of items that you might find helpful when working with reports in this lesson:

➤ When an Access Report is in Design or Layout View, you can quickly select the Report object by clicking the Report Selector. The Report Selector is the little square box in the top-left corner of a report that is opened in Design View.

➤ You can use the F4 key to open the Property Sheet at any time (but must be supported in the current context).

➤ The Access Status Bar displays a description of any selected property in the Property Sheet.

➤ You can use the Shift+F2 key combination to open the Zoom dialog when a property value is selected in the Property Sheet.

Step-by-Step

1. Open Access 2010 from the Windows Start menu. The Access Backstage will open in the Access window.

2. In the Backstage, click the New option on the left-hand menu and then click the Sample Templates option to show a list of the built-in templates.

3. Click the Northwind template option in the middle of the list of templates to select it.

4. In the right panel of the Backstage, optionally select a name and location for the new database application.

5. Click the Create button to create the new database application from the template. The Northwind database application will open in the Access window.

6. Close any forms that open when the database is created, so that no database objects are open in the Access window.

7. In the Navigation Pane, click the title bar where it says Northwind Traders and select the Object Type View option. This will change the view in the Navigation Pane to Group on Object Type.

8. In the Navigation Pane, expand the Tables group and click the `Invoices` table to select it.

9. On the Ribbon, click the Create tab to select it and then click the Report button. This creates a new `Invoices` report.

10. On the Report Layout Tools Format Ribbon, click the View button and select the Design View option from the fly-out menu. This switches the report to Design View mode.

11. If the Property Sheet does not open automatically, press the F4 key to open the Property Sheet pane.

12. Click the Format tab on the Property Sheet to select it. Select the `Caption` property value in the Property Sheet and type in the value **Invoices Report**. The `Caption` property value is what is shown as the title for the report window when the report is open in Report View or Print Preview View modes.

13. Once the value has been typed in, click the Save button in the top-left corner of the Access window to save the report. The name `Invoices` is fine, so just click OK when the Save As dialog is presented.

Congratulations, you have now set a property value manually by typing in the specific property value. To see the `Caption` property in action, simply switch the report to Report View mode and notice that the title of the report shows as Invoices Report. Now switch back to Design View mode to continue with this lesson and set properties using the other methods that the Access Property Sheet provides.

14. With the entire report selected in the Property Sheet, click the Format tab to select it. Then, click the value field for the `Allow Layout View` property, which specifies whether the report can be switched to Layout View mode.

15. Notice that there is a down arrow button on the right side of the field. Click this pull-down menu button and select the `No` option.

16. Click the Save button in the top-left corner of the Access window to save the new setting.

Congratulations, you have now set a property value by selecting an option from the pull-down menu. To see the `Allow Layout View` property turned off, simply click the View button on the Report Design Tools Design Ribbon and notice that there is no option available to switch the form to Layout View mode.

17. In the Property Sheet, click in the value field for the `Record Source` property. As noted previously, the `Record Source` property specifies which data source is tied to the report.

18. Notice that there is a button on the right side of this field with an ellipsis (the ". . ." text), which is called the Builder button. Click the Builder button.

19. Because this report already has the `Record Source` property set to a data source, Access presents you with a dialog asking if you want to create a query based upon the `Record Source`. Click the Yes button and a new query is opened in Design View mode in the Access window.

20. Double-click the * (star) field in the `Invoices` field list to add it to the query in the Query Designer.

21. Close the new query by clicking the X button on the top right of its window. You will be prompted to save the changes, so just click Yes. The new SQL statement will be added to the `Record Source` property for the report.

Congratulations, you now have now successfully set a property using the Access Query Designer. To verify this is working correctly, click in the value field for the `Record Source` and press the Shift+F2 key combination to open the Zoom dialog. You should see the text "SELECT Invoices.* FROM Invoices;" which is the SQL Statement that you created in the previous steps. If you switch the report to Report View mode, you will now see all the records in the `Invoices` table shown in the report. Using any of the methods described here is quick and easy to do using the Property Sheet and the various tools it provides.

SUMMARY

Setting the properties of reports, or the properties for controls that the report contains, is a vital part of building reports in an Access database application. Throughout this lesson, you explored several of the more common options for setting report properties using the Property Sheet. Depending on which specific property you are working with, some properties allow you to select the property value option from a list and many properties provide builder options for creating the property value. In all cases, the user can always type in the value that is desired for the property, and in many cases, it is required. As you become more familiar with the Access Report and various control properties, you'll also become more accustomed to using the Property Sheet and may find that one day you cannot live without it! Working with report properties is a snap in Access 2010!

 Please select Lesson 43 on the DVD to view the video that accompanies this lesson.

44

Report Sorting, Grouping, and Totals

Another very important part of building reports in Access is displaying the data in the report in the manner that you want it to be displayed. Often this requires that you sort and group the data to get the desired output in the report. For example, you may want to create a report for your Customers table that sorts and groups each customer shown in the report by the first letter of their last names. Fortunately, Access 2010 provides the Group, Sort, and Total pane to make it very easy to manipulate the way the data in a report is displayed. This lesson discusses the basics of working with the data in Access reports and provides an overview of how to use the Group, Sort, and Total pane.

LESSON SETUP

To begin working with reports with the Group, Sort, and Total pane, you must have a report to work with in a database and preferably some data to work with in that report. You can easily create a new report or just use an existing one that is already in a database; it doesn't really matter for the purpose of this lesson. The important part in this lesson is that the report has some data.

SHOWING DATA IN ACCESS REPORTS

In previous lessons, you used the Access Field List pane to drag and drop fields from preexisting tables into reports, so that the data from those fields would be displayed in the report. When the user performs this drag-and-drop operation from the Field List, Access is simply creating a new TextBox control and placing it in the Detail section of the report, setting the Control Source property for the TextBox to the selected field to tie the control to that data source. The Detail section of the report determines how data is to be displayed for multiple records and is the part of the report that is used when adding controls that are to display multiple records. This is because the `Detail` section of a report is repeated for each record in the data source that is tied to the report. Working with Group levels is much the same, and in this case, Group levels are added to the report as embedded `Detail` sections.

The really interesting thing about the `Detail` section for reports is that there can actually be multiple embedded `Detail` sections within a report, which provides several features for displaying the data in that report, such as grouping the data values. Multiple embedded group levels can be added to further group data within the `Detail` section and each of these groups can have its own header and footer for adding controls. The `Detail` section, supports up to 10 levels of embedded groups. However, it is important to note that you will only see the `Detail` section headers when in Design View mode (not in Layout View). In Layout View mode you see the data contained within the `Detail` section only, not the headers.

Also, several Access standard section types can be added to a report, each of which is used for a very specific purpose. These sections include the Report Header, the Page Header, the Page Footer, and the Report Footer. As each section's name suggests, the controls and data shown in each of these predefined section types only shows the data on that part of the report. For example, any controls in the Report Header section are shown only one time at the top of the report, and any controls placed within the Page Header section of the report appear on each printed page of the report. Although these particular sections are not actually accessible from the Group, Sort, and Total pane, the Access Ribbon provides entry points for working with them.

THE GROUP, SORT, AND TOTAL PANE

Originally introduced in Access 2007, the Group, Sort, and Total pane replaced the Grouping and Sorting dialog in previous versions of Access. As you may have gathered by now, the Group, Sort, and Total pane allows the user to visually sort, group, and total datasets that are shown in a report. The pane provides a number of new benefits for working with reports, such as allowing the user to see the visual changes in the report as modifications are being made in the pane. This is all in addition to the functionality that the old Sorting and Grouping dialog provided. Figure 44-1 shows the Group, Sort, and Total pane in Access 2010.

FIGURE 44-1

 If you are not familiar with the Sorting and Grouping dialog, do not worry! The Group, Sort, and Total pane in Access 2010 is very easy to use and this lesson covers all the basics.

Opening the Group, Sort, and Total Pane

You can open the Group, Sort, and Total pane whenever a report is open in either Design View or Layout View mode. Once in the correct View mode, open the Group, Sort, and Total pane using either of the following methods:

➤ Click the Group & Sort button on the Design tab of the Report Design Tools Ribbon.

➤ Click the Group & Sort button on the Design tab of the Report Layout Tools Ribbon.

Once you open the Group, Sort, and Total pane, you can begin using it to sort, group, and total data in the report. To close the pane when finished, click the X button in the top right of the pane, click the Ribbon button again, or use the key combination one more time — all of these methods will close the pane. However, because the pane is context-sensitive, meaning that it only shows when a report is open in the proper mode and the report is displayed in the Access main window, I often just leave the pane turned on until there is a specific need to turn it off.

Sorting Data in Reports

One of the most common features that the Group, Sort, and Total pane provides is the ability to quickly select and sort a field in the report. For example, you might want to have a `Contacts` report sort on the last names and then the first names of the people listed in the report. Using the Group, Sort, and Total pane to add sorts to a report is very easy in Access 2010. To add a new sort setting to a report, complete the following steps:

1. Open the desired report in either Layout or Design View mode.

2. Open the Group, Sort, and Total pane.

3. Click the Add a Sort button on the pane.

4. Choose a field name for which to create a sort.

5. Choose whether the sort should be ascending or descending.

Once a sort has been added to the report, records will begin sorting in the order (from top to bottom) that fields have been listed in the Group, Sort, and Total pane. Also, it is not necessary that the field actually be shown on the report to sort on it — as long as the field is included in the `Record Source` of the report, it can be sorted! If you need to remove a sort, simply click the X button to the right of the sorted field listing in the Group, Sort, and Total pane.

Grouping Data in Reports

Another very useful feature in an Access report is the ability to create groups for records that contain fields with non-unique values. For example, you might want to create a `Contacts` report that groups the contacts by their state name, so that the report shows all of the contacts by each state they live in. The Group, Sort, and Total pane makes creating groups on reports very easy. Follow these steps:

1. Open the desired report in either Layout or Design View mode.

2. Open the Group, Sort, and Total pane.

3. Click the Add a Group button on the pane.

4. Choose a field name for which to create a group.

5. Optionally, choose a sort for that field.

Once the new group has been added to the report, a new group level section will be added for the field. At that point, you can begin adding controls to this section of the report and the section will be repeated for each unique value for the record. Just like with sorts, it is not necessary that the field actually be shown on the report to group on it — as long as the field is included in the Record Source of the report, it can be grouped! If you need to remove a group, simply click the X button to the right of the grouped field listing in the Group, Sort, and Total pane.

Adding Totals to Reports

The last major feature of the Group, Sort, and Total pane to examine is the ability to add a control (to show the totals for selected fields in the report). For example, maybe you want to create a Contacts report that lists a count of all of the records (contacts) on the report. Using the Group, Sort and Total pane, it is very easy to create a totals row in the report, and you have several options for providing different types of totals, such as summing the values of the field or just simply counting the records. Complete the following steps to use the Group, Sort, and Total pane to add a control to show totals for a specific field:

1. Open the desired report in either Layout or Design View mode.

2. Open the Group, Sort, and Total pane.

3. If the desired field is already sorted or grouped, click that sort or group level in the Group, Sort, and Total pane to select it. Then click the More option on the selected sort or group level to expand and show all of the options.

4. Depending on the field, the third or fourth option from the left on the sort or group level will display the menu for adding a total for the field. To show the Totals menu, simply click the down arrow to the right of the Totals option on the sorting or grouping menu.

5. Select the desired options to add a control to display the totals for the field.

However, these steps assume that the desired field already has a sort or group level to be able to add a top-level total for that field. It is often much simpler to add a totals control from the Ribbon, especially when the report does not need any sort or group levels. Adding a totals control from the Ribbon is extremely easy. Follow these steps:

1. Open the desired report in either Layout or Design View mode.

2. Click the desired field control that should be totaled.

3. On the Design tab of either the Report Layout Tools or Report Design Tools Ribbon, click the Totals button to expand the Totals menu.

4. Select the desired totals option for the field. Depending on the data type of the field, some totals options will be enabled or disabled accordingly.

Once the desired totals option has been chosen from the menu, a new `TextBox` control will be added to the report to display the totals value. Of course, at the point, you can adjust the control and manipulate its properties to the desired settings. All Access did to create either of these totals controls is create a new `TextBox` control on the report and set a few properties for that control, the `Control Source` property being the most important of these.

Other Options on the Pane

Finally, aside from just sorting, grouping, and totals, the Group, Sort, and Total pane also provides several other options related to these features. These options include items such as adding Header and Footer levels for the sort of group level, adding a title control to the sort or group level, and even selecting how the records should be distributed within the sort or group level between printed pages. These options can be displayed by clicking the More option for any sort or group level in the Group, Sort, and Total pane. Any of these options can be selected as any other option is selected in the Group, Sort, and Total pane.

TRY IT

In this lesson, you use the Group, Sort, and Total pane to add some sorting and grouping to a report. This example guides you through the steps necessary to complete this task and attempts to illustrate how to use the Sort and Grouping pane features to build reports. Sample files are available on the book's DVD and website.

Lesson Requirements

For this lesson, the example steps use the Northwind database application created from a template. This example focuses primarily on building the report itself and showing the data in different configurations using the tables and data from the sample Northwind database application.

Step-by-Step

1. Open Access 2010 from the Windows Start menu. The Access Backstage will open in the Access window.

2. In the Backstage, click the New option on the left-hand menu and then click the Sample Templates option to show a list of the built-in templates.

3. Click the Northwind template option in the middle of the list of templates to select it.

4. In the right panel of the Backstage, optionally select a name and location for the new database application.

5. Click the Create button to create the new database application from the template. The Northwind database application will open in the Access window.

6. Close any forms that open when the database is created, so that no database objects are open in the Access window.

7. In the Navigation Pane, click the title bar where it says Northwind Traders and select the Object Type view option. This will change the view in the Navigation Pane to group on Object Type.

8. In the Navigation Pane, expand the Tables group and click the `Customers` table to select it.

9. Click the Create Ribbon tab to open the Create Ribbon and then click the Report button. A new report based on the `Customers` table will be created and opened in Layout View mode.

10. Click the `ID` column header in the report to select the entire `ID` column and then press the Delete key. The `ID` column will be removed from the report.

11. Repeat the previous step to remove all fields/columns from the report, except the `Company`, `Last Name`, `First Name`, `City`, `State`, and `Zip` fields.

12. On the Report Layout Tools Format Ribbon, click the Group & Sort button to open the Group, Sort, and Total pane.

13. In the Group, Sort, and Total pane, click the Add a Group button to begin adding a new group level to the report.

14. For the new group, select the `State` field from the menu.

Congratulations, you have now successfully created a group level for the `State` field in the report. Once the Group on State option is selected, the layout of the `State` column will be moved all the way to the left of the report, and each unique `State` field value will only be shown once and the corresponding records for that `State` will be shown under it. Also notice that by default, the `State` field is also sorting on ascending values. Figure 44-2 provides an example of what this report might look like.

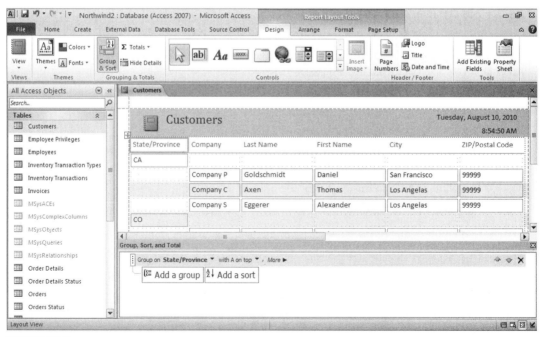

FIGURE 44-2

15. Next, click and drag the `Company` field to the right so that it is between the `First Name` and `City` columns.

16. In the Group, Sort, and Total pane, click the Add a Sort button.

17. On the Sort menu, choose the `Last Name` field.

Congratulations, you have now successfully sorted on the `Last Name` field of the report. Notice that the `Last Name` column under each `State` is now sorted by ascending value. Because the report is in Layout View mode, you see all of these updates with the data values as the changes are made, which is one of the major benefits to working in Layout View mode.

18. To add a totals control for the number of customers by state, in the Group, Sort, and Total pane, click the More button to expand the options for the `State` group level.

19. Click the down arrow to the right of the With ID Totals option to expand the Totals menu for the group level.

20. On the Totals menu, for the Total On option, choose the `Last Name` field option from the list.

21. For the Type option, select the Count Record option from the list.

22. Click the check box to select the Show in Group footer option. A new field will be added below the `Last Name` values for each state showing the number of records in that group.

23. Click the Save button in the top left of the Access window to save the report. When prompted for the report name, type in the value **Customers by State** and click the OK button.

24. Click the X button on the top right of the report to close it.

Congratulations, you now have now successfully created a report that uses the sorting, grouping, and totaling features of Access to display the data contained within the `Customers` table. To see this report in action, double-click the `Customers by State` report in the Navigation Pane to open the report in Report View mode and to see all of the data contained in the report. Optionally, you can switch the report to Print Preview mode to see what the printed pages of the report look like with the sorting, grouping, and totals. Creating sorting, grouping, and totals for a report is extremely quick and easy to do using the Group, Sort, and Total pane.

Finally, one last note: I recommend switching the report to Design View mode and examining the layout and controls to see how Access created this report using the Layout View mode designer and the Group, Sort, and Total pane. Remember, it is possible to create all of this functionality manually, without using the Group, Sort, and Total pane, by adding controls and setting the proper values to their properties in Report Design View mode. However, using the Access designer tools is often much easier and faster than manually creating the controls and setting the property values individually.

SUMMARY

Sorting, grouping, and totaling field values in Access reports is a very important part of building high-quality, descriptive reports. Using the Group, Sort, and Total pane in Access 2010, the user can quickly add and manipulate the way that data is shown in the report, using an Access visual designer. Sort levels allow the user to adjust the order in which the records are displayed in the report. Group levels allow the user to group records by the values stored in a field. And adding a totals row to the report or to a group level in the report is a great way to show off your data to the reader. Sorting, grouping, and totaling is a truly powerful and useful feature of Access 2010.

 Please select Lesson 44 on the DVD to view the video that accompanies this lesson.

45

Using Macros in Reports

As you've seen in previous lessons, macros are a big part of Access databases and can be extremely easy to create. Just as with forms, using Macros in reports can provide powerful functionality, without all the complexity of having to write and maintain VBA code. This lesson discusses the basics of working with macros using the new Access 2010 Macro Designer, and how macros can be applied to reports and their controls.

LESSON SETUP

To begin working with macros in reports, you must have a report to work with in a database. Every report contains the same Events methods, so it doesn't really matter what kind of report you use, except for Web Report objects. They are somewhat different and are for use with SharePoint and Access Web Applications specifically, but for this lesson, you should use normal Access Report objects. You can easily create a new report or just use an existing one that is already in a database; it doesn't really matter for the purpose of viewing the report's events and building macros for this lesson.

MACROS IN ACCESS

The term *macro* in Access refers to a set of functionalities provided by Access that can be executed when the macro is called. Macro objects can have one or more of these actions that execute in sequence when the macro is called. The best part about macros is that building them is as easy as choosing items from a list, just like when using the Property Sheet.

As you already know, two types of Access Macro objects exist: Named Macro objects and Embedded Macro objects. These two types of macros are basically the same, with a few distinct differences, and you will examine both types in this lesson and learn how both types can be applied to reports.

Named Macros

Named Macro objects, also known as standalone macros, are the Access Macros that are created as database objects. These are the base type of Macro object that Access 2010 provides. Each of these macros has a name attached to it, so that the macro's name can be called to execute the macro, from any place in the database application where calling macros is allowed. This allows macros to be shared by multiple forms or reports. Named Macro objects are separate entities from other objects in the database and exist as a separate database object, without necessarily depending on other database objects.

Embedded Macros

Embedded Macro objects are macros that live directly within another database object. These macros also consist of one or more actions, but these macros are part of the parent object and execute actions based on the events occurring within the parent object. The nice part about using Embedded Macros is that the Access Report Designer makes it very easy to embed macros in any object with just a few clicks. However, one drawback to embedded macros is that you may find yourself making the same macro over and over again, with just minor differences in the objects. In any case, the Access Report Designer makes it quick and easy to embed macros into your reports.

The Access 2010 Macro Designer

The new Access 2010 Macro Designer is the place for building macros in Access. The Access Macro Designer has been designed to make it easy to create macros, either Named or Embedded, and works very well for building macros in your reports. The Access Macro Designer provides a UI (user interface) where all of the possible macros can be selected from a list. Once an action is selected, the designer provides a list of parameters as well as the available settings for many of these parameters. This Access 2010 Macro Designer is shown in Figure 45-1.

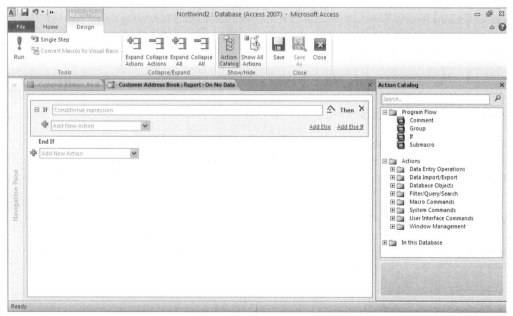

FIGURE 45-1

When an Embedded Macro is created, it is always immediately tied to the Event method for that the database object, being either a form or report. For example, you might create an Embedded Macro to open a form when the `On Click` event of a button is fired. Once the particular event is triggered, the macro's actions are executed in sequence from top to bottom, as they are shown in the Macro Designer. Data can be passed between these macros using `TempVars`, temporary variables for use in macros. Of course, if the macro only consists of one action, this doesn't really matter, but if there are multiple actions (and there often are), you can specify the order of actions by ordering the list of macros from top to bottom appropriately. Embedded Macros live in the module behind the form or report in which they are embedded, which is the primary difference between them and Named Macro objects.

New Macro Features in Access 2010

In addition to these previously existing features of macros, Access 2010 provides several brand new features for macros: conditional branching, an updated designer UI, IntelliSense in the Macro Designer, and an enhanced Action Catalog. The conditional branching features are provided by the if/else macro actions available in Access 2010. The new layout and look of the Macro Designer makes it easier to read and build macros very quickly. The IntelliSense feature both increases productivity and reduces the chances of errors by providing a list of available options when typing text into the fields in the Macro Designer. And it's easier than ever to choose actions from the Action Catalog. Although it may not sound like all that much on paper, these new Access 2010 features make it easier than ever to build macros in Access.

Adding Macros to Reports and Controls

Named Macros are probably the easiest kind to tie to the events of a report or its controls. Simply select the control on the report and, using the Property Sheet, locate the specific event to which you wish to add the macro. Click the down arrow in the event's value field in the Property Sheet and select the Named Macro you want to use. Alternatively, you can just type the name of the Named Macro into the value field for the event in the Property Sheet. In either case, the Named Macro is executed every time the chosen event has been raised.

Embedded Macros are always added to report and control Event methods, which is also accomplished by using the Property Sheet. In fact, you've already created a number of Embedded Macros if you followed all the steps in the previous lessons and probably already know how easy it is to do! To add an Embedded Macro to a form or control Event method, simply click the "..." (Builder) button in the Property Sheet for the desired event and choose the Macro Builder option. The Macro Designer will be opened to create a new macro, if one does not already exist for the Event method. If a macro already exists for the Event method, the Macro Designer will open the existing macro in Edit mode, so that it may be modified. When you're done adding the macro actions and setting the various properties, simply close the Macro Designer and the macro will be added to the report. Once you save the modified report, all changes to the macro will be persisted to the report object. Embedding macros in Access reports is probably the more common method used for creating macros in Access and extremely easy to accomplish.

ENABLING MACROS IN ACCESS

As mentioned in previous lessons in the book, the security features of Access, by default, block VBA code and certain unsafe macros from running until the database is in a trusted state. However, this does not block all macros from running; only unsafe macros are blocked from executing when the database is in disabled mode. Once the database is opened in a trusted state, typically by clicking the Enable button on the Access Security Bar, all code and macros can run freely, without deterrence from Access application security. The following sections describe some of the differences between safe and unsafe macros.

Safe Macros

Safe, or trusted, macros are macro actions that do not actually change the objects or data in the database and that cannot modify or change settings on the machine on which the application is running. For example, opening an Access report (all else being equal) does not actually change any data in the database; by itself, it does not modify or change any settings on the machine. It simply displays the report for the user to see. Therefore, a macro such as this can be considered trusted, because it cannot actually affect the database or machine in any way.

The major benefit to using trusted macros is that the database is not required to be trusted/enabled to actually execute these macro actions. Because they are deemed safe, Access will run them regardless of the Access application security state. If your database can function without code or unsafe macros, this will potentially save the user of the application the extra step of having to enable the database every time the application is invoked. However, the scope and overall feature set of trusted macros is fairly limited, and you may find that unsafe/untrusted macros are required for many common database operations.

Unsafe Macros

Unsafe, or untrusted, macros are macros that can perform actions that can potentially change the database objects, data in the database, or the settings on the machine on which the database is running. This is truly the essence of the power of unsafe macros, though — they can do so much, with so little effort. These macros can add/modify/delete data, run action queries, save changes to database objects, and so forth. And though unsafe macros are powerful, they come at the cost of requiring the database to be in a trusted state before these actions can be executed, because they can pose a risk of malicious programming to end users. You can always spot an unsafe macro in the Macro Designer by the Warning icon to the left of the name of the macro action, as shown in Figure 45-2.

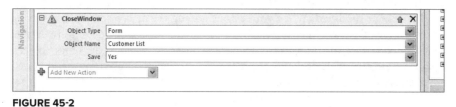

FIGURE 45-2

TRY IT

In this lesson, you create some Embedded Macros for a report using the methods described previously. Getting familiar with creating report and control events is a great way to learn more about the Access 2010 Macro Designer and how it is used. Complete the following example to accomplish this task. Sample files are available on the book's DVD and website.

Lesson Requirements

For this lesson, the example steps use the Northwind database application created from a template. However, the Northwind database is not necessarily required to complete this lesson; you can use just about any database application that contains a table with some fields and data. This example focuses primarily on how to create Embedded Macros for reports, and not necessarily the specific report objects or data in the database being used.

Step-by-Step

1. Open Access 2010 from the Windows Start menu. The Access Backstage will open in the Access window.

2. In the Backstage, click the New option on the left-hand menu and then click the Sample Templates option to show a list of the built-in templates.

3. Click the Northwind template option in the middle of the list of templates to select it.

4. In the right panel of the Backstage, optionally select a name and location for the new database application.

5. Click the Create button to create the new database application from the template. The Northwind database application will open in the Access window.

6. Close any forms that open when the database is created, so that no database objects are open in the Access window.

7. In the Navigation Pane, click the title bar where it says Northwind Traders and select the Object Type view option. This will change the view in the Navigation Pane to group on Object Type.

8. In the Navigation Pane, expand the Reports group to show the reports that already exist in the database.

9. Right-click the `Customer Address Book` report and choose the Design View option to open the report in Design View mode.

10. Press the F4 key to open the Property Sheet, if it is not already open.

11. Click in the value field in the `On No Data` property to select it and then click the "..." (Builder) button.

12. The Choose Builder dialog will open, so select the Macro Builder option and click the OK button. The macro designer will open.

13. From the macro action list, select the `MessageBox` option. The parameters for the `MessageBox` macro action will be expanded.

14. For the `Message` parameter, type in the value **This report does not have any data to show, it will now be closed.**

15. For the `Title` parameter, type in the value **No Data for Report.** The first action of this Embedded Macro is now ready to go.

16. For the next macro action, select the `CloseWindow` option from the action list. The parameters for the `CloseWindow` macro action will be expanded.

17. For the `Object Type` parameter, select the value `Report`.

18. For the `Object Name` parameter, select the value `Customer Address Book`.

19. The embedded macro actions are now set correctly and ready for use. Click the X button to the left of the macro's window tab to close the designer. When prompted to save, click the Yes button.

20. Now click the Save button on the top left of the Access window to save the report, because the new macro has been successfully applied.

21. Click the X button next to the tab for the report to close it. You are now ready to test it out!

Congratulations, you have now successfully created an embedded macro for a report. This macro will display a message for the user to see, saying that the report has no data to show, when that is the case. To verify this macro functionality is working in the application, complete the following steps:

22. In the Navigation Pane, click the `Customer Address Book` report to open it. Once the report has been opened, notice that it has a lot of data — in the form of `Customer` table records — to show the user.

23. Click the X button to the right of the report tab to close it.

24. In the Navigation Pane, right-click the `Customer Address Book` report and choose the Design View option to open the report in Design View mode.

25. Press the F4 key to open the Property Sheet, if it is not already open.

26. Make sure the Report object is selected in the Property Sheet, then click the Data tab to select it.

27. For the `Filter` property, type in the value **City='Boulder'.**

28. For the `Filter On Load` property, choose the Yes option.

29. Click the Save button in the top-left corner of the Access window to save the changes to the report's properties.

30. Right-click the document tab for the report and choose the Report View option to switch the report to the normal Report View mode.

Congratulations! You have successfully created some Embedded Macros for an Access report object. Because the `Customers` table does not have any records that contain the name `Boulder` in the `City` field, the report opens, but the message box, which you created in the Embedded Macro in the previous steps, is opened. Click the OK button to close the message box and the report. Notice that the report is now closed too, along with the message box, as specified in the Embedded Macro. Note that because you added the filter to this report, from now on, every time it is opened, you will see this message box. You may want to remove the filter, so that the message is not always shown for this report — only when it truly doesn't have any data to display.

SUMMARY

Using macros in reports is a great way to add functionality to any report without having to write VBA code. Both named and embedded macros can be used in reports, depending on how you design the specific macros. Just remember that it is important to require that the user of the application enable the database when unsafe macros are in use. And Access supports a wide variety of macro actions, several of which are new to Access 2010, and the new macro designer is easier than ever to use. Macros provide a powerful set of features that can be used to enhance any Access report.

For more information about working with macros, see the upcoming macros lessons later in this book, starting with Lesson 46, which discusses working with macros much more in depth. Although this lesson is a basic overview, you should have a good understanding of how to begin using macros in Access 2010 reports.

 Please select Lesson 45 on the DVD to view the video that accompanies this lesson.

46

Creating Macros in Access 2010

As you've seen in previous lessons, Access 2010 provides the ability to create Macros to execute simple functionality in a database application, without having to write code. This is accomplished through the use of the Macro Builder, which has been completely overhauled along with the other macro features in Access. This lesson guides you through the basics of creating macros using the Access 2010 Macro Builder and discusses the highlights of its features.

LESSON SETUP

Creating macros is very easy and requires very little knowledge of Access. You should already be familiar with Access databases and have a basic knowledge of the major database object types. To begin creating macros in Access, you only need an empty database to build standalone macros. However, it helps to have other database objects, such as forms and reports, to utilize many of the macro features that are available.

THE THEORY OF MACROS

Macros in Access are nothing more than a set of predefined actions that can be called, very easily, to perform their designated tasks. Often viewed as a simpler alternative to writing VBA code, literally hundreds of common macro operations can be executed without ever having to write a single line of code. For example, there are macros to open and close database objects, filter forms and reports, and even start the common built-in Access wizards and dialogs. The true advantage to macros is that the Macro Builder makes it very easy to select any of these actions from a list and then set their properties, directly within the designer. This effectively removes the need to know how to write code in VBA; it also reduces the chance for mistakes when creating an application's logic. The drawback is that macros are much less flexible than VBA code, provide much less overall functionality, and can have serious complexity issues as they grow in size. However, their simplicity and constantly expanding feature set make them a powerful feature that every developer should know about and utilize when it makes sense.

Enabling Macros

At this point in the book, you should be well aware of the Trust Bar, and the difference between enabled and disabled modes. Because certain macros are considered unsafe, which is discussed more in the upcoming lessons, some macros will not execute in disabled mode. The database is required to run in enabled mode to properly execute those particular macros. The user only needs to click the Enable Content button on the Trust Bar in Access to do so. Once the database has been enabled, all macros — regardless of trust status — should execute properly.

Creating a New Macro

Creating a new macro in Access is done in typically one of two ways. The first method, which creates a standalone macro, is to click the Macro button on the Create tab of the Ribbon. The second method, which creates an embedded macro, is to enter the Macro Builder by using the Builder button for object events on the Property Sheet. Although these are not the only methods for creating macros, you're sure to use both of them frequently if you plan to use macros in your database applications, which I recommend doing when possible.

THE ACCESS 2010 MACRO DESIGNER

The Access 2010 Macro Designer is more like a form in Access, where you fill in all of the fields, and that reacts to the chosen settings. This new designer also improves the ability to read and understand macro logic and flow, while providing the simplest interface yet. Figure 46-1 shows the Access 2010 Macro Designer.

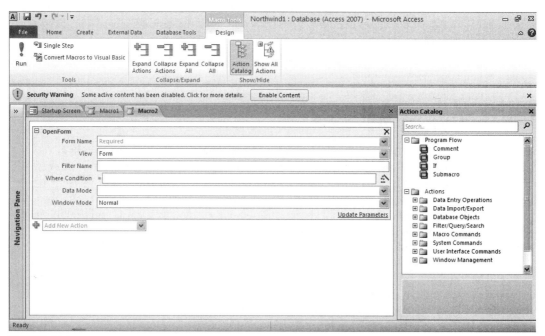

FIGURE 46-1

The Macro Tools Ribbon

The Access 2010 Macro Designer provides the Macro Tools Ribbon as part of the designer package. The Macro Tools Design Ribbon (the sole macro Ribbon) provides a few nice features for debugging and working with macro logic, as well as converting macros to VBA code. The latter can be quite helpful when learning to write VBA code. Figure 46-2 shows the Macro Tools Ribbon.

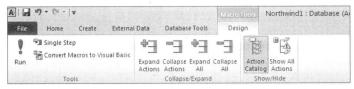

FIGURE 46-2

The Actions Catalog Pane

The Access 2010 Macro Designer provides the Actions Catalog Pane as part of the designer package. This pane provides a list of all macro actions, tools for Program Flow, and a list of your custom macros. Figure 46-3 shows the Actions Catalog Pane.

FIGURE 46-3

EXECUTING MACROS

All macros, in one way or another, are executed as a result of an event being fired. A macro is first set to an event, either specifying it by name or embedding it into the object; it is automatically executed when the event is fired. For example, the OpenForm macro can be embedded in a form behind the OnClick event for a Button control. Any time the button is clicked, the OpenForm macro is executed and the form it specifies is opened. This is really what makes macros so easy — you just set them to an event and presto, the action just works!

The Macro Tools Ribbon also provides the Run button for executing macro actions without having to set them to an event. The Run button can execute a given macro — usually for testing purposes to ensure that the macro actions are working as expected. Once the Run button has been clicked, the macro is executed as though it had been triggered from an event. Using the Run button to debug macros can save a lot of time when repeatedly executing the same macro for testing.

TRY IT

In this lesson you build a few Macros using the Access 2010 Macro Designer. Now that you know a little about macros in Access 2010 and the new Macro Designer, building them should be very simple and only take a few minutes. Sample files are available on the book's DVD and website.

Lesson Requirements

For this lesson, the example steps use the Northwind database application created from a template. However, the Northwind database is not required to complete this lesson; you can use just about any database application. You should be familiar with creating new databases and understand the basic Access objects, but no prior knowledge of macros is required to complete this lesson.

Step-by-Step

1. Open Access 2010 from the Windows Start menu. The Access Backstage will open in the Access window.

2. In the Backstage, click the New option on the left menu and then click the Sample Templates option to show a list of the prebuilt database templates.

3. Choose the Northwind option from the list of templates and click the Create button on the right side of the screen to create the sample database application. The new Northwind database will open in the Access window.

4. On the Create tab on the Ribbon, click the Macro option. This creates and opens a new standalone macro in Design View.

5. In the Action pull-down menu, choose the MessageBox option. This expands four properties options for the MessageBox macro.

6. For the Message property, type **Hello World of Macros.** For the Title Property, type **Hello World**. This is what appears in the MessageBox when it is executed.

7. Click the Save button on the top left of the Access window. For the name of the new macro, type in **Hello World**. The new macro will be saved. Go ahead and close it.

8. On the Create tab on the Ribbon, click the Form Design option. This creates and opens a new form in Design View.

9. On the Form Tools Design Ribbon, click the Button option to select it and then click the top right of the form to drop a new Button control on it. A new button is added to the form.

10. Press the F4 key to open the Property Sheet, if it is not already open.

11. With the new Button control selected, change the Name property on the All tab to **btnHello**.

12. Click the Event tab of the Property Sheet and click the down arrow for the value field of the OnClick event. Select the Hello World macro so that the field shows Hello World as the value of the OnClick event.

13. In the Selection Type pull-down menu on the Property Sheet, choose the Form option to select the entire form.

14. For the OnActivate event, click the "..." (Builder) button and choose the Macro Builder option. This opens a new embedded macro for the form in the Macro Designer.

15. In the Action pull-down menu, choose the MessageBox option. This expands four properties options for the MessageBox macro.

16. For `Message` property, type **This Form Has Been Activated**. For `Title` property, type **Form Active**.

17. Save and close the embedded macro.

Congratulations; you have successfully created a brand new, fully functional set of working macros. You were able to create both a standalone macro, which was called by name, and an embedded macro, which was embedded directly into a form. To test these macros, open the form in Form View. A message box pops up saying that the form has been activated. Click the OK button on the pop-up and then click the button you created on the form. A message saying `Hello World of Macros` pops up. Both of these new macros are working great.

SUMMARY

The Access 2010 macro builder provides all the tools necessary to quickly build macros for your database applications. The designer makes it easy to build macros by choosing from a list of options. It also provides the Macro Tools Ribbon and Action Catalog to quickly find and build macro logic. Set macros to events by using the Property Sheet, and executing those macros only requires firing the desired events. The Access 2010 macro builder is a surprisingly powerful feature, considering its extreme ease of use.

 Please select Lesson 46 on the DVD to view the video that accompanies this lesson.

47

Macro Types and Security

Now that you are familiar with how to create macros using Access 2010, you have a number of basics to consider. The macro security built into Access is very important to understand, so that your macros will run properly when executed. Also, it is important to understand the difference between embedded macros and standalone macros. This lesson discusses these concepts and provides some examples of working with these features in Access 2010.

LESSON SETUP

The only requirement for this lesson is that you understand how to create macros in Access 2010, as discussed in the previous lesson. Otherwise, this lesson does not require any previous specific knowledge of macros or Access 2010.

MACRO TYPES

Access 2010 has three types of macros: *Macro database objects*, *Embedded Macros*, and *Data Macros*. Though the differences between these types are somewhat minor, you should be aware of some important distinctions. This section discusses each type of macro and the key differences between the macro types.

Macro Database Objects

Macro database objects, often referred to as *standalone macros*, are the standard macro objects available in an Access database file. These macro objects are created when you choose the Macro option from the Create Ribbon. These macros are named and are called by name wherever their logic needs to be executed. The nice thing about standalone macros is that they are global to the database and can be called from anywhere that calling a macro is allowed, making them extremely reusable. For example, you can create a macro to open a specific form and then create multiple buttons, presumably on different forms throughout your applications, to open the specified form as needed. What makes standalone macros different than embedded macros is that they are separate database objects and not necessarily tied to any other object in the database.

Embedded Macros

Embedded macros are macros that are embedded directly in the module of a form or report. Embedded macros are created by using the Macro Builder option from the Property Sheet when building an event handler for a control on a form or report. These macros are specifically tied to the event in the form or report in which the macro is defined. Embedded macros are part of the code module for the form or report and they live in that module specifically, and because they are part of that module, they cannot be called from other modules or locations. Other than that fact, embedded macros are essentially the same as standalone macros and supply the same set of actions. Embedded macros are most effective when you need to add a quick macro behind an event that doesn't need to be shared across multiple event handlers.

Data Macros

Data Macros are new to Access 2010 as part of the feature set included with the new Access Web Applications on SharePoint. As of the Office 2010 release, the new Access Services package that is part of SharePoint Server 2010 allows the creation of a new special kind of Access SharePoint application, known as an Access Web Application. The new Data Macros feature of Access allows the developer to create macros that are specific to working with SharePoint tables, often regarded as somewhat similar to database triggers by the Access team. Data Macros allow the developer to add macro logic to the events of a SharePoint table. For example, a macro could be used to normalize the data when the record is submitted. Regardless of the specific task, Data Macros are a very handy feature for working with table events, but are only allowed with SharePoint tables in an Access Web Application.

MACRO SECURITY

The most important feature of Access 2010 to consider when building macros is Macro Security. Originally introduced in Access 2003, Access application security is designed to prevent any untrusted database application from executing both code and certain macros that are deemed unsafe or that could potentially cause a security issue on the client machine. This section discusses the difference between safe and unsafe macros, and what it means to be designated as such.

Safe Macros

Macro actions that do not potentially cause a security issue are called *safe macros* and are considered trusted in the database automatically. For this reason, only safe macro actions can be executed without security errors, regardless of the trust level of the Access client program executing the database application. The majority of macro actions are deemed safe, and these types of macros do things like open and close database objects, set filters, and move focus to controls. However, you may find that safe macros are quite limiting in a database application, because they cannot execute actions that modify data in the database or generally change the database file (or other files and objects on the machine). Still, the feature set supported by safe macros is pretty broad and you will undoubtedly use lots of safe macros throughout your applications.

Unsafe Macros

Conversely, there is a set of macros that provide a number of very powerful features, such as updating data, calling code or other macros, or even simply setting certain options in the database. These types of macro actions are known as *unsafe macros*. Unsafe macro actions are deemed untrustworthy because they can cause security issues due to their potential to make changes on the local machine. For this reason, unsafe macro actions will not be executed unless the database application is in a trusted state. Unsafe macros are easily identifiable by the warning icon that is shown next to the macro action name in the Access 2010 Macro Designer. When an unsafe macro action is selected by the developer, the yellow warning icon is shown directly to the left of the macro action name text. Figure 47-1 shows what the warning icon for unsafe macros looks like.

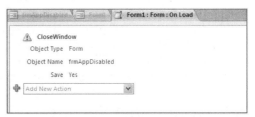

FIGURE 47-1

It is important to consider that whenever an unsafe macro is used in an application, the user of the application will be required to enable, or trust, the database application before the macro can be executed. It will not necessarily be evident to the user that this is the case upon simply opening a database application, because the Trust Bar is always shown regardless of whether the database actually contains untrusted objects. It is always a good idea to program some UI logic into the application to let the user know that the database uses macros and that the application requires that the user enable the content for the application to operate correctly.

 Even then, it is generally not recommended to ever trust an Access database application if you do not trust the developer. Remember, the most important thing here is that as soon as the database application has been trusted by the user, it has the potential to do serious damage to your computer.

Enabling Macros

At this point in the book, you should be well aware of the Trust Bar, and the difference between enabled and disabled modes. Enabling a database is quite simple to do, because the user only needs to click the Enable button on the Trust Bar in Access. When a database has been enabled by the user, it will be closed and reopened; so again, it always helps to tell the user to trust the database as soon as it is opened in Access. But again, beware and always know your database source before you enable it; once the database has been enabled, any and all macros and code will execute without discrimination and could potentially cause security issues for your computer.

Trusted Locations

It is also worth mentioning the trusted locations feature of Office 2007 and up. A trusted location is a folder on the machine that is designated as a safe location and any Office document run from that location will automatically be run in trusted mode. This can be very useful, because the user of a database application would not be required to click the Enable button each time the application is run from this location. However, there is a security concern in the fact that you don't want to just blindly run unknown applications from a trusted location. Trusted locations can also be set with a registry key, so it is easy to automate creating a trusted location during installation of the database application. In most cases, the trusted locations feature of Office can reduce the amount of overhead and headache for Access users by automatically enabling their database applications.

Access Runtime Security

Finally, one last item about the Access Macro Security features to consider: when running macros from an Access Runtime database application. When the Access Runtime is used to execute a database application, the database application must be trusted by the user to be opened. If the application is not trusted, the database application is automatically exited and the user will not be allowed to enter or work with the application.

A handy trick when using unsafe macros (and code) is to force the user to enable the application by making it an Access Runtime application, which is discussed in more detail in Lesson 62. Although the Access Runtime can be a great method of requiring the user to enable the application before it can be executed, be aware of how the Runtime works and, specifically, the differences between executing a database application under the Access program and the Runtime.

TRY IT

In this lesson, you build some macros to illustrate the difference between safe and unsafe macros. The following example walks you through the steps necessary to build some simple macros to show how both types of macros can be used in a database application. Sample files are available on the book's DVD and website.

Lesson Requirements

For this lesson, the example steps use a new, blank database to complete the tasks at hand. However, you can use just about any database application for this task, because you will be building all of the functionality from scratch. You should be familiar with the different types of database objects and how to create them to complete this lesson. This example focuses primarily on building some simple macros in a database, and does not necessarily require any specific data, database objects, or prior knowledge of building macros.

Hints

The following is a list of items that you might find helpful when completing this lesson:

➤ Unsafe macro actions are denoted by a warning icon shown just to the left of the macro action in the Macro Designer.

➤ Renaming an `.accdb` file extension to `.accdr` automatically forces the application to use the Access Runtime when launched from Windows Explorer.

➤ The F4 hotkey opens the Property Sheet.

Step-by-Step

1. Open Access 2010 from the Windows Start menu. The Access Backstage will open in the Access window.

2. In the Backstage, the Blank Database option should be selected by default. If not, click on the New option on the left pane, and click the Blank Database option to select it.

3. Optionally, choose a name and click the Create button on the right panel to create the new blank database. The new database will open in the Access window.

4. Close the default table that is created and opened automatically. It is not needed for this example.

5. On the Create Ribbon, click the Form Design option. This creates and opens a new form in Design View mode.

6. Press the F4 key to open the Property Sheet, if it is not already open.

7. On the All tab of the Property Sheet, set the `Caption` property to the value **Main Form.**

8. From the Form Design Tools Design Ribbon, drop a new `Label` control onto the form. Double-click the control and type in the value **This is the main application form.** This will be the hypothetical main starting form for the database application.

9. Click the Save button on the top left of the Access window. When prompted for the name, type **frmMain** and click the OK button. Close the form; it will be used again shortly.

10. On the Create Ribbon, click the Form Design option again. This creates another new form in Design View mode.

11. Click the Save button on the Quick Access Toolbar. When prompted for the name, type **frmAppDisabled** and click OK. This form is saved immediately, because it will be referenced in the following steps.

12. To add an Embedded macro to this form, click the Event tab of the Property Sheet and click the "..." (Builder) button for the `OnLoad` event for the form. The Choose Builder dialog will be invoked, so just choose the Macro Builder option. The Macro Designer will open in the Access window.

13. For the Macro action, choose the If option. This expands the `If` macro criteria.

14. For the condition field, the text box to the right of the `If` action label, type in **CurrentProject.IsTrusted**. This tells the macro to examine the `IsTrusted` property of the `CurrentProject` object to see if the application has been enabled and if Access is in a trusted state.

15. In the Add New Action field, just below the `If` action, choose the `OpenForm` option.

16. For the Form Name, type in **frmMain**, the form that you created earlier.

17. To add another macro action to this group, choose the `CloseWindow` action in the Add New Action pull-down just below the `OpenForm` macro.

18. For the Object Type, choose the `Form` option. For the Object Name, type **frmAppDisabled** (which is this form).

19. Close the new macro and choose Yes at the save prompt. You are taken back to the form.

20. From the Form Design Tools Design Ribbon, drop a new `Label` control onto the form. Double-click the control and type in the value **Application disabled, please click the Enable button to enable this application.**

21. Close and save the form. This form will now be used as the startup form for the database when the database is opened.

22. Click the File tab of the Ribbon to open the Access Backstage. On the left pane, click the Options option at the bottom. This opens the Access Options dialog.

23. In the Access Options dialog, click the Current Database option on the left pane to show the current database option in the right pane.

24. For the Display Form option, choose `frmAppDisabled`. This sets the `frmAppDisabled` form as the Startup Form in the database.

25. Click OK to close the Access options.

Congratulations, you have successfully created an application-disabled form for a hypothetical database application. If you close and reopen the database, the `frmAppDisabled` form will be shown as soon as the database is opened, telling the user that the application needs to be enabled before it will work correctly. Once the database has been enabled, the `frmAppDisabled` form will be closed and the hypothetical start form for the application will be opened. If you close the database, rename the file extension to `.accdr`, and then reopen the database, you'll notice that instead of the `frmAppDisabled` form, you are presented with an Access Security Notice. Clicking the Open button on the Security Notice dialog opens the application, and the `frmMain` form will be opened, because the application is trusted. Creating this form to verify an application's trusted mode using safe macros embedded in a form only takes a few minutes to set up, yet is extremely useful.

SUMMARY

Although the differences in the types of macros is minor, Data Macros are by far the most different, when compared to both standalone and embedded macros. All of these macros are subject to the Access 2010 Macro Security features and it is important to understand when a macro can be executed, and probably more importantly, when it cannot. Unsafe macros will only be executed when the database application is in a trusted state. There are several methods for attaining a trusted state, either by the end user trusting it manually, trusting it automatically by placing it in a trusted location, or by forcing the user to trust it by making it a Runtime application. No matter which kinds of macros you choose to use in a database application, they are sure to be easy to use and provide powerful features.

 Please select Lesson 47 on the DVD to view the video that accompanies this lesson.

48

Macro Parts

Now that you're familiar with the basics of creating macros in Access 2010, this lesson reviews the parts of a macro. Macros consist of four basic parts: name, actions, arguments, and conditions. Although all these parts are not always used when creating a macro, the macro action and its parameters must always be specified. In addition to these four parts, macros also have a couple of other features that are worth noting. For example, `TempVars` allow you to store and retrieve data within a macro. This lesson discusses Access 2010 macros parts and provides some examples of how to build macros, using the Access 2010 Macro Designer, with each of these components.

LESSON SETUP

The only requirement to this lesson is that you understand the basics of macros in Access 2010, as discussed in the preceding two lessons. Otherwise, this lesson does not require any other specific knowledge of Access.

MACRO CHANGES IN ACCESS 2010

As mentioned earlier, Access 2010 has had a major overhaul to the Macro Designer tools. In previous versions of Access, the Macro Designer looked much more like the Table Designer: a grid-based layout where the user filled in the macro's values. This grid contained five columns, though only three were shown by default: Macro Name, Condition, Action, Arguments, and Comments. The user created a macro by adding a new row to the grid and filling in the appropriate values. Each row in the grid represented a different macro, which would be executed in sequence from top to bottom, assuming the conditions allowed execution. Although all of these options are still available in Access 2010, the designer's layout is very different.

Upon creating a new macro in Access 2010, users are taken to a macro design surface, where they can select an action from a list. Once the action has been selected, the action's parameter controls are expanded and the available options are shown. Additionally, a second action list menu is shown, just below these parameters, so users can add actions to the macro. This new layout also allows the new conditional branching features to group macros visually in an indented section, where all actions within that section belong to the group. The theory is that the new Macro Designer makes it easier to read and understand the logic of a macro. All the parts of a macro in Access, and the changes in 2010, are discussed in the following sections.

MACRO NAMES

A macro name is used to call and execute a given macro. The macro name can simply be placed in any location a macro can be called in a database application, such as the value for an event method in the Property Sheet. However, the way macro names are specified has changed in Access 2010, compared to the previous versions. In Access 2007 and prior, the user could specify a macro name for an action, or group of actions, directly within the macro object (though the field for this option was hidden by default). This allowed a macro object to contain any number of different macro actions, all of which could be called directly by name. In Access 2010, the macro name is specified by the name that is used for the macro object for standalone macros. Embedded macros cannot be directly assigned a name, and thus cannot be called directly by any name. This new design simplifies calling macros, because the macro names are macro object names, and individual actions within the macro object can no longer specify, or be called by, a designated name.

MACRO ACTIONS

Macro actions are the actions that can be specified within the macro object. These actions carry out the specified tasks for the actual macro. Many different macro actions are available and can be viewed in the Action pull-down menu on the Macro Designer surface or in the Action Catalog Pane for the Macro Designer. By default, only safe macros are shown in the pull-down menu; however, the user can turn on all macros by clicking the Show All Actions button on the Macro Tools Design Ribbon. Also, some of the macros in Access 2010 have been renamed from the previous versions of Access; however, the overall actions should remain the same.

Specifying an action from the list is accomplished by expanding the pull-down menu and selecting the desired macro. Or, the user can begin typing a macro name into the Action field. The new Access 2010 Macro Designer provides IntelliSense and will show a list of actions based upon the values typed. Once an action has been selected, the macro parameters expand to allow the user to set the values. Once the values have been set, the macro is ready to use. Building the macros from the list of actions is just that easy. Figure 48-1 shows the pull-down list displaying the macro actions for a macro.

MACRO PARAMETERS

Macro parameters are the options available for a particular action. The parameters are specified by either selecting a value from the pull-down menu option or typing in the desired value. The specific macro parameters that are available depend on the specific macro being called, because these are the particular options of a macro action; but in general these are things such as a form name, a `Where` condition, or the values for a specific command.

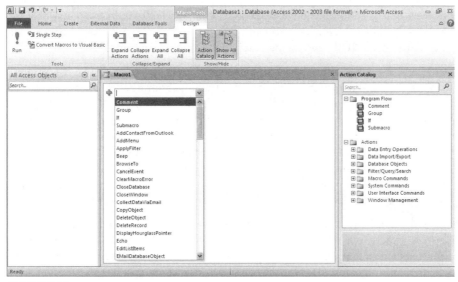

FIGURE 48-1

The parameters for a given action are not visible until the macro has been selected from the pull-down menu. Once the macro action name has been selected from the list, the grouping for the parameters is expanded so the user can begin to set the values. Not all macros require that all parameters be set. Access 2010 makes it very easy to determine which parameters are required: All required parameters show the word `Required` in the value field. Figure 48-2 shows the expanded parameters for a macro action once the action has been selected in the Macro Designer.

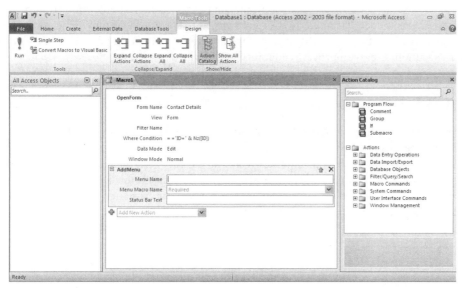

FIGURE 48-2

MACRO CONDITIONS

Macro objects can also contain conditions, which specify whether a particular macro action should be executed. However, macro conditions have also changed in Access 2010. In previous versions, the macro conditions were specified as an expression and that macro action would be executed if that expression were true. In Access 2010, specifying macro conditions is very different.

The Access 2010 Macro Designer allows the user to specify if, else if, and else conditional branching statements. To use one of these, simply select the item from the list of actions. Of course, else if and else can be used only if the if condition is used first. Once if or else if has been chosen for the action, the expanded parameters allow the user to specify a standard expression for the condition. The added benefit to this change is that it helps improve readability and makes it easier to create the logic of the macro (by grouping the actions within the if/else if/else statement block). Although the way conditions are specified in Access 2010 is different, the expression part of the condition statement is essentially the same as previous versions; any valid expression can be specified for the condition.

It is important to understand how if, else if, and else statements work. An if/else if/else block consists of exactly one if statement to start the block, followed by zero or more else if statements, and finished by zero or one else statements, in that order. During macro execution, each statement condition is tested, from the top down, and the first statement found true will have its actions executed. For example, when the if condition is failed, any subsequent else if conditions are tested; if none are true, the actions within the else statement will automatically be executed. However, if one of the previous if or else if conditions is true, then only the actions within that statement will be executed and the rest of the if/else if/else block will be skipped.

MACRO GROUPS

Also new to Access 2010: the Group macro action. Grouping macros simply allows the user to expand and collapse a set of actions. To create a group, simply select the Group option from the list of macro actions. The expanded parameter options allow you to specify the group name, along with the macro actions that are to be part of the group. It is important to note that grouping macros does not affect their execution; it only improves readability within the designer.

MACRO XML

Another set of features added as part of the Access 2010 release are the new Macro XML features. Macro XML allows the user to load macros from, and save macros to, an XML string. This new feature allows users to share macros with one another freely and easily. There was no easy way to do this in previous versions of Access. To quickly get the XML for any macro, simply highlight the desired actions and press Ctrl+C to copy the macro. Then the Macro XML can be pasted into a text document as an XML text string. The following is an example of the OpenForm macro:

```
<?xml version="1.0" encoding="UTF-16" standalone="no"?>
<UserInterfaceMacros xmlns=
```

```
       "http://schemas.microsoft.com/office/accessservices/2009/11/application">
         <UserInterfaceMacro MinimumClientDesignVersion="14.0.0000.0000">
           <Statements>
             <Action Name="OpenForm">
               <Argument Name="FormName">Contact Details</Argument>
               <Argument Name="WhereCondition">="ID=" &amp; Nz([ID])</Argument>
               <Argument Name="DataMode">Edit</Argument>
             </Action>
           </Statements>
         </UserInterfaceMacro>
       </UserInterfaceMacros>
```

To create a new macro from some existing Macro XML text, simply do the reverse of the previous steps. Highlight the desired Macro XML text, press Ctrl+C to copy the text to the Windows Clipboard, open a new or existing macro in Design View, and press Ctrl+V to paste the XML into the Macro Designer. The actions will be added to the macro, based on the pasted XML.

MACRO COMMENTS

Another Access 2010 feature change to macros involves how comments are used in macros. Comments in macros can be employed to provide any text information the user desires, such as how and why a macro was built. Comments in macros do not affect their execution. Because the Comment field is no longer available, to add a comment to a macro in Access 2010, simply select the Comment option from the list of macro actions. The only parameter for this macro is the comment text itself, which you can type right into the expanded text box after selecting the action. Comments are just another Access feature that helps improve macro development and usage.

MACRO TEMPVARS

Added as part of the Access 2007 release, TempVars are variables that can be used during macro execution. Their use is considered safe, so the database does not need to be enabled to read from, and write to, them. There are exactly three macro actions for working with TempVars:

➤ SetTempVar — To create a new, or set an existing, TempVar.

➤ RemoveTempVar — To delete a single TempVar.

➤ RemoveAllTempVars — To delete all existing TempVars.

The nice thing about TempVars is that they are global to the application and can be used in expressions anywhere in the database application and even called directly from VBA code. The Application.TempVars collection stores all of the TempVars in the database and can be used to access these variables in VBA code. However, one major limitation is that a database application is limited to a maximum of 255 TempVars in memory at any given time. Although that limitation is very important, most database applications do not need that many variables in memory at any given time. The benefits of using TempVars typically outweigh the drawbacks, especially considering they are the only built-in variable mechanism for use with macros in Access.

In terms of general usage, TempVars can only be used during the normal execution of a database application and do not exist in memory otherwise. That is to say, once the database has been closed, all TempVars are deleted. Tempvars only exist in the current instance of the Access application and the values are not automatically persisted to other memory when the application is exited. So, as a guideline for usage: The applications starts, you create new TempVars by calling SetTempVar in your macros, use them throughout your macros calling them using the TempVars collection, and when the application is exited, all the TempVars are destroyed. Working with TempVars in macros is really just that easy.

TRY IT

In this lesson you build a few macros using each of the macro parts that are discussed in this lesson. The following example walks you through the steps necessary to build some simple macros and illustrates how each of the parts of a macro can show how a macro is built in Access 2010. Sample files are available on the book's DVD and website.

Lesson Requirements

For this lesson, the example steps use the Northwind database application created from a template. However, the Northwind database is not necessarily required to complete this lesson; you can use just about any database application. This example focuses primarily on building some macros that use each of the macro parts discussed previously.

Hints

The following items might be helpful when completing this lesson:

➤ Unsafe macros are denoted by a warning icon, shown just to the left of the macro action in the Macro Designer.

➤ Clicking the Show All Actions button on the Macro Tools Design Ribbon shows all available macro actions in the macro action list.

Step-by-Step

1. Open Access 2010 from the Windows Start menu. The Access Backstage will open in the Access window.

2. In the Backstage, click the New option on the left-hand menu and then click the Sample Templates option to show a list of the built-in templates.

3. Choose the Northwind option from the list of templates and click the Create button (on the right side of the screen) to create the sample database application. The new Northwind database will open in the Access window.

4. On the Create Ribbon, click the Macro option. This creates and opens a new standalone macro in Design View.

5. Click the Save button (on the top-left corner of the Access window) to save the new macro. For the name, type **CloseAllForms**.

6. In the Action pull-down menu, choose the If macro. The parameters for the If macro will expand.

7. For the Condition field, type **[Forms].[Count] > 0** in the text box to the right of the If macro action. This condition states that if the number of open forms in the database application is greater than 0, run the following steps.

8. Add a new action to the If statement by choosing the CloseWindow option from the Action pull-down inside the If statement. This expands the parameters for the CloseWindow macro.

9. For the object type, choose Form. For the object name, type in the value =[Forms](0).[Name]. This statement returns the name of the first open form in the database application.

10. Add another new action to the If statement by choosing the RunMacro option from the next action pull-down inside the If statement. This expands the RunMacro macro parameters.

11. For Macro Name, choose the CloseAllForms option (which is actually this macro).

12. Click the Save button and close the macro.

Now you have successfully created a macro that recursively calls itself to close all forms in the database. If you open a few forms and then run this macro, all of the forms will be closed. Continue by adding a little more functionality here.

13. On the Create Ribbon, click the Macro option. This creates and opens a new standalone macro in Design View.

14. Click the Save button (on the top-left corner of the Access window) to save the new macro. For the name, type **OpenHomeForm**. The macro will be saved.

15. From the Action list, choose the Comment option. This expands a new Comment macro, so for the value type **Close All Existing Open Forms**.

16. From the action list, choose the RunMacro option. This expands the RunMacro macro parameters.

17. For Macro Name, choose CloseAllForms. This ensures that all the forms have been closed prior to opening the Home form.

18. From the action list, choose the OpenForm option. This expands the OpenForm macro parameters.

19. For the Form Name, choose the Home option. The macro is now complete, so click the Save button (on the top left of the Access window) to save the macro.

20. To show the Macro XML, click the OpenForm macro section and press Ctrl+C. Then open a new instance of Word (or some other text editor) and press Ctrl+V. The Macro XML for the OpenForm macro will be pasted.

21. Close the macro; it is ready for use.

Congratulations; you have successfully created a couple of macros, using each of the parts discussed in this lesson. If you open a few forms in the database and then run the OpenHomeForm macro, all forms in the database will close and the Home form will open for the user to work with.

Although this is just a brief overview of each of these parts, using them in an Access database is pretty much the same, no matter how you look at it. Remember that to get really good using macros, practice building them in applications. Also, search the Web to see other macros. With the new Macro XML features of Access 2010, there are bound to be thousands of great macros out there that you can use by simply copying and pasting them into your applications!

SUMMARY

The macro features have been greatly improved in Access 2010, and building each of the parts of a macro has never been easier. This lesson reviewed each of the major parts of macros in Access 2010: macro names, macro actions, macro parameters, macro conditions, macro comments, macro groups, Macro XML, and TempVars. Macro names, actions, parameters, conditions, and comments are the five basic parts of a macro in Access 2010. Macro groups are a new construct for expanding and collapsing a set of macros in the Macro Designer. Also new to Access 2010, Macro XML can create, save, reuse, and even share your macros. Finally, TempVars are a built-in mechanism for variables in macros that can store and retrieve data during macro execution. Understanding each of these macro parts and how to use each within a database application will ensure high-quality macro design as well as robust functionality for your Access database applications.

 Please select Lesson 48 on the DVD to view the video that accompanies this lesson.

49

Building Macros

Now that you're familiar with the different parts of macros in Access 2010, this lesson reviews building more complex, multi-step macros. Often, it is useful to build macros that execute more than just one macro action at a time and, as you'll see, building these steps is an art. As a macro performs more actions, the number of places the macro can fail increase exponentially, thus increasing the overall likelihood of your database application behaving in unexpected ways. These types of failures are often referred to as *bugs* in the application and programmers often take great care in preventing these sorts of problems from occurring. Learning how to properly handle problems that can occur will save both you and your application users a lot of time and frustration. This lesson discusses how to design multi-step macros, handle macro errors, and use logic branching and loops in macros to provide application functionality.

LESSON SETUP

The major requirement for understanding this lesson is that you should already be familiar with the basic parts of macros in Access 2010 and how to build them, as discussed in the previous lessons. Otherwise, this lesson does not require any other specific knowledge of Access 2010.

CREATING MULTI-STEP MACROS

Macro actions are really just granular operations that can be executed in a macro. In most cases it is desirable to put together several of these actions to build some operational logic into a database application. This concept is known as a *multi-step macro*. Although the benefits to putting these actions together are boundless, making it all work together can be confusing and the possibility for failures increases with each step added. When building multi-step macros, it is a good practice to complete each of the items in the following list:

1. Define what the overall macro will do.
2. Decide the actions required to get to the final result.

3. Consider the errors that could result from each action.

4. Design error handling to handle possible errors.

5. Build the logic for the macro by adding each of the actions.

6. Test the macro logic. If bugs are found when testing, repeat Steps 2 through 4 as needed.

Although these steps comprise the basic procedure for building macros, it is easier said than done. For example, it is hard to know exactly which problems can occur for any macro action. Testing your macros in different contexts will definitely be the key to making sure they work well. Fortunately, Access 2010 makes it very easy to build in error handling, debug, and test your macros.

HANDLING ERRORS IN MACROS

Because it is difficult to know exactly what can go wrong at any given time in a database application, especially one that is very complex, it is important to have solid error handling in a macro. In previous versions of Access, it was much more difficult to build in proper error handling, but this experience has been much improved in Access 2010, by providing a suite of features for working with macro errors. The `MacroError` object exposes information about any macro errors that may have occurred during macro execution. Also, there are exactly three macro actions for working with macro errors: `OnError`, `SingleStep`, and `ClearMacroError`. Although these four pieces may not seem like all that much on the surface, they are the basic building blocks for building powerful error handling into your macros.

The MacroError Object

The `MacroError` object is a member of the `Access.Application` class and it provides six properties that contain information about a given error. The following is a list of each of these properties and a description of the information that property provides:

➤ **ActionName** — The name of the action where the error occurred.

➤ **Arguments** — The parameters of the action when the error occurred.

➤ **Condition** — The condition under which the macro was executing.

➤ **Description** — The actual error message for the error.

➤ **MacroName** — The name of the macro where the error occurred.

➤ **Number** — The number assigned to the specific error.

The `MacroError` object can be called in any place an expression is allowed in Access. Also, the `MacroError` object can be accessed from VBA code as well, so that you can build applications with both macros and code to provide seamless error handling. The `MacroError` object does not contain any other methods or events.

The OnError Action

The `OnError` macro action is used to handle an occurrence of the `MacroError` object being set and is probably the most used action of all these error handling actions. The `OnError` action has two parameters:

➤ **Go To** — Specifies what should happen when the error occurs. It has three options: `Next`, `Macro Name`, and `Fail`. `Next` specifies moving on to the next macro action without any regard to the error. `Fail` specifies stopping and exiting the macro. `Macro Name` specifies jumping to the provided sub-macro.

➤ **Macro Name** — Specifies the name of the macro to go to when an error occurs, if the `Go To` parameter is set to the `Macro Name` option.

To use the `OnError` action, simply call the action before calling any action for which you want to catch errors. Any subsequent macro calls will be subject to that `OnError` action, so it is not necessary to make a specific call to `OnError` for every macro action called. To change the error handling procedure during the course of a macro, simply call the `OnError` macro action again and set it to the desired values. The `OnError` action is designed to allow the developer to catch any error that occurs and specify how that error should be handled.

The SingleStep Action

The `SingleStep` macro action allows the developer to explicitly define a breakpoint in a macro, which will open the Macro Single Step dialog. The `SingleStep` macro does not take any parameters and simply opens the dialog whenever the action is executed. This allows the developer to manually debug a macro from a specific point, and is very helpful when stepping through each action of a macro is not desired.

The ClearMacroError Action

Finally, the `ClearMacroError` macro action simply clears the current macro error by resetting the `MacroError` object. We recommend calling this method once you have successfully handled an error manually, before moving on to the next operation. This action does not take any parameters and to provide seamless error handling with VBA, the `DoCmd` object also provides the `ClearMacroError` method to perform the same operation from within VBA code.

LOGIC BRANCHING IN MACROS

The ability to branch code is very important in error handling routines. For example, in the case of one error, you might want to take one action, but in the case of a different error, you might want to take a different action. Fortunately, Access 2010 provides the `If`, `Else if`, and `Else` actions for constructing branching statements in macros, as mentioned in the previous lesson. Because the `If` statement can be used to specify a condition in which a macro is executed, the developer can check for conditions like this:

```
[MacroError].[Number] = 100 or [MacroError].[Description] = "Some Error Message".
```

A more subtle but powerful feature supported, as a result of the ability to branch, is the ability to create loops!

LOOPING IN MACROS

Though there are no built-in constructs for looping in macros, three features in macros make it possible to build loops: the ability to branch, the ability to use `TempVars`, and the ability to run a macro by name. For example, consider each of the more common types of loops and how they can be constructed using the features in Access 2010:

➤ **Do loop theory:** Do loops first execute a block of code and then check a condition, and if true, repeat that same code. A macro that performs a set of actions and then checks a condition before calling the `RunMacro` action on itself could be used to simulate a Do loop.

➤ **While loop theory:** While loops check a condition and if it evaluates as true, it will repeat a block of code. A macro that checks a condition before performing a set of actions and then calling the `RunMacro` action on itself could be used to simulate a While loop.

➤ **For loop theory:** For loops work much like While loops in the respect that they first evaluate a condition and if it returns true, they execute a block of code. However, in addition, For loops often allow the creation and modification of variables directly within the construct. In Access, one could use `TempVars` within the macro to simulate this behavior.

The key to any of these types of loops is the fact that Access allows *macro recursion*, the process of a macro calling itself to continue its execution. In each of these cases, the entire macro itself is the only loop. It should also be noted that the `RunMacro` action provides two parameters to allow the user to specify exactly how many times a macro should be executed: `Repeat Count` and `Repeat Expression`. Using any of these options creatively will allow the database application developer to simulate looping in macro actions, even though there is no direct support or action provided for looping in the base set of macro actions in Access 2010.

DEBUGGING MACROS

Finally, the last major feature of building macros to discuss is the ability to directly debug macros in Access 2010. The Single Step option, which is found on the Macro Tools Design Ribbon, can be toggled on and off to allow the developer to step through and halt on each action of a macro. When the Single Step option is enabled for a macro, every time a macro action is executed, the Macro Single Step dialog is shown. This is also the same dialog that is shown when a macro error occurs. Figure 52-1 shows the Macro Single Step dialog.

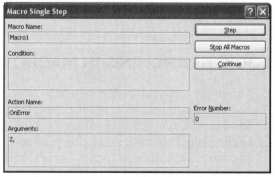

FIGURE 49-1

The Macro Single Step dialog provides all of the information that the `MacroError` object provides, except for the Description: the Macro Name, Condition, Action Name, Arguments, and Error Number are all supplied. This dialog provides three buttons:

➤ **Step** — Continues but then halts on the next action.

➤ **Stop All Macros** — Stops execution of all macros and returns to the database application. This is the only option available when this dialog is raised due to an error.

➤ **Continue** — Continues normal execution of the macro.

Single stepping a macro is quite easy to do. Just run the macro with the Single Step option enabled and the dialog will be raised each time a macro action is encountered in the macro. The only thing that is missing is an immediate window in this dialog to check the values of objects at any given point; however, you could simply use the immediate window in VBE, which is discussed in Lesson 51. The ability to debug macros is a powerful and useful feature, as you are sure to find as you build macros in your database applications.

TRY IT

Now that you have an understanding about how to build multi-step macros and have learned about the more complex features of working with macros, try building some more macros to do some error handling in an application. The following example walks you through the steps necessary to build such a macro and attempts to illustrate how each of the macro parts discussed here can be used. Sample files are available on the book's DVD and website.

Lesson Requirements

For this lesson, the example steps use the Northwind database application created from a template. However, the Northwind database is not necessarily required to complete this lesson; you can use just about any database application. This example focuses primarily on building some macros that employ error handling and the other features discussed earlier.

Hints

The following is a list of items that you might find helpful when completing this lesson:

➤ Clicking the Show All Actions button on the Macro Tools Design Ribbon shows all available macro actions in the macro action list.

➤ Clicking the Single Step button on the Macro Tools Design Ribbon enables single stepping for all macros.

➤ The database application must be enabled for unsafe macros to run without error.

Step-by-Step

1. Open Access 2010 from the Windows Start menu. The Access Backstage will open in the Access window.

2. In the Backstage, click the New option on the left-hand menu and then click the Sample Templates option to show a list of the built-in templates.

3. Choose the Northwind option from the list of templates and click the Create button on the right side of the screen to create the sample database application. The new Northwind database will open in the Access window.

4. On the Create Ribbon, click the Macro option. This creates and opens a new standalone macro in Design View.

5. Click the Save button on the top-left corner of the Access window to save the new macro. For the `Name`, type **ShowCustomError**. The macro is saved to the database.

6. From the Action list, choose the `If` macro option. The parameters for the `If` macro are expanded.

7. For the condition, type in the value [MacroError].[Number] = 2950. Adding this conditional statement executes the condition if a Divide by Zero error occurred.

8. From the action list inside the `If` block, choose the `MessageBox` macro action. The parameters for the `MessageBox` macro are expanded.

9. For the `Message` parameter, type in the value **Dividing by zero is not allowed!** For the `Title` parameter, type in the value **Error**.

10. For the `If` block, choose the `Add Else` option on the bottom left of the block when it is selected. This expands an `Else` statement for the `If` block.

11. From the action list inside the `Else` block, choose the `MessageBox` macro action. The parameters for the `MessageBox` macro are expanded.

12. For the `Message` parameter, type in the following value:

```
="Error Occurred! Number: " & [MacroError].[Number] & ". Message: " &
[MacroError].[Description]
```

13. For the `Title` parameter, type in the value **Error**.

14. Finally, outside of the `If` block, select the `ClearMacroError` option from the action list. This clears the macro error no matter which statement is used and it is cleared for any error, but you can put this inside the `If` block if you want to clear errors on a per-condition basis. In this case, you only call this one time, instead of for each condition.

15. Click the Save button on the top left of the Access window; the custom error message macro is now complete. Close the macro once it has been saved.

16. On the Create Ribbon, click the Macro option. This creates and opens a new standalone macro in Design View.

17. Click the Save button on the top-left corner of the Access window to save the new macro. For the name, type **LoopToDivideByZero**. The macro is saved to the database.

18. From the Action list, choose the `SetTempVar` option. This expands the `SetTempVar` parameters.

19. For the `Name` parameter, type **LoopCount**. For the `Expression` parameter, type:

```
=[TempVars]("LoopCount") - 1
```

This expression will set the value of the `LoopCount` TempVar to one less than the last time this macro was called, like a countdown in a `For` loop.

20. Choose the `If` option from the action list to create a new `If` block. The `If` parameters will be expanded.

21. For the `Condition`, type in the value:

```
[TempVars]("LoopCount") >= 0
```

22. From the Action list inside the `If` block, choose the `MessageBox` macro action. The parameters for the `MessageBox` macro will be expanded.

23. For the `Message` value, type:

```
= "100 divided by # of loops left = " & 100/[TempVars]("LoopCount")
```

24. For the `Title` value, type **Divide by Zero Example**. The `MessageBox` macro is now complete.

25. From the next Action list inside the `If` block, choose the `RunMacro` macro action. The parameters for the `RunMacro` macro will be expanded.

26. For the `Macro Name`, choose the `LoopToDivideByZero` option, which is this macro. Click the Save button and close the macro; it is now complete.

Now, when the `LoopToDivideByZero` macro is called, the recursive loop works all the way until the `LoopCount` TempVar gets to zero, at which point it will cause an error and show the custom error message that you just created. Finally, to add the last piece to this example, create one last macro.

27. On the Create Ribbon, click the Macro option. This creates and opens a new standalone macro in Design View.

28. Click the Save button on the top-left corner of the Access window to save the new macro. For the name, type **CreateError**. The macro will be saved to the database.

29. Choose the `OnError` option from the action list. The `OnError` parameters will be expanded.

30. For the `Go To` option, choose **Macro Name**. For the `Macro Name` option, type in the value **HandleErrors**.

31. Choose the `SetTempVar` option from the action list. The `SetTempVar` parameters will be expanded.

32. For the `Name`, type in the value **LoopCount**. For the `Expression`, type in the value 3. This sets the initial value for the `LoopCount` variable.

33. Choose the `RunMacro` option from the action list. The `RunMacro` parameters will be expanded.

34. For the `Macro Name`, choose the `LoopToDivideByZero` option. This is the initial call to start the loop.

35. Choose the `SubMacro` option from the next action list. The `SubMacro` parameters will be expanded.

36. For the `SubMacro Name`, type in the value **HandleErrors**.

37. From the action list inside the `SubMacro` block, choose the `RunMacro` option. The `RunMacro` parameters will be expanded.

38. For the `Macro Name`, choose the `ShowCustomError` macro that was created first. This will show the error message once the error has been hit.

39. Finally, click the Save button and close the macro. The `CreateError` macro is now complete and ready for use.

Congratulations, you now have successfully created several complex macros that simulate a loop recursively, cause an error, and then handle that error with a custom message using a branching statement. If you run the `CreateError` macro, you can see the error handling message occur. If you enable Single Step, you can walk through each macro action using the Macro Single Step dialog to see how the error occurs. Building complex macros can provide powerful functionality in any database application with just a few clicks and keystrokes.

SUMMARY

Constructing complex macros is a tricky business, but Access 2010 makes it easier than ever before. The new error handling features allow developers to trap and manipulate macro execution during an error. Logic branching allows developers to build code to handle and branch their macros, based on the current state in the application. Looping can be accomplished by building macros that recursively call themselves. Debugging macros is a snap using the Single Step macro option and action, which can integrate seamlessly into a database application. Access 2010 finally provides all the tools necessary for making macros first-class citizens in an Access database application.

 Please select Lesson 49 on the DVD to view the video that accompanies this lesson.

50

Data Macros in Access 2010

New to Access 2010, Data Macros are macros that allow the developer to apply macros to table-level events. Several different types of Data Macros exist and creating them is somewhat different than traditional macros. Now that you're familiar with some of the more advanced features of macros in Access, this lesson discusses Data Macros and how they can be created and applied to your applications.

LESSON SETUP

The only requirement to this lesson is that you understand how to use and create macros in Access 2010, as discussed in the previous lessons. Otherwise, this lesson does not require any other specific knowledge of Access.

THE THEORY OF DATA MACROS

The purpose of the Data Macro feature is to provide a macro that takes a user-defined action before or after an event occurs on the table. Because Data Macros are applied to table-level events, they are often compared to SQL triggers. Data Macros are different from standard Macro objects and embedded macros, because they provide only a limited set of macro actions.

In addition to being simply called from table events, Data Macros can also be called by name from the `RunDataMacro` macro action, which was added as part of the Access 2010 release. Although the number of table events available prohibits me from discussing each one individually, it is important to understand how these Data Macros work with these events and how Data Macro actions can be applied to these events.

EVENTS FOR DATA MACROS

As mentioned, Data Macros are applied to table-level events, and Access 2010 supports five table events. The table-level events can be broken down into two basic categories: before events and after events. There are two before events, `Before Change` and `Before Delete`, and three after events, `After Insert`, `After Update`, and `After Delete`. The corresponding event is raised either before or after a modification has been applied to the table. For example, you could set a local variable to denote that a delete action has occurred, after a delete action occurs on a table. No matter which events or actions you choose, creating Data Macros is just as easy as creating other macro objects.

CREATING DATA MACROS

Creating Data Macros in Access 2010 is somewhat different than other macros. Although the user still uses the Macro Designer feature to build the macro actions, the way in which the macros are assigned to the table events is different. In Access 2010, events are added to tables in one of two ways. The first is by selecting the event name on the Table Tools Table Ribbon (instead of the Property Sheet), which is available when a table is open in Datasheet View mode. Once the event button on the Ribbon has been clicked, the Access Macro Designer opens and you can create the macro itself. When a macro has been saved and set to one of these table events, the event will be highlighted in the Ribbon. The second method for applying a Data Macro to a table is accomplished by selecting the Create Data Macro option under the Table Tools Design Ribbon, while the table is open in Design View mode. Either method is sufficient for quickly adding a Data Macro to a table.

The Data Macro feature in Access 2010 also allows the creation of Named Data Macros. Clicking the Named Macro button on the Table Tools Table Ribbon allows the creation of a Named Data Macro for the table that can then be called up again by other events, macros, or VBA code. When creating a Named Macro, you can specify custom parameters to be used in the macro, much like a function in VBA code. Creating Data Macros in Access 2010, both named and otherwise, requires only a few steps of work.

RUNNING DATA MACROS

You should know by now that macros are executed in one of two ways: implicitly, as a result of an event being triggered that the macro is tied to; or explicitly, by calling the macro from another macro or through VBA code. For example, when a macro is run implicitly, it is because an event has been triggered that the macro was tied to, such as an update event occurring on the table after the user has added some data. Implicit macro calls are the method in which most macros are likely to be triggered and begin executing the macro. However, as with other macros, Data Macros can be called explicitly, yielding a number of benefits, and there are a couple of methods for doing so.

Data Macros can be named so that they may be called explicitly by other macros or in VBA code. When called, the Data Macro is specified in the form `<Table Name>.<Named Data Macro>`. For example, a macro by the name of `InsertMacro` for the `Customers` table would be called in the following form: `Customers.InsertMacro`. The `RunDataMacro` could be called with the `Customers.InsertMacro` as a macro parameter for the action, so that the macro applied to the `InsertMacro` event could be executed from anywhere. Explicitly calling a macro can also be accomplished by calling the `RunDataMacro` method of the `DoCmd` object in VBA code. The following is an example of how to write this code:

```
DoCmd.RunDataMacro Customers.InsertMacro
```

TRY IT

In this lesson you build a simple Data Macro and learn how the macro can be applied to the events of a table. Now that you have a basic understanding of what Data Macros are and how they can be applied to table events, building a Data Macro should be very simple. The following example walks you through the steps necessary to build a simple Data Macro and attempts to illustrate how Data Macros can be applied to the events of a table. Sample files are available on the book's DVD and website.

Lesson Requirements

For this lesson, the example steps use the Northwind database application created from the template. However, the Northwind database is not necessarily required to complete this lesson; you can use just about any database application. This example focuses primarily on building a Data Macro that will require the use of an existing table.

Step-by-Step

1. Open Access 2010 from the Windows Start menu. The Access Backstage will open in the Access window.

2. In the Backstage, click the New option on the left-hand menu and then click the Sample Templates option to show a list of the built-in templates.

3. Choose the Northwind option from the list of templates and click the Create button on the right side of the screen to create the sample database application. The new Northwind database will open in the Access window.

4. Close the Login dialog for the Northwind 2010 template once it has been opened.

5. Click the Shutter Bar on the Navigation Pane to expand it. Click the top of the Navigation Pane to switch it from the Northwind Traders custom group to Object Type. The Access object groups will be shown in the Navigation Pane.

6. Double-click the `Customers` table to open it in Datasheet View mode.

7. Click the Table tab of the Table Tools Ribbon to select it. Then click the After Update button to add a Data Macro to the After Update event for the table. The Macro Designer will open.

8. For the macro action, select the `If` option. For the condition, type in the following text:

   ```
   Nz([E-mail Address], "") <> "".
   ```

9. This condition requires that an e-mail address exists for the record, before the conditional actions are executed for this macro.

10. For the action contained inside of the `If` block, select the `SendEmail` macro action. The parameters for the action will be expanded.

11. For the To parameter, type in the value: **=[E-mail Address]**.

12. For the Subject parameter, type in the value: **Northwind Account Information Updated**.

13. For the Body information you could specify any string of data that you like. For this example, use the following string:

```
="Dear " & [First Name] & " " & [Last Name] & ", " & Chr(13) &
    "Your account information has been updated. " & Chr(13) &
    "Sincerely," & Chr(13) & "Northwind Traders"
```

The `Chr(13)` inserts a new line into the e-mail body in those locations.

14. The macro is now complete. Close the Macro Designer and choose Yes when prompted to save the changes to the macro.

Congratulations, you now have successfully created a Data Macro that sends an e-mail automatically to a person in the `Customers` table when his or her record has been updated. You can verify that the macro is working by adding your personal e-mail address to one of the customer records in the `Customers` table. Once you have added your e-mail address, an e-mail will be sent from your current machine to the e-mail address supplied in the table. A powerful feature for any Access database application, created in just a few minutes, and only two macro actions were required to make this functionality possible!

SUMMARY

Data Macros in Access 2010 are an awesome new addition to the macro features of Access. Data Macros allow the developer to add business logic in the form of macros to the five new table events exposed by Access 2010, something that was not possible in any previous version of Access. Though the available events are somewhat limited in scope, the overall power afforded by Data Macros greatly overcomes any drawbacks or limitations they may have. Data Macros are the perfect feature for building business logic into table events.

 Please select Lesson 50 on the DVD to view the video that accompanies this lesson.

The Visual Basic Editor

Before looking at how to write VBA code, you should be familiar with the Visual Basic Editor (VBE) feature of Access. VBE is included with Access, along with most of the other Office applications, and is the application that is used to write Visual Basic for Applications (VBA) code for an Access database application. The VBA programming language is a derivative of the Visual Basic language, and is most similar to Visual Basic 6.0. VBE provides a number of different tools and is much like other Microsoft code editors, so if you've used other Microsoft code editors such as Visual Basic 6.0 or Visual Studio .NET, you'll feel right at home in VBE. This lesson discusses the basics of VBE and how to use it to create VBA code. Figure 51-1 provides an image of VBE.

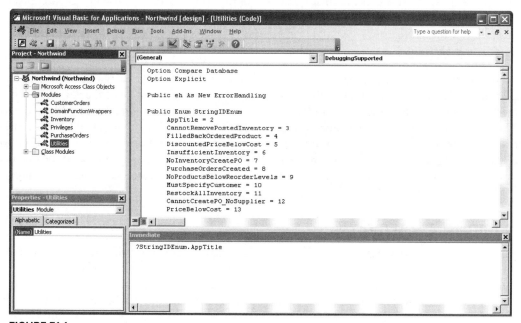

FIGURE 51-1

LESSON SETUP

The lesson is designed to provide information about the Visual Basic Editor and how to use it with Access 2010. You should be familiar with creating databases and creating the basic objects provided by an Access database. Otherwise, this lesson does not require any other specific knowledge of Access or writing VBA code.

STARTING VBE

VBE is built directly into the Access 2010 product, and Access provides several different methods for starting VBE:

➤ Clicking the Visual Basic button on the Create Ribbon.

➤ Choosing the Code Builder option from the Choose Builder dialog for an event from the Property Sheet.

➤ Selecting a pre-existing event in the Property Sheet that contains VBA code.

➤ Pressing the Alt+F11 key combination to open VBE.

➤ Pressing the Ctrl+G key combination to open the Immediate window.

➤ Creating a new Module or Class Module from the Create Ribbon.

Once VBE has been started, you can begin writing code. VBE has many different parts available to help you work with VBA code. Each key component that you are likely to use in VBE is called out in the following sections.

The Code Window

Probably the most important piece of VBE is the Code window. The Code window is the location that shows the actual code files in VBE, and is located right in the middle of the editor. When a module is open in VBE, it is shown in the Code window and the user can edit the code in the file. The Code window also provides IntelliSense for code objects when writing the code, which means that the methods, properties, events, and enumerations for an object are shown in an option list at certain times when writing code in VBE. VBE also allows multiple Code windows to be open at the same time, so that the user can quickly switch between windows. Figure 51-2 shows an image of the VBE Code window.

The Immediate Window

Another extremely handy feature in VBE is the Immediate window. When the Immediate window is open, it is located just below the Code window. The Immediate window allows the user to write some code and run it, without having to put it inside a module. Using the Immediate window, you can quickly run a piece of code, set or get the value of a variable, call a function or method belonging to an object, and so on. The Immediate window is often used for debugging purposes, or to quickly get or set the value of a variable. Figure 51-3 provides an image of the Immediate window.

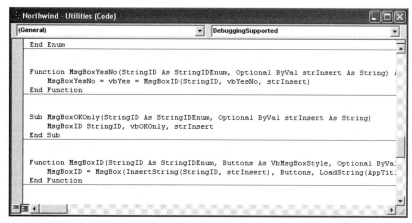

FIGURE 51-2

FIGURE 51-3

Opening the Immediate Window

You have a few methods for opening the Immediate window in VBE:

➤ Choosing the Immediate window option from the View menu in VBE.

➤ Using the Ctrl+G key combination. This works anywhere from within Access, not just in VBE.

➤ Clicking the Immediate window icon on the VBE toolbar.

By default, the Immediate window is located on the bottom of the VBE window, but can be moved to whatever location is desired, like any other pane or window in VBE.

Executing Commands

Executing commands in the Immediate window is very easy to do. For example, you could examine the number of tables contained in the database by getting the value of the Count property for the TableDefs collection for the CurrentDb object. To do this, simply type ? (a question mark, which is shorthand for PRINT) and then the property in the Immediate window:

```
?Application.CurrentDb.TableDefs.Count
```

When you press the Enter key after typing this statement, the number of tables in the database that is currently open in Access is returned in the Immediate window. For example, in the case of the Northwind database, the value of 33 is returned. You can do this while code is halted or even executing in the database application. The Immediate window is extremely handy for quickly getting and setting values.

The Object Browser

The next feature to examine in VBE is the Object Browser. The Object Browser allows the user to examine any code object that is already referenced by the VBA code project. The Object Browser shows the methods, properties, collections, enumerations, and events that any code object contains and is a good way to find out more about any given object. For example, I often use the Object Browser to find the parameters for any given method. The Object Browser can also be used to search for objects by name or for specific words or letters in object names. Figure 51-4 provides an image of the Object Browser window.

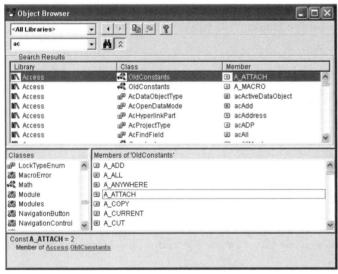

FIGURE 51-4

Opening the Object Browser

You can open the Object Browser window in VBE in several ways:

➤   Choosing the Object Browser option from the View menu in VBE.

➤   Using the F2 key when the VBE Editor is open.

➤   Clicking the Object Browser icon on the VBE toolbar.

When the Object Browser window is opened, it will be in window mode in the VBE Code window area. You can maximize the window to encompass the entire section and it can be sized just like any other window to fit however you like. The Object Browser window can even be docked to any side of the VBE window, just like any other window inside VBE.

Showing Hidden Objects

Some code objects are marked as hidden, or have methods or properties that are hidden, and are not shown by default in the Object Browser. However, it is possible to show hidden objects in the Object Browser by right-clicking anywhere in the Object Browser window and choosing the Show Hidden Objects option from the context menu. This option can be used to toggle on and off the Show Hidden Objects option for the Object Browser. Once the option has been selected, all objects, methods, properties, events, and so on that are hidden are shown in the Object Browser in a light gray font. Although it is very useful to see these hidden objects sometimes, it is also equally as useful to not have them cluttering up the Object Browser dialog, so the option is available for the user to decide whichever option they require.

The Project Explorer

The Project Explorer pane shows all of the code modules contained within a VBA code project. By default, the Project Explorer window is opened automatically and shown in the top-left corner of the VBE window. It can also be opened from the View menu and from the VBE toolbar, just as with the Object Browser and Immediate window. Each form or report that has a code module (i.e. contains code or macros) is required to have its own module and the Project Explorer can be very handy for opening the code module for any given object in a database. To open any module shown in the Project Explorer, simply double-click it. The module will open in the Code window. Figure 51-5 provides an image of the Project Explorer window.

FIGURE 51-5

The References Dialog

Any code object that is used in a VBA project must have a project reference store to that code library's physical code file, which is typically a DLL (Dynamic Link Library) or a TLB (Type Library) file. The References dialog is used to view, set, and remove any references for the VBA code project for a given Access database application. To open the Reference dialog, simply select the References option from the Tools menu in VBE. Figure 51-6 provides an image of the References dialog.

By default, several object libraries are set in a new Access database and are shown in the References dialog. The items that have checks to the left of their names are code objects that are already referenced in the VBA code project. By default, an ACCDB-format

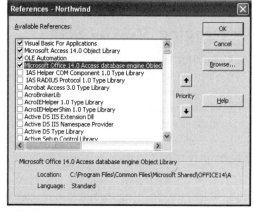

FIGURE 51-6

database created in Access 2010 automatically has four references: Visual Basic for Applications, the Access 14.0 Object Library, OLE Automation, and Access 14.0 Database Engine, all of which allow the user to work with the VBA and Access code objects in the Access database application. To add a reference to any additional code library in the list, simply check the box next to it and the reference will be added to the project. Unchecking any of the checked items removes the reference from the code project. If the library is not already in the list, you can always browse to the desired library by clicking the Browse button and then navigating to the library file in the Open File dialog. Working with references in VBE is just that easy!

DEBUGGING CODE

Arguably the most powerful and widely used features of VBE are the code debugging features. Using VBE, you can halt the execution of code, step through code line by line, and break at any specified location to help determine the state of the executing code at any time. This is extremely useful for resolving problems that may occur during the execution of your database application code. Several debugging features are available in VBE, each of which I discuss in the next sections.

Setting Breakpoints

Breakpoints are used to specify a location to halt the execution of code. To set a breakpoint, click the gray strip on the left-hand side of the Code window, directly next to a line of code. A red circle will be placed in the gray strip and the line of code will be highlighted in red to denote the breakpoint. Once code execution reaches that line of code, it will be halted and VBE will be opened so that the user may complete any number of operations that are allowed while the code is halted, such as check the state of variables or other code objects, change the state of things by setting values, begin stepping through the code line by line, or even start writing new code right on the spot. However, it is important to note that not every line of code can have a breakpoint set for it, such as variable declarations or Option statements. But most other code statements support breakpoints, and they are likely to be very useful to you when building and debugging your VBA code.

Debugging Step by Step

Once code execution has been halted, it is often helpful to step through the code line by line, and VBE provides several features for such operations. Specifically, VBE provides three different stepping features: Step Into, Step Over, and Step Out. In addition to stepping through code, VBE also provides the ability to continue execution, halt execution, and stop execution of code. Each of these items is discussed in the following sections.

Stepping Into Code

The ability to step into code allows the user to see every line of code executed. When code execution is halted and the Step Into option is selected, the debugger will go to the next line of code that is to be executed, even if it exists in another file or method. This allows the developer to examine the code in a line-by-line fashion, as it gets executed by the Access application. Three distinct methods exist for stepping into code when execution has been halted by the debugger:

➤ Selecting the Step Into option from the Debug menu in VBE.

➤ Selecting the Step Into option from the Debug toolbar in VBE.

➤ Pressing the F8 key.

However, this only includes code written by the user, which is contained within the database. VBA functions and other code libraries for which you do not have the source code cannot be stepped into.

Stepping Over Code

The ability to step over code allows the user to quickly walk every line of code executed in a VBA function. When code execution is halted and the Step Into option is selected, the debugger will go to the next line of code that is to be executed in that function. If the current line of code is a function call to another function, it will not be stepped into. Instead, it will be executed as normal and then code execution will again be halted on the next line of code in the current location. Three distinct methods exist for stepping over code when execution has been halted by the debugger:

➤ Selecting the Step Over option from the Debug menu in VBE.

➤ Selecting the Step Over option from the Debug toolbar in VBE.

➤ Pressing the Shift+F8 key combination.

Stepping Out of Code

The ability to step out of code allows the user to finish execution of the current function. If there is more code following the function call, execution will be halted on the next line of code after exiting the function. If that is the end of the code in the database, the database application will continue to execute as normal. Three distinct methods exist for stepping out of code when execution has been halted by the debugger:

➤ Selecting the Step Out option from the Debug menu in VBE.

➤ Selecting the Step Out option from the Debug toolbar in VBE.

➤ Pressing the Ctrl+Shift+F8 key combination.

Continuing Code Execution

Once code has been halted, VBE provides the user with the option of continuing normal code execution, as though it had never been stopped, called the Run option. Of course, if another breakpoint is encountered after continuing, it will be halted as normal. This is useful for debugging long blocks of code, where you do not want to step though everything line by line or if you simply just want to continue on. The Run option also allows the user to simply select a function, by placing the cursor in it, and then immediately run it by choosing the option. Three distinct methods exist for selecting the Run option:

➤ Selecting the Run option from the Run menu in VBE.

➤ Selecting the Run option from the Standard toolbar in VBE.

➤ Pressing the F5 key.

Pausing and Stopping Code Execution

VBE also provides the option to halt code execution, with the Break option. When selected, this halts code execution on the current line and is very useful for when code is taking long periods of time to execute, or when an infinite loop has been encountered. Three distinct methods exist for selecting the Break option:

➤ Selecting the Break option from the Run menu in VBE.

➤ Selecting the Break option from the Standard toolbar in VBE.

➤ Pressing the Ctrl+Break key combination.

Stopping code execution is just as simple: Press the Stop button from the VBE toolbar. When code execution is stopped, the code is reset and you will not be able to continue further from the last code location. Instead, you must start the code over again to begin executing the block of code when needed. Whether it be pausing or completely stopping code execution, VBE makes it extremely easy to do using the built-in commands.

TRY IT

In this lesson you use VBE to work with and debug some existing code. Now that you have a basic understanding of the Visual Basic Editor and some of the features it provides, working with some simple VBA code should be very easy. The following example walks you through the steps necessary to run and debug code in VBE and attempts to highlight how to use the key features of VBE discussed in this lesson. Sample files are available on the book's DVD and website.

Lesson Requirements

For this lesson, the example steps use the Northwind database application created from the template. However, the Northwind database is not necessarily required to complete this lesson; you can use just about any database application. You should be familiar with creating new databases and new database objects; otherwise no prior knowledge of writing VBA code is required. This example focuses primarily on working with some existing code to show how VBE can be used, so this example only requires a database that contains some VBA code.

Hints

The following might be helpful when working with VBE:

➤ Access must have code enabled in a database before you can run code in VBE.

➤ The Alt+F11 key combination can be used anywhere within Access to open VBE.

➤ The Ctrl+G key combination can be used anywhere within Access to jump to the Immediate window in VBA.

➤ The F2 key can be used to open the Object Browser when VBE is open.

Step-by-Step

1. Open Access 2010 from the Windows Start menu. The Access Backstage will open in the Access window.

2. In the Backstage, click the New option on the left-hand menu and then click the Sample Templates option to show a list of the built-in templates.

3. Choose the Northwind option from the list of templates and click the Create button on the right side of the screen to create the sample database application. The new Northwind database will open in the Access window.

4. On the Security Bar, click the Enable button to enable the database. This allows you to run code in this instance of the Access database application.

5. Press the Alt+F11 key combination to open VBE. VBE will open with the Northwind code project loaded.

6. In the Project window, expand the Northwind project. This will show folders for the three kinds of modules under it.

7. Expand the Microsoft Access Class Objects folder. This will show the modules in the Northwind project when expanded.

8. Double-click the `Form_Inventory List` module to open it. The code window will open with the VBA code for the module shown in it.

9. Notice that the code in the `Form_Inventory List` module has a method called `MsgBoxOKOnly`, which is not a standard VBA method. To find out more about it, press the F2 key to open the Object Browser.

10. Once the Object Browser is open, type in the value **MsgBox** and press Enter. The Object Browser will show all results for objects that contain the word MsgBox. Notice that the third result from the top of the Object Browser results is MsgBoxOKOnly, and that it is a member of the `Utilities` class of the Northwind code project.

11. Double-click the MsgBoxOKOnly result in the Object Browser. This opens the Code window to this method in the Utilities module that is included in the Northwind database application.

Congratulations, you have now successfully opened VBE, used the Project Explorer to find a code file in the VBA project in the database, and opened that code file in the VBE Code window. You were then able to successfully open the Object Browser and use it to search for code contained within the current project. Using VBE to work with code files is just that easy, but what about debugging? These next steps take you through the process of debugging a code file.

12. Close the Utilities Code window to go back to the Object Browser.

13. Close the Object Browser to go back to the `Form_Inventory List` Code window.

14. Click the gray strip next to the fifth line of code, to set a breakpoint for the line of code that says `If Not Me![Qty To Reorder] > 0 Then`. This sets a breakpoint and highlights the code in red.

15. On the Windows Task Bar, click the Access item to bring the main Access window to the front, so you can see it.

16. Click the Navigation Pane to expand it.

17. In the Navigation Pane, click the Inventory & Purchasing group to expand it.

18. Double-click the `Inventory List` form to open it in the Access window.

19. The `Inventory List` form will show all of the inventory information for each of the products in the database. Also notice that this form has a Purchase button on it for each record. Click the Purchase button for the first item in the list.

20. Notice that instead of all of the code executing, VBE is opened to the breakpoint set in Step 14 and execution of the code is halted.

21. Hover the mouse's I-beam pointer over the `RestockSuccess` variable. Notice that the IntelliSense popup is shown and provides a value of `RestockSuccess=19`. This is the current value of the variable and this feature is extremely useful in VBE for quickly figuring out the current values of variables.

22. If the Immediate window is not already open, press the Ctrl+G key combination to open it.

23. In the Immediate window, type in the value **?Me![Qty To Reorder]** and then press Enter. The Immediate window returns the value of `0`. This is how the Immediate window can be used to quickly check the value of objects while debugging code.

24. Press the F8 key to step into the current line of code. Notice that the current code cursor is moved to the next line of code and that the previous line of code was executed. This is how to step into code, and walk the code line by line.

25. Press the F8 key to step into the current line of code. Notice that this time the Utilities Code window is opened and code is halted on the `MsgBoxOKOnly` subroutine. This is because you stepped into the `MsgBoxOKOnly` subroutine in the previous line of code in the other file. When the code is present in the database, stepping into the code will take you to the code's definition file in the code project.

26. Press the F5 key to continue on with normal code execution. The code continues and you are eventually taken to a message in the main Access window.

Congratulations, you have successfully used VBE to debug some code. You set a breakpoint, executed code to that breakpoint, viewed some variable values using both the Immediate window and the VBE IntelliSense features, and stepped through that code. Debugging code sections is really nothing more than this and usually, using these features, you will be able to find errors in the code and where they occur, so that you can easily and quickly make changes. Using VBE to debug code is a piece of cake and an extremely powerful feature in Access.

SUMMARY

The Visual Basic Editor is an integral part of Access 2010 and required for building and working with VBA code in an Access database. VBE provides a host of features such as, but not limited to, the Code window, the Object Browser, the Immediate window, and the Project Explorer, all of which were examined in this lesson. The debugging features are likely to be the features in VBE that you use the most. Now that you understand the basics of setting breakpoints and stepping through code, debugging your own applications with VBE should be a snap!

 Please select Lesson 51 on the DVD to view the video that accompanies this lesson.

52

Introduction to VBA

Visual Basic for Applications (VBA) is a programming language that is included with Access and most of the other Office 2010 products. VBA allows a user of Access to write a kind of Visual Basic code to provide custom functionality for a database application. VBA is very closely tied to all of the Office applications and makes it very easy to create custom code that works directly with a specific Office application and the code objects contained within it. Although you've already created some VBA code in previous lessons, these next several lessons discuss creating VBA code in much more depth.

LESSON SETUP

This lesson is designed to provide information about the Visual Basic programming language and the basics of writing VBA code. You should be familiar with creating databases, working with the basic objects in an Access database, and the Visual Basic Editor. Otherwise, completing this lesson does not require any other specific knowledge of Access or VBA code.

WRITING VBA CODE

Writing VBA code is by far the hardest part of learning to use Access, but the rewards are endless. Using VBA code, you can program almost any functionality desired into an Access database application. Now that you have a pretty good understanding of the major features that VBE has to offer and how it can be used, you can put that knowledge to use and begin learning how to write VBA code.

Visual Basic for Applications is a derivative of Microsoft's Visual Basic programming language, and is almost identical to Visual Basic 6.0 (VB6). Although differences exist between VBA and VB6, the syntax (how the language is constructed and written) is almost exactly the same. Also, most of the keywords, operators, and functionality are the same as well. So, if you are already familiar with VB6, learning VBA will be very easy for you. But, if you don't know

VB6 already, these next few lessons will provide many examples about how to write VBA code and work with Access using VBA. There is no need to worry about having a pre-existing knowledge of VB6 to review and complete the steps in these lessons; all of the basics you need to know about writing VBA code will be discussed here.

Creating Modules

Before you can begin writing VBA code in an Access database application, you must first create a module to write the code in. A module is where the VBA code in a database lives, and most databases have lots of them, even if you aren't directly aware of them. There are several different kinds of modules in Access 2010: a Module database object, a Class Module database object, and Form and Report Modules. Module and Class Module objects can be created from the Create Ribbon, by choosing the corresponding option under the Macros & Code group. Form and Report Modules can be created explicitly, but are usually created automatically when the user chooses the option to embed code or macros in a form or report. Code in any given module is specific to that module, and many rules exist about how modules can reference each other's code. Either way, you'll need a module before you can begin creating code.

Modules are most commonly created by clicking the Module or Class Module button on the Create Ribbon. Clicking either of these buttons creates a new object in the database and opens the Visual Basic Editor to allow the developer to begin writing code in the module. However, the module will not actually be saved to the database until you press the Save button in VBE or close VBE and choose the Yes option when prompted to save the module. When saved, you must supply a name for the module, and in the case of a class module, this name is the name of the class itself. Either way, creating a new module is extremely easy using the options on the Create Ribbon.

Creating Subroutines

Subroutines are the simplest type of code procedure available in VBA, and are declared using the Sub keyword. You have probably already created a few subroutines if you have completed many of the previous lessons in this book. In VBA, a Sub does support parameters, but does not allow return values. A Sub can be specified with a code access modifier, such as Public, Private, or Friend, which are used to determine what other code can access this subroutine. Subs must be terminated with the End Sub keywords. A Sub can be exited at any time in the method by issuing the Exit Sub statement. The following code provides two different examples of subroutines:

```
Sub ShowInfo()
  MsgBox "Some information to show in a message box", vbInformation
End Sub


Public Sub Add(iLeft as Integer, iRight as Integer)
  MsgBox "The result is: " & (iLeft + iRight), vbInformation
End Sub
```

The first of these two subroutines, named ShowInfo, simply shows a message box with some information; it does not take any parameters. The second subroutine, named Add, takes two parameters, adds them together, and shows the result in a message box. A Sub is a quick way in VBA to build a code routine that does not need to return a value.

Creating Functions

Functions are quite similar to subroutines in VBA, except that functions can also return a value. Functions are declared by using the keyword `Function`. Functions also support parameters and can be scoped as `Public`, `Private`, or `Friend`. Functions must be terminated with the keywords `End Function`, and can be exited at any time by issuing the `Exit Function` statement. To return a value from a function, you must also specify the return type in the function declaration and set the function name to the return value, before exiting the function. The following code provides an example of two different functions:

```
Public Function HelloWorld()
   MsgBox "Hello World of VBA!", vbInformation
End Function


Private Function Add(iLeft as Integer, iRight as Integer) as Integer
   Add = iLeft + iRight
End Function
```

The first of the previous two functions, named `HelloWorld`, simply outputs a message box again. However, it is the second of these two functions that is much more interesting. The `Add` function takes two integer parameters, adds them together, and then returns the result by setting the `Add` function name to the sum of the parameters. Functions are most useful when you need to return a value, after executing a block of code that you want to use in multiple locations throughout the code project.

VBA Keywords and Reserved Words

Like all programming languages, VBA has a number of keywords that are used to specify constructs of the programming language and are often required when building code statements. Because these words are required for specific purposes, keywords and other reserved words cannot be used for any other purpose, such as a variable name. For example, the keyword `If` is used to specify the beginning of an `If` block, and cannot be used for any other purpose. The following code provides an example of defining a variable, using the `Dim` and `As` keywords:

```
Dim iCount As Integer
```

The preceding code statement contains four words: two keywords, `Dim` and `As`; one variable name, `iCount`; and one data type, `Integer` (which in this case is also a keyword, as it is one of the base data types in the language). As you can see, the keywords of the language are used to build statements in the language, and they have many different purposes. VBA actually has more than 100 keywords and other reserved words, and are far too numerous to list in their entirety here. However, you can find a complete list of VBA keywords and their definitions in the VB6 *Programmer's Reference* in the MSDN library at `http://msdn.microsoft.com/en-us/library/aa338157(VS.60).aspx`.

Adding Comments to Code

One very useful, but simple, part of the VBA programming language is the ability to add comments to code. Code comments are nothing more than notes that can be placed in code to provide some sort of information to developers who are reading your code. When the code is executed the comments are skipped completely.

To add a comment to VBA code, simply prefix the text with a single quote. Any text to the right of a single quote is treated as a comment, until the end of the line. The following code shows a comment on the first line and after the code on the second line:

```
' Declare an Object variable
Dim oAnObject As New Object ' Create a New instance of the Object
Dim iCount as Integer
```

Notice that the comment only extends to the end of the line and the third line is a separate line of code. Comments in VBA code cannot span multiple lines; each line must be prefixed with a separate single quote to declare the comment statement.

VBA Data Types

Data types in a programming language determine what kind of data values can be represented by a particular variable. Different types of data require different storage mechanisms and can have different kinds of operations applied to them. For example, both `Integer` and `String` data types can be used to store a number, but `String` objects cannot be added in the same manner that `Integer` objects can be added together. Table 52-1 provides a list of the 12 basic data types in VBA, the values they can represent, and how they map to Access table field data types.

TABLE 52-1: VBA Data Types to Access Table Field Data Types

VBA TYPE	VALUES	ACCESS FIELD DATA TYPE
Boolean	False (0) or True (–1).	Yes/No
Byte	Integer values of 0 to 255.	Number—Byte field size
Currency	Fixed-point numeric values of –922,337,203,477.5808 to 922,337,203,685,477.5807.	Currency
Date	January 1, 100 to December 31, 9999.	Date/Time
Decimal	Floating-point values of –79,228,162,514, 264,337,593,543,950,335 to 79,228,162, 514,264,337,593,543,950,335 when no decimal places are used. Represents up to 28 decimal places of precision with values from –7.9228162514264337593543950335 to 7.9228162514264337593543950335.	Number—Decimal field size
Double	Floating-point values of –1.79769313486232E308 to 1.79769313486232E308 or –4.94065645841247E-324 to 4.94065645841247E-324.	Number—Double field size
Integer	Integer values of –32,768 to 32,767.	Number—Integer field size

VBA TYPE	VALUES	ACCESS FIELD DATA TYPE
Long	Integer values of −2,147,483,648 to 2,147,486,647.	Number—Long Integer field size
Object	Can represent any data type or class, used for generically storing any type of data.	OLE Object
Single	Floating-point values of −3.402823E38 to 3.402823E38 or −1.401298E−45 to 1.401298E−45.	Number—Single field size
String	A string of text characters.	Text or Memo
Variant	Can represent any data type, just as an Object type can, but can also evaluate the difference between null and empty.	OLE Object

Although this list covers only the basic VBA data types, literally thousands of different data types exist, in the form of all the various classes in all of the libraries included with Access and Office. Also, VBA provides the ability to create custom, user-defined classes to allow developers to create their own data types, which you will see in Lesson 55. But for now, familiarize yourself with these basic data types, because they will be the basis for a lot of your VBA code.

Variables in VBA

Variables are a way of temporarily storing, retrieving, and manipulating some kind of data in a program. Variables in VBA are typically created based on a data type to declare the kind of data that will be stored in the variable. The data type could be one of the kinds shown in the previous section, any of the thousands of data types or code objects allowed in VBA, or even a user-defined data type. The kind of data you need to store in the variable will usually dictate which data type you will use for the variable.

Several kinds of variables are allowed in VBA: Locals, Globals, Constants, and Literals, and where and how a variable is defined will determine what kind of variable it is. VBA also allows the creation of an array, which is a variable to store any number of values of the same data type, which is considered a collection of values. Lesson 54 discusses variables in VBA in much more depth, but for now, it is good to have a basic understanding of what they do and how they work.

To create a new variable you can declare it in the VBA code, though declaring variables is not required. To declare a variable in VBA, simply use the `Dim` keyword, followed by the desired variable name. Optionally, the `As` keyword can be specified, followed by the data type name, to specify a type for the variable, which is always recommended, but not required. If the data type is not declared, VBA determines which type of data to use by the data stored in the variable. The following code provides an example of declaring several variables:

```
Dim MyVariable
Dim iCount As Integer
Dim strMessage As String
```

The preceding code declared (created) three variables, named `MyVariable`, `iCount`, and `strMessage`. Notice that for the first one, a data type was not declared. The second two both have data types, which are `Integer` and `String`, respectively. These data types determine what kind of data can be stored in the variable. If no data type is defined, as in the case of the first variable, that variable is of type `Variant`, which is a type of data that can represent any data type. Although that may sound great on the surface, `Variant` data types are necessarily the end all to variable types and the functionality they provide comes at a cost. I recommend always creating variables using a proper data type, based upon the values that will need to be stored. `Variant` types may not always work as expected, and there are possible performance considerations when using a `Variant`. Regardless of which data type you decide to use, declaring the variable is accomplished as shown above.

Once you have a variable created, you can use that variable to store and retrieve the data contained within it. For example, you might want to store some data in the variable for later use. The following code provides an example of assigning (storing) data to each of the variables that were declared in the previous code example:

```
MyVariable = #1/10/2010#
iCount = 10
strMessage = "This is my string data"
```

This code shows how to assign data values to the variables that were previously declared. Once you have data stored in a variable, you can use that variable anywhere in code that shares the scope of the variables (which means they are accessible from that location in code), instead of having to use literal data values in those locations. This is really all you need to know to start using variables, and you can do lots of things with them, like perform math or other operations on them, call functions with them, or even call their methods, if their data types support any. The next few sections discuss more about working with variables in different ways, but Lesson 54 discusses variables in much more depth.

VBA Operators

Once you have a variable, you need to work with that variable in different fashions, which is where operators come into play. Operators are a part of the VBA language that allow specific operations to be performed upon one or more variables. For example, the + (plus symbol), known as the *Addition Operator*, is used to add the value of two variables and returns the result. The following code provides an example of using the + operator on two literal values:

```
Dim iCount As Integer
iCount = 5 + 6
```

When the second code statement executes, the + operator adds the 5 and the 6 together and returns the result. Notice that the second line of code actually uses two operators: the + and the = operators. Once the value of 11 is returned by the + operator, the value should be assigned to something, so assign it to the `iCount` variable that was declared on the first line of code in the preceding example. The assignment is accomplished with the = operator, which assigns the value of 11 to the `iCount` variable. As mentioned in the previous section, a variable can be used in place of a literal value in code, and most of the time you will use operators directly on variables instead of just literal values. To add to the preceding example, the following line of code could be added to subtract a value from the `iCount` variable:

```
iCount = iCount - 3
```

In the preceding code statement, the value of 3 was subtracted from the iCount variable, using the – operator, known as the *Subtraction Operator*. However, operators can do much more than just simple arithmetic operations. For example, VBA offers sets of both Comparison and Boolean logic operators for deriving information about data and even asking questions for conditional branching operations, such as If statements. To continue to add to the previous examples in this section, the following code provides an example of using a comparison operator for an If statement in VBA:

```
If iCount < 10 Then
   iCount = 0
End If
```

This code example uses the < (less than) conditional operator to test the iCount variable to see if it is less than the value of 10 and if so, execute code to assign the iCount variable to the value of 0. In fact, the last three lines of code are made up of two operators, four keywords, and four variables, two of which are literal values. The following lines of code provide an example of using the And Boolean operator, combined with some conditional operators, to create an If statement which evaluates multiple conditions:

```
If iCount < 10 And iCount > -10 Then
   iCount = 0
End If
```

In this code example, the Boolean And operator requires that the value stored in the iCount variable be both greater than –10 and less than 10 before the If block will execute. Hopefully, by now you are getting the hang of VBA code and can see the usefulness of operators in the language. Lesson 53 is devoted to discussing all of the operators provided by the VBA language, but for now, you should have a basic understanding of what operators are and how they work in VBA.

Branching in VBA

VBA supports branching in code, which is the ability to jump to different code locations, usually based on a condition. VBA supports four types of branching statements: If statements, Case statements, Goto statements, and GoSub statements. This section discusses each of these branching statements and provides an example of how each can be used.

If Statements

Probably the most familiar to people, the If statement allows the user to specify a Boolean logic statement to determine if a block of code should be executed. Additionally, the user can specify one or more ElseIf statements, optionally followed by an Else statement. The ElseIf statement is used to check an additional condition if the previous conditions failed. Else does not require any condition and its code is run if all previous conditions failed. The If and ElseIf statements are always followed by the condition and then the Then keyword to specify the statement. Finally, If blocks are always terminated by the End If statement. The following code shows the structure of the simplest If block:

```
If iCount < 5 Then
   ' Execute the code in this block
End If
```

This statement simply compares a literal value to a variable, and if this condition results in `True`, the code contained within the `If` block will be executed. The following code is a more advanced example of an `If` block, which uses multiple `ElseIf` statements and an `Else` statement:

```
Dim iUserInput As Integer
iUserInput = -1

If iUserInput = 5 Then
   ' Execute some code
ElseIf iUserInput > 0 And iUserInput < 10 Then
   ' Execute some different code
ElseIf iUserInput < 0 Then
   iUserInput = 1
Else
   ' If all other conditions fail, execute this block
End If
```

After the preceding code has been executed, the second `ElseIf` statement will be executed and the `iUserInput` variable will be set to the value of 1. `If` statements are extremely common and you are likely to use them often in your VBA code.

Select Case Statements

The next kind of branching statement to examine is the `Select Case` statement. The `Select Case` statement allows the user to specify an expression that will be followed by a series of `Case` statements, which takes a possible result for the expression to match to. The `Case` with the matching value is executed. If no `Case` value is matched and a `Case Else` is specified, the `Case Else` is executed instead; otherwise no `Case` is executed. The `Case` statements can specify a single value or range of values. The code in the `Select Case` statement can be exited immediately at any time by calling the `Exit` statement. Finally, the `Select Case` statement must be terminated by the `End Select` statement. The following code provides an example of a `Select Case` statement in VBA:

```
Dim iUserInput As Integer
iUserInput = 5

Select Case iUserInput
   Case 1
      ' Execute some code
   Case 2, 3, 4
      ' Executed some different code
   Case 5 To 10
      ' Execute a third set of code
   Case Else
      ' If all other conditions fail, execute this block
End Select
```

After this code is executed, the third `Case` statement will be executed. Also, it is important to note that a `Case` statement behaves just like an `If/Else If/Else` block and the developer may only specify literal values for the conditions. Although not as widely used as `If` statements, `Select Case` statements can be a good way to replace long `If` blocks.

Goto Statements

A Goto statement is an unconditional branching statement used to jump to a label specified in code. To use the Goto statement, simply specify the Goto keyword followed by the label name to jump to. To specify a label, simply type a label name, followed by a colon. Once the Goto statement is executed, the code will immediately begin executing from the line that the label is placed on. The following provides an example of using a Goto statement:

```
Dim iCount As Integer
iCount = 5

My_Label:
If (iCount > 0) Then
  iCount = 0
  Goto My_Label
End If
```

Once this code has been executed, the If statement will be entered the first time, the value of the iCount will be updated to 0, and the code will jump back to the My_Label label and restart execution from there. Of course, the second time the If condition is tested, the result will be False, so the block will be skipped. Goto statements are the branching statements provided by VBA when no condition is required.

 It is generally not recommended to use Goto statements in VBA code; instead, write a Function or Sub to replace the desired functionality. This is because it is often considered very difficult to trace and debug code which contains a large number of Goto statements.

GoSub Statements

Finally, the last type of branching statement, and by far the least used, is the GoSub statement. The GoSub statement provides the ability to embed subroutines within a procedure. This provides several benefits, probably the most important of which is the ability to condense code that appears multiple times within a procedure into one location, without having to make a separate full Sub or Function call, which is just slightly more computationally expensive, although generally more recommended.

To call the GoSub statement, simply provide the name of the embedded subroutine, which must exist within the current procedure. To declare the embedded subroutine, simply create a line with any name you want to use, and then make sure that the block is completed with the Return keyword. The following code provides an example of using the GoSub statement in VBA code:

```
Public Sub MyExample()

    Dim iCount As Integer
    iCount = 5

    ' If the condition is met, execute the embedded sub
    If (iCount > 1) Then
```

```
      GoSub MyEmbeddedSub
   End If

   GoSub MyEmbeddedSub ' Execute the block of code again automatically

   ' Exit Sub to prevent falling through to the next code
   Exit Sub

   ' The Embedded Sub definition
   MyEmbeddedSub
      iCount = iCount + 1
      MsgBox "The count was updated"
   Return

End Sub
```

Note that the `Exit Sub` statement was called in the preceding code, but it is not required and if not used, the embedded subroutine code would be executed one more time.

The preceding code attempts to illustrate how `GoSub` can be used to abstract a block of code used multiple times within a procedure, but this is not the only use. Although extremely useful, `GoSub` statements are widely discouraged and generally misunderstood by the programming community. In fact, the statement was included in the VBA language as support for the old Microsoft Basic features. But, with the release of the Visual Basic .NET, the `GoSub` statement has been completely phased out of the language. Although it is little known, the `GoSub` statement can be useful when used effectively.

Loops in VBA

VBA supports looping in code, which is the ability to repeat a block of code while or until a condition is met. VBA provides four types of loops: `Do` loops, `While` loops, `For` loops, and `For Each` loops. This section discusses each of these types of loops and provides some examples of how they can be used in VBA code.

While Loops

The simplest loop in VBA is the `While` loop. A `While` loop allows the user to loop over a block of code until the specified condition is met. The `While` statement requires only the `While` keyword and a Boolean conditional statement to declare the loop. The `Wend` keyword must be used to terminate the loop statement, but the `Exit` statement can be used to break the loop at any time. The following code provides an example of using the `While` statement:

```
Dim iCount As Integer
iCount = 0

While (iCount < 3)
   iCount = iCount + 1
Wend
```

In this example, when the `While` statement is reached, the condition is evaluated, and because it is found to be `True`, the code block inside the loop is executed. Once the `Wend` statement is reached, the `While` condition is evaluated again, and the code is executed again until the condition is `False`. For this particular code, the `While` loop is executed three times before the block is finally exited.

Do Loops

VBA provides the Do statement for creating the Do loop programming construct. Two kinds of Do loops exist: a Do loop where the code is executed one time before the condition is checked, and a Do loop where the condition is checked before the loop is executed. Both the While and Until keywords can be used to specify the condition and the statement is always terminated by the Loop keyword. The following code provides an example of creating a Do loop that evaluates the condition, before the loop is executed:

```
Dim iCount As Integer
iCount = 0

Do While (iCount < 3)
   iCount = iCount + 1
Loop
```

In this code, when the Do loop is reached, the While condition is evaluated and found to be True and the code inside the block is executed. Once the Loop statement is reached, the block is restarted and the condition is evaluated again, which continues until the condition is False. For this particular code, the Do loop is executed three times before the block is finally exited. But, as mentioned, there is also another, more common method for constructing a Do loop. The following code provides an example of creating a Do loop that runs once before the condition is evaluated:

```
Dim iCount As Integer
iCount = 0

Do
   iCount = iCount + 1
While (iCount < 1) Loop
```

The preceding code only executes the Do block the first time, and when the condition is evaluated, it is True, so the block is not looped again. Also, it is worth noting that the Until keyword could replace the While keyword in both previous examples, and the code would still be valid in the VBA programming language.

For Loops

The next type of loop to discuss in VBA is the For loop statement. The For loop in VBA allows the user to loop a block of code a specified number of times and provides an Integer type variable that is typically used within the loop. To declare a For loop, use the For keyword, followed by a new variable name for the Integer counter, followed by the = operator, and end with the range that specifies the number of times the loop is to be executed. The For block is terminated by the Next statement, which can be optionally followed by the name of the variable to update after the block has completed execution. The following code provides an example of how to create a For loop using VBA:

```
For i = 1 to 3
   MsgBox "Loop #" & i
Next i
```

In this code, the block within the `For` loop executes three times, each time showing a message box denoting the iteration of the loop. The loop can be exited immediately at any time by calling the `Exit For` statement. `For` loops are extremely common and very useful when you need a counter type of variable in your loop.

For Each Loops

The final type of loop in VBA to discuss is a `For Each` loop. A `For Each` loop is used to iterate through an array or collection of objects. Each object in the array or collection is visited during the loop, unless specifically exited early. To declare a `For Each` loop, use the `For Each` keywords, followed by a new variable name for working with the items of the collection, followed by the `In` keyword, and end with the name of the array or collection object to be iterated. The `For Each` block is terminated by the `Next` statement, which is the `Next` keyword optionally followed by the item variable name. The following code provides an example of how to create a `For Each` loop using VBA code:

```
Dim iIntArray(5) As Integer
Dim iItem As Integer

For Each iItem In iIntArray
    iItem = 0
Next iItem
```

In this code, the block within the `For` loop executes five times, once for each item in the `iIntArray` array, setting the value of each item to `0`. A `For Each` loop can be exited immediately at any time by calling the `Exit For` statement, as with other `For` loops.

Option Statements

The `Option` statement allows the user to specify certain compiler settings for the VBA code. Many of these statements are widely used and often recommended. There are not very many of them, so they are easy to remember, and they do all sorts of things, such as specify how text should be compared and require that all variables be specifically declared before they can be used. Table 52-2 provides a list of VBA `Option` statements and their descriptions:

TABLE 52-2: Option Statements

OPTION	DESCRIPTION
Base	Specifies whether the lower bound of user-defined arrays should start at `0` or `1`, which is `0` by default. Example: `Option Base 1`
Compare	Specifies the type of `String` comparison operation to use by default. Valid values are `Binary` (default), `Text`, and `Database`. Example: `Option Compare Database`
Explicit	Requires that all variables in the module be explicitly declared. This option is highly recommended by the VBA community, because it can greatly reduce the chance of common coding mistakes, such as variable name typos. Example: `Option Explicit`

OPTION	DESCRIPTION
Private Module	Blocks sources outside of the project from referencing properties, methods, and events within the module, even if they are explicitly marked as Public. Example: Option Private Module

These Option statements must be declared before any subs or functions in the module, and are specific to the module only. Each of the different options can be used together, but multiple instances of the same Option statement in the same module with different option values are not allowed. The following is just one example of a set of Option statements that could be specified at the top of a VBA code module:

```
Option Explicit
Option Private Module
Option Compare Database
```

Calling Subroutines

Now that you are familiar with most of the basic constructs of the VBA language, it is time to examine how subroutines can be called. There are actually several different manners in which a subroutine can be called and all are valid. To call a subroutine, simply specify the name of the Sub followed by any parameters that are passed in. The parameters themselves must be separated by commas. The following code provides an example of calling the ExportXML subroutine:

```
' Call the ExportXML subroutine
ExportXML acExportForm, "Order Details", "C:\test.xml"
```

There is nothing really special about this code; it simply calls the ExportXML method with the specified parameters. But what happens if two subroutines have the same name and the same type of parameters? Which one will be run? The answer to that is very tricky and will depend on the situation, but in general, to resolve these sorts of issues, prefix the parent class name onto the beginning of the object to reference the specific method that is desired. For example, you could prefix the ExportXML subroutine with its parent class, the Application object, to ensure that definition of the ExportXML subroutine is used:

```
' Call the ExportXML subroutine, prefixed with the Application class
Application.ExportXML acExportForm, "Order Details", "C:\test.xml"
```

Using the ByVal Keyword

One last thing to understand about calling subroutines is how the parameters are treated. By default, parameter objects are passed ByRef, which means that if the parameter is modified within the subroutine, the changes will be propagated to the caller's object, even after the subroutine has exited, but only if the parameter is a complex data type, not a value (base) data type. The ByVal keyword can be specified before the parameter name in the subroutine definition to specify that the routine not modify the original variable in any way. The following code provides an example of using the `ByVal` parameter modifier when defining a subroutine:

```
Public Sub DoNotModifyParam(ByVal oSomeParam as Object)
 ' Modifying the oSomeParam doesn't change the caller's values for the object
End Sub
```

Using the ByRef Keyword

Because basic data types, such as `Integer` and `String`, are always passed `ByVal` for subroutines, one might expect that using the `ByRef` keyword would allow the parameter to be passed by reference through a subroutine. This is not true and it will not work for forcing a non-complex data type to be passed by reference to a subroutine. This functionality is only supported in functions, which allow non-complex data types to be passed by reference through the function's parameters.

Calling Functions

The other kind of procedure that can be called is a `Function`, and it has a number of differences in the way the code is written. The biggest difference is that functions can provide a return value, which can optionally be assigned to a variable by the caller. This section discusses the basics of calling functions in VBA code.

Getting Return Values

Assigning return values from a function call is quite simple, but slightly different than a call to a subroutine. When assigning a return value, the user must supply the variable name and assignment operator, before the function call. The following code provides an example of calling the `ColumnHistory` function:

```
Dim strHistory As String
strHistory = ColumnHistory("Customers", Notes, "")
```

Notice that there are at least two differences here from calling a `Sub`: the first, already discussed, is that the return value has been assigned to the `strHistory` variable. The second is that parentheses must be used when specifying the parameters. Other than those minor differences, calling functions is much like calling subroutines.

Using the Set Keyword

If the return value from a function is a complex data type, the `Set` keyword must be used at the beginning of the statement. The following code provides an example of calling the `CreateForm` function, which returns a `Form` object:

```
Dim frmNewForm As Form
Set frmNewForm = CreateForm()
```

If the `Set` statement is not used, the code will generate a compile error that says `Invalid use of property`, which can be fairly confusing if you are not aware of what the error message means. Also, notice that the previous code does not specify any parameters for the `CreateForm` function, even though it takes two parameters which already have default values making them optional. When no other value is desired for an optional parameter, the parameter value can be left completely blank.

The IntelliSense list provided when the `CreateForm` *function name is typed into the VBE Code window shows the parameter names for the function surrounded by square brackets. That is how you know that the parameters are optional, and if not specified, will automatically use their default values.*

Using the Call Keyword

Functions can be called without having to set the return value to anything, essentially discarding the return value. In this situation, the `Call` keyword is required at the beginning of the statement; otherwise you will receive a compile error. The following code provides an example of calling the `CreateReport` function without getting the return value:

```
' Call a function and discard the return type
Call CreateReport()
```

In this code, the `CreateReport` method is simply called and the reference to the report that is created is just discarded. Although it is not generally recommended to discard return values, sometimes they are just not required and it does not make sense to write code to get them when they will not be used.

Using the ByVal Keyword

Finally, the last difference between functions and subroutines is that all data types are passed by reference by default for functions in VBA, including the primitive (base) data types. Using the `ByVal` keyword in the parameter's definition allows the developer to specify that the parameter be passed by value only. The following code provides an example using the `ByVal` keyword for a parameter of a function:

```
Public Function MuckWithMessage(ByVal strMessage as String)
  ' The strMessage parameter can be modified here
  ' and any changes will not be visible to the caller
End Function
```

In this code, even if the developer explicitly sets the value of the `strMessage` parameter inside the function, the caller of the function will never see any such change. The `ByVal` keyword is a contract, assuring the caller that the variable will not be modified by the function.

Help with VBA Code

As mentioned, VBA is probably the single hardest feature to learn in Access, and even Access programmers with 15 years of experience often need to look up things about VBA or find out more information about features that they are not familiar with. Not knowing how code objects and their methods work can often be the cause of not building VBA code properly. Fortunately, both Access and VBA have built-in help that provides tons of great information about all kinds of different topics about each Office product. Simply press the F1 key from anywhere within either Access or VBE and Office Help will be presented. From there, you can search help topics, both those included with the product and topics found at `http://office.microsoft.com`.

In addition to the help available for Access and the VBA language, Microsoft also provides an incredible repository of resources for working with VBA, Access, and almost all other Microsoft products, which is called the MSDN library and has been mentioned on numerous occasions throughout this book. You can find the MSDN free online VB6 programmer's reference at `http://msdn.microsoft.com/en-us/library/aa338032(VS.60).aspx`. Also, many websites are devoted to programming VBA code using Access and have lots of great information and code examples. If you ever get really stuck on something in VBA and just can't find it anywhere else, try searching for an answer using one of the major Internet search engines — you're sure to get millions of hits!

TRY IT

In this lesson you write some sample VBA code. Now that you have an understanding about the basic parts of the VBA language, try writing some VBA code. The following example walks you through the steps necessary to build some VBA code in an Access database application and illustrates how the code can be used within the application. Sample files are available on the book's DVD and website.

Lesson Requirements

For this lesson, the example steps use a blank database created from scratch. You should be familiar with creating a new database and new database objects to complete these steps. However, a blank database is not necessarily required to complete this lesson; you can use just about any database application. This example focuses primarily on building some VBA code and does not require any existing objects or other knowledge of VBA in Access.

Step-by-Step

1. Open Access 2010 from the Windows Start menu. The Access Backstage will open in the Access window.

2. In the Backstage, click the New option on the left-hand menu and then click the Blank Database option.

3. Optionally, choose the file name and location and click the Create button on the right side of the screen to create the new blank database application. The new database will be created and opened in the Access window.

4. Close the default table that is created; once the new database has been opened, you won't need it for this lesson.

5. Click the Create tab on the Ribbon to open it.

6. On the Create Ribbon, click the Module option. This creates a new module in the database and opens it in VBE.

7. Once VBE has been opened, click the Save button on the top left of the VBE toolbar. The Save As dialog will open.

8. For the Module Name, type **ModMath**. Then click OK to save the data. The module will now be saved in the database.

9. Notice that the `Option Compare Database` statement is already present in the new module. To add your own `Option` statements, put the cursor just below the existing `Option` statement and type the following: **Option Explicit**. This is added so you are required to explicitly declare all variables within this module.

10. Press the Enter key three or four times to add a few new lines to the file, so that you can create a new function.

11. Type the following code for the function:

```
Public Function Add(iLeftVal As Double, iRightVal As Double) As Double

   Add = iLeftVal + iRightVal

End Function
```

12. This code adds two Integer types together and has now been created. All you need now is a user interface for the code.

13. Save and close VBE. You will be taken back to Access.

14. On the Create Ribbon, choose the Form Design option to create a new form in Design View mode.

15. Click the Save button to save the new form. For the name of the form, type **frmCalculate** and click OK. The form will be saved to the database.

16. On the Form Tools Design Ribbon, click the Text Box control option to select it, and then click the form to drop a new Text Box control on the form.

17. Again, click the Text Box control option on the Ribbon to select it, and then click the form just below the previous control to add a second Text Box control to the form.

18. Click the Button control option on the Form Design Tools Ribbon to select it and then click the form just below the previous Text Box control to add the button to the form. The Command Button Wizard will be invoked, so just press the Cancel button.

19. Delete the Label controls for both of the Text Box controls; they are not needed for this example.

20. Hit the F4 button to open the Property Sheet if it is not already open.

21. Click the first Text Box to select it, so that its properties are shown in the Property Sheet. Select the All tab and change the Name property value to **txtInput1**.

22. Click the second Text Box to select it, so that its properties are shown in the Property Sheet. Select the All tab and change the Name property value to **txtInput2**.

23. Click the Button control to select it. Change the Name property value to **btnCalculate**. Change the Caption property value to **Calculate**.

24. Click the Event tab of the Property Sheet to select it. Click the "…" (Builder) button for the On Click property value. This invokes the Choose Builder dialog, so choose the Code Builder option and click OK.

25. VBE will be invoked with an `OnClick` event method added for the Button control. Add the following code to the `OnClick` event method:

```
MsgBox ModMath.Add(txtInput1, txtInput2)
```

26. Click the Save button to save everything. Once saved, close VBE. Then close the new form and choose OK when prompted to save.

Congratulations, you now have successfully created a form that uses custom code in a user-defined module. To verify the code is working correctly, simply double-click the `frmCalculate` form in the Navigation Pane to open it. Once it has been opened, type a numeric value into each Text Box and then click the Calculate button. A message box will open, showing the sum of the two values entered into the Text Box controls. The new custom code works, and it only took a few lines of code!

SUMMARY

VBA code is one of the most powerful and flexible features in Access, and most of the other Office products for that matter. The VBA language is simple enough, and this lesson has reviewed all of the major parts of the language. This lesson discussed creating modules, creating and calling functions and subroutines, declaring and using variables, using operators, the various branching and loop statements in VBA, and working with `Option` statements. These pieces of VBA make up the basics of the language and just knowing these items, you can easily begin writing VBA code without a hitch! The next few lessons discuss much more about writing VBA code and examine many features of the language in greater depth.

 Please select Lesson 52 on the DVD to view the video that accompanies this lesson.

53

Using Operators in VBA

Now that you have a pretty good understanding of the basics of VBA and how to write VBA code, it is time to examine all of the operators available in the VBA programming language. Though the number of operators is limited, they provide a plethora of functionality and are required quite often. As you saw in the previous lesson, operators serve many purposes, from arithmetic operations to logical operations. This lesson describes all of the operators available in the VBA language and provides examples of how they can be used.

LESSON SETUP

This lesson is designed to provide detailed information about the operators provided by VBA code. You should already be familiar with the basics of using operators from the previous lesson and know the basic parts of writing VBA code. Otherwise, this lesson does not require any other specific knowledge of Access.

VBA OPERATORS

As you have already seen, operators are a big part of the VBA programming language. Operators allow the user to perform a specific operation on one or more variables, depending on the type of operator that is used. For example, the + (addition) operator is used to add the values of two variables and returns the result. VBA offers close to 40 different operators, each of which serves a specific purpose, as shown in the next several sections.

Assignment Operators

VBA supports a number of assignment operators, but they are all derived from one basic assignment operator, which is the equal operator, denoted by the = (equal symbol) character. The equal operator simply assigns the value on the right side of the equal sign to the variable on the left side of the equal sign. For example, the following code assigns a literal value to a string variable:

```
' Assign a literal string to a variable
strMessage = "It is easy to assign values!"
```

Once this statement has been executed, the strMessage variable will contain the literal string that was supplied. The assignment operator is the operator that is used the most in VBA, and you will likely assign many values throughout your VBA code. Table 53-1 is the complete list of assignment operators allowed in VBA.

TABLE 53-1: VBA Assignment Operators

OPERATOR	DESCRIPTION
=	Assigns the value on the right side of the operator to the variable on the left side. Example: iCount = 5
^=	Raises the variable on the left side of the operator to the power represented by the value on the right side of the operator and assigns the result. Example: iCount ^= 5
*=	Multiplies the variable on the left side of the operator by the value on the right side of the operator, and assigns the result back. Example: iCount *= 5
/=	Divides the variable on the left side of the operator by the value on the right side of the operator and assigns the result, as a Double value. Example: iCount /= 5
\=	Divides, using integer division, the variable on the left side of the operator by the value on the right side of the operator, and assigns the result as an Integer value. Integer division is the process of dividing two numbers and keeping the integer result while truncating the decimal remainder value. Example: iCount \= 5
+=	Adds the variable on the left side of the operator to the value on the right side of the operator, and assigns the result. Example: iCount += 5
-=	Subtracts the value on the right side of the operator from the value stored in the variable on the left side of the operator, and assigns the result. Example: iCount -= 5
<<=	Shifts the bits stored in the variable on the left side of the operator toward the higher bit direction, the number of times listed by the value on the right side of the operator, and assigns the result. This operation is the equivalent of multiplying by two. Example: iCount <<= 5
>>=	Shifts the bits stored in the variable on the left side of the operator toward the lower bit direction, the number of times listed by the value on the right side of the operator, and assigns the result. This operation is the equivalent of dividing by two. Example: iCount >>= 5
&=	Concatenates the String variable on the left side of the operator with the value on the right side of the operator, and assigns the result back to the String variable. Example: strMessage &= "Concat more strings"

Comparison Operators

VBA supports seven comparison operators to perform Boolean logic operations on variables: Equal To, Not Equal To, Greater Than, Greater Than or Equal To, Less Than, Less Than or Equal To, and Like. These operators yield Boolean values, either True or False, that indicate if the type of comparison was true for the values being compared. The following code provides an example of comparing two numbers and returning the result:

```
Dim bResult As Boolean
bResult = 5 > 10
```

Once this code has executed, the bResult variable will contain the value False, because 5 is not greater than 10. Table 53-2 is the complete list of comparison operators allowed in VBA.

TABLE 53-2: VBA Comparison Operators

OPERATOR	DESCRIPTION
=	**Equal To** — Returns True if the values are equal, otherwise False. Example: If iCount = 5 Then
<>	**Not Equal To** — Returns False if the values are equal, otherwise True. Example: If iCount <> 5 Then
>	**Greater Than** — Returns True if the value on the left side of the operator is greater than the value on the right side of the operator, otherwise False. Example: If iCount > 5 Then
>=	**Greater Than or Equal To** — Returns True if the value on the left side of the operator is greater than or equal to the value on the right side of the operator, otherwise False. Example: If iCount >= 5 Then
<	**Less Than** — Returns True if the value on the left side of the operator is less than the value on the right side of the operator, otherwise False. Example: If iCount < 5 Then
<=	**Less Than or Equal To** — Returns True if the value on the left side of the operator is less than or equal to the value on the right side of the operator, otherwise False. Example: If iCount <= 5 Then
Like	**Like** — Valid for String comparisons only. Usually used for validating data or performing wildcard searches on String objects. Note: All valid wildcard operators are described in Table 53-7. Example: If strMessage Like "###" Then

Of course, to use these operators on a variable, the variable's data type must support the operator, but in general, all of the basic types support all of the comparison operators. Also, many non-basic types also support comparison operators, but on a case-by-case basis.

Arithmetic Operators

VBA supports seven arithmetic operators, for performing basic mathematical operations on number data types. Basic arithmetic operations are very important in any programming language to compute new values. The following code provides an example of adding two literal values together and storing the result in a variable:

```
Dim iSum As Integer
iSum = 5 + 10
```

Once this code has executed, the iSum variable will contain the value 15, as a result of addition of the two numbers, due to the use of the addition operator in the code. Table 53-3 is the complete list of arithmetic operators allowed in VBA, their description, and their order of precedence (1 being the highest):

TABLE 53-3: VBA Arithmetic Operators with Precedence Order

OPERATOR	DESCRIPTION	PRECEDENCE
^	**Exponential operator** — Raises the value on the left side of the operator to the power of the value on the right side, and returns the result. Example: 5^2 would return 25.	1
*	**Multiplication operator** — Multiplies the value on the left side of the operator by the value on the right side, and returns the result. Example: 5*2 would return 10.	2
/	**Division operator** — Divides the value on the left side of the operator by the value on the right side, and returns the result, as a Double value. Example: 5/2 would return 2.5.	2
\	**Integer division operator** — Divides the value on the left side of the operator by the value on the right side, and returns the result, as an Integer value, and remainder is truncated from the resulting value. Example: 5\2 would return 2.	3
Mod	**Modulus arithmetic operator** — Returns the remainder from a division operation, as an Integer value. Example: 5 Mod 2 would return 1.	4
+	**Addition operator** — Adds the value on the left side of the operator to the value on the right side, and returns the result. Example: 5 + 2 would return 7.	5
−	**Subtraction operator** — Subtracts the value on the right side of the operator from the value on the left side, and returns the result. Example: 5 − 2 would return 3.	5

Again, to use these operators, the variable's data type must support the operator, but in general, all of the basic number types support all of the arithmetic operators. Also, some non-basic types also support arithmetic operators, but on a case-by-case basis.

It is important to remember that with operators, there is precedence, or an order in which operations occur. For example, the code 2+12/2 would return the value of 8, because the 12/2 operation would occur first, because it has a higher precedence, and then the addition of the value of 2 would occur second, producing a result of 8. Of course, surrounding any equation in parentheses will ensure that operation, or set of operations, executes first, overruling any precedence that might otherwise take place.

Bitwise Operators

VBA supports eight bitwise operators for performing basic bitwise operations, and in some cases logical operations, on a data type. Bitwise operations allow the developer to manipulate the actual bit values stored in a variable. In a bitwise operation, each individual bit is compared with the corresponding bit in the same position, but in the second variable, and the result is returned based on the particular logic used to compare the bits. The following code provides an example of ANDing two numeric values together in a bitwise operation and storing the result in a variable:

```
Dim iResult As Integer
iResult = 5 AND 1
```

Once this code has executed, the iResult variable will contain the value 1. The bitwise AND operation sets only the lowest bit in the result, because the lowest bit is the only 1 bit in common for both the number 5 and the number 1. Thus the AND comparison returns a value of 1.

Additionally, most bitwise operators are binary operators, meaning those operators require two values to perform the operation on, but the NOT operator is unary, meaning that it only requires one value to operate on, the value to the right of it. Table 53-4 is the complete list of bitwise operators allowed in VBA and their descriptions, including their unary or binary status.

TABLE 53-4: VBA Bitwise Operators

OPERATOR	DESCRIPTION
And	Binary — Returns 1 for each bit that has 1s for both values being compared, otherwise 0. Example: 5 & 3 would return the value 1.
Not	Unary — Returns 0 for each bit that has a 1, and 1 for each bit that has a 0. This essentially flips the bits in the variable. Example: For a Byte value of 0, Not 0 would return the value 1.
Or	Binary — Returns 0 for each bit where both comparing bit values are 0, otherwise 1. Example: 5 Or 3 would return the value 7.
Xor	Binary — Returns 0 for each bit where compared bit values are either 0 or both 1, otherwise returns 1 for each set of bits that don't match. Example: 5 Xor 3 would return the value 6.

continued

TABLE 53-4 *(continued)*

OPERATOR	DESCRIPTION
<<	Binary — Shifts the bits for the value on the left side of the operator toward the higher bit direction, the number of times denoted by the Integer value on the right side of the operator, and returns the result. Bits shifted out are lost and all bits shifted in are 0s. Example: 3 << 1 would return the value 6.
>>	Binary — Shifts the bits for the value on the left side of the operator toward the lower bit direction, the number of times denoted by the Integer value on the right side of the operator, and returns the result. Bits shifted out are lost and all bits shifted in are 0s. Example: 3 >> 1 would return the value 1.

Again, to use the bitwise operators, the variable's data type must be supported by the operator, but in general, the basic integer number types that are integer form support all of the bitwise operators well. Also, some non-basic types also support bitwise operators, but on a case-by-case basis.

Logical Operators

Some bitwise operators can also be used as logical operators, and a couple of other specific logical operators are available in VBA. A logical operator applies Boolean logic to a Boolean expression or data type. For example, the value of True ANDed with False results in the value False. The following code provides an example of ANDing two Boolean values together in a bitwise operation and storing the result in a variable:

```
Dim iResult As Boolean
iResult = True AND False
```

Once this code has executed, the iResult variable will contain the value False, because logical AND requires both values to be True for it to return True. Table 53-5 is the complete list of logical operators allowed in VBA and their descriptions, including their unary or binary status.

TABLE 53-5: VBA Logical Operators

OPERATOR	DESCRIPTION
And	Binary — Returns True if both values being compared are True, otherwise False. Example: True And False would return the value False.
Not	Unary — Returns the opposite of the value applied to: False if the value is True, otherwise True if the value is False. Example: Not False would return the value True.
Or	Binary — Returns False if both values compared are False, otherwise True. Example: True Or False would return the value True.
Xor	Binary — Returns False if both values are the same, otherwise True. If both values are True or both values are False, it returns False, otherwise True. Example: True Xor False would return the value True.

OPERATOR	DESCRIPTION
AndAlso	Binary — Returns `True` if both values being compared are `True`, otherwise `False`. However, if the value on the left side of the operator is `False`, then the value on the right side of the operator is not evaluated, saving time, and is the difference between the `And` and `AndAlso` operators. This is a form of a "short circuit operator." Example: `True AndAlso False` would return the value `False`.
OrElse	Binary — Returns `False` if both values compared are `False`, otherwise `True`. However, if the value on the left side of the operator is `True`, then the value on the right side of the operator is not evaluated, saving time, and is the difference between the `Or` and `OrElse` operators. This is a form of a "short circuit operator." Example: `True OrElse False` would return the value `True`.

And remember, logical operators can only be applied to Boolean expressions or values; otherwise the bitwise operators will be used instead.

String Operators

VBA provides several string operators for performing a number of operations on a string. There are really two kinds of operators: string concatenation operators and wildcard operators. This section discusses both of these types of string operators.

Concatenation Operators

Surprisingly, VBA actually provides two string concatenation operators, which are used to join two strings together. The following code provides an example of using both of these operators:

```
Dim strMessage As String
strMessage = "Using the ampersand " & "is one method for concatenation"
strMessage = "Using the plus sign " + "is the second method"
```

These operators by definition are always binary, meaning they always operate on two values, which are the values being concatenated. Table 53-6 provides a list of both `String` concatenation operators and their descriptions:

TABLE 53-6: VBA String Concatenation Operators

OPERATOR	DESCRIPTION
&	Returns a `String` object containing the `String` on the right side of the operator appended to the end of the `String` on the left side. If both objects are not strings, or cannot be expanded to string values, then the statement will generate a compile error. Example: `"The " & "code"`
+	Returns a `String` object containing the `String` on the right side of the operator appended to the end of the `String` on the left side. Allows variables of different types to be concatenated together, as a `String` value. Supported types are: `String`, `Byte`, `Short`, `Integer`, `Long`, `Single`, `Double`, and `Decimal`. Example: `"The " + 5`

In general, using the + concatenation operator is much looser, but there are a number of rules and it is often considered somewhat dangerous, because exactly how it performs the concatenation will depend on the types that it is concatenating. It is usually recommended to just use the & operator to concatenate strings, until there is a specific need to use the other.

Wildcard Operators for Strings

VBA provides several string wildcard operators, which can be used in a number of places. Wildcards are often used when specifying the criteria for a query, to make the search more generic. Also, these operators can be used in conjunction with the Like comparison operator to specify rules for a comparison. The following code provides an example of using the * (star) operator in conjunction with the Like operator:

```
Dim strMessage As String = "This is a message"
Dim bResult As Boolean
bResult = strMessage Like "*message"
```

Once this code has been executed, the value of True is returned to the bResult variable. Table 53-7 provides a list of all of the wildcard operators and their descriptions.

TABLE 53-7: VBA String Wildcard Operators

OPERATOR	DESCRIPTION
*	Specifies 0 or more characters of any type. Example: "*a*" matches any string with at least one lowercase a character in it.
?	Specifies a single character of any type. Example: "a?" matches any two-character string beginning with a lowercase a character.
#	Specifies a single numeric (0-9) character. Example: "1##" matches any three-character string that starts with the number 1.
[CharList]	Specifies a single character of the type listed in the CharList parameter. The CharList parameter will accept multiple values and ranges. Example: "a[A-Za-z]" matches any two-character string that starts with a lowercase a and has either an uppercase or lowercase letter as the second character.
[!ChaLlist]	Specifies excluding a single character of the type listed in the CharList parameter. The CharList parameter will accept multiple values and ranges. Example: "a[!0-9abc]" matches any two-character string that starts with a lowercase a and does not contain a numeric character or lowercase a, b, or c as the second character.

Using the Like operator with wildcards is extremely useful for data validation when inputting values into a table. But remember, they can only be used for comparing String objects.

Other Operators

Finally, VBA provides two other operators that don't fall into any other category, but are very useful within the language: the `AddressOf` operator and the `GetType` operator. The following code provides an example of calling the `GetType` operator:

```
' Get the Type info for an Integer type
Dim tIntType As Type
tIntType = GetType Integer
```

Once this code has executed, the `tIntType` variable will contain the type information for the `Integer` data type. Table 53-8 provides a list of both operators and their descriptions.

TABLE 53-8: Other VBA Operators

OPERATOR	DESCRIPTION
AddressOf	Unary — Returns the address of a procedure name on the right side of the operator. Used when creating a delegate to reference the given procedure, so it can be called directly from the delegate. Example: `AddressOf MyFunctionName`
GetType	Unary — Returns a `Type` object containing the type information of the data type name specified on the right side of the operator. Example: `GetType Long`

If you don't completely understand how these operators work, it is okay. These particular operators are used for very advanced VBA programming concepts and will not be used throughout the rest of this book. Just know that they exist; the day may soon come when you do need to use them!

TRY IT

In this lesson you write some VBA code that uses a few operators. Now that you know all of the operators that VBA provides and how they can be applied in code, the only thing left to do is to try them out in some basic VBA functions. The following example walks you through the steps necessary to build some code that performs bit operations, using `Xor` operator, on two variables and returns the value for the user to see. Sample files are available on the book's DVD and website.

Lesson Requirements

For this lesson, the example steps use a blank database created from scratch. However, a blank database is not required to complete this lesson; you can use just about any database application. You should be familiar with creating a new database and database objects to complete this lesson. This example focuses primarily on building some simple VBA code and does not require any other specific knowledge of Access.

Step-by-Step

1. Open Access 2010 from the Windows Start menu. The Access Backstage will open in the Access window.

2. In the Backstage, click the New option on the left-hand menu and then click the Blank Database option.

3. Optionally, choose the file name and location and click the Create button on the right side of the screen to create the new blank database application. The new database will be created and opened in the Access window.

4. Close the default table that is created; once the new database has been opened, you won't need it for your purpose.

5. Click the Create tab on the Ribbon to select it.

6. On the Create Ribbon, click the Module option. This creates a new module in the database and opens it in VBE.

7. Once VBE has been opened, click the Save button on the top left of the VBE toolbar. The Save As dialog will open.

8. For the Module Name, type **ModMath,** then click OK to save the data. The module will now be saved in the database.

9. Notice that the Option Compare Database statement is already present in the new module. To add your own, put the cursor just below the existing Option statement and type the new Option statement: **Option Explicit.** This is added so you are required to explicitly declare all variables.

10. Press the Enter key three or four times to add a few new lines to the file, so that you can create a function.

11. Type the following code for the function:

    ```
    Public Function lXor(iLeftVal As Long, iRightVal As Long) As Long

        lXor = iLeftVal Xor iRightVal

    End Function
    ```

12. The code to perform the exclusive OR operation on two Long data values has been created, now all you need is a user interface for the code.

13. Click the Save button to save the module and then close VBE. You will be taken back to Access.

14. On the Create Ribbon, choose the Form Design option to create a new form in Design View mode.

15. Click the Save button to save the new form. For the name of the form, type **frmCalculate,** then click OK. The form will be saved to the database.

16. On the Design Ribbon of the Table Design Tools group, click the Text Box control option to select it, and then click the form to drop the Text Box control on the form.

17. Again, click the Text Box control option on the Ribbon to select it, and then click the form just below the previous control.

18. Click the Button control option on the Ribbon to select it and then click the form just below the previous Text Box control to add the button to the form. The Command Button Wizard will be invoked, so just press the Cancel button.

19. Delete the Label controls for both of the Text Box controls; they are not needed for this example.

20. Hit the F4 button to open the Property Sheet if it is not already open.

21. Click the first Text Box to select it, so that its properties are shown in the Property Sheet. Select the All tab and change the Name property value to **txtInput1**.

22. Click the second Text Box to select it, so that its properties are shown in the Property Sheet. Select the All tab and change the Name property value to **txtInput2**.

23. Click the Button control to select it. Change the Name property value to **btnCalculate**. Change the Caption property value to **Calculate**.

24. Click the Event tab of the Property Sheet to select it. Click the "..." (Builder) button for the On Click property value. This invokes the Choose Builder dialog, so choose the Code Builder option and click OK.

25. VBE will be invoked with an `OnClick` event method added for the Button control. Add the following code to the `OnClick` event method:

```
MsgBox ModMath.lXor(txtInput1, txtInput2)
```

26. Click the Save button to save everything. Once saved, close VBE. Then close the new form and choose OK when prompted to save.

Congratulations, you now have successfully created a form that uses custom code that employs the `Xor` operator. To verify the code is working correctly, simply double-click the `frmCalculate` form in the Navigation Pane to open it. Once it has been opened, type a numeric value into each text box and then click the Calculate button. A message box will open, showing the result of an exclusive OR computation of the two values entered into the Text Box controls. The `Xor` code works with only a few lines of code!

SUMMARY

Operators are a critical part of any programming language and play a huge role in VBA code development. VBA offers a wide variety of operators: assignment, arithmetic, comparison, logical, bitwise, string, and a couple of others. The operators provide a wide variety of functionality that could only be otherwise accomplished by the development of many, many more routines. These operators are quite easy to use and will come in handy as your VBA skills get more use.

 Please select Lesson 53 on the DVD to view the video that accompanies this lesson.

54

Using Variables in VBA

As you've seen in the previous two lessons, variables play a critical role in VBA programming and as such, deserve a detailed explanation of the different kinds of variables and how they can be used. Although you have already used variables in many places throughout this book, it is important to discuss the different kinds of variables and what the differences mean in the VBA code. It is important to understand that where and how a variable is declared will determine how it can be used in VBA code. This lesson is devoted to discussing the kinds of variables allowed in VBA and what the differences are between them.

LESSON SETUP

This lesson is designed to provide information about using variables in VBA and the different kinds of variables it provides. You should be familiar with Access databases, creating modules, and the basics of VBA programming to complete this lesson. Otherwise, this lesson does not require any other specific knowledge of Access.

VARIABLES IN VBA

Variables in a programming language are a way of temporarily storing, retrieving, passing, and manipulating data in code. Variables in VBA are typically declared with a data type, called a *Class*, to denote the kind of data that will be stored in the variable, though explicitly specifying the data type is not required in VBA. When a variable is declared without a type, it is automatically given the type `Variant`, which can store any type of data by implicitly casting it to the data type of the assigned value. Several kinds of variables are allowed in VBA: globals, locals, constants, and literals. VBA also allows the creation of enumerations and arrays, which are specific types of variables. The following sections discuss each of these types of variables and show how they can be used in VBA code.

Global Variables

Global variables are variables that are defined at the module or class level, outside of any Sub, Function, or Event. Because they are global to the module, any Sub, Function, or Event contained within the module has the ability to access global variables. Global variables can be Public or Private. When Public, objects outside of the module will have access to the variable, but when Private, only members of the module can access the variable. All variables, not just globals, are defined by using the Dim keyword (when Public or Private is not used), followed by the variable name, and optionally followed by the as keyword and the data type for the variable. The following code could be added at the top of a code file to declare some global variables:

```
Dim varTemp
Dim strMyString As String
Private iCount As Integer
Public oSomeData As Object
```

All four of the variable declarations, except for the first, specify the data type for the variable. The last two specify the access modifier, which is Public or Private, instead of the Dim keyword. All of these are valid variable declarations for global variables.

It is also important to consider how the access modifiers work. When the Public keyword is used, the global variable may be used by objects outside of just the immediate module. The Private keyword stipulates that only objects within the module can access the variable and it is not usable by objects outside of the class. For modules in Access, when not specified otherwise, all global variables are Public by default. In class modules, when not specified otherwise, all global variables are Private by default. This is just one of the major differences between modules and class modules, and considering how global variables can be accessed with each will be very important when writing VBA code.

Local Variables

Local variables are variables that are defined within a Sub, Function, or Event. Because they are defined within a procedure, they are local to that procedure and are not usable outside that procedure. That is to say, local variables can only be used by code within the procedure they are defined in and are lost once the procedure has been exited. Local variables are defined in much the same manner as globals, except that locals do not have an access modifier (that is, they are not specified as Public or Private). However, non-basic type local variables, including Object and Variant types, must be set to an instance of an object before they can be used, whether that instance is pre-existing or brand new. Thus, VBA provides the New keyword that can be used to define a new instance of the object when the variable is declared, which is placed between the As and the data type for the variable.

The following code could be added within a Sub or Function to declare some local variables:

```
Dim varTemp
Dim strMyString As String
Dim oSomeData As New Object
```

These declarations look, and are, very similar to the global variable declarations that you saw previously. Notice that the last declaration uses the New keyword to specify a new instance of the Object type. All of these are valid variable declarations for global variables. And technically, unless the Option Explicit statement is used, you do not have to declare variables at all in VBA! Just start using them in code and it will work. Even though not declaring variables is allowed, I always recommend using the Option Explicit statement in every module, to ensure all variables are declared and to reduce the risk of coding errors.

Accessing Variables

Once a local or global variable has been created, you will want to write to and read from it during code execution. To set the value of a variable in code, simply issue a statement with the form of the variable name, then the equal sign, and finally the value to set the variable to. The following code provides an example of assigning a value to an Integer type variable:

```
iCount = 5
```

To read from a variable, simply use that variable in place of other values. For example, you could read the value from the previous code line and create a statement to add it to itself and assign that sum to another variable. The following code illustrates such an example:

```
iAnotherVariable = iCount + iCount
```

Reading from and writing to variables is just that simple. However, it should be noted that in the case of complex variable types, you will need to use the Set keyword to assign to the object. For example, the following code declares an object of type Database and assigns the object returned from the CurrentDb method to it.

```
Dim dbMyDatabase as Database
Set dbMyDatabase = Application.CurrentDb
```

Creating New Instances for Complex Types

Variables that are one of the 12 basic data types, except for Variant and Object types, automatically have an instance created for them when they are declared. However, Object, Variant, and all other types, except for enumerations, must be set to an instance of that type before they can be used. This instance can be new or pre-existing, but you will get an Object Not Set error if you try to access a variable that is not bound to an instance, otherwise known as a null variable. To create a new instance of most types (some types you are not allowed to create a new instance of for specific reasons), simply use the New keyword. The New keyword can be used when the variable is declared, or at any other time you want to create a new instance of a given data type. The following code provides a couple of examples of creating a new instance of an Object data type:

```
Dim oTempObject As New Object
oTempObject = New Object
```

However, when declaring the non-basic data types, using New is not required; it is only used when a new instance of the object needs to be created.

Literal Values

Another important type of variable to examine is literal values. Literal values are simply the hard-coded values specified directly in code. The following code provides an example of setting literal values in VBA code:

```
' Assigning a number
Dim iCount as Integer
iCount = -1

' Assigning a string - Note: strings must be surrounded by quotes
Dim strMessage As String
strMessage = "This is a string"
strMessage = "Now assigning a different message"
strMessage = strMessage & " - Now concatenating to the last message"

' Assigning a Date - Note: dates are surrounded by pound signs
Dim dtStartDate As Date
dtStartDate = #8/13/2009 12:15 PM#
```

This code provides a few simple examples of how literal values can be assigned to variables in code. Notice that for each of the variables that were defined, the code is slightly different depending on the data type. When setting the literal value of a number type, such as an `Integer` or `Double`, one only has to specify the number to be used. However, for a `String` or a `Date` variable type, the user must surround the literal value in quotes or pound signs (respectively), which are the two special cases for assigning literal values to the basic types discussed earlier. Specifying literal values is very important in VBA code for setting variable values.

Constants

A constant is a type of variable that cannot be modified. There are two kinds of constants in VBA: constants that VBA provides and constant variables that the user defines. Constant values that VBA provides include `vbNewLine` or `vbNullChar`, which are variables that can be used in the place of the literal values to remove the need to use literal, hard-coded values over and over again in code. For example, the following code uses the `vbNewLine` constant to supply a new line character in a string:

```
strMessage = "The operation has been cancelled." & vbNewLine & _
             "Press OK to continue."
```

As such, the user can also define constant values that can be used in place of literal values throughout code. This is often very handy when you want to specify the literal value of a variable one time and then use that value throughout the code, while specifically disallowing any changes to that variable. To create a constant variable, use the `Const` keyword, followed by the variable name, assignment operator, and literal value to be set to the constant. The following code provides a few examples of declaring constant variables:

```
Const strApplicationTitle = "My Super Access App"
Public Const iDaysInWeek = 7
Private Const dtFiscalStartDate = #9/1/2010#
```

Enumerations

An enumeration in VBA is a data type that maps keywords to integer values of the Long data type, removing the need to use the hard-coded values directly in code by instead specifying one of the options. Although an enumeration is really a type of data and can have user-defined types created, enumerations have characteristics that are similar to variables and should be discussed at this point. Enumerations are used throughout VBA, as well as many other programming languages and libraries, and are extremely common, so this section covers their basics.

Using Enumerations

An enumeration is an object that contains a set of options, in which each option maps to one of the values of a Long data type for the VBA language. If you've worked with VBA before, you've probably used enumeration values on many different occasions. For example, the AcCommand object is an enumeration that is used to store values for a list of Access dialogs and command options. The RunCommand method, which is a member of the Application object, takes an option value from the AcCommand enumeration and executes the command that the specified option is mapped to. The following code is an example of calling the RunCommand method with the acCmdSaveAs member of the AcCommand enumeration to invoke the Save As dialog:

```
RunCommand AcCommand.acCmdSaveAs
```

In this case, the acCmdSaveAs option was prefixed with the AcCommand class name, but that is not necessarily required. You could have just as easily called this option by itself, and VBA will have no problem resolving it, because the project already has a reference to the Access Object Library. In this particular case, the acCmdSaveAs dialog maps to the value of 21, so you could have also called the RunCommand method with the parameter value of 21 and you would get the same result. The following code provides examples of both calling the enumeration option alone, and calling the method with the value of the enumeration option:

```
RunCommand acCmdSaveAs
RunCommand 21
```

Both of the preceding lines of code will produce the same result. Using enumeration option values in VBA code is just that easy!

Creating Enumerations

VBA provides the ability to create user-defined enumerations, to allow creating your own group of options that can be used as a data type. The Enum keyword in VBA is used to declare an enumeration, followed by the name string for the enumeration, which is terminated by the End Enum statement. The individual options are defined within the block by specifying the option name, the = operator, and the option value. For example, the following code illustrates how an enumeration can be declared in VBA:

```
Enum DaysOfTheWeek
    [_MinValue = 0]
    Sunday = 0
    Monday = 1
    Tuesday = 2
```

```
    Wednesday = 3
    Thursday = 4
    Friday = 5
    Saturday = 6
    [_MaxValue = 6]
End Enum
```

Notice that the preceding code example creates an enumeration for the days of the week and maps each to a Long data type value. Also, notice that there are two additional members: MinValue and MaxValue, and that they are enclosed in square brackets and prefixed with an underscore. When prefixed with an underscore, the member is marked as hidden, and will not be shown in the IntelliSense in VBE by default, unless hidden objects are turned on. The square brackets are used to make the underscore character valid.

Once a custom enumeration has been declared, it can be used in code just like any other enumeration object. The following code provides an example of defining a variable of the custom Enum type and shows how it can be set:

```
' Declare and set the custom Enum type
Dim dowDay As DaysOfTheWeek
dowDay = DaysOfTheWeek.Sunday
```

Really, that is all there is to it. Once the preceding code has been executed, the dowDay variable will contain a value of 0, which is the value that the Sunday option maps to in the declaration of the enumeration. Also, it should be noted that once an enumeration has been added to a module, it becomes a Class module, which is discussed more in the next lesson.

VBA Arrays

Finally, the last kind of variable to examine is an array variable. An array is a set of variables of the same type, stored as a group. Each item in the array can be accessed individually, but the array also provides other operations, specific to the array. VBA supports two kinds of arrays: static and dynamic. This section discusses both, and provides examples of accessing and working with the array items.

Static Arrays

Static arrays are arrays where the number of items contained in the array is fixed, and not changing. Declaring static arrays is much like declaring other variables, except for one major difference: When declared, the upper boundary index must be specified with the variable name. The following code is an example of the declaration of a static array of Integer elements:

```
Dim arrIntegersArray(10) As Integer
```

Note that this looks exactly like a normal variable declaration, except that there is a number specified in parentheses after the variable name. Although one might assume this means create an array of 10 elements, the number 10 actually specifies the upper boundary index of the array, and the lower boundary automatically starts at index 0, unless an Option Base statement in the module specifies otherwise. So, that means that the previous array declaration really has 11 elements, items 0 through 10. As such, the user can directly specify either boundary index for the array when it is declared. The following code provides some more examples of array declarations, where the upper and lower boundary indexes of the array have been specified:

```
Dim arrResultValues(0 to 9) As Long
Dim arrDaysInWeek(1 to 7) As Date
Dim arrPositions(-50 to 50) As Double
```

Notice that the arrPositions array defines negative values for array indexes, which is allowed in VBA, so the array actually has 101 elements available in it. Because the bounds are specified as a Long value, the maximum number of elements in an array is 4,294,967,296, or 2 to the 32nd power, because a Long data type in VBA is four bytes in size. However, because a Long can represent negative values as well, the maximum upper and minimum lower index values allowed are 2,147,483,647 and –2,147,483,648, respectively. These values specify not only the boundaries of the array, but the size of the array itself, albeit indirectly. It is also important to consider the amount of available memory on the machine when allocating large arrays, because VBA must be able to allocate the requested size for the array in memory, and if it is not available, an error will be returned. For example, if you request an array of 4,294,967,296 elements that are of Integer type, because each element is four bytes in size, the program will need to allocate 16 GB of memory, which is a lot of memory even by today's standards and would most likely eat up all of the memory on the machine! All of the array examples shown here so far are fixed in size when declared, but VBA also allows for dynamic arrays to be created as well.

Dynamic Arrays

A dynamic array is an array that can change in size, but not in data type. When a dynamic array is declared, the bounds are not specified. Instead, the ReDim keyword is used to declare the size of the array when needed. The following is an example of a declaration and ReDim statements for a dynamic array:

```
' Declare the dynamic array
Dim arrMyDynamicArray() As Integer

' Set the size of the array
ReDim arrMyDynamicArray(10)

' Set a new size for the array
ReDim arrMyDynamicArray(-50 To 50)
```

Notice that the first statement simply declares the array variable, with the parentheses, but does not provide the bounds. The second statement, which includes the ReDim keyword, actually completes the memory allocation for the array. It looks a lot like a normal Dim statement, except that it does not specify the data type for the array, because it was already defined in the array declaration. The neat thing about a dynamic array is that you can call ReDim as many times as you like for it, and change the size of the array as many times as desired. Each time the ReDim statement is used, the memory that was previously stored in the array is lost to that array, although you could always assign the data to another object before calling ReDim. Dynamic arrays are most useful when the number of elements to be stored in the array is not known until run time of the application.

Multi-Dimensional Arrays

A multi-dimensional array is an array that has more than one set of indexed dimensions. Up to this point in the lesson, all of the arrays discussed have been one-dimensional, meaning only one set of indexed values is used to reference elements within the array. However, it is possible to declare an array with multiple indices by separating each set of index values with a comma in the array declaration. For example, consider a Cartesian map that has X and Y coordinates; one could easily implement storage for a map's data in a two-dimensional array, and then reference the items in the map array by using the X and Y indices. The following code provides an example showing how to create some multi-dimensional arrays:

```
Dim arrMap(10, 10) As Object
Dim arrSpatialPoint(1 To 10, 1 To 10, 1 To 10) As Long
```

Multi-dimensional arrays can also be declared dynamically and still conform to the other rules of normal arrays, such as maximum size. The only real difference is how the array is declared and how the array items can be accessed.

Accessing Array Values

Once you have an array declared, reading from and writing values to the elements of the array are quite easy. The number surrounded by parentheses following the array variable name is used to specify the index of an element in the array when reading from or writing to the array. The following code provides an example of declaring an array and then reading from and writing to the fifth element within it:

```
' Declare the Array
Dim strMessage(1 To 10) As String

' Assign a value to the fifth element of the array
strMessage(5) = "This is the element's value string"

' Show the value of the fifth element in the array in a message box
MsgBox strMessage(5)
```

The preceding code example shows how to access the elements of a one-dimensional array, and for accessing a multi-dimensional array, it is much the same, except that again the indexes are separated by a comma. The following code provides an example of accessing the values in a multi-dimensional array:

```
' Declare the multi-dimensional Array
Dim strMap(1 To 10, 1 To 10) As Long

' Assign a value to an element of the array
strMap(5, 5) = 100

' Show the value of the element in a message box
MsgBox strMap(5, 5)
```

Arrays are very useful in VBA and simple to understand. Arrays are also the only ordinal data structure that VBA provides, so they are likely to be used in your code often.

TRY IT

In this lesson, you create some code that uses several different types of variables. Now that you know all about the different kinds of variables in VBA and how they can be applied, try building some code using these variables. The following example walks you through the steps necessary to build some VBA code and attempts to illustrate how the different kinds of variables can be used in code. Sample files are available on the book's DVD and website.

Lesson Requirements

For this lesson, the example steps use a blank database created from scratch. However, a blank database is not necessarily required to complete this lesson; you can use just about any database application. You should be familiar with creating a new database, creating database objects, and the basics of working with VBE and VBA, as discussed in the preceding lessons.

Step-by-Step

1. Open Access 2010 from the Windows Start menu. The Access Backstage will open in the Access window.

2. In the Backstage, click the New option on the left-hand menu and then click the Blank Database option.

3. Optionally, choose the File Name and Location and click the Create button on the right side of the screen to create the new blank database application. The new database will be created and opened in the Access window.

4. Close the default table that is created; once the new database has been opened, you won't need it for your purpose.

5. Click the Create tab on the Ribbon to select it.

6. On the Create Ribbon, click the Class Module option. This creates a new module in the database and opens it in VBE.

7. Once VBE has been opened, click the Save button on the top left of the VBE toolbar. The Save As dialog will open.

8. For the Class Module Name, type **ModUtility**, then click OK to save the data. The module will now be saved in the database.

9. Notice that the `Option Compare Database` statement is already present in the new module. To add your own, put the cursor just below the existing `Option` statement and type the new `Option` statement: **Option Explicit**. This is added so you are required to explicitly declare all variables.

10. Press the Enter key two or three times to add a few new lines to the file to create a global variable.

11. Type the following line of code to declare a global, constant variable:

     Const MAX_DAY_VALUE = 6

12. Press the Enter key three or four times to add a few new lines to the file to create a custom enumeration.

13. Type the following code for the enumeration:

```
Enum DaysOfTheWeek
  [_MinValue = 0]
  Sunday = 0
  Monday = 1
  Tuesday = 2
  Wednesday = 3
  Thursday = 4
  Friday = 5
  Saturday = 6
  [_MaxValue = 6]
End Enum
```

14. Press the Enter key two or three more times to add a few new lines to the file to create a new subroutine.

15. Type the following code for the subroutine:

```
Public Sub ShowDay(dowDay As DaysOfTheWeek)

  ' Check to make sure the value is not too large
  If dowDay > MAX_DAY_VALUE Then
    MsgBox "The Day Value of: " & dowDay & " is TOO LARGE"
    Exit Sub
  End If

  ' Otherwise, show the day of week name value
  Select Case dowDay
    Case Sunday
      MsgBox "Today is Sunday"
    Case Monday
      MsgBox "Today is Monday"
    Case Tuesday
      MsgBox "Today is Tuesday"
    Case Wednesday
      MsgBox "Today is Wednesday"
    Case Thursday
      MsgBox "Today is Thursday"
    Case Friday
      MsgBox "Today is Friday"
    Case Saturday
      MsgBox "Today is Saturday"
    Case Else
      MsgBox "The Day value is NOT recognized!"
  End Select

End Sub
```

16. Save and close VBE. You will be taken back to Access.

17. On the Create Ribbon, choose the Form Design option to create a new form in Design View mode.

18. Click the Save button to save the new form. For the name of the form, type **frmShowDay**, then click OK. The form will be saved to the database.

19. On the Design Ribbon of the Table Design Tools group, click the Text Box control option to select it, and then click the form to drop the Text Box control on the form.

20. Click the Button control option on the Ribbon to select it and then click the form just below the previous Text Box control to add the button to the form. The Command Button Wizard will be invoked, so just press the Cancel button.

21. For the Label control of the Text Box control, type in the value **Enter a Number (0-6)**.

22. Hit the F4 button to open the Property Sheet if it is not already open.

23. Click the first Text Box to select it, so that its properties are shown in the Property Sheet. Select the All tab and change the Name property value to **txtInput**.

24. Click the Button control to select it. Change the Name property value to **btnShowDay**. Change the Caption property value to **Show Day**.

25. With the button still selected, click the Event tab of the Property Sheet to select it. Click the "..." (Builder) button for the On Click property value. This invokes the Choose Builder dialog, so choose the Code Builder option and click OK.

26. VBE will be invoked with an `OnClick` event method added for the Button control. Add the following code to the `OnClick` event method:

```
Dim muUtil As New ModUtility
muUtil.ShowDay txtInput
```

Because the `ModUtility` is a class module, a local variable needs to be created with a new instance of it, so that it can be used.

27. Click the Save button to save everything. Once saved, close VBE. Then close the new form and choose OK when prompted to save.

Congratulations, you've created some custom code that uses three kinds of variables: a global, a local, and an enumeration. To see that this code is working, simply open the frmShowDay form, type an integer value into the Text Box, and click the Show Day button. A message will be shown telling the user what day value was entered. However, note that because your code requires that the Text Box contain an integer value, if any other value type is used, such as a string value, an error message will be shown. Also, it is worth noting that the previous code does an implicit cast from type `String` to type `Long` in the `Select Case` statement, because the `DaysOfTheWeek` enumeration has an underlying value of `Long`. Regardless, the code still works as expected, sloppy or not, because VBA is smart enough to make it all work out!

SUMMARY

Variables are one of the key foundations of the VBA programming language, and understanding how they work and can be used is critical to building high-quality database applications. This lesson explored all of the basic kinds of variables that the VBA programming language offers: globals, locals, literals, constants, enumerations, and arrays. Each of these variable types has its own purpose and is easy to use, depending on what you need the variable to do. Although this has been a brief overview of variables and is by no means all the possible information about variables, you should have a good enough understanding of them to at least begin creating applications that utilize their features. But, the best method for learning to use variables is practice — you now have the knowledge, see what you can do with it!

 Please select Lesson 54 on the DVD to view the video that accompanies this lesson.

55

Creating Class Modules

Up to this point, you have used the basic data types and a few other classes that are part of Access and VBA (Visual Basic for Applications), but it is also possible to create your own data types using VBA, called a *class*. A class is a means of encapsulating related functions and data. Creating a user-defined class is very useful, because it allows users to create their own data types for specific tasks. For example, someone might create an Error class to provide functionality related to dealing with errors for the application. Think about all of the Access objects you have used so far throughout this book; those are all classes too. In fact, most modern-day programming languages provide some sort of method for creating user-defined types. Regardless of the application, you are sure to create plenty of class modules when building VBA code in Access.

LESSON SETUP

This lesson is designed to provide in-depth information about creating user-defined classes in VBA. You should be familiar with Access databases, creating modules, and basic VBA programming. Otherwise, this lesson does not require any other specific knowledge of Access.

CREATING A NEW CLASS MODULE

The easiest method for creating a new user-defined VBA class in Access is to create a new class module in the database. To create a class module using Access 2010, complete the following steps:

1. Open the database that you want to create the class in using Access 2010.

2. On the Create Ribbon, click the Class Module button to create the new class module object. Once the class module is created, VBE (Visual Basic Editor) will open.

3. Click the Save button to immediately save the new class module to the database.

4. You will be prompted to choose a name, so type in the desired class name (this will be the actual name of the class object; these examples use the name clsCounter) and click OK. The new class module will be saved to the database.

Once a class module has been created, you can begin writing code for the class and use it in your other VBA code. However, it is important to note that no code can be executed in the database unless the Access database session has code enabled.

Creating Properties

The first type of member of a class is a class property. User-defined classes can have properties that act like the properties of other code libraries, such as the Connection property of the CurrentProject class that the Application object provides. Typically there is an underlying private member variable in the class to store the data for this property. Member variables in a class feel a lot like properties, providing access to a variable that is accessible to the scope of the class (and even outside of the class if marked Public), but are different in a number of ways. For example, the designer of the class could create a private global variable within the class, to be used by a property later on, by adding the following code to the top of the class module.

```
' Declare a member variable in a class
Private g_count as Integer
```

However, member variables are not the same as a property of a class. The difference is that the Property construct allows the developer to specify how the getting and setting of the property is to be accomplished, by implementing Get and Let statements within the property declaration. To declare a property in VBA code, simply use the Property keyword, followed by either the Get or Let statement, directly before the variable name in the declaration statement for the Get and Let statements. The following code provides an example of declaring a Get statement for a property named iCount.

```
' Declare a Get statement for a Public iCount property
Public Property Get iCount() as Integer

' Return the value of the underlying variable
iCount = g_count

End Property
```

Implementing the Let statement is much like the Get statement, except the statement takes one parameter — the value to be set to — and does not return any value. The following code provides an example of declaring the Let statement for a property named iCount.

```
' Declare a Let statement for a Public iCount property
Public Property Let iCount(ByVal iNewValue as Integer)

    ' Set the value of the underlying variable
    g_count = iNewValue

End Property
```

The nice thing about properties in VBA is that the Get and Let constructs allow the developer to specify how the property can be used. The Get construct allows the user to define code to execute when the property is accessed. Similarly, the Let construct defines how the property is set to a new value. If either of them is not specified, then that functionality is not allowed for the property. For example, if the property defines `Get`, but not a `Let` method, the users of the class will only get the value from the property, but will not be able to set the value directly. Properties are a great way to control access to a member variable in a user-defined class.

Creating Methods

Creating class methods is just like creating functions and subroutines in a standard module. The only difference is that these functions and subroutines are members of the class, and inherit many important structural properties due to this fact. But for now, they can be considered basically the same.

To create a `Sub` that is part of the class, simply define it inside the class file as you would any other `Sub`, but ensure that you use a code access modifier, such as `Public` or `Private`, to explicitly define code access for the `Sub`. The following code provides an example of creating a `Sub` in a class module.

```
Public Sub ClearCount()

    ' Set the iCount property to zero
    iCount = 0

End Sub
```

This code simply sets the `iCount` property to a value of `0`. Of course, functions can be created too, providing all of the functionality that a function allows. The following code provides an example of creating a function in a class module.

```
Public Function IncrementByOne() As Integer

    ' Increment the g_count property by 1
    g_count = g_count + 1

    ' Set the return value for the function
    IncrementByOne = g_Count

End Function
```

This function simply increments the `g_Count` property by 1 and then returns the new value. But more importantly, it illustrates how a function can be created in a class module. Regardless of how you create them, you are sure to build classes that use lots of functions and subroutines with them.

Creating Events

The last type of class object is the `Event` method. Events are a type of method for a class that is defined within the class; it is raised when some action in the class has occurred, at which point the `Event` methods associated with that event are executed. For example, the `Form` class has an `Open` event and whenever the form is opened, the `Open` event is raised. The developer of the form has the option to implement the `On_Open` event method, which will be called whenever the `Open` event is raised.

So, events in VBA really have three parts:

➤ Creating the event.

➤ Raising the event.

➤ Creating an event handler method that is called when the event is raised.

This section describes how to create custom events for a user-defined class.

Declaring Event Methods

Before an event can be implemented, it must be declared within the class module. The declaration for the event consists of the following in this order:

➤ The `Public` or `Private` keyword

➤ Then the `Event` keyword

➤ Then the desired event name

➤ Then the parameters for the event method

Typically they are declared at the top of the class module file. The following code provides an example of declaring an `Event` method for a class module:

```
' Declare the Event method
Public Event OnChange(ByVal iValue As Integer)
```

Raising Events

Once the `Event` has been declared for the class, the class should explicitly raise the `Event` everywhere it occurs within the class. For example, the `clsCounter` class should raise the `OnChange` event every time the value of the `iCount` property changes. To raise the event, simply create a code statement that starts with the `RaiseEvent` keyword and is followed by the call to the event method. The following code provides an example of modifying the previous `Let`, `ClearCount`, and `IncrementByOne` methods to incorporate the `OnChange` event for the class.

```
Public Property Let iCount(ByVal iNewValue as Integer)

   ' Set the value of the underlying variable
   g_count = iNewValue

   ' Raise the OnChange event for the class
   RaiseEvent OnChange(iNewValue)

End Property


Public Sub ClearCount()

   ' Set the iCount property to zero
   iCount = 0
```

```
    ' Raise the OnChange event for the class
    RaiseEvent OnChange(iCount)

End Sub


Public Function IncrementByOne() As Integer

    ' Increment the g_count property by 1
    g_count = g_count + 1

    ' Raise the OnChange event for the class
    RaiseEvent OnChange(g_count)

    ' Set the return value for the function
    IncrementByOne = g_count

End Function
```

Notice that each of these three methods in the preceding paragraph raise the OnChange event. This means that event handlers tied to the OnChange event will be executed whenever any of these methods are invoked and any user-defined code for this event will be executed as well. It is easy to implement an event handler in VBA code, but I must discuss using a class in code before I can show you how to implement the classes' events.

USING A CLASS MODULE

Once the class module has been implemented, it will be ready to use in code. Using a custom class is just like using a complex data type, such as a Variant type object. First it must be declared, and optionally instantiated as a new instance of the object, before it can be used. Once an instance is created, you can access properties, call methods, and implement events for the class with little effort. This section discusses how to accomplish each of these tasks for a user-defined class object.

Creating a New Instance

The first thing to do with a class is to create an *instance* of it. In most cases, you will use the New keyword to declare a new instance of a class or other complex data type in VBA. When declaring a new instance of a class, place the New keyword between the As keyword and the data type name in the declaration statement. The following code provides an example of declaring a new instance of the clsCounter class created in the previous sections of this chapter.

```
    ' Declare a new instance of the clsCounter class
    Dim ctrMyCounter As New clsCounter
```

Remember, before a user-defined class can be used, it must be instantiated. If the object is not instantiated prior to use, you will get runtime error number 91: Object variable or With block variable not set. You are likely to see this error often when developing in VBA, so be aware that it often means that the variable that was accessed was not previously set to an instance of the object, new or otherwise.

Accessing Properties

Getting and setting the properties of a user-defined class is no different than getting or setting the properties of any other object. To set a property, simply set the property to some value. The following code provides an example of setting the iCount property from the preceding clsCounter class.

```
' Declare a new instance of the class
Dim ctrMyCount As New clsCounter

' Set the iCount property of the class
ctrMyCount.iCount = 10
```

Similarly, getting the value of a property is just as easy. Simply set the property to some variable or apply the property to some method. The following code builds on the preceding example, illustrating how to read from the iCount property that was previously set in the following code.

```
' Declare a variable to store the count in
Dim iTheCount As Integer

' Get the iCount property of the class
iTheCount = ctrMyCount.iCount
```

And remember, to get and set the values of a property, the class must implement both the Get and Let statements; otherwise, the operation will be unavailable for the property and produce a compile error if attempted.

Calling Methods

Just as with class properties, calling methods for user-defined classes is exactly the same as calling the methods of other objects in VBA. For Sub type methods, the user can simply call the following in order:

➤ The variable name

➤ A . (dot operator)

➤ The method name

➤ Optionally, include any parameters to the Sub

The following code builds on the previous two examples to provide an example of calling the ClearCount Sub of the clsCounter class.

```
' Call the ClearCount sub
ctrMyCount.ClearCount
```

Likewise, calling a Function member of a user-defined class is just like calling the functions of any other object, as described in Lesson 52. The following code adds to the previous three code samples to provide an example of calling the IncrementByOne function of the clsCounter class.

```
' Call the IncrementByOne function
iTheCount = ctrMyCount.IncrementByOne()
```

Either way, calling the methods of a user-defined class is extremely easy and just like calling other functions or subroutines.

Implementing Event Methods

If an object, such as a user-defined class, provides events, these events can be wired up by the class user. However, this requires a special declaration of the class that contains the events being implemented. But once the declaration has been created, you can implement the events in a user-defined class just as you would with any other object. This section discusses the basics of declaring and implementing events for user-defined classes.

Declaring WithEvents

To begin using the events provided by a class, as mentioned previously, a special declaration of the object is required. Specifically, the variable for the instance of the class must be declared using the keyword WithEvents. It is important to note that WithEvents must be declared within a class module and it must be declared at the module level (that is, global to the class). The following code provides an example of declaring a global variable for the clsCounter class using the WithEvents keyword inside of a new class module.

```
' Declare the clsCounter class variable using WithEvents
Private WithEvents ctrMyCount As clsCounter
```

Implementing Class Events

Once WithEvents has been declared, the event handler method can be implemented so that the handler code will execute when a given event is raised. The following code provides an example of implementing the OnChange event of the clsCounter class to show a message box containing the value of the current counter every time the value changes.

```
' Declare the OnChange event for the ctrMyCount variable
Private Sub ctrMyCount_OnChange(ByVal iValue As Integer)

    ' When the value changes, show a message box with the new value
    MsgBox "Changed to: " & iValue

End Sub
```

TRY IT

In this lesson you build a user-defined class module in an Access database application. By now, you should have a good knowledge of what classes are, how user-defined classes can be created, how to create the various members that classes support, and how to use each of those objects in code. The following example walks you through building a class and illustrates how each of its components can be used in VBA code. Sample files are available on the book's DVD and website.

Lesson Requirements

For this lesson, the example steps use a blank database created from scratch. However, a blank database is not required to complete this lesson; you can use just about any database application. You should be familiar with creating new database objects, using the Visual Basic Editor, and writing basic VBA code to complete this lesson.

Step-by-Step

1. Open Access 2010 from the Windows Start menu. The Access Backstage will open in the Access window.

2. In the Backstage, click the New option on the left-hand menu and then click the Blank Database option.

3. Optionally, choose the file name and location and click the Create button (on the right side of the screen) to create the new, blank database application. The new database will open in the Access window.

4. Close the default table that is created; once the new database has been opened, you won't need it.

5. Click the Create tab on the Ribbon to select it.

6. On the Create Ribbon, click the Class Module option. The class module will be created in the database and opened in VBE.

7. Once VBE has opened, click the Save button on the top left of the VBE toolbar. The Save As dialog will open.

8. For Class Module Name, type **clsCounter**. Then click OK to save the data. The module will be saved in the database.

9. Notice that the Option Compare Database statement is already present in the new module. To add your own `Option` statement, place the cursor just below the existing `Option` statement and type **Option Explicit**. This is added as a safety measure so that the developer is required to explicitly declare all variables.

10. Press the Enter key three times to add a few more lines to the file to create a member variable. Then type the following line of code to declare a member variable for the class:

    ```
    Private g_count As Integer
    ```

11. Press the Enter key three times to add lines to the file to declare events for the class. Then type the following code to declare an `OnChange` event method:

    ```
    Public Event OnChange(ByVal iValue As Integer)
    ```

12. Press the Enter key three more times to add lines to the file to create `Let` and `Set` methods for a class property. Then type the following code to create the `Public iCount` property:

    ```
    ' Declare a Get statement for a Public iCount property
    Public Property Get iCount() As Integer
    ```

```
' Return the value of the underlying variable
iCount = g_count

End Property


' Declare a Let statement for a Public iCount property
Public Property Let iCount(ByVal iNewValue As Integer)

   ' Set the value of the underlying variable
   g_count = iNewValue

   ' Raise the OnChange event for the class
   RaiseEvent OnChange(iNewValue)

End Property
```

13. Press the Enter key three more times. Then type the following code to implement a Sub and Function for the class:

```
' Declare a Sub
Public Sub ClearCount()

   ' Set the iCount property to zero
   iCount = 0

   ' Raise the OnChange event for the class
   RaiseEvent OnChange(iCount)

End Sub


' Declare a Function
Public Function IncrementByOne() As Integer

   ' Increment the g_count property by 1
   g_count = g_count + 1

   ' Raise the OnChange event for the class
   RaiseEvent OnChange(g_count)

   ' Set the return value for the function
   IncrementByOne = g_count

End Function
```

14. Save and close VBE; you are done implementing the clsCounter class. The new class code will be saved and you will be taken back to Access.

Congratulations; you created a new user-defined class in VBA. The clsCounter class can be used to store a counter value and retrieve that value when needed. To verify that the code is working correctly, implement some more code to call this code.

15. On the Create Ribbon, click the Class Module option. The class module will be created in the database and opened in VBE.

16. Once VBE has been opened, click the Save button on the top left of the VBE toolbar. The Save As dialog will open.

17. For the Class Module Name, type **clsTestClass**. Then click OK to save the data. The module will be saved in the database.

18. Add an `Option Explicit` statement to this code file by typing in the value **Option Explicit** at the top of the code file. This is added so the developer is required to explicitly declare all variables.

19. Because you will be implementing the `OnChange` event created in the `clsCounter` class, add the following code just below the Option Explicit statement to declare `WithEvent` for the class:

```
Private WithEvents ctrMyCount As clsCounter
```

20. To implement the `OnChange` event in the `clsTestClass`, add the following code:

```
' Declare the OnChange event for the ctrMyCount variable
Private Sub ctrMyCount_OnChange(ByVal iValue As Integer)

    ' When the value changes, show a message box with the new value
    MsgBox "Changed to: " & iValue

End Sub
```

21. Add one more method to actually call into the `clsCounter` class to trigger the `OnChange` event. Add the following code to the class file:

```
Public Sub TestEvent()

    ' Create a new instance of the clsCounter class
    Set ctrMyCount = New clsCounter

    ' Trigger the OnChange event by setting the value of the iCount property
    ctrMyCount.iCount = 10

End Sub
```

Congratulations; you have created another user-defined class that implements the `clsCounter` class's `OnChange` event. To see this code in action, complete a few more steps and the application will be ready to use!

22. On the Create Ribbon, choose the Form Design option to create a new form in Design View mode.

23. Click the Save button to save the new form. For its name, type **frmShowExample** and click OK. The form will be saved to the database.

24. On the Design Ribbon of the Table Design Tools group, click the Button control option on the Ribbon to select it; then click the form to add a new button to the form. The Command Button Wizard will be invoked, so click the Cancel button.

25. Press the F4 button to open the Property Sheet if it is not already open.

26. Click the Button control to select it. Change the `Name` property value to **btnTest**. Change the `Caption` property value to **Test Event**.

27. Click the Event tab of the Property Sheet to select it. Click the "…" (Builder) button for the On Click property value. This invokes the Choose Builder dialog, so choose the Code Builder option and click OK.

28. VBE will create an `OnClick` event method for the Button control. Add the following code to the `OnClick` event method:

```
' Declare a new instance of the clsCounter class
Dim ctrMyCount As New clsTestClass

' Call the TestEvent method of the class
ctrMyCount.TestEvent
```

29. Click the Save button. Once saved, close VBE.

30. Close the new form and choose OK when prompted to save.

Congratulations; you've created two user-defined classes, which implement properties, methods, and events. If you open the form and click the Test Event button, the `iCount` property of the `clsCounter` class will be set to the value of `10` and the `OnChange` event will be fired. Because the `OnChange` method was implemented to show a message box with the `iCount` variable's current value, the message box will be presented to the user. Creating and using user-defined classes is truly a simple task using VBA code.

SUMMARY

Classes are a huge part of VBA and knowing how to build user-defined classes is extremely useful. This lesson discussed how to create, instantiate, and use a class module in VBA. Specifically, this lesson reviewed the basics of creating user-defined classes; creating properties, methods, and events; and even discussed how those events could be called from another class. If you plan to continue writing VBA code in your Access database applications, you are likely to create many more classes — they are a great way to build VBA objects that other code can easily work with. Plus they encapsulate related functionality.

 Please select Lesson 55 on the DVD to view the video that accompanies this lesson.

56

The Access Object Model

VBA provides the ability to work with the Access 2010 program directly, through the use of the Access Object Model. The Access Object Model is a collection of classes that are designed specifically to allow the developer to use Access features using directly in VBA code. For example, say you want to open a database in the Access program using VBA code; the developer could call the `OpenCurrentDatabase` method to accomplish this task. The Access Object Model provides the ability to create instances of the Access program, open and close database files, interact with database objects, and even run the Access wizards and other features of Access 2010. This lesson discusses the Access Object Model and shows how it can be used in VBA code.

LESSON SETUP

This lesson is designed to provide some basic information about using the Access Object Model. You should be familiar with Access databases, creating modules, and the basics of VBA programming. Otherwise, this lesson does not require any other specific knowledge of Access.

THE ACCESS APPLICATION OBJECT

The `Access.Application` object is the basis for working with all functionality within the Access program. By default, every database created in Access has a reference set to the Access Object Model in the VBA code project. For example, databases created by Access 2010 automatically have a reference set to the Microsoft Access 14.0 Object Library. This reference is what provides the ability to use Access objects, such as the `Application` class or the `DoCmd` class, in an Access database application without having to do anything special to use these Access objects. All functionality that can be used from the Access program in VBA code is part of the `Access.Application` object.

The object that refers to the current instance of the database loaded in the Access program is the global variable named `Application`, and is the type `Access.Application`. You can use the `Application` object to work with all of the functionality for the current instance of the database loaded. For example, you can call the `Application.DoCmd.OpenForm` method to open a form in the current instance of the database. The `Application` object contains a multitude of functionality and because it contains all functionality for Access, you will likely use this object often in your VBA code.

In addition to using the `Application` object to manipulate the current instance of the Access program, any number of other instances of Access can also be created. This is accomplished by creating new instances of the `Access.Application` object. By creating a new instance of Access, you can load other databases or perform operations in Access that, for example, require no database to be open, instead of having to perform this functionality in the current instance of Access. The following code provides an example of creating a new instance of the `Access.Application` object and opening a `Database1.accdb` file.

```
Public Sub OpenAccess()

    ' Create a new instance of Access
    Dim appAccess As New Access.Application

    ' Make the instance visible to the viewer
    appAccess.Visible = True

    ' Open a database in the instance
    appAccess.OpenCurrentDatabase "C:\Database1.accdb"

End Sub
```

The preceding code does three things: creates a new instance of the `Access.Application` object, sets the instance of Access to visible (so that the user can see it in Windows), and finally, opens a database from the local hard drive (or throws an error if the database file is not present at the specified location). Working with other instances of the Access program is just as easy as working with the current instance of the program, in this case, by using the new instance of Access stored in the `appAccess` variable, instead of the current instance of Access stored in the `Application` global variable.

The CurrentDb Function

The `CurrentDb` object is a member of the `Application` object that returns an object of type `Database`, representing the instance of the database open in that instance of Access. The `CurrentDb` function returns the currently open database in Access as a `Database` type object. The `Database` object provides all of the functionality for working directly with the data objects in a database file. For example, the `TableDefs` collection provides classes and functionality for working with the tables in a given database file. The following code provides an example of a function that returns the number of tables in the database, by calling both the `CurrentDb` method and accessing the `Count` property of the `TableDefs` collection, all in one line of code.

```
Public Function GetTableCount() As Integer

    ' Return the table count using the CurrentDb object
    GetTableCount = Application.CurrentDb.TableDefs.Count

End Function
```

This code simply returns the Count property for the TableDefs collection, which is nothing more than an array of Table objects for working directly with the tables in the database file. Knowing that the CurrentDb method returns a database object, the VBA compiler is smart enough to allow the TableDefs object to be called directly from the end of the CurrentDb method. The CurrentDb method is extremely useful for working with data aspects of an Access database application and you will likely use it often if you plan to programmatically work with Table and Query database objects.

The CurrentProject Object

The CurrentProject class is a member of the Application object that is a collection of all of the code objects in the current instance of a database. The CurrentProject class provides all of the functionality for working directly with the Form, Report, Macro, and Module database objects in a database file. For example, the AllForms collection provides classes and functionality for working with the forms in the database file. The following code provides an example of a function that returns the number of forms in the database, using both the CurrentProject and AllForms objects.

```
Public Function GetFormCount() As Integer

    ' Return the form count using the CurrentProject object
    GetFormCount = Application.CurrentProject.AllForms.Count

End Function
```

This code simply returns the Count property for the AllForms collection, which is an array of Form objects for working directly with the forms in the database. The CurrentProject object is extremely useful for working with code aspects of an Access database application and you will likely use it often if you plan to programmatically work with forms, reports, macros, and/or modules in a database application.

The DoCmd Object

The DoCmd object is a member of the Application object and provides a set of methods for performing common operations in Access. For example, the OpenReport method is a member of the DoCmd object and can be used as a simple procedure for opening Report objects from a database in Access. The following code provides an example of calling the OpenTable method of the DoCmd object to open a database table in the current instance of Access.

```
Public Sub OpenTable()

    ' Open a table in the database
    Application.DoCmd.OpenTable CurrentDb.TableDefs(0).Name

End Sub
```

This code simply opens the name of the first table that is returned by the TableDefs collection. The DoCmd object is extremely useful for quickly performing common operations in Access, but often does not provide all of the low-level functionality you would get by working with the actual individual objects directly. Even still, the DoCmd object is used quite often and is very easy to use.

The RunCommand Method

The RunCommand method is a member of the Application object and is provided to perform common operations that do not require any parameters and are typically features of the Access program. The RunCommand method can perform literally hundreds of operations, such as opening various Access dialogs to undo and redo functionality. The RunCommand method is exposed under both the DoCmd and Application classes. It takes just one parameter, a value from the AcCommand enumeration object, which specifies the operation to be executed. For example, the following code uses the RunCommand method to open the Access Options dialog by specifying the acCmdOptions member of the AcCommand object.

```
Public Sub OpenAccessOptions()

    ' Open the Access Options Dialog
    Application.RunCommand AcCommand.acCmdOptions

End Sub
```

When the preceding OpenAccessOptions Sub is called, the RunCommand method simply opens the Access Options dialog. Although this is only a small example of what the RunCommand method is capable of, it is representative of the kind of functionality that this method supports. Also, it is important to understand that much of the functionality supported by the RunCommand object is specific to the current context of the database application. For example, calling acCmdUndo shows an error message if there is nothing to undo! Regardless of the functionality that is required, the RunCommand object is sure to be easy to use and used often in your database applications.

TRY IT

In this lesson you use the Application object to perform some common operations in Access. The following example walks you through the steps necessary to build some code using the Application object and attempts to illustrate how it can be used in VBA code. Sample files are available on the book's DVD and website.

Lesson Requirements

For this lesson, the example steps use the Northwind database application created from a template. However, the Northwind database is not necessarily required to complete this lesson; you can use just about any database application that contains some database objects. This example focuses primarily on writing some code that uses the Access Object Model code objects.

Step-by-Step

1. Open Access 2010 from the Windows Start menu. The Access Backstage will open in the Access window.

2. In the Backstage, click the New option on the left-hand menu and then click the Sample Templates option to show a list of the built-in templates.

3. Choose the Northwind option from the list of templates and click the Create button on the right side of the screen to create the sample database application. The new Northwind database will open in the Access window.

4. Enable code in the Northwind database application by clicking the Enable button on the Access Security Bar. Code will be enabled in the application and the `Northwind Login` form will open.

5. Close the `Login` form for the Northwind database once it has been opened. You will not need it for this example.

6. Click the Create tab on the Ribbon to select it. The Create Ribbon will be shown.

7. Click the Form Design button on the Ribbon to create a new form. The new `Form` object will open in Design View mode and the Form Design Tools Design Ribbon will open.

8. Click the Button control option on the Design Ribbon and click the top left of the form to drop a new `Button` control on the form. The Command Button Wizard will open, so just click the Cancel button to close it.

9. Press the F4 key to open the Property Sheet, if it is not already open. Make sure that the properties for the new `Button` control are shown in the Property Sheet.

10. On the All tab of the Property Sheet, change the Name property to **btnOpenOptions**.

11. Change the value of the `Caption` property to **Show Access Options**.

12. Resize the button so that all of the `Caption` property text can be seen on it.

13. Click the Event tab of the Property Sheet to select it.

14. Click the "…" (Builder) button for the On Click event. The Choose Builder dialog will be shown, so select the Code Builder option and click OK. VBE will open and a new `OnClick` method will be created for the `btnOpenOptions` button.

15. Add the following code to the new `OnClick` event method:

```
' Open the Access Options Dialog
Application.RunCommand AcCommand.acCmdOptions
```

16. Click the Save button on the top left of the Access window. When prompted for the form name, type **Test Form** and click OK. The form and code will be saved in the database.

17. Close VBE and you will be taken back to the Access window.

18. Click the Button control option on the Design Ribbon and click just below the previous `Button` control to drop another new `Button` control on the form. The Command Button Wizard will open, so just click the Cancel button to close it.

19. Press the F4 key to open the Property Sheet, if it is not already open. Make sure that the properties for the new `Button` control are shown in the Property Sheet.

20. On the All tab of the Property Sheet, change the Name property to **btnOpenCustomers**.

21. Then, change the value of the `Caption` property to **Customers Table**.

22. Resize the button so that all of the `Caption` property text can be seen on it.

23. Click the Event tab of the Property Sheet to select it.

24. Click the "..." (Builder) button for the `On Click` event. The Choose Builder dialog will be shown, so select the Code Builder option and click OK. VBE will open and a new `OnClick` method will be created for the `btnOpenCustomers` button.

25. Add the following code to the new `OnClick` event method:

```
' Open the Customers table
Application.DoCmd.OpenTable "Customers"
```

26. Click the Save button on the top left of the Access window. The form and code will be saved in the database.

27. Close VBE and you will be taken back to the Access window.

Congratulations, you've now created two button controls to perform some common operations in an Access database application. The first button will open the Access Options dialog and the second will open the `Customers` table. To verify this functionality is working, simply switch the form to Form View mode and then click the buttons; they should open their respective objects appropriately!

SUMMARY

The Access Object Model provides the ability to work with Access programmatically in VBA code. By default, all Access databases have a reference to the Access Object Model. The `Access.Application` object provides all of the functionality necessary for working with the Access program and the database that is open within it. Using the objects provided by the `Application` class and the Access Object Model, it is possible to accomplish almost any functionality possible within the Access program in a programmatic fashion.

Please select Lesson 56 on the DVD to view the video that accompanies this lesson.

57

Working with DAO

Data Access Objects (DAO) is a set of classes for working directly with the data objects of an Access database, and most commonly, the `Table` and `Query` objects of a database. The DAO collection of classes are specific to Microsoft Access and are used directly within the Access Object Model to provide the functionality for working directly with Access data objects. Although DAO provides quite a bit of functionality, this lesson provides a brief overview of using DAO to add, modify, and delete data in an Access database application.

LESSON SETUP

This lesson is designed to provide a basic overview of working with DAO to access data using VBA code. You should be familiar with Access databases, creating modules, and the basics of VBA programming. Also, this lesson uses some strings that are written in the SQL language, so having an understanding of SQL language and how to build SQL statements will aid in better understanding the uses of DAO, though it is not necessarily required. Otherwise, this lesson does not require any other specific knowledge of Access.

THE DAO OBJECT MODEL

The DAO object model contains 15 major object types: `DBEngine`, `Workspace`, `Database`, `TableDef`, `QueryDef`, `Recordset`, `Container`, `Relation`, `Field`, `Index`, `Parameter`, `Document`, `User`, `Group`, and `Error` objects. All of these classes together provide a great deal of functionality for working with many different aspects of an Access database. However, in the interest of sticking to the basics, this lesson focuses on only a few of these objects — the minimum objects required for working with data in a database. Table 57-1 provides a description of the three DAO objects this lesson examines.

TABLE 57-1: DAO Objects in This Lesson

OBJECT	DESCRIPTION
Database	A class designed to represent a database, providing methods for working directly with the data objects of an Access database.
Recordset	A class designed to represent a set of data within a DAO Database object, providing methods and properties for working directly with the individual fields and pieces of data contained in the dataset.
Field	A class to work with a field of a table contained in the Database object, providing methods and properties for working directly with field objects.

Using just these objects, the user can create VBA code to read, write, and manipulate the data in an Access database, as you will see in the following sections.

Referencing DAO

DAO is the preferred data access API (Application Program Interface) for use in an Access database application, and as such, all new databases created in Access 2010 automatically have a reference set to DAO. However, this was not always the case in previous versions of Access, and if you are using databases created in previous versions, they may not necessarily have references configured to use DAO. Also, DAO objects have fairly generic names that can conflict with the names of objects in other classes, namely the ADO (ActiveX Data Objects) Object Model. This section discusses how to verify, and set if needed, references to DAO and how to properly reference DAO objects in VBA code.

Setting References to DAO

Before you can begin working with DAO objects in VBA code, the VBA code project must have a reference set to DAO. By default, new databases created in Access 2010 automatically have a reference set to DAO. However, if you are unsure whether the database contains a reference to DAO, simply check the References dialog in VBE (the Visual Basic Editor). The DAO reference name for Access 2010 is titled `Microsoft Office 14.0 Access database engine Object Library`. If this reference, or a similar reference, is not present in the VBA project, you can add it by completing the following steps:

1. With the database open in the Access window, press the Alt+F11 key combination to open the VBE.

2. On the VBE's Tools menu, select the References option. This opens the References dialog.

3. All references that are already set in the database are shown at the top of the References dialog, with their check boxes checked. If the DAO reference is not present at the top, simply scroll down to it (the references are in alphabetical order) and check its check box to select it.

Once the DAO reference has been added to the VBA code project, writing code to use DAO objects is just a matter of pressing the keys.

Referencing DAO Objects in VBA Code

As mentioned, DAO object names are pretty generic and DAO objects can have the same names as objects in other libraries. The order of the references in the VBA project also specifies the precedence of the reference, and the higher a reference is positioned in the References dialog the higher its precedence over any lower references to objects of the same name, when the parent class is not explicitly specified. If two objects have the same class name, conflicting declarations of that class will result in the class with higher precedence being used. For this reason, it is always recommended to prefix object names with the DAO class name when declaring them to explicitly ensure that the class from the DAO object library is used. The following code provides two examples of declaring DAO Database objects.

```
' Generically define a Recordset object
Dim rsSomeRecordset1 As Recordset

' Explicitly define a DAO Recordset object - Preferred
Dim rsSomeRecordset2 As DAO.Recordset
```

Both variable declarations in the preceding code declare objects of type Recordset, and in a code project that only contains references to DAO, they will both be of type DAO.Recordset. However, the first declaration, for the variable named rsSomeRecordset1, could possibly be of a type other than DAO.Recordset, because the DAO type name is not explicitly specified. If another library with a Recordset class is referenced and higher in the reference list order than the DAO type library, then rsSomeRecordset1 will not be type DAO.Recordset. Whenever possible, always prefix class names with the library names when declaring variables to explicitly declare the object, as shown in the second variable declaration in the preceding code.

The DAO Database Object

The DAO Database object is the basis for working with the objects in an Access database. Access makes it very easy to get a reference to the database that is already open in the Access instance by calling the CurrentDb method of the Application object. As mentioned in Lesson 56, the CurrentDb method returns a DAO.Database object to the database open in the Access instance. The following code provides an example of getting a Database object using the CurrentDb method.

```
' Declare a DAO Database object
Dim dbCurrent As DAO.Database

' Get the Database object from the current instance of Access
Set dbCurrent = Application.CurrentDb()
```

The second line in the preceding code simply sets the dbCurrent variable to the Database object returned by the CurrentDb method. Once you have an instance of the Database object to work with, you can read and write data, as you will see next.

Using DAO to Work with Data

The DAO.Recordset object is the primary class used for working with data in an Access database. Gathering data in a Recordset will allow navigation and manipulation of that dataset. This section discusses using the DAO.Recordset object to add, modify, and delete records in the database.

Opening Recordsets

The first thing to do with a `Recordset` is to open it, usually loading it with a set of data. A number of methods exist for opening new or existing `Recordset` objects in DAO, but this example uses a SQL statement to open an existing table object in the database. The `OpenRecordset` method is a member of the `DAO.Database` class that allows the user to quickly open a `Recordset` object based on a table, query, or a SQL statement against the data in the database. The `OpenRecordset` method takes four parameters: `Name`, `Type`, `Options`, and `LockEdit`, the last three of which are optional. The following code provides an example of opening a `Recordset` object based on the `Customers` table of the Northwind sample database.

```
' Declare variables for the Database and Recordset objects
Dim db As DAO.Recordset
Dim rs As DAO.Recordset

' Get the Database object for the current instance of Access
Set db = Application.CurrentDb

' Open the Customers table in a Recordset object
' Note: This code assumes that the Northwind database is open already
Set rs = db.OpenRecordset("Customers", dbOpenTable)
```

Once this code has been completed, the `rs` variable will be loaded with the `Customers` table from the Northwind database. Notice that only the name of the table and the type of object were required to open the `Recordset`, and could have just have easily been done with other existing data objects in the database, including tables, linked tables, and queries. Once the `Recordset` has been opened, you can begin navigating and manipulating the records within it, as you will see in the following sections.

Navigating Recordsets

Once a `Recordset` object has been opened, you will want to be able to navigate through the records to access and manipulate their data. Every `Recordset` has a cursor that points to a record in the `Recordset`, or otherwise no record, in which case it points to either `BOF` (Beginning Of File) or `EOF` (End Of File). A number of methods and properties are built into DAO for moving the current record cursor in the `Recordset`, so that you can access all its records easily. This section discusses the basics of how to navigate a `DAO.Recordset` using the built-in methods.

The RecordCount Property

The `RecordCount` property of a `Recordset` returns a `Long` value denoting the number of records that are currently loaded in the `Recordset` object. This property is often used in a conditional statement when looping through a set of records, or to just know how many records are in the set.

The BOF and EOF Properties

The `Recordset` provides two very important properties that can be used when navigating records, which are the `BOF` and `EOF` properties. The `BOF` and `EOF` properties return `Boolean` values denoting whether the current record cursor is before the beginning or after the end of the records in the `Recordset`. If `BOF` is `True`, the cursor is before the records in the `Recordset` and not currently pointing to any record. If `EOF` is `True`, the cursor is after the end of the records in the `Recordset` and not currently pointing to any record. These are often used to check the position of the current record cursor to make sure it is not outside of the bounds of the contained data when navigating through records.

The Move Methods

The five different move methods for moving the current record cursor between records in a `Recordset` are described in Table 57-2.

TABLE 57-2: The Move Methods of the DAO Recordset Class

METHOD	DESCRIPTION
Move	The `Move` method moves the current record cursor forward the specified number of records in the `Recordset`, based on the current position. It takes two parameters: `Rows`, specifying the number of records to move, and `StartBookmark`, which optionally specifies the location at which to start, if the current position is not desired.
MoveFirst	The `MoveFirst` method moves the current record cursor to the first record in the `Recordset`.
MoveLast	The `MoveLast` method moves the current record cursor to the last record in the `Recordset`.
MoveNext	The `MoveNext` method moves the current record cursor to the next record in the `Recordset`.
MovePrevious	The `MovePrevious` method moves the current record cursor to the previous record in the `Recordset`.

Using these methods is extremely easy to do in VBA code. The following code provides an example of looping through all of the records in the `Customers` table from the Northwind database, using the `MoveFirst` and `MoveNext` methods.

```
' Declare variables for the Database and Recordset objects
Dim db As DAO.Recordset
Dim rs As DAO.Recordset

' Get the Database object for the current instance of Access
Set db = Application.CurrentDb

' Open the Customers table in a Recordset object
' Note: This code assumes that the Northwind database is open already
Set rs = db.OpenRecordset("Customers", dbOpenTable)

' Check to make sure that there are records
If rs.RecordCount > 0 Then
```

```
' Move to the first record
rs.MoveFirst

' Loop through each of the records
While Not rs.EOF

    ' Do some operation on each record here
    ' Then move to the next record
    rs.MoveNext

Wend

End If

' Close and Destroy the Recordset variable
rs.Close
Set rs = Nothing
Set db = Nothing
```

The preceding code simply opens a `Recordset` with the `Customers` table data, moves to the first records, and then walks through each record in the `While` loop. If the user moves past the end or before the beginning of a `Recordset`, the corresponding `BOF` or `EOF` property will be set to the value of `True`. Navigating a `DAO.Recordset` using the move methods is very easy, but they are not the only methods for moving through a `Recordset`, as you will see next.

The AbsolutePosition Property

The `AbsolutePosition` property of the `Recordset` object is a `Long` value that can be used to get or set the position of the current record cursor for the `Recordset`. If you get this property, it returns a `Long` integer value denoting the record number in the `Recordset` to which the current record cursor points. The following code provides an example of getting this property.

```
Dim iRecordNumber As Long
iRecordNumber = rs.AbosolutePosition
```

This code gets the position value of the current record cursor and stores it in the `iRecordNumber` variable. When setting this property, it will automatically set the position of the current record cursor to the corresponding record. The following code provides an example of setting the `AbsolutePosition` property.

```
rs.AbsolutePosition = 10
```

The preceding code sets the `AbsolutePosition` property to the value of `10`, which in turn moves the current record cursor to the tenth record in the `Recordset`. Setting the `AbsolutePosition` property can be extremely useful when you already know exactly which record you want to jump to in the `Recordset`.

Finding Records

The last methods for navigating through a `Recordset` to discuss in this lesson are the find methods. Several different methods exist for finding records in a `Recordset`, depending on the set of criteria you wish to use to find the record. Table 57-3 provides the method name and description of each of the find methods available in the `DAO.Recordset` class.

TABLE 57-3: The Find Methods of the DAO Recordset Class

METHOD	DESCRIPTION
FindFirst	Finds the first record in the Recordset to match the Criteria parameter.
FindLast	Finds the last record in the Recordset to match the Criteria parameter.
FindNext	Finds the next record in the Recordset to match the Criteria parameter, based on the current record cursor position.
FindPrevious	Finds the previous record in the Recordset to match the Criteria parameter, based on the current record cursor position.
Seek	Faster than the other find methods, but can only be used on Table type Recordset objects, because it uses the table's indexes to find the specified record. The Seek method takes up to 14 parameters: Comparison, the operator to use for the key comparison, and up to 13 keys to compare.

Each of these methods, except for Seek, takes exactly one parameter: Criteria, the criteria for the find statement, which is a SQL Where clause without the Where keyword on the front of it. The following code provides an example of searching for a customer name in the Customers table of the Northwind database.

```
' Declare variables for the Database and Recordset objects
Dim db As DAO.Recordset
Dim rs As DAO.Recordset

' Get the Database object for the current instance of Access
Set db = Application.CurrentDb

' Open the Customers table in a Recordset object
' Note: This code assumes that the Northwind database is open already
Set rs = db.OpenRecordset("Customers", dbOpenTable)

' Check to make sure that there are records
If rs.RecordCount > 0 Then

  ' Find the first record with the First Name of John
  rs.FindFirst = "[First Name] = 'John'"

End If

' Close and Destroy the Recordset variable
rs.Close
Set rs = Nothing
Set db = Nothing
```

After the preceding code executes, the current record cursor for the Recordset will be moved to the first record that is found where the First Name field is equal to the value of John. Also, if the find method does not find a match for the criteria, the NoMatch property of the Recordset object will be set to the value of `True`. Using the find methods can be extremely useful when you need to move the current record cursor directly to a specific record in the set, but you do not know the exact record number.

Reading Data Values

Once the current record cursor is positioned on a record, you can read the data values stored in that record for use in your VBA code. When you are reading these values out of the record, you are reading them from the `Fields` collection of the `Recordset` class. Also, when you are reading data out of the `Fields` collection, you are reading the data from the record that the current record cursor points to at that moment. Several different methods exist for writing the code to read the value out of a field, both implicitly and explicitly, as follows:

```
Dim strFirstName As String

' Examples of reading the data from the Recordset fields Implicitly
strFirstName = rs![First Name]
strFirstName = rs("First Name")
strFirstName = rs(4)

' Examples of reading the data from the Recordset fields Explicitly
strFirstName = rs.Fields("First Name")
strFirstName = rs.Fields(4)
```

All of the methods shown in the preceding code set the `strFirstName` variable to the same value — the value of the `First Name` field for the record to which the `Recordset` currently points. None of these methods is really better than the others per se, and they all work the same way in this case, but the last two lines of code are often preferred because they are the most explicit of the entire example, are probably easiest to read and understand, and do not require VBA to have prior knowledge of the data type to explicitly index the `Fields` collection.

Modifying Data Values

Modifying the values of the data in a `Recordset` is almost as easy to accomplish as reading values from the `Recordset`, but with a couple more steps. Before a record can be edited, the `Edit` method must be called to enable editing for the `DAO.Recordset` object. Also, once all edits to the record have been completed, the user must call `Update` to commit the changes to the `Recordset` object. The following code provides an example of updating the `First Name` field of a record in a `Recordset` object.

```
' Declare variables for the Database and Recordset objects
Dim db As DAO.Recordset
Dim rs As DAO.Recordset

' Get the Database object for the current instance of Access
Set db = Application.CurrentDb

' Open the Customers table in a Recordset object
' Note: This code assumes that the Northwind database is open already
Set rs = db.OpenRecordset("Customers", dbOpenDynaset)
```

```
' Check to make sure that there are records
If rs.RecordCount > 0 Then

    ' Find the first record with the First Name of John
    rs.FindFirst = "[First Name] = 'John'"

    ' Check to make sure that a match was found
    If Not rs.NoMatch Then

        ' Enable Editing in the Recordset
        rs.Edit

        ' Change the value of the First Name field
        rs("First Name") = "Bill"

        ' Commit the changes to the Recordset
        rs.Update

    End If

End If

' Close and Destroy the Recordset variable
rs.Close
Set rs = Nothing
Set db = Nothing
```

This code example simply opens a Recordset with the Customers table of the Northwind database, finds the first record where the First Name field is equal to John, and then updates that value to Bill. Notice that before the record is edited, the code calls the Edit method, and then it also calls the Update method once the record edit has been completed. Conversely, the user could discard the changes to a record by calling the CancelUpdate method, instead of the Update method.

Adding New Data

In addition to modifying existing data, it is often useful to add new records to a Recordset, and as such, the AddNew method is provided to allow the user to explicitly add a new record to the Recordset. Just as with modifying data, the Update method should also be called once the new record's field values have been set to commit the new record data to the Recordset object. The following code provides an example of adding a new record to the Customers table of the Northwind database:

```
' Declare variables for the Database and Recordset objects
Dim db As DAO.Recordset
Dim rs As DAO.Recordset

' Get the Database object for the current instance of Access
Set db = Application.CurrentDb

' Open the Customers table in a Recordset object
' Note: This code assumes that the Northwind database is open already
```

```
Set rs = db.OpenRecordset("Customers", dbOpenDynaset)

' Check to make sure that there are records
If rs.RecordCount > 0 Then

    ' Enable AddNew to add a record to the Recordset
    rs.AddNew

    ' Add the values for the fields of the record
    rs("First Name") = "Geoff"
    rs("Last Name") = "Griffith"

    ' Commit the new record to the Recordset
    rs.Update

End If

' Close and Destroy the Recordset variable
rs.Close
Set rs = Nothing
Set db = Nothing
```

After the preceding code executes, a new record will be added to the Customers table, containing the name value of Geoff Griffith. Conversely, you could have discarded the new record by calling the CancelUpdate method, instead of the Update method. Adding and modifying records is much the same in DAO, with just a few differences in method calls.

Deleting Data

The last type of Recordset modification to discuss is how to delete records from a DAO.Recordset object. Actually, deleting a record from a Recordset is quite easy to do and is accomplished by calling the Delete method. The Delete method removes and discards the record pointed to by the current record cursor from the Recordset, effectively deleting it from the database. Once a record has been deleted, the current record cursor still points to the deleted record (though trying to access its data generates an error). You must move the current record cursor away from the deleted record. After that, it is no longer accessible at all. The following code provides an example of calling the Delete method of the Recordset class.

```
' Declare variables for the Database and Recordset objects
Dim db As DAO.Recordset
Dim rs As DAO.Recordset

' Get the Database object for the current instance of Access
Set db = Application.CurrentDb

' Open the Customers table in a Recordset object
' Note: This code assumes that the Northwind database is open already
Set rs = db.OpenRecordset("Customers", dbOpenDynaset)

' Check to make sure that there are records
If rs.RecordCount > 0 Then
```

```
' Find the first record with the First Name of John
rs.FindFirst = "[First Name] = 'John'"

' Check to make sure that a match was found
If Not rs.NoMatch Then

  ' Delete the Record
  rs.Delete

End If

End If

' Close and Destroy the Recordset variable
rs.Close
Set rs = Nothing
Set db = Nothing
```

The preceding code opens the Customers table from the Northwind database, finds the first record with the First Name field value of John, and then deletes that record from the Recordset. Notice that you are not required to call the Update method after calling the Delete method. Once the record has been deleted, it will be gone, so it is very important to be careful when using the Delete method.

Closing Recordsets

Once you have completed working with a Recordset, it is always a good idea to close it to destroy references to those records and help eliminate possible data locking issues when multiple sources are accessing the same set of data. To do this, the DAO.Recordset class provides the Close method. The Close method does not take any parameters and calling it simply closes the Recordset. Once the Recordset has been closed it can be reopened again at any time, and with different options, using the Open method. However, once you are completely done with a Recordset and have closed it, it is typically recommended to set that variable to the value of Nothing to discard the reference to that Recordset object. The following code provides an example of how to properly open and close a Recordset object.

```
' Declare variables for the Database and Recordset objects
Dim db As DAO.Recordset
Dim rs As DAO.Recordset

' Get the Database object for the current instance of Access
Set db = Application.CurrentDb

' Open the Customers table in a Recordset object
' Note: This code assumes that the Northwind database is open already
Set rs = db.OpenRecordset("Customers", dbOpenTable)

' Do some operations on the Recordset here

' Close and Destroy the Recordset variable
rs.Close
Set rs = Nothing
Set db = Nothing
```

The last three lines of the preceding code really illustrate the point that is being made here. Calling `Close` and then setting the `Recordset` variable to `Nothing` properly releases all objects associated with that `Recordset`. Also, it is always a good idea to release the `Database` object, so the final line of code sets the `db` variable to `Nothing` as well. This is the proper method for fully closing and releasing the variables that were created at the beginning of this code block.

More Information about DAO

As mentioned earlier, DAO is a huge library and the sheer number of objects and methods can be a little overwhelming at times. Don't worry. The MSDN online library has an extensive collection of information about the DAO Object Model in Access 2010 and it is found at `http://msdn.microsoft.com/en-us/library/ff841598.aspx`. I highly recommend becoming familiar with and utilizing the resources of the MSDN library if you intend to use a lot of code in your Access applications. The MSDN provides volumes of information about almost all Microsoft programs as well as tons of sample code and tutorials. I cannot stress enough how invaluable a resource the MSDN library has been to me in my career, and I urge you to read more about the DAO objects and Access 2010 when needed.

TRY IT

In this lesson you use the `DAO.Database` and `DAO.Recordset` classes to navigate and modify some data in the `Customers` table in the Northwind database. The following example walks you through the steps necessary to build a form to allow a user to see and modify this data using a `DAO.Recordset` object. Sample files are available on the book's DVD and website.

Lesson Requirements

For this lesson, the example steps use the Northwind database application created from a template. However, the Northwind database is not necessarily required to complete this lesson; you can use just about any database application that contains some database objects, most importantly a table with some data. This example focuses primarily on writing some code that reads and writes data to a table in the database.

Step-by-Step

1. Open Access 2010 from the Windows Start menu. The Access Backstage will open in the Access window.

2. In the Backstage, click the New option on the left-hand menu and then click the Sample templates option to show a list of the built-in templates.

3. Choose the Northwind option from the list of templates and click the Create button on the right side of the screen to create the sample database application. The new Northwind database will open in the Access window.

4. Enable code in the Northwind database applications by clicking the Enable button on the Access Security Bar. Code will be enabled in the application and the `Login Dialog` form will open.

5. Close the `Login` form for the Northwind 2010 template once it has been opened.

6. Click the Create tab of the Ribbon to select it. Then click the Form Design button to create a new form in Design View mode. A new form will open in Design View mode.

7. Press the F4 key to open the Property Sheet.

8. Set the properties for the new form as shown in Table 57-4.

TABLE 57-4: Form Property Settings

PROPERTY	VALUE
Record Source	\<Empty>
Caption	Customer Details
Record Selectors	No
Navigation Buttons	No

9. Click the Save button on the top left of the Access window to save the new form. When prompted for the name of the form, specify **frmCustomerDetails,** then click OK. The new form will be saved to the database.

10. On the Form Design Tools Design Ribbon, click the Text Box button to select it and then click the top left of the new form. A new `TextBox` and its `Label` control will be added to the form.

11. Double-click the new `Label` to select the text in it and change it to the value **First Name.**

12. Click the `TextBox` control to show its properties in the Property Sheet and modify its name value to **txtFirstName.** This `TextBox` will be used to show the first name of the current record selected by your form.

13. On the Form Design Tools Design Ribbon, click the Text Box button to select it and then click just below the previous `TextBox` control. Another new `TextBox` and `Label` control will be added to the form.

14. Double-click the new `Label` to select the text in it and change it to the value **Last Name.**

15. Click the `TextBox` control to show its properties in the Property Sheet and modify its name value to **txtLastName.** This `TextBox` will be used to show the last name of the current record selected by your form.

You could repeat the preceding three steps for each of the fields in the Customers *table, to show more data on the form. However, for this example, just these two fields are sufficient.*

16. On the Form Design Tools Design Ribbon, click the Text Box button to select it and then click just below the previous `TextBox` control. Another new `TextBox` and `Label` control will be added to the form.

17. This time, delete the new `Label` by clicking it to select it and then pressing the Delete key. You will not need this `Label` control for this example.

18. Click the `TextBox` control to show its properties in the Property Sheet and modify its name value to **txtRecordNumber**. This `TextBox` will be used to show the current record number selected in the form.

19. In the Property Sheet, switch the Selection Type pull-down menu to the Form option. This selects the entire form in the Property Sheet.

20. On the Event tab of the Property Sheet, click the "…" (Builder) button for the `OnOpen` event for the form. This invokes the Choose Builder dialog, so just select the Code Builder option and click OK. VBE will open with a new `OnOpen` event method created for the form.

21. At the top of the module (outside of the new `Event` method), add the following lines of code:

```
Private rsRecords As DAO.Recordset
Option Explicit
```

This code declares a global `Recordset` variable that you will use to store the data behind the form and an `Option Explicit` statement that requires that all variables explicitly be declared.

22. Next, add a function that will update the `TextBox` control's values on the form. Add the following code just above the new `OnOpen` event method code:

```
Private Sub UpdateUI()

    If (Not rsRecords.BOF) And (Not rsRecords.EOF) Then
      txtFirstName = rsRecords("First Name")
      txtLastName = rsRecords("Last Name")
      txtRecordNumber = (rsRecords.AbsolutePosition + 1) & _
                " of " & rsRecords.RecordCount
    Else
      txtFirstName = ""
      txtLastName = ""
      txtRecordNumber = "None"
    End If

    ' Set focus to the txtFirstName
    txtFirstName.SetFocus

    ' Hide the Save button
    btnSave.Visible = False

End Sub
```

This code updates the `TextBox` control with the data that is currently selected in the global `rsRecords` `Recordset` object.

23. For the OnOpen event that was created, add the following lines of code:

```
Private Sub Form_Open(Cancel As Integer)

    ' Open the Customers table in the form
    Set rsRecords = Application.CurrentDb.OpenRecordset( _
                "Customers", dbOpenDynaset)

    ' Read the set of records into the Recordset
    rsRecords.MoveLast
    rsRecords.MoveFirst

    ' Update the Form with the current data
    UpdateUI

End Sub
```

24. Then add the following Sub code to create a Close event for the form:

```
Private Sub Form_Close()

    ' Close the form and clean up
    rsRecords.Close
    Set rsRecords = Nothing

End Sub
```

This code will clean up the form when it is closed.

25. Switch back to the Access window by clicking on it in the Windows taskbar.

26. On the Form Design Tools Design Ribbon, click the Button control button to select it and then click the top left of the new form.

27. Add seven new buttons to the form. Set the Name and Caption properties for each button via the Property Sheet, using the values shown in Table 57-5.

TABLE 57-5: Button Property Settings

BUTTON	NAME	CAPTION
Button1	btnMoveFirst	First
Button2	btnMovePrev	Prev
Button3	btnMoveNext	Next
Button4	btnMoveLast	Last
Button5	btnNew	New
Button6	btnEdit	Edit
Button7	btnSave	Save

28. These buttons will be used to provide the functionality for the form and allow the user to interact with the dataset behind the form.

29. Once the buttons have been added and their properties have been set, add the code for each button. Create an On Click event for the First button and add the following code for it:

```
Private Sub btnMoveFirst_Click()

  If rsRecords.RecordCount > 0 Then

    rsRecords.MoveFirst

  End If

  ' Update the Form with the current data
  UpdateUI

End Sub
```

30. Create an On Click event for the Prev button and add the following code for it:

```
Private Sub btnMovePrev_Click()

  If (Not rsRecords.BOF) And _
    rsRecords.AbsolutePosition > 0 Then

    rsRecords.MovePrevious

  End If

  ' Update the Form with the current data
  UpdateUI

End Sub
```

31. Create an On Click event for the Next button and add the following code for it:

```
Private Sub btnMoveNext_Click()

  If (Not rsRecords.EOF) And _
    (rsRecords.AbsolutePosition < (rsRecords.RecordCount - 1)) Then

    rsRecords.MoveNext

  End If

  ' Update the Form with the current data
  UpdateUI

End Sub
```

32. Create an On Click event for the Last button and add the following code for it:

```
Private Sub btnMoveLast_Click()
```

```
If rsRecords.RecordCount > 0 Then

    rsRecords.MoveLast

End If

' Update the Form with the current data
UpdateUI

End Sub
```

33. Create an On Click event for the New button and add the following code for it:

```
Private Sub btnNew_Click()

    ' Add a new record
    rsRecords.AddNew

    ' Update the form
    txtFirstName = ""
    txtLastName = ""
    txtRecordNumber = "New"

    ' Hide the Edit button and Show the Save button
    btnEdit.Visible = False
    btnSave.Visible = True

    ' Set focus to the txtFirstName
    txtFirstName.SetFocus

End Sub
```

34. Create an On Click event for the Edit button and add the following code for it:

```
Private Sub btnEdit_Click()

    ' Turn on editing for the record
    rsRecords.Edit

    ' Hide the New button and Show the Save button
    btnNew.Visible = False
    btnSave.Visible = True

    ' Set focus to the txtFirstName
    txtFirstName.SetFocus

End Sub
```

35. Create an On Click event for the Save button and add the following code for it:

```
Private Sub btnSave_Click()

    ' Update the Data from the form
    rsRecords("First Name") = txtFirstName
```

```
        rsRecords("Last Name") = txtLastName

        ' Persist the changes
        rsRecords.Update

        ' Show the Edit and New buttons and Hide the Save button
        btnEdit.Visible = True
        btnNew.Visible = True

        ' Update the Form with the current data
        UpdateUI

    End Sub
```

36.   Click the Save button on the top left of the Access window. This form is now ready for use!

Congratulations, you've now created a form that uses a `DAO.Recordset` object to allow the user to work with and manipulate data within the form. To verify this code is working, simply open the form in Form View mode. Once the form is opened, the first record in the `Customers` table will be shown in it. You can move through the records using the `First`, `Prev`, `Next`, and `Last` buttons. You can add a new record to the table by clicking the `New` button, and you can edit the current record by clicking the `Edit` button. All of the functionality necessary to work with a set of data in the database can be accomplished using the DAO object library!

SUMMARY

DAO is the preferred method in Access 2010 for working with the data in a database programmatically in VBA code. DAO provides all of the functionality necessary to read, modify, add, and delete data from the tables of a database, via the `DAO.Recordset` object. In addition, the `DAO.Recordset` object provides a number of methods for navigating the records in any type of data object in an Access database. DAO is an extremely simple, yet flexible method for working with data programmatically in any Access database application. And again, I urge you to learn more about the DAO Object Model by reading about the subject on the MSDN library.

 Please select Lesson 57 on the DVD to view the video that accompanies this lesson.

58

Access Application Settings

Throughout this book so far, each chapter has discussed working with individual objects inside of a database, but Access also provides the ability to manipulate application-level and database-level settings. These settings can affect the Access program, the database application, or both, and it is important to understand how they can be used. This lesson discusses the basics of working with the settings for individual databases and the Access program itself.

LESSON SETUP

The lesson is designed to provide a basic overview of working with the Access application settings. The only requirements are that you be familiar with Access databases and the different database objects to begin working with the application and database settings. Otherwise, this lesson does not require any other specific knowledge of Access.

THE ACCESS OPTIONS DIALOG

The Access Options dialog is where all of the magic happens for Access properties (settings), at both the application level and the database level. You can open the Access Options dialog from the Access 2010 Backstage by clicking the Options button on the bottom-left side of the window. Figure 58-1 shows the Access Options dialog in Access 2010.

Once the Access Options dialog has been opened, the user can work with most of the application-level and database-level settings. The Access Options dialog is divided into two parts: the left side, which provides tabs for the various categories for the program settings, and the right side, which shows the individual settings for each category when any given tab on the left is selected. This dialog is very important because this is where you typically go to manually set some settings in Access or for the database that is currently loaded. Some database settings are set in other parts of the program, but not many! This section examines setting both kinds of settings: application level and database level, using the Access Options dialog.

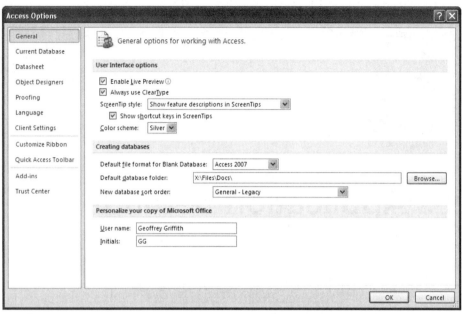

FIGURE 58-1

Access Program Settings

The Access program settings are properties that affect the Access 2010 application itself. Although these often affect the database that is loaded in the Access program, these settings are actually part of the Access program, and not the specific database that is loaded. These are settings like the default folder path for new databases created by Access and what font to display in the Query Builder. These settings don't typically affect the functionality of the database directly. There are far too many to list and describe each of these properties individually in this chapter. The General, Datasheet, Object Designers, Language, Client Settings, Customize Ribbon, Quick Access Toolbar, Add-ins, and Trust Center tabs provide the Access program settings. Really, these are all of the tabs except the Current Database tab, which controls the database-level settings. When any of these tabs is selected, the properties in its category are shown in the right pane of the Access Options dialog. To set any of these properties, simply supply or choose the desired value. Once you click the OK button, the new property setting is applied. However, some properties require that you restart Access before the change is visible. Setting either the application or database properties is just that simple!

Changing many of the settings in the Access Options dialog requires that the Access program be restarted before the changes will take effect.

Access Database Settings

Probably the most interesting and most used properties in the Access Options dialog are the database property settings. These are the database property settings that are specific to the active Access database application. These properties consist of settings like the Startup Form and the Application Title for the database. These properties can be set either through the Access UI or through VBA code, which is discussed next.

Setting a Database Property

All of the database property settings that can be set through the Access UI are found on the Current Database tab of the Access Options dialog. The following are the steps necessary for setting Access database properties via the Access UI:

1. Open any existing database in Access 2010, or just create a new database.

2. Click the File Ribbon tab, if it is not already selected, to open the Access 2010 Backstage.

3. On the left panel of the Backstage, click the Options button on the bottom of the panel. This opens the Access Options dialog.

4. On the Access Options dialog, click the Current Database tab on the left side of the window. This will show the various database properties that can be set in the Access UI.

5. Select a value for the property. In the case of the Northwind database, you could select the `Customer List` form for the `Display Form` (Startup Form) property by selecting it from the pull-down.

There really isn't much to setting these properties other than specifying the desired values. The database will most likely need to be closed and reopened before the changes to the database will be persisted to that Access database, depending on the option that is selected.

As mentioned previously, in a few instances certain database properties can be set through the Access UI, but cannot be set through the Access Options dialog. For example, the Encrypt Database with Password feature is a database-specific setting, but the option is actually set from the Info tab of the Access 2010 Backstage, and not the Access Options dialog. In most cases, the entry points for settings like these are mostly in the Access Backstage, and only a handful of these database properties are not listed in the Access Options dialog.

Working with Database Properties in VBA Code

In addition to setting database-specific properties through the Access Options dialog, the user can also set properties through VBA code. In fact, when a database property is set through the Access UI, Access is really just calling code to set the property on the database. Users can do this using VBA code in the exact same manner, and even create their own custom database properties, using the same property storage mechanism, but which are also only accessible through code. Moreover, it is important to note that even some Access database properties can be accessed only through code and not through the Access UI. Using VBA code to work with database properties is the most comprehensive method for working with database-specific properties and settings.

Getting Database Properties

The `Properties` collection of the `DAO.Database` class is where all database properties are stored and accessed using the Access Object Model. The `Property` object in the database consists of a `Name`, a `Value`, a `Type`, and a `DDL` component setting in the property, also called a `Property`. You can call up any of these properties of the `Property` object to get its value. For example, you can run the following code in the VBE Immediate window to get the `Name` property value of the first database property in the collection:

```
?Application.CurrentDb.Properties(0).Name
```

In the case of the Northwind database, this returns the value `Name`, which is specifying that this is the `Name` property of the database. To see the value for this property, call either of the following lines of code in the Immediate window:

```
?Application.CurrentDb.Properties(0).Value
?Application.CurrentDb.Properties("Name").Value
```

Both of these code statements return the same value, which is the value of the database name and full file path in this case. Although the preceding text specifies using these lines of code in the Immediate window to see these values, they could also be used in code just as easily, without specifying the `?` character at the front of the code (which is just the query symbol used by the Immediate window).

Setting Database Properties

Setting database properties is a little more involved than reading properties and probably a little more complex than one might expect at first, but is easily accomplished with a few more lines of code. When creating a new database-level property, the user is required to call the `CreateProperty` method of the `DAO.Database` class for the current database, as opposed to just creating a new instance of the `Property` class and appending it to the `Properties` collection. When calling `CreateProperty`, the user typically supplies three parameters with this method: the `Name`, the `Type`, and the `Value`. However, these parameters are not required because they have default values; but it usually doesn't make sense to create a property without a name, value, or type setting. Also, the type setting can be a number of options. See the MSDN for information about each of the different types allowed. Once the new `Property` object has been created, you must call the `Append` method of the `Properties` collection to add the new property to the database. The following code provides an example subroutine that could be created to add `String` type properties to the database.

```
Public Sub SetDbProperty(strName As String, strValue As String)

    ' Declare variables to store the Database and Property objects
    Dim db As DAO.Database
    Dim prp As Property

    ' Get the current instance of the Database object in Access
    Set db = Application.CurrentDb()

    ' Create the new Property using the instance of the Database
    Set prp = db.CreateProperty(strName, dbText, strValue)

    ' Append the new property to the Properties collection
```

```
        Application.CurrentDb.Properties.Append prp

    End Sub
```

The preceding code block creates a couple of variables, gets a reference to the `DAO.Database` object for the current database, creates a new property of type `dbText` with the specified `Name` and `Value` properties, and then appends the new `Property` object to the database. Although this is a little more complex than one might expect for creating a custom database property, it is still very easy to do in VBA code.

TRY IT

In this lesson you use the Access Options dialog to set the Display Form database setting. Then you verify the new setting, both by reopening the database and using code in the VBE Immediate window. The following example walks you through the steps necessary to complete these tasks for working with Access database properties. Sample files are available on the book's DVD and website.

Lesson Requirements

For this lesson, the example steps use the Northwind database application created from a template. However, the Northwind database is not necessarily required to complete this lesson; you can use just about any database application that contains some forms. This example focuses primarily on working with the database properties, and not necessarily the objects or data in the database.

Step-by-Step

1. Open Access 2010 from the Windows Start menu. The Access Backstage will open in the Access window.

2. In the Backstage, click the New option on the left-hand menu and then click the Sample Templates option to show a list of the built-in templates.

3. Choose the Northwind option from the list of templates and click the Create button on the right side of the screen to create the sample database application. The new Northwind database will open in the Access window.

4. Enable code in the Northwind database application by clicking the Enable button on the Access Security Bar. Code will be enabled in the application and the `Login Dialog` form will be opened.

5. Close the `Login Dialog` form for the Northwind 2010 template once it has been opened.

6. Click the File tab of the Ribbon to open the Access 2010 Backstage.

7. In the pane on the left side of the Access Backstage window, click the Access Options button on the bottom of the pane. This opens the Access Options dialog.

8. Click the Current Database category on the left side of the Access Options dialog. The database-level properties and settings will be shown on the right side of the dialog.

9. For the Application Title property, type in the value **Custom Northwind Title**. This title will now show at the top of the Access window, starting the next time the application is opened.

10. For the Display Form property, choose the `Customer List` option. This automatically opens the Customer List form every time the database is opened in Access.

11. Click the OK button on the Access Options dialog to save the new setting and close the dialog.

12. A message will be shown that the user must close and reopen the database to see the changes take effect. Just click OK to dismiss the message.

13. Press the Ctrl+G key combination to open the Immediate window in VBE.

14. Type the following code into the VBE Immediate window and press the Enter key:

```
?Application.CurrentDb.Properties("StartUpForm").Value
```

The value of `Customer List` should be returned, now that you've updated the `Display Form` property in the Access Options dialog.

15. Close VBE and close out Access. The new Application Title and Display Form database-level properties have now been persisted to the database.

Congratulations, you've now set some database-level properties and were able to verify the settings were persisted using the VBE Immediate window. To verify the changes in the Access UI, simply open the database again. Once it has opened, the `Customer List` form will open by default. Additionally, the title bar of the Access window will say `Custom Application Title`, instead of the normal database file name. Also, it is worth noting that after setting the properties in the Access Options dialog, the changes were viewable immediately in the `Properties` collection, just not in the instance of Access, which had to be restarted to see the changes. You now know how to set both the application and database properties using both the Access 2010 UI and VBA code.

SUMMARY

Access properties store settings for both the database application and the Access program itself. Both types of properties can be set through the Access UI or in VBA code and are very important, in one way or another, to the operation of an Access database application. Additionally, the user can even create custom database properties, using VBA code, that are set at the database level, just as with any other database property setting. Although these properties would not be settable through the Access UI, they could be used in code just as any other database property could. Regardless of the method chosen, Access 2010 and VBA make it very easy to work with the Access application and database properties.

 Please select Lesson 58 on the DVD to view the video that accompanies this lesson.

59

Customizing the Navigation Pane

Originally introduced in Access 2007, the Access Navigation Pane replaced the previous database window and is much more customizable and flexible than its predecessor. Not only does the Navigation Pane allow the user to see the database objects by an Object Type grouping, but it also provides many other types of groupings, allows users to create custom categories and groups, and to expand and collapse those groups, and even allows database objects to have aliases to show different names than their actual object names in the database. This lesson discusses the basics of building custom Navigation Pane settings and attempts to show how they can be applied to an Access database application.

LESSON SETUP

This lesson is designed to provide a basic overview of working with the Access Navigation Pane settings. The only requirements are that you be familiar with the different types of database objects and you have a database (such as the Northwind database) to begin working with the Navigation Pane settings. Otherwise, this lesson does not require any other specific knowledge of Access.

THE NAVIGATION OPTIONS DIALOG

The Access Navigation Pane provides an entry point to the Navigation Options dialog, which is the Access UI for working with all of the Navigation Pane options. The following steps describe how to open the Navigation Pane options in Access 2010:

1. Open any database in Access 2010.

2. If the Navigation Pane is not expanded, click it to expand the pane so that you can see the database objects in the pane.

3. In the space inside the Navigation Pane where there is no object shown, right-click the pane to show the context menu. It is very important that you right-click an empty space in the pane and not a database object.

4. On the Navigation Pane context menu, select the Navigation Options item in the list.

Notice that this dialog has two list panels: one on the left, which is the Categories panel, and the one on the right, which is the Groups panel. These panels allow the user to modify and delete old Navigation Pane categories and groups. They allow the user to specify which groups are visible in the Navigation Pane, as well as show the hidden and system objects in the database. This section discusses how to create and work with these Navigation Pane settings.

The Navigation Pane Settings

Following are the four main types of settings in the Navigation Pane options dialog:

➤ Category Settings — Contain the various sets of groupings that can be shown in the Navigation Pane for a database application, whether they are user-created or predefined by Access.

➤ Group Settings — Determine the names of the groups of each Category, and whether or not that group is shown in the Navigation Pane.

➤ Display Option Settings — Allow the user to show or hide hidden and system objects, as well as the Navigation Pane Search Bar.

➤ Click Behavior Settings — Allow the user to specify objects opening on a single or a double click.

Other than that, this dialog only has OK and Cancel buttons. Using just these features, you can create many different Navigation Pane view options and even multiple sets of settings. The options are almost limitless.

Creating a Custom Category

The first thing to do when creating a custom Navigation Pane setting is to create a new Category. The Category name is the name that is shown at the top of the Navigation Pane when a category is selected. By default, all databases have two Categories: Tables and Related Views and Object Type. To create a new custom Category, complete the following steps:

1. Click the Add Item button on the Navigation Options dialog. This creates a new Category object in the left list panel.

2. Type in the name desired for the Category object.

3. Once the desired name has been added, press the Enter key to complete creating the new Category.

Once the new Category has been created, it will only have one group, so you will need to create those next. If you want to rename or delete a Category, simply click the desired Category and click the Delete Item or Rename Item button, respectively. Also, each Category object has an up and down arrow button, so that the user can arrange the ordering for showing the Category options. There is not much more to working with custom Navigation Pane Category objects.

Creating Custom Groups

Creating custom Group objects in the Navigation Options is just as easy as creating Category objects, except that a Group is defined within a Category object. The Group name is the name of the objects in the Navigation Pane under which all desired database objects placed in that Group are shown. By default, the Navigation Pane provides one group automatically for a custom Category, which is the Unassigned Objects group. All database objects are in this group automatically, until they have been assigned to another group, which will need to be completed by the developer of the Navigation Pane settings. To create a custom Group, complete the following steps:

1.   Click the Add Group button on the Navigation Options dialog. This adds a new Group object to the right list panel and it will be selected.

2.   Type in the desired name for the Group object.

3.   Once the desired name has been added, press the Enter key to complete creating the new Group.

Once one or more custom Group objects have been created, you can begin adding those objects to groups; see the following section in this chapter. Notice that each of the Group objects has a check box to the left of it, which toggles the Group object's visibility. Each Group object also has up and down arrows to the right of it so that the user can set the ordering of the groups in the Navigation Pane from top to bottom. Adding the database objects to the various groups is actually done in the Navigation Pane itself, so you will need to close the Navigation Options dialog by clicking the OK button to save the settings.

Adding Objects to Custom Groups

Once custom Group objects have been created in the Navigation Pane, the user can begin adding the database objects to the Group objects. To begin working with a new Category in the Navigation Pane after it has been created in the Navigation Options dialog, select the Category name in the pull-down menu at the top of the Navigation Pane. This switches the view in the Navigation Pane to show the Group objects for the chosen Category in the pane. As mentioned previously, when a new Category is created, all database objects are stored in the Unassigned Objects group. To add those database objects to another group, simply drag the object from the old Group to the new Group in the Navigation Pane. The object will be added to the new group, and the object's icon will show a little arrow in the bottom-left corner, denoting it is a shortcut. Once the item has been added to a custom Group object, it will be shown in that Group as long as the Group is visible in the Navigation Pane. Also, when a custom Category is selected in the Navigation Pane, deleting a database object from a custom Group will simply return to the Unassigned Objects Group, and not delete the object from the database. The user must delete the object from the Unassigned Objects Group to remove it from the database completely, when a custom Category in the Navigation Pane is shown. And, of course, moving a database object between Group objects is as easy as dragging it from one Group to another.

Putting all objects that you don't want users to interact with directly into a Group and hiding that Group is a great way to hide database objects from the user, but should not be considered a form of security. Hiding groups in the Navigation Pane in no way stops users from finding those objects if they know enough about Access.

Creating Custom Object Names

Once a database object has been assigned to a custom Group, that object becomes a shortcut and can be given a custom name. To create a custom name for any shortcut object, simply right-click the shortcut object and choose the Rename Shortcut option. This allows the user to supply a custom name for the object, which is only shown in the Navigation Pane and in no way affects the real object name in the database. But remember, custom object names can only be applied to shortcut objects in custom, user-defined Group objects.

TRY IT

In this lesson you use the Navigation Options dialog to create a custom Category and some custom Group objects for the Navigation Pane. Then you add the database objects to these Groups and create some custom names for those objects. The following example walks you through the steps necessary to accomplish each of these tasks using the Northwind database application. Sample files are available on the book's DVD and website.

Lesson Requirements

For this lesson, the example steps use the Northwind database application created from a template. However, the Northwind database is not necessarily required to complete this lesson; you can use just about any database application that contains a few database objects. This example focuses primarily on building custom Navigation Pane settings, and not necessarily the objects or data in the database.

Step-by-Step

1. Open Access 2010 from the Windows Start menu. The Access Backstage will open in the Access window.

2. In the Backstage, click the New option on the left-hand menu and then click the Sample Templates option to show a list of the built-in templates.

3. Choose the Northwind option from the list of templates and click the Create button on the right side of the screen to create the sample database application. The new Northwind database will open in the Access window.

4. Close any forms that open for the Northwind 2010 database once it has been created.

5. Click the Navigation Pane bar on the left side of the Access window to expand it.

6. Collapse all of the groups in the Navigation Pane so that none of the database objects are visible.

7. Right-click the blank area inside of the Navigation Pane. The context menu will open.

8. In the Navigation Pane context menu, click the Navigation Options choice. This opens the Navigation Options dialog.

9. Click the Add Item button on the Navigation Options dialog. This creates a new Category object.

10. Type in the Category name: **Customers**. Press the Enter key once you have completed typing. The new Category will be added.

11. Click the Add Group button on the Navigation Options dialog. This creates a new Group object.

12. Type in the Group name: **Forms**. Press the Enter key once you have completed typing. The new Group will be added.

13. Click the Add Group button on the Navigation Options dialog again. This creates a new Group object.

14. Type in the Group name: **Reports**. Press the Enter key once you have completed typing. The new Group will be added.

15. Click OK on the Navigation Options dialog. The dialog will close and you will be taken back to the Access window.

16. At the top of the Navigation Pane, select the new Customers Category option from the pull-down menu. The Navigation Pane's view will be changed to only show the three Category objects.

17. From the Unassigned Objects Category, drag the `Customer List` form into the custom Forms Group. The Customer List form will be added to the Reports group.

 Notice that it is very difficult and cumbersome to scroll down and find the `Customer List` *form in the huge list of database objects that are part of the Northwind database application. This is exactly the reason you might want to create custom Navigation Pane settings for a database application.*

18. Right-click the `Customer List` form and choose the Rename Shortcut option on the context menu. The form name will be selected for renaming.

19. Type in the new name: **Customers**. Then press the Enter key. The object will be renamed.

20. Next, scroll down to `Customer Address Book` report, click it, press and hold the Ctrl key, and then click the `Customer Phone Book` report to select both of them at the same time.

21. Drag both reports up to the custom Reports Group at the top of the Navigation Pane. Both reports will be added to the Group.

22. Collapse the Unassigned Objects group, so that the objects under this group are no longer visible.

23. Right-click the blank area inside of the Navigation Pane. The context menu will open.

24. In the Navigation Pane context menu, click the Navigation Options choice. This opens the Navigation Options dialog.

25. In the Categories list panel, click the Customers Category to select it. This shows the Group objects in the right list panel.

26. Click the check box to deselect it for the Unassigned Objects Group. This hides the Unassigned Objects Group from the user's view in the Navigation Pane.

27. Click OK on the Navigation Options. The dialog will close and you will be taken back to the Access window.

Congratulations, you have now successfully created a custom Navigation Pane setting to allow your users to work with the Customers form and report objects for the Northwind database. The next time the database is opened, the user will see the last Category option that was set in the Navigation Pane. And, of course, the user also has the ability to flip between different Navigation Pane categories by using the pull-down menu at the top of the Navigation Pane.

SUMMARY

Creating custom Navigation Pane settings is a great way to make it easy to work with the objects of any database application. Creating custom navigation Categories and custom Groups is easily accomplished through the Navigation Options dialog. The Navigation Options dialog provides the user with the ability to show hidden and system objects, as well as hide and unhide the Group objects. Database objects can be added to a custom Group object by dragging them from one group to another, and database objects in custom Groups can have custom shortcut names. And creating custom Navigation Pane settings only takes a few short minutes. Building custom Navigation Pane categories and groups can be extremely helpful for a database application user, and is recommended when the application contains a large number of database objects.

 Please select Lesson 59 on the DVD to view the video that accompanies this lesson.

60

Customizing the Ribbon

The Ribbon is the new menu system for Office that was originally introduced in Office 2007, replacing the previous Windows-style menus in all of the Office applications. If you've programmed database applications with custom Command Bar objects in versions of Access prior to 2007, you can still use those Command Bar objects in your database applications with Access 2010. However, the Ribbon is designed to be much more powerful and user-friendly, and is now the new standard for building a customized menu system into an Access database application. Throughout this book so far, you've used the Ribbon to perform or set all sorts of commands, from creating new database objects to working with the various database tools. This lesson discusses how to build custom Ribbons to provide user-defined functionality as well as disable the normal Ribbons in a given database application, using Access 2010.

LESSON SETUP

The lesson is designed to provide a basic overview of working with the Access Ribbon settings. The only requirements are that Access 2010 is installed, you are familiar with the different types of database objects, and you have a general knowledge of what the Ribbon does and how it works. Otherwise, this lesson does not require any other specific knowledge of Access.

THE CUSTOMIZE RIBBON OPTIONS

New to Access 2010 is the Customize Ribbon tab in the Access Options dialog, which provides the various Customize Ribbon options available in the UI. Using this new dialog, the user can create new Ribbon tab or new groups in new or existing Ribbons, rename new or existing Ribbon objects, change the ordering of Ribbons in the Access UI, add/remove commands from any Ribbon, and enable/disable entire Ribbons themselves. The Customize

Ribbon tab in the Options dialog is extremely useful for working with the Ribbons built into the Access program and for building user-defined Ribbons. Figure 60-1 shows the Customize Ribbon tab of the Access Options dialog.

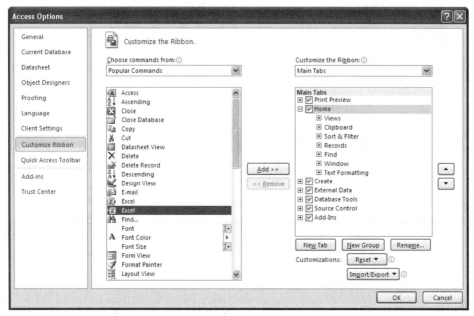

FIGURE 60-1

However, a number of limitations exist with Ribbons when using the Customize Ribbon dialog. First, this dialog does not allow the user to build and define custom command functionality, such as a button to open a user-defined form; for that kind of functionality, the user needs to take a few more steps, which are discussed shortly. Second, any changes made in this dialog are only for the Access program on that user's machine, and not the instance of the database, which means that even if you create a custom Ribbon for a database using this dialog, the Ribbon is not tied directly to that database and will not be persisted on other users' machines by default. The Customize Ribbon tab in the Access Options dialog itself is just a UI for building new Ribbons from existing functionality and for working with Ribbons in the current Access installation, but don't underestimate this dialog either! It is extremely useful if you plan to build Access database applications with a customized menu scheme. The Ribbon settings can be exported and imported at will and an Access database application can take advantage of that functionality by loading custom Ribbons for the database itself. This lesson examines some simple methods for creating such custom Ribbons for an Access database application, with a little help from the Customize Ribbon settings.

Opening the Customize Ribbon Dialog

The first thing to do to begin building a custom Ribbon is to open the Customize Ribbon tab on the Access Options dialog, as described in the following steps:

   1. Start Access 2010. This can be with or without a database application loaded; the database itself is not required, though it may be helpful for reference when choosing the Ribbon options.

2. Click the File tab to show the Access 2010 Backstage.

3. On the left panel of the Backstage, click the Access Options button at the bottom of the menu. This opens the Access Options dialog.

4. Click the Customize Ribbon tab on the left side of the Access Options dialog. The shows the Customize Ribbon options.

Once the Customize Ribbon dialog is open, the user can begin working with the various Ribbon settings that this dialog provides, such as creating a brand new Ribbon.

The Customize Ribbon Settings

The Customize Ribbon tab consists of two parts: the Command buttons that Access 2010 provides, which is the left half of the dialog, and the Ribbon options, which is the right half of the dialog. These pieces provide a number of operations, but typically, this dialog is used for editing existing Ribbons and creating new Ribbons. This section discusses the basics of both of these options.

Modifying Existing Access Ribbons

The right half of the Customize Ribbon dialog is the location for working with existing Ribbon objects. There is a pull-down menu for the different categories of Access Ribbons, a list control for displaying the Ribbons in the selected category, and a number of buttons for building and modifying the existing Ribbons in Access. Commands are selected in the list on the left side of the dialog and then added to the selected Ribbon on the right side of the dialog by clicking the Add button. Similarly, commands on the different Ribbons can be removed by selecting the desired command and clicking the Remove button. Ribbon Tabs and Groups can be renamed by selecting the desired Ribbon in the list on the right and then clicking the Rename button. This will highlight the text for editing, allowing the user to supply a new name for the Tab or Group object. New Groups can be created and then have commands added to them by choosing a Ribbon and then clicking the New Group button. The positions of commands, Groups, and even Ribbon Tabs can be adjusted by selecting the desired object and then clicking the up and down arrows to position the objects in the desired order. And, of course, Ribbons can be enabled and disabled by selecting the check box just to the left of each Ribbon name. Working with the existing Ribbon Tabs is quite simple to do with this dialog, but remember, these changes are persisted to the Access program itself, and only on that machine.

Creating New Custom Ribbons

Users can create brand new Ribbons, which show up as separate Tabs, by clicking the New Tab button. This allows the user to add groups and predefined Access commands to the Ribbon at will. Also, this can be a great starting point for creating some Ribbon XML for which you will add the custom code later.

Exporting the Current Ribbon Settings

Once the desired customizations to the Ribbon have been created, they can be exported to an external file, which is in XML format. This is handy for sharing Ribbon settings with other users, saving a static copy of your current Ribbon settings, or even creating some Ribbon XML as a starting point for building a custom Ribbon system for an Access database application. To export the current settings, complete the following steps:

1. Once the desired Ribbon settings have been created in the Customize Ribbon dialog, click the Import/Export button. This shows the pull-down menu for the button.

2. On the Import/Export pull-down menu, select the Export All Customizations option. This opens the File Save dialog.

3. Choose a name and location for the file and click the Save button.

The new Ribbon XML file, with the file extension .exportedUI, will be created at the specified location. This file can then be opened in a text or XML editor for viewing and editing. However, before it can be used as a user-defined Ribbon, the first mso:cmd node should be removed from the XML. The following code is an example of some custom Ribbon XML created using the Access 2010 Customize Ribbon dialog that can be used as a user-defined custom Ribbon.

```
<mso:customUI
   xmlns:mso="http://schemas.microsoft.com/office/2009/07/customui">
  <mso:ribbon>
    <mso:qat/>
    <mso:tabs>
      <mso:tab id="mso_c1.15EDDB66" label="Test"
               insertBeforeQ="mso:TabCreate">
        <mso:group id="mso_c2.15EDDB66" label="Options"
                   autoScale="true" />
      </mso:tab>
      <mso:tab idQ="mso:TabCreate" visible="false"/>
      <mso:tab idQ="mso:TabExternalData" visible="false"/>
      <mso:tab idQ="mso:TabDatabaseTools" visible="false"/>
      <mso:tab idQ="mso:TabSourceControl" visible="false"/>
      <mso:tab idQ="mso:TabAddIns" visible="false"/>
    </mso:tabs>
  </mso:ribbon>
</mso:customUI>
```

This file can then be opened and edited in any XML or text editor. Exporting the Ribbon settings using Access 2010 is easier than ever before!

Resetting the Ribbon

Once the Ribbon customizations and been created and saved (exported), it is common to reset the Ribbon back to its normal settings for Access, so that all of the commands are available again. The Customize Ribbon dialog provides the Reset button to quickly reset the Ribbon options. This button offers two options: Reset Only Selected Ribbon Tab and Reset All Customizations. These options are pretty self-explanatory — the first resets the currently selected Ribbon and the second resets the entire Ribbon. Resetting the Ribbon options is quick and easy using Access 2010.

Importing Ribbon XML for a Database

Users can import custom Ribbons just as easily as they can be exported using Access 2010. The Customize Ribbon dialog provides the Import Customization File option on the Import/Export Ribbon pull-down menu for loading a custom Ribbon from file. To load a custom Ribbon from file, complete the following steps:

1. Open Access 2010. This can be with or without a database open.

2. Click the File tab to open the Access 2010 Backstage.

3. On the left panel of the Backstage, click the Options button on the bottom. This opens the Access Options dialog.

4. On the left panel of the Access Options dialog, click the Customize Ribbon button. This shows the Customize Ribbon options.

5. Click the Import/Export button and choose the Import Customization File option. This opens the File Open dialog.

6. Select the desired Ribbon customization file and then click the Open button. You will be prompted to confirm loading the new Ribbon, so click OK.

The custom Ribbon will be loaded automatically, and all of the old settings on the Ribbon will be removed. Using the Customize Ribbon dialog to load Ribbons in Access 2010 is very simple, but not the only method for loading custom Ribbons in Access, as you will see shortly.

CUSTOM RIBBON COMMANDS

Now that you have a pretty good understanding of the basics of working with the existing Ribbon functionality that Access 2010 provides, it is time to examine building custom Ribbon commands. A number of methods exist for building custom Ribbon commands, but for this lesson, the purpose is to describe a simple method for creating simple Ribbon buttons that perform some user-defined functionality. This can be accomplished using expressions, macros, or even VBA code, as shown in this section.

Adding Controls to the Ribbon XML

A number of different Ribbon controls can be used for a custom Ribbon commands: Menus, Separators, Buttons, Toggle Buttons, Split Buttons, Check Boxes, Combo Boxes, Drop Downs, Edit Boxes, Labels, Dialog Box Launchers, and even Ribbon Groups. Any of these control types can be added, as XML, to the custom XML file that was exported from the Customize Ribbon dialog to quickly create a customized Ribbon. For example, adding the following XML to the `mso:group` node inside the `mso:tab` node in the custom Ribbon XML file adds a button to the specified group in the specified Ribbon:

```
<mso:button id="btnRibbonButton1" label="Button Name" />
```

In this XML code, mso:button is the Ribbon control type, the id attribute is the name of the control (as called in code), and the label attribute is the name that is displayed on the Button control in the Ribbon. Once the Button control has been specified, the user can add a number of additional attributes to specify the behavior of the Button control. Although many different attributes are supported by each of the control types, this section discusses a few of the more common attributes for the mso:button Ribbon control type.

The onAction Attribute

Probably the most important attribute for the mso:button control is the onAction attribute. The onAction attribute specifies the action that is to be executed when the Button control is clicked. This action can be specified as an expression, a macro, or even a VBA function. Each of these options is quite easy to specify, although each is slightly different, as illustrated in the next few sections.

Using Expressions for the onAction Event

The onAction event attribute allows the use of an Access expression as the value of the action to be executed. To use an expression, simply specify the expression text as the onAction attribute value. The following XML code provides an example of using an expression for the onAction attribute:

```
<mso:button id="btnButtonExpr" label="Show MsgBox"
          onAction="=MsgBox('This is an Expression')" />
```

Once this action has been executed, a message box will be displayed for the user to see. Of course, this will require that a database be loaded in the current instance of Access, but will work even if the database is not in a trusted state.

Using Macros for the onAction Event

The onAction attribute also allows the user to execute macros. This means that when the button is clicked, the macro will be executed. The following XML code is an example of calling a Macro object named OpenCustomersForm for the onAction attribute:

```
<mso:button id="btnButtonMacro" label="Execute Macro"
          onAction="OpenCustomersForm"/>
```

Once the button has been clicked, the macro will be executed for the user. Of course, this will require that a database be loaded in the current instance of Access and, depending on the Macro actions, require the database to be in a trusted state.

Using VBA Code for the onAction Event

Finally, the onAction attribute allows the user to define a VBA method as the value of the attribute. This means that the VBA code will be executed when the button is clicked. The following XML code is an example of calling a VBA method named CustomVBACode for the onAction attribute:

```
<mso:button id="btnButtonVBA" label="Execute VBA Code"
          onAction="CustomVBACode"/>
```

However, this will require a `Public Sub` called `CustomVBACode` to be created in a module in the database. In addition, the subroutine created will be required to accept a single parameter of type `IRibbonControl`, which requires that a reference be set in the database to the Microsoft Office 14.0 Object Library. The following code provides an example of how this `Sub` could be written.

```
Public Sub CustomVBACode(ctlSender As IRibbonControl)

    ' Write some custom code here
    MsgBox "Custom VBA code has been executed"

End Sub
```

Once the button has been clicked, the code will be executed for the user. Of course, this will require that a database be loaded in the current instance of Access and require the database to be in a trusted state to execute the code.

Setting a Custom Ribbon for a Database

Now that you know how to create custom Ribbons and even add custom commands to them, it is time to examine one of the several methods in which a Ribbon can be applied to a particular database, instead of the Access program itself. This consists of two parts: applying the Ribbon to the database itself and then setting that Ribbon to be the default Ribbon for the database. Both of these steps are extremely easy to do using Access 2010, and the experience is much improved over the previous 2007 version of Access.

The USysRibbons Table

The `USysRibbons` table can be created in an ACCDB file (Access 2007 file format or higher) to specify custom Ribbon settings. However, this table is not part of a database by default and therefore must be created by the user before it can be used. To create the `USysRibbons` table, create a new table with that name, containing the fields shown in Table 60-1.

TABLE 60-1: The USysRibbons Table Fields

FIELD NAME	FIELD TYPE	DESCRIPTION
RibbonName	Text	The name of the Ribbon that is specified in the `RibbonXML` field for this record.
RibbonXML	Memo	The actual Ribbon XML text to be used for this custom Ribbon.

Once this table has been created in the database, you can begin creating custom Ribbons for the database application by adding records to this table. Then simply provide a name and the Ribbon XML for the custom Ribbon in their corresponding fields, and the custom Ribbons will be ready to use in the database application, but there is one last step — enabling the custom Ribbon for the database.

Applying the Ribbon to the Database

Once the USysRibbons table has been created and the desired Ribbons have been added to it, the user can then select the default Ribbon to be used by the database in the Access Options dialog. If you've just created the table and records, you must close and reopen the database before Access will recognize the changes and the custom Ribbons. To select the default Ribbon for the database, complete the following steps:

1. With the database containing the custom Ribbons open in Access, click the File tab of the Ribbon to open the Access 2010 Backstage.

2. On the left panel of the Backstage, click the Options button, found at the bottom of the Access window. This opens the Access Options dialog.

3. On the Access Options dialog, click the Current Database tab to show the options for the current database settings.

4. Scroll down to the Ribbon and Toolbar Options section and select the desired Ribbon from the Ribbon Name pull-down menu.

5. Click OK and the options will be persisted. You will be presented with a message stating that the new changes will not be applied until the database is closed and reopened, so just click OK to dismiss the message.

The selected Ribbon will now be applied as the default Ribbon for the database. The next time you open the database, that custom Ribbon will be shown, and not the normal Access Ribbon. Setting a custom Ribbon couldn't be any easier — it is building the custom Ribbons that is the tricky part!

TRY IT

In this lesson you create a custom Ribbon and some custom VBA code to provide some custom menu functionality for an Access database application. The following example walks through the steps necessary to accomplish this task using the Northwind database application created from a template. Sample files are available on the book's DVD and website.

Lesson Requirements

For this lesson, the example steps use the Northwind database application created from a template. However, the Northwind database is not necessarily required to complete this lesson; you can use just about any database application that contains some database objects. This example focuses primarily on building a custom Ribbon, and not necessarily the objects or data in the database.

Step-by-Step

1. Open Access 2010 from the Windows Start menu. The Access Backstage will open in the Access window.

2. In the Backstage, click the New option on the left-hand menu and then click the Sample Templates option to show a list of the built-in templates.

3. Choose the Northwind option from the list of templates and click the Create button on the right side of the screen to create the sample database application. The new Northwind database will open in the Access window.

4. Close any forms that open for the Northwind 2010 database once it has been created.

5. Click the Create tab of the Ribbon to select it. The Create Ribbon will be shown.

6. Click the Module button under the Macros & Code group all the way on the right side of the Ribbon. A new Module database object will be created and VBE will open.

7. On the top right of the VBE window, click the Save button to save the new module. You will be prompted for a name, so type in the value **ModCustomRibbon** and click OK. The new module will be saved to the database.

8. Click the Tools menu and select the References option. This opens the References dialog.

9. In the References dialog, scroll down and select the Microsoft Office 14.0 Object Library option and click OK to save the changes. This will add the reference to the database.

10. Add the following subroutine to the module:

```
Public Sub CustomRibbonCode(ctlSender As IRibbonControl)

    MsgBox "Your code has been executed!"

End Sub
```

11. Click the Save button and close VBE. You are done with it for now. You will be taken back to the Access window.

12. On the Create Ribbon, click the Macro button under the Macros & Code group. A new Macro object will be created and Macro Designer will open.

13. In the Macro Action pull-down, choose the OpenForm macro option. This expands the OpenForm parameters.

14. For the Form Name, choose the Customer List form. Then close the Macro Builder. Choose Yes on the Save Macro dialog, and for the Macro Name, type in the value **OpenCustomers** and click OK. The new macro will be saved to the database.

15. Click the File tab of the Ribbon to open the Access 2010 Backstage.

16. On the left panel of the Backstage, click the Options button at the bottom. This opens the Access Options dialog.

17. On the Access Options dialog, click the Customize Ribbon option on the left panel. This shows the Customize Ribbon options.

18. From the Customize the Ribbon pull-down menu on the right, select the All Tabs option. This shows all of the built-in Access Ribbon tabs in the right list box.

19. Uncheck all of the Ribbon tab options. This hides all of the existing Access Ribbons.

20. Select the Main Tabs option from the pull-down. This hides all of the contextual Ribbon tab options in the right list box.

21. Click the New Tab button to add a new custom Ribbon tab to the Ribbon.

22. Click the new tab in the right list box to select it and click the Rename button. The Rename dialog opens for editing the name of the object.

23. For the new name, type in the value **Custom**. Then press the Enter key. The new tab will be renamed Custom.

24. Click the New Group control (that was created with the New Tab object) to select it and click the Rename button. The Rename dialog opens for editing the name of the object.

25. Type in the value **Options** and press the Enter key. The New Group object will be renamed Options.

26. Click the Import/Export button and choose the Export All Customizations option from the pull-down menu. The File Save dialog will open.

27. Browse to a location you can remember, such as your desktop, and then click the Save button to save the file. The custom Ribbon XML file will be saved to the specified location and you will be taken back to the Access Options dialog.

28. Click the Reset button and choose the Reset All Customizations option. A dialog requesting confirmation of the reset will be presented, so just click the Yes button. The Ribbon XML has already been saved to the file.

29. Click OK to close the Access Options dialog. You are done using the Customize Ribbon dialog for now.

30. Open the Ribbon XML file that was just saved. Notepad or Visual Studio will both work well for this.

31. Reformat the XML if needed, so that it is easy to read and understand.

32. Remove the first `mso:cmd` XML node, which says:

```
<mso:cmd app="Access" dt="0" />
```

33. Find the `mso:group` node with the attribute `label="Options"` and replace it with the following XML node:

```
<mso:group id="grpOptions" label="Options" >
  <mso:button id="btnButtonExpr" label="Use Expr"
      onAction="=MsgBox('You have executed an expression')" />
  <mso:button id="btnButtonMacro" label="Use Macro"
      onAction="OpenCustomers" />
  <mso:button id="btnButtonCode" label="Use VBA"
      onAction="CustomRibbonCode" />
</mso:group>
```

34. Now that the Ribbon XML is ready to go, switch back to the Access window.

35. On the Create Ribbon, click the Table Design option. This creates a new table in Design View mode.

36. For the first field name, type in the value **RibbonName**. For the data type, choose the Text option.

37. For the second field name, type in the value **RibbonXML**. For the data type, choose the Memo option.

38. Click the Save button on the top left of the Access window to save the new table. For the table name, type in the value **USysRibbons**, then click OK to save the table to the database.

39. When prompted to create a primary key, click Yes. You will be taken back to the Access window.

40. Switch the new table to Datasheet View mode by clicking the View button on the Table Tools Design Ribbon. The table will open in Datasheet View.

41. For the first record of the table, type in the value **Custom** for the RibbonName field.

42. Copy the Ribbon XML that was exported and modified and paste it into the RibbonXML field for the first record. The next custom Ribbon will be ready to use.

43. Close the database to persist all settings. Then reopen the database in Access.

44. Click the File tab to open the Access 2010 Backstage.

45. On the left panel of the Backstage, click the Options button near the bottom. This opens the Access Options dialog.

46. Click the Current Database tab to show the settings and options for the current database.

47. Scroll down to the Ribbon and Toolbar Options section. In the Ribbon Name pull-down, choose the Custom option.

48. Click OK on the Access Options dialog. You will be informed that the settings will not be persisted until the database is closed and reopened. Click OK to dismiss the message.

49. Close Access again and then reopen the database. This time you will notice that the custom Ribbon that you created is shown, instead of the normal Access 2010 Ribbon.

Congratulations, you have now successfully created a custom Ribbon to allow your users to work with some custom menus in the Northwind database. This menu has three buttons: one that uses an expression, one that calls a macro, and one that calls VBA code. To verify that this functionality is working, try clicking any of the buttons. The appropriate action will be executed. Of course, the button that runs the VBA code requires that the database have code enabled before it will execute correctly. No matter which method is selected, building custom Ribbon functionality in Access could not be any simpler!

SUMMARY

Custom Ribbons are the perfect method for creating custom menus for any database application. This lesson discussed how to create custom Ribbons using Access 2010. The ACCDB file format supports the creation of the USysRibbons table, a table used by Access to define and store custom Ribbon data to be used by the current database. The Access 2010 Customize Ribbon dialog provides all sorts of different features for creating, exporting, and importing custom Ribbon XML files. This custom XML can then be stored in the USysRibbons table to provide custom Ribbon menus for the Access database application. As you can see, building custom Ribbons is a very powerful feature of Access 2010 and this lesson only touches on the very basics of this subject. For more information about building custom Ribbons using Access 2010, see the *Access 2010 Programmer's Reference* book, published by Wiley, the Microsoft Office website at http://office.microsoft.com, or the MSDN library at http://msdn.microsoft.com.

 Please select Lesson 60 on the DVD to view the video that accompanies this lesson.

61

Customizing the Backstage

Completely new to Access 2010, and many of the other Office 2010 applications, is the Office Backstage. The Backstage replaces the Access 2007 Getting Started screen and is intended to be the new user interface for launching new sessions of Access, as well as replace the previous File menu, providing common database and file-related tasks. The really cool thing about the Office 2010 Backstage is that it is highly customizable, much like the Ribbon. Although there is no UI for building custom Backstage settings, the user can build a custom Backstage using XML code, just as with the Ribbon. This lesson discusses the basics of adding some customizations to the Access 2010 Backstage.

LESSON SETUP

The lesson is designed to provide a basic overview of building customization into the Access Backstage. The only requirements are that you be familiar with the different types of database objects and that you have a general knowledge of what the Backstage does and how it works. Knowing what XML is and how it works will also be helpful for this lesson, but is not required.

THE ACCESS 2010 BACKSTAGE

Upon launching the Access 2010 program without a database application, you will immediately see the new Access 2010 Backstage and have likely seen it countless times throughout the lessons in this book. As you are aware, tabs on the left side show the various Backstage pages. Each of these pages contains controls to provide some program or database-level functionality, such as saving or creating a new database.

The Backstage allows the user to create custom pages and add controls to those pages, much like the Ribbon. This is accomplished by adding customizations to the USysRibbons table.

The USysRibbons Table

The USysRibbons table can be created in a database file to specify custom Backstage settings (just like the Ribbon). However, this table is not part of a database by default and therefore must be created by the user before it can be used. To create the USysRibbons table, create a new table with that name, containing the fields shown in Table 61-1.

TABLE 61-1: The USysRibbons Table Fields

FIELD NAME	FIELD TYPE	DESCRIPTION
RibbonName	Text	The name of the Ribbon that is specified in the RibbonXML field for this record.
RibbonXML	Memo	The actual Ribbon XML text to be used for this custom Ribbon.

Once this table has been created in the database, you can begin creating custom Backstage settings for the database application by adding records to this table. Then simply provide a name and the Ribbon XML (which I discuss shortly) for the custom Backstage settings, and the custom Backstage will be ready to use in the database application once it has been enabled for the database.

The <backstage> Tag

Customizing the Backstage begins with using the <backstage> tag. The <backstage> tag is the root node that must be specified to begin working with the Access Backstage, and all customizations that are specified for the Backstage are specified within this tag. The <backstage> tag is placed within the <customUI> tag XML that was used for customizing the Ribbon in the previous lesson. The following code provides an example of the base XML that is required to be specified with the USysRibbons table to begin customizing the Backstage.

```
<customUI xmlns="http://schemas.microsoft.com/office/2009/07/customui"
        onLoad="OnLoad">
    <backstage>
    </backstage>
    <ribbon>
    </ribbon>
</mso:customUI>
```

Notice that the <backstage> tag is placed within the <customUI> tag, making it a sibling node to the Ribbon tags discussed in Lesson 60 about custom Ribbons. This means that the custom Backstage UI is specific to the Ribbon UI that is specified in the Access Options, and can therefore be switched at will, either through the UI or through code. And of course, specifying a custom Backstage component does not require the user to specify a custom Ribbon; they are completely independent of each other.

Creating a New Backstage Tab Control

The Backstage allows the creation of Tab controls, such as the tabs on the left side of the Backstage window. Each Tab control is specified with the <tab> tag and provides a surface for adding other controls to the Backstage. In addition to specifying a `<tab>` tag, the use must also specify which Tab column is to be used. Two types of columns exist: the first column and second column tabs, which are specified with the `<firstColumn>` and `<secondColumn>` tags, respectively. The following code provides an example of the XML that could be used to specify both kinds of tabs.

```xml
<customUI xmlns="http://schemas.microsoft.com/office/2009/07/customui"
    onLoad="OnLoad">
  <backstage>
    <tab>
      <firstColumn>
      </firstColumn>
      <secondColumn>
      </secondColumn>
    </tab>
  </backstage>
</customUI>
```

Adding Controls to Tabs in the Backstage

Once the base XML has been specified for the Backstage UI settings, you can begin adding controls to the Backstage design surface. The Backstage provides a number of different controls that can be used: Button, Category, Group, GroupBox, HyperLink, ImageControl, LayoutContainer, RadioGroup Task, TaskFormGroup, and TaskGroup controls. Though far too many controls exist to provide examples for each in this lesson, examining how the Button control works is sufficient to show how controls can be added to the XML code for the Backstage. The following code provides an example of how to create the XML code for creating a new Backstage Tab and adding a couple of Button controls in various locations on that Tab in the Backstage.

```xml
<customUI xmlns="http://schemas.microsoft.com/office/2009/07/customui"
    onLoad="OnLoad">
  <backstage>
  <tab id="tabTab1" insertAfterMso="TabInfo" label="Test">
    <firstColumn>
      <group id="grpGroup1" label="Group1">
        <primaryItem>
          <button id="btnButton1" label="Button1" />
        </primaryItem>
        <topItems>
          <layoutContainer id="lytLayout1" layoutChildren="vertical">
            <button id="btnButton2" label="Button2" />
          </layoutContainer>
        </topItems>
      </group>
    </firstColumn>
  </tab>
  </backstage>
</customUI>
```

Adding Code to Controls

Once you have some controls added to the Backstage, you can add functionality to those controls. Just like the Ribbon, with the Backstage you can use pre-existing Access functionality, expressions, macros, and even VBA code to provide functionality for your Backstage controls. Just like with the Ribbon controls, adding the functionality to the Backstage controls is exactly the same. By using the onAction attribute in the Backstage control's XML, you can specify what action should be executed when that Button control is clicked. For example, you could define a Button control in the Backstage with the following XML code:

```
<button id="btnMyButton" label="MyButton" onAction="MyVbaSub" />
```

Notice that the onAction attribute in this XML code specifies the name MyVbaSub. As mentioned earlier, this can be a number of different types of things such as an expression, macro, or, in this case, a user-defined VBA method. To create the MyVbaSub method for this control, simply create a module with the following subroutine declaration in it:

```
Public Sub MyVbaSub(ByVal Control As IRibbonControl)

End Sub
```

MyVbaSub, along with all other Ribbon and Backstage onAction method definitions, takes one parameter: the control parameter. It is of type IRibbonControl, which is the control itself. And, of course, adding this code requires a reference in the VBA project be set to the Microsoft Office 14.0 Object Library, to provide support for the Backstage control types. Adding custom functionality to the Backstage controls is just the same as adding custom functionality to Ribbon controls!

Applying the Custom Backstage

Once the USysRibbons table has been created and the desired custom UI records have been added to it, the user can then select the default Ribbon to be used by the database in the Access Options dialog. If you've just created the table and records, you must close and reopen the database before Access will recognize the changes and see the custom UI records. To select the default Ribbon for the database, which includes the Backstage settings, complete the following steps:

1. With the database containing the custom Ribbons open in Access, click the File tab of the Ribbon to open the Access 2010 Backstage.

2. On the left panel of the Backstage, click the Options button (at the bottom of the Access window). This opens the Access Options dialog.

3. On the Access Options dialog, click the Current Database tab to show the options for the current database settings.

4. Scroll down to the Ribbon and Toolbar Options section and select the desired Ribbon from the Ribbon Name pull-down menu.

5. Click OK and the options will be persisted. You see a message stating that the new changes will not be applied until the database is closed and reopened, so click OK to dismiss the message.

The selected Ribbon and Backstage will now be applied as the default for the database. The next time you open the database, that custom Backstage will be shown, and not the normal Access Backstage. Setting a custom Backstage couldn't be any easier — building the custom settings is the tricky part!

More Resources

This lesson offers an extremely brief overview of customizing the Ribbon. *The Access 2010 Programmer's Reference*, published by Wrox, dedicates an entire chapter to discussing Backstage customization and talks in depth about the controls that can be used. In addition, the Microsoft and MSDN websites provide lots of resources for customizing the Access 2010 Backstage. For more information about the Backstage, start at `http://technet.microsoft.com/en-us/library/ff468686.aspx`.

TRY IT

In this lesson you create a custom Backstage Tab control that contains a Button control that provides some custom functionality for an Access database application. The following example walks through the steps necessary to accomplish this task using the Northwind database application created from a template. Sample files are available on the book's DVD and website.

Lesson Requirements

For this lesson, the example steps use the Northwind database application created from a template. However, the Northwind database is not necessarily required to complete this lesson; you can use just about any database application that contains some database objects. This example focuses primarily on building custom Access Backstage settings, and not necessarily the objects or data in the database.

Step-by-Step

1. Open Access 2010 from the Windows Start menu. The Access Backstage will open in the Access window.

2. In the Backstage, click the New option on the left-hand menu and then click the Sample Templates option to show a list of the built-in templates.

3. Choose the Northwind option from the list of templates and click the Create button on the right side of the screen to create the sample database application. The new Northwind database will open in the Access window.

4. Close any forms that open for the Northwind 2010 database once it has been created.

5. Click the Create tab of the Ribbon. The Create Ribbon will be shown.

6. Click the Module button under the Macros & Code group all the way on the right side of the Ribbon. A new Module database object will be created and VBE will open.

7. On the top right of the VBE window, click the Save button to save the new module. You will be prompted for a name, so type in the value **modBackstage** and click OK. The new module will be saved to the database.

8. Click the Tools menu and select the References option. This opens the References dialog.

9. In the References dialog, scroll down and select the Microsoft Office 14.0 Object Library option and click OK to save the changes. This will add the reference to the database.

10. Add the following subroutine to the module:

```
Public Sub CustomBackstageCode(ByVal Control As IRibbonControl)

    MsgBox "Your code has been executed!"

End Sub
```

11. Click the Save button and close VBE. You are done with it for now. You will be taken back to the Access window.

12. On the Create Ribbon, click the Table Design option. This creates a new table in Design View mode.

13. For the first field name, type in the value **RibbonName**. For the data type, choose the Text option.

14. For the second field name, type in the value **RibbonXML**. For the data type, choose the Memo option.

15. Click the Save button on the top left of the Access window to save the new table. For the table name, type in the value **USysRibbons** and click OK to save the table to the database.

16. When prompted to create a primary key, click the Yes button. You will be taken back to the Access window.

17. Open Word or some other XML or text editor and create the following XML code (this code is included with the sample files for this chapter in the RibbonXML.txt file):

```
<customUI xmlns="http://schemas.microsoft.com/office/2009/07/customui"
    onLoad="OnLoad">
    <backstage>
      <tab id="tabTab1" insertAfterMso="TabInfo" label="Test">
        <firstColumn>
          <group id="grpGourp1" label="Group1">
            <primaryItem>
              <button id="btnButton1" label="Test"
                      onAction="CustomBackstageCode" />
            </primaryItem>
          </group>
        </firstColumn>
      </tab>
    </backstage>
</customUI>
```

18. Highlight this XML code and press the Ctrl+C key combination to copy the code to the clipboard.

19. Switch back to the Access 2010 window by clicking it in the Windows taskbar.

20. In the Navigation Pane, double-click the new USysRibbons table to open it in Database View mode.

21. For the first record of the table, type in the value **Custom1** for the `RibbonName` field.

22. Paste the custom Backstage XML into the `RibbonXML` field for the first record by pressing the Ctrl+V key combination while the cursor is inside the field. The next custom Ribbon will be ready to use.

23. Close the database to persist all settings. Then reopen the database in Access.

24. Click the File tab to open the Access 2010 Backstage.

25. On the left panel of the Backstage, click the Options button near the bottom. This opens the Access Options dialog.

26. Click the Current Database tab to show the settings and options for the current database.

27. Scroll down to the Ribbon and Toolbar Options section. In the Ribbon Name pull-down, choose the Custom1 option.

28. Click OK on the Access Options dialog. You will be informed that the settings will not be persisted until the database is closed and reopened. Click OK to dismiss the message.

29. Close Access again and then reopen the database. This time you will notice that the custom Ribbon that you created is shown, instead of the normal Access 2010 Ribbon.

Congratulations; you have successfully created some custom Backstage settings and functionality to allow your users to work with some custom menus in the Northwind database. To verify that this code is working, click the File tab of the Ribbon to open the Access Backstage. Notice that there is a Tab control on the left panel called Test. If you click the Test tab, it reveals a Button control called Test. If you click the Test button, a message box is shown, stating that the code has been executed. Building custom Backstage layouts and functionality is a new and powerful method for providing custom functionality to users in Access 2010.

SUMMARY

Building a custom Backstage is the perfect method for creating custom database-level functionality, adding a launching point for a Help program, creating an About page for your application, or just about anything else you can dream up for it. The custom Backstage XML settings are created much like the custom Ribbon settings, in an XML format which specifies the controls and the layouts for the customizations. These settings are then added to the `USysRibbons` table, so that they can be applied directly to the database, via the Access Options dialog.

 Please select Lesson 61 on the DVD to view the video that accompanies this lesson.

62

The Access Runtime

One of the largest complaints from Access users is that anyone who wants to run an Access application must have some version of Access installed. Not true! The Access Runtime is a program that can be freely distributed to users to allow them to run Access applications, without having to have the full version of Access installed. Although the Access Runtime does not provide the full functionality and features of the Access program itself, it does allow Access database applications to be run on the user's machine when Access is not present. However, you have a number of items to consider when using the Access Runtime, as you will see shortly. This lesson discusses the basics of the Access Runtime and attempts to illustrate how these concepts can be applied to an Access database application.

LESSON SETUP

This lesson is designed to provide a basic overview of the Access Runtime and how it can be used. By now, you should have a good knowledge of all the different kinds of database objects and how they can be used in a database application. Now you will see how these objects function under the Access Runtime, so it is very helpful to have a good knowledge of all of the parts of Access for this lesson.

THE ACCESS RUNTIME OVERVIEW

The Access Runtime is a royalty-free, redistributable package provided by Microsoft to allow Access developers to distribute their Access applications to users who do not currently have Access installed on their machines. The Runtime package is an installer that installs all of the components necessary to run Access database applications, though it does not include the features of the Access program itself. It only provides a shell in which to execute Access database applications, and a number of differences exist between full Access and the Runtime.

Access 2010 versus the Access Runtime

The Access program itself provides all of the features for creating, modifying, and deleting data and database objects in a given database file. The Access program provides literally hundreds of features, such as the Navigation Pane, most of the built-in Ribbon functionality, the Property Sheet, the Field List, and so on, to allow the user to build database applications within the Access program. Using the Access Runtime to execute a database application, the user only sees the shell Access window, without any of the bells and whistles found in the Access program. For this reason it is important to consider a number of different database application design aspects when employing the Access Runtime for a database application.

Considerations when Using the Runtime

When a database application is executed in Runtime mode, the user sees a very different Access window, because most of the major features that are included in Access are not available with the Runtime. The following is a list of the major features of Access that are *not* included in the Access Runtime:

➤ The Navigation Pane

➤ Most of the built-in Ribbons functionality

➤ Most of the Backstage tools and features

➤ The Design Task Pane, including the Field List and the Property Sheet

➤ The Visual Basic Editor

➤ The built-in wizards or other Access dialogs

However, although this may seem like most of the features you are used to using in the Access program, the Runtime is still sufficient to run database applications with the proper planning. The following is a list of items to consider when building Access Runtime applications:

➤ You can create custom navigation, either through Forms or custom Ribbons and Backstage settings, to allow the user to navigate to the forms, reports, and optionally data, in the application.

➤ You should test all code and macros to ensure that they work the same way in the application when executed in Runtime mode.

➤ You can ensure that custom features added to the Ribbon have their own separate, custom Ribbon XML provided for the database.

➤ You can set a Display Form in the Access Options dialog or implement the AutoExec macro for the database to open some initial database object as a launching point within the application.

One other difference to be aware of: When a database application is executed in Runtime mode, a dialog requires the user to trust the database application before it can be executed, if the application is not already stored in a trusted location. Otherwise, if the user declines to allow the application to run in trusted mode when presented with this dialog, the database will be automatically exited, without executing any of the functionality in the database application. So, any database application executed in Runtime mode is automatically running in trusted mode and can perform all operations that are allowed when the database application is in trusted mode, assuming those specific features are supported by the Runtime. Although the major differences to consider when using the Runtime are listed here, there may be other issues as well. It is very important to fully test an application under the Runtime to ensure it is working properly prior to distribution. With proper planning, design, and testing, the Runtime can be an extremely powerful tool for distributed Access database applications.

Benefits to Using the Access Runtime

Utilizing the Access Runtime provides a number of very useful benefits. The following is a short list of the major benefits that the Access Runtime provides:

➤ Having the Runtime installed does not require that Access be installed to execute Access database applications.

➤ The Runtime is a good way of hiding all the features in the Access client from the user, when it is not desirable for the user to see them. However, this should not be used as a form of security in your application, because executing in Runtime mode by itself does not necessarily stop or protect the user from opening the database file in full Access.

➤ You can be sure that an application functions as expected on all machines, by ensuring that a specific version of the Runtime is being used (and not just any old version of Access, which can vary slightly in functionality from version to version).

➤ The Access Runtime is much more lightweight and has a much smaller hard-drive memory requirement than the full Access 2010 install.

➤ Users with older versions of Access can use database applications created in new versions of Access by installing the newer version of the Runtime.

Using the Access Runtime can be a very effective solution for providing support for Access database applications, and best of all, it is free to everyone.

BUILDING RUNTIME APPLICATIONS

Building Access database applications that use the Runtime is very easy to do and just like building other database applications, but they must be built and tested with the considerations discussed in the previous section. Access Runtime applications are nothing more than regular database applications and you use all of the normal Access tools to put together the database application, adding a few extra steps at the end to make the application execute under the Runtime. This section discusses the minimum steps required to build an application that uses the Access Runtime.

Getting the Access Runtime

The first thing to do is to get the Access Runtime package that you will be distributing with the applications. Although Access 2010 comes with the ability to test against the Runtime, it does not directly include the Runtime package itself. Although a number of methods exist to acquire the Access Runtime package, the easiest is to just download it from the Microsoft website at `http://www.microsoft.com/downloads/details.aspx?familyid=57a350cd-5250-4df6-bfd1-6ced700a6715&displaylang=en`.

The installer package for the Access Runtime can be downloaded from this site and then directly installed on any Windows machine freely, per the license agreement for the Runtime distributable package (as shown during installation). Once the executable file has been downloaded from the site, you will be ready to begin testing database applications against it and distributing it with your applications.

Enabling the Access Runtime

Although you can test directly against the Access Runtime, it is often easier to do initial development testing against the Runtime components included with Access 2010. Using just the normal installation of Access 2010, it is possible to simulate all of the behavior that the Access Runtime will exhibit and all of the features it provides. Several methods exist for enabling Runtime mode using Access 2010, but the two most common are using the ACCDR file format and running the database with the /runtime command-line switch. Using both of these options is quite easy to do, and each option is examined in the following sections.

The ACCDR File Format

Originally introduced with the release of the ACCDB file format in Access 2007, utilizing the ACCDR file format is the preferred method for creating and testing Runtime database applications. The ACCDR file format is exactly the same as the ACCDB file format, except for two minor differences: The first is that the file extension for the database file is .accdr, and the second is that any file with this extension run by Access will automatically execute in Runtime mode. The corresponding MDR file format is also available for database applications built using one of the legacy MDB database file formats, but MDR is only supported for the MDB 2000 file format databases and beyond. However, even though these two requirements seem simple, it is not as easy to create an ACCDR file as one might think.

As it turns out, creating an ACCDR file is a little trickier than you might initially expect. By default, file extensions for known file types (file types that are already associated with some installed program, such as Access 2010 in this case) are hidden in Windows 7, Vista, and XP. In addition, Access 2010 does not provide any option for saving a database file under this extension, so the user must perform the operation manually, from within the Windows environment. To create an ACCDR file using an existing ACCDB file, complete the following steps:

1. From the Windows Start menu, choose the My Computer option to open it.

2. Press the Alt key to enable the old menus, if using Windows 7 or Vista. This opens the menu in the My Computer window. For Windows XP machines, you can skip this step completely.

3. From the Tools menu, choose the Folder Options option. This opens the Folder Options dialog.

4. Click the View tab of the Folder Options dialog to see the View options.

5. Uncheck the option that says Hide Extensions for Known File Types. This shows the file extensions at the ends of the filenames in Windows.

6. Click OK to save the changes and go back to the My Computer window.

7. In My Computer, navigate to the directory with the ACCDB file that is to be created as an ACCDR file. Notice that that filename now shows the .accdb file extension.

8. Right-click the file and choose the Rename option. This highlights the filename for editing.

9. Change the file extension to .accdr and then press the Enter key to complete the change. The file extension will be changed, and you can optionally re-enable hidden file extensions at this point, though if you enable file extensions once in Windows, it is more than likely that you'll do it again!

Once the Access database file's extension has been renamed to ACCDR, simply double-clicking the file opens it in Runtime mode. This is also the reason why this is the preferred method for running in Runtime mode, because it automatically forces the use of Runtime mode, regardless of whether the user has just the Runtime installed or a full version of Access.

The /runtime Command-line Switch

The other very common, and probably easier, method for executing a database application in Runtime mode is by using the /runtime command-line switch when opening the database file. For example, if you installed Access to the default location, you could call the following code from any command prompt in Windows to open a file named Contacts.accdb from the root of the C: drive:

```
"c:\Program Files\Microsoft Office\Office14\MSACCESS.EXE"
/runtime c:\Contacts.accdb
```

Using the /runtime switch forces Access to open the database file in Runtime mode, but it is often difficult to type in this long string every time the database needs to be opened in Runtime mode. For this reason, it is often very useful to create a Windows Shortcut file that uses the /runtime switch to automate this task. The following steps describe how to create a shortcut to a hypothetical Contacts.accdb file on the root of the C: drive:

1. On the Windows desktop, right-click a location where there isn't a file present to open the Windows desktop's context menu.

2. On the context menu, choose the New option and then choose the Shortcut option on the New fly-out menu. This opens the Create Shortcut dialog.

3. On the Create Shortcut dialog, click the Browse button and browse to the database file. Then click the Next button.

4. Choose a name for the shortcut file and then click the Finish button. The new shortcut will be created on the Desktop.

5. Right-click the new shortcut file on the Windows Desktop and choose the Properties option. This opens the Properties dialog for the file.

6. For the Target setting of the shortcut, specify the following:

```
"c:\Program Files\Microsoft Office\Office14\MSACCESS.EXE"
/runtime c:\Contacts.accdb
```

where the Contacts.accdb file is the name and location of the database for which you are creating the shortcut.

7. Click OK to apply the changes to the shortcut's properties and dismiss the dialog.

The shortcut is now ready for use. If you double-click it, the database application opens in Runtime mode because the Target contains the /runtime command switch. This method of invoking a database application in Runtime mode can be very beneficial during the development phase of the application, because it is less time-intensive compared to continually changing the extension of the file between ACCDR and ACCDB for testing the application's features in Runtime mode.

Testing with the Access Runtime

Once a database application has been created and you want to distribute it with the Access Runtime, it is highly recommended that you test the application in Runtime mode to ensure that it is working properly and that all features run as expected. For example, because the Navigation Pane is not present, it is especially important to ensure that the user of the application has the ability to get to all forms and reports within the application. This is accomplished by creating a solid UI for the application, which is often attained by implementing application navigation through things like forms and custom Ribbons. Once the application has been tested and found to be working properly, you can rest assured that users of the application will see the same functionality.

DEPLOYING RUNTIME APPLICATIONS

The last major item to discuss in regard to the Access Runtime is deployment of the Runtime to users. It is not all that uncommon for an Access database application to be distributed by simply transferring the database file to others. Because everything in the application is usually already contained within a single file, it is extremely easy to transfer a database application, or even a shortcut file, in this manner. However, that still requires that the users somehow get a copy of the Access Runtime, if they do not already have Access installed. A number of methods exist for deploying the Access Runtime and the most common options are described in the following list:

➤ Require the users of the application to manually download and install the Runtime from the Microsoft website as needed. This is probably the simplest method for developers, because it does not require any additional work on their part, but might be somewhat difficult or unachievable for the users of the application, depending on their level of skill, requirements for the application, and environment in which the application is being deployed.

➤ Manually distribute the Access Runtime file with the database application. This requires that the users get two files instead of one with the application, and that they potentially install the Runtime before they can run the application. But transferring an additional file is extremely easy to do and only requires that the developer download the Runtime before distributing it directly with the application.

➤ Build a setup package through Access 2010 that includes the Access Runtime and installs it, if necessary, when the database application is created. Although this option requires the most work on the part of the developer of all these deployment scenarios, it is the most streamlined option for the user and makes the database application feel more like a professional piece of software with its own installation package.

No matter which method for deploying the Access Runtime is chosen, deploying and installing the Runtime with an application is likely to be the least of your problems during the life cycle of the database application, because Access makes installing and using the Runtime so easy to do!

TRY IT

In this lesson you create both a shortcut file and an ACCDR file for an existing database application to illustrate how easy it is to utilize the Access Runtime. The following example walks through the steps necessary to accomplish this lesson, using the Tasks database application created from a template. Sample files are available on the book's DVD and website.

Lesson Requirements

For this lesson, the example steps use the Tasks database application created from a template. However, the Tasks database is not necessarily required to complete this lesson; you can use just about any database application that contains some database objects. This example focuses primarily on working with an Access database executing in Runtime mode, and does not necessarily require the objects or data in the Tasks database.

Step-by-Step

1. Open Access 2010 from the Windows Start menu. The Access Backstage will open in the Access window.

2. In the Backstage, click the New option on the left-hand menu and then click the Sample Templates option to show a list of the built-in templates.

3. Choose the Tasks template option at the bottom of the list of templates to select it.

4. Click the folder next to the filename in the right panel of the Backstage. This opens the File New Database dialog.

5. Select your Desktop as the folder location for the new file and optionally choose a name for the new database. Then click OK to apply the settings. You are taken back to the Access window.

6. Click the Create button. The new Tasks database application will be created from the template.

7. Close out Access because the application has now been created. You will work with the new file in Windows.

8. On the Windows Desktop, notice that the `Tasks.accdb` file is now present.

9. Right-click a location away from any files and select the New option from the context menu and then choose the Shortcut option from the New fly-out menu. This opens the Create Shortcut dialog.

10. On the Create Shortcut dialog, click the Browse button and browse to the `Tasks.accdb` database file on your Desktop. Then click the Next button.

11. For the shortcut name, type **Tasks Application** and click the Finish button. The new shortcut will be created on the Desktop.

12. Right-click the new shortcut file on the Windows Desktop and choose the Properties option. This opens the Properties dialog for the shortcut file.

13. For the Target setting, type the following command:

```
"c:\Program Files\Microsoft Office\Office14\MSACCESS.EXE"
/runtime %userprofile&\Desktop\Tasks.accdb
```

 This Target value assumes that Access has been installed to the default location on the C: drive and that the database application is named `Tasks.accdb` and is located on the current user's Desktop.

14. Click OK to apply the changes to the shortcut's properties and dismiss the dialog.

Congratulations, you have just created a new Windows shortcut that will run your database application in Runtime mode. To verify this is working, double-click the shortcut. You'll see a message stating that there is a potential security concern and that the publisher of the application cannot be verified. Just click OK to trust and start the application. The Tasks application will open in Runtime mode. Notice that none of the Access Ribbons, except for the file tab for the Backstage, or the Navigation Pane are present; only the `Tasks List` form is open. By now, hopefully, you are beginning to see the differences between executing a database application in Runtime mode and in Access itself.

However, as noted earlier in the lesson, this only opens the database file in Runtime mode when the application is started from the shortcut. Next, you modify the file extension to force the application to execute in Runtime mode:

15. Go back to the Windows Desktop to see the `Tasks.accdb` file again.

16. Click the Start menu and choose the Computer option. (In Windows XP and earlier, it is called My Computer.) This opens the Computer window. Press the Alt key to show the legacy Windows menus at the top of the window.

17. On the Tools menu, choose the Folder Options option. This opens the Folder Options dialog.

18. On the Folder Options dialog, click the View tab to select it.

19. Under the Advanced Settings group, click to uncheck the Hide Extensions for Known File Types option. This will show file extensions in Windows for all files.

20. Click OK to apply the settings and close the dialog, then close the Computer window. You will be taken back to the Desktop.

21. Right-click the `Tasks.accdb` file and choose the Copy option on the context menu. This creates a copy of the database file on the Windows clipboard.

22. Right-click away from any files in this folder and choose the Paste option to paste a copy of the file to the Desktop. A new copy of the database file will be created.

23. Right-click the new database file and choose the Rename option. This highlights the filename for editing, so type in the new value of **Tasks.accdr** and then press the Enter key. The file will now be renamed.

Congratulations, you have now successfully renamed the Access database application's file extension to .accdr to make it a Runtime database file. To verify the change is working, double-click the database file to open it. Again, the security dialog will be presented, so just click the Open button to open the application. The database will open in Runtime mode and the Tasks List form will be shown. Again, notice that the standard Access Ribbons and the Navigation Pane are no longer present. Now that the file extension has been renamed, you can be assured that the database application is running in Runtime mode.

SUMMARY

Creating Access database applications that are designed to execute under the Access Runtime is extremely powerful for distributing database applications, but comes with a few trade-offs. Access database applications that execute under the Runtime can be extremely cost-effective for users, especially when the user requires that application run on a large number of machines that do not otherwise have or require Access to be installed. However, because the features that are part of the Access program, and not an individual database, are not available in Runtime mode, much more planning and development are required on the part of the creator of the database application. At the minimum, the developer is required to build custom navigation directly into the application, because the Navigation Pane, among other Access features, is not available in Runtime mode. But, more times than not, the benefits of using and the cost of developing for the Access Runtime are an acceptable expense for a widely used, distributed database application.

 Please select Lesson 62 on the DVD to view the video that accompanies this lesson.

What's on the DVD?

This appendix provides you with information on the contents of the DVD that accompanies this book. For the latest and greatest information, please refer to the ReadMe file located at the root of the DVD. Here is what you will find in this appendix:

➤ System Requirements

➤ Using the DVD

➤ What's on the DVD

➤ Troubleshooting

SYSTEM REQUIREMENTS

Most reasonably up-to-date computers with a DVD drive should be able to play the screencasts that are included on the DVD. You may also find an Internet connection helpful for searching Microsoft's online help and for downloading updates to this book. Finally, the system requirements for running Access are much greater than those for simply running a DVD.

If your computer doesn't meet the following requirements then you may have some problems using Access.

➤ PC running Windows XP, Windows Vista, Windows 7, or later

➤ A processor running at 1.6GHz or faster

➤ An Internet connection

➤ At least 1GB of RAM

➤ At least 3GB of available hard disk space

➤ A DVD-ROM drive

You may be able to run Access using a slower processor or with less memory, but things may be slow. I highly recommend more memory: 2GB or even more if possible. (I do fairly well with an Intel Core 2 system running Windows 7 at 1.83 GHz with 2GB of memory and a 500GB hard drive.)

USING THE DVD

To access the content from the DVD, follow these steps.

1.   Insert the DVD into your computer's DVD-ROM drive. The license agreement appears.

*The interface won't launch if you have autorun disabled. In that case, click Start ⇨ Run (For Windows 7, Start ⇨ All Programs ⇨ Accessories ⇨ Run). In the dialog box that appears, type **D:\Start.exe**. (Replace D with the proper letter if your DVD drive uses a different letter. If you don't know the letter, see how your DVD drive is listed under My Computer.) Click OK.*

2.   Read through the license agreement, and then click the Accept button if you want to use the DVD.

The DVD interface appears. Simply select the lesson number for the video you want to view.

WHAT'S ON THE DVD?

Each of this book's lessons contains a "Try It" section that lets you practice the concepts covered by that lesson. The "Try It" includes a high-level overview, requirements, and step-by-step instructions explaining how to build the example program.

This DVD contains video screencasts showing my computer screen as I work through key pieces of the "Try It" from each lesson. I don't always show how to build every last piece of a "Try It" program.

I recommend using the following steps when reading a lesson:

1.   Read the lesson's text.

2.   Read the "Try It" overview, requirements, and hints.

3.   Read the step-by-step instructions. If the program you wrote doesn't satisfy all of the requirements, use these instructions to improve it.

4.   Watch the screencast to see how I handle the key issues.

5.   Try to write a program that satisfies the requirements.

Sometimes a screencast mentions useful techniques and shortcuts that didn't fit in the book, so you may want to watch the screencast even if you feel completely confident in your solution.

After finishing with the "Try It" section, I recommend that you work through the exercises (or at least skim them and figure out how you would solve them). You can also download all of the book's examples, "Try It" solutions, and exercise solutions at the book's website.

TROUBLESHOOTING

If you have difficulty installing or using any of the materials on the companion DVD, try the following solutions:

➤ **Reboot if necessary.** As with many troubleshooting situations, it may make sense to reboot your machine to reset any faults in your environment.

➤ **Turn off any anti-virus software that you may have running.** Installers sometimes mimic virus activity and can make your computer incorrectly believe that it is being infected by a virus. (Be sure to turn the anti-virus software back on later.)

➤ **Close all running programs.** The more programs you're running, the less memory is available to other programs. Installers also typically update files and programs; if you keep other programs running, installation may not work properly.

➤ **Reference the ReadMe.** Please refer to the ReadMe file located at the root of the DVD for the latest product information at the time of publication.

CUSTOMER CARE

If you have trouble with the DVD, please call the Wiley Product Technical Support phone number at (800) 762-2974. Outside the United States, call 1 (317) 572-3994. You can also contact Wiley Product Technical Support at `http://support.wiley.com`. John Wiley & Sons will provide technical support only for installation and other general quality control items. For technical support on the applications themselves, consult the program's vendor or author.

To place additional orders or to request information about other Wiley products, please call (877) 762-2974.

INDEX

Symbols

. (period), field names, 58
& (ampersand)
    Input Mask, 84
    string concatenation operator, 403–404
&= , assignment operator, 398
<> (angled brackets)
    field expressions, 157
    Input Mask, 84
    Validation Rule, 83
* (asterisk)
    arithmetic operator, 400
    wildcard operator, 404
*= , assignment operator, 398
\ (backslash)
    arithmetic operator, 400
    Input Mask, 84
\= , assignment operator, 398
^ (caret symbol), arithmetic operator, 400
^= , assignment operator, 398
" " (double quotes)
    Input Mask, 84
    Query Design View, 181
= (equals sign)
    assignment operator, 398
    comparison operator, 399
    equals operator, 384
    Validation Rule, 83
! (exclamation mark)
    bang operator, 263
    field names, 58
    Input Mask, 84
> (greater than symbol), comparison operator, 399
>> , comparison operator, 399
>>= , assignment operator, 398
>= , comparison operator, 399
>= , field expressions, 157
(hash mark)
    Input Mask, 84
    wildcard operator, 404

< (less than symbol), comparison operator, 399
<< , bitwise operator, 401
<<= , assignment operator, 398
<= , comparison operator, 399
– (minus sign)
    arithmetic operator, 400
    subtraction operator, 385
–= , assignment operator, 398
( ) (parentheses), arrays, 416
+ (plus sign)
    addition operator, 384
    arithmetic operator, 400
    string concatenation operator, 403–404
+= , assignment operator, 398
? (question mark)
    Input Mask, 84
    wildcard operator, 404
/ (slash), arithmetic operator, 400
/= , assignment operator, 398
[ ] (square brackets)
    field names, 58
    prompt method, 151
_ (underscore), naming schemes, 47

A

AbsolutePosition, 444
accCmdUndo, 436
ACCDA, 7
ACCDB, 6, 15–21
.accdb, 15
ACCDE. See Access Compiled Database
ACCDR, 6, 492–493
ACCDT. See Access Database Template
Access Compiled Database (ACCDE), 6
Access Data Collection Replies, 137
Access Data Project (ADP), 7
Access database engine (ACE), 117

Access Database Template (ACCDT), 6
Access Font dialog, 25
Access Object Model, 433–438
Access Runtime, 489–498
    ACCDR file format, 492–493
    application navigation, 288
    macro security, 344
    /runtime, 493–494
    testing, 494
Access Services, 342
Access.Application, 356, 433–434
AcCmdSaveAs, 413
AcCommand, 413
ACE. See Access database engine
actions, 348
Action Catalog, 253, 329, 337, 348
Action queries, 16–17, 173, 174
ActionName, 356, 359
ActiveX, 234
ActiveX Data Objects (ADO), 216, 440
Add, 380
Add & Delete, 48
Add a Group button, 324
Add a Sort button, 325
Add Existing Fields, 296
Adding totals, 151
AddNew, 447–448
AddressOf, 405
ADO. See ActiveX Data Objects
ADP. See Access Data Project
Advanced button, 125
After Delete, 364
After Insert, 364
After Update, 364
All Access Objects, 38
All Records, 103
All tab, 228, 313
Allow Form View property, 269, 271
Allow Layout View, 316
Allow Value List Edits, 90–91

Allow Zero Length, 73, 82, 175
Anchor properties, 245–246
AND, 157
And, 401, 402
AndAlso, 403
API. *See* Application
  Program Interface
appAccess, 434
Append Only, 73
Append queries, 143, 149, 173–177
    Action Queries, 173
    Design Ribbon, 174–175
    settings, 175
    SQL View, 175
Application, 422, 441
application, 433–434
application navigation, 287–292
    Access Runtime, 288
    Button controls, 289
    ComboBox, 289
    forms, 288–289
    ListBox control, 289
    Navigation Pane, 287–288
    Ribbon, 288
    TextBox, 289
Application Parts button, 49
Application Program Interface
  (API), 440
application tables, 16
Application.DoCmd
  .OpenForm, 434
Application.TempVars, 351
Arguments, 356, 359
arithmetic operators, 400–401
Arrange Ribbon, 303
Arrange tab
    Form Design Tools Ribbon, 218
    Form Layout Tools Ribbon, 207
    Report Layout Tools Ribbon,
      294, 295
arrays, 414–416
arrPosition, 415
as, 263
assignment operators, 397–398
Attachment control, 234
Attachment data type, 68, 234
AutoNumber, 16, 46, 68, 96, 136,
  174, 175
Available Templates, 12
Avg(), 163
Avg queries, 151

B

back-end databases, 130
background, 303

Backstage, 6, 10, 31–35, 315
    Access Options dialog, 25
    Access Runtime, 490
    controls, 32–34, 483–484
    customization, 34, 481–487
    MSDN library, 485
    onAction, 484
    templates, 331, 365, 375
    USysRibbons, 481–482
<backstage>, 482–484
Backstage View, 31
backups, 180, 185, 187
bang operator, 263
Base, 390
Before Change, 364
Before Delete, 364
bitwise operators, 401–402
blank databases, 10–11
BOF, 442–443
Boolean, 118, 442
Boolean data type, 382
bound fields, 91–92
bound forms, 215–216
Bound Object Frame control, 234
bound reports, 302–303
bound subforms, 243, 244
bound subreports, 243
branching, 385–388
    conditional, 253, 329
    logic, 357–358
Break, 374
breakpoints, 372, 377
btnGo, 266
bugs, 355
Builder, 150, 331, 336
button commands, 24, 32, 168.
    See also specific buttons
Button control, 233, 289
ByRef, 391–392
Byte, 49, 66, 382
ByVal, 391–392, 393

C

calculated fields, 17, 59, 68, 180
Calendar control, 234
Call, 393
camel case, 47
CancelUpdate, 447
Caption, 73, 315
Cartesian joins, 142
cascading deletes, 114, 186
cascading updates, 114
Category
    drop zone, 281
    Navigation Pane, 464

Category Settings, 464
Change Row Source Type, 90
[!CharList], 404
Chart Field List, 280
Chart Wizard, 279
CheckBox control, 234
child records, 186
child tables, 111–113
Choose Builder dialog, 257
classes
    events, 423–425
    instances, 425
    methods, 423, 426–427
    modules, 421–431
    properties, 422–423, 426
    variables, 409
Class Module, 260, 380, 421
ClearCount, 424
ClearMacroError, 357
Click, 266
Click Behavior Settings, 464
Close, 449–450, 453
CloseWindow, 332
clsCounter, 421, 426, 427
code
    Backstage controls, 483–484
    debugging, 372–374
    syntax, 262
    VBA, 379–394
Code Builder, 313
Code window, 368, 393
Collect Data Through E-Mail
    Messages Wizard, 135–140, 137
colors, 297, 303
columns, 303
Column Headings, 163–164, 199
COM, 234
ComboBox, 91, 97, 289, 290
comments, 351, 381–382
Compact & Repair Database, 33,
    187, 193
Compact and Repair tool, 185
Compare, 390
comparison operators, 83, 385, 399
compound keys, 46, 108
concatenation
    field expressions, 150
    operators, 403–404
    queries, 91
    strings, 17
Condition, 356, 359
conditions, 350
conditional branching, 253, 329
Connection, 422
Const, 412
constant variables, 81, 383, 409, 412
Contact Details, 40

Contacts.accdb, 493
context menu, 40
contextual tabs, 24
Continue, 359
Continuous Form "Multiple
    Items," 209
controls. *See also specific controls*
    Arrange Ribbon, 303
    Backstage, 32–34, 483–484
    default properties, 237
    Design Ribbon, 294, 303
    Design View, 246
    Form Layout Tools Ribbon,
        207, 218
    forms, 233–241
    Help, 237–239
    Layout View, 246
    layouts, 303
    macros, 235, 253, 329
    Navigation Pane, 219
    parameter queries, 168
    properties, 237, 296, 305
    Property Sheet Pane, 219
    reports, 302
    Ribbon, 24, 473–475
    XML, 473–475
Control Source, 302, 319
controlSource, 290
Count, 358
Count queries, 151
Create Data Macro, 57, 364
Create New List Wizard, 50
Create Relationship Wizard, 49
Create Ribbon, 45
    Class Module, 380, 421
    Datasheet forms, 271
    Macros & Code, 147
    Multiple Item forms, 270
    Navigation Pane, 274
    PivotChart, 279
    Query Design button, 148,
        180, 187
    quick forms, 206
    Quick Reports, 293
    Report button, 324
    Single Item form, 270
    Split forms, 272
    Table Design button, 56
    Visual Basic button, 368
Create tab, 24, 216, 255, 274, 282,
    315, 336, 451
CreateForm, 392–393
CreateProperty, 460
Creating a Linked Table, 131
Criteria row, 151, 156–157
cross joins, 142

Crosstab queries, 143, 149, 163–164,
    197–203
    Design View, 198–199
    Query Design View, 199
    settings, 199
    Update queries, 180
Crosstab Query Wizard, 198
Crosstab Wizard, 143
Currency data type, 67–68, 382
Current Database tab, 459
CurrentDb, 434–435, 441
CurrentDB Execute, 174
CurrentProject, 422, 435
cursor, 311
Custom Command Bars, 25
customization
    Backstage, 34, 481–487
    groups, 41, 465
    Navigation Pane, 463–468
    Ribbon, 25–26, 469–480
    ...databases, 475–476
Customize Input Mask Wizard,
    83–84
Customize Ribbon, 25–26, 469–472
CustomVBACode, 475

D

DAO. *See* Data Access Objects
DAO.Database, 460
DAO.Recordset, 441
DAP. *See* Data Access Page
data
    aggregation, 161–165
    external
        Excel, 122–123
        tables, 121–127
        XML, 123–124
    groups, 161–165
    integrity, 103, 113, 114
    scrubbing, 122
    sorting, 321
    validation, 79–87
Data Access Objects (DAO),
    439–456
    MSDN library, 450
    references, 440–441
    VBA, 441
Data Access Page (DAP), 15
Data Collection, 135–140
Data Definition Language (DDL),
    101, 119
data definition queries, 16–17
Data Definition SQL, 17
Data drop zone, 281
data macros, 19, 342, 363–366

Data Source, 206, 296, 302
Data tab, 228, 312, 332
data types. *See also specific data
    types*
    data integrity, 103
    Excel, 122
    fields, 58–59, 65–70
    parameters, 169
    properties, 237
    table fields, 48–49
    variables, 409
    VBA, 382–383
Database, 440, 441
databases. *See also specific
    database types*
    back-end, 130
    blank, 10–11
    naming schemes, 46–47
    objects, 15–21, 39
    properties, 459–461
    Ribbon customization, 475–476
    settings, 459–461
    templates, 11–12
Database Engine, 372
Database Tools Ribbon, 107
Database Tools tab, 24
Datasheet, 209, 270–271
Datasheet View, 16, 17, 45–53, 243
Date(), 81, 157–158
Date, 382, 412
DateAdd(), 81
Date/Time, 67, 81, 162, 234
DateValue(), 163
dbText, 461
DDL. *See* Data Definition Language
debugging, 358–359, 372–374
Decimal, 49, 67, 382
Decimal Places, 73
default properties, 237
Default Value, 73, 80–82
Default View, 72, 269
DefaultView, 270, 272
DELETE, 187
Delete, 448–449
Delete button, 48, 187
Delete Columns, 150
Delete queries, 143, 185–190
    backups, 185, 187
    cascading deletes, 186
    child records, 186
    database applications, 185
    Design View, 187
    DISTINCT, 186
    normalization, 185
    referential integrity, 186
    SQL View, 187–188
    testing, 186

Delete Rows, 150
Description, 72, 356
Design Ribbon, 57
  Append queries, 174–175
  controls, 303
  Field List Pane, 294, 303
  footers, 303
  headers, 303
  PivotChart, 279
  Property Sheet Pane, 294, 303
  Report Design Tools
    Ribbon, 303
  Report View, 294
  themes, 303
  View, 174, 303
  Web Browser control, 265
Design tab, 235
  Form Design Tools Ribbon, 217
  Group & Sort button, 321
  Properties button, 296
  Property Sheet Pane, 305, 310
  Report Design Tools Ribbon,
    305, 310, 321, 322
  Report Layout Tools Ribbon,
    294, 296, 310, 322
  themes, 297
Design View, 305, 331. *See also*
  Query Design View
  controls, 246
  Crosstab queries, 198–199
  Delete queries, 187
  Detail, 320
  Document tab, 217
  Field List Pane, 218–219
  Form Design Tools Design
    Ribbon, 24
  forms, 18, 215–240
    controls, 236
  Group, Sort, and Total Pane, 321
  Make Table queries, 192
  Navigation Pane, 219, 305
  parameter queries, 168–169
  PivotChart, 279
  Property Sheet Pane, 219
  Report Selector, 314
  reports, 19, 301–308
  Subform/Subreport control, 245
  Table Design button, 45
  tables, 16
  Update queries, 180
  View, 217, 315
desktop shortcuts, 5
Detail, 319–320
Dim, 263, 383, 415
Disabled Mode, 19
Display control, 90

Display Option Settings, 464
DISTINCT, 161, 162, 175, 180, 186
DLL. *See* Dynamic Link Library
Do, 389
docking/undocking, 310–311
DoCmd, 357, 365, 435
Document tab, 217
Double, 49, 67, 382, 412
drill down, 124
drop zones, 280–282
dynamic arrays, 415
Dynamic Link Library (DLL), 371

E

Edit, 446, 455
Edit List Items dialog, 90–91
Edit Relationships dialog, 109–114
  join types, 112
  referential integrity, 110–111
  relationship modification, 113
Edited Records, 103
Else, 357
else, 350
Else if, 357
else if, 350
ElseIf, 385–386
embedded macros, 19, 327
  events, 329
  forms, 251–258
  Macro Builder, 342
  modules, 342
  Report Designer, 328
Enable button, Security Bar, 17, 258,
  330, 375, 450
Enable Content, 12, 33, 336
Encrypt with Password, 33
End If, 385
End Sub, 380
Enum, 413
enumerations, 413–414
EOF, 442–443
error handling, 356–357
Error Number, 359
Event, 410, 423–425
events
  classes, 423–425
  data macros, 364
  embedded macros, 329
  forms, 18
  functions, 262
  methods, 427
  named macros, 329
Event tab, 228, 256, 312
Excel, 122–125, 131, 200

Excel Spreadsheet Wizard, 131
Execute, 174
Exit button, 32
Exit Function, 381
Exit Sub, 388
Explicit, 390
export
  Make Table queries, 191
  Ribbon settings, 471–472
Expression, 73
expressions, 81, 150, 163, 474
Expression Builder, 81–82, 150, 313
Extensible Markup Language
  (XML), 123–124, 350–351
  Ribbon controls, 473–475
external data
  Excel, 122–123
  tables, 121–127
  XML, 123–124
External Data Ribbon, 125,
  130–131, 137, 200
External tab, 24

F

Fail.Next, 357
Field, 440
fields. *See also specific field types*
  bound, 91–92
  data definition queries, 17
  data types, 58–59, 65–70
  expressions, 150, 163
  forms, 219
  indexes, 96
  modifying, 103
  naming schemes, 58
  PivotChart, 280–281
  primary keys, 60
  properties, 59–60, 71–78
  queries, 150
  Table Design View, 58–60
  tables, 16, 48
    data types, 48–49
    indexes, 117–120
  value list, 89–93
Field, Record & Table Events, 57
Field List Pane
  Access Runtime, 490
  Data Source, 296
  Design Ribbon, 294, 303
  Design tab, 217
  Design View, 218–219
  forms
    controls, 236
    fields, 219

Layout View, 208
Record Source, 218, 219, 296, 304
Show All Tables, 304
SQL statements, 304
TextBox, 319
Field Properties, 56, 59–60, 80–84, 90
Field Size, 73
Fields, 446
files, 15–16
    types, 6–7
File Ribbon tab, 459
File tab, 24
Filter, 72
    drop zone, 281
Filter On Load, 72
Find, 445
Find Duplicates queries, 143
Find Unmatched queries, 143
FindFirst, 445
FindLast, 445
FindNext, 445
FindPrevious, 445
First, 454
floating-point decimals, 49, 67
fonts, 297, 303
footers, 207, 294, 303, 320
For, 389–390
For Each, 390
foreign keys, 46
    lookup tables, 95
    normalization, 108
    one-to-many relationship, 111
    tables, 142
    Update queries, 179
FORM, 274
forms, 18. *See also specific forms*
    application navigation, 288–289
    bound, 215–216
    controls, 233–241
    Datasheet, 270–271
    Design View, 215–240
    embedded macros, 251–258
    fields, 219
    HTML, 137–138
    InfoPath, 137
    Layout View, 205–213
    macros, 253
    Multiple Items, 270
    parameter queries, 168
    PivotChart, 273
    PivotTable, 273
    properties, 227–232
        PivotChart, 281–282
    quick, 206

Record Source property, 17, 209, 215
references, 151
Single Item, 269–270
types, 209–210, 269–277
unbound, 215–216
VBA, 259–267
Form Design Tools Ribbon, 24, 217–218, 235
Form Layout Tools Ribbon, 207–208, 218, 235
Form Layout View designer, 205–213
Form Module, 260, 262
Form View, 256
Form Wizard, 270, 271
Format(), 157, 162–163
Format Ribbon, 303, 315, 324
Format tab, 208, 218, 228, 294, 295, 312, 315
Friend, 380, 381
frm, 47
frmLocations, 97
FROM, 158, 187, 192, 200
Function, 381, 387, 410
functions
    calculated fields, 17
    Default Value, 81
    events, 262
    return values, 392
    SQL View, 152
    standard modules, 20
    VBA, 381, 392–393

G

Get, 422–423
Get External Data, 131
GetType, 405
global variables, 383, 409, 410
globally unique identifier (GUID), 67
Go To, 357
GoSub, 387–388
Goto, 387
graphical user interface (GUI), 17
groups
    customization, 41, 465
    data, 161–165
    macros, 350
Group, Sort, and Total Pane, 305, 319–326
    Design View, 321
    grouping data, 321–322
    Layout View, 321, 325
    reports, 321–323
Group & Sort button, 321, 324

GROUP BY, 158, **162, 163,** 192, 200
Group By queries, **151,** 156
Group Settings, **464**
GUI. *See* graphical user interface
GUID. *See* globally unique identifier

H

hardcoding, 80–81
HasModule, 260–261
HAVING, 158, 162, 192
headers, 207, 294, 303, 320
Heavyweight Form objects, 260
Help
    Backstage, 34
    controls, 237–239
    properties, 314
    VBA, 393–394
Home Ribbon, 206, 294
Home tab, 24
Horizontal Anchors, 245–246
hotkeys, 27
HTML form, 137–138
Hyperlink data type, 68

I

iCount, 381, 384, 387, 422, 423, 426
If, 357, 381, 385–386
if, 350
Image control, 234
IME Mode, 74
IME Sentence Mode, 74
Immediate window, 368–370, 376
Import Wizard, 121–122, 124
Import/Export Ribbon, 473
IncrementByOne, 424
indexes
    data definition queries, 17
    DDL, 119
    fields, 96
        tables, 117–120
    Table Design View, 118
    tables, 16
        fields, 117–120
    VBA, 119
Indexed, 74, 175
Indexes button, 118
Info tab, 33
InfoPath forms, 137
inner joins, 112, 142
Input Mask, 74, 83–84
Insert Columns, 150

INSERT INTO
    Append queries, 175
    AutoNumber, 174
Insert Rows, 150
instances, 411, 425
Integer, 49, 66, 381, 382, 384, 412
IntelliSense, 253, 313, 329, 376, 393
INTO, 192
Invalid use of property, 392
IRibbonControl, 475, 484
.iso, 3

J

JOIN, 158
joins, 109
    Cartesian, 142
    relational databases, 142
    Select queries, 156
    types, 112
JOINS, 158
Joins, 192
junction tables, 112

K

Key Violations, 175
keyboard shortcuts, 27
keywords, 381

L

Label control, 233, 236, 256
Lag Triangles, 163–164
Last, 454–455
Layout View, 18
    Allow Layout View, 316
    controls, 246
    Detail, 320
    Field List Pane, 208
    forms, 205–213
        controls, 236
    Group, Sort, and Total Pane,
        321, 325
    Navigation Pane, 294
    PivotChart, 279
    reports, 19, 293–299, 314
    Subform/Subreport control, 245
    View, 294
left joins, 112
Let, 422–424
Lightweight Form objects, 260
Like, 399, 404
Line control, 234

Link Child Field, 72
Link Master Fields, 72
linked tables, 16, 129–134
    Excel, 131
    imports, 130–131
    permissions, 130
    security, 130
    SharePoint lists, 131
lists. *See also* Field List Pane
    Allow Value List Edits, 90–91
    Chart Field List, 280
    Create New List Wizard, 50
    Edit List Items dialog, 90–91
    queries, 91–92
    SharePoint, 45, 50, 131
    tables, 91–92
    values, 89–93
List Box, 91, 97
List Items Edit Form, 90–91
ListBox control, 289
literal variables, 383, 409, 412
local tables, 16
local variables, 383, 409, 410–411
LockEdit, 442
locks, 102–103, 180–181
logic branching, 357–358
logical operators, VBA, 402–403
Login Dialog, 450
Long, 383, 413, 414
Long Integer, 49, 66
Lookup data type, 69
lookup fields, 89–91
Lookup tab, 60, 90
lookup tables, 95–99
loops, 358, 388–390

M

macros, 19, 341–342. *See also
   specific macro types*
    Action Catalog, 329
    actions, 348
    building, 355–362
    CloseWindow, 332
    comments, 351
    conditions, 350
    conditional branching, 329
    controls, 235, 253, 329
    creating, 335–339
    database objects, 19
    debugging, 358–359
    enabling, 336, 343
    error handling, 356–357
    executing, 337
    Form View, 256

    forms, 253
    groups, 350
    IntelliSense, 329
    logic branching, 357–358
    loops, 358
    MessageBox, 331
    multi-step, 355–356
    names, 348
    onAction, 474
    parameters, 348–349
    parts, 347–354
    recursion, 358
    reports, 327–333
    security, 330, 342–344
        Access Runtime, 344
    TempVars, 351–352
    trusted locations, 344
    UI, 329
    VBA, 335
    XML, 350–351
Macro Builder, 253, 256, 335
    Builder, 331, 336
    Choose Builder dialog, 257
    embedded macros, 342
    Property Sheet Pane, 313, 329
Macro button, 336
Macro Designer, 252–253, 328–329,
    336–337, 350
    Action Catalog Pane, 337, 348
    changes, 347–348
    Macro Tools Ribbon, 337
    parameters, 328
Macro Name, 357, 359
Macro Single Step dialog, 358–359
MacroError, 356–357, 359
Macros & Code, 147
Macro-to-VBA converter
    button, 253
Make Table queries, 149, 191–195
Manage Data Tasks, 125
Manage Replies button, 137
many-to-many relationship, 110,
    111–112, 180
Max, 143
Max queries, 151
MaxValue, 414
MDA, 7
MDB, 6
.mdb, 15
MDE, 7
Me, 263
Memo, 66, 82, 83
Message Ribbon, 137
MessageBox, 331
methods, 18, 423, 426–427
Mid(), 179

Min, 143
Min queries, 151
MinValue, 414
Mod, 400
Modal Dialog, 209
Modal forms, 272–273
modules, 20, 260, 342, 380, 421–431
Month(), 163
More Commands, 25
More Fields button, 48
Move, 443–444
MoveFirst, 443
MoveLast, 443
MoveNext, 443
MovePrevious, 443
MSDN library, 314, 450, 485
multi-dimensional arrays, 416
Multiple Item forms, 270
multiple tables, 156
multi-step macros, 355–356
Multivalued data type, 69
My_Label, 387
MyVariable, 384

N

Name, 442, 461
names
    data macros, 364
    databases, 46–47
    fields, 58
    macros, 348
Name AutoCorrect, 101–102
Name field, 311
named data macros, 364
named macros, 19, 251–252, 327, 328, 329, 341–342
Named Ranges, 131
natural keys, 46
navigation. *See* application navigation
Navigation Buttons, 289
Navigation control, 234
Navigation Options dialog, 40–42
    custom groups, 41
    hidden objects, 41
    Navigation Pane, 463–464
    Search Bar, 40–41
    system tables, 42
Navigation Pane, 37–44
    Access Runtime, 490
    application navigation, 287–288
    Category, 464
    context menu, 40

controls, 219
Create Ribbon, 274
customization, 463–468
database objects, 39
Design View, 219, 305
expanding and collapsing, 39
form controls, 236
grouping types, 38–39
Layout View, 294
linked tables, 131
Navigation Options dialog, 463–464
Object Type, 255, 315, 324, 331
objects, 465–466
quick forms, 206
Quick Reports, 293
Report View, 325
Shutter Bar, 365
Subform/Subreport control, 244
Subreport, 305
views, 38–39
new, 263
New button, 455
New Query dialog, 198
New tab, 33
New Values, 74
Next, 357, 390, 454
No Locks, 103
normalization, 107–108, 113, 179, 185
Not, 401, 402
Now(), 81
Number, 48, 49, 66–67, 356

O

Object, 383, 410–411
objects, 245, 260
    Navigation Pane, 465–466
    VBA, 263
Object Browser, 237, 262, 370–371, 375
Object Dependencies, 57, 102
Object Library, 372
Object Type, 255, 315, 324, 331
Office Clipboard Pane, 25
OLE Automation, 372
OLE Object data type, 68
On Click, 454–456
onAction, 474–475, 484
OnChange, 424–425
OnClick, 258, 337
OnClick OpenForm, 337
OnError, 357
one-to-many relationship, 109, 111

one-to-one relationship, 109, 111
OnLoad, 18, 345
OnOpen, 453
On_Open, 423
Open, 423
Open button, 32
OpenAccessOptions Sub, 436
OpenForm, 337
OpenRecordset, 442
operators, 81, 384–385, 397–407. *See also specific operator types*
Option Base, 414
Option Button control, 234
Option Explicit, 411, 452
Option Group control, 234
Option statements, 390–391
Options, 442
Options button, 32
Options dialog, 25, 26, 457–461, 469–470
Or, 401, 402
Order By, 72
ORDER BY, 158, 163, 192
Order By On Load, 72
OrElse, 403
Orientation, 72
orphan records, 107, 168
Other tab, 228, 313
Outlook, 137

P

Page Footer, 320
Page Header, 320
page numbers, 303
Page Setup Ribbon, 304
Page Setup tab, 294, 295
parameters
    data types, 169
    macros, 348–349
    Macro Designer, 328
    OnError, 357
    Required, 349
parameter queries, 167–171
Parameter Request dialog, 167, 168
PARAMETERS, 169, 199
parent tables
    child tables, 113
    one-to-many relationship, 111
    many-to-many relationship, 112
    primary keys, 113
pass-through queries, 149
permissions, 130
Pessimistic Locking, 103
PIVOT, Crosstab queries, 200

PivotChart, 279–285
    fields, 280–281
    forms, 209, 273
    Subform/Subreport control, 244
PivotChart Tools Ribbon, 280
PivotChart View, 16, 17, 18, 280
PivotTable, 200, 209, 244, 273
PivotTable View, 16, 17
Pop-up forms, 272
Prev, 454
primary keys, 46, 60, 96, 113
    Autonumber, 16
    Excel, 122
    lookup tables, 95–96
    many-to-many relationship, 112
    normalization, 108
    one-to-many relationship, 111
    tables, 142
Print Preview View, 18–19, 315
Print tab, 33–34
Private, 380, 381, 410, 423
Private Module, 391
Program Flow, 337
Project Explorer, 371
prompt method, 151
properties
    Anchor, 245–246
    classes, 422–423, 426
    controls, 296, 305
    data types, 237
    databases, 459–461
    Datasheet forms, 271
    default, 237
    Design View, 45
    fields, 59–60, 71–78
    forms, 18, 227–232
        controls, 236–238
        PivotChart, 281–282
    Help, 314
    MSDN library, 314
    Options dialog, 457
    PivotChart, 281
    reports, 309–317
    standard modules, 20
    Status Bar, 314
    Subform/Subreport control, 246
    tables, 71–78
    VBA, 71
Properties, 460
Properties button, 208, 296
Properties Sheet, 71–72, 156
Property, 422
Property Sheet Pane, 208,
    309–313, 332
    Access Runtime, 490
    Builder, 336
    Caption, 315

control properties, 296
controls, 219
Design Ribbon, 294, 303
Design tab, 217, 305, 310
Design View, 219
Event tab, 256, 312
forms, 227–228
    controls, 236
Format tab, 312, 315
Macro Builder, 313, 329
named macros, 329
PivotChart, 281
Properties button, 296
Selection Type, 265
Status Bar, 315
TextBox, 451
Value field, 311, 313, 316
VBA, 261
Public, 380, 381, 410, 423
Public Sub, 475
Publish to Access Services, 33

Q

QAT. See Quick Access Toolbar
qry, 47
qryLocations, 97
queries, 16–17. See also specific
    query types
    Adding totals, 151
    concatenation, 91
    Criteria row, 151
    data aggregation, 162–163
    Data Collection, 136
    Datasheet View, 243
    fields, 150
    forms, 18
    indexes, 118
    lists, 91–92
    lookup fields, 90
    Query Design View, 147–153
    Query Wizard, 141–145
    Record Source, 316
    Sort row, 151
    SQL, 141
    SQL View, 152, 163
    types, 143
Query Builder, 458
Query Design button, 148, 180, 187
Query Design Ribbon, 148
Query Design View, 16–17, 151
    " " (double quotes), 181
    Crosstab queries, 199
    Properties Sheet, 156
    queries, 147–153
    Query Design Ribbon, 148

Query Parameters dialog, 199
Query Setup, 150
Query Type, 149
Record Locks, 180–181
Results, 148
Run, 149
Select queries, 156
Show Table dialog, 148
Show/Hide, 150
Sort row, 151, 163
Update queries, 180–181
Use Transactions, 180–181
View, 149
Query Designer, 96, 97
Query Parameters dialog, 199
Query Setup, 150
Query Tools Design Ribbon, 169,
    180, 187, 192
Query Type, 149, 192
Query Wizard, 141–145
QueryDef, 167
Quick Access Toolbar (QAT), 25
quick forms, 206
Quick Launch Toolbar, 5
Quick Reports, 293
Quick Start, 49
quick styles, 303

R

RaiseEvent, 423–424
RDMS. See Relational Database
    Management System
Read Only When Disconnected, 72
Recent tab, 33
Record Locks, 180–181
Record Selectors, 216
Record Source
    Field List Pane, 218, 219,
        296, 304
    forms, 17, 209, 215
    queries, 316
    Quick Reports, 293
    recordsets, 216
    reports, 17, 302–303
    Select queries, 142
    SQL statements, 296, 316
    Value field, 316
Recordset, 440–450, 452
    AddNew, 447–448
    Close, 449–450
    Delete, 448–449
    Find, 445
    Move, 443–444
    Update, 446–448
    values, 446–447

recordsets, 180, 216
Rectangle control, 234
recursion, 358
reDim, 415
references, 151, 440–441
References dialog, 371–372, 440
referential integrity, 107, 110–111,
    113, 114, 186
Relational Database Management
    System (RDMS), 107
relational databases, 46, 96,
    107–108, 142
relationships, 107–116, 118
Relationship Tools, 107
Relationships, 57, 109–114
RemoveAllTempVars, 351
RemoveTempVar, 351
Rename Shortcut, 466
Repeat, 358
Repeat Expression, 358
Replication ID, 67
reports, 18–19
    bound, 302–303
    Control Source, 302
    controls, 302
    Data Source, 302
    Design View, 301–308
    Detail, 319–320
    Group, Sort, and Total Pane,
        321–323
    Layout View, 293–299, 314
    macros, 327–333
    properties, 309–317
    Property Sheet Pane, 309–313
    Record Source, 17, 302–303
    unbound, 302–303
Report button, 324
Report Design Tools Ribbon,
    303–304
    Design tab, 305, 310, 321, 322
Report Design View Designer,
    301–308
Report Designer, 328
Report Footer, 320
Report Header, 320
Report Layout Tools Ribbon,
    294–297, 310, 322
    Format Ribbon, 315, 324
Report Module, 260, 380
Report Selector, 314
Report View, 18, 294, 315, 325, 332
Required, 74, 82, 175
Required, 349
reserved words, 47, 381
Reset button, 472
Result Type, 75
Results, 148

Return, 150
return values, 392
Ribbon, 23–30. See also specific
    Ribbons
    Access Options dialog, 26
    Access Runtime, 490
    application navigation, 288
    command customization,
        473–476
    Create tab, 216, 255, 274, 282,
        315, 336, 451
    customization, 25–26, 469–480
        databases, 475–476
    Drop Zones button, 282
    form controls, 235
    hotkeys, 27
    Options dialog, 469–470
    QAT, 25
    Reset button, 472
    sections, 25
        expanders, 25
    settings
        customization, 471
        export, 471–472
    tables, 16
    XML, controls, 473–475
RibbonName, 475, 482
RibbonXML, 475, 482
right joins, 112, 142
Row Headings, 163–164, 199
Row Source property, 89, 90
Row Source Type, 91
rows, 303
RowSource, 290
RowSourceType, 290
ruler, 217
Run, 149, 187, 192, 337,
    373–374
RunCommand, 413, 436
RunDataMacro, 363–365
RunMacro, 358
/runtime, 493–494

S

safe macros, 330, 342–343
SampledAt, 162
Save, 455–456
Save & Publish tab, 34
Save button, 32
Save Database As button, 32
Save Import Steps, 124
Save Object As button, 32
Save property, 257
Saved Imports button, 125
Search Bar, 40–41

security
    linked tables, 130
    macros, 330, 342–344
        Access Runtime, 344
        VBA, 264
Security Bar, 12, 17, 258, 330,
    375, 450
Seek, 445
SELECT, 158, 161, 162, 163
    Append queries, 175
    Crosstab queries, 200
    Make Table queries, 192
Select Case, 386
Select queries, 16–17, 143, 149,
    155–160
    Criteria row, 156–157
    joins, 156
    multiple tables, 156
    Query Design View, 156
    Record Source property, 142
    SQL View, 158
Selection Type, 265
Series drop zone, 281
SET, 181
Set, 392, 411
SetTempVar, 351
setup.exe, 3
SharePoint, lists, 45, 50, 131
SharePoint Server, 342
SharePoint Site Wizard, 131
SharePoint Web Applications,
    309, 342
shortcuts, 5, 27
Show All Tables, 304
Show Date Picker, 75
Show Hidden Objects, 371
Show Table dialog, 148, 150
Show/Hide, 57, 150
ShowInfo, 380
Shutter Bar, 39, 365
side-by-side installations, 2
Single, 49, 67, 383
Single Form, 209
Single Item forms, 269–270
SingleStep, 357
Smart Tags, 75
Sort row, 151, 163
Source Object property, 244
Split Form, 209, 256, 271–272
Splitter Bar, 271, 311
SQL. See Structured
    Query Language
SQL statements, 296, 304, 316
SQL View, 16–17
    Append queries, 175
    Crosstab queries, 199–200
    Delete queries, 187–188

SQL View *(continued)*
  field expressions, 163
  Make Table queries, 192–193
  parameter queries, 169–170
  queries, 152, 163
  Select queries, 158
  Update queries, 181
standalone macros. *See*
  named macros
standard modules, 20
Start menu, 5
State field, 324
Status Bar, 314, 315
Step, 359
Step Into, 372–373
Step Over, 373
Stepping Out, 373
Stop, 374
Stop All Macros, 359
strHistory, 392
String, 48, 383, 384, 412
strings
  concatenation, 17
  operators, 403–405
strMessage, 384, 393
Structured Query Language (SQL),
  101, 119, 141. *See also* SQL
  statements; SQL View
Sub, 380, 387, 392, 410, 423, 453
Sub datasheet Expanded, 72
Sub datasheet Height, 72
Sub datasheet Name, 72
subforms
  bound, 243, 244
  unbound, 243, 244
Subform/Subreport control, 234,
  243–249
Subreport, 305
subreports, unbound, 243
subroutines, 20, 262, 380, 391–392
Sum, 143
Sum(), 164
Sum queries, 151
Support tab, 34
surrogate keys, 46
system requirements, 2
system tables, 16, 42
Systolic, 162

tabs. *See also specific tabs*
  Backstage, 32, 33–34
  Property Sheet Pane, 312–313
  Ribbon, 24
Tab control, 234

tables, 16. *See also specific*
  table types
  calculated fields, 59
  data definition queries, 17
  Datasheet View, 45–53, 243
  Design View, 16
  external data, 121–127
  fields, 48
    data types, 48–49
    indexes, 117–120
  foreign keys, 142
  forms, 18
  lists, 91–92
  locks, 102–103
  lookup fields, 90
  modifications, 101–105
  primary keys, 16, 142
  properties, 71–78
  relationships, 107–116
  renaming, 101–102
  Table Design View, 55–63
  templates, 49
  temporary, 191
Table Design button, 45, 56
Table Design View
  Field Properties, 56, 59–60
  indexes, 118
  tables, 55–63
Table tab, 365
Table Tools Design Ribbon, 60, 118
Table Tools Fields Ribbon, 48
Table Tools Ribbon, 47–48, 365
Table Tools Table Ribbon, 364
Tabular Document mode, 246
tbl, 47
tblLocations, 97
tblPressures, 162
templates
  Backstage, 331, 365, 375
  databases, 11–12
  tables, 49
temporary tables, 191
TempVars, 329, 351–352, 358
testing
  Access Runtime, 494
  Delete queries, 186
  Update queries, 181
Text, 66, 82, 83, 263
Text Align, 75
Text Format, 75
Text Formatting, 25
Text Import Wizard, 125
TextBox, 233, 236, 256,
  263, 451
  application navigation, 289
  Control Source, 319
  Field List Pane, 319

themes
  Design Ribbon, 294, 303
  Design tab, 297
  Form Layout Tools Ribbon, 207
  Report Layout Tools
    Ribbon, 297
Then, 385
TLB. *See* Type Library
Toggle Button control, 234
Tools for Working with Office
  tab, 34
Tools section, 57
TOP, 175
Top Values property, 156
Totals, 162
  Group, Sort, and Totals Pane,
    322–323
Totals menu, 322
Totals queries, 163
TRANSFORM, 199
Tree View, 124
True/False, 197
Trust Bar, 336, 343
trusted locations, 17, 344
trusted macros, 254, 330, 342–343
Type, 442
Type Library (TLB), 371

U

UI. *See* user interface
unbound forms, 215–216
unbound reports, 302–303
unbound subforms, 243, 244
unbound subreports, 243
underlying object, 245
Unicode Compression, 75
Union queries, 17, 149, 152, 180
Unique Values property, 156
unsafe macros, 330, 343
untrusted macros, 254, 330, 343
Update, 446–448
Update button, 180
Update queries, 143, 149, 179–183
  backups, 180
  Design View, 180
  Query Design View, 180–181
  SET, 181
  settings, 180–181
  SQL View, 181
  testing, 181
Use Transactions, 180–181
user interface (UI), 15
  macros, 253, 329
USysRibbons, 475, 481–482
Utilities Code window, 376

V

Validation Rule, 72, 75, 82–83, 175
Validation Text, 72, 75, 83
Value, 163–164, 311, 313, 316
Value, 461
values
    arrays, 416
    lists, 89–93
    Recordset, 446–447
VALUES, 175
variables. *See also specific*
    variable types
    accessing, 411
    classes, 409
    data types, 409
    instances, 411
    TempVars, 329,
      351–352, 358
    VBA, 383–384, 409–420
Variant, 383, 384, 410
VBA. *See* Visual Basic for
    Applications
VBE. *See* Visual Basic Editor
vbNewLine, 412
vbNullChar, 412
Vertical Anchors, 245–246
View
    Design Ribbon, 174, 303
    Design View, 217, 315
    Home Ribbon, 206, 294
    Layout View, 294
    Make Table queries, 192
    Query Design View, 149
    Report Layout Tools Format
      Ribbon, 315
views. *See also specific views*
    forms, 18
    Navigation Pane, 38–39
    queries, 17
    reports, 18–19
    tables, 16
View Properties, 40
Views section, 57
Visual Basic button, 368
Visual Basic Editor (VBE), 16, 19,
    260, 367–377
    Access Runtime, 490
    Break, 374
    breakpoints, 372, 377

Code window, 368
    IntelliSense, 393
debugging, 372–374
Design Ribbon, 303
Immediate window,
    368–370, 376
Object Browser, 237, 262,
    370–371
Project Explorer, 371
property data types, 237
References dialog,
    371–372, 440
Run, 373–374
starting, 368
Step, 372–373
Stop, 374
Utilities Code window, 376
VBA, 261
Visual Basic for Applications (VBA),
    19–20, 372
    arithmetic operators, 400–401
    arrays, 414–416
    assignment operators, 397–398
    bitwise operators, 401–402
    branching, 385–388
    code, 379–394
    comments, 381–382
    comparison operators, 399
    concatenation operators,
      403–404
    DAO, 441
    data types, 382–383
    database properties, 459–461
    ElseIf, 385–386
    forms, 259–267
      controls, 237
    functions, 381, 392–393
    Help, 393–394
    If, 385–386
    indexes, 119
    keywords, 381
    logical operators, 402–403
    loops, 388–390
    macros, 335
    Macro-to-VBA converter
      button, 253
    modules, 260, 380
    objects, 263
    onAction, 474–475
    operators, 384–385, 397–407

Option statements, 390–391
properties, 71
Property Sheet Pane, 261
reserved words, 381
security, 264
string operators, 403–405
subroutines, 380, 391–392
variables, 383–384, 409–420
VBE, 261
While, 388
wildcard operators, 404

W

warnings, 174, 257
Web Browser control, 234, 265
Web Report, 309
Web tables, 16
Wend, 388
WHERE, 158, 162
    Crosstab queries, 200
    Delete queries, 187
    Make Table queries, 192
    PARAMETERS, 169
Where, 445
Where Condition property, 256
While, 388
wildcard operators, 404
Windows Explorer, 5, 6
WithEvents, 427
Worksheets, 131

X

XML. *See* Extensible
    Markup Language
Xor, 401, 402

Y

Yes/No, 118

Z

Zoom Builder, 312
Zoom dialog, 247, 312, 315

WILEY PUBLISHING, INC.
END-USER LICENSE AGREEMENT